Black Body

Women, Colonialism, and Space

Radhika Mohanram

PUBLIC WORLDS, VOLUME 6
UNIVERSITY OF MINNESOTA PRESS
MINNEAPOLIS • LONDON

Published simultaneously by the University of Minnesota Press
111 Third Avenue South, Suite 290
Minneapolis, MN 55401-2520
http://www.upress.umn.edu

and Allen & Unwin
9 Atchison Street
St Leonards NSW 1590
Australia
http://www.allen-unwin.com.au

Printed and bound by KHL Printing Co Pte Limited, Singapore

Library of Congress Cataloging-in-Publication Data

Mohanram, Radhika.

  Black body: women, colonialism, and space/Radhika Mohanram.
  p. cm— (Public worlds: v.6)

  Includes bibliographical references.
  ISBN 0-8166-3542-0 (hc).—ISBN 0-8166-3543-9 (pbk).
  1. Body, Human—Social aspects. 2. Body, Human—Symbolic aspects.
  3. Group identity. 4. Feminism—Australia. 5. Feminism—New Zealand.
  6. Indigenous peoples—Australia. 7. Indigenous peoples—New Zealand.
  8. Postcolonialism. I. Title. II. Series.
  HM636.M64 1999

306.4—dc21   99-26268

Contents

Acknowledgments

I wish to thank the following institutions for supporting this project: the Humanities Research Centre at the Australian National University; the Institute for Research on Women and Gender at Stanford University; the Southwestern Institute for Research on Women at the University of Arizona; the Beatrice M. Bain Research Group at the University of California, Berkeley. Without the generous grants that all these institutions provided for me over summers and during my sabbatical semester, this book would not have been done at all. In particular I want to thank the University of Waikato which has supported my scholarship for the past five years.

I also wish to thank the following colleagues and friends associated with these various institutions for giving me feedback on my ideas, reading bits of or all of this book, and encouraging me on this project: Tracy Bowell, Margaret Burns, Simon Burrows, Debi Cain, Ralph Crane, Annabel Cooper, Ann Curthoys, John Docker, Subash Jaireth, Margaret Jolly, Rosann Kennedy, David Lumsden, Karen Offen, Fiona Paisley, Jindy Pettman and Angela Woolacott. In particular, I wish to thank Michael Goldsmith and Louise Allen, the latter of whom, putting aside her own work, made substantive remarks on the penultimate draft. My thanks to my colleagues, Marion de Ras, Hilary Lapsley, and Catherine Kingfisher in the Department of Women's and Gender Studies at the University of Waikato, for their support through the duration of this work. I also wish to thank Margaret Wilson and Anna Yeatman for being my Antipodean mentors. I wish especially to thank Emma Cotter, Liz de Loughrey, Robert Con Davis, Terry Threadgold and Elizabeth Weiss and the editing staff at Allen & Unwin for working with me on the final drafts.

Finally, my thanks to my mother for giving me the gift of time to write, and to my sister and brother and their families for lending me their homes and their cars while I was in California. This book is dedicated to them.

Introduction

The genesis of this work initially appears circumstantial and
tangential. In 1993 I immigrated to New Zealand after having
lived in the US for over eleven years. My stay in the US I
experienced always as temporary and tenuous, a feeling attributed to being for the most part in graduate school on a student
visa, later on a work permit. In the years I lived and worked
in the US, I became a statistic, one of the 142 076 530
non-immigrants granted temporary domicile in that country in
the 1980s. My peers in graduate school and at my workplace
granted me the identity of the Indian national because the last
place I had lived in was India. When I moved to New Zealand,
one short overnight trip between San Francisco and Auckland
saw me recategorized by New Zealanders from Indian to
American. American and Canadian citizens living and working
in New Zealand now claim me as one of their own, a North
American. New Zealanders categorize me as American on
hearing a sort of American accent, and align me with US
imperialist aggressions. In the Antipodes, in academia specifically, through a process of displacement I have become a
representative of the multicultural and multiracial, metropolitan
superpower of the Northern hemisphere. What the INS (Immigration and Naturalization Services) failed to give me—an
American identity—was bestowed upon me in absentia by New
Zealand. I had to be dislocated from the US to become
identified as an American, just as I had to leave India to

become Indian. When I went back to the US to attend the 1995 Modern Languages Association Conference and on my sabbatical in 1996, ironically I was always categorized as a New Zealander. Since Americans generally don't know how a New Zealander is supposed to look and sound—they never hear the American in my voice—I soon embodied the little known and 'quaint' status of the New Zealander in the US.

In a further twist, after I arrived in New Zealand I was referred to as 'black'—which threw me into utter confusion as I had shaped my adult identity as a minority in the US labelled 'brown'. This continual recategorization—from 'unmarked' to 'brown' to 'black'—goes beyond a classification of race; these terms contain within them the social, economic and cultural history, as well as the markers of the places of domicile, of the subject. When visiting in India, even when dressed in traditional Indian clothes, the movements of my body, my walk, my body language, mark me as not completely Indian. The way my body holds itself and occupies space betrays its prolonged sojourn in non-Indian spaces and in unfamiliar landscape features. This destabilisation, from unmarked Indian, to a minority brown, to an immigrant black, forced me to analyse my own notions of raced hierarchies, embodied nations, bodily identity and mobility, and led to the writing of this work.

It is a critical commonplace to suggest that in a postmodern, transnational theory-world, notions such as a 'pure' national or racial identity are anachronistic or outmoded concepts, since a postmodern understanding of identity is based on a comprehension of nation and race as arbitrary or as a political construct. Yet subjects have a close relationship with the landscape that surrounds them, a relationship which shapes their bodies and perceptions, forms their knowledge and informs their sense of aesthetics. Such an awareness suggests that place and landscape are not inert but things which actively participate in the identity formation of the individual. Not only does a sense of place participate in the construction of a perception of physical identity, it is also central to the formation of racial identity. The category of the 'black body' can come into being only when the body is perceived as being out of place, either from its natural environment or its national boundaries. A black body in apartheid South Africa or in Uganda would not be understood as black in quite the same way as it would be in Western countries. Yet the different meanings of blackness are also metonymically linked with each other. In the eighteenth and nineteenth centuries, colonialism and the racial categories it produced were largely expressions of white bodies from Western hemispheres recreating and reworlding non-Western regions of the world. Colonialism and racial categories constituted a territorialization of place/landscape. In the twentieth century multicultural/multiracial countries, together with terms such as 'racial diversity' (especially within metropolitan spaces with their attendant race and refugee problems), are a result of mostly non-Western subjects being perceived as being out of the place to which they 'naturally' belong.

Throughout this work I use the terms 'black' and 'white' as binary opposites. Such a usage is considered outdated, especially in current practices of expanding the term 'black' to mean something beyond an essentialized identity. Blackness is perceived in its heterogeneity in the works of a variety of theorists, and signifies differently when used as a marker of race in different parts of the globe. For instance, within the definitions of a literary theorist such as Joyce Ann Joyce in the US, black is used as an essentialized racial identity and refers in particular to the history of slavery in the US and the metonymic links of this identity to blacks in the African continent.[1] In *The Black Atlantic*, Paul Gilroy posits the notion of an 'intercultural and transnational formation' which links black communities, despite political and cultural differences. Thus in Gilroy's work Africa, Europe, the Caribbean, Latin America and the US function as specific points in a network in which fifteen million slaves moved about. Yet the notion of blackness goes beyond its historically specific link to slavery and is also the transfer of an idea of resistance and decolonization.[2] For Stuart Hall, black identity in Britain had to be learnt at a certain moment in British history. His agenda has been to highlight the complex nature of essentialized notions of blackness by perceiving it in its heterogeneity, so it cannot be contained by the singular marker 'black'.[3] In Britain this term specifically refers to people of both the African and South Asian diasporas. Or, as Kobena Mercer puts it, 'we are here because you were there'.[4] While there might be an essentialized link to blackness among people of African descent, as in the UK, at specific moments in the 1970s and 1980s the Aboriginal peoples of Australia and the Maori of New Zealand have also embraced the term 'black' to describe themselves.[5] While younger generations of people of Indian subcontinent descent in Britain embrace this categorization as it forges them a political, specifically British identity, for Indians in India, who have their own notions of race hierarchies and racism, to be deemed black is anathema; Indians in the US are categorized/categorize themselves as 'brown', or as a 'model minority'. In effect the term black goes beyond a connection to the African continent.

Notions of black seem to reproduce the dichotomy of white/black and refer to an essentialized identity. While I fully support Gilroy, Hall and Mercer's agenda of reading black in its complexity and heterogeneity, the focus of this project is rather to trace the process of representation in a variety of discourses and texts central to Western notions of identity. The notion of representation traditionally presumes reality to be the presence behind it. In the age of post-structuralist thought, we all concur that reality itself is a discursive construct. Since Saussure we accept that words and signs are defined not by essential, intrinsic properties, but by differences from other signs and through binary opposites. I attempt to read the discursive nature of blackness which is constructed in order to function as a binary opposite to whiteness, and to bring the latter into meaning. My analysis underscores quite insistently that blackness is a discursive practice exercised by the confluence of history, culture, economics, geography and language, which conditions the *enunciative* function. In this work I will attempt to show the links between the body, geography and the enunciative function of blackness.

Further, this work attempts to tease out a theory of identity from within the context of place/landscape rather than from the traditional models of identity formation and development which emphasize temporality. Earlier models emphasize a structure of maturation or development which follows a temporal frame. Within liberal democratic discourse, with its emphasis on human rights and justice, John Locke's notion of identity contains a definite hierarchy of development. Within psychoanalytic discourse Freud and Lacan, too, insist on a developmental, maturational model which is temporal and hierarchical. For instance, in Lacan, the subject follows progressively from a non-individuated identity at birth into the Symbolic. My alternative approach of foregrounding place is called for because place is normally perceived as a passive, abstract arena in which events occur. However, place/landscape is saturated with relations of domination which are relevant to the construction of identity. Metaphors which attest to the mutual interrelationship between the identity of the subject and that of place include position, location, situation, centre-margin, liminal space, and dominant-subordinate. In other words, theories of identity cannot be articulated merely from aspects of power or development (First/Third World, developed/developing) without bringing the concept of place/landscape within this equation, because power and development are anchored spatially as well.

I also explore the woman's body within this work as it links notions of embodiment (in terms of race and gender) with that of place. Woman's body intersects place, race and gender, as indicated in Freud's description of woman as the 'dark continent', or in Plato's *Timeaus*, where the woman is place, *chora*, 'unnameable, improbable, hybrid, anterior to naming, to the One, to the father, and consequently maternally connoted'.[6] Luce Irigaray, too, suggests that woman functions as place for man: 'A doubling, sought after by man, of a female *placenessness*. She is assigned to be place without occupying a place. Through her, place would be set up for man's use but not hers.'[7]

My emphasis on foregrounding the submerged concept of place/landscape will also show the connections among the various strands in postcolonial studies: the politics of place/displacement, the concept of diasporic identity vs. indigenous identity, the identity of woman in the nation and the spatial construction of femininity, the identity of the black body and its natural relationship to nature and landscape as opposed to that of the white body and its relationship to knowledge.

By not analysing sexuality at any length in this work, I have established a heterosexual imperative, always the premise of liberal democratic discourses of the nation and of the woman. Blackness is perversion unto itself in anthropological and geographical discourses, just as the woman's body is perverted within the psychoanalytic framework. Since every chapter in this work examines and reads the nature of representation in a variety of texts, my own text has reproduced the heterosexual imperative which marks the original texts.

The first part of the work comprises three theoretical chapters and deals with the construction of the body within discourse and theory. First, I examine discourses on the body; then I look at discourses on identity; and finally I examine the marked, sexed body. At the level of representation, the discursive formations of the marked body primarily function to unmark the norm. All these discourses on the marked body are ultimately about the dominant, hegemonic, white male body.

In contrast to theories of identity which follow a model of temporality, the first theoretical chapter deals with the construction of knowledges and the territorialization of identity through land or spatiality. This chapter examines terms such as 'indigene', 'native' and 'nation' within this context. It juxtaposes theories of nomadism and diaspora in the production of identity to examine the part played by place and landscape within the term 'identity'. I further examine questions such as: How is bodily identity processed? and: How is the racialized body produced by landscape? I juxtapose Lévi-Strauss' chapter on 'The Science of the Concrete' in *The Savage Mind*, on the relationship between the savage and 'his' environment, its fauna and flora, and the white and black bodies in Alfred Crosby's work, *Ecological Imperialism*, with that of the unmarked man in Maurice Merleau-Ponty's chapter on motility in *Phenomenology of Perception*. The unmarked man's body comes into being only within metaphysical space, whereas the black (male) body can be located only within fauna and flora.

Chapter 2 should be read in conjunction with the previous one, as this work functions like a mosaic. If the previous chapter examined academic discourses on the body and knowledge, this chapter examines the relationship between representation and identity. It looks at *bodily* identity within liberal democratic discourse, psychoanalytic theory and postcolonial theory. Here I analyse John Locke's chapter on identity in *An Essay Concerning Human Understanding*, Freud's 'Ego and the Id' and Frantz Fanon's *Black Skin, White Masks*, and consider what they mean by bodily identity. In particular, I juxtapose Locke and Freud with Fanon to tease out the implications of their schema of identity in the construction of the racialized body. My selections of Locke and Freud are not arbitrary. Prior to its usage in Locke's *An Essay*, the term 'identity' was used within logic and algebra, rather than to describe an individual within the discourses of social sciences or the humanities. Furthermore, this work was immensely influential in the Enlightenment movement in England and on the Continent. Most importantly, his work is the cornerstone of the discourse of liberal democracy which underpins Western democracies and nationalisms. The section on Freud—the father of psychoanalysis—is also useful since psychoanalytic frameworks have contributed vastly to an understanding of identity, identification, self/other and same/other. In the last section of Chapter 2 I cull the metaphors of place in Fanon's text, which seem to indicate an alternative consideration of identity formation which has been influential in postcolonial theory. The analysis of bodily/embodied identity within liberal democratic and psychoanalytic traditions reveal that the black body (as well as the female body) is out of place in these theoretical discourses.

In Chapter 3 I use Fanon's evocative 'Algeria Unveiled' to discuss how the gendered body is positioned within the nation. I examine, in particular, women's positioning within the discourse of the nation. If woman is the scaffolding upon which rests the identity of the nation and its male citizens, what do you do with her materiality? The figure of the woman is symptomatic of all that is occluded in the discourse of the nation. I also examine the analogical nature of race and gender within theoretical discourse where each of these categories function interchangeably, yet isolated from each other.

The second part of the work uses the theoretical approaches described in the first part to discuss identity formation (both of nation and individual subject) in New Zealand and Australia, two postcolonial nations which are currently debating a number of issues related to questions of embodied, racial and national identity. I examine how the reintroduction of the notion of place/landscape shifts our perceptions of terms such as 'settler', 'indigenous', 'diasporic' and 'postcolonial', and how a discourse of place is also a continual dialectic between subject and object.

Chapters 4, 5 and 6 deal with femininity in the Antipodes, a term which I find rich in meaning, for it not only means 'the opposite side of the globe' but also 'diametrically opposite to anything' as the *Oxford English Dictionary* defines it. This term has been resonant for me because my enterprise of tracking blackness and the woman's body has been an attempt to read the diametric opposition which this term signifies.

Chapter 4 is in two parts. In the first part I consider how theories travel just like people and how they are differently manifested in new cultures, new lands and new aesthetics. This chapter also deals with the hegemony of paradigms and frameworks of race and the nation produced in the Northern hemisphere, most particularly in the US and in the UK, and their appropriateness and significance in the more sparsely populated settler colonies in the Southern hemisphere. I also examine the situatedness of knowledge or traces of place in theoretical frameworks and the changes undergone by bodies of theoretical frameworks when they move from one place to another. The second part of the chapter deals with Maori (indigenous) feminist theory in Aotearoa/New Zealand and Maori feminists' essential constructions of themselves in their relationship to landscape. It first explores the significance of landscape in the aesthetic/intellectual/political formation of identity, then argues that any evocation of landscape itself is metaphorical in that it suggests an originary loss of land. I argue that notions of indigenousness which imply the political strategies of the indigene are premised on an unproblematic relationship between the land and the indigene. By mediating the concept of indigenousness through the framework of nationalism, I complexify the signification of 'indigene'. Such a reading will reveal that the originary meaning of land valorized in association with the indigene is a political construct rather than a natural relationship. In relation to such an argument, Maori feminism fits seamlessly within a postcolonial context, but with a difference; Maori feminism, if read within the framework of nationalism, reveals Maori feminists to be not in an uncontaminated continuum with a pre-contact era but rather to be enmeshed within a neo-patriarchy which is a product of colonialism.

My selection of the topic of Chapter 5 occurred after a trip to Australia. While browsing through a tourist shop in Canberra's Botanic Gardens I came across abridged copies— children's versions—of Sally Morgan's *My Place*. These books were excerpts with titles such as *Gladys Corunna's Story* and *Arthur Corunna's Story*. Seeing these works confirmed for me the historical importance of *My Place* to Australia, its very commodification in a tourist trap in Canberra emphasizing its importance in the embodiment of Australia. Chapter 5 deals with Aboriginality in *My Place* and tracks the relationship between identity mediated through race and that through class. It also examines the embodiment of multicultural Australia and the notion of miscegenation contained within history and within the term 'multiculturalism'.

Chapter 6 discusses the construction of white femininity in the Antipodes. I felt the need to work on this antipodean difference because notions of white femininity resonate with historical, political and national differences. I could be accused of homogenizing Australian with New Zealand white femininity here, but what I have attempted to do is to examine the relationship between domestic ideology and imperialism in the age of Victoria, and to show how this connection manifested itself in the letters of two pioneer women in the 1850s, Rachel Henning in Australia and Charlotte Godley in New Zealand.

The third section of this book is the conclusion and briefly examines how postcolonial theory, which is always about the interrogation of race, place and identity, can itself be inflected by changing landscapes. Chapter 7 deals with the dominance of postcolonial theories by scholars from India settled in the West, and with the differences between postcolonial theory produced by Indian scholars living in the West and by those living in India, their different positionalities in the larger culture in which they live, and the impact of their proximity to India in their epistemology and writing. The political/cultural space occupied by Indian academics in India is premised on the notion of essence and their location in India as having created their Indian identity. They insist on epistemological purity in the production of indigenous theories on identity. In contrast, the Indian academic in the West always insists on her identity as a product of discourse, produced in the interstices of the discourses of race, the status of minorities, and the socio-economic and the juridical as it affects the non-white immigrant in the West. The Indian academic in the West sees herself as an effect of these discourses rather than a cause. Ultimately, the debate between these sets of theorists is significant in that it subverts the neat demarcations within Western epistemology between indigenous and settler, First World and Third World, white and non-white, and North and South itself. Identity itself proves to be an indeterminacy which prevents authoritative closure.

The coda sums up the debates in this work and deals with how postcolonial discourse opens up new lands of theory. It briefly describes the significance of postcolonial discourse to an analysis of race, place, the body and identity.

There is no linear argument contained in this work. As previously stated, it functions as a mosaic, individual pieces with integrity intact in a larger pattern. Each chapter functions as a whole, and can be read individually. Alternatively, you can read the book in a linear fashion from start to finish. I hope you do both.

PART I

In theory

1

The cartography of bodies

At first glance I seem to be comparing apples and oranges here, two texts from two different discourses. First, an anthropological text, Claude Lévi-Strauss' 'The Science of the Concrete', which distinguishes between science and magic, the different forms of classification and their relationship to human development; and second, a text on biogeography, Alfred Crosby's exciting work *Ecological Imperialism,* which is an analysis at the interface of biology, geography and European colonial expansion.[1] While seeming to have nothing much in common in terms of their disciplines, they dovetail and mingle with each other in that both texts develop and analyse the notion of man's relationship with his environment, how learning and knowledge formation is linked to landscape, fauna and flora, and how 'autochthony', or springing out of the soil, constructs indigenousness and links bodies to their specific environments. Race, place and knowledge are inextricably linked in these texts. It is a commonplace to point out that the concept of race has always been articulated according to the geographical distributions of people. Racial difference is also spatial difference, the inequitable power relationships between various spaces and places are rearticulated as the inequitable power relations between races.

In this chapter I read Lévi-Strauss' text in juxtaposition with Crosby's because I want to examine the bodies which are formed in the two. I want to suggest that there is a double

3

move in both these texts, in that there is an embodiment of blackness with a simultaneous disembodiment of whiteness, a disembodiment accompanied by two other tropes at the level of discourse. First, whiteness has the ability to move; second, the ability to move results in the unmarking of the body. In contrast, blackness is signified through a marking and is always static and immobilizing.

Body and national landscape

I lay the groundwork for reading Lévi-Strauss and Crosby by citing some well-known assertions about bodily identity and geography. Notions of autochthony and bodies belonging to specific places are peculiar constructions of disciplines like geography and anthropology, which were institutionalized in the last few decades of the nineteenth century, the period of high imperialism in Western Europe. I draw attention to this minor detail, not to do any ritualistic fingerpointing at these disciplines, but to suggest that these notions became formalized within the construct of the nation in the nineteenth century. Raced bodies, nations, ideas about places, passports and visas all emerged in the nineteenth century and are inextricably linked. Senses of place are linked with ideas of national identity as well as with the hierarchy of nations.

Furthermore, bodies are specifically linked with nations. For instance, in Germany concepts such as 'fatherland' and 'blood and soil' are linked to the imagining of the perfect German body, as George Mosse has amply demonstrated.[2] The conflation of bodies and nation is implicit in a myriad texts written in the late nineteenth and early twentieth centuries, as in Rupert Brooke's famous poem 'The Soldier': 'If I should die, think only this of me:/That there's some corner of a foreign field/That is for ever England.' Here the English body is a metaphor for England and becomes interchangeable with it. The distinction between body and the place in which it originates implodes. Interestingly, this concept contains within it a colonializing move, in that the dead English soldier's body buried in a foreign field recreates the foreign land as English. According to Liisa Malkki, the close relationship between body and home is further manifest in non-discursive practices.[3] For instance, when going into exile, people carry a handful of soil from their country or, in a reverse move to Brooke's poem, people who die in foreign places are often transported to their home nation (27). Here the buried body dissolves to dust, to earth, but it must mingle only with like or familiar dust and earth. As Malkki points out, this relationship between soil or the earth and body manifests itself in botanical metaphors: 'people are often thought of, and think of themselves, as being rooted in place and derive their identity through their rootedness . . . Motherland and fatherland, aside from their historical connotations, suggest that each nation is a grand geneological tree, rooted in the soil that nourishes it' (27–8).

Additionally, while the body is closely aligned with the soil and botany, so is the nation closely tied to its landscape. By this I mean that one of the functions of nationalism is to intensify feeling for the landscape. Though the features of hills, mountains, rivers, oceans and deserts are common to a number of countries, each nation prefers to consider its own geographical features as unique. Some national anthems celebrate scenic splendours or nature's bounties. For instance, the Indian national anthem links the variety of landscape features and terrains within its borders to its heterogeneous people and cultures. The American national anthem celebrates the vastness of its landscape, 'from sea to shining sea' representing the breadth of the country from the Atlantic seaboard to the Pacific. David Lowenthal points out that '[n]ationalist impulses reveal the novel charms of otherwise unsung landscape features'.[4] In such a reading the bog is perceived as the mystique of Ireland; the poet Seamus Heaney celebrates 'an idea of the bog as the memory of the landscape, or as a landscape that remembered everything that happened in and to it' (as cited in Lowenthal; 17). Here the landscape functions as a scribe recording the passage of history of the nation and its people. The emotion attached to the landscape relates to its ability to release memory, allowing the past to exist simultaneously with the present. Thus there is a metonymic link between bodies, landscape and nation, in that they are all contiguous; in the examples cited above, they function to temporarily replace one another. Within enunciation, the reference to the landscape makes the reader/viewer think of the nation; the nation, in

5

turn, links it to its people. Each of these terms (landscape, nation, people) derives its value and significance from the others but none is subordinate to the others. Each term recalls the others but does not replace them; their distinction is as important as their similarity. Within the context of displacement from one's nation, often an encounter with a compatriot or a familiar feature of landscape powerfully and painfully evokes the other terms.

Lowenthal further explains that '[n]ational landscape tastes have largely rural roots and a populist democratizing bent . . . Nationhood for most Europeans came when they were still rural, linking peasant emancipation with national sovereignty' (29–30). In Lowenthal's definition, nations and people's relationship with nature/landscape becomes a modern construct, in that the emotion of nationalism supposedly mediates our relationship with our geography. Such an approach to nationalism is implicit in most modern theories of the nation. For instance, Miroslav Hroch suggests that nations are formed because of a memory of a common past, a common linguistic and cultural background which enables communication between the group, and a conception of the equality of all members of the group which is organized as a civil society.[5] For Benedict Anderson, a print culture and a system of transportation which increased the mobility of people facilitated nation-building.[6] For Etienne Balibar, the institution of administrative and fiscal centralization in a monarchy led to the origins of national formation.[7]

While I am in agreement with all these theorists, I suggest that in all of their theories, the contours of landscape and the particularities of the environment, which also are part of nation- and community-building, are subsumed under the term 'territory' which needs to be administered by the people. This discursive shift from national landscape to territory also shifts the latter's position from active to passive. The specificity of the experienced environment gives way to the generalities of the nation, which must be governed. This slippage of meaning from landscape to nation functions within an economy of conscious and unconscious systems, primarily through metaphoric substitution. The landscape which initially unites bodies and creates an identity through place becomes repressed in the formation of the nation. Landscape features or geographical contours always underpin the meaning of a nation and the formation of national boundaries. But in this repression the term 'landscape' becomes meaningless without the mediation of the political construct of the nation. The thews and sinews of the body shaped by our relationship to our specific environment are covered over by the forging of a national identity. In other words, the discourses of nationalism subscribe to a different form of embodiment (as in race/ethnicity) which requires the foregoing of an embodiment mediated through nature: our bodily relationship to our landscape is repressed so that we may come into coherency via the nation. Notions of race are a part of nationalistic discourse.

Lévi-Strauss and embodiment

It is with these foregrounding words that I analyse Lévi-Strauss' 'The Science of the Concrete'. I want to examine the notion of embodiment and disembodiment in this work, which I think is intimately connected to the knowledge acquired through, and meaning-formation in, landscape. In 'The Science of the Concrete' the tropes of seeing, knowing, and classifying converge to construct the 'engineer' and the 'bricoleur'. The former is characterized by his ability to abstract, the latter is inventive; he 'make[s] do with "whatever is at hand"' (17). This work begins with the tabulation, classification and enumeration of the plants, weeds, animals and birds of indigenous peoples and an analysis of their ability to construct concepts. For instance, the Hanunoo of the Philippines, who chew betel leaves, identify four varieties of the areca nut and eight substitutes for them, as well as five varieties of betel leaves and five substitutes. In the Tyuku archipelago even children can identify the types and the sex of trees from wood fragments; members of the Native American Seminole tribe can identify 250 species and varieties of plants; the Navajos, 500; the Hanunoo 2000; the Negritos of the Philippines can identify 45 types of ground-mushrooms and ear-fungi (4–7). The list is overwhelming, and Lévi-Strauss proves that there is a close relationship between the native and 'his' environment.[8]

While the native's epistemology is derived from the natural

world of the environment, the metropolitan inhabitant's system of knowledge is different. As a second step, Lévi-Strauss cites Smith Bowen, who was doing field-work on an African tribe. As she began learning their language she was taught a large number of botanical names and specimens. Lévi-Strauss points out that 'she was unable to identify them, not because of their exotic nature but because she had never taken an interest in the riches and diversities in the plant world' (6). The native, on the contrary, took such interest for granted. Thus, the knowledge production of the African tribe is located not within a developmental discourse but within their close proximity to their environment. In contrast, Smith Bowen is suggested as being urban as she is disinterested in features of botany. In this step Lévi-Strauss does not hierarchise tribal knowledge and metropolitan ways of knowing. However, there is a clear distinction between the native and the metropolitan visitor, in that the latter is always white in Lévi-Strauss' text.[9]

Yet when he links ways of knowing with scientific thought, Lévi-Strauss' work becomes problematic, not for what he says, but for the effects of his analysis. As mentioned earlier, Lévi-Strauss distinguishes between the bricoleur and the engineer, who employ two different modes of scientific thought. The bricoleur uses perception and imagination and the engineer uses concepts. The bricoleur has 'a set of tools and materials which is always finite and is also heterogenous because what it contains bears no relation to the current project' (17). The bricoleur is the indigenous 'scientist' who uses intuition, imagination and signs. In contrast, the engineer uses abstract thoughts, concepts and scientific knowledge: 'It may be said that the engineer questions the Universe while the "bricoleur" addresses himself to a collection left over from human endeavours, that is a subset of culture' (19). The bricoleur works within the science of the concrete, the engineer within the science of the abstract.

Besides a certain construction of nature in this work, what is problematic about Lévi-Strauss' classification is that the engineer is located within a metropolitan modernity which appears to result in an abstraction and a removal from the 'natural' environment, the plants, trees, insects, birds and beasts. Such a removal also results in the production of different forms of knowledge. In terms of locale, the metropolis functions as the binary opposite to the 'natural' environment. But does one stop becoming a native in 'un-natural' environments? Conversely, does being a bricoleur locate one in an early neolithic moment of development? Such a notion is certainly implicit when Lévi-Strauss suggests that the native who is also capable of categorising like his counterpart in modernity does so intuitively rather than through rationale. Onions, garlic, turnips, radishes and mustard are grouped together intuitively even though botany separates *Liliaceae* from *Cruciferae*. Lévi-Strauss states: 'In confirmation of the evidence of the senses, chemistry shows that these different families are united on another plane: they contain sulphur' (12). The bricoleur's system of categorization is indicated by Lévi-Strauss in indigenous Siberian peoples' medicinal practices: among others, spiders and whiteworms are swallowed as a cure for sterility, macerated worms for rheumatism, loach and crayfish for epilepsy, contact with a woodpecker's beak is recommended for toothache and so on (8–9). The logic behind this last is that the woodpecker's beak and a man's tooth are 'seen as "going together"' (9). What is evident in Lévi-Strauss' comparison of the bricoleur and the engineer is not that one categorizes and the other does not, but rather that the basis for categorization is different. One has intuition (as is evident in the example of the sulphurous plants) to guide him; the other scientific proof. The bricoleur is able to make connections between the resemblances and make meanings materialise from possibilities. The engineer is seen as a more advanced model in that he forces the materialization of meanings from concepts which do not resemble each other in the first place.

To sum up, the distinction between the two functions at two levels in the text. First, at the level of language, wherein the bricoleur is entrapped in the web of nature, fauna and flora, and the magical world. The engineer, however, is discursively connected to the laws of physics and chemistry in anthropological discourse. Second, the difference between the bricoleur and engineer starts functioning within a discourse of development rather than one of difference—the bricoleur's intuitive knowledge and mythological thought is primitive in comparison to the engineer's ability to think in the abstract.

Furthermore, in this text, the bricoleur is always raced as black; the engineer white.

But what is the relationship between whiteness and the environment, the engineer and nature? In *Imperial Eyes*, Mary Louise Pratt suggests a different trajectory for the Western individual's relationship with nature.[10] In Pratt's narrative of events there is a definite shift in 1735 in Western natural history with the publication of Carl Linné's (Linnaeus') *The System of Nature*, which came up with a classification system for all plants 'known and unknown according to the characteristics of their reproductive parts' (24). Linnaeus categorized plants according to 26 basic configurations of stamens and pistils which could even include those plants unknown to Europe. The implied 'chaos' of the natural world was brought to order by this classification. Here the premised chaotic nature of the natural world is a retroactive construct whose sole function is to be a binary opposite to the order of Western classification. It is precisely Linnaeus' system of classification, which was able to bring order to what is not yet known, that underpins the difference between the bricoleur and the engineer. While the bricoleur could classify only perceived differences and similarities (as in the connection between the woodpecker's beak and a man's tooth), the engineer's abstract system could classify plants not yet known or seen. For Pratt, this planetary systematization of nature dovetailed with two other totalizing projects, the circumnavigation of the globe and the mapping of all the coastlines in the world. The classification of plants thus became the counterpart of the mapping of coastlines—as it were the mapping of surfaces. Eventually Linnaeus' classificatory system included the animal kingdom (including man, classifying *Homo sapiens* into six varieties: the wild man, the American, European, Asiatic, African and the monster). Pratt points out that this systematization was not only European discourse about non-European worlds but an urban discourse about non-urban worlds; it was also a bourgeois discourse about peasant worlds, because Linnaeus' system intersected with urban intervention in agricultural production, 'seeking to rationalize production, increase surpluses, intensify exploitation of peasant labor, and administer the food production on which the urban centers utterly depended' (35). It is in this intersection that the difference between the bricoleur and the engineer perhaps rests. The bricoleur envisaged in his classificatory relationship with nature is seen as pre-capitalistic, in contrast to the engineer who is located within modernity and capitalism.

I want to pick up on merely one aspect of the difference, that of the discourse of incarceration and its opposite, freedom to move. Arjun Appadurai locates the binary opposition between the indigene and the European produced in Linnaean discourse within the usage of the term 'native', which for him functions as a respectable substitute for terms like primitive.[11] Appadurai points out that while the etymology of the word native indicates a person who is born in and thus belongs to a certain place, in practice it refers to only those people who belong to certain parts of the world at a distance from the metropolitan West. Indeed, among the varieties of definitions of the term native in the *Oxford English Dictionary* are: 'one born in bondage'; or 'one of the original or usual inhabitants of a country, as distinguished from strangers or foreigners; now esp. one belonging to non-European and imperfectly civilized or savage race'; or as 'a coloured person, a black'. For Appadurai, this tying of the native to their particular place or environment results in their incarceration in discursive practice:

> Natives are those who are somehow confined to places by their connection to what the place permits. Thus all the language of niches, of foraging, of material skill, of slowly evolving technologies, is actually also a language of incarceration. In this instance confinement is not simply a function of the mysterious, even metaphysical attachment of native to physical places, but a function of their adaptations to their environments.(37)

In Appadurai's reckoning they become prisoners of a mode of thought, as the bricoleur so obviously is. The science of the concrete ultimately becomes the space of incarceration and, in extension, the place of blackness.

Crosby and the trope of mobility

If the Lévi-Strauss text represents the native (read: black) as pre-capitalistic as well as influenced by magical thought, unable

11

to think abstractly but able to categorize, enmeshed and shaped physically and intellectually by his environment as well as imprisoned within it, how are whiteness and nature represented? For this, I must turn to Crosby's text *Ecological Imperialism*, which tracks the natural habitat of the Western European. Alfred Crosby posits the question, why do European emigrants and their descendants live in such diverse places as Canada, the United States, Brazil, Argentina, Uruguay, Australia and New Zealand? Crosby's analysis shows that all these countries lie in similar latitudes on both sides of the equator. They are all almost completely in the temperate zone and so have roughly similar climates, which has led to the intense cultivation of wheat and the production of cattle, enough to produce huge surpluses. These factors led to the whitening of what Crosby calls the Neo-Europes. Crosby gives us some astonishing statistics: between 1820 and 1930, over 50 million Europeans, or one-fifth of the entire population of Europe in 1820, migrated to the Neo-Europes (5). Between 1750 and 1930 the population of the Neo-Europes increased by almost 14 times, whereas that of the rest of the world increased by only 2.5 times. Between 1750 and 1930, while Asians increased 2.3 times in population, Caucasians increased by over 5 times. This surge in population resulted in the acquisition of 30 million square kilometres of land outside Europe by the Caucasians. These statistics call into question the positing of Asia and Africa as 'overpopulated' in this century.

This fecundity of Caucasians is linked to the fecundity of the soil in the Neo-Europes in Crosby's work. The geographical advantages to the Neo-Europes sounds like a description from a real estate catalogue. Their location in the temperate zone—between the Tropics and 50 degrees latitude North and South—means that these places have high photosynthetic potential, abundant sunlight, plentiful water and an eight-month growing season, which has resulted in the production of huge surpluses of food (295–308). Crosby constructs a narrative of the creation of the Neo-Europes—or Europe away from Europe—due to three distinct advantages that Caucasians had over the indigenes of these latitudes: the neolithic revolution came earlier to Europe (and Asia); being from densely populated areas, Europeans (and Asians) have developed greater immunity to infections; European (and a large proportion of Asian) bodies also had the ability to digest milk, which enabled them to take up a pastoral life, raise cattle and stave off starvation, which people in the past were constantly threatened with.

Crosby's Neo-European, unlike his indigenous counterpart in Lévi-Strauss who is shaped by his surroundings, in fact shapes his environment to his advantage. Crosby draws a list of geographical conquests and how their biota were reprogrammed so they could be Europeanized. For instance, in the Canaries, the Spaniards imported species of Old World plants and animals that were doing well in the Mediterranean. Cattle, camels, rabbits, pigeons, ducks, honeybees, grapevines, pears, apples, melons and, most importantly, sugar were all introduced by the Spaniards. In the process of Europeanization, the Guanches, natives of the Canaries were all obliterated. This narrative of Europeanization was repeated from Virginia to New South Wales, and from Brazil and Argentina to New Zealand. The Europeans brought with them plants, trees, and even weeds on the soles of their shoes (for instance, the Old World peach and orange trees achieved weed status in North America). Even grass was brought from the Old World to plant in the New as it held up to cattle better. William Penn, for whom Pennsylvania is named, grew some Old World grass in his courtyard. Europeanization required the native biota to give way to the imported plants and hard-hoofed cattle which provided the protein so desperately craved by the settlers. Ultimately, the weeds or the exotica saved the topsoils of the Neo-Europes, which were unsuited to the hooves, shoes, and felling of native forests by the Caucasians. Similarly, horses, sheep, cattle, honeybees, pigs and rats, too, were knowingly and unknowingly imported to the Neo-Europes, as were Old World diseases such as smallpox, chickenpox and measles, diphtheria, trachoma, whooping cough, bubonic plague, malaria, typhoid, cholera, amoebic dysentery and influenza. The Neo-Europes and their indigenous inhabitants, geographically isolated from the Old World for many centuries, had not built any immunity towards the exotic weeds, plants, diseases and people they fell prey to. The only New World disease transported to the Old World was venereal syphilis.

Reading Crosby, we can see that in his analytic framework there is a metonymic link between the virginal helpless lands of the New World, the fauna, flora and native birds, and the recently neolithic and helpless indigenes. This paradigmatic group recedes and is obliterated by the onslaught of the diseases, weeds, feral horses, pigs, rats and Europeans, who are all also metonymically linked as the oppositional paradigmatic group of signifiers. The Europeans prove too powerful for the indigenes. What is disturbing to me is not what Crosby says, for he records historical facts, but rather how he says it. Once again the indigene and his environment are held immobile against the repeated onslaught of the settler, who alone has the ability and freedom to move and change his landscape. Even the settler's diseases and the fauna and flora, the latter normally fixed and rooted to the earth, move along with him. Most importantly, Europe as a trope travels as well, and reproduces Europe in non-European spaces. In Crosby's narrative, if Caucasians were once indigenous to Europe, Europe becomes located not in a fixed geographical space on the globe any more but from 50 degrees North and South to the tropics of Capricorn and Cancer on both sides of the equator. Again, if the Caucasians are in pursuit of protein, which would become a surplus in the Neo-Europes, neither Asians, Middle Easterners nor Africans in this text seem to crave protein.

What troubles me in Crosby's narrative is if Africans, Asians and Middle Easterners were subject like the Europeans to the same diseases, same weeds, and same ability to digest milk—at least most of them—why did they not travel and Asianize or Africanize other parts of the globe? Crosby almost anticipates this question in his simple suggestion that people stay in the climates and geographical environments they are familiar with. So I suppose since the equatorial regions were fully occupied and all of *terra nullius* was in the temperate zones, it was left to the Europeans, the inhabitants of the temperate zone, to 'discover' and settle Neo-Europes. One could say that in Crosby the desire to move and to travel seems to be characteristic only of those indigenous to the temperate zones. By being indigenous to the temperate zones they are transformed into citizens of the world, thus detaching themselves from their indigenous status. The rest of us are immobile, pinned, raced and incarcerated in our particular spaces.

Ultimately, we can see in Crosby's analysis that this Europeanisation of the Neo-Europes also leads to the disjunction between the Caucasian and the environment. Liisa Malkki astutely questions the cultural forms of certain questions after witnessing the linking of the rainforest and indigenous people. She asks,

> Why should the rights of 'Indigenous People' be seen as an environmental issue? Are people 'rooted' in their native soil somehow more natural, their rights somehow more sacred, than those of other exploited and oppressed people? And one wonders, if an 'Indigenous Person' wanted to move away, to the city, would [he or she quit being indigenous]? (29)

Here we see that the ecological immobility of the indigenous person as a discursive botanical construct functions to locate the settler as mobile, free, taking his environment with him in ships, boats, planes, and on the soles of his shoes. While the indigene's body comes into being and is shaped by native bioregions, the settler as exotica spreads like a weed but becomes disembodied not only because he is not in his native bioregion, but also because the Europeanization of the Neo-Europes makes the European the Universal Subject. The very term 'universal' suggests a subject who is able to take anyone's place, to occupy any place, a process that occurred in the transformation of the Neo-Europes. The Caucasian is disembodied, mobile, absent of the marks that physically immobilize the native.

The embodiment of disembodiment

What I have suggested so far is that there are terms metonymically linked with the settler and the native, two terms for each. For the settler they are 'mobility' and 'disembodiment'; for the native they are 'incarceration' and 'black embodiment'. Such a statement is a theoretical commonplace reproducing Cartesian notions of the mind/body split, wherein Lévi-Strauss and Crosby's blackness and whiteness assume the status of the Cartesian body and the mind respectively. In the Sixth Meditation in particular, Descartes finalizes the distinction between the body and mind.[12] For him the body is divisible and can be distinguished between its parts whereas the mind cannot:

15

'And although the whole mind seems to be united to the whole body, yet, if a foot or an arm, or any other part is separated from my body, it is certain that, on that account, nothing has been taken away from my mind . . .' (164). This subordination of the body and its predication to the mind is amplified in his most famous pronouncement in the fourth chapter of *Discourse on Method*: 'I think, therefore I am.' Here he concludes: 'that if I had only ceased to think, although all the rest of what I ever imagined had been true [of having a body, a world, and a place] I would have no reason to believe that I existed' (54). Thus the notion of Universality which I referred to earlier, which de-materializes and de-biologizes the body, and unhinges it from a specific place (an implicit premise in Crosby and Lévi-Strauss' Western or white body) is in continuum with Descartes' understanding of the identity of the mind, in that in Cartesian thinking the condition of the body is unimportant and soon falls out of sight due to the primacy of the mind. Linking Descartes with Lévi-Strauss and Crosby's disembodiment of whiteness suggests that within discourse the indigene functions as the body and the Caucasian as the mind.

Within the context of racial discourse then, can whiteness only ever be disembodied? Is mobility and knowledge predicated on the dematerialization of the body? Is there a framework which also embodies whiteness? In this next section I will read a fragment of Maurice Merleau-Ponty's *Phenomenology of Perception*, a text which, though normally never contextualized within postcolonial studies, is rich for its connection of the body with the environment. In this text, Merleau-Ponty reverses the Cartesian subordination of the body and locates it as primary for the perception of the world and the formation of knowledge. Elsewhere Merleau-Ponty suggests that '[p]erceptual behaviour emerges from relations to a situation and to an environment which are not merely the working of a pure, knowing subject . . .'[13] Whereas the disembodiment of whiteness for Crosby and Lévi-Strauss grants it the subject position (and, by extension, blackness as the object of inquiry), for Merleau-Ponty bodies are never just subject or object. He states that what prevents the body 'ever being an object, ever being "completely constituted" is that it is that by which there are objects. It is neither tangible nor visible insofar as it is that which sees and touches'.[14]

He asserts that since the body leads to the perception of objects, it has to be located as subject; it cannot itself be objectified completely.

In the chapter 'The Spatiality of One's Own Body and Motility', Merleau-Ponty connects the relationship between the body, perception of space and movement which obliquely refers to the themes of race and place raised by Crosby and Lévi-Strauss. In three steps—the meaning of the body image, the body's symbiotic relationship with landscape, and the acquisition of habit—Merleau-Ponty theorizes on *all* bodies, black and white. This chapter is suggestive and interesting in that it embodies whiteness in the same terms as blackness. Body image itself is located in movement in that an awareness of the body is possible only through its dynamic nature and in the tasks that it does (100). Its awareness of its spatiality can come into being only through its interaction with a situation, not through its location in a static space. This development of body image and spatiality is central for its comprehension of being 'in-the-world' (101) and provides it perspective and the ability to see, judge and rationalize.

Merleau-Ponty also suggests that there is a symbiotic relationship between the body and landscape in that 'a knowledge of place . . . is reducible to a sort of co-existence with that place . . .' (105). He points out that a marking of boundaries is necessary to give a sense of organization to the world, thus building 'into the geographical setting a behavioural one, a system of meanings outwardly expressive of the subject's internal activity' (112). Thus body image and embodiment, the sense of one's body and an awareness of physicality, are located within one's environment. Application of Merleau-Ponty's system to discourses on nationalism suggests that feelings of patriotism, fondness for one's country, the love of a familiar landscape, all go beyond an emotion, as Benedict Anderson would have it, and are specifically a physical response because our body functions optimally and has a sense of well-being within a familiar geographical setting. Certainly, such a theme can be construed in a reading of Merleau-Ponty's chapter, for he suggests a link between the symbolic and the visual: 'Visual contents are taken up, utilized and sublimated to the level of thought by a symbolical power which transcends them' (127). Indeed, the visual aspect of landscape results in the construction of its meaning; this construction in turn elevates the landscape to the status of symbol, giving rise to a wealth of emotion in the subject, all of which are mediated through the body.

Finally, Merleau-Ponty links the formation of habit and habitual movement of the body and one's location in an environment, and suggests that 'the acquisition of habit [is] a rearrangement and renewal of the schema' (142). For him, since the body is not merely an object, acquiring a habit constantly revises and renews the understanding of the body. The body mediates with the world and actively participates in it. As such, for him, 'our [habits are] not long-established custom' (146) because such a theorization of the body locates it in the passive, a ground *upon* which habits are formed. He uses the example of the body learning to dance, which once learnt constantly re-enacts the originary spontaneity; the habit of dance recomposes the body, which rearranges itself anew in this situation and reveals its constant renewal only in motility.

Merleau-Ponty thus absolutely insists on embodiment in place and the mutually interdependent relationship between the body, identity and place. Furthermore, knowledge formation is linked not to the body as object, but body as subject, in that it is absorbed and analysed only via the body. Finally, he suggests that bodies are shaped by one's environment and landscape and a sense of this is grasped only when it is in motion. As such his framework would find the correlation between mobility and disembodiment in Lévi-Strauss' text untenable, for mobility is central to embodiment in Merleau-Ponty's theorizing.

Does Merleau-Ponty's notion of the body speak for all sorts of bodies then: white/black, male/female, young/old, to name a few of the binaries? His theorizing suggests a commonality of experience and shaping to the bodies which defies the existence of binaries which are constructed within relationships of power. If all bodies responded in similar ways to features in the environment, then there should be a community among them. However, one can see that instead, the existence of power inequities in categories such as race, class and gender suggest otherwise. For instance, Iris Marion Young suggests that the anonymous body theorized by Merleau-Ponty reflects an absence of gendered existence in its construction.[15] For young, feminine bodies experience phenomenal space different to that which masculine bodies experience. Furthermore, feminine bodies experience themselves as objects. Among further differences, women generally are more timid about their bodies and see space as an enclosure. More recently, Shannon Sullivan points out that cultural specificities also participate in shaping our bodies.[16] She cites the example of an Asian student who refuses to make eye contact with her by tilting her head deferentially, thus indicating her respect for authority. Sullivan as American could read the student's body as indicating shiftiness and inattentiveness; she concludes that the student's body in this case must also be read as having a particular culture, nationality and gender.

To this extent, Merleau-Ponty's theorization of the body and its experience of movement seems to be race and gender specific. If whiteness and maleness can be experienced corporeally at all, then it is via Merleau-Ponty's framework. However, his framework seems to locate whiteness in a *metaphysical space*, and confers upon it the ability to contemplate on physical things, abstract objects, values, necessities and facts. The distance between Merleau-Ponty's articulation of the phenomenology of perception and Lévi-Strauss' engineer is very short indeed. Within metaphysical space the broad structures of reality are examined but the examination is always race and gender specific. In contrast, the native is incarcerated in *physical* place and caught in the web of nature, categorizing facts but unable to analyse, perceiving material reality but unable to abstract. The contrast between the native in physical space and the white male is that between 'meaning' (for others) and 'knowing' for the self, and the power differential therein.

Bodies and representation

And it is Frantz Fanon's anger that speaks to me finally. In *Black Skin, White Masks*, he points to the inadequacy of the analysis of the corporeal schema without contextualizing it within a historical-racial schema as well.[17] His sense of the body is provided for him not by:

> 'residual sensations and perceptions primarily of a tactile, vestibular, kinesthetic and visual character' but by the other,

the white man, who had woven me out of a thousand details, anecdotes, stories. I thought what I had in hand was to construct a physiological self, to balance self, to localize sensations . . . [Instead the words that follow me are], 'Look a Negro . . . Mama, see the Negro! I am frightened!' (111–12)

Fanon rages over the fact that the black body is only ever represented, never experienced. Such a secondary experience of the body is different from the experience of the anonymous body in Merleau-Ponty's work. In his definition of motility Merleau-Ponty constructs objects prior to their representation and suggests that the body learns to move towards objects which call out to it (138). For Merleau-Ponty, body and object seem to be pure entities unmediated by any Lacanian sense of desire, loss, and lack or issues of representation. Here Merleau-Ponty's body is one imbued with agency, outside and alongside language, representation and the body as a discursive construct. Fanon's anger, however, suggests that the black body is never a body with agency; it is always only a discursive construct.

Lévi-Strauss and Crosby's representations of the black body must be read within the context of their positioning of themselves in relation to their positioning of the native. In her critique of Foucault and Deleuze in 'Can the Subaltern Speak?', Gayatri Spivak clarifies the two different meanings of the verb 'to represent'.[18] She suggests that in their desire to give a voice to the masses by being their spokespersons, Foucault and Deleuze refuse to analyse the role of the intellectual as influenced by dominant ideology. According to Spivak, the two philosophers assume the transparency of the role of the intellectual who merely voices the concerns of the subaltern masses by functioning as their proxy, by representing them, but who himself is devoid of any agency. She states that: 'Two senses of representation are being run together: representation as "speaking for", as in politics, and representation as "re-presentation", as in art or philosophy' (275). Representation in art and philosophy suggests that reality is the underlying presence. Conflating representation as proxy with representation as removed from reality by using the same verb, to represent, she argues, suggests that the person who speaks for the masses also speaks the truth and speaks within reality. Such a conflation of the two senses of the verb also results in a lack of examination of what is essentially a power relationship between the intellectual and the masses, for the intellectual is also a product of dominant ideology and thus cannot be transparent or devoid of any markers of self-interest.

In such a reading of the discourse and scholarship on embodiment, Merleau-Ponty's body cannot quite theorize blackness adequately, for the black body is only within representation a construct of scholars like Lévi-Strauss and Crosby (and myself, for I too am implicated in this construction of blackness as a theorizable discursive construct). If the verb 'to represent' is used in the sense of proxy by Lévi-Strauss et al. in their representations of blackness, then their enterprise fails to represent blackness except as homogenized and within a power relationship. If, instead, the verb is used in the sense of art and philosophy, as in 're-present', or with reference to a pre-existing presence of reality and truth, then again their intentions go askew and the referential relationship between representation and the real becomes unhinged. Instead of re-presenting the native, their theorizations are more pertinent to the encoding, disembodying and mobilizing of whiteness. In their analysis, representations of blackness become parasitic on further representations of whiteness in an infinitely circular and regressive pattern.[19] The homogenization and representation of blackness covers over Lévi-Strauss et al.'s own imbrication in an uncritical acceptance of dominant ideology. Ultimately, in this line of reading, there is indeed a convergence of Merleau-Ponty's work with Lévi-Strauss' and Crosby's, for the motility of the body with agency and outside of representation, appears to be reserved for the white (male) body.

The discourse within which blackness is embodied, however, goes beyond that caused by the politics of representation for it is connected to the perception of space as well. In *The Production of Space*, Henri Léfèbvre analyses the way space is normally perceived and suggests that it is normally read as a text. He says that: 'To underestimate, ignore and diminish space amounts to the overestimation of texts, written matter, and writing systems, along with the readable and visible, to the point of assigning these a monopoly on intelligibility'.[20]

It is such a reading of the representation of space/place that allows it to be schematized as measurements and maps,

21

and as the product of writing. This perception of place is demanded by imperialism, which does not take into account the dynamic, dialectical nature of space which is suggested in its use in everyday life. As Ian Buchanan points out, '[s]ince space is produced by its occupants, and the nature of space changes with the actions of the occupiers, its present—its everyday-ness—can never be mapped'.[21] It is only through a consideration of the everyday-ness of space that agency becomes visible in the black body. The heterogeneity of the embodiment of blackness is effaced alongside that of the account of the quotidian, the everyday-ness of space, and are both reduced to mere representations. The everyday-lived-in-ness of black bodies in their environment is effaced along with the everyday-ness experience of dynamic space. To put it in another way, representation can only occur within relationships of power. At the level of discourse, the signifier never fully approximates the signified within language and representation. To this extent the discursive construction of blackness is metonymically linked to the schematization of space and the function of the signifier.

To sum up, within specific texts (Lévi-Strauss and Crosby) there is a construction of blackness as being trapped within the web of nature whereas the white body has the freedom of movement. Such a freedom also disembodies whiteness. This construction of the black body freezes it as a pre-modern, pre-capitalist construction, which in turn enables whiteness to be located within capitalism as well as modernity. The anonymous body constructed by Merleau-Ponty in his theorization of embodiment and motility seems to appear outside the politics of representation. In the next chapter I will work with two texts from John Locke and Sigmund Freud, who both work intensely on the notion of bodily identity. In so doing I want to examine further the relationship between representation and the formation of identity.

The embodiment of blackness

I have before me the fragments of three seemingly disparate texts from three different writers working within three theoretical frameworks, who all define identity as corporeal. The three writers are of three different national origins, from two different centuries, two different professions, and of two different colours, white and black. They are similar only in the sense that they are all men. They are John Locke, Sigmund Freud and Frantz Fanon. First John Locke, the English physician-turned-philosopher, who in 1690 underscored the centrality of identity as somatic. In *An Essay Concerning Human Understanding*, he states: 'the identity of the same *man* [sic] consists . . . in nothing but a participation of the same continued life, by constantly fleeting particles of matter, in succession vitally united in the same organized body' (444).[1]

Locke's emphasis on the importance of categorizing identity through somatic sameness must be situated within its historical and cultural framework—the English Enlightenment. In 'Identifying Identity', Philip Gleason indicates that the word 'identity' was coopted from within the terminologies of logic and algebra by politico-philosophic discourse, initially by Locke and then by David Hume, in their discussions of the distinction between mind and body, human and animal.[2] For Locke, identity is encapsulated within the same body which functions as a bag or vessel that contains life and grants identity to the individual as well as separating him from other humans and animals. However, while identity is located within the sameness of the body, this notion of sameness can be purchased only by the effacement of the physiological differences that wear and tear, aging and the passage of time can bring upon the body.

While the timeless body is emphasized within the concept of identity, Locke simultaneously insists on the body as being located within temporality when he defines identity as coming into being when we compare *'anything as existing at any determined time and place'* with *'itself existing at another time'* (Locke's emphasis; 440). The continuity of forms proves their existence. This notion of continuity takes us back to the etymological root of 'identity' (from Latin *idem*, meaning 'the same'). The history of the individual—the individual within linear temporality—proves the continued existence of a person or thing: 'one thing cannot have two beginnings of existence, nor two things one beginning; it being impossible for two things of the same kind to be or exist in the same instant, in the very same place; or one and the same thing in different places' (440). Thus within Locke's chapter on identity, temporality is under-scored, yet simultaneously denied, especially within the context of the changes wrought upon the body by the ravages of time. The form of the aging body itself is located as static, the same, perceived as unchanging. It is the mind that is analogically bound to time which gets to rove and to change.

I now want to make temporal and geographical shifts by juxtaposing Locke's words beside some excerpts from Sigmund Freud's definitions of bodily identity. *The Ego and the Id*, written in 1923, contains the oft-cited line that the ego is 'first and foremost, a bodily ego; it is not merely a surface entity, but is itself the projection of a surface'.[3] Freud, here, distinguishes between the cutaneous and the representation of the bodily frame, the material sense of the body as opposed to (mis)identifications. He emphasizes the binary structure of identity taking his reader beyond the literal to the metaphorical, from a singular body to the dually-perceived body, split between the somatic and the symbolic. Freud adds a footnote to this 1923 text:

> The ego is ultimately derived from bodily sensations, chiefly from those springing from the surface of the body. It may

thus be regarded as a mental projection of the surface of the body, besides, as we have seen above, representing superfices of the mental apparatus. (26)

The ego, though composed of bodily sensations, is also a 'projection', a 'represent[ation]' of that same body. Freud collapses differences between real and represented, originary and secondary, with regard to bodily sensations. Identification is always already misidentification. The Cartesian mind/body split gets scrambled. By collapsing the difference between the two senses of the body Freud simultaneously underscores the dual comprehension of the body. Within a Freudian mapping of the ego/body, in opposition to Merleau-Ponty, there can be no one-to-one correspondence between the body's surface and a direct sensation of it, for the body's surface is always mediated through a perception of it. Such a theorization is necessary for Freud, since within the psychoanalytic framework the ego is read as outlining the erotogenicity of bodily zones and organs.[4]

I draw attention to identity and the ego within Freudian psychoanalytic traditions because Freud's mapping of the narcissistic/bodily ego becomes the cornerstone for Lacan's connections between the corporeality of identity and specular (mirrored) perceptions of it.[5] The child passing through the mirror-stage transforms its sensations of itself as an anatomical and physiological object to become a cultural/social entity. The body becomes the visual perception of it rather than an experience, the sensation of space/place it previously occupied is important only insofar as it gives the subject historical perspective. As within the philosophical discourse of Locke, so also in Freudian psychoanalytic discourse, the body as materiality with its own logic and agency gets left behind within static space, a punctuation mark in the maturation and socialization process of the subject. However, there is a slight difference: while Locke's historiography is linear, Freud and Lacan's are always conferred in retrospect, in a loop as opposed to a strictly linear trajectory.

I want to complete the collage by referring to the third selected text before I analyse what can be teased out by this juxtaposition. I again move geographically, now to Algeria to the hospital at Blida-Joinville and the words of its director and resident psychiatrist, Frantz Fanon. I again choose familiar sentences, words which are oft-cited. Curiously in this instance, Fanon discusses neither his identity as a black subject of French colonialism in Antilles, his place of origin, nor his current location in French Algeria, but rather an incident during his sojourn in France. I refer, of course, to the famous incident in the fifth chapter of *Black Skin, White Mask*s when a white child, its sex unspecified upon seeing Fanon in his blackness audibly exclaims to its mother, 'Mama, see the Negro! I'm frightened!'[6] Fanon's response:

> [my] corporeal schema crumbled, its place taken by a racial epidermal schema . . . I took myself far off from my own presence, far indeed, and made myself an object. What else could it be for me but an amputation, an excision, a hemorrhage that splattered my whole body with black blood? (112)

Here Fanon points to the negrophobia hovering over European/metropolitan spaces and within Western ontology/epistemology which results in his experience of his body as 'a triple person' (112): he occupies space; he experiences his body; and to the white child, he appears as 'the evanescent other, hostile but not opaque, transparent, not there, disappeared' (112). Here a representation of him also makes him disappear. Fanon's physical response to what his body signifies is 'nausea' (112). He states, 'All I wanted was to be a man among other men. I wanted to come lithe and young into a world that was ours and to help to build it together' (112–13). Fanon rages against the strictly epidermal identity bestowed upon blacks in colonized and metropolitan spaces which is different from the corporeal schema normally reserved for whites. Instead of the 'residual sensations and perceptions primarily of a tactile, vestibular, kinesthetic, and visual character' (Jean L'Hermitte as quoted by Fanon; 111) which is the legacy inherited by the white corporeal schema, what is bestowed upon blacks is a historical-racial schema woven out of a 'thousand details, anecdotes, stories' (Fanon; 111). If the corporeal/bodily ego provides perspective for the white man, as Freud and Lacan would have it, the black man is pure representation for Fanon.[7] The black man is hypervisible yet invisible simultaneously, but he himself lacks 'perspective'.

Instead he functions to grant a perspective to the white man. If the corporeality of (white) man grants him equality and political space, and if the civil state is the metaphor par excellence of the rational bent of man, as Locke espouses in his political philosophy, for Fanon this very corporeality of black man and his particular sense of his body prevents them from achieving this state of equality. At best, it locates his alterity (otherness), but an alterity constructed precisely by Western ontology/epistemology. In a passage where Fanon conflates Greek with the notions of Western and whiteness, he says:

> Yes, we are—we Negroes—backward, simple, free in our behavior. That is because for us the body is not something opposed to what you call the mind. We are in the world . . . Emotive sensitivity. *Emotion is completely Negro as reason is Greek.* (Fanon's emphasis; 126–7)

The white man transcends and transforms the body into will and rationale, a perception and a perspective, whereas the black man embodies the Body. Though the Negro functions as other to the White, however, it is within this location of otherness that a trace of alterity can be found: 'The white man had the anguished feeling that I was escaping from him and that I was taking something with me . . . [I]t was obvious that I had a secret' (128).

Blackness functions in two different senses here. First, if the black man is a construction connoting the body, and the black epidermis a fictive representation composed of a thousand details and anecdotes, blackness is also the constitutive condition, enabling Western epistemology as well as Western ontology. Yet secondly, blackness is simultaneously a substitution for, as well as the displacement of, a blackness in the alternative sense that Fanon hints at. For Fanon the blackness composed through anecdotes is itself a metaphor for the blackness that remains a secret, and is inarticulable in the corporeal fabric of the black body. The supplementary nature of Fanon's blackness must be excluded for the internal coherence of a system divided into blacks and whites to function, a system defined from the vantage point of whiteness.

I have juxtaposed these three texts, one from the liberal humanist framework (Locke), one from the psychoanalytic framework (Freud), and one from a postcolonial framework (Fanon), because all three traditions are familiar and because they bespeak the reproduction of the Nature/Culture divide: identity as self-reflection; identity as gendered; and identity as other. In all three traditions identity is written on the material body, yet there is a difference in the way bodies materialize. My selections of Locke and Freud are not arbitrary. As mentioned earlier, the term 'identity' prior to its usage in Locke's *An Essay* was used within logic and algebra rather than to describe an individual within the discourses of social sciences or the humanities. Furthermore, Locke's text was immensely influential on the Enlightenment movement in England and the Continent. His work, most importantly, is the cornerstone of the discourse of liberal democracy which underpins Western democracies. Freud—the father of psychoanalysis—is also useful here since the psychoanalytic framework has contributed vastly to an understanding of identity, identification, self/other and same/other. Fanon, read contrapuntally against Locke and Freud, creates a trace of an embodiment which falls outside of liberal democratic and even psychoanalytic discourse.

In this chapter I will examine how the body functions discursively within the concept of identity. Given that the body/skin is the visible site of difference, I will examine the way in which embodiment is languaged within liberal democratic and psychoanalytic discourses. Reading Locke and Freud backwards, via Fanon, inscribes a trace of another form of the body, not unlike Derrida's concept of 'différance'. Embodiment within the frameworks of Freud and Locke would then indicate a closure of presence in a system that produces whiteness (and its opposite, blackness). These binary terms also suggest an originary embodiment which simultaneously dispels any notions of originary and secondary in that it is a discursive effect of these terms and can manifest itself only in traces. The body in both Locke and Freud seems to function as the point of (non) origin of identity and race. My intention in reading bodily identity in Locke and Freud is to tease out the occluded black body in space/place—that which is simultaneously theorized and which exists in the traces and interstices of Locke and Freud's works.

Bodily identity in Locke

Locke's chapter 'Of Identity and Diversity', first published in the second edition of *An Essay Concerning Human Understanding*, was written on the urging of William Molyneux, a member of Trinity College, Dublin, who shared a collegial relationship with Locke.[8] Within Locke's own lifetime, his work was translated into French and Latin and occasioned much response from contemporary scholars in Britain and Europe. I wish to underscore the influence that *An Essay* has exerted, its impact on philosophical and political thought in its attempt to forge an account of human knowledge. My juxtaposition of Locke with Fanon is one which I hope will tease out the 'collusive forms of European knowledge', as Robert Young describes the Enlightenment project in *White Mythologies*, and its implication in the history of European colonialism.[9] In short, I hope to trace the relationship between Locke's *Essay* and Fanon's *Black Skin, White Masks*.

'Of Identity and Diversity' is contextualized within the ongoing debate on the doctrine of the natural immortality of the soul.[10] In his two-volume work on Locke's *Essay*, Michael Ayers writes:

> In the light of criticism of traditional views of what a *man* is, Locke then proceeded to offer his own careful definition of a *person*: 'a thinking, intelligent Being, that has reason and reflection, and can consider it self as it self, the same thinking thing in different times and places'. He wished to derive the principle of individuation of a 'thinking thing' from the nature of thinking itself: it is 'that consciousness, which is inseparable from thinking, and it seems . . . essential to it. It being impossible for anyone to perceive without perceiving that he does perceive.' (emphasis in original)[11]

It is within this context of individuation and distinction, between the thinking thing and the nature of thinking, that Locke had to establish the centrality of the body. References to the body as the scaffolding upon which identity and difference rest are numerous in Locke's chapter. In one instance he insists on the mutual interdependence of the body and soul in the construction of identity. He states:

> For should the soul of a prince, carrying with it the con-
> sciousness of the prince's past life, enter and inform the body
> of a cobbler, as soon as deserted by his own soul, every one
> sees he would be the same *person* with the prince accountable
> only for the prince's actions: but who would say it was the
> same *man*: but he would be the same cobbler to everyone
> besides himself. (Locke's emphasis; Book II: 457)

Here identity is located not only in the consciousness of the
subject or person but in the perception that everybody else
has of the subject. In this instance, society, on seeing the
subject, sees the cobbler, notwithstanding the princely soul
lodged within a cobbler's body. Here consciousness is placed
as secondary to identity, the somatic form being the deciding
factor of identity.[12] I want to emphasize this passage because
the prioritizing of the body in the passage described above
and elsewhere earlier slips from view as Locke continues his
dissertation on identity.

The passage from Locke with which I began this chapter
in its entirety states:

> Identity of the same Man consists . . . in nothing but a
> participation of the same continued Life, by constantly fleet-
> ing Particles of matter, in succession vitally united to the
> same organized Body. He that shall place the identity of man
> in anything else, but like that of other animals, in one fitly
> organized body, taken in any one instant, and from thence
> continued, under one organization of life, in several succes-
> sively fleeting particles of matter united to it, will find it hard
> to make an embryo, one of years, mad, and sober, the same
> man by any supposition, that will make it possible for Seth,
> Ismael, Socrates, St. Austin, and Caesar Borgia to be the
> same man. (Book II: 444)

Alexander Campbell Fraser in annotating this passage points
out that Locke makes a distinction between physical identity
and moral or personal identity. For both Locke and Fraser
the difference between the two lies with the former kind of
identity being located in his physical senses and the latter in
the continued self-consciousness (444).

This slippage of the concept of identity leading from the
awareness of the body to a self-consciousness parallels the
maturation process of the rational man who progresses from
body to mind, and becomes the cornerstone of Locke's

theoretical framework. Locke locates bodily identity as necessary to separate man from beast in the construction of civil society within liberal humanist thought and also provides the grounds for authorizing individuated identity, permeated with a consciousness and a sense of history. Nevertheless, notwithstanding his insistence on the importance of the body, he suggests that it is ultimately consciousness that must be valorized over the former.

What must be noted in this distinction between the two types of identity is that it reproduces the Cartesian mind–body split. A series of binary opposites starts functioning: bodily identity vs. identity with consciousness; body vs. mind; being vs. becoming; senses vs. reason. Furthermore, Locke's framework locates the body within static space and time, and the mind or consciousness as having the ability to transform, to grow, and to develop. Yet this effect is achieved peculiarly, in that in the passage quoted above there is an overabundance of words denoting body, 'one fitly organized body', 'particles of matter', 'one organization of life', 'an embryo', 'same contained life', and 'same organized body', all of which seemingly emphasize the solid, material corpus only to undermine it as less important in the hierarchy of mind and body and their function in the civil state.

Why insist on the centrality of the body to the civil state only to locate it promptly as less important?[13] It is within the context of this gradual occlusion of the body that Ed Cohen points out that identity in Locke is predicted on 'the enduring sameness of "the body."'[14] Cohen states: ' "identity" evokes the sameness of human differentiation *across time* by collapsing the processes of time into an unchanging and highly idealized notion, "the same organized body"' (77). The continuity of the body comes into being by elision of the ravages of time on it. This elision produces two effects: the gradual unmarking of the body and a perception of a homogeneity in all bodies, and the attendant idealization of the body. This idealization of the body leads to making 'qualitative distinctions' between the different sorts of human beings and their different bodies (77). Cohen's assertion that Locke achieves the idealization of the body by freezing it outside of time is extremely pertinent to any analysis of racialized, sexed or sexualized bodies in that there is an ideal body implied within Locke's framework which functions as the norm. This ideal body can be achieved only by placing 'the body' outside of history, by ignoring historical events such as colonialism and slavery, and facts such as racism and sexism; in short, by ignoring the cultural and historical constructions of the body.

Of beasts, birds and bodies

To summarize my argument so far: I have stated that Locke's simultaneous temporalizing and detemporalizing of identity causes the body to come into relief only to be erased promptly, I have also suggested that this approach to identity creates an idealized, unmarked body. I will come back to this point later but first I would like to examine the process through which Locke constructs his argument in *An Essay*, because I think an exposition of the process through which the body drops out of sight in his work will also reveal the way the black body functions within discourse and culture, through representation and invisibility. To put it another way, the relationship between Fanon and Locke's notions of identity becomes clear only by examining the process of metaphorization that the body undergoes.

The argument that Locke develops carefully thus far falters during his re-telling of a story in Sir William Temple's *Memoirs of What Passed in Christendom from 1672–79*. This story, told to Sir William Temple by someone who knew a Dutch Prince Maurice in Brazil, was about the latter's encounter with a talking parrot. Upon meeting the Prince and a number of other Dutchmen, the parrot exclaims, 'What a company of white men are here!' (446). In the conversation that ensues between Prince Maurice and the parrot, the latter confesses to having the job of looking after the chickens ('*Je garde les poulles*'). The Prince laughs at this and the parrot retorts, 'I know well enough how to do it' ('*Je scai bien faire*') (447). This odd story once mentioned is ignored by Locke, who uses it merely to suggest that it is not rationality but the body that makes the human, for otherwise there could not be much difference between a dull rational man and a very intelligent, rational parrot (446). Michael Ayers points out that for Locke this story serves to illustrate the shortcomings of the traditional definitions of man as a rational animal or of his identity being located in the soul (Ayers, vol. 2: 260). Locke renarrates the story as a rhetorical strategy to position himself and the logic of his own argument.

I would like to focus my attention not so much on what Locke says but rather how he says it, not on the contents of his discussion of identity, but rather on its grammar. I want to read the 'Prince Maurice and the parrot story' within the context of analogy, metaphor and displacement wherein occurs the transfer of psychic investment from one, often unacceptable, element to another culturally more acceptable one. In 'White Mythology' Jacques Derrida reiterates that '[m]etaphor has always been defined as the trope of resemblance; not simply between signifier and signified, but between what are already two signs, the one designating the other'.[15] Within such a definition, the parrot story functions as metaphor, not for Locke's definitions of identity, but to distinguish his framework from those others who locate identity within rationality. Here the story is used to function in an analogy: Rationality is to man as irrationality is to bird. Locke merely transposes the second term with the fourth in order to poke fun at such reasoning: Rationality is to bird as irrationality is to man. This strategy underscores the inadequacy in the argumentation of those philosophers who locate identity within the notion of rationality and not the body.

However, far from disproving his opponents, a peculiar displacement occurs in Locke's own work. As Kaja Silverman explains in *The Subject of Semiotics*, the process of displacement 'invests an innocent and often unimportant object with the affect which properly belongs to one which is taboo'[16] (63). Reading the parrot story within the structure of displacement, it is possible to ask a series of questions: Why insist on the importance of the body in order to ignore it promptly? Why is the selected story so far removed from the source, read by Locke in a book by an author who heard it elsewhere about a fantastic/colonized space such as Brazil? Why does the parrot only notice white men in the room? Why is there such a series of translations? That is to say, Locke renders in English the story of a parrot reportedly talking in Portuguese ('Brazilian'), translated by interpreters both Dutch and Brazilian for Prince Maurice, who in turn narrates the story in

33

French. What is this story so elaborately saturated with its own fictiveness, doing in an otherwise soberly argued philosophical text? The story, in short, deliberately draws attention to itself.

Instead of recording Locke's objections, the parrot story takes on a life of its own in *An Essay*. Alexander Campbell Fraser cites Stewart's *Elements* in which the author records that 'more than one of [Locke's] admirers seemed to recollect little else which they had learned from that work than the story of this parrot' (Locke, vol. 1: 446). In his essay on Locke, Paul de Man, too, points out that 'examples used in logical arguments have a distressing way of lingering on with a life of their own'.[17] In the next section I will examine how this parrot story takes on a life of its own and calls into question the status of the body in Locke.

Displacements and effects

I want to examine the relationship between the human and the bestial body and the function of displacement in the parrot story. The human body in Locke is used as contrast to the parrot in order to draw a firm boundary between the human and the animal/bird. A definite hierarchy of man over bird/beast is also established at this juncture. However, having valorized the body, Locke then proceeds to deny it, insisting that it is consciousness and not the body that grants man his identity: 'For, since consciousness always accompanies thinking, and it is that which makes every one to be what he calls self, and thereby distinguishes himself from all other thinking things, in this alone consists personal identity . . .' (449). But when Locke quickly bypasses the body to now locate identity in consciousness, the body falls from being the signified to the signifier. The text now posits consciousness as the signified and the body in a subordinate relationship to it.

The body drops away from significance altogether along with the body of the parrot when Locke uses another example in his argument, of the loss of a person's hand not substantively changing his identity (452–3). The argument now shifts from the insistence on the somatic to the discursive and from the physiological to the psychological.[18] In this shift, the body, that which is the constitutive condition for the appearance of consciousness in the argument, is lost. The body as sign completely repressed, along with the body of the parrot, joins the ranks of the animal kingdom. It is this process of displacement that renders the body itself to become a signifier, not of the human, but of the animal kingdom, the bestial.[19] The body originally signifying difference now achieves a more ambiguous character in that it now means that which functions to call the conscious subject into being. Thus the body takes on the status of 'prior to signification'. In this shift in meaning and status, the body is othered, objectified by the emphatic claim on consciousness. The 'man of consciousness' has to separate himself from the bestial body, which transforms from signified to signifier to sign, so that he is primary in a hierarchy of man over beast, consciousness over body. The body as used by Locke is located in some primordial time where forms are necessary to separate man from beast. But once man's hierarchy over the beast (via his body) is established, it is consciousness that is valorized.

Structurally, the status of the body shifts considerably in Locke's narrative: from being central it is revealed as marginalized; from being definitive it is revealed as being undesirable in the subsequent development of his framework; from being used obviously in separating man from beast or bird it shifts to being part of the repressed. It is this movement, this shift, which accounts for the way that the material human body is assimilated with the bestial body. In 'Race Under Representation', David Lloyd says:

> The constitution of any metaphor involves the bringing together of two elements into identity in such a manner that their differences are suppressed. Just so, the process of assimilation, whether in bringing two distinct but equivalent elements into identity or in absorbing a lower into higher element as by metastasis, requires that which defines the difference between the elements to remain over as residue. Hence although it is possible to conceive formally of an equable process of assimilation in which the original elements are entirely equivalent, the product of assimilation will always necessarily be in an hierarchical relation to the residual, whether this be defined as, variously, the primitive, the local or the merely contingent.[20]

In Locke the body thus devolves in the hierarchy of the beast, the human and consciousness. From being superior to the beast it becomes the beast. Like the animal, the body ultimately is used pejoratively; it functions only to give credibility to consciousness.

The unmarked body

I want to go back now to Ed Cohen's essay wherein he suggests that within the context of bodily identity, Locke 'produces the idealized body as both the ground and the guarantee for making qualitative distinctions between "kinds" of human beings' (77). Cohen's analysis at first glance might appear at odds with the way I have analysed the Lockean body. Indeed, on the one hand in Locke there is an implicit idealized body—unmarked—produced at the intersection of all that is desirable (age, race, sex, sexuality and wealth); on the other hand there is a discomfort altogether with the materiality of the body. This gap—the valorization of the body only to emphasize its undesirability—must be read as a product of the usage of the term 'identity', not only within notions of representation, but also within discourses of political philosophy and empiricism. Cohen correctly pinpoints that within the liberal democratic framework of identity used by Locke, the disposition of bodies as they 'mark out the locus of the self . . . is circumscribed by a tradition of . . . "possessive individualism"' (77). Cohen cites C.B. Macpherson to point out that within this tradition, 'individuals are defined primarily as proprietors of their fleshly incarnations, who are consequently entitled to rights only as the owners of themselves' (77–8). The body has no identity on its own except insofar as it is property, functioning as object to provide subject status to the individual.[21] In his analysis of Hobbes and Locke, Macpherson implies a connection between the unmarked and the poor or racialized body:

> If men are by nature equally rational, in the sense of equally capable of looking after themselves, those who have fallen permanently behind in the pursuit of property can be assumed to have only themselves to blame. And only if men are assumed to be equally capable of shifting for themselves, can

it be thought equitable to put them on their own, and leave them to confront each other in the market without the protections which the old natural law doctrine upheld. (245)

It is in its function in the interstices of ontology and political philosophy that the body becomes property. If body is property, the differential capacities of individuals are marked on the body itself. The kind of 'man' you are is visible at a glance. Property grants invisibility—an ideal—to the body and poverty makes it visible. Poverty therefore is to be abhorred within liberal democratic discourse as it draws attention to the body. For the rich white man the mind spills over into the body, making it disappear altogether; for the black and/or poor man, it is the body that is highlighted.

In another context, in *The Threshold of the Visible World*, Kaja Silverman discusses her anxiety at the presence of the homeless in Telegraph Avenue at Berkeley, California, and attributes two reasons for her puzzling response, both of which deal with the concept of specularity. The first she attributes to the lack of ideality that the homeless people embody. They have 'bodies that are calloused from sleeping on the pavement, chapped from their exposure to sun and rain, and grimy from weeks without access to the shower' (26). But the second reason is more complex in that the homeless in Berkeley dispel any myth that she, Silverman, herself is corporeally herself. Instead, she adds, '[the homeless bodies] show me that, if homeless, I would precisely no longer be "myself"'(27). This statement if anything replicates the Lockean schema for bodies, properties and identities. Poverty drains one of identity, as identity in its purest form is steeped in consciousness, which brings about detachment and objectivism. Poverty reverts us to being the visible body and as being subject to the body, and as object, without padding, protection or consciousness.

Returning to Macpherson's *The Political Theory of Possessive Individualism*, we find this statement:

> The seventeenth-century bourgeois observer could scarcely fail to see a deep-rooted difference between the rationality of the poor and that of the men of some property. The difference was in fact a difference in their ability or willingness to order their own lives according to the bourgeois moral code. But to the bourgeois observer this appeared to be a

difference in men's ability to order their lives by moral rules as such. (245–6)

Hence, bodies become visible or invisible only through the vectors of power and economics and the meaning imputed to these within cultural knowledge systems. The visual nature of poverty functions thus: it becomes the underside of an indexical relation through which the bourgeois observer comes into an identity. The negative aspects of embodiment are displaced completely onto the poor body. The poor body's obvious visibility puts it in closer proximity to the 'brute', and to the animal kingdom generally. His visual immediacy locates the poor man as incapable of the development of consciousness.

Underpinning Locke's notion of identity is the discourse of developmental categories. Within the Lockean schema of power and property, the distance between the discourse of race and that of class is very short indeed, at this juncture in my reading. The term 'racialized body' can be used interchangeably with the term the 'poor body' in that neither has an idealized, invisible body, nor do they have a proper identity. The proper, ideal subject is one with property but no body.

Before I stop analysing Locke, I want to make one final point about the ambiguous and contradictory status of the body in his schema, to suggest that the idealized body in Locke and his insistence of the superiority of consciousness itself is a manifestation of the anxiety encoded within the disembodied subject. This belief in the superiority of consciousness yoked to that of anxiety is manifested through a proclamation of a disavowal of difference, for an admission of difference would rob consciousness of its hierarchical status. The disavowal of difference is central to the validity of the discourse of development/evolution; as long as the latter underpins the logic of identity, the Lockean subject can avoid being reminded of his own body and his bestial materiality.

In a further move, Locke's discourse of development simultaneously suggests that the marked body—marked through race, gender or poverty—is a product of traits internal to the body, just as the beast is inhuman because of its body. The bestial, poor or black marked body cannot transcend itself to consciousness. It is this double move of disavowing difference (between marked and unmarked bodies) and the simultaneous insistence of difference (between man and beast) that allows for the unmarked body to be presented as prior to consciousness, and as originary. What the unmarked body manages to occlude by this double move is the fact that notions of marked and unmarked, embodied and disembodied, are all social relationships of domination and exploitation. This occlusion allows the body to pass the unmarked self as a natural trait, internal to itself, and leads to disembodiment.

Only by keeping the racialized body or the sexed body in view can we read Locke's unmarked body, which grants identity to the individual. Only such a juxtaposition of the marked and the unmarked will allow for the reading of the process through which the body unmarks itself. In the chapter 'The Fact of Blackness', Fanon suggests the same dynamics at play:

> Ontology—once it is finally admitted as leaving existence by the wayside—does not persuade us to understand the being of the black man. For not only must the black man be black; he must be black in relation to the white man . . . The black man has no ontological resistance in the eyes of the white man. (110)

This citation is not to suggest that the black body is pure materiality but rather to point to its discursive construction. As Fanon says: *'It is the racist who creates his inferior . . . It is the anti-Semite who makes the Jew'* (Fanon's emphasis; 93).

The body has a peculiar ontological status within Locke's liberal democratic Enlightenment discourse. I have argued that his compulsion to unmark the body results in the othering of any body which is visible because of its economic status, race or gender. These othered bodies are precluded from participating in the rational discourse of the human and of consciousness in Locke, which attempts to expel any traces of the somatic from its midst. These othered bodies by dint of their visibility cannot 'progress' into consciousness. They remain static and their status as mere bodies is underscored, thus creating anxiety for rational subjectivity. Within this context, Fanon's body, both the same and not the same—must be rendered abject: 'I am given no chance. I am over-determined from without. I am the slave not of the "idea" that others have of me but of my own appearance' (116).

The Freudian body

From the discourse of liberal democracy I move to the psychoanalytic framework, which has elaborated the concepts of identity and identification at great length. In this section I will briefly summarize Freud's view on bodily ego prior to reviewing a recent work on racialized somatic identity by Sander Gilman, which uses a psychoanalytic framework to discuss the relationship between race and gender in Freud.[22] Finally, I will juxtapose Fanon with Freud to analyse the structural space occupied by the racialized body within Freud's concept of a bodily ego. As Diana Fuss has recently pointed out, notwithstanding his prolific writing on a variety of topics, Freud never published a full length work on identity, hence his theorizing on bodily identity has to be culled from a variety of sources.[23] They are, among others, *The Ego and the Id* for notions of consciousness and how it is constructed through an interaction between the id and the superego, *Group Psychology and the Analysis of the Ego* for how group ties are made, 'On Narcissism: An Introduction' for the theorization of bodily identity and the internalization of bodily contours, and 'Mourning and Melancholia', which is significant for its analysis of how certain body parts are idealized.[24] As within Locke's text, the Freudian schema (especially in *The Ego and the Id*) reiterates the emphasis on consciousness as the site of the rational human being, but here the notion of 'consciousness' is itself complexified in that it functions as an antonym to the 'unconscious'. I have chosen to examine these works, rather than *Totem and Taboo* or *Moses and Monotheism*, for the analysis of the black body because I want to suggest that the black body is located not in the texts of the 'primitive' but rather in the interstices of the texts on identity, the body and gender. Furthermore, as Sander Gilman suggests, the issue of the racialized body is displaced onto the discussions of gender within the Freudian schema because gender functions as a metaphor for race in Freud's work.

Freud's theorizing of bodily identity contains the two distinct readings of the ego, the realist and the narcissist. Within his framework there is a conflation of the ego with bodily identity in that the body is seen to mediate and assist in the formation of the outline of the ego, and vice versa.

The ego and bodily identity cannot be considered separately as the two are mutually interdependent. To summarize, in the realist view of the ego, outlined especially in the initial sections of *The Ego and the Id*, the contours of the ego are formed as a result of the battering the body receives from the id (governed by the pleasure principle and seeking antisocial and sexual impulses) and reality, which is exerted externally on the subject. The ego comes into being by mediation between the two conflicting elements, one which seeks only pleasure, the other which demands a social harnessing of that pleasure. The ego functions to bring peace between pleasure and reality, to bring the subject into the social, while allowing him to experience some pleasure and satisfaction.

Freud uses a metaphor of a horse and its (male) rider to explain the delicate role that the ego plays:

> Thus in its relation to the id it is like a man on horseback, who has to hold in check the superior strength of the horse; with this difference, that the rider tries to do so with his own strength while the ego uses borrowed forces. The analogy may be carried a little further. Often a rider, if he is not to be parted from his horse, is obliged to guide it where he wants to go; so in the same way the ego is in the habit of transforming the id's will into action as if it were its own. (*SE* 19: 15)

In this analogy the central role of the pre-social and pre-existent id in the formation of the ego is emphasized. Indeed, the ego which is influenced so profoundly by the id is simultaneously a product of the process of differentiation inaugurated by external reality. Hence there is no one-to-one correspondence between the body and the ego—the anatomically experienced body is a product of the ego's enmeshing with external reality. To this extent one cannot locate the body as originary (à la Locke) and the ego as secondary. The formation of the ego and the sense of bodily contours is simultaneous. The id which only seeks pleasure is harnessed in the formation of the ego.

The shift in the discourse on the ego occurs when Freud discusses its relationship with the id. The narcissistic ego forms when it loses erotic object-choices. In this instance, the ego attempts to seduce the id by assuming the features of its lost erotic object and forces itself 'upon the id as a love-object and [tries] to make good the id's loss by saying: "Look, you can love me too—I am so like the object"' (*SE* 19: 20). In playing the role of the lost object-choice, the ego becomes that which it plays, leading Freud to suggest that the ego itself is a composite of lost erotic objects. This view of the ego leads Diana Fuss to suggest that '[i]dentification operates as a mark of self-difference, opening up a space for the self to relate to itself as a self, a self that is perpetually other' (2).[25] This theme of loss and identification, which is at the heart of the construction of the ego, calls into question the 'reality' of the external world, the reality of reality, in that the ego is more a compensation—a coping mechanism—for the loss of a departed love-object than a product of 'reality'. Thus in *The Ego and the Id* Freud appears to vacillate over defining exactly what the ego is, something that stands between two opponents, reality and the id, or something that is not particularly distinguishable from its own internal processes.

It is this latter view he amplifies in the earlier essays, 'On Narcissism' written in 1914 and 'Mourning and Melancholia' written in 1915 and published in 1917. In these the ego is drawn as fluid and as a warehouse of libido (ego-libido) waiting for appropriate object-choices upon which it can invest the libido (object-libido). The libido is finite, and, if invested on beloved objects, depletes the ego. Object-libido depletes ego-libido. In this version of events the ego does not really partake in external reality since its primary goal, not unlike the id, is the obtaining of pleasure. If love is reciprocated the libido-deprived ego is reinvested with the cathexis from this other and expands back into a self-esteem. If love is not returned, the ego suffers and falls into a melancholia.[26]

While the love-object is normally another person, Freud points out that it is possible to invest libido to parts of one's own body as if external to them. In 'On Narcissism: An Introduction' he makes a distinction between primary narcissism, which is defined as a period of 'self-contentment and inaccessibility' (*SE* 14: 89) that one undergoes in infancy, and narcissism in adults who have 'suffered' in their libidinal development, such as perverts, homosexuals and women (*SE* 14: 88–9). The difference between the two lies in the intervening phase when the baby learns to locate sexual instincts in another who brings satisfaction to the ego-instincts. This normative transition is only possible in the heterosexual male. Perverts, most women and homosexuals merely intensify their original narcissism and make themselves their own object-choice, causing difficulties in the process of identification.[27] Like the realist ego, the narcissistic ego (especially that which bestows libido on to the subject's body parts) brings the body into being, gives it a shape and coherence, and allows it to come into representation.

The raced/sexed body

The following story was narrated to me by an anthropologist friend, who while doing fieldwork in Niue had stayed with a family which had only daughters.[28] In order to have a son the family recategorized one daughter as a son. The entire community accepted this recategorization until her 'true' sex was 'discovered' by a white New Zealand rugby coach who saw her in the boys' shower after practice along with other boys. Pointing at her, the coach exclaimed, 'What's that girl doing in a boys' shower?' Everybody present, including the one who had been born a girl, turned and stared in the direction pointed at by the coach. My re-telling of this story is not to discuss how gender identification comes into being in Niue or how Niuean gender identifications enter modernity (through the Western white New Zealander), but rather to ask the question, What do we see when we look? *The Ego and the Id* supplies this answer partially by indicating that what we perceive as the materiality of the body is really a culturally orchestrated or mediated event. The body is always already only within representation.[29]

A recent work which explores the question 'What does Freud see when he looks?' and which on one level deals with the black body within the Freudian framework, is Sander Gilman's *Freud, Race, and Gender*. Gilman's reading of the black body in the Freudian framework is premised on Freud's preoccupation with his Jewish identity and his desire to express it in a pre-Second World War Austrian/German cultural context which was intensely anti-Semitic. Gilman posits the transference of the (male) Jewish body (connoted as 'black' in

Freud's Vienna) onto the female body within Freud's theoretical work on gender and sexuality. Gilman's authoritative reading of Freud completely resituates our comprehension of his essays on 'Femininity', 'Female Sexuality' and 'Some Psychical Consequences of the Anatomical Distinction between the Sexes', especially when Gilman points out that the slang/colloquial term for the clitoris in *fin de siècle* Vienna was *Jud* (Jew), a term which was also used to refer to the circumcized penis of the Jew. Knowing this fact shifts our reading of Freud's framework of the female body as being an elaboration of the same/male, as Luce Irigaray analyses in *Speculum of the Other Woman.*[30]

Gilman cites a number of parallels which render the feminine body as an analogy of the male Jewish body. For instance, the unknowability of the Jew (in the dominant discourse of turn-of-the-century Vienna) was paralleled by the perception of unknowability of the woman. Again, the rhetoric of scientific discourse linked these unknowabilities (37). The mind and body of the Jew were also considered parallel to the mind and body of woman. Furthermore, the dominant scientific discourse (with which Freud aligned himself) was pejorative about the dark, diseased Jew (38), characteristics Freud displaced onto the woman in his several essays on woman and femininity. Finally, as Gilman puts it, there was a 'pejorative synthesis of both bodies [woman and Jew] because their "defective" sexual organs reflected the *fin de siècle* Viennese definition of the essential male as the antithesis of the female and the Jewish male' (39). Gilman adds that since Freud was writing as a Jew who was part of a 'neutral' scientific community, a neutrality that was anti-Semitic, there was a political urgency implicit in his desire to dislocate the subject from its sexed/raced anatomy (41–2). Indeed, in 'Femininity' Freud is insistent in locating the difference between men and women not on their anatomical differences but on the knowledge of castration, an act which is symbolic but especially so because both males and females are innately bisexual. Although Freud argues for the castration complex as psychical and not physical, the knowledge of the castrated body is itself dependent strictly on the anatomical.[31] The woman knows she is castrated. To this extent, Gilman's brilliant reading of Freud, from complexifying our understanding of the father of psychoanalysis as a victim of anti-Semiticism (and thus freeing him from the accusation of reading woman as man), reimplicates him as having the blind spot that Irigaray reads in his work. Previously, 'Femininity' was read by Irigaray within the context of Freud's inability to read alterity. Reading Gilman we realize that Freud wasn't reading woman at all. From being read in a biased way she is now not even considered worthy of being read at all. She is always a metaphor for somebody else.

Ultimately, Gilman's reading of Freud and the black body reveals certain problems deep within the Freudian framework. First, the actual materiality of woman's bodies cannot be theorized and must be denied so that the black body can come into being within representation; and second, the black body itself is denied its existence in that it must cross-dress as woman to come within representation and theorization. Though carrying the burden of race and gender, the (unsexed) black body and the (unraced) woman's body are really not there, but are rather the constructs by which male Viennese identity can come into inscription. Both the black and the female bodies are very much social, political and racial constructions.

The Freudian body revisited

At this juncture I revisit the status of the body and its precise relationship with the ego in *The Ego and the Id* and 'On Narcissism' because I want to trace how the materiality of the body slips into being a cultural representation and re-examine those oft-cited lines in *The Ego and the Id*: 'The ego is first and foremost a bodily ego; it is not merely a surface entity, but is itself a projection of a surface' (*SE* 19: 16). After reminding us of his definitions of the unconscious in the first chapter, Freud defines the ego: 'in each individual there is a coherent organization of mental processes, and we call this his [sic] ego. It is to this ego that consciousness is attached' (*SE* 19: 7). At this point, Freud emphasizes the ego as part of the mental processes rather than being attached to the body. He reiterates this point by stating that 'consciousness is the *surface* of the mental apparatus; that is, we have ascribed it as a function to a system which is spatially the first we reached from the external world—and spatially not only in the functional sense but, on this occasion, also in the sense of anatomical dissection' (Freud's emphasis; *SE* 19: 9). Here Freud starts refining his definition of which part of the ego is the body by pinpointing consciousness as that which mediates between sense perception of the anatomy and the objects in the outer-world which bear down upon the body. At this juncture the body is purely a surface and does not refer to the internal/psychical agitations that it may be subjected to from within. Soon he makes a place for the 'internal perceptions of the ego' (*SE* 19: 11) by aligning it with the id: 'The ego is not sharply separated from the id: its lower portion merges into it' (*SE* 19: 14). Freud constructs the ego as participating with the id in order to make room for the repressed to 'communicate with the ego through the id' (*SE* 19: 14). As a result, the body becomes the site upon which both internal and external perceptions are enacted on its surface: 'It is *seen* like any other object, but to the *touch* it yields two kinds of sensations, one of which may be equivalent to the internal perception' (Freud's emphasis; *SE* 19: 15). There is a peculiar split in the body here in that it has become two different entities forever separated by, first, the way it is perceived as an object and, second, the way it feels, a split which is central to Lacan's articulation of bodily identity in the mirror stage. Freud sutures the split in the body/text by stating that pain plays a part in the way we gain an idea of our body. In other words, internal pain shapes our perception of external reality.[32]

I want to concentrate on the status of the body, not as it comes into being via pain but through two different elisions in the language of Freud's text. The first slip occurs in *The Ego and the Id*, when Freud discusses the relationship between the ego and superego and he prioritizes the latter. The superego, which functions like the Althusserian notion of ideology,[33] is perpetuated through the authority of church, school, state and language (*SE* 19: 24–5). The superego is central to the perpetuation of the species. The body conflated with the ego can materialize only through the influential superego. This conflation occurs in several steps in the Freudian text. First, the body is perceived as similar to but not the same as the ego; then the text increasingly removes the demarcation between the two. There is a conflation in language too; just as the body and the perception of it is both internal as well as external in the first part of *The Ego and the Id*, soon the ego itself is formed externally and internally: 'we shall have to say that not what is lowest but also what is highest in the ego can be unconscious' (*SE* 19: 17). The ego and the body thus become interchangeable terms—in this way the material body is displaced by the ego. Further, physical pain, which Freud had suggested previously gave an idea of the body, is now subsumed under the internal pain of self-criticism and conscience.

The second elision of the body occurs when Freud describes the relationship between the ego and the superego and the strong influence of the latter over the former. The superego's alignment with cultural forces of church, school, state and language soon renders the ego (and by extension, the repressed body) as a materialization of culture rather than something even remotely connected to the biological body. This elision occurs in a strategy not unlike Lacan's positing of the Imaginary as an imaginary retroactive construct which can be activated only via the Symbolic.[34] The ontology of the body shifts in a similar way in Freudian discourse. What is posed as the material body prior to representation is really a machination of that cultural force—the superego— which ensures the perpetuation of the species. What is an effect of the superego is passed off as prior to it for the sake of a distinction and demarcation between the ego and the superego.

A third elision occurs when Freud points out that the superego partakes of the id, 'the internal world'. The id which was the site of the raging inferno of the libido and the pleasure principle, 'which contains the passions' (*SE* 19: 15), is suddenly conflated with the ego-ideal or 'everything that is expected of the higher nature of man. The ego-ideal represents the father and exercises moral censorship' (*SE* 19: 27). Freud does point out that the ego-ideal is 'the heir of the Oedipus complex' (26) and 'what belonged to the lowest part of the mental life of each of us is changed through the formation of the ideal, into what is highest in the human mind by our scale of values' (*SE* 19: 26). Here the input of the subject's body, the id, is completely expunged in the repression of the Oedipus complex. In short, his narrative on the construction of the ego and the superego contains no body at all, notwithstanding his insistence that the ego is a bodily ego. The body dematerializes in the wake of the construction of the ego; eventually Freud suggests that the ego itself is given shape by the superego.

But what about the body? How, where and why is it displaced and replaced? The bias against the body is revealed in 'On Narcissism'. Here Freud isolates perverts, homosexuals and most women who in their choice of love-object reveal their narcissism (vol. 14: 88), in a difference from the normative male whose object-choice is his mother/substitute and reveals an anaclitic type of desire. Women and other perverts are fascinated with their own appearance and 'develop a certain self-contentment' (*SE* 14: 88). These perverts experience their bodies at variance from the normative way which requires a superimposition of the bodily form by the ego which, in turn, is influenced by the superego. Alternatively, the perverted woman is frozen at the stage of the body, unable to mature any further and incorporate the superego adequately. As Freud states in his essay 'Femininity':

> In the absence of fear of castration the chief motive is lacking which leads boys to surmount the Oedipus complex. Girls remain in it for an indeterminate length of time; they demolish it late and even so, incompletely. In these circumstances the formation of the super-ego must suffer; it cannot attain the strength and independence which give it its cultural significance, and feminists are not pleased when we point out to them the effects of this factor upon the average feminine character.(*SE* 23: 129)

In short, it is the fear of the loss of a bodily part that causes the boys to transcend the body and incorporate the superego. Having no body part to lose, always already mutilated, the girl gains no fear, no proper sense of cultural injunctions. She cannot incorporate the superego; she cannot attain to culture as a subject. She is perverted and it is in the body of the perverted woman that the 'body' stubbornly appears to exert a will of its own, refusing to comply with the demands of culture. This connection between castration (anxiety) and lack of moral development can extend to the black man as well, in that his marked body reveals his mutilated identity. His black body marks his lack as internal to him.

In her reading of the body in Plato, Judith Butler points out that his schema is possible only by excluding women, slaves or racialised others, children and animals, for their bodies bespeak irrationality; their irrational bodies function to produce and underscore the Greek (Western) male body as the rational choice. She says:

> This is a figure of disembodiment, but one which is nevertheless a figure of a body, a bodying forth of a masculinized rationality, the figure of a male body which is not a body, a figure in crisis, a figure that enacts a crisis it cannot fully control. This figuration of masculine reason as disembodied body is one whose imaginary morphology is crafted through the exclusion of other possible bodies.[35](48–9)

Thus there is a continuum in the representation of the body in Western culture, from Plato through Locke and Freud, which demands the expunging of the body for the construction of subject status. Yet the dematerialization of the body—its unmarking—is possible only for a select group of subjects. The rest remain the body in excess, be it the black body, or the perverse female body. The unmarked body is put forward as the norm.

However, marking also functions as exteriority. If the body functions to locate the borders of the ego and superego, as I explained previously, the site at which it is represented is also the site of its erasure. It is in the skewing of the ontology of the body—posited as materially prior to the formation of the ego and the superego when it is an effect—that the Freudian schema reveals the body to be in a trace; the depicted body is a displacement of something else, which leaves traces of itself in the body in representation. That which has been excluded from the parameters of the ego and the superego functions as an exteriority to mark the boundaries of coherence of a cultural force, a coherence which can be purchased only by accepting the rule of the ego and the superego, who between themselves violently erase the body only to re-posit a version of it, to domesticate it within their schema. The body has to be excluded—to function as exteriority—for the perpetuation of the species. In Freud's schema, the body becomes a fetish object for its own missing self.

Body without culture

Notwithstanding Freud's insistence on the centrality of the physical, material body with its sensitive epidermis and the receptiveness and resonances of the rest of its senses, it is the culturally constructed ego and superego which materialize the sense of the body. Notions of interiority and exteriority—the drawing of borders on the body—also set up hierarchies which are formed by and, in turn, form the superego. In the rule of the superego and through the works of Plato through Locke, those humans who are white, male and normatively heterosexual prevail over those who are not.

Furthermore, despite their insistence on identity as being embodied, in their simultaneous denial of its importance both Locke and Freud reveal their deep discomfort with the body. In their discomfort is revealed their hierarchization of body and mind, body and consciousness, body and the superego. In their works the body moves from its status of being material to being a notion, and eventually being a mere trace, the existence of which must be read in the spoor it leaves behind, the spoor of their arguments. The body just will not go away. It is bestial. The body narcissistically fixated on its materiality and physicality is a pervert, a woman, a black. In *Bodies That Matter* Butler raises the question 'What about the materiality of the body?', a question she cannot pursue. Since language itself is a representation, how can the theorists theorize (through language) the body outside of representation, outside of meaning, outside of culture? There is an inevitability to the displacements and slippages in the Lockean and Freudian texts.

But it is the very effacement of the body in Freud and Locke that undoes their work. To echo Derrida, the body as a mere trace displaces and dislocates; it is its own excess; it refers beyond itself.[36] Their easy erasure of the body belies the material solidity of the physical body itself, a materiality which is visible, palpable and tangible. I want to suggest that the body in philosophic/psychoanalytic discourses functions as différance, especially in the tiresome way in which it lingers on long after it is expunged. On the one hand, it lends itself to the construction of hierarchies of body/mind, body/consciousness and further differences, yet, on the other, the very effects of these differences refer to a point of origin. As Derrida puts it, 'Différance is the nonfull, nonsimple origin; it is the structured and differing origin of differences' (141). The body functions as both trace and presence, materiality and absence. The body within representation itself is a manifestation of this (non)originary body.

I want to suggest that it is within the context of displacement and trace that the black body comes into being. In the developmental schema ascribed to identity by Locke and Freud, the visible body is located as bestial, perverted or feminine. Locke and Freud's notion of maturation and development hinges on the unmarked body, the disembodied. I want to record various interjections from Fanon here:

> The Negro is the genital. His body is black, his language is black, his soul must be black too. (180)

Again:

> . . . one is no longer aware of the Negro but only of a penis; the Negro is eclipsed. He is turned into a penis. He *is* a penis. (170)

or:

> There are times when the black man is locked into his body. Now 'for a being who has acquired consciousness of himself and of his body, who has attained the dialectic of subject and object, the body is no longer a cause of the structure of consciousness, it has become an object of consciousness'. (225)

If the 'Body' can only exist as trace, its ontological spoor is left on the black body. In fact it is the process of displacement that allows the Negro/female/perverted body to come into being. They are the body. They cannot attain the dialectic of subject and object, cannot transcend their materiality.

The space–time continuum

In this final section I would like to examine terms such as 'interiority'/'exteriority', 'metaphor'/'displacement', all of which

51

as tropes of spatiality point to the elided term 'place' within the construction of identity and subjectivity. I want to move my argument into the direction of place because a concept such as a 'black' body can come into meaning only by returning this elided term to the foreground. In other words, 'black' can only resonate with the meaning that it does when it is considered to be geographically and socially in or out of place. To put it in yet another way, 'black' signifies differently in Uganda or South Africa than it does in Oakland, California or Auckland, New Zealand. In each situation the signifier 'black' resonates with the history, culture and power dynamics that are particular to that place. Yet the significance of 'place' is often subsumed under the rubric of 'the politics of location'. Such a term emphasizes history and temporality—its politics— over the sense of place, the influence of its landscape in the construction of identity, and the materiality of place.

The rhetorical strategy of displacement which is so important in Locke and Freud erases the notion of spatiality in the construction of identity and relocates it within the discourse of temporality. The structure of displacement itself contains within it the trope of travel, of a forward and a sideways motion which transfers the affect of one thing to another, one emotion to another. That which is intrinsic to an element prior to its subjection to displacement is lost from sight in the motoring forth of meaning. The emphasis has moved from place to the linear movement of time and history. As I have suggested, it is the rhetorical effect of displacement in Locke that allows for a hierarchy of the man with consciousness to be established over a human body. Similarly in Freud, though the body is the medium through which the external is perceived by the subject, ultimately it is an external cultural force posing as an internal—the superego—that helps shape the ego as well as the body. In both these theories the body is located in static space and does not partake in the schema of development. To that extent, identity or subjectivity within Locke or Freud is impossible without the trope of travel, displacement and the function of temporality. I suggest that inherent within the structure of displacement itself is an insistence of the prioritizing of the temporal over the spatial which allows for meaning to be motored forward. Only such a displacement will eventually allow for the human body to be placed within a developmental model or within an evolutionary framework. This construction of identity allows gendered (white) male subjects to enter temporality, modernity, progression and development. It also functions to create a hierarchy wherein the bodies of women, perverts and blacks occupy a more ambiguous space, marked as primitive, undeveloped, forever aspiring to play 'catch-up' with their straight white male counterparts, who are already situated in modernity.

Ernesto Laclau puts forward a similar claim in *New Reflections on the Revolution of our Time,* when he makes the distinction between two different notions of temporality, that which is internal to the closed system of spatiality and that which is dynamic and part of history. For Laclau, '[p]olitics and space are antinomic terms. Politics only exist insofar as the spatial eludes us' (68). Space and time thus become mutually exclusive terms.[37] In 'Space, Time, and Bodies' Elizabeth Grosz indicates how space becomes place.[38] She points out that space is not 'an empty receptacle' (92); however she argues it cannot be perceived without any objects within it to give it perspective: 'It is our positioning within space, both as the point of perspectival access to space, and also an object for others in space, that gives the subject a coherent identity and an ability to manipulate things, including its own body parts, in space' (92). In this, Grosz follows a Lacanian mode of thought by suggesting that space gives perspective, but unlike Laclau she does not locate space and time as antonyms. In fact, unlike in Laclau, she believes that within philosophical conceptions of time and space, the latter is valorized over the former. For Grosz, in fact, 'time is represented only insofar as it is attributed certain spatial properties' (97). I would like to modify Grosz's statement by pointing out that time resembles space because of the motion of displacement—the affect which properly belongs to space is displaced onto time in this instance. I want also to add that metaphysical notions of space and time do not seem to consider the concept of power which permeates notions of place as well as identity, as Michel Foucault has indicated in a number of his works.[39] While Laclau's premise is that all space is static and detemporalized to a certain extent, I would argue that place functions in two ways: first, the materiality of place, its landscape and the formation of our aesthetics influences the construction of identity. Second, place is simultaneously enmeshed within systems of power and domination, as are identity and subjectivity. To deny the importance of spatiality in favour of temporality constructs a lopsided theory of identity which inevitably locates an individual only within a model of development and posits such a model as 'natural', while simultaneously covering over the vectors of power within which the human is enmeshed. The signification of black is always spatially and temporally bound, even if this term is normally perceived only within its temporal framework.

I shall let Fanon have the last words here, to posit the significance of place in the consideration of blackness. In one instance he refers to the replication of the hierarchy in the metropolis in Martinique: 'The process [of hierarchization] repeats itself with the man of Martinique. First of all his island: Basse-Pointe, Marigot, Gros-Marne, and opposite, the imposing Fort-de-France. [Most importantly], the negro who knows the mother-country is a demigod' (19). In yet another instance, he indicates the connection between displacement and the whitening of blackness: 'The colonized is elevated above his jungle status in proportion to his adoption of the mother country's cultural standards. He becomes whiter as he renounces his blackness, his jungle' (18). Displacement and the elevation in hierarchy resound throughout Fanon's work. Here he discusses the Antillean Negro in Senegal, who is deemed superior to the Senegalese Negro: 'On one side he has the Europeans, whether born in his own country or in France, and on the other he has the Senegalese . . . At such times, one no longer knows whether one is *toubab* [European] or "native"' (26). Ultimately, the Negro 'symbolizes the biological' (167), for the term Negro evokes the following responses: 'biology, penis, strong, athletic, potent, boxer . . . savage, animal, devil, sin' (166).

The centrality of place in the construction of identity is evoked everywhere in *Black Skin, White Masks*. The Negro is visible and invisible, signifying the body—the lost materiality of whiteness, and vilified for it while also evoking a nostalgia for the lost white body. The signification of place is complexified beyond an ordinary understanding of it as a geographical point on the map. It signifies postcoloniality: the loss of identity through territorialization and loss of place, yet also the presence of an identity, undescribable, indigenous. 'Place' signifies the loss of language through the process of colonialism, yet a simultaneous alterity of consciousness suggesting the undertow of indigenous identity seeping through, and restructuring colonized identity; finally, 'place' suggests identity by being in place and the sense of blackness manifested through being dis-placed.

What I have examined in this chapter is the displacement of the body in liberal democratic discourse and in psychoanalytic discourse, while postcolonial theory seems to represent the lost body. I have pointed out that theories of identity which emphasize temporality occlude the construction of identity and knowledges within and through place. I have also suggested that the phenomenon of displacement in representations of the body represses spatiality in favour of temporality of identity. In the next chapter I want to follow up on this binary structuring of spatiality and temporality and concentrate on the embodiment of women; an embodiment which, within the contexts of the nation and nationalistic discourse, functions as the ground upon which men erect their identity within the nation.

3

Woman–body–nation–space

I read with bewilderment two texts on Algerian women published some 28 years apart: Frantz Fanon's fascinating essay written in 1959, 'Algeria Unveiled', on the discursive shifts of the veil worn by Algerian women during the freedom struggle in Algeria, and Marie-Aimée Hélie-Lucas' interview 'Bound and Gagged by the Family Code', published in 1987.[1] The first text celebrates the role played by the Algerian woman—including her coming into subjectivity during the freedom struggle:

> The Algerian woman is at the heart of the combat. Arrested, tortured, raped, shot down, she testifies to the violence of the occupier and to his inhumanity.
>
> As a nurse, a liaison agent, a fighter, she bears witness to the depth and density of the struggle. (Fanon, 66)

He concludes this essay: 'Side by side with us, our sisters do their part in further breaking down the enemy system and in liquidating the old mystifications once and for all' (67). Despite the way he places the Algerian woman at the heart of the freedom struggles, Fanon is nevertheless blind to the irony that she comes into subjectivity only at the moment she is arrested, raped, tortured and shot. The Algerian woman who fights alongside the Algerian man in Fanon now gives way to Hélie-Lucas' text, which traces her increasingly restricted circumstances just two decades after the freedom struggle wherein she was central. By 1987 she is constrained in major ways by the passage of the Islamic Family Code in the Algerian Constitution. Among other rights seized from her, she loses her right to marry—she has to be 'given' in marriage; she loses her right to her children if divorced; she loses her right to divorce; she loses her right to keep her illegitimate child; she loses her right to adopt children (4–9). The Algerian woman who was crucial to the revolution, who carried grenades and guns, who helped kill the enemy, is written out of the Islamic Family Code. The circumstances under which Hélie-Lucas gives her interview underscore her own deteriorating rights: she originally gave it in 1984 for the British journal *Trouble and Strife* under the pseudonym Nadine Claire, 'for fear of reprisal from the Algerian authorities' (3). In short, the Algerian woman who comes into subjectivity via her nation in Fanon's text now functions to suggest that coming into subjectivity and having agency are two different things. In Hélie-Lucas's text she is located in the passive at every turn: loses her right to marry but is to be married, loses her right to divorce but can be divorced.

As these different texts suggest, I am faced with a particular problem when I contemplate the role of the woman in the nation, the woman with agency. I have to pull together disparate theoretical frameworks, that of nation and nationalism and that of feminism, which seem antithetical to each other. There is a plethora of material theorizing woman and femininity within the context of gender studies, but not very much within the context of nation, as if woman were disembodied and desexualised within the nation. If traces of her subversion, resistance and agency are found everywhere in the feminist theorizing of her within gender studies, there is no trace of resistance, subversion or agency within discourses of the nation. In 'Reading *The Satanic Verses*', Gayatri Chakravorty Spivak suggests that

> 'Agent' and 'subject' are different codings of somethings we call being . . . The question of free will should not be inscribed within arguments from subject-production; it is rather to be seen in connection with the presupposition of individual agency in collectivities. (231)[2]

In 'Nationalism, Gender, and Narrative', R. Radhakrishnan suggests that 'the women's question . . . is constrained to take on a nationalist expression as a prerequisite for being considered "political"' (78).[3] Through being subordinated within discourses of the nation, the woman as agent virtually disappears except insofar as she upholds the nation.

It is a commonplace that discourses on the nation presume an idealized, gendered (read 'male') citizen. For instance, Benedict Anderson in *Imagined Communities* suggests that 'in the modern world everyone can, should, will "have" a nationality as he or she "has" a gender', thus indicating that both nationality and gender are constructions which are retroactively posited as essences (16).[4] This also suggests that both notions, gender and nationality, can come into being only within a system of differences—that is, in relation to what they are not. Furthermore, gender and nationality in Anderson's definition are intricately enmeshed and implicated within each other, in that if masculinity and femininity can come into being only through negation, then inbuilt into these two are notions of nationality as well.[5] Though Anderson is inclusive of both genders early on ('as he or she "has" a gender'), he later refers to the 'deep and horizontal comradeship [of the] *fraternity*', thus emphasizing only men (emphasis added; 16). Other examples of the visualizing of the citizen as male abound. For instance, Ernest Gellner notes, '*Men* are of the same nation if and only if they recognize each other as being from the same nation (emphasis added).'[6] In his early piece 'What is a Nation?', Ernest Renan suggests, 'A large aggregate of *men*, healthy in mind and warm of heart creates the kind of moral conscience which we call a nation' (emphasis added).[7]

Nowhere is the heirarchy between male and female citizens more implicit than in its construction of sexuality. For instance, in his work on German nationalism and its construction of gender and sexuality, George Mosse suggests that German national identity between the two world wars was predicated on manly bodies because any trace of effeteness (be it the Jewish or the homosexual body) bespoke a nation in decay, deterioration and crisis.[8] In this schema women played the specific role of upholding masculinity in man, and helped to reproduce it. Indeed, Mosse states, 'nationalism had a special affinity for male society and together with the concept of respectability legitimized the dominance of men over women' (67). In his work on Greek homosexuality, *One Hundred Years of Homosexuality*, David Halperin insists upon the connection between the notion of democracy and the idealized body in early Greek society:

> For [the production of a democratic body] entailed not only the distribution to all the male citizens of an irrefutably 'masculine' body but the appropriation of the actual bodies of individual women for the purposes of male sexual pleasure. Moreover, to define the body of the male citizen as socially and sexually assertive was also to reinscribe the traditional definition of *the female body as socially and sexually submissive* in the very structures of Athenian democracy; it was to tie the status of Athenian women even more closely to *the social significance* of their bodies.[9] (emphasis added)

Thus, the notion of (Athenian) democracy is hierarchized, embodied and gendered. While my choice of examples here might seem specific and pertinent only to early Greek democracy or to German fascism, I want to argue strongly that the nation is always embodied, and the idealized body within any nationalistic discourse is always gendered. The woman is central to the nation in that she plays a part in literally reproducing it (as in bodily reproduction); however, her role is marginalized in that she is located as devoid of agency as a 'woman within the nation', though she might gain access into the nation from within the context of race, class, sexuality, age, etc. It is important to acknowledge also that, within the discourse of the nation, the woman is always configured only within the family, and the latter, far from being the realm of the private and outside the purview of the state, is very much an extension of it.[10]

In *Woman–Nation–State*, Nira Yuval-Davis and Floya Anthias directly address the issue of the woman's role within the nation.[11] Notwithstanding that the historical, religious and cultural specificities which locate women multiply, all these specificities function to position women similarly in the nation, i.e., the desire for racial and national homogeneity. Yuval-Davis and Anthias suggest that women are located as biological reproducers of ethnic groups; as reproducers of the *boundaries* of ethnic/racial/national groups; as transmitters of the ideology and the culture; as signifiers of ethnic/racial/national differences; and as participants in national, economic, political and military struggles (emphasis added; 7). In their work, the woman's body embodies difference, both through race and as maps/boundaries of groups, and is spatialized to some extent.

The (unequal) relationship between women and the nation, or gender and nation, is poignantly and particularly visible in postcolonial societies in which colonized peoples have had to imagine and fight for their nation which has, in its turn, located women within a nationality, but not within agency. Kumari Jayawardena attests to this position by pointing out that in the Third World:

> It has variously been alleged by traditionalists, political conservatives and even certain leftists, that feminism is a product of 'decadent' Western capitalism; that it is based on a foreign culture of no relevance to women in the Third World; that it is an ideology of women of the local bourgeoisie; and that it alienates or diverts women from their culture, religion and family responsibilities on the one hand, and from the revolutionary struggles for national liberation and socialism on the other.[12]

Not unlike Radhakrishnan, Jayawardena concludes that women's movements which demand agency for women 'do not occur in a vacuum but correspond to, and to some extent are determined by, the wider social movements of which they form part' (10). To that extent women's causes and rights have to subordinate themselves within the broader issue of nationalism.

I want to set the scene of this chapter by juxtaposing the two texts on Algerian women I mentioned earlier and analysing the effect created therein. Questions provoked by this juxtaposition are: What did the revolution do to shift Algerian women discursively? Did they have agency? What does their clothing and their veil signify for the French men and for the Algerian men in Fanon? And what does it signify for the Algerian women of the Revolution? What was the discursive shift made by 'woman' three decades later? How does this shift influence our re-reading of Fanon via Hélie-Lucas? I hasten to add that this chapter is neither about Algeria nor Fanon's corpus nor Islam, but is rather an examination of the agency of the woman in the nation as represented in Fanon's 'Algeria Unveiled'. In the longer first section I will examine the discursive construction of the woman's role within Fanon's text while, in the shorter second section I will analyse her role within the (democratic) nation. Accordingly, I will examine theorists such as Carole Pateman and Rosi Braidotti.[13] In *The Sexual Contract*, Pateman examines the notion of contract, the cornerstone of a liberal democracy. She posits that repressed out of the text of contract is the sexual contract, that which actually genders the 'neutral' notion of contract and results in the different positionings of man and woman in citizenship, employment and marriage. In *Nomadic Subjects*, Rosi Braidotti celebrates women's tenuous relationship to the nation and the rights of citizenship. I will conclude by discussing via the theories of Irigaray and Lacan how the positioning of the woman's body as given within psychoanalytic discourses on gender is useful in shedding light on the relationship between the woman, her body, place, and nation.

White men saving black women from black men

In the introduction to this chapter I suggested, via Yuval-Davis and Anthias, that the woman's body, at some level, is like maps of/within the nation in that it has triple functions: to encode boundaries, to reproduce sameness, and to reveal difference simultaneously. In this section, I wish to analyse the relationship between gender and nation within the context of identity by examining Fanon's 'Algeria Unveiled', suggesting that the spatializing discourse on women is especially important to gendered national identity in Fanon's text.

The war of liberation in Algeria lasted from 1954 to 1962 and ended 130 years of French colonization. Initially only men were revolutionaries but the urgency of the situation led to 'the decision to concretely involve women' (Fanon; 51). In another context (that of the Indian independence movement), Ketu Katrak succinctly sums up the rationale for including women in the (Indian) freedom movement: 'after all, nearly half of the population could not be left out of a national struggle'.[14] Fanon, however, locates the inclusion of women in the Algerian independence movement well before 1954, back in the 1930s when the French administration urged Algerian women to come out from behind the veil (37). Traditionally the veil was worn by the young Algerian woman as she came to maturity. In a move that anticipates the Foucauldian view that prohibition in fact constructs and instigates desire, Fanon suggests that the veil, 'previously, an undifferentiated element in a homogenous whole', was pinpointed by the French as an indicator of backwardness, and caused it to acquire 'a taboo character' (47). For the Algerians the suggested unveiling took on the meaning of 'a cultural destruction' (49).

Fanon traces the shifting discursivity of the veil on the woman through the Algerian war of liberation, wherein first it was a signifier of tradition and culture; the French desire to unveil woman revealed their intention to bring her into modernity. As the independence struggle intensified, women joined up as revolutionaries and deliberately unveiled themselves so they could have more access to the French and be successful in the resistance movement. In yet another stage, when the French became suspicious of unveiled women, they donned their veils again so they could strap weapons secretly to their bodies. The veil underwent yet another marked shift in that it now read ambiguously, as both traditional and revolutionary, patriotic yet unfeminine.

In 'Algeria Unveiled', the Algerians' clothing functions as the prime indicator of difference for the French. Fanon opens this essay with these lines: 'The way people clothe themselves, together with the traditions of dress and finery that custom implies, constitutes the most distinctive form of a society's uniqueness, that is to say the one that is most immediately perceptible' (35). While the Algerian man was identifiable by his fez or turban or *djellaba*, which varied according to whether he was urban or from the countryside, the Algerian woman was visible in her veil.[15] While men's clothing was heterogenous, woman's homogenous clothing located her as the timeless essence of Algeria, unchanging through history, time and generations. Significantly, her location within a timeless space invites the French discourse of Enlightenment and modernity. Fanon says:

> The behavior of the Algerian was very firmly denounced and described as medieval and barbaric. With infinite science, a blanket indictment against the 'sadistic and vampirish' Algerian attitude toward women was prepared and drawn up . . . Algerian women were invited to play 'a functional, capital role' in the transformation of their lot. (38)

Thus the French strategy was one of constructing binaries. They located themselves in modernity and history and all Algerians as locked in a past that had yet to deal with rationality and science and represented the role of 'traditional'. Algerian woman, in turn, embodied and became a metaphor for the timeless essence of Algerians. Algeria, Algerian woman, and the veil are first metonymically linked; secondly they become metaphors for each other. Strategically then, in order for Algeria to be brought into the Enlightenment identity of the West, it was the woman who had to be persuaded first. 'Every kilo of semolina distributed [to indigent and famished women] was accompanied by a dose of indignation against the veil and the cloister' (38). In Fanon's narration of French strategies, availability of plentiful food was equated with progression and the French.

The French construction of the Algerian woman was thus: 'white men were saving black women from black men',[16] a sentence which dovetails with the Algerian man's construction of her: 'An unveiled Algerian girl who "walks the street" is very often noticed by [Algerian] young men who behave like young men all over the world . . . She is treated to unpleasant, obscene, humiliating remarks' (53). The Algerian man who allowed his wife to unveil was 'prostituting' her, 'exhibiting her, abandoning a mode of resistance' (40). In the dialectical complicity of these two constructions of the Algerian woman, her veiled body is sexualized and fought over by Islam and France equally. Within the context of Indian women under colonialism Gayatri Spivak observed: 'Imperialism's image as the establisher of the good society is marked by the espousal of the woman as object of protection from her own kind. How should one examine the dissimulation of patriarchal strategy which apparently grants the woman free choice as subject?' (299) Instead of emphasizing her free choice as subject, the French unveiling of Algerian woman reinscribes her into another form of patriarchy.

However, Fanon attributes a different reason for the French desire to unveil Algerian woman; for them Algeria was 'a womanless society' (67) in that it was 'altogether commonplace to hear a European confess acidly that he [had] never seen the wife of an Algerian he [had] known for twenty years' (41). She, however, could see him from behind her veil. Fanon

63

interprets: 'This woman who sees without being seen frustrates the colonizer. There is no reciprocity. She does not yield herself, does not give herself, does not offer herself' (44). Though the sentiment is expressed in sexual terms, the frustration over the veiled Algerian woman becomes a synecdoche for the whole Algerian experience for the French: to be seen but cannot see.

But why this desire to see what lies beneath the veil? How does woman veiled equate to 'a womanless society' in Fanon? Does her veil make her invisible to the French? In her reading of 'Algeria Unveiled', Anne McClintock suggests that 'Fanon recognizes the colonial gendering of women as symbolic mediators, the boundary markers of an agon that is fundamentally male'.[17] McClintock insists on 'colonial conquest as an erotics of ravishment' (364). Along the same lines, Diana Fuss suggests that 'in the discourse of colonial imperialism and the discourse of national resistance, the veiled Algerian woman stands in metonymically for the nation. In both instances, the woman's body is the contested ideological battleground, overburdened and saturated with meaning' (150).[18] While McClintock and Fuss make convincing arguments on the meaning of the woman's body and her function as an ideological battleground for French and Algerian men, I want to concentrate on the unpacking of the trope of surveillance—to see and not to be seen—a trope which gets reversed for French men in Algeria.

The structure of surveillance is inherent to colonialism in that the colonizing force maintains authority as much through surveillance, spying, controlling and constructing the behaviour and identity of the colonised as it does through its militaristic force. In his magnificent chapter on Jeremy Bentham's architectural design of the Panopticon, Foucault underscores the disciplinary nature of surveillance whence it:

> serves to reform prisoners, but also to treat patients, to instruct schoolchildren, to confine the insane, to supervise workers, to put beggars and idlers to work. It is a type of location of bodies in space, of distribution of individuals in relation to one another, of hierarchical organization, of disposition of centres and channels of power, which can be implemented in hospitals, workshops, schools, prisons.[19]

Foucault describes Bentham's architectural plan which will render surveillance easy and efficient: a circular building on the periphery and a tower at the centre. The tower becomes the point from which observation takes place, from which every point in the interior of all the cells in the circular building becomes visible. The observer is invisible always and the inhabitants of the cells always subject to scrutiny. The purpose of the Panoptic is 'to induce in the inmate a state of consciousness and permanent visibility that assures the automatic functioning of power' (201). Soon, regardless of whether he is actually observed or not, the inmate presents the desired behaviour, all caused by the architectural design. For Foucault, the structure of the Panopticon was inherent not just to prisons but also to hospitals, workplaces and educational institutions; it participated in the disciplining of the body by altering behaviour, and by increasing the points of contact of power. In this structure, power is no more rigid and heavy-handed, but internal to the construction of the subject itself. Foucault insists that Bentham's work was relevant not only to late eighteenth-century England, but is the very schema of Enlightenment and modernity in its distribution of discipline and power, capital and economy. It is a 'calculated technology of subjection' (221). Its architectural plan goes beyond the prison system to all bodies in space, permeating the structure of factories, schools, barracks and hospitals (228).

I draw attention to Foucault's text because the notion of the Panopticon is so intimately connected to the construction of knowledges and power. Within colonial discourse, surveillance and knowledge are metonymically linked. There is a remarkable similarity between the desired effect of English education in India in T.B. Macaulay's infamous 'Minute' on education, and Foucault's analysis of Bentham's Panopticon. In the oft-quoted lines of Macaulay: 'We must at present do our best to form a class who may be interpreters between us and the millions we govern; a class of persons, Indian in blood and colour, but English in taste, in opinions, in morals and in intellect.'[20]

A number of critics and theorists have commented at length on the ideological function of the English language and literature in making its subject people accept the hierarchy of imperialistic forces.[21] Gauri Viswanathan points out that 'humanist functions traditionally associated with the study of literature—for example, the shaping of character or the development of the aesthetic sense or the discipline of ethical thinking—are also essential to the process of *sociopolitical control*'.[22] Jenny Sharpe points out that 'the human-making project of inculcating Western tastes and values was inseparable from the profit-making enterprise of creating new markets for English manufactures'.[23] For Sharpe, the imperialist's agenda was always to see a smooth transition from colonialism to neocolonialism; as Macaulay himself puts it, it was better that 'Indians were ruled by their kings but wearing our broadcloth, and working with our cutlery, than that they were performing *salaams* to English collectors and English magistrates, but were too ignorant to value or too poor to buy, English manufactures' (as cited in Sharpe; 142). Political ideology for Macaulay is underpinned by economic gain rather than a need for colonialism. Economic gain, in turn, is connected to the disciplining of the body—and mind—of the Indian.

Additionally, the establishment of English/literary studies in India was linked not only to ideological conquest but also to function as a Panopticon—by ensuring the production of discipline. Commerce and the English language, discipline and modernity, are intricately intertwined for Macaulay: 'It may safely be said, that [English literature] is of far greater value than all the literature which three hundred years ago was extant in all the languages of the world together . . . It is likely to become the language of commerce throughout the seas of the East' (360). Macaulay urges that English be taught so Indians can learn European science. He offers the case of Russia, which by learning European languages came into modernity only three generations ago: 'I cannot doubt that they will do for the Hindoo what they have done for the Tartar' (360). In another work, Fanon laments:

> Every colonized people . . . every people in whose soul an inferiority complex has been created by the death and burial of its local cultural originality—finds itself face to face with the language of the civilizing nation; that is with the culture of the mother country . . . To speak a language is to take on a world, a culture.[24]

But learning a new language and taking on a new world is a form of disciplining also. English language and literary studies function as a Panopticon in that these become an internal functioning of the subject people, shaping them for maximum economy, training them, giving them access to an accumulated and centralized knowledge. As Foucault states, 'it is not that the beautiful totality of the individual is amputated, repressed, altered by our social order, it is rather that the individual is *carefully fabricated in it*, according to a whole technique of forces and bodies' (emphasis added; 217). The study of English language and literature thus renders the Indian subject both docile and useful to England beyond the age of colonialism into the age of neocolonialism in the late twentieth century. The disciplining of the Indians must masquerade as the desire to bring Indians into modernity. The Panoptic nature of English/literary studies must masquerade as benign aesthetics.

I must now articulate this obvious link between surveillance, knowledge and discipline in colonial discourse to interpret the French desire to unveil Algerian women. My analysis must respond to questions such as: How is this link between surveillance, knowledge and discipline nullified by the veiled women in Fanon's text? And most importantly: Why is the struggle for power conducted over the bodies of Algerian women? And, finally: What status do the French women have in Algeria?

The meaning of the French discomfort with veiled Algerian women resides in the metonymic link between surveillance and knowledge. If knowledge formation is Panoptic in structure—the discipline which comes with being always visible—so also is colonial identity predicated on vision. Within the structure of surveillance the one who sees is invisible, but the one who is seen, the colonized in this case, is always subject to scrutiny. Within the context of colonialism, visible racial difference plays a fundamental role in the conferring, or the taking away, of identity. David Lloyd suggests that the visual index is central to colonialism and racism in that the superiority of the colonizer can be legitimized only through immediately perceptible visual difference.[25] In colonial discourse, whiteness 'legitimates a violent assertion of superiority by way of appeal to developmental categories: against the achieved identity of the white man, the black appears as being in greater proximity

67

to childhood or animality' (74). In this instance, black is metonymically linked to the savage, the baboon, with their obvious difference to the white man. Visual difference is central to colonial discourse, as is evident in the confusion and distress that the Englishman Charles Kingsley displays when he sees poor Irish. In his oft-quoted letter to his wife he says, 'But I am haunted by the human chimpanzees I saw along the hundred miles of horrible country . . . [T]o see white chimpanzees is dreadful; if they were black, one would not feel it so much, but their skins, except where tanned by exposure, are as white as ours.'[26] His repeated, insistent usage of the Irish as chimpanzees reveals his anxiety at his physical similarity to the Irish without the visual indicator of the difference between black and white. McClintock, too, suggests that notions of visual difference in colonialism are located within a discourse of development and commodity, or as she calls it, 'commodity racism' (209). In fact, Macaulay's urging that English be taught so the Indians could reach modernity and rationality and learn European science is very much within the framework of development which is underpinned by markers of visual difference in colonialism. Learning English will make the Indians more like the English, anglicized, but still different. As Homi Bhabha points out, the difference between being English and being anglicized is located in the visual.[27]

At another level, the French desire to unveil the Algerian woman also signifies within the trope of surveillance. The immediacy of visual difference implicit in the veil, however, is simultaneously disavowed by that very veil. Her difference is now, contradictorily, located as invisible, impossible to discern at a glance, and conferring a lack of difference. The veil allows her to bypass the circuit of knowledge formation based on visual immediacy. In fact the presence of the veil causes the reverse to happen. The French might have colonized Algeria, but in the process it is the Algerian who has become opaque. Her very opacity contributes to the fantasizing: 'A strand of hair, a bit of forehead, a segment of an "overwhelmingly beautiful" face glimpsed in a streetcar or a train, may suffice to keep alive and strengthen the European's persistence in his irrational conviction that the Algerian woman is the queen of all women' (Fanon; 43).

It is this nullifying of the desired effect of the surveillance that frustrates the French in 'Algeria Unveiled'. The scene of fantasy is also the site of instability in the text in that the deployment of power implicit in the Panoptic structure—the power which resides with the viewer—reverses itself, and it is the French who are now subject to scrutiny, exhibited to Algerians due to their imposition of the French culture, language and education system. They are known. In this reversal there is a metaphoric shift in the text and the Algerian women occupy the place recently vacated by the French, primarily because of their ability to see while not being seen. The French who now have assumed the position of the Algerian women are feminized in their passivity, mastered and possessed by the gaze of the women.[28]

In a further step, in her refusal to be subject to his gaze, the veiled Algerian woman calls into question the right of the French man to possess her and, by extension, possess Algeria. She negates the legitimacy of colonialism. In her refusal to be seen, in her refusal to be surveyed and dominated, the Algerian experience for the French becomes an incomplete one, in that the difference emphasized by the Algerian body is simultaneously disavowed by the impenetrable veil. Algeria is a place of partial presence for the French and ambivalently signifies both comforting familiarity as well as threatening, menacing difference, becoming a place of reversals. The veiled Algerian woman disrupts French authority because she prevents the completion of their gaze. The incomplete gaze can only result in a partial panoptic of Algeria—only men in a womanless society.[29] Why Algerian women were fought over by French and Algerian men becomes clear. For the Algerians, her veiled status represents the failure of French colonialism; for the French, her unveiling would signify the success of colonialism.

White women–black men

If the structural function of white men unveiling the Algerian woman was to save the black woman from black men, what would save white women from black men? What would save white women from white men? Or didn't they need saving? Did French women in Algeria come into being only within the context of race and not within gender? In examining the relationship between the structural positioning of French women and Algerian men, I suggest that in the mimetically dialectic relationship between white men and black women, and white women and black men, the latter two identities are structurally aligned with each other. Earlier, following a discussion of Spivak's ideas, I suggested that between colonial patriarchy and indigenous patriarchy the Algerian woman as subject is muted, as are the French women in Algeria for Fanon.

French women in Algeria receive scant mention in 'Algeria Unveiled'. If whiteness equates with modernity, the first mention of white women in this text belies the equation. In a footnote, Fanon explains that:

> certain unveiled Algerian women turn themselves into perfect Westerners with amazing rapidity and unexpected ease. European women feel a certain uneasiness in the presence of these women. Frustrated in the presence of the veil, they experience a similar impression before the bared face, before that unabashed body which has lost all its awkwardness, all timidity, and become downright offensive . . . The European woman has no choice but *to make common cause with the Algerian man* who had fiercely flung the unveiled woman into the camp of evil and of depravation. (emphasis added; 44)

If white men compete with Algerian men for their rights over Algerian women, Fanon suggests that in a reversal of order, French women compete with 'enlightened' Algerian women for sexual rights over French men. In opposition to their male counterparts who wish for women unveiled, the French women, in fact, demand visual difference in the maintenance of the veil. To this extent the veil signifies differently yet again; now it functions as a shroud which will keep the black women out of sight, not because of tradition but because of sexual competition.

In Fanon's text French women are marginal to the conflict between imperialism and the freedom struggle. Recent scholarship[30] on the role of European women within colonialism has attempted to examine the traditional reading of (white) women as having caused the loss of empire by their petty insistence on maintaining strict racial and class boundaries in the colonies and their reproduction of dominant colonial ideology in their relationship with colonized women.[31] Feminist scholars, however, working within the context of British colonialism, indicate the difficult structural position occupied by European women in the colonies in that colonialism underscored a masculine ideology through its 'military organization and processes, its rituals of power and hierarchy, its strong boundaries between the sexes'.[32] Claudia Knapman also suggests that, unlike the stereotype of the racist, white women actually had more contact with and more tolerance of the non-white.[33] In these works European women had a positive, though invisible, role to play within the colonial enterprise in that they made colonialism less brutal, more humane even, with their work among the blacks. In their decidedly secondary status to white men, white women in the colonies could themselves have agency only via race, especially since the embodiment of colonial domination was masculinity. If notions of European masculinity and femininity necessarily shifted in the colonies, under imperialism with its exaggerated sense of male domination and female dependency, the desire of French women to retain the veil of the Algerian woman can also be interpreted as their deferral of confronting their own powerlessness and their own gender oppression.

There are three other brief mentions of the French woman in Algeria in Fanon's text: once to suggest that European women attempt to embellish their appearance in a contrast to their colonized sisters who conceal their imperfections with the veil (45); a second indicating that European women too joined the freedom struggle in Algeria (61); the third recounting an incident when five members of the National Liberation Front were caught; a French woman clerk in Birtouta 'waved their photographs in front of their shop, shrieking: "They've been caught! They are going to get their what you call'ems cut off!"' (56). The reference to castration of the black man—a form of punishment fantasized in interracial rape/sex—suggests that the raped body is Algeria, feminized, the rightful property of the French (men). While the Algerian woman becomes metonymically linked to Algeria through the trope of rape, the jubilant French woman is neutered in that she signifies not through her gender and sexuality but only through her race.

In fact it is the French men who have the rape fantasies according to Fanon: 'In the dream, the [Algerian] woman-

71

victim screams, struggles like a doe, and as she weakens and faints, is penetrated, martyrized, ripped apart' (46). In another context, Jenny Sharpe suggests that 'when deployed as a concept-metaphor for imperialism, "rape" does not designate the penetration and control of a female colonial body; rather it designates the emasculation of a male one' (155).[34] Within the context of Fanon's text, the Algerian men never pose a sexual threat to either the French or the Algerian women. Their relationship with and control over the veiled women is always only readable specifically within the context of maintaining tradition and culture, and not within sexual relations. It is the French men who are sexually potent, the Algerian women being the passive recipients of this potency. If, as Ella Shohat and Robert Stam suggest, colonized people function as body rather than mind (just as the colonized world was perceived as raw material, rather than as mental activity),[35] it is the Algerian woman who functions as body, masterminded by the French man. In contrast, both French women and Algerian men signify not via their sexuality but through their race; they are sexually neutered in the text. The structure of sexual potency within which the French men are located must be read contrapuntally,[36] in that it can signify only through the attenuation of Algerian male sexuality by the winning over of Algerian women by French men.

At another level, arguments based on gender relations are made to underscore Algerian men's lack, and their lack of fitness for independence and self-determination. Within this context, the status of Algerian women is never an issue. What is at stake in her unveiling is suggesting the inferiority of Algerian man. Under the guise of championing female emancipation, French men reinscribe her within another form of sexism—an 'emancipated' Algerian woman would also signify as working for the cause of French imperialism. Unveiling Algerian women was finally about French masculinity. Empire could function only through the emasculation of Algerian man. To a large extent resistance to unveiling must be read within the context of resistance to emasculation. In their signification through race, not sexuality, Algerian men are not the opposites of their racially and sexually complete French counterparts but rather their incomplete forms, forms which fit in neatly with the discourse of development as generated by the Enlightenment and modernity.[37] The relationship between colonizer and colonized therefore goes beyond the discourse of race, including within it the complex interplay of racialized, gendered and sexualized positions.

Algerian women unveiled

> Everywhere, I think, not only here in Algeria, women fight and work for their country as much as men do but eventually they get very little out of it. Men don't like independent women with opinions of their own.
>
> Mme Hamdi in *Both Right and Left-Handed*

There is a metonymic link between the veil, Algerian women and Algeria itself, in that the colonization of Algeria is equated with the unveiling of its women. As Fanon says, the woman unveiled, 'disclosed to the eyes of the colonialists [sic] horizons' until then forbidden, and revealed to them, piece by piece, the flesh of Algeria laid bare' (42). From being metonymically linked, the Algerian woman becomes a metaphor for the colonized land itself, embodying the Algerian landscape. In the sequence nation, citizen, patriots, Algeria is the signified, and the Algerian woman is initially just one of the signifiers. Soon, through the trope of veiling and unveiling, she is suddenly rendered the nation's synecdoche—a part for a whole. Metaphorized in this way, she becomes interchangeable with the nation. At one level she becomes the signified to be fought over between French and Algerian men. At another level, through the process of metaphorization, her similarity/homogeneity with the nation is underscored; but that which gives her agency and subjectivity—her womanliness, her individuality—is lost, left behind as residue. Within the discourse of nationalism there is a slippage in the meaning of the Algerian woman—from sign to signifier to signified, or from metonymy to synecdoche to metaphor. It is this instability within the process of signification that causes the French men and women and the Algerian man to read/fix her differently. For the French man she functions as object/other, underpinning his subjectivity and knowledge formation; for the French woman she functions doubly: initially as competition, and eventually

73

as vulnerability displaced; for the Algerian man controlling her becomes an assertion of his masculinity, his potency.

But what could the veil mean for the Algerian woman in Fanon's text? Her perception of the veil is indicated in Fanon's text only at the moment she unveils herself for the sake of the revolution. I want to examine in particular his spatialization of gender and its connection to the veil. In one instance he suggests, '[t]he veil covers the body and disciplines it, tempers it, at the very time when it experiences its phase of greatest effervescence. The veil protects, reassures, isolates' (59); the young Algerian girl coming into maturity is veiled so that the two instances become inextricably braided for her—the womanly body as needing protection, needing veiling. Fanon adds that her unveiling of herself for the sake of the revolution results in:

> an impression of her body being cut up into bits, put adrift
> . . . When the Algerian woman has to cross the street, for
> a long time she commits errors of judgement as to the exact
> distance to be negotiated . . . The absence of the veil distorts
> the Algerian woman's corporal pattern. She quickly has to
> invent new dimensions for her body, new means of muscular
> control. (59)

Just as her veiled face causes the reversibility of the trope of surveillance for French men, her covered body conditions her vision itself in that the relationship between her body and her surrounding is mediated by the veil. The very materiality of her body; the sensations experienced by it in its environment, are cloaked by and negotiated through the veil.[38] Unable to perceive her own body without the veil, she experiences herself as invisible, incapable of being seen. Her perception of her covered body is in continuum with that of the French man. In a further step, her experience of her invisibility also shifts her very ability to see. Her womanly perspective, initially shaped by her veiled body, has to reorient and relearn how to negotiate spaces. Notions of her femininity, her body and her self as constricted and bounded by the veil undergo a shift through the unveiling.

Furthermore, Fanon's description of her bodily sensations replicates the dichotomy between the public and the private, a traditional division within Western feminism. Traditionally, the spatial segregation of public and private is gendered, the domestic perceived as woman's space, the world outside is the domain of the man. In *The Disorder of Women*, Carole Pateman suggests that this gendering of realms has its origins in liberalism, which distinguishes the public from the private sphere, making them totally independent.[39] While on the one hand liberalism presumes that every human being regardless of their gender can compartmentalize their lives according to such categories, on the other the division into public and private is neatly superimposed on the older patriarchal argument that women are closer to nature and men to culture. Thus the binary division of private and public neatly replicates the gendered difference of nature and culture. Pateman adds that such an interpretation of public and private is problematic, as these terms make no distinctions between cultures, nor allow for historical shifts in their meanings.

As a number of feminist critics have pointed out, the spatializing of gender relations manifests itself not only in the division of labour but also in the workplace, in architecture and in social relations. Among others, Doreen Massey points out, 'It's not just the spatial [that] is socially constructed; the social is spatially constructed too' (6). Daphne Spain suggests, 'Spatial arrangements between the sexes are socially created, and when they provide access to valued knowledge for men while reducing access to that knowledge for women, the organization of space may perpetuate status differences' (3). Sara Mills suggests that '[t]he architectural constraints and ideological strictures on women's movements within the colonial zone [are] important in shaping a notion of a woman's place and contribute to a sexualizing of space' (142).[40] All of them agree that the strict division between public and private is never unproblematic because race, class and history play a major role in the complexifying of this binary structure, and suggest that gendered spatial divisions and the experience of space is always culture specific. In Fanon's text, it is the French who construct the veiled woman as being 'humiliated, sequestered, cloistered' (38). In fact, in Henrietta Moore's words such a reading is brought about because:

> the ruling or dominant groups in society always present their
> culture both as natural and as the culture of the whole society

. . . The plurality of culture and the existence of alternative interpretations and values are not usually emphasized in the symbolic analysis of space, or indeed in the symbolic analysis of any form of cultural representation.[41]

As Fanon says, '[t]he Algerian woman's ardent love of home is not a limitation imposed by the universe' (66). Indeed Fanon suggests that she opts for it willingly.

In examining the construction and imbrication of gender, race, sexuality and culture through the spatial metaphors in Fanon's text I would suggest that the difference between the construction of French and Algerian women lies within notions of race, for otherwise as women they would be in alignment with each other. If Fanon describes the veil as protecting, reassuring and isolating the Algerian woman, then it is also metonymically linked with the Algerian man whose role consists of ensuring that his wife is not exposed. Where earlier I suggested that the veil, as part of her clothing, is a metaphor for the woman, I now suggest that it also functions as a substitute for the Algerian man's physical presence. Unveiling her is simultaneously to banish his presence from her life. In this metonymic linking of the veil to the Algerian man it once again shifts in meaning. If previously it functioned to inscribe her femininity, his very linking with it also feminizes him.

Fanon also uses the trope of the veil to indicate racial/colonial demarcations, a commonplace segregation in colonial discourse, as Mary Louise Pratt, John Noyes, and Gayatri Spivak have indicated.[42] Within colonial discourse the colonizer empties the (colonized) landscape of its original meanings and produces new knowledge, meaning and history about it. This in turn produces clear boundaries between the place occupied by the colonizers and that by the colonized. While the maintenance of boundaries reveals the deployment of power and colonial anxiety about maintaining racial boundaries, it becomes obvious that racial lines also construct notions of gender while being constructed by those same notions. In a metonymic link to the veil, Fanon suggests that the *Kasbah* (the Arab town) is itself a 'protective mantle', an 'organic curtain of safety [around] the native' (51). If the veil is a protective enclosure, so too is the Kasbah, in opposition to the European city which Fanon clearly indicates is 'not the prolongation of the native city' (51), adding that the bounding of 'the native city' by the European city is also an 'immobilizing' of it (52). There is no interaction between the two cities except via the 'charwoman' (52), an interaction which reinscribes class and racial demarcation and not gender. The unveiled Algerian woman's foray into the European city as a revolutionary forces her to overcome inner resistances and to 'remove something of the shame that is attached to it' (52). Being without her veil in the European city is like being naked (59).

Leaving the protective mantle of the Kasbah and going into the European city shifts the unveiled Algerian woman's very notion of femininity and regenderizes her in a continuum with the Algerian man who within colonization is feminized as long as he is under cover, under the mantle of the Kasbah, and in disguise in the European city. The Kasbah itself, a metaphor for the veil, is a feminine space for the French as long as it is perceived as an enclosure. As a consequence, entry into the European city shifts gender constructions for both the Algerian man and the woman. Fanon uses a copulative metaphor when he describes the revolutionary Algerian woman in the European city who '*penetrates* a little further into the flesh of the Revolution' (emphasis added; 54). Such regenderizing also reembodies her. Unveiled and in the European city: 'The shoulders of the unveiled Algerian woman are thrust back with easy freedom. She walks with a graceful, measured stride . . . Her legs are bare . . . and her hips are free' (58). The power within gender relations also become less clear. Fanon indicates that the young Algerian woman's patriarchal father, on discovering his daughter's participation in the revolution, follows 'in her footsteps' (60) and supports the revolutionary cause.

Ultimately, 'Algeria Unveiled' and *A Dying Colonialism* (of which it forms a part), at some level note the dissipation of the practice of traditional patriarchy. In a footnote in 'Algeria Unveiled', Fanon records that '[t]he Algerian's age-old jealousy, his "congenital" suspiciousness have melted on contact with the Revolution . . . The militant man discovers the militant woman, and jointly they create new dimensions of Algerian society' (note 14). This change goes beyond the unveiling of woman and shifts in gender relations, affecting familial relationships in general. In the chapter on 'The Algerian Family', Fanon suggests that through colonialism and the revolution, all Algerian members 'gained in individuality' and faced 'new choices, new decisions' (99). Instead of the son following in the footsteps of the father, the revolutionary son sets the example for the father. The sexualized, veiled daughter 'was replaced by the militant, the woman by the *sister*' (Fanon's emphasis; 108). The revolutionary younger brother set the example to the older brother (110); 'The Algerian couple . . . became considerably more close knit in the course of this Revolution' (113). In sum, in Fanon's text colonialism is connected to patriarchy; the overthrow of colonialism results in the overthrow of patriarchy as well.

Notwithstanding the overthrow of patriarchy/colonialism, ultimately the text discursively constructs Algerian women rather peculiarly, especially in its theme of the spacing of people. Spatial divisions function as signifiers of racial as well as gendered difference: under both colonial rule and patriarchy, Algerian women's movements are controlled and restricted. The right to mobility is located primarily with French men and women and, to a lesser extent, Algerian men. The veiled Algerian woman occupies the static, timeless space signified under the term 'traditional'. Veiled, she functions diacritically, as the negative term which must and can always only function as comparison to the Algerian man. Unveiled and in Western garb she functions in a similar way to enhance the masculine potency of the French man. In both instances she herself is devoid of agency and is incapable of coming into representation. She can only be represented. But unveiled and revolutionary she inscribes herself as subject and as other, forcing both the French and the Algerian man to function in relation to her. But how long does it last?

Woman–Body–Nation–Space

It is Fanon's optimism followed by the sobering tones of Hélie-Lucas' interview that causes bewilderment. It is the very ambiguity brought about by the respacing and the gendering of Algerian women through the unveiling, the revolutionary activities and the penetration into the European city—this fundamental shift bringing instability to tradition—that brings about the reprisals recorded in Hélie-Lucas' text. In her reading of Mahasweta Devi's fiction, Gayatri Spivak points to the seamless narrative produced by the decolonizing nation, which somehow reproduces the ideology of colonization,[43] when she says: 'the political goals of a new nation supposedly are determined by a regulative logic derived from the old colony, with its interest reversed: secularism, democracy, socialism, national identity, and capitalist development' (106). In the narrative of the new nation, however, 'the consumer elite is being constituted as the definitive citizen' (109). Left out of the status of citizenship are those who cannot be categorized as the consumer elite. This occlusion is recorded in Hélie-Lucas' text, when she suggests that in the construction of the national narrative of the definitive Algerian, the woman is excluded. There is no proper place for her in the new nation-space. Nalini Natarajan suggests that the heterogenous nature of the nation can be homogenized only through the figure of the woman who is essentialized and located as prior to history.[44] This unchanging quality attributed to woman also contributes to and legitimizes the construction of the definitive citizen, the ideal national subject.

Another way of reading the status of Algerian women in this disjunction between Fanon and Hélie-Lucas, is to trace the slippage between the problematic and the thematic, the two different levels in the structure of the body of knowledge about colonialism/postcolonialism. In defining these terms Partha Chatterjee[45] suggests that the thematic 'refers to an epistemological as well as ethical system which provides a framework of rules for establishing relations between elements; the problematic, on the other hand, consists of concrete statements about possibilities justified by reference to the thematic' (38). Chatterjee suggests that in postcolonial countries, decolonization is normally just on the political arena, not in the epistemological or representational level. Terms such as 'agency' and 'subjecthood', so central to decolonization, are historically specific to the European Enlightenment, but need not signify in identical ways in previously colonized countries. To that extent, notions of agency and subjecthood do not percolate downwards beyond that of political freedom from colonial masters. To explain within the scope of the problematic the Algerian demand for independence suggests an internalization of Enlightenment categories such as progress, modernity and individualism. Within the scope of the thematic, progress and modernity as interpreted by the Enlightenment are just not historically specific in the same way in Algeria. Algeria might selectively use Enlightenment categories of independence and freedom for its nation, but not necessarily for its women. Hence the restriction of Algerian women in Hélie-Lucas' text. This slippage between the thematic and the problematic, this disjunction in postcolonial nationalism, is enacted on Algerian women's bodies rather than on Algerian men, suggesting that it is at the very level of their embodiment that the women function in specific ways in the nation.

While I realize the need for historical and cultural specificity, in the rest of this chapter I will begin to speculate on how women function in the structure of the democratic nation. For Carole Pateman, that which underpins a democratic nation or any civil society is the notion of contract intrinsic to issues of citizenship, employment, marriage, et cetera, in any democratic state that is based on the claim that all 'individuals are free and equal to each other or that individuals are born free and equal' (39). Pateman juxtaposes the works of Hobbes, Locke and Rousseau, among others, and analyses how women are located within civil society. Classic contract theory presumes that individuals subordinate themselves to civil law; subordination itself is contractual between equal individuals. Thus the notion of contract is central not just to issues of citizenship but of employment as well. Pateman examines the construction of gender within contract theory and suggests that while notions of contract underscore its basis as a construction for the collective benefit of individuals, women themselves are located as being prior to civil society, unchanging and 'born into subjection' (41).

The conundrum faced by women is that while the notion of the individual is theoretically considered to be free of gender bias, within marriage the woman contracts to give up her freedom in order to obey her husband. Pateman explains: 'A (house)wife remains in the private domestic sphere, but the unequal relations of domestic life are "naturally so" and thus do not detract from the universal equality of the public world' (117). In contracting into marriage, the woman in particular agrees to assume a disadvantageous position. Because contract (for men) is predicated on the public/private divide, Pateman suggests that women's lives are governed by the sexual contract, that 'which both establishes the orderly access to women and a division of labour in which women are subordinate to men' (119). Ultimately the sexual contract is not unlike the contract between slaves and their masters, in that their chief function is to enhance the quality of life for the patriarchy. Though Pateman's mapping of race onto gender is problematic, her underscoring, that the public world of men is perceived as constructed and within the confines of the trajectories of historical time whereas the notion of contract locates women as prior to history and even to construction, as 'natural', and static in her status, is useful. In short, her body, which locates her in the realm of the private, also deprives her of the full status of citizenship.

If woman's links to the nation are weak, if they don't have equal rights with their male counterparts, if their citizenship is on shaky grounds, is their inequality necessarily negative? This tenuousness of a woman's relationship with the nation-state causes Rosi Braidotti to evoke the words of Virginia Woolf: 'As a woman I have no country, as a woman I want no country, as a woman my country is the whole world' (as quoted in Braidotti, 21). Braidotti strongly advocates a 'postmodern feminist nomadism', the latter term informed by Deleuze and Guattari's usage of nomadism as a critical consciousness. The central issue of Braidotti's thesis is 'the interconnectedness between identity, subjectivity, and power . . . By what sort of interconnections, sidesteps, and lines of escape can one produce feminist knowledge without fixing it into a new normativity?' (31). In order to bring about a defamiliarization to notions of identity she finds a nomadic consciousness useful in that it 'combines coherence with mobility' (31) and allows her to rethink the unified, unitary subject: 'As an intellectual style, nomadism consists not so much in being homeless, as in being capable of recreating your home everywhere' (16). Braidotti differentiates between the exile, the migrant and the nomad. While the first is constructed politically, the migrant is perceived within the context of economically disadvantaged groups (22). Though Braidotti decries Woolf for advocating a liberating homelessness for women on the one hand, the trajectory of her own intellectual movements—from Italy, to Australia, to France, to the Netherlands—valorizes that same sort of homelessness. She shows her preference for places of transit—transit lounges at railway stations, airports—which for her are 'oases for non-belonging' (18). She likens the interrogatory role of Women's Studies as a discipline within the academy to the critical consciousness generated by being nomadic.

While intellectually I can appreciate her post-structuralist agenda of dismantling and destabilizing identities, for me Braidotti's work is haunted by a scene which she describes and then discards—black immigrants waiting in the transit zone of the Paris International Airport, not allowed entry into France. Braidotti herself obviously gains entry easily. She might valorize nomadism and debiologize the body—'the body . . . [is] a point of overlapping between the physical, symbolic, and the sociological' (4), but a lot of black women cannot be perceived beyond the body. The literal aspect of nomadism—the ease of and the right to mobility—is reserved for women with strong passports. Women with weak passports are normally confined within their borders. Braidotti's ease of movement across borders reveals the unmarked European body. This aspect of nomadism is ultimately a metaphor for having access to a nomadic consciousness. For a lot of unprivileged women, their traditions and their nations are often their only conduit to agency and self. As Caren Kaplan says: 'Some of us may experience ourselves as minor in a world that privileges the masculine gender. But our own centrality in terms of race, class, ethnicity, religious identity, age, nationality, sexual preference, and levels of disabilities is often ignored in our own work. All women are not equal . . .'[46]. Despite Braidotti's determination to be unfixed, she reproduces an unmarked fixity in that she disregards that at some level the material reality of the body also fixes it racially, culturally and socially. This fixity always reveals a certain positionality, an occupation of a certain tract of land. Her advocation of a post-structuralist nomadism—the demand for unfixing and for oppositionality—can work as a strategy only for some. The rest are always already fixed, arrested, pinned into position.

What I am suggesting here is that the woman's body is coded not only racially, culturally, sexually and socially but also nationally, embodying the nation as well, carrying on and through her body the marks of the position occupied by the nation she represents in the hierarchy among nations. It is the imbrication of the woman's body with the nation/national landscape that interests me. In her early work, *The Lay of the Land*, Annette Kolodny suggests a rationale for the feminization of the landscape in the newly colonized and settled US:

> gendering the land as feminine was nothing new in the sixteenth century; Indo-European languages, among others, have long maintained the habit of gendering the physical world and imbuing it with human capacities. What happened with the discovery of America was the revival of that linguistic habit on the level of personal experience . . . [P]erhaps, the connections are more subtle still; was there perhaps a *need* to experience the land as a nurturing, giving, maternal breast, because of the threatening, alien, and potentially emasculating terror of the unknown?[47] (Kolodny's emphasis)

In short, the woman's body functions as a mediator for the male citizens to experience the landscape and the nation as nurturing, comforting and familiar. Given that her body functions to mediate the connection between the male citizen and nation, a female citizen cannot experience the national landscape in an identical way to her male counterpart, in that her body functions to nurture him. But who would nurture her?

Luce Irigaray extends this line of reasoning in her analysis of the woman's problematic relationship to place.[48] For Irigaray, the maternal body is experienced as place, skin and envelope for the growing fetus/baby. The maternal body also functions as the basis, the nature, of form and matter (37). The maternal body braids place, form and matter: 'Place is thus not the thing but that which permits the thing to be insofar as the thing can exist in and outside place' (30). So the individual's experience of his self is always in relation to place/the maternal body—either as part of it or separate from it. The woman's relationship with place is fraught in that she *is* the place, separated from her own place. As Irigaray puts it, 'She is or ceaselessly becomes the place of the other [the man] who cannot separate himself from it. Without her knowing it or willing it, she is then threatening because of what she lacks: a 'proper' place' (10–11). In short, she is; she does not have.

I conclude by pursuing the line of argument evoked by the two basic verb forms 'to be' and 'to have', the difference between them, and the construction of gendered subjectivity within the nation. Within the context of gender theory, Jacques Lacan in 'The Signification of the Phallus' explains the difference between the mutually exclusive verb forms 'to be' and 'to have'.[49] He says: 'the relations [between the sexes] will turn around a "to be" and a "to have", which by referring to a signifier, the phallus, have the opposed effect, on the one hand, of giving reality to the subject in this signifier, and, on the other, of derealizing the relations to be signified' (289).

At the risk of grossly oversimplifying, for Lacan the verbs 'to be' and 'to have' are gendered/sexed positions which are constituted with reference to the phallus. The phallus, which is not to be perceived as interchangeable with the penis even though there is a close connection between the two, culturally signifies authority and power; the phallic order governs exchange relations and culture. In anthropological discourse, Lévi-Strauss describes the phallus as the very condition of culture in that it stands for both the object of exchange within social networks as well as the rules which influence and govern the exchange of objects.[50] Within psychoanalytic discourse the phallus is linked with the subject coming into signification and language. It is through his relationship and positioning to the phallus that the subject ascends to the position of 'I' in language and discourse. In sum, the phallus represents power, is at the basis of culture and social networks, and at the very foundations of language and subjectivity.

Lacan, who derived his notion of being and having the phallus from Freud's description of heterosexual relations in 'On Narcissism: An Introduction', suggests that women *are* the phallus as men *have* them. By this he means that both sexes desire the phallus in the same way. The girl's greatest realization in her heteromaturation process is that, though herself castrated, she can accede to the phallus via the man, by becoming the object of his desire, by reflecting and representing male desire; in short by becoming the phallus. As Judith Butler suggests, 'For woman to "be" the Phallus means . . . to reflect the power of the Phallus, to signify that power,

to "embody" the Phallus, to supply the site to which it
penetrates, and to signify the Phallus through "being" its
Other, its absence, its lack, the dialectical confirmation of its
identity' (44). In his turn, the man's possession of the phallus
can be affirmed only through the woman's desire for him. He
can confirm that he has it not only through her lack but
through her desire of him. Thus, though being and having
the phallus are (normally) mutually exclusive, they are also
intersubjective, for as Elizabeth Grosz suggests, 'it is only by
means of the other that one's possession of or identity with
the phallus can be confirmed. To have or to be the phallus
entails having a place within a circuit in which the other's
desire plays a crucial part' (133).

While Lacan makes the distinction between 'to be' and 'to
have' strictly within the context of sex/gender and heterosexuality, I would like to speculate that a similar circuit of
relations exists between the nation, male citizen and female
citizen. Just as the phallus suggests power, authority, and the
constitution of the subject, and is at the basis of culture, so
is the nation in the constitution of the subject. In such an
analogy the nation functions as phallus. Notions of sexuality,
masculinity, and femininity are governed by nationalistic discourses. To that extent, the nation/culture determines what is
masculine and femininist just as much as does the unmarked
notion of the Oedipus complex. In a related context, Sneja
Gunew suggests that since language constructs subjectivity, a
migrant's movement from one country to another, one language to another must, of necessity, shift, repress and
reconstruct their subjectivity.[51] The nation not only determines
gender relations but also embodies them racially to a
large extent: except in the case of immigrants, one can
normally discern compatriots at a glance. Within this paradigm,
the woman 'is' the nation in that her function, literally, is
to reproduce it and maintain its boundaries. As Anthias and
Yuval-Davis point out, her body must be used to maintain
ethnic/racial/national differences. She also embodies the
nation, for without her cooperation the nation dies. While she
embodies it she does not really have it, in that it is only in
recent times that her citizenship has stabilized: a woman
marrying an 'alien' until recently automatically lost claims to
her citizenship. As for the male citizen, his easy alliance with

85

the nation can be mediated only via the woman's body. He needs the woman/nation to confirm his patriotism, his national identity. Her attachment to the patronymic grants the woman a minimum of subjectivity, agency and power within the nation. In the (edited) words of Butler: 'Hence, "being" the [nation] is always a "being for" a masculine subject who seeks to reconfirm and augment his identity through the recognition of that "being for"'(45).

The construction of masculinity and femininity has to be read at the intersection of theories of nationalism as much as through gender theory. To see a global continuum in woman's oppression is no longer acceptable, as it does not take issues of race, class, sexuality, age, location and so on into consideration. Furthermore, such a move locates the woman outside of history, in a moment before time began. Locating her strictly within discourses of the nation is also problematic, as this merely codes her racially/culturally, and not within the context of gender relations. An analysis of the woman's role within the nation should interconnect her history with that of the nation while simultaneously examining the specific constructions of gender and sexuality within that nation/culture.

PART II

In the Antipodes

4

The memory of place: Maori nationalism and feminism in Aotearoa/New Zealand

In the fascinating chapter 'Traveling Theory', in *The World, the Text, and the Critic,* Edward Said speculates on how theoretical frameworks, born in response to a particular event or political situation, reemerge in a different manifestation when they shift from one place to another, one time to another.[1] The passage through time and space results in overlays of contexts and resistance until the theory is transformed in the new context. My question is: How pertinent are theoretical frameworks produced in the more densely populated Northern hemisphere, with routinely mobile academics, to those of us living in the Southern hemisphere? This population differential has significantly contributed to the hegemony of scholars and theoretical frameworks produced in the North. The scholar in the South is faced with a difficult choice—either use frameworks which reveal their Northern bias or be read only locally.

It is with these cautionary words that I want to embark on the topic of Maori (indigenous) feminism which I see as a construction of Maori nationalism rather than a derivation of the feminist movement in Aotearoa/New Zealand. I will begin by posing a series of questions: What part does a person's relationship to the (imagined) contours of land and place play in any discourse on nationalism? What are the specific roles played by women and the women's movement in the rhetoric of the nation? What is the form of nationalism (e.g., Maori nationalism) constructed not on identity as Benedict Anderson has suggested, but rather through difference as Partha Chatterjee suggests?[2] Is Maori nationalism constructed on the basis of identity or difference?

Metropolitan paradigms of the Northern hemisphere

This discussion of indigenity and indigenous feminism is framed within the intellectual ambit of two central essays, Chandra Mohanty's 'Cartographies of Struggle' and Ella Shohat's 'Notes on the 'Post-colonial', which within different contexts shed light on what indigenousness entails.[3] Mohanty's essay, among other things, attempts to redefine Third World women, not within the context of geographical contours, but within 'particular socio-historical conjunctures' (2). Mohanty perceives a commonality between the struggle of women in the Third World and that of women of colour in the First World, in that they are all products of the 'internationalization of economies and of labour' (2):

> With the rise of transnational corporations which dominate and organize the contemporary economic system, however, factories have migrated in search of cheap labour, and the nation-state is no longer an appropriate unit for analysis. In addition, the massive migration of ex-colonial populations to the industrial metropolises of Europe to fill the need for cheap labour has created new kinds of multiethnic and multiracial social formations similar to those in the US. Contemporary postindustrial societies, thus, invite cross-national and cross-cultural analyses for explanation of their own internal features and socioeconomic constitution.(2)

In this schema, Third World women (or 'women of colour', Mohanty using the two terms interchangeably) become a political category in an imagined community, as Benedict Anderson also defines the term, with its implications of community and alliances between the ethnically and racially different Third World women. By subordinating the notion of the Third World to that of a political category, and one determined by an internationalization of economy, Mohanty destroys any clear-cut demarcations between the First and Third Worlds. To her they are not just a division of space but also suggestive of one group (First World) being read through tropes of progression, modernity and Westernization and the other through themes of poverty, illiteracy, tradition and backwardness. In her argument the First World exists in the Third, and vice versa. Such a theoretical move also allows for a unity among Third World women in that their identity is constituted via their relation to racist, colonialist/neo-colonialist and sexist structures rather than by their particular geographic location.

Mohanty's argument, empowering though it is to Third World women, is problematic on two counts. First, in its haste to demarcate itself from First World feminism, it symptomatically reproduces the homogenizing effect of the Third World which she herself finds problematic in her extremely influential essay, 'Under Western Eyes'.[4] In this essay she castigates those First World feminists who have homogenized women in the Third World, reading them as poor, illiterate, traditional and suffering. Furthermore, she perceives this reading as one which splits the globe into two unequal halves *vis-à-vis* power, wherein Western/First World women's definitions of their less fortunate and poorer sisters of colour is merely to empower themselves and to derive an identity for themselves, while simultaneously situating themselves as primary in the equation. Her redefinition of women of colour to include those in the First World, which is defined by a global economy, while it takes care of the problematic division of the two hemispheres (Western and non-Western), nevertheless reaffirms Third World women as poor and united in their struggle for survival, regardless of their location on the globe. The very structure against which Mohanty argues in 'Under Western Eyes'—a homogenized Third World and an equivalent First World—somehow remanifests itself in 'Cartographies of Struggle'.

This criticism of Mohanty's essay is not to deride her argument completely. However, I do think the second problem or limitation in her essay needs to be addressed. This is that while alliance through a common context of struggle is particularly meaningful in a multicultural, ethnically diverse country such as the US or the UK, it does not resonate in the same way in a bicultural nation such as Aotearoa/New Zealand. In the last census in 1991, which revealed a total population of around 3.5 million, Pakeha (white, Anglo-Celtic)

New Zealanders accounted for about 80 per cent of the population, Maori (indigenous) New Zealanders for about 10–12 per cent, the rest (consisting of Pacific Islanders, Asians and non Anglo-Celtic white) being categorized as Other. Attention must be drawn to the population breakdown because New Zealand is the only white-settler nation other than South Africa which contains a large proportion of indigenous people. This ethnic balance has resulted in a call for biculturalism[5] or partnership sharing between Maori and Pakeha, unlike Australia which, because of its greater ethnic diversity and decimated Aboriginal population (between 1–2 per cent), has gone the way of multiculturalism. Such clear demarcations in the racial groups make it easier to think of Aotearoa/New Zealand as a bicultural rather than a multicultural nation. Mohanty's argument about a common context of struggle theoretically ought to build possible alliances between the various 'black'/women—Maori, Asian, Pacific Islander—but, in reality, no such alliance appears. Instead, Asians in particular are perceived as usurpers of that which rightfully belongs to Maori, rather than being perceived as similar victims of the global economy. The prevailing feeling among Maori has been that the inclusion of Asian women in the equation will render New Zealand a multicultural nation, completely bypassing indigenous rights and biculturalism. Multiculturalism would be regarded by Maori as likely to prise them from their *tangata whenua* or 'first-people' status and reposition them as just another minority in this 'common context of struggle'. It is their special status in Aotearoa/New Zealand that leads Maori feminists to build alliances with Pakeha feminists rather than with their Asian or Pacific Islander counterparts.[6] Maori feminists' relationships with Pakeha feminists is mediated by the presence of the Treaty of Waitangi, a point I will elaborate on shortly.

Multiculturalism vs biculturalism

I dwell here on Mohanty's essays because they are symptomatic of the notion of multiculturalism particularly as practised in the US. For instance, multiculturalism as defined by the Chicago Cultural Studies Group functions:

to rethink canons in the humanities—to rethink both their boundaries and their function . . . to find the cultural and political norms appropriate to more heterogenous societies within and across nations, including norms for the production and transmission of knowledges.[7]

Within such a move, as Berube indicates in 'Public Image Limited', multiculturalism includes ethnics such as Asians, Latino/as, Blacks, indigenous peoples, along with a motley of other disenfranchised groups who are united in their opposition to Western values, the West and eurocentrism.[8] Also included in this notion of opposition is the premise of the assimilation of more established ethnic groups such as Italians, Eastern Europeans and Jews within the dominant group in the US. Underpinning the notion of multiculturalism in the US is the desire for racial equality across its population. Only such an interpretation of multiculturalism (as the equality of all racial groups) would even allow for generalized opposition to eurocentrism. It is also this underlying understanding of multi-culturalism that allows Mohanty to see alliances among all the disenfranchised women of the world, in that they are all victims of eurocentrism. This reading also allows her to locate Native American women as yet another minority in the US.

However, notions of multiculturalism are interpreted dif-ferently in the Antipodes, particularly in Australia and New Zealand, in that its premise is located not within issues of race and racism as in the US but within migration patterns that manifest themselves racially. Within the context of Aus-tralian multiculturalism, Sneja Gunew comments that 'racism is constructed as much in terms of those who are non-Anglo as in terms of those who are non-white. One needs to recall here that Italians were designated "blacks" around the second world war and that Arab-Australians are described so now and one hears of Australian-Greeks speak of themselves as "black".'[9] Blackness or race, then, is a category which serves to trace the recentness of migration to Australia rather than functioning merely as an ascription of colour. Multiculturalism in Australia therefore functions not so much against euro-centrism (or anglocentrism) but rather to include 'ethnic diversity'. It is precisely this definition of multiculturalism based on ethnic immigration that has demoted Aboriginal

Australians to the status of ethnicity, bypassing the central issue of their land rights. And it is precisely the centrality of land rights to indigenous Maori and the history of migration patterns specific to Aotearoa/New Zealand that allows the Maori to demand a definition of the state as bicultural rather than multicultural. As I noted earlier, the higher percentage of Maori—10–12 per cent—as compared to Aboriginal Australians or Native Americans, in addition to an immigrant population predominantly from Great Britain (80 per cent), allows New Zealand to bypass multiculturalism altogether. Furthermore, in New Zealand the distinction between Maori and Pakeha is based on the provisions of the Treaty of Waitangi, signed in 1840, which secured Aotearoa/New Zealand as part of the British Empire. To put it another way, what is meaningful and sensible (within limitations) in the American context and within Mohanty's argument is historically specific only to the US and does not transfer well into another framework with a different history.

In 'Notes on the "Post-colonial"', Ella Shohat raises a similar question about the inappropriate usage of terms and frameworks. Shohat says the term 'Third World' has been superseded by 'post-colonial'. Addressing the problems adherent to the superimposition of the new term, Shohat points out that 'post-colonial':

> collapses very different national-racial formations—the United States, Australia, and Canada, on the one hand, and Nigeria, Jamaica, and India on the other—as equally 'post-colonial'. Positioning Australia and India, for example, in relation to an imperial center, simply because they are both colonies, equates the relations of the colonized white settlers to the Europeans at the 'center' with that of the colonized indigenous populations to the Europeans. (102)

Shohat's challenge to the concept denoted by 'post-colonial' is a pertinent response to Mohanty's notion of Third World feminism, because the latter leaves no space for the struggles of Native American women, dominated by both multinational corporations of the US and other feminists of colour. Mohanty's postcolonial feminism prevents recognition of the specificity of Native American women's struggles which, in the name of the common context of struggle, is erased in a different form of hegemonic violence.

Shohat's essay is satisfying to the Antipodean reader especially when she acknowledges the failure of metropolitan syncreticism:

> Post-colonial theory's celebration of hybridity risks an anti-essentialist condescension towards those communities obliged by circumstances to assert, for their very survival, a lost and even irretrievable past. In such cases, the assertion of culture prior to conquest forms part of the fight against continuing forms of annihilation . . . The question . . . is not whether there is such a thing as an originary homogenous past, and if there is whether it would be possible to return to it, or even if the past is unjustifiably idealized. Rather the question is: who is mobilizing what in the articulation of the past, deploying what identities, identifications and representations, and in the name of what political vision and goals? (110)

Here Shohat castigates the promotion of the notion of hybridity so intrinsic to postcolonial strategies of identity formation, and reads it within the context of syncreticism rather than in the way Homi Bhabha originally used the term.[10] Shohat rightly points out that the retrieval of an originary past goes hand in hand with postmodern awareness that the originary past is a retroactive construct. This dichotomy is especially evident when the indigene anachronistically skews chronology by using the technology of the late twentieth century to re-evoke a glorious and lost past culture—for instance, the indigenous Kayapo in the Amazon using video cameras to preserve a memory of their culture. The irony of such a move merely underscores that the indigene is a deliberate retroactive construct rather than someone locked in her past. To that extent, the indigene is as much a product of syncreticism as are hybrid/syncretic theorists such as Mohanty.

While Shohat's criticism of postcolonial theory's condescension towards nativism is warranted given the political agenda of indigenous peoples, there is a problem with her argument. In her haste to disturb clear-cut distinctions between postcolonials (who are read as hybrids) and the indigenous (normally with a nostalgia for a glorious, precolonial past), she situates the latter as postmodern and syncretic as well. In her bid to equate the indigene with the postcolonial, she displaces them from their relationship to their land and disrupts patterns of identity formation based on landscape and place. Furthermore, such a postmodern, postcolonial imposition of hybridity or syncreticism on native cultures and their geographic space prohibits political agency from that very space.

Spatial identity

Shohat's move is theoretically sound given the criticism which traditional anthropology has suffered. For instance, Arjun Appadurai in 'Putting Hierarchy in Its Place' makes the argument that '[t]he link between the confinement of ideology and the idea of place is that the way of thought that confines natives is itself somehow bounded, somehow tied to the circumstantiality of place' (38). Appadurai proceeds to argue that, within traditional Western anthropological discourse, this notion of the native's attachment to the fauna and flora of their place is tied to a perception that native patterns of thought are specifically linked to their landscape (38). This perception he argues, leads to the incarceration of the native (38). In an extension of this argument, Akhil Gupta and James Ferguson in 'Beyond "Culture": Space, Identity, and the Politics of Difference' suggest that to theorize natives as pure and uncontaminated prior to Western intervention is completely erroneous because:

> Colonialism . . . represents the displacement of one form of interconnection by another. This is not to deny that colonialism, or an expanding capitalism, does indeed have profoundly dislocating effects on existing societies. But by always foregrounding the spatial distribution of hierarchical power relations, we can better understand the process whereby a space achieves a distinctive *identity* as a place. Keeping in mind that notions of locality or community refer both to a demarcated physical space *and* to clusters of interaction, we can see that the identity of a place emerges by the intersection of its specific involvement in a system of hierarchically organized spaces with its cultural construction as a community or locality.[11]

In so saying, Gupta and Ferguson correctly indicate the involvement of traditional anthropological discourse with the hierarchization of spaces—Western as primary and non-Western as secondary.

While Gupta and Ferguson, Appadurai and, by implication Shohat, make an undeniable assertion, there is an unexplained issue here. Is any attachment to a particular fauna, flora and landscape displayed by the native merely a construction of the Western anthropologist? Most importantly, in what context is the native's deliberate evocation of their relation to land to be taken? There is a long and illustrious tradition of people's attachment to place forming the basis for nationalistic feelings. In *Imagined Communities*, Benedict Anderson associates the primordial sense of identity (of a culture) through place to our perception of the 'primordialness of language' itself. Anderson points out that '[n]o one can give the date for the birth of any language. Each looms up imperceptibly out of a horizonless past' (144). The implications of this are that our sense of cultural identity is intertwined not only with our relationship to and rootedness in the land, but also that our use of our language is, in turn, rooted to particular tracts of land. Anderson gives the example of the singing of the national anthem for our experience of place and identity, a phenomenon which I discussed in Chapter 1 on the cartography of bodies: 'No matter how banal the words and mediocre the tunes . . . people wholly unknown to each other utter the same verses to the same melody' (145). By singing about their land people achieve a common identity which has its basis in national boundaries and demarcation.

Anderson argues that our structuring of identity and our relationship to place is not limited to national anthems alone. He also points to our use of the language of kinship—'Motherland', 'Fatherland', *patria*—and the importance of this in the definition of our cultural identity. This use of kinship terms, he suggests, indicates bondedness through blood which establishes or structures our relationship to our country or place of origin. The terms we use for home—'homeland', *heimat*—also act to territorialize our identity, denoting 'something to which one is *naturally* tied' (emphasis added; Anderson, 143). In the article 'National Geographic', Liisa Malkki, too, points out that the relationship between people and place is often established through discursive as well as non-discursive practices; for example, the custom of kissing the ground when people return to their country of origin. Another example she supplies is people taking a handful of soil from their country when going into exile. Malkki also points out that the rooted-ness of people to land is 'often specifically conceived in plant metaphors' (34). Malkki argues that the reason for the use of arborescent language in our construction of (ethnic) identity is seen in the connection between family identity (family tree) and origin and national identity: 'Motherland and fatherland, aside from their other historical connotations, suggest that each nation is a grand genealogical tree, rooted in the soil that nourishes it. By implication, it is impossible to be part of more than one tree' (28). All this underscores that there is a naturalized relationship between one's place and one's self.

Maori sovereignty

Having argued for the native's attachment to the fauna and flora of their place, I might appear to set the clock of scholarship back, ignore the ravages of colonialism, and deny the existence of the logic of late capitalism which posits a single world economy. However, I merely want to state that what is posited by scholars such as Appadurai and Gupta is an either–or argument—either accept the native as a construct of the metropolitan West or incarcerate him. I would like to suggest an alternative framework in an analysis of the identity of the indigenous New Zealander, one in which the Maori deliberately reconstruct and re-evoke their native identity through their relationship with their land, a relationship dic-tated by Western settlers. By deliberately mimicking[12] the identity demanded of them by Pakeha, Maori aim to achieve specific political goals. I want to look at just two examples, both of which oscillate around issues of land.

The first example comes out of the formation of New Zealand as a state and as part of the British Empire. This event was organized around the Treaty of Waitangi,[13] signed in New Zealand in 1840. Prior to Western intervention, Maori were a heterogenous group, consisting of a number of tribes (*iwi*) with chiefs. The Treaty signed by a number of Maori chiefs (but not all) in Article 1 ceded 'to Her Majesty, the Queen of England, absolutely and without reservation all the rights and powers of sovereignty' which these chiefs exercised or possessed over their territories. In return, in Article 2 the Queen confirmed and guaranteed:

> to the chiefs and tribes of New Zealand and to the respective families and individuals thereof the full exclusive and undisturbed possession of their Lands and Estates, Forests Fisheries and other properties which they may collectively or individually possess so long as it is their wish and desire to retain the same in their possession.

Article 2 also demanded that Maori land be sold only to the Crown. In addition to granting the tribes the use of their lands, in Article 3 the Queen also extended her protection to the Maori and granted them 'all the rights and privileges of British subjects', namely, citizenship. The Maori who signed over the sovereignty/governorship did so believing that the 'shadow of the land goes to the Queen but the substance remains with us'.[14]

Article 2 of the Treaty, which oscillates around the use of land, has been under intense disputation ever since 1840. The Crown reneged on the honouring of the Treaty soon after it was signed. As a result of the Land Wars of the 1850s and 1860s the Crown, in violation of Article 2 of the Treaty, directly confiscated three million acres and indirectly confiscated sixteen million acres of Maori land in the North Island. The confiscation of land did not just economically dispossess Maori of land but also dispossessed them of their kin and the presence of their ancestors which the land represented. From the mid–1970s there has been a movement in New Zealand to honour the Treaty once more and make reparation for the loss and damage suffered by the Maori. A Waitangi Tribunal, of both Maori and Pakeha, has been set up to investigate claims against the Crown. The concluding act of reparation will be the formal legalization of biculturalism as policy in New Zealand and the acknowledgment of the equal partnership between Maori, with their rights as the *tangata whenua*, and Pakeha as the dominant group of white settlers.

The second example also arises from the issue of land. Here I make reference to the Maori practice of burying the placenta and the umbilical cord of a newborn baby in the ancestral land. This practice is particularly meaningful in that the word for land and placenta is the same, *whenua*. In this custom, land functions as more than a repository of memories or a signifier of economic values. It works to assign an individual identity to the Maori native as well as to indicate her place among her kin and her ancestors, a continuing cultural practice that can be seen as what Shohat describes as a 'fight against continuing forms of annihilation'. This custom has shifted in meaning and became layered with a certain poignancy since the Maori were denuded of land after the dishonouring of the Treaty. Another way of looking at this custom is to record it as an example of the 'unchanging' ways of the Maori, which renders them 'predictable' and safe.

Juxtaposing these two examples will show the strategies of Maori nationalism. The continuing tradition of burying the placenta represents Maori nationalism as timeless and unchanging, whereas signing the Treaty of Waitangi suggests just the opposite—their adaptability to new ways of constructing identity. Both ploys are necessary in the growing bid for Maori nationalism. In oppositional nationalism, a braiding of the unchanging and the changing, the predictable and the political, the Maori plays the role that is expected of her by being timeless and unchanging in her ways while simultaneously going beyond the role assigned to her, being overtly political. By deliberately 'incarcerating' themselves in their relationship to land, Maori form the contours of the pan-Maori nationalistic movement in Aotearoa/New Zealand.

Maori feminism and Maori nationalism

In the first part of this chapter, I pointed out the complex meaning adherent to the notion of indigene, made an argument for the derivation of identity through land, and also attempted to give some background information on New Zealand. This rather long preamble has been necessary because Treaty issues in New Zealand have to be perceived as just a part, though a significant part, of the larger issue of Maori nationalism, for two reasons: first, and most important, for biculturalism to be taken seriously, for Aotearoa/New Zealand is not yet a bicultural society, despite the existence of the Treaty, a legal document. Second, only an acceptance of Maori nationalism will allow for a perception of a contextually specific origin and agenda for the Maori feminist movement. In the second half of the chapter I locate Maori feminism as having derived from Maori nationalism, which allows for the visibility of racial divisions (Maori vs. Pakeha) rather than the gender divisions (men vs. women) which structure the traditional model of Western feminism.

Within New Zealand the land and sovereignty issues are inextricably intertwined within the feminist movement. In her article 'Maori Sovereignty: A Feminist Invention of Tradition', Michele Dominy links the two movements by suggesting that the Maori Land March of 1975 led by Dame Whina Cooper, the Bastion Point Occupation by the Maoris in 1978 and the protests against the South African Springbok Rugby Tour in 1981 were linked with the emergence of feminism.[15] To recapitulate: in 1975 Dame Whina Cooper marched from Te Hapua, in the north of the North Island, to the capital, Wellington, in the south of the North Island. Basing her politics on the premise that for a Maori to be landless is tantamount to being deprived of an identity, she marched to Wellington to present a statement of Maori rights to the government.

The Bastion Point Occupation represented a challenge to the Crown's underhanded ways of acquiring Maori land during the late 1800s. In 1976 the Government announced plans to build a major high income housing development on what was originally Maori land. In response, Maori protestors occupied Bastion Point for 506 days and demanded the return of 180 acres of land to their ownership. Around this action, Maori women challenged their men for equality within the movement. In her article on the experience of Maori women at Bastion Point, Jan Farr wrote: 'The women by sheer persistence, perseverance and by their over-all ability to organize, participate and show results for their efforts, managed to evolve from a merely supportive or back-up role (for men), to a dynamic role in active leadership.'[16]

According to Dominy, the last incident which contributed to forging an identity for Maori feminism was the Springbok Rugby Tour in 1981. Many New Zealanders were opposed to the tour of the South African team, not only because it was not integrated but because Maori players in the New

Zealand All Blacks rugby team had previously been refused permission to tour South Africa. Sir Robert Muldoon, the then Prime Minister, despite intense opposition from Maori and Pakeha alike not only permitted the Springboks to tour New Zealand but also provided police and army support for the team at a cost of $8 million. While Maori who marched against the Tour immediately saw the parallels between apartheid in South Africa and racism in New Zealand, a number of Pakeha needed some persuasion. Donna Awatere wrote:[17]

> The relationship between black and white political groups will in the long run depend on how well whites can identify and work against injustice to black people. Very few will. Yet racism is a global phenomenon, not particular to one country and it must be fought globally, wherever it is. And it is here. In New Zealand. But anti-racism isn't fashionable like feminism, or full of intrigue like anti-capitalism, although it includes both feminism and the class struggle. Emotionally, fighting overseas racism must be easier to cope with for whites. (12)

Dominy points out that the protests against the Tour gave prominent roles to both Maori and Pakeha women, who often marched in the frontlines and were equally physically assaulted by government forces (250). Furthermore, the protests against the Springbok Rugby Tour questioned the notion of a homogenous identity for Aotearoa/New Zealand and ripped the white nation apart. Finally, it heightened Pakeha awareness of racism in their own country against the indigenous population for the first time and forged ties between Maori and Pakeha to consider a bicultural identity for Aotearoa/New Zealand.

Maori feminism within Pakeha feminism?

Michele Dominy also suggests that the Bastion Point occupation and the anti-Tour movement not only reconfigured traditional gender relations for Maori but also reconstituted notions of colour and race. She suggests that a direct consequence of Bastion Point was the adoption of the manifesto 'Gonna Share with all our Black sisters/The Right to be Black/The Right that was taken from us like the land' (248–9) at the national *hui* (gathering) of Maori women in 1980. In this move, Black does not signify a racial ascription, but in its inclusion of all Maori, Pacific Islanders and Indians, signifies a marker of political alliance instead (249). For Dominy feminism becomes a Black woman's revolution and all men, Maori and Pakeha, are conflated 'as owners and perpetrators of oppressive institutions, governments and systems' (Farr as quoted in Dominy, 248).

It is a commonplace in feminist theory to suggest a natural alliance between the disenfranchised, a line of argument premised on simple notions of oppositionality wherein the dominative (read: masculinist) power in a socio-juridical system is first located; this identification results in alliances between all marginalized groups who interrogate and oppose that cultural authority. This alliance is indicated by Bill Ashcroft et al. in *The Empire Writes Back*:

> Women in many societies have been relegated to the position of 'Other', marginalized and, in a metaphorical sense, 'colonized', forced to pursue guerilla warfare against imperial domination from positions deeply embedded in, yet fundamentally alienated from, that *imperium*. They share with colonized races and peoples an intimate experience of the politics of oppression and repression, and like them they have been forced to articulate their experiences in the language of their oppressors.[18]

While such an alliance of the marginalized is often undeniable and fruitful, there are some problems with Dominy's reframing of the indigenous rights movement in Aotearoa/New Zealand as feminist. First, because of the structure of binary opposites— men vs. women—Maori men become metonymic extensions of Pakeha men. Only such a structuring would permit sisterhood in the Pacific and foster the positioning of women as oppositional. While Dominy's location of Pakeha men as the hegemonic group in Aotearoa/New Zealand is appropriate, to equate Pakeha men with Maori men is inadequate within a socioeconomic category which always remanifests itself as a racial category. Awatere herself critiques left-wing academics elsewhere, 'Left-wing groups analyse the basic contradictions in terms of the class-struggle. In their analysis issues of sovereignty, race and culture fade into marginality'.[19] In the privileging of gender over race and culture Dominy foregrounds one form of difference (men vs. women), but she glosses indifferently other forms of disenfranchisement, those which occur on the grounds of race and culture.

The second problem in this analysis is that the indigenous rights movement becomes framed within the feminist struggle. Dominy indicates the subordination of Maori nationalism to feminism in the following:

> Their identities as Maori and as women share aspects of each other, and both identities at times join in opposition to white male-dominated culture. In particular Maori activist women work to *redefine and recreate their cultural tradition*, rejecting certain aspects of Pakeha culture and the imposition of Western aspects of ethnicity . . .' (emphasis added; 238).

In the guise of uncovering 'true' Maori identity ('rejecting . . . the imposition of Western aspects of ethnicity'), Dominy's argument slides in a hierarchy where only 'activist' Maori women redefine and recreate their cultural tradition, a move in which activist Maori women are seen to take their cue from the feminist struggle and reinvent tradition, as do their Pakeha counterparts. Dominy thus offers a Western model of identity politics to explain the awakening of political awareness among Maori women.[20] In this additive model, indigenous women, led by their Pakeha counterparts discover their identity as oppressed women prior to their awareness of their identity as oppressed Maori women.

Most importantly, this continuum between Pakeha and Maori women under the rubric of feminism in Dominy's analysis reveals the underlying premise of the resituation of the latter as minority rather than *tangata whenua*, an issue central to the growing nationalism and political construction of Maori.[21] This subordinates the specificity of their wider struggle to women's issues in general in New Zealand. For example, it draws attention away from the Treaty to relocate Maori women as any other minority women, as an economic and ethnic category without any other primary identity.

Maori women within Maori nationalism

Another way of analysing this series of events is from within the context of the role of women within nationalism. Such a reading is warranted in that Maori feminism, as much as it coincides with the New Zealand Women's movement, also intersects in 1970 with the formation of the Nga Tamatoa, a predominantly male action group whose primary function was to preserve *maoritanga* ('things Maori'), and the Maori Organization for Human Rights, a protest group formed as a response to the 1967 Maori Affairs Amendment Act. The growing leadership of Maori women is further contextualized within the organization Te Roopu O te Matakite ('those with foresight') in which Dame Whina Cooper played a part. The important point is that the assertions of Maori women ought to be read within the growing pan Maori nationalism and not merely as a metonymical extension of the white women's movement in Aotearoa/New Zealand. While Dame Whina Cooper played the leading role in the 1975 Land March, Dominy notes that no other woman functioned as an 'official' leader in either the Bastion Point Occupation in 1977–78 or in the 1981 Springbok Tour. If in 1975 a Maori woman played the leading role in the Maori political landscape, why not in 1977–78 or in 1981? This is not to suggest that Maori women of calibre were just unavailable in the latter two events and that Dame Whina Cooper was the only woman with recognizable leadership qualities; for a more fruitful explanation, I would argue instead for a re-examination of Maori women's leadership in light of the role of women in nationalistic struggles.

Women and nationalism

It is a commonplace to suggest that women function in very specific ways within a newly emergent nation-state or within a growing nationalism. Theorists such as Carole Pateman suggest that within the notion of citizenship, the state constructs men and women in gender specific ways. In *Woman–Nation–State*, Floya Anthias and Nira Yuval-Davis indicate the complex relation that the woman has to the state,[22] pointing out that women:

> on the one hand, . . . are acted upon as members of collectivities, institutions or groupings, and as participants in the social forces that give the state its given political projects

105

in any particular social and historical context. On the other hand, they are a special focus of state concerns as a social category with a specific role (particularly human reproduction). (6)

Anthias and Yuval-Davis proceed to enumerate the various functions of women within the context of the nation: as biological reproducers of members of ethnic collectivities; as reproducers of the boundaries of ethnic/national groups; as central participants in the ideological reproduction of the collectivity and as transmitters of its culture; as signifiers of ethnic/national differences—as focus and symbol in ideological discourses used in the construction, reproduction and transformation of ethnic/national categories; as participants in national, economic, political and military struggles (7). In this they suggest that women are the state in that they reflect and embody its power yet also function as the site upon which the nation confirms its own masculine, powerful identity. In other words, women as members of the collectivity are the nation yet they simultaneously function as the objects, the maternal bodies, upon which the state literally reproduces itself. Women function as the basis, the logic upon which the state names itself.[23] To this extent, Dame Whina Cooper's leadership in the Land March as well as the lack of 'official' leadership of women at Bastion Point and during the Springbok Tour are not acts of individual agency. Their visibility and assertion is an orchestration precipitated by the requirement of the Maori nation.

Read within the context of growing Maori nationalism and the conscious formation of *maoritanga* and *tikanga Maori* ('Maori knowledge'), the emergence of Maori women becomes a logical outcome. Charged with being reproductive members of Maoridom, women's roles become prominently etched. Maori women have not only maintained racial/ethnic boundaries, they have also transmitted its culture while participating in its economic and political struggles. The growing awareness of *maoritanga* and its organization resulted in increasingly prominent roles for the women. As such, one can read this series of events (the Land March, the Bastion Point Occupation, and the Springbok Tour) which found women in assertive roles as being connected to the resurgence of Maori nationalism and the deliberate imagination of the Maori nation-state.

Within the context of women and nationalism I wish to cite Partha Chatterjee's influential article, 'The Nationalist Resolution of the Women's Question',[24] in which he examines the shifting role of women in the nationalist struggle in British India to overthrow British rule. According to Chatterjee, Indian nationalism went beyond a political struggle for power and permeated every aspect of the material and spiritual life of the people (238). He argues that the binary opposition of colonizer/colonized, white/brown, Western/Eastern reproduces itself in yet another dichotomy: material (outer)/spiritual (inner), with Britain identified as the visible numerator and India as the submerged denominator:

> The material/spiritual dichotomy, to which the terms 'world' and 'home' corresponded, had acquired . . . a very special significance in the nationalist mind. The world was where the European power had challenged the non-European peoples, and by virtue of its superior material culture, had subjugated them. But it had failed to colonize the inner essential identity of the East which lay in its distinctive, and superior, culture. That is where the East was undominated, sovereign, master of its own fate. For a colonized people, the world was a distressing constraint forced upon it by the fact of its material weakness. It was a place of oppression and daily humiliation, a place where the norms of the colonizer had perforce to be accepted. (239)

Chatterjee adds that within this divided world the colonized had to learn the sciences from the West to match their power over the material world. But in order to do so, 'the crucial need was to protect, preserve and strengthen the inner core of its national culture, its spiritual essence . . . In the world, imitation of and adaptation to western norms was a necessity; at home they were tantamount to annihilation of one's very identity' (239).

The implications of the production of such a binary of outer and inner are obvious and superimposed on the construction of gender as well. The man participates in the profanity of the outer whereas the woman represents the inner, functioning as caretaker and guardian of the traditional and the indigenous. Though the woman may participate in the outer world, she is reinscribed within a new form of patriarchy, different to the patriarchy of indigenous tradition in that it is inflected with colonialism as well as nationalism. My underscoring of this Indian model of nationalism is not to suggest that it is the only or the originary form of Third World nationalism, but rather an attempt to understand Dominy's perception of the change among Maori women being faced with an either-or solution: 'either accepting traditional constraints or risking their old affiliations' (245). I would argue instead that this assertion of a female identity among Maori women that Dominy notes is a requirement of the mobilization of the nationalistic struggle for sovereignty. In the significant roles played by women in the nation, where they signify both its boundary and difference, as well as the maternal body upon which the Maori nation defines and predicates itself, women's roles gain in importance and visibility. To attribute it to global feminism alone would be to erase the centrality and significance of Maori nationalism.

Within this context of the misuse of the category 'global feminism' I want to draw attention to just one example under intense contestation in the 1980s, namely the debate over speaking rights on the *marae* (a far more complex version of a Town Hall but with spiritual connotations; the *marae* is a building which symbolizes the tribe) where traditionally women have the specific role of greeting and men of speaking. Reading these structured roles within Western paradigms of what constitutes agency (speech rather than the ritual of greeting) led to the debate whether women should speak on the *marae* or not. As Kathie Irwin says in 'Towards Theories in Maori Feminisms': 'For many Maori, having the right to speak on the marae is not an issue and never has been. It is viewed as Pakeha women's preoccupation, which is irrelevant to Maori.'[25] The ritualized nature of speaking on the *marae* consists of several parts, however: *karanga* ('greeting'), *waiata* ('song'), *tangi* ('mourning') and *whaikorero* ('speech-making'). 'Protagonists in this debate have recognized only whaikorero as speaking' (12). In short, the forms of speaking in which women participate have not been recognized by Pakeha feminists as no equivalent categories exist within Pakeha feminism. Irwin is indignant that 'the frustrations of the feminist movement were visited upon individuals and institutions alike. The *marae*, the central most important institution in Maoridom, became a target for the visitation for some of this feeling' (10). While Irwin rightly identifies the inadequacy of Pakeha-centric feminism to categorize, comprehend and explain the specificities of Maori practices, it is evident that in this entire debate over the right of *whaikorero* on the *marae* there has been no major shift in gender roles for the postcolonial Maori; this is not unlike Indian nationalism, in which women have their own role to play in the maintenance of inner spirituality of indigenous social-cultural-spiritual life. Irwin herself admits that a Pakeha man 'who is tauiwi [stranger, foreigner], not a speaker of the language, or *tangata whenua* in a Maori sense of this word, is allowed to stand and *whaikorero* on the *marae atea* simply because he is a man' (17).

To clarify this point about gender roles, I cite Chatterjee again. He continues to explain the reinscription of women's roles in growing Indian nationalism:

> . . . the 'spirituality' of her character had also to be stressed in contrast with the innumerable surrenders which men were having to make to the pressures of the material world. The need to adjust to the new conditions outside the home had forced upon men a whole series of changes in their dress, food habits, religious observances and social relations. *Each of these capitulations now had to be compensated by an assertion of spiritual purity on the part of women.* They must not eat, drink or smoke in the same way as men; *they must continue the observance of religious rituals which men were finding it difficult to carry out*; they must observe the cohesiveness of family life and the solidarity to the kin which men could not now devote much attention. The new patriarchy advocated by nationalism conferred upon women the honour of a new social responsibility, and by associating the task of 'female emancipation' with the historical goal of sovereign nationhood, bound them to a new, and yet entirely legitimate, subordination. (emphasis added; 248)

Chatterjee indicates that in the nationalistic struggle it was necessary to mobilize the women, who constituted half the Indian population. Yet mobilization for Indian emancipation did not necessarily include Indian women's emancipation. They had to be reinscribed within a new form of patriarchy, one carrying the markers of both colonialism and nationalism. The recognition of their value as Indians to the nation precluded their autonomous identity as women. Their importance was explained to them via their complementary roles to Indian men. Similarly in Aotearoa/New Zealand, the debate over the *marae* did not result in any specific changes in women's right to *whaikorero*. As Irwin points out, having the right to speak is not an issue—what is emphasized is the significant complementary role that women play on the *marae* as well as the maintenance of gender roles. I do not suggest that Chatterjee's model precisely describes Maori gender roles; rather that in this instance, Maori women are relocated in their traditional space on the *marae*. The point I am making is that women function as metaphor for the nation and therefore become the scaffolding upon which the men construct national identity. In their construction of Indianness, Indian men constrained Indian women in specific ways. Similarly, I think Maori men construct the Maori nation as female in order to reflect their own identity. There is no agency where Maori women construct themselves autonomously, as separate from Maori men or the Maori nation.[26] All these thematics and configurations of identity are implicated within each other.

The text of Maori sovereignty

> The only thing that remains believable is the cave of one's own dwelling, for the present [is] still permeable by legend, still touched with shadows . . . Memory is the anti-museum: it cannot be localized. Its remains can still be found in legend.
>
> Michel de Certeau, *Practices of Space*

Having provided a framework which reveals the overlapping of Maori nationalism and Maori feminism, I now want to discuss Donna Awatere's *Maori Sovereignty*, which is inflected with issues of postcoloniality as well as nationalism and reveals the inscription of women within this historical configuration.

Serialized between June 1982 and February 1983 in *Broadsheet*, the well-circulated feminist journal, Donna Awatere's three articles, 'The Death Machine', 'Alliances' and 'Beyond the Noble Savage', reappeared in 1984 in *Maori Sovereignty*, with the inclusion of a fourth chapter, 'Exodus'. Together these four essays became the central articulation of sovereignty issues in New Zealand from a Maori perspective and generated debate from feminists and non-feminists, Maori and non-Maori alike. In fact, as Awatere herself notes in the second essay 'Alliances', '[a] number of Wellington feminists have protested at the publishing of [chapter one, 'Death Machine'] in *Broadsheet*' (43). She adds 'the *Maori Sovereignty* issue was a keynote article in relations between white and Maori women. Yet the cover of *Broadsheet* for that month was globules representing pink and white tits. This is an insult to Maori women and to the Maori people' (45). This reveals the deep divide between white and Maori feminism in Aotearoa/New Zealand in the early 1980s, not unlike the statements made by feminists of colour elsewhere in the world. While this text generated critical attention and discussion in the 1980s, in the current decade it is relegated to the pages of history, a punctuation mark in the feminist debates in New Zealand, at most garnering references in footnotes. By the late 1990s the text has fallen into obscurity primarily because Awatere is held suspect both as a feminist and as a Maori nationalist, due to her association with Roger Douglas' political party, Association of Consumers and Taxpayers (ACT), which advocates self-reliance and individual accountability. Both Maori and liberal Pakeha find her new political affiliation a complete reversal of her previous argument for Maori sovereignty.

Notwithstanding the author's unpopular affiliations, *Maori Sovereignty* is a rich text inviting interpretation. Constituted through two competing genres, the main text is interrupted by an alternate text, composed of photographs and their accompanying captions; the two texts combine to ensure the primacy of context over pure text, demanding shifting multiple interpretations. The murmur of voices and meanings constantly contextualize as well as destabilize each other to provide a new understanding of the text, land rights and Aotearoa/New Zealand's legacy of biculturalism. The photographs function to construct a history of the pre-contact pure Maori, but the whole enterprise is marked with contamination. As photography itself is a post-contact phenomenon, this underscores the idea that attempting to locate the precolonial is always already marked with the postcolonial, since all knowledge of the precolonial emerges from within the last three hundred years. Awatere can to some extent be accused of being (as Spivak

describes in 'Who Claims Alterity?') 'the new culturalist alibi, working within a basically elitist culture industry, insisting on the continuity of a native tradition untouched by a Westernization whose failures it can help to cover, legitimizes the very thing it claims to combat'[27].

In fact, Awatere's text is not about the glory days of pure Maori in brave and beautiful hermetically-sealed Aotearoa. It maps out a picture of Maori as a community in interconnected spaces, demonstrated by three photographs in particular. The photograph on page 14 of the text is of a landscape inscribed with meaning by Maori, not Pakeha. In the long shot the background fades at a distance, indicating the full landscape and plenitudinous life led by the pre-contact Maori. The ground is pockmarked by what the caption indicates are kumara pits circa 1899 (post-Treaty). The text continues:

> Continuous cropping tropical plants were adapted to the colder climate. Storage pits provided for a seasonal growing and a year-round food supply. Soils were made suitable where

necessary by transporting huge loads of manuka to the garden
site and burning it there. In the South Island, kumara gardens
were planted facing north to catch the sun and networks of
stone walls protected crops and divided whanau plantings.
(16)

The photograph on page 16 is of a Maori woman surrounded
by mutton birds which are being cleaned in preparation for
winter food storage in the South Island. The caption that
accompanies it not only records the exclamation of a British
immigrant on Ruapeke Island at how fresh the preserved *nga
titi* was nine months later, but also contains another significant
comment:

> Titi were a vital source of food along the Southern Coasts
> along Foreaux Strait where it was too cold for kumera
> growing. They were taken in the autumn and preserved for
> the winter. A British immigrant on Ruapuke Island in the
> 1820s described how the roasted titi were kept airtight in
> split sheets of kelp. He reported that they were as fresh as

113

the day they were put in, when eaten eight months later. From other reports it seems Otago and possibly Canterbury Maori had hunting rights to certain mutton bird islands to the south. Title to an area of land by inheritance or conquest did not preclude other whanau, hapu or iwi having rights to the same land for a different purpose. The primary right was to live on and cultivate the land, but others might have the right to snare birds in particular trees, or set nets at a particular spot in the whitebait season. (16)

I draw attention to these sentences as they are significant in my argument a little further on, but for now it is enough to say that both these photographs, along with various others in the text, serve to draw a picture of Maori ways, methods of organization and economy prior to colonization (as much as photographs from within the colonizing period can possibly record such events).

The third picture I have selected appears on page 48, a photograph of *Te-Toki-a-Tapiri*, a war canoe, damaged, fated to be burned by the Navy but 'spared at the last minute by the Collector of Customs at Onehunga', which now rests in the Auckland Museum. This photograph thus becomes a metaphor for Maori, brave and ferocious in the war of the 1860s, but eventually defeated and preserved only in memory and museums. This is one of the last photographs in the book which records precolonial Maori sovereignty, appearing to function as a dirge lamenting the time that was and a land inscribed only by Maori.

But do these photographs really mark the waning years of a once proud indigenous people? A re-examination of the pictures and the captions produces an alternative interpretation, a reading which suggests a marked awareness of the Maori of the 1980s and 1990s as postcolonial, living in the arena of postmodernity and global capitalism. To read these photographs as the sad remnants of an autonomous (read: 'precapitalist') Maori suggests that they were a static localized people in a primordial time violated by colonialism and global capitalism. Yet the kumara pits and the *nga titi* preservation photographs and the organization of land suggests a different story, that of the Maori as politically and economically organized in precolonial days. There was no 'autonomous' primeval economy but rather a community of interconnected space,

Te-toki-a-Tapiri. Maori attempts to defend and hold onto their land in the wars of the 1860s led to them being called 'Enemy' by the white settlers and soldiers alike. As part of the assault on the Enemy, General Cameron ordered that all Maori canoes in the Auckland area be destroyed. Canoes were vital to the local trade in food, for transport and the mana of the people. Over 60 were towed to Onehunga and burned by the Navy. One great war canoe, Te-Toki-a-Tapiri (its damaged prow shown above) was spared at the last minute by the Collector of Customs at Onehunga. It is now in the Auckland Museum.

people who traded with one another, who manufactured, who formed an interconnected community: North Island with the South, Aotearoa with Australia and Polynesian islands, their canoes used for trade and transport of food and people. 'Precontact' New Zealand had already been contacted by other people of colour; it was not hermetically sealed; Maori were not insular people but an interconnected community living already to some extent beyond a purely local economy. As I mentioned before, Akhil Gupta and James Ferguson indicate: 'Colonialism . . . represents the displacement of one form of interconnection by another . . .'. (9)

This notion of spaces being hierarchically interconnected is fundamental to the construction of the nation, as is indicated by the arbitrariness of national boundaries on the map, separating and connecting one country with another. Yet nationalism also requires a process of forgetting the political act encoded in spatial boundaries in order for nationality to re-emerge as essence, race and individual. Nation as a merely political construct must be forgotten for the production of nationalistic feelings.

Distribution of space/place in Aotearoa/New Zealand

Finally, I want to discuss briefly the implications of Awatere's definition of Maori sovereignty. She initiates the debate over this issue very early in the text by defining Maori sovereignty as:

> the Maori ability to determine our own destiny and to do so from the basis of our land and fisheries. In essence, Maori sovereignty seeks nothing less than the acknowledgement that New Zealand is Maori land, and further seeks the return of that land. At its most conservative it could be interpreted as the desire for a bicultural society, one in which taha Maori receives an equal consideration with, and equally determines the course of this country as taha Pakeha.(10)

Here Awatere is upholding the conditions of the Treaty which had allocated the lands, forests and fisheries to Maori which they individually or collectively owned. By echoing the language of the Treaty ('our land and fisheries'), Awatere reveals her strategy of argument. First she evokes the Treaty when she refers to the postcolonial Maori reconfigured as one people by the Treaty, not a loose conglomerate of different tribes. Secondly, by evoking the Treaty she draws attention to Article 2, that which was systematically reneged on by Pakeha. In referring to Article 2 (which specified that the Crown would leave undisturbed the land owned by Maori), she slides in the reminder that, in fact, all land in Aotearoa/New Zealand once belonged to Maori. It works strategically in that she first upholds the law only to remind the law of its own lawlessness and unfairness.

Having defined the issue of sovereignty, she says:

> Maori sovereignty has always been a thread of belief, commitment and desire, seen in the bloody defence of our land, in the Ringatu movement, Kotahitanga, Kingitanga. Set against our people has been the united strength of white people. The Maori now seeks to break that unity in the interests of justice for the Maori people . . . All immigrants to this country are guests of the tangata whenua, rude visitors who have by force and corruption imposed the visitor's rules upon the Maori . . . This country is Maori land. (34–5)

Now Awatere appeals to the morality of this issue; far from being a history of 'rebellion' against the Crown—the history designated to defeated peoples—she attempts to redress this historical rendition of her people, to resituate and reread the Ringatu and Kingitanga movements. This becomes her decolonizing gesture, a strategy which becomes an amalgam of evoking then refuting the knowledge arising from colonization and suggesting that the truth lies elsewhere.

In Awatere's last chapter, 'Exodus', her definition of sovereignty becomes meaningful when she posits a politics of inclusion:

> The elemental forces of Maoridom are based on human connections, on the dynamics of human exchange, of pooling resources and pulling together, of mutual exchanges of thought and actions, of interweaving and interlocking patterns of human connections, of all skills, knowledge, talent and 'things' belonging to the group not the individual. (101–2)

While seeming to write only to Maori in this chapter, in this repetition of the term 'human' she opens it up to Pakeha as well. By including Pakeha through human connections, mutual exchanges of thought and actions, the paradox is revealed: when Awatere posits sovereignty, she posits a biculturalism, not one that is about Maori being granted their rights due to the 'generosity' of Pakeha, but one, in fact, already part of Maori cultural values which dictate, demand inclusion and connection and mutual exchanges of thought and action. It is biculturalism initiated not by Pakeha but by Maori, sharing that which is theirs with others.

The Treaty, the photograph of the *nga titi* and its caption about the division of land and the chapter 'Exodus' suggest the indigenizing of Aotearoa/New Zealand precisely by including

117

difference, by 'interweaving and interlocking patterns of human connection'. The *nga titi* caption suggests that more than one tribe of people can have rights over the land—some to cultivate, some to fish and some to snare birds—and that Aotearoa/New Zealand has place for all these people. By asserting Maori sovereignty, Awatere's text redefines it as indicative not of naked power and aggression but as one suffused with sharing. By sharing and interconnecting, Maori values proliferate rather than diminish. The meaning of biculturalism itself shifts in that, instead of addressing issues pertinent to Maori and Pakeha only, it includes all issues pertinent to Maori and non-Maori alike.

The two conclusions of *Maori Sovereignty*

Ultimately, the photographs in *Maori Sovereignty* provide the key which makes the heteroglossic text (the text of the double-voiced discourse) visible. Without the photographs of the warriors, the way of life, the women, the families, the children, *Maori Sovereignty*, far from being one of the central documents of decolonization would be instead the discourse of the defeated. The photographs contextualize the unique ideology and the world of the Maori. This resituation of Awatere's words via the photographs gives them a moral suasion and transforms them into a re-imagination of a 'new' conceptual system in its complex interrelationships, consonances and dissonances.

Via these photographs I come back to my earlier questions: How are Maori women re-imagined in *Maori Sovereignty*? How are Maori women located in the Maori nation? How do the photographs of the women in the last chapter, 'Exodus', vary from those in previous chapters? I suggest that the key to unlocking the 'woman question' in *Maori Sovereignty* lies in the anomaly of the conclusion of the text. Quite simply, there are two conclusions, 'Beyond the Noble Savage', which functions as the conclusion of the *Broadsheet* version, and 'Exodus', the last chapter when it was republished as a book; we are left to question the significance of the two conclusions. What is the purpose of having a false ending ('Beyond the Noble Savage') which functions as disconfirmation, first falsifying reader expectations only to point to an unexpected route and yet another conclusion?

Read within the context of narrative theory—and *Maori Sovereignty* is a narrative, retelling the story of Maori with pictures and words—endings are very important to the way we read a text. Closures contain within them the key to the interpretations of the beginnings and the middle. For instance, Frank Kermode points out in *The Sense of an Ending* that conclusions are fundamental to the way in which the reader perceives patterns in the work and in life around her.[28] In *Closure in the Novel*, Marianna Torgovnick states 'Endings, closures reveal the essences of [the work] with particular clarity; to study closure is to re-create and re-experience [the work] with unusual vividness'.[29] By positing two conclusions Awatere deliberately draws attention to closure in *Maori Sovereignty*.

The answer to this dilemma is simple. The two conclusions work differently. The audience that 'Beyond the Noble Savage' is aimed at is obviously Pakeha; the photographs in this chapter function as a lament, a wail indicating the slow defeat of a people, their attempts to assimilate, their creation of a hybrid identity. The history referred to in the photographs is set in the end of the nineteenth and the beginning of the twentieth centuries. The photographs are mostly of male leaders, Tawhiao Te Wherowhero, Te Kooti Rikirangi, Te Whiti o Rangomai, Rua Kenana and Wiremo Tahupotiki Ratana, to name a few. In addition, there are photographs of Parihaka, a village on the Waimate Plains in the process of being pillaged, bone pendants carved in prison, Maungapohatu, Rua Kenana's settlement before and after being ransacked, Rua in chains. Towards the end of this sad tale are a few photographs of women, one taken at a *hui*, 'probably taken at Ngaruawahia', two of Te Puea, one with a young girl, another with Pirihia Katipa, and others which do not portray women alone.

The photographs of 'Exodus' sit in contrast to those in 'Beyond the Noble Savage'. The audience that this chapter addresses is not Pakeha but Maori, and the tone is one of hope of victory. With just one exception, there are no photographs of individual men or women. They are in groups, photographs of Nga Tamatoa, the disruption of Waitangi Day celebrations in 1972 in which men are depicted. There are

119

also large photographs of women which fill whole pages (there is very little text in this chapter): large photographs of young Maori women learning Maori; striking photographs of Eva Rickard and other women leading the Tainui Awhiro protest in Raglan; several photographs of Dame Whina Cooper, again with other women; and photographs of Maori women leading the Anti-Tour Protest March in Gisborne. The only photograph of a sole woman is of Tungia Baker. The last photograph is of the *hikoi* stopped on the bridge at Waitangi by police, 6 February, 1984. If 'Beyond the Noble Savage' overwhelmingly represents male Maori leadership, 'Exodus' overwhelmingly represents Maori women in the struggle for the nation.

Awatere's situation of women, the role and position she would have them occupy, lies in the contrast to the photographs the two conclusions put forward. Notions of agency and individual will in the struggle for freedom are the predominant themes in the last two chapters of *Maori Sovereignty*. The male leaders pictured alone, successful briefly, but eventually defeated, jailed, now dead, are a contrast to the women leading in community, leading with family, friends, supporters, tribe. The category of leadership in 'Exodus' has changed face. Perhaps it is time for this category to shift in meaning in order to bring freedom and equality to Maori. To a large extent, this capacity of inclusiveness, the politics of inclusiveness, read along the racial lines in the previous section of this essay is visible among the women leaders of the Maori nation. The leadership of women as suggested in *Maori Sovereignty* is not individual leadership, but a leadership of a collective female identity. Leadership now indicates a new society, of equality of women with their men, not at the cost of their men. The women in these pictures, exhorted and made responsible for building the new Maori nation, do so collectively. Only in this move can the agency of women in the nation become visible.

In conclusion, I am cognisant of the fact that my discussion carries all the marks of the fact that I am neither Pakeha nor Maori but an Asian settled in New Zealand, evident through the style of analysis and my subjective positioning. I have argued that the theory that has travelled does not in most cases resemble its progenitor. To that extent my use of metropolitan theories from the Northern hemisphere in order to critique them as well as to construct my own argument has been inevitable. Feminist theories which arise out of indigenous nationalisms are inevitably different from their metropolitan counterparts. Only an acknowledgment of their historical specificity will allow for the encoding of Maori feminisms as arising from Maori nationalism.

Place in My Place:
embodiment, Aboriginality
and Australia

Sally Morgan's autobiography[1] calls out to me to flesh out the embodiment of the Aboriginal and the Australian which are constructed by it. As I read Morgan and the criticism generated by her work, I wonder about the politics that surround the act of a non-Aboriginal—and, in this instance, a non-Australian as well—writing on a text on Aboriginality. A number of responses have been published around this issue in the wake of Bain Atwood's article on Morgan's text.[2] For instance, Jackie Huggins, an Aboriginal academic, insists: 'I detest the imposition that anyone who is non-Aboriginal can define my Aboriginality for me and my race. Neither do I accept any definition of Aboriginality by non-Aboriginals as it insults my intelligence, spirit and soul and negates my heritage' (459). Again, when Subash Jaireth, a non-Aboriginal academic, argues for his right to dialogue on this work, he is severely admonished by Jo Robertson for his use of a Bakhtinian framework which '[n]either considers situations of unequal power relations, nor accounts for epistemic violence' ('Authority and Authenticity'; 145). Robertson suggests that Jaireth's inclusion of Morgan's text within the society of discourse gives rise to questions of domination and power, oppression and the silencing of Aboriginal voices on Aboriginal texts, in that there are 'traditional Aboriginal restrictions and prohibitions on the circulation of and the transmission of information' ('Authority and Authenticity'; 147). Robertson's admonishment extends to me as well, as I am positioned in continuum with Jaireth. As I read this work, I wonder about the difference between being indigenous and black and being postcolonial and black. When did I, a postcolonial, stop being indigenous? When I left India? When the British left India? How do I, a black postcolonial, sometimes categorized as indigenous Indian, read Morgan's text? What is invested in my act of reading this particular text? Our readings, Morgan's and mine, whether categorized as indigenous or postcolonial are both the effects of racial discourses.

I turn to Gayatri Spivak's 'A Literary Representation of the Subaltern' to authorize my reading of Sally Morgan to counteract Jackie Huggins' criticism of non-Aboriginal readings of Aboriginal texts and find that it cannot be so easily done.[3] Instead I learn a lesson from Spivak:

> The position that only a subaltern can know the subaltern, only women can know women and so on, cannot be held as a theoretical presupposition either, for it predicates the pos-sibility on identity . . . [In fact] knowledge is made possible and is sustained by irreducible difference, not identity. What is known is always in excess of knowledge. (253–4)

For Spivak a symbiotic relationship between (Aboriginal) knowledge and (Aboriginal) identity is also a 'figure of the impossibility and non-necessity of knowledge' (254), in that knowledge-production is predicated on a subject-object rela-tionship. Only an objectification of Aboriginality would permit Bain Atwood and Suresh Jaireth to write about it, to rewrite themselves as subjects. Spivak's admonition extends to me as well, as a reader of Morgan's text. In turn I too am implicated in the objectification of Sally Morgan's life in this reading, in that I have to admit that this chapter is a rewriting of myself as subject (and Morgan as object), being inflected by my postcolonial understanding, enframed within my perception of postcolonial theory as grand theory in the interpretation of this work. This chapter is as much about my positioning as it is about my understanding of Morgan's text. I want to add my voice to that of others responding to one of the most important Australian texts in recent times, one written not just for Australia alone.

To make my aggrandizement of an Aboriginal text worse, if the act of reading is an objectification, I seem to be doing so not to a piece of fiction but to Sally Morgan's autobiography. The autobiography is an intensely problematic genre. On one hand it is a text, to be read like a piece of fiction, but on the other it categorizes itself as 'truth', being the life story of the writer. The demarcation between textualizing and truth, lived life and a reconstruction, breaks down in this genre. In 'Autobiography as Defacement' Paul de Man suggests that one of the problems inherent within the autobiography is its very elevation to the status of genre with its implications of aesthetics and history.[4] However, unlike other genres such as the novel, the epic and so on, which are fictional in nature (and therefore appropriate to aestheticization), the autobiography,

> seems to belong to a simpler mode of referentiality, of representation, of diagesis. It may contain lots of phantasms and dreams, but these deviations from reality remain rooted in a single subject whose identity is defined by the uncontested readability of his [sic] proper name. (920)

Truth writing is perceived to be categorized within a simpler mode of referentiality, unmediated by language, narrative techniques or deliberate aestheticization. To this extent my reading of Morgan's work, which interrogates so intensely the question of what makes the Aboriginal, is also my reading of Aboriginality, for this genre is implicated in 'truth' production. De Man suggests a way out of this impasse (of reading the autobiography solely to locate authenticity and 'truth' in the subject) by pointing out that it is the autobiographical project that determines the life of the writer itself who, like the writer of fiction, is 'governed by the technical demands of self-portraiture' (920). As a result of following the dictates of portraiture, the author specularizes himself/herself and functions as a trope of a linguistic structure, an effect of language (922). It is this troping that forces the reader to judge the authenticity of the life described: 'The study is caught in this double motion, the necessity to escape from the tropology of the subject and the equally inevitable reinscription within a specular mode of cognition' (923).

To complexify matters in any consideration of Morgan's text, yet another problem of genre looms in the fact that *My Place* does not fall easily within traditional notions of autobiography, the book is not just the construction of her own Aboriginal identity but also a tracing and textualization of her entire family's identity, containing within it the autobiographies of her uncle Arthur Corunna, her mother Gladys Corunna and her grandmother Daisy Corunna; also interspersed are stories of the 'mob' from Corunna. The Sally constructed by the text[5] is a composite of all these various stories and autobiographies. To that extent, it comes closer to the sub-genre of the testimonio, that which Doris Sommer suggests 'strives to preserve or to renew an interpersonal rhetoric' as opposed to the autobiography which 'strains to produce a personal and distinctive style as part of the individuation process'.[6] Unlike the autobiography, which emphasizes the exemplary life led by the autobiographical subject, the testimonio tends to construct the collective subject enmeshed in a social struggle. John Beverley suggests the 'testimonio constitutes an affirmation of the individual self in a collective mode [and therefore] . . . involves a sort of erasure . . . of the textual presence, of the author'.[7] In this erasure of authorial singularity and the advancement of a collective identity, the testimonio which is autobiographical in form also undercuts the primary purpose of the autobiography; the collective subject constructed by the testimonio opens up the relationship between reader and the autobiographical subject and demands a complicity and identification from its readers 'by engaging their sense of ethics and justice—with a popular cause normally distant, not to say alien from their immediate experience' (99). Sommer differentiates even further when she suggests:

> The testimonial 'I' does not even invite us to identify with it. We are too different, and there is no pretense here of universal or essential human experience . . . The singular represents the plural not because it replaces or subsumes the group but because the speaker is a distinguishable part of the whole . . . It is a translation of a hegemonic auto-biographical pose into a colonized language that does not equate identity with individuality. It is thus a reminder that life continues at the margins of Western discourse, and continues to disturb and challenge it. (emphasis added; 108; 111)

The testimonio functions to locate the reader differently: 'Once the subject of the testimonial is understood as the community made up of a variety of roles, the reader is called in to fill one of them' (118).

Read within the context of the testimonio, Sally, the autobiographical subject, is both subject and interlocutor in turn, interviewing her grandmother's brother Arthur Corunna, her mother Gladys and her grandmother Daisy, recording their lives and reading them while contextualizing them within hers, and vice versa. To this extent, the reader and Sally are aligned, equally interpellated by the project to recover her life and her racial identity. As Sommer and Beverley suggest, the testimony produces complicity and lateral identifications. Arthur, Gladys, and Daisy Corunna's Aboriginality functions doubly: first, to endow Sally with it and to envelope, to surround, her in it; second, the reader's participation in the community ensures validation. Unlike in the traditional autobiography, the reader is differently positioned and reads the life of an entire community when reading *My Place*. Yet this work is sufficiently aligned with the hegemonic genre of the Western autobiography for Sally and her family not to be rendered as alien, foreign, totally other.

To add a further point to the notion of community in this text, I suggest that just as a melange of voices of family members is necessary for its construction, so also are a mosaic of texts which are necessary to my imputation of meaning to Sally's life. This text and my reading of it interacts with, and reaccentuates, a number of texts about Australia. Uncovering those other texts will force the readers of *My Place* to resituate it and the discursive matrix with which it interacts and to examine the diverse subject positions available, not only to Sally in the text, but to 'Australia' as well.

At another level, *My Place* also constructs a hierarchy of bodies, first introduced when she passes her Aboriginality as Indian to explain her physical difference to her schoolmates: first, the 'Aussie' body, presumably white and Anglo-Celtic; then the Italian, Greek or Indian (38)—the multicultural though black body; and finally, the Aboriginal—the blackfella— whose true race and status are culturally/racially supposed to be written on their bodies. In the construct of Australia in *My Place*, everyone's bodies are inscribed by race and class. The work traces the life of Sally Morgan who lives with her mother, grandmother and siblings in Western Australia. Growing up in the 1950s, Sally loses her (white) father, a soldier in World War II, who was intensely troubled by his experiences in a concentration camp in Germany. Initially locating her sense of difference within a discourse of class, Sally slowly realizes that her family is Aboriginal. The rest of the work proceeds to locate the black side of her family and to inscribe their unrecorded lives. Sally's deliberate evocation of her Aboriginality also carries a history of her body. Intersected with the 'I' of Morgan's text is Australia's history, both white settler and Aboriginal; Sally's pursuit of the truth of her body conjoins Australia's history.

Within this context of relationships and texts, Aboriginality and the embodiment of history, I intend to unravel the texts contained within *My Place*, not to conduct a source study, but to examine the legacy from which it is written, to examine the discourses which construct Australia and Aboriginality because both these notions are important to Morgan's text. I begin with two intertextual references and their social location and relevance to *My Place*, its construction of a history via the theoretical framework of Mikhail Bakhtin, and follow up by showing how discourses on Australia are imbricated within my understanding of Sally's bodily history.

Bakhtin and intertextuality

The influence of Mikhail Bakhtin's theoretical framework on the narrative led Julia Kristeva to coin the term 'intertextuality'.[8] In the essay 'Word, Dialogue, and Novel', Kristeva suggests that 'any text is constructed as a mosaic of quotations; any text is the absorption and transformation of another. The notion of *intertextuality* replaces that of intersubjectivity, and poetic language is read as at least *double*'[9] (Kristeva's emphasis).

For Bakhtin, any utterance can only acquire meaning in relation to other utterances and the utterances of an other, all of which are in constant interaction with each other.[10] This lack of fixity in meaning is primarily due to heteroglossia, the prime condition of language which prioritizes context over text. In short, at any given time and place, any utterance is grounded socially, historically and intellectually.[11]

It is this specificity of the grounded utterance that causes it to have a different meaning under different conditions. The notion of intertextuality naturally follows, in that all writing is a composite of other writing and draws on and reinflects the multiplicity of discourses that circulate in any society/ culture at any given time. Simon Dentith suggests that '[t]he Bakhtinian notion of heteroglossia . . . radically transforms the questions of sources, making them a matter not just of individual influences or borrowing, but of the socially located languages that each and every text manages in its own particular way . . .' (95). Kristeva, too, suggests, 'If it is admitted that any signifying practice is a transposition of diverse signifying systems (an inter-textuality), it will be understood that its "site" of enunciation and its denoted "object" are never unique, full and identical to themselves, but are always plural . . .' (as cited in Dentith; 96).

Kristeva's coinage of the term 'intertextuality' underscores the negotiation of meaning with other texts that any writing undergoes in order to be productive. This new relocation of the text is termed 're-accentuation' by Bakhtin. In the conclusion of 'Discourse in the Novel', Bakhtin points out that readers need not necessarily recognize the irony, parody or 'some other preexisting "qualified" intonation' of novels written in a bygone era (*The Dialogic Imagination*; 416). Though the modern reader may not have a basic knowledge of the dialogic background from which the novel emerges, it is resituated, accentuated anew to suit the reader; the dialogizing background shifts continually; in other words, the novel is recontextualized to suit the modern reader. To this extent not only does a text evoke other texts but each generation which reads it is differently grounded in a political, historical and intellectual sense and therefore reads it freshly, with new and reaccentuated nuances. To this extent, Morgan's text is haunted by the presence of a number of other texts on Australia, and I want to underscore that, regardless of whether she was aware of the hovering presence of these references, all these texts negotiate the meaning of *My Place* and the meaning of Australia for me.[12]

High Victorianism and *My Place*

Though *My Place* is replete with other references (for example, Enid Blyton and comparisons to Albert Facey's *A Fortunate Life*), I am concentrating on references to Victorian texts because I want to trace the overlapping of territories and the intertwining of British and Australian histories central to the analysis of this work. Gayatri Spivak suggests in 'Three Women's Texts and the Critique of Imperialism',

> It should not be possible to read nineteenth century British literature without remembering that imperialism, understood as England's social mission, was a crucial part of the cultural representation of England to the English. The role of literature in the production of cultural representation should not be ignored. These two obvious 'facts' continue to be disregarded in the reading of nineteenth century British literature.[13]

In *Culture and Imperialism*, Edward Said also argues for a contrapuntal reading of the imperial and the colonial text to draw out 'what is silent or marginally present or ideologically represented . . . in such works'.[14]

The single reference to Charles Dickens' *Great Expectations* occurs in Gladys Corunna's story. Until this moment her life/story constantly evokes the fiction of high Victorianism. For instance, Charlotte Brontë's *Jane Eyre* is evoked in the story of the school, Parkerville Children's Home, that Gladys is farmed out to as a child not yet five. There she meets her friend Iris who falls ill and dies, not unlike Jane Eyre's friend, Helen Burns in Lowood, the school that she is sent out to in Brontë's novel. Gladys says, 'I remember one night hearing Iris cough and cough . . . When I woke up in the morning Iris was gone' (242). Later she finds out the truth about her friend when she comes across her grave. At her tears, another one of the residents of Parkerville comforts her, 'It's all right . . . Your friend is happy in heaven' (245). These lines mirror the scene of Helen Burns in her deathbed who says, 'I believe: I have faith. I am going to God . . . [to the] region of happiness'.[15] In their canonical feminist reading of *Jane Eyre*, Sandra Gilbert and Susan Gubar interpret Helen Burns' life within the context of renunciation, one of few structural spaces allotted to women and girls, which gives them voice.[16] Gilbert and Gubar state that Helen Burns is 'the ideal—defined by Goethe's Makarie—of self-renunciation, of all consuming (and consumptive) sprituality' (345–6).

Both Jane Eyre and Gladys Corunna's stories underscore the centrality of a class analysis for a critique of Britain and Australia, for it is their poverty that subjects them to the nightmarish horror of their childhoods at these charity schools—but with a difference. Jane's escape from poverty is predicated on colonialism. First, she inherits an abundance of money from an uncle who makes his fortune from a sugar plantation in Madeira; then she marries Mr Rochester, who comes into his wealth via his first marriage to Bertha Mason, a wealthy heiress from the West Indies. Jane and Mr Rochester's achievement of self-suffiency and individualism in the Victorian era is dependent on slavery and plantations, as Spivak so convincingly argues. In contrast, having been born in the colonies and being of mixed blood, Gladys Corunna can only escape from poverty through extreme hard work, holding two menial jobs simultaneously, while trying to pass as white. Gladys is shipped out to Parkerville Children's Home not because of poverty, but precisely because she is of mixed race and subject to Australia's assimilationist policy.

Gladys Corunna also makes passing references to Hollywood films watched at the school which are at the intersection of Dickens and race. These films are 'quite heart-rending tales about gypsies stealing a child from a family. Of course by the end of the film, they'd all be reunited. I really identified with those films' (246). Gladys evokes what Freud calls the 'Family Romance' wherein the child constructs 'a correction of actual life', daydreaming a 'fulfillment of wishes'.[17] Gladys' desire to be restored to her rightful parents is a peculiar, plaintive amalgam of Hollywood and Freud, colonialism and racism, her Family Romance encoding the colonial practice of Aboriginal children being forcibly removed from their parents. Echoed everywhere in Gladys Corunna's life story is her lost paternity, her 'wounded genealogy'.[18] On one hand the gypsies, ironically, are metaphors for the colonial state which forcibly removed children from their Aboriginal parents, as Arthur, Daisy and Gladys Corunna's stories all attest. On the other, the very mention of gypsies racializes, or brings the race element into visibility, a situation which could otherwise pass for being merely about class, as Jane Eyre's Lowood experience underscores. Certainly Gladys reads yet another incident within the discourse of class rather than race when she evokes Dickens' *Great Expectations.*[19] In a peculiar scene she describes her relationship with two English women in Australia, Miss Button and Miss Lyndsay, the latter of whom produced cake from a glass cabinet: 'The first time I'd had a cake from Miss Lyndsay, I'd taken a bite straight away and found to my horror, that my fancy pink cake had cobwebs inside' (258). This image of the cake is underscored in that it does not happen just once but every cake she is given by Miss Lyndsay is filled with cobwebs: 'I kept going back, she kept giving me cakes and they always had cobwebs in them' (258). Gladys explains it within the context of her constant hunger as a child in Parkerville Children's Home, but to me the repeated references to cobwebs in the cake draws attention to and underscores her story's connection to *Great Expectations*, Dickens' novel about Australia and Empire. The cake crammed with cobwebs directly refers to Pip's visit to Miss Havisham, who had been jilted at the altar many years previously and in whose house all the clocks had been stopped to record the moment of her trauma. On a long yellow table, Pip sees the bride-cake: '[A]s I looked along the yellow expanse out of which I remember its seeeming to grow, like a black fungus, I saw speckle-legged spiders with blotchy bodies running home to it, and running out from it . . .' (113). This image of the cake, of time arrested, of history frozen, links Dickens' and Morgan's works on Australia. Gladys Corunna and Pip are positioned structurally similarly in the two texts and *My Place* is Gladys Corunna's great expectation. At one moment in *Great Expectations*, the transported convict Magwitch, illegally in England, tells Pip the young protagonist, 'I lived rough, that you should live smooth' (337), indicating the inextricable link between mother country and colony, class and race. The evocation of Dickens functions doubly. First, it thematically links *Great Expectations*, often categorized as a detective story, with *My Place* which, has been repeatedly likened to detective fiction. At their centres is a search for identity which is also linked to the search for a missing father. In this next section I want to read *Great Expectations* against *My Place* to see how race is troped as class in Morgan's text.

131

Reading the two works contrapuntally also draws direct attention to the close relationship between mother-country and colony which is central to Australia's social and racial history.

Paternity and identity

In Dickens' work, Pip is bestowed with two fathers; his biological father, Philip Pirrip, dead and buried at the start of the novel, and Abel Magwitch, the criminal transported to Australia who becomes his secret benefactor. Philip Pirrip is mentioned twice, both times in passing, both at his graveside. It is at his father's graveside that Magwitch the escaped criminal makes his first appearance and seeks Pip's help. Eleven years later Pip, apprenticed to his blacksmith brother-in-law, is bestowed money by a mysterious benefactor whom he assumes to be Miss Havisham. This windfall elevates him from the status of skilled labourer to that of moneyed gentleman. Magwitch, a 'lifer' in Australia, illegally returns to England and informs Pip that he is the benefactor: 'Look'ee here Pip. I'm your second father. You're my son—more to me nor any son. I've put away money, only for you to spend' (337). The rest of the novel deals with Pip coming to terms with the violent, illegal nature of his paternity and the identity it shapes. Though he renounces his ill-gotten inheritance, he accepts Magwitch's paternal role and stays by him as he dies in prison.

The relationship between missing/dead fathers and sons is central to Dickens' novels, as *Oliver Twist, Our Mutual Friend, David Copperfield, Dombey and Son* and *Bleak House* indicate. Anny Sadrin explains the relationship between money and fathers and sons in Dickens: 'The father's money as much as the father's name, the patrimony as much as the patronymic, must be handed over at the appointed hour; it is the son's viaticum, the father's parting gift to the new pilgrim on the brink of his journey.'[20] For Sadrin, paternity and genealogy is at the core of the son's sense of identity. In *Great Expectations*, Magwitch inherits the mantle of fatherhood and shapes Pip's identity while he also embodies the social horror associated with criminality and transportation. The horror of Australia becomes interchangeable with the horror of Magwitch; the site of transported prisoners and the flouting of the class system become intertwined. Magwitch tells Pip that his revenge on class, that which led him to a life of crime in England, is 'to know in secret I was making a gentleman. The blood horses of them colonists might fling up the dirt over me as I was walking. [But my response to them is], "All on you owns stock and land; which on you owns a broughtup London gentleman"' (339). Paternity as ownership and patrilineage as class are all inextricably linked in Magwitch's revenge. Magwitch becomes monstrous not only for his criminal status and his breaking of the law but for his illegal visit to England and his manipulation of Pip, and most especially for his perversion of class. (Displaced) paternity which must uphold the law, in this novel, perverts the very basis of the law by scrambling the boundaries of class. In Dickens' England, law and class are tightly braided.

Incest and miscegenation

If this trope of paternity is located within illegality and class boundaries, *My Place* introduces a third element within it—that of race. As in Dickens, this work is replete with fathers who are missing. For instance, Sally's father is emotionally missing in the early chapters because of his experiences in World War II. Sally and her siblings are not fathered but mothered. Alternately, fathers either cannot be named or they are illegal. Arthur Corunna has two fathers, his white biological father, Howden Drake-Brockman, and his Aboriginal father whose two wives Howden shared. By underscoring the excess of fathers the text suggests its opposite. The very excess of fathers signals the disavowal of paternal responsibilities.

But it is Gladys Corunna's story that again implies the violent nature of fatherhood. Like Pip's search for his benefactor, her quest for her father is central to her story as well as to Daisy Corunna's stories. Gladys and Daisy's genealogies follow two different trajectories in that when Sally pursues the truth of paternity, she is given two different versions. First, there is the version given by the Drake-Brockmans. Judy Drake-Brockman informs her that Gladys Corunna's father was Jack Grime and Daisy Corunna's father was Maltese Sam (154–7). This genealogy is confirmed by Judy's mother, Alice

Drake-Brockman, in whose house Daisy Corunna worked as a domestic servant from the age of fourteen (168). These facts are refuted repeatedly by Sally's Aboriginal family members, who suggest that Daisy Corunna's father is Howden Drake-Brockman (157, 221). Daisy herself names Howden as her father (162).

The disavowal of fatherhood is underscored in Gladys' life in that her paternity is a 'blank' on her birth certificate (152). In fact, it is the very refusal to name him that indicates who he may be in *My Place*. The clues to Gladys' paternity can only be inconclusive, for the only person who can identify him—her mother, Daisy—refuses to name him (162). In her narrative, Daisy says: 'Everyone knew who [Gladdie's] father was, but they all pretended they didn't know . . . You didn't talk about things, then. You hid the truth' (340). Yet clues abound in the text. In Arthur's version, Gladys was born in December 1927 and it was Howden who 'saw Daisy's baby before he died. They called her Gladys' (203). At another juncture, Arthur says, 'You see, Howden was a lonely man. I know, one night at Ivanhoe, we both got drunk together and he told me all his troubles. He used to go down to Daisy's room at night and talk to her. I can't say no more. You'll have to ask her' (158).

What transpires in Daisy's room can only be guessed at in the text's refusal to speculate. The text deliberately draws attention to its strategy of refusal to articulate when Sally first suggests—and then denies—that Howden Drake-Brockman could be both Gladys' grandfather and father. In this scene she persuades her mother to stand beside a photograph of Jack Grime in front of the mirror. The result: 'Well that was a dead loss. You don't look anything like him.' Then she picks up a photograph of Howden and holds it beside her mother: 'My God . . . Give him black, curly hair and a big bust and he's the spitting image of you' (237). Illicit paternity can be represented only through the in-between image of drag—neither quite masculine, nor quite feminine, neither quite father, nor quite grandfather. Notwithstanding the attempt at inscription, the text promptly erases it. When Gladys asks Sally, 'You don't think it's possible he was my father?' she responds, 'Anything's possible. But he couldn't be yours as well as Nan's. You know, features can skip a generation' (237).

Despite Sally's shying away from further inquiry, the trace of incest starts pervading the text.

But why can unnameable paternity manifest itself only through the trope of drag? In *Gender Trouble*, Judith Butler suggests that the common understanding of sex/gender is that the true anatomical status of the body is manifest in our gender specific behaviour.[21] But the performance of drag dispels any such understanding in that performers behave contrary to their anatomical truth, problematizing the natural continuum between sex and gendered behaviour and revealing that the assumption of gendered behaviour is always already only a performative act that every subject enacts. The performative nature of gender underscores its status as fiction; gendered behaviour reveals itself to be 'a stylized repetition of acts' (137). If the performance of drag deconstructs notions of gendered behaviour, in a further step it deconstructs the notion of anatomical truth itself. In fact, anatomical truth is as fictive as gendered behaviour.

Butler's notion can explain the figure of Howden Drake-Brockman with black curly hair and a big bust. This trope of drag establishes that in the genealogy of the body, there is 'the anatomical truth', that is, the maternal body from which the subject is issued. But paternity is always a performance, an enactment, a naming or misnaming through birth certificates, family stories, history, and clues of likenesses in photographs; it is a model of identity which accrues power by positing itself as truth and concealing its performative nature. Maternity and paternity are always at a disjunction. While the naming of the paternal is valorized in the search for identity, it is the bodily truth, the materiality of the maternal body, that is sustained. Sally realizes this when she laments her lack of Aboriginal knowledge as embodied in the women of her family: 'Where are Lilla and Annie and Rosie and Old Fanny? Where are the women in my family, are they all right?' (227).

It is also the betwixt-and-between trope of drag which scrambles demarcations between the real and the representation that notions of incest and miscegenation can be inscribed. The cultural injunction against incest is fundamental to the production of language and representation for, as Lacan says, 'without kinship nominations, no power is capable of instituting the order of preferences and taboos that bind and weave the yarn of lineage through suceeding generations'.[22] The incest taboo must be upheld in order to differentiate between family members and others and this can be done only through linguistic categories which name the father and the mother. In *My Place*, the refusal to name the father permits an incest. In its turn the refusal to name the incest prevents its very representation in the text. Ultimately, incest and the non-differentiation of identity are unrepresentable, uninscribable and can only be achieved through the in-between body of a woman superimposed by the image of a man in the text.

Miscegenation, too, contains within it the structure of non-differentiation in that it collapses the difference between white and black. Multiple reasons existed for the taboo of miscegenation: not only did it control white women's as well as black sexuality but also contained within it the horror of racial indeterminacy.[23] In 'Biological Degeneration' Nancy Stepan suggests that in the early nineteenth century the predominant opinion among scientists was that though all humans were of the same species, environmental influences caused degeneration which created the different racial groups.[24] By the mid-nineteenth century, however, there was a shift in the way degeneration was considered, in that now it was suggested that all racial varieties formed distinct types and could not transform into each other (97). Stepan adds that with the abolition of slavery, racial biology became 'a science of boundaries between groups and the degenerations that threatened when these boundaries were transgressed' (98). Within this context, racial indeterminacy, a visible signifier of degeneration, itself bespoke a racial degeneration. The British anatomist Sir William Lawrence believed that racial mixing brought about a physical and moral 'deterioration' of the European, whereas it improved the quality and the status of the darker varieties (as cited in Stepan 107).[25]

This anxiety of disavowal and 'deterioration' is present in *My Place* as well. The taboo of miscegenation is enacted in every denial by the Drake-Brockmans that Gladys Corunna is related to them. Gladys explicates the consequences of miscegenation: 'I suppose, in hundreds of years' time, there won't be any black Aboriginals left' (306). The disavowal is always linked to an avowal, for whiteness cannot be enacted without the presence of blacks; whiteness requires blackness to come

into being, but must also simultaneously disavow it to constitute itself visually. A disavowal of blackness too is linked to
racial indeterminacy in the text. As Gladys says:

> Our colour dies out; as we mix with other races, we'll lose
> some of the physical characteristics that distinguish us now.
> I like to think that no matter what we become, our spiritual
> tie with the land and the other unique qualities we possess
> will somehow weave their way through to future generations
> of Australians. (306)

Other examples of the disavowal of blackness abound in the
text. For instance, light coloured Aboriginal children are
removed from their Aboriginal families; Daisy Corunna constantly denies that their family is Aboriginal; this denial is
always coupled with the insistence that the Corunnas are white,
as in the scene where she refers to her whiteness to the rent
collector (107); she dislikes Cyril, Sally's friend who stays with
the family for a period, because his habits will cause the
neighbours to 'think there's blackfellas living here!' (122).

Race and class

Great Expectations is central to my reading of *My Place* because
both texts draw attention to the problematic figure of the father
and the troublesome nature of paternity. Gender and race
boundary transgressions are related to illegitimate and unbridled paternal sexuality in Morgan's text. Finally, the disavowal
of racial indeterminacy is at the core of the problem of
representation in the text, with the effect that the horror of
racial determinacy has to be displaced to remanifest itself in
disguise elsewhere. The focus of this next section is that given
the disavowal of blackness in *My Place*, how can it be inscribed
at all there? In my view, racial difference can be inscribed
only through the discourse of class. Sally, as a child, constantly
wonders about her difference from her classmates, a difference
that can only be articulated through an awareness of class.
For instance, the discourse of class is present when in Grade
3, Sally could pinpoint her petit-bourgeois classmates based
upon the kind of lunches they brought to school: 'They had
pieces of salad, chopped up and sealed in plastic containers.
Their cake was wrapped neatly in grease-proof paper, and

they had real cordial in a proper flask.' In contrast, the students who were as poor as she 'drank from the water-fountain and carried sticky jam sandwiches in brown paper bags' (37). Again, when Sally and her mother decide to wallpaper the lounge, Gladys buys only eight rolls of Paisley print wallpaper from the specials bin and 'reasoned that it was better to have one feature wall of Paisley print than none at all. It would give [their] place a bit of class' (118).

A metaphoric process—the transferring of intensity of meaning from one element to another—functions in the level of race/class here. Since race cannot be inscribed in *terra nullius*—a point I will elaborate on shortly—racial difference in the text comes into being via class difference.[26] The interchangeable tropes of class and race are embodied through Gladys and Sally in that they function as reversed mirror images. The trajectory of Gladys' life follows a gradual attenuation of identity via race and an assumption of class. Her early life is constructed through her Aboriginality, but life after her marriage to her white husband is constructed through class. For instance, as a young woman she declares her Aboriginality to a woman at the bus-stop. The woman's response: 'You can't be . . . Oh you poor thing . . . What on earth are you going to do?' (278). This scene is in contrast to her decision after her husband's death to 'definitely not tell the children they were Aboriginal' because she is afraid that the Welfare Department would take them away from her, as she had been taken away from her mother, who in turn had been taken away from her mother (304–5). Gladys equates Aboriginality with families torn asunder. Thus, assuming a white working-class identity bespeaks socially upward mobility for her. For Sally, however, the trajectory of her identity leaves classed difference behind to take on racial difference. When she finds out that their family is Aboriginal, she applies for an Aboriginal scholarship because she 'desperately wanted to do something to identify with [her] new-found heritage' (137). Her Aboriginality leads her to research her family story and to work on an autobiographical project. If Gladys disembodies herself from her raced history through a framework of class discourse, Sally re-embodies herself through Aboriginal history and substitutes class with race. In short, the first half of the work emphasizes class and the second half race.

The tropes of class and race themselves function as metaphors in *My Place* in that they are understood not to be mutually exclusive, but interchangeable and supplementary. Sally's discourse of race is predicated on her experience of class difference; Gladys' experience of class is predicated on her raced difference. So if race underpins class so does class underpin race. In her analysis of the analogous nature of race and gender, Nancy Stepan suggests that 'interactive metaphors bring together a *system* of implications[;] other features previously associated with only one subject in the metaphor are brought to bear on the other'.[27] Thus my rereading of *My Place* causes me to interpret Sally and her siblings sleeping five in a bed via the framework of both class *and* race. In his work on metaphor, Paul Ricouer suggests, 'In order that a metaphor obtains, one must continue to identify the previous incompatibility *through* the new incompatibility . . . "Remoteness" is preserved within "proximity". To see *the like* is to see the same in spite of, and through, the different'.[28]

While Ricouer emphasizes the principle of metaphor as being located in the similarity between two elements, David Lloyd astutely points out that metaphorization contains within it the principle of assimilation in that the differences between the two elements must be suppressed. This results in a hierarchical relationship between the two elements, for the one being assimilated leaves its difference behind.[29] The dominant element does not undergo any substantial changes. As Lloyd puts it, '[d]ifferences that in the first instance have no meaning and no law come to signify negatively under the law of identity that produces them' (73).

And it is from within the masquerading, mimicking, and passing of race as class that the two texts of High Victorianism are resituated by *My Place*. Like Dickens' *Hard Times*, Brontë's *Jane Eyre*, too, offers a critique of the contemporary education system for girls. Thus *Jane Eyre* functions as a template for Gladys' early life; in its simultaneous articulation of race and class, *My Place* also functions as the excess and slippage of the Brontë novel. Gladys' life might mirror Jane's upward mobility but simultaneously questions it because it ignores the centrality of colonialism in its positioning as master-text. Gladys' life emerges from the blind spot in Jane, Mr Rochester and St John Rivers' lives, and ultimately refuses to be representational of it. By mimicking *Jane Eyre* through Gladys' life, *My Place* articulates historical, cultural, racial, and colonial differences always present in the subterranean regions of the imperial text, but subject to interdiction. Similarly, *My Place* reinscribes the interdiction of the discourses of race/colonialism that *Great Expectations* is subject to. The English class system might be subverted by Magwitch, a subversion which can occur only through the disavowal of race and its close links to and interchangeability with class. England can become an imperial power in Europe only by colonizing those spaces which lie beyond Europe; it can become an empire only by sending its Magwitches to Australia; Magwitch can prosper only at the expense of the Aboriginals; class boundaries can be erased, as Magwitch wills it, only through the production of racial boundaries between white and black. Ultimately the themes of incest and miscegenation which haunt *My Place* act as metaphors for the relationship between England and the 'Australia' it constructs—at the underside of colonialism and racial difference is incest and miscegenation. When *My Place* destabilizes racial boundaries through the hybrid Sally, all the interdictions of imperialism and class, and the practice of transporting convicts, become visible in the text to reveal colonialism as structured by more than a simple binary of colonizer/colonized. In inscribing Gladys' life as difference, the text of 'Australia' reveals itself to be a palimpsest. Etched faintly and underpinning the discourses of imperialism and class is that of race.

The history of the body

In examining the imbrication of *My Place* within two texts of High Victorianism, the golden era of British colonial expansion, I applied Bakhtin's notion of reaccentuation, which decontextualizes a work out of its specific historical and cultural milieu to make it burst forth with new meaning. I would, however, prefer to think of my reaccentuation of *Great Expectations* and *My Place* not so much as a dehistorization but as a rehistorization which allows the history of power relations under erasure in Dickens to become visible, made possible by reading *Great Expectations* against a colonial text.

In my tracing of the discourse of race manifesting itself as class I have also attempted to show how the body gets both dehistoricized and debiologized, while the discourse of class which speaks in the name of race dislocates the body from its racialized history. The contours of the body must become unmarked within the discourse of race, which speaks from within economic relations. Similarly, its trajectory of pursuing the meaningful life and its thematic of individualism, the genre of the autobiography is traditionally predicated on the body coming into meaning only by disappearing, in that disembodied bourgeois identity and subjectivity are emphasized in the exemplary life. To that extent, the frameworks of class and autobiographical discourse both demand that the body fall out of view. In *My Place*, the task that Sally faces is to rebiologize and racialize the body-in-difference by negotiating her way through discourses which distance themselves from the body.

In the rest of this chapter, I will briefly locate the Aboriginal body within the context of *terra nullius*, a concept central to the context of Australian colonization, before I show Morgan's specific strategies of fleshing the Aboriginal/Australian bodily history.

In *Subjectivity, Identity, and the Body*, Sidonie Smith points out that the 'universal' subject comes into being only by escaping 'all forms of embodiment' (6). Locating a shift in the seventeenth century in the relationship between body and identity, Smith cites Cartesian dichotomies of mind/body which resulted in the body being restrained and repressed: '[t]he banishment or splitting off to the margins of the conscious self of what now becomes a "supplementary body" invites on the one hand a neutralization of the body through a self-censoring that functions to contain, control the body's "dangerous passions."'[30] The universal subject who is disembodied is always already gendered as male. To that extent women function as the body. Judith Butler explains that the disembodiment of 'man' is conditional upon women occupying their body. She states that 'if woman are only their bodies, if their consciousness and freedom are only so many disguised permutations of bodily need and necessity, then women have, in effect, exclusively monopolized the bodily sphere of life'.[31] Smith adds that woman not only occupies the place of the body but is identified almost entirely by her social roles, which converge with her body (12–13). Importantly, it is from within the context of body and social role that women's autobiographies are written. Woman as body is an antonym to the demands of the traditional autobiography which is predicated on the establishment of the disembodied self. In a further complication of woman as body, Sally has to encode her Aboriginality which is just not present in the foundation of Australia.

The black body in the autobiography faces the same interdiction that the woman's body does, an interdiction which is compounded in the term *terra nullius*. In the period of colonial expansion, European nations agreed that territory could be acquired by conquest, by cession, or if it was deemed *terra nullius*. This term literally means 'land of no one', in that it is territory which does not belong to any recognized international entity.[32] Territory was categorized as *terra nullius* if the original occupants were perceived as not having any (Westernized) social or political/legal organization. Title to *terra nullius* could be had either by the first European state to 'discover' it or through planting a cross, flag or royal insignia. Within this context *Terra Australis Incognita* became subject to British occupation. The preliminary naming of the Australian continent as *terra nullius* functions to categorize the Aboriginals either as an extension of the flora, fauna and wildlife, or on a lower scale of the evolutionary ladder than the European settlers. I draw attention to these obvious points because I want to underscore the dovetailing of the discourse of international law and colonial expansion with that of biological discourses of race and degeneration, as well as that of aesthetics. For instance, Sir Francis Bacon in 1620 classified people of colour 'discovered' by Renaissance Europe according to their production of art—if one compares the life of men from civilized Europe with those in barbaric New India a difference will be perceived: 'And this difference comes not from the soil, not from climate, not from race, but from the arts'.[33] Again, as Nancy Stepan notes, from the late eighteenth century the notion of degeneracy was yoked particularly to the definition of species ('Biological Degeneration'; 97). All these sets of discourses are mutually interdependent in the production of the binary of civilized Europe and the uncivilized, unoccupied *terra nullius*, waiting for the arrival of Europe.

Kay Schaffer suggests that:

> the history of Australia was built on the notion of the land as *terra incognito, terra nullius* —unknown, untamed, unoccupied and open to the progressive mastery of colonization. That process of colonization relied upon the imagined absence of indigenous peoples, and also at the same time inscribed them in 'our' history as remnants of a static primordial past.[34]

I want to examine briefly the production of the indigene through the dynamics of naming Australia *terra nullius*, a term that demands the mapping and the knowing of this continent. J.B. Harley suggests that 'maps are never value-free images' because they require a selection of their content; in the chosen styles of representation and of conceiving and articulating the human world maps both prompt and exert influence upon particular sets of social relations,[35] thus pointing to the close relationship between mapping and the powerful in society. In his reading of Mercator's seventeenth-century *Atlas*, Jose Rabasa notes the historical links between the dominant Eurocentric organization of geographical space which 'institute[s] a systematic forgetfulness of antecedent spatial configurations'.[36] It is the naming of the Australian continent as *terra nullius* that makes possible the anteriority of the West, as Graham Huggan has demonstrated.[37] Gayatri Spivak suggests that within the context of colonialism the European self 'obliges the native to cathect the space of the Other on his home ground. He is worlding their own world which is far from mere uninscribed earth anew, by obliging them to domesticate the alien as Master'.[38] Renaming Australia as *terra nullius* not only forces the Aboriginal to domesticate the alien as Master but, in a step further, to virtually disappear as humans, to become a part of the fauna and flora; naming Australia *terra nullius* demands the disavowal of the black body and the disavowal of black as human because the very legality of the term is contingent upon the bestowal of non-human status to black and indigenous Aborigines. This notion of black as non-human is hinted at in *My Place* when Gladys Corunna admits to being called a 'mongrel' (143) because she is Aboriginal.

Within discourses of race, Aboriginality is predicated on skin colour. Judith Butler suggests a way to locate the underpinning of power dynamics in the context of gender in *Gender Trouble* which is pertinent to a reading of race through the significance of skin colour:

> [t]hat penis, vagina, breasts and so forth are *named* sexual parts is both a restriction of the erogenous body to those parts and a fragmentation of the body as a whole. Indeed, the 'unity' imposed upon the body by the category of sex is a 'disunity', a fragmentation and compartmentalization, and a reduction of erotogenicity. (114)

Extending this line of argument to the category of race suggests that skin, the largest organ, determines racial affiliations in their entirety and produces social meaning and narrative cohesion to (racial) difference. To this extent, there is an epistemological violence to the organ 'skin' which is shaped by the violence of history but is located as natural and prior to history. The racial difference of Aboriginality becomes a retroactive construct, created both by white settler history and the notion of *terra nullius* which, in fact, locate themselves as a product of racial difference and, therefore, legitimate.

Encoding her Aboriginality is particularly fraught for Sally because she not only passes as Indian, Greek or Italian but also starts losing her pigmentation around her neck and shoulders (82). Notwithstanding her ability to pass as immigrant, the incident where one of the deacons of the Youth Group of the church she attends asks her to 'stop mixing' with his daughter because as an Aboriginal, she is 'a bad influence' (102), reveals how the social meaning of Aboriginality covers over the violence through which such a meaning is produced. Here the meaning imposed on her body and her nature is one predicated on her 'racial difference'. Racial difference, in this instance, is a product of fetishization in that though she doesn't look visibly Aboriginal, Aboriginality is bestowed upon her in its fulness of social meaning by the deacon for whom she appears nothing but Aboriginal.

I wish to pursue this notion of fetishization in my discussion of Sally's strategies of embodiment. In *The Politics and Poetics of Transgression*, Peter Stallybrass and Allon White point to the close relationship between fetishization and repression in that the former privileges and encapsulates within it a nostalgia for the thing/being which was located as full but is now lost, and the latter is obvious, crude, vulgar and in need of refinement.[39] Stallybrass and White point out that both repression and fetishization, though antonyms, are part of the same 'civilizing process'. Both these terms are likely to occur in any attempt to think through the body. Both disembodiment and embodiment 'partake of the same mystification' (192). This dual meaning of the body in the civilizing process is particularly evident in the incident where Sally applies for and receives an Aboriginal scholarship at University. Later she gets into trouble with the scholarship authorities because they receive a complaint that she is not quite Aboriginal. Here the two meanings of the body converge—the scholarship authorities nostalgically demand the Aboriginal body, yet simultaneously hold her suspect, crude and vulgar because her body can pass. If previously she is not quite white, now she is not quite black.

Sally makes two distinct steps to embody history—the history of miscegenation—in her autobiography. First, she places the Aboriginal. Stallybrass and White suggest that the body is a composite of 'social formation, symbolic topography and the constitution of the subject' (192). For them place is central for the construction of the body and goes beyond just a geographical location. It contains within it 'a mode of discursive production and also a psychic content' (196). In this line of thinking, each place/structural space is saturated with its own history and is placed in a hierarchy with other places/structural spaces, an analysis useful within the context of *My Place* because the discourse of class which structurally superimposes that of race makes both race and class resonate with and through each other. If the suburb of Manning where Sally grows up is discursively saturated by its particular social neighbourhood, where children ate school lunches of Vegemite and jam sandwiches, it is compared to the neighbouring suburb of Como where children get nicer lunches and live in houses with carpets on floors and tidy gardens. The school lunches are an extension of, and reproduce, the hierarchies of the places of their production. Another example of places being discursively saturated and consequently hierarchized is the schoolroom, where one of Sally's classmates insists on spelling b-o-t-t-o-m as b-u-m, much to the disgust of the school teacher 'who disliked anything even slightly earthy' (95). Here the school becomes the site where uncivilized children are brought into civilization and a bourgeois sensibility.

Within this context of place saturated with meaning and its relationship to the racialization of identity I want to briefly discuss Sally and her family's trip to the North and their return to Corunna Downs (219–34). The trip is enframed by Sally's realization of her Aboriginality. As she reaches Port Hedland, the first question asked of her is: Which way do you go by, the blackfella's way or the white man's way? To this she responds 'the blackfella's way' (219). As she returns she concludes by realizing she had acquired an 'Aboriginal consciousness' (233). Returning to the land of her forebears and to Corunna and seeing the intricate web of her Aboriginal side of her family is a 'spiritual and emotional pilgrimage' (233). It also becomes a trip of re-embodiment.

I want to suggest that the trip North complicates notions of place, the segregation of bodies, and the strict demarcation of races in that the North and Corunna in particular, and Manning, all become sites of miscegenation or race mixing. As Arthur Corunna states within the context of the interdependent relationship in Corunna Downs: 'We all belonged to each other. We were the tribe that made the station. The Drake-Brockmans didn't make it on their own' (181). Pioneer history has black history at its foundations. History and place themselves become the sites of miscegenation. Furthermore, the North, far from being a hermetically sealed site of the Aboriginals, becomes the site of Australian history. As one old full-blooded Aboriginal woman says: 'You don't know what it means, no one comes back. You don't know what it means that you with light skin want to own us.' Sally reverses this sentiment to suggest that it means a lot to her that they would own her as well (228–9). The offsprings of miscegenation are racially mixed subjects, spatially intersecting histories, and the intellectual intertwining of ideas and traditions.

Sally expresses the predicament faced by subjects who are the products of hybrid bodies and histories when she is questioned over her right to have an Aboriginal scholarship: 'What did it mean to be Aboriginal? I'd never lived off the land and been a hunter and gatherer. I'd never participated

146

in corroborees or heard stories of the Dreamtime . . . I hardly knew any Aboriginal people. What did it mean for someone like me?' (141). Here the notion of miscegenation reveals itself to be underpinned by a demand and insistence for racial purity, a homogenous body/politic, and a unitary history. Within such a context, a hybrid always proves herself to be problematic in that she is a representative of a race/body dislocated from place and history, though very much a product of that history. Morgan represents a breed of people outside of place and time, a pure materiality which cannot participate in spatiality or the linearity of time.

In *Colonial Desire*, Robert Young suggests an alternative reading of hybridization in that it consists 'of the forcing of a single entity into two or more parts, a severing of a single object into two, turning sameness into difference . . . [It] makes difference into sameness, and sameness into difference, but in a way that makes the same no longer the same, the different no longer simply different' (26). The hybrid, in its simultaneous similarity and difference, creates the shock of recognition in the different and strangeness in the familiar all at once, forcing a dislocation and renegotiation of meaning. To this extent, Sally is Aboriginal even though she might not have participated in corroborees or heard stories of the Dreamtime. As one of the men in the trip north describes people like her: 'Light coloured ones wanderin' around not knowing they black underneath' (222). If light skinned people are really black, the converse can also be true—black-skinned people can also partake of whiteness. Hybridity thus also undermines the visual markers of difference on the skin which normally reveals the 'truth' of racial affiliations. If Sally is black via her grandmother and mother, she is simultaneously white, as were her father and her grandfather before her. This simultaneous embodiment of whiteness is underscored when we are informed that their (white) grandmother did not like her (black) grandchildren and did not let them in the house. Yet she liked Sally's brother Billy, who was 'the image' of his father. Notwithstanding their bodies encoding racial difference, in this instance Billy reveals sameness-in-difference; their bodies thus transform rigid oppositions between white and Aboriginal bodies and create 'a radical heterogeneity, discontinuity, the permanent revolution of forms' (Young; 25).

147

This dislocation of hybridized bodies from spaces and bodily affiliations in *My Place* results in a rethinking and rearticulation of racial difference itself. Furthermore, the text resituates the notion of embodiment itself. If previously there were three sorts of bodies—white, Aboriginal and the indeterminate one of Greek, Italian or Indian—soon there are only two—white and Nyoongah. For Daisy Corunna, 'everyone dark [was] Nyoongah. Africans, Burmese, American Negroes were all Nyoongahs. She identified with them . . . because they shared the common bond of blackness' (138). This homogenization of the black body is also fundamental to its dispersion and dissemination, so much so that the black body of Aboriginality, far from having disappeared, appears in the heart of bourgeois life in the text. If the 'individual' of the autobiography is disembodied and devoid of content, any form of colourfulness bespeaks the Nyoongah body. Thus the boy who refers to the word b-o-t-t-o-m as b-u-m; Sally's difference from her peers in her love of animals and birds, her visions, her hearing of birdsong; Arthur Corunna's love of animals and refusal to separate a young animal from its mother; Sally's criticism of the Australian health system which separates the patient as individual from the patient as body; all become an inscription of the body, of the Nyoongah consciousness. The mess and clutter of Sally's home is the mess and clutter of the body. Nyoongah is the trope of the body that Australia has distanced itself from, the body as residue in the construction of Australia. Through her body, Sally re-embodies Australia.

6

Britannia's daughters: race, place, and the Antipodean home

The argument for this chapter evolved from a question which I asked a historian friend on a trivial detail in Charlotte Godley's *Letters from Early New Zealand*.[1] Soon after her arrival in Wellington in 1850, only ten years after the signing of the Treaty of Waitangi which established New Zealand as the newest colony in the extremities of the British Empire in the South Pacific, Charlotte Godley wrote to her mother on 28 April of the difficulty of obtaining furniture for their new home. The entire house itself had been brought over from England by Lord Petre's son who had since moved away from Wellington. The garden consisted of 'sweet briar, honeysuckle, clove pinks, and white moss roses and other real English plants, scarcely yet out of flower' (31). There was a 'good plot of English grass in front' (32). In this replication of an English garden in a house brought from England, the Godleys, in pioneer spirit, constructed makeshift furniture: for a dining table, a flour barrel with a packing case lid on top covered over by a tablecloth; for a dressing table for Mrs Godley, the same; for a cupboard for Mr Godley the case itself 'with a bit of calico round' (33). They have to resort to these measures because anything that resembles furniture is 'so dear and bad and tables, chairs, etc., not to be had ready made' in early New Zealand (33). Instead of being impressed by their pioneer ingenuity, I had questions: Why must Britain be replicated in the structures of New Zealand homes, in the gardens, in the streets which remind Mrs Godley of Hastings, in the names of places, Christchurch, Dunedin (the old name for Edinburgh), Riccarton, New Plymouth? Couldn't she make do without a dresser? Without a cupboard?

At one level, this is the reality of imperialism, the naming and the worlding of the colonized world. Using the Heideggerian concept of the reworlding of the world in art, Gayatri Chakravorty Spivak points to the close links of this concept to colonial enterprise in that the colonizer is authorized to remake colonial spaces in the image of the mother country and to occlude extant, local history in the renarrating and remaking of places. This remaking and reworlding is premised on the notion of the colonial space as uninscribed earth. In Spivak it is the epistemic violence of the reworlding that is emphasized.[2] At another level, the replication of home and its aesthetic familiarity bespeaks comfort for the settler population. The alien and unfamiliar must be domesticated, must become familiar. Home and nation must be evoked. New Zealand must function as Britain, yet Britain as a *tabula rasa*—a blank page—for her people in the diaspora to inscribe their lives upon. If there is a reworlding of New Zealand, it offers the settlers the opportunity of rebirthing and living their lives anew, though always in the image of Britain.

The tropes of home and familiarity are also important in *The Letters of Rachel Henning*, which were written from Australia between 1853 and 1882.[3] Rachel Henning had a specific role to play in the home she shared with her brother Biddulph in the Australian bush and later with her husband, Deighton Taylor. Her description of her sitting room in New South Wales reveals the imbrication of the trope of home with the trajectory of imperialism. Her books were purchased in Bristol, her chair is from America, the matting on her floor is from India. In both Charlotte Godley and Rachel Henning's letters there is a braiding of home, imperialism, and Victorian femininity.

Charlotte Godley (1821–1907) and Rachel Henning (1826–1914) were not only contemporaries of each other but also of Queen Victoria. They were of the same middle-class provenance—Godley's father was the younger son of Lord Aylesford and Rachel Henning's father was chaplain to HRH the Duke of Cambridge. Both came to the Antipodes in the same decade, Godley to New Zealand in 1850 and Henning to Australia in 1854. The resemblance stops here: Rachel Henning was unmarried and except for a return to England between 1856–61, lived the rest of her life in Australia. She married Deighton Taylor at age of 40. Charlotte Godley, on the other hand, married John Godley at the age of 25 in 1846; she lived in New Zealand for only three years before returning to Britain.

To some extent, Charlotte Godley's short sojourn in the Antipodes tied her to the pages of the political history of New Zealand in ways in which Henning's immigrant status did not tie her to that of Australia. For instance, a statue of Godley's husband John stands to this day in Cathedral Square in Christchurch, a settlement he had helped found in his involvement with the Canterbury Association. The Canterbury Association was specifically formed by Edward Gibbon Wakefield to settle Church of England followers in the new province of Canterbury; the intention was to settle a complete segment of English society with all classes and professions represented, with Church and school, so that a civilized community could be formed. John Godley was selected as Chief Agent of the Canterbury Association to prepare the grounds for the first settlers. His assignment was for three years.

In contrast, Rachel Henning had lost her father at the age of fourteen, her mother at nineteen, and being the oldest child had taken charge of the household. When her brother, Biddulph, turned nineteen, poor health and economic reasons necessitated that he emigrate to Australia. Biddulph and their sister Annie left for Australia in 1853. Rachel followed in 1854, returned to England in 1856 and returned again to Australia to settle permanently in 1861. Her chief role was to help Biddulph run his station in Australia. Biddulph, enterprising and successful, was most often the subject of her letters to their sister Henrietta. Like Godley, Henning had no direct role to play in the imperial/colonial enterprise. She was not independently wealthy and needed Biddulph's approval when she became engaged to Deighton Taylor, who was almost ten years her junior.

The worlds of the Victorian man and woman were clearly separate. The men made the decisions and partook of the political, public life while women were located in the private, the traditional divide. That Victorian women were located in the realm of the private, lacked agency, and became metonymic extensions of the home, is testified to by works such as Coventry Patmore's *The Angel in the House*. Though such a discursive move essentializes all women and makes their love of home an innate characteristic, I want to argue that Victorian femininity was a specific product of Victorian political history, especially imperialism and that Victorian femininity was constructed by Britain's imperial enterprise as much as it was by notions of womanhood. To this extent, the concept of femininity that second wave feminists in the 1960s fought against is as much a product of imperialism as it is rooted in a Victorian domestic ideology that was merely reinscribed after the Second World War. This chapter will attempt to analyse the relationship between the three terms 'imperialism', 'home', and 'Victorian femininity'. I will examine Godley and Henning's letters in particular to suggest that the imperial expansion of Britain in the Victorian age and the Victorian domestic ideology were two sides of the same coin, mutually interdependent and absolutely essential for the construction of Britannia. Godley and Henning are Britannia's daughters, sent to the Antipodes because they had a specific role to play in Britain's imperial enterprise. My juxtaposition of the two is not arbitrary but deliberate. Some important questions that arise out of this juxtaposition are: Was there a difference in the construction of emigrant femininity between women who were married and women who were not? If Victorian domestic ideology underscored the need for women to marry, what part did Henning's spinster status play in the construction of her identity as (white) woman? Does a Victorian woman who settles in the Antipodes think about home differently to one who is away for only three years? To put it another way, does she negotiate with her new landscape differently to one who leaves home only temporarily? And, finally, how is whiteness encoded in emigrant femininity?

Class and Victorian femininity

Both women's early letters describe their fellow passengers on their voyages, descriptions which reveal their awareness and reproduction of classed differences. For instance, Henning's letters from aboard ship are replete with references to 'several commercial gentlemen, or rather not gentlemen, and a little Scotchman, who looks more polished' (50); at another instance, she refers to a Mrs Westgarth who 'looks like a lady, but I have never heard her speak' (20); again, she refers to a Mrs Hake, 'who is handsome and speaks like a lady. *But* her husband, Tregenna [a cousin] says, is a linen-draper in Sydney' (emphasis added; 20). Charlotte Godley refers to a Miss Borton as 'neither aristocratic nor very bright' (3), as though one quality could make up for the other; again, describing another group, 'an Englishwoman [who] has been in service with Lady Ponsonby' and another girl who used to be 'a ladies' maid', she concludes, 'these form with one or two more the aristocracy of the *forecabin*' (emphasis in original; 12). These and a myriad other references in their letters to the stupidity of servants or their refusal to know their place suggest their own class affiliations. In yet another instance, Henning refers to the lack of priorities in a servant who won a doll in a raffle. The doll was large, dressed as a bride, and Jane, the servant, wished to take it with her to Sydney. Henning comments sarcastically: '[the doll] certainly is a highly useful article for a general servant' (77). Rachel Henning feels that though Jane is a good servant—for Australia, that is—she would not be able to retain her job for even a week in England. In the hierarchy of servants, obviously a generalist like Jane does not rank very high. In another instance Henning points to the sheer carelessness of servants, giving as example the continually smashed crockery (129). Servants are no different in New Zealand; either they dress inappropriately, or they are 'countrified-looking girls with rough hair, and no caps . . .' (73). In short, as Godley suggests, 'the whole subject of maid-servants [is] one of the great miseries of human life in New Zealand' (56). Here the very term 'human' is encoded as being middle-class or above.

Although the Victorian domestic ideology is structured by class in that it is braided with the rise of the middle class in the late eighteenth and early nineteenth centuries, the concept of femininity itself is devoid of classed affiliations. In *White, Male, and Middle-class*, Catherine Hall refers to the origins of domestic ideology and suggests that the Evangelicals (in particular, the Clapham Sect) were very influential in the development of distinct definitions of public and domestic life in the late eighteenth and early nineteenth centuries.[4] This particular group was connected to both the aristocrats and the manufacturing class, and saw the demise of the mores of eighteenth-century notions of femininity located in the aristocracy; they also influenced the birth of femininity within industrial capitalism. In the wake of the French Revolution across the Channel and of a rising, industrial, capitalist bourgeoisie in Britain, the Evangelicals condemned aristocratic women and women of the gentry who were educated only in dressing well, dancing and singing. Within the context of a changing political and economic scenario, the Evangelicals argued for a return to a daily spiritual life, resituating woman as the repository of domestic ideals. She was supposed to morally regenerate the nation. The domesticity of woman was underscored and a good woman was 'modest, unassuming, unaffected and rational' (87). While they felt upper- and middle-class women should be trained to be morally excellent, to be good daughters, wives and mothers, poor women would be trained to be industrious, frugal, diligent and good managers. By redefining femininity, the Evangelicals instituted a bourgeois ideal of the family which functioned to obscure 'class relations, for it came to appear above class . . . Nature decreed that all women were first and foremost wives and mothers' (92).

The relationship between the economy, the nation and the particular construction of femininity is also explored by Nancy Armstrong in *Desire and Domestic Fiction*.[5] She analyses the semiotics of conduct books of the eighteenth and nineteenth centuries which instructed women on how to be good wives, good managers—in short, how to be domesticated. She suggests that because men as a group were fragmented between being designated as being from town or country, rich or poor, upper class or labouring class, it was women who bound these factions together by being 'free of bias toward an occupation, political faction, or religious faction' (69). Armstrong locates such a construction of the woman in the domestic ideal because of the need for conduct books. The fragmentation among men, had it permeated to women, would have required books written for specific audiences. Armstrong furthermore links the bringing together of various social groups of men to the eventual formation of the middle class, which didn't exist in Britain until the nineteenth century.[6]

But if women are located as prior to class, if they were metonymic extensions of the home, and the moral centre of the ideal of the family, how can we explain the classed nature of Henning's and Godley's comments? In *Uneven Developments*, Mary Poovey also argues that despite this construction of the woman as the bedrock of Victorian society, the Victorian notion of femininity itself abounded with contradictions.[7] Though woman, idealized, was perceived as domestic, virtuous and moral in the nineteenth century, in the ideology of the sixteenth, seventeenth and eighteenth centuries she was perceived as the 'site of willful sexuality and bodily appetite' (9) and the embodiment of flesh and desire, impulses and passion (9–10). These earlier discourses commingled with the Victorian perception of woman to render her as needing the control of man, needing his protection. Within the cultural and political arena, woman was interpreted as being governed, not by reason, like men, but by the biological demands of her body. Her femininity was her maternity. Her productiveness was her reproductiveness. Therefore she could not contribute economically or politically to the nation. Poovey points out that:

> In producing a distinction between kinds of labor (paid versus unpaid, mandatory versus voluntary, productive versus reproductive, alienated versus self-fulfilling), the segregation of the domestic ideal created the illusion of an alternative to competition; this alternative, moreover, was the prize that inspired hard work, for a prosperous family was the goal represented as desirable and available to every man.(10)

Thus, while notions of manhood signified man's participation in the social, political and economic world, woman encapsulated home, reproduction and the moral values that the nation desired. Here, the difference between the sexes followed a schema of binary qualities which supposedly complemented each other.

It is a commonplace to point out that notions of hierarchy in binary terms deconstruct, switch places, and resituate the meanings and power differentials between the two terms in their signification. The binary terms in this instance are

'Victorian man' and 'Victorian woman', with the man signifying variations in race, region and class, and the woman, whose
only function was to embody her difference from man but not
any of the variations among her sex. The primary term,
'Victorian man', is able to signify change and differences which
accrue meaning in culture only if 'Victorian woman' as
secondary term remains unchanging and constant. Of course,
even the simplest strategy of deconstruction indicates that the
primary term is structurally the secondary term, because its
meaning is dependent on what is designated as the secondary
term. Thus the superiority of the primary term is revealed to
be a construction. The Victorian woman is located as unchanging, not because she is innately so, but so her male counterpart
can signify distinctions and differences. To this extent her
identity is porous in that she, too, partakes of the distinctions
of her male counterpart. To suggest that a middle-class man
encodes his classed position, but that his wife or daughter
does not, makes no sense at all. As Pierre Bourdieu suggests,
'the primary forms of classification owe their specific efficacy
to the fact that they function below the level of consciousness
and language, beyond the reach of introspective scrutiny or
control of the will'.[8] Within such a reading, Henning and
Godley inevitably cannot help their classed responses. Far from
experiencing a sisterhood with servants, their class of origin
and that of their spouse prevents them from overidentifying
with working-class women.

This narrative of evoking and erasing differences falters
slightly and reconfigures itself differently once in Godley's text,
when a Maori man asks John Godley the charge for Charlotte
Godley to iron his shirts. Charlotte offers to do four shirts at
twopence each. She says: 'Indeed, though I say it, they were
so well done that I began to think I have an undeveloped
talent for laundry work' (313). In this incident, notwithstanding
racial difference, it appears that Maori men are metonymic
extensions of white settler men and white women that of Maori
women. However, this story is quickly recontextualized within
the ignorance of hygienic matters among Maori, for though
the Maori woman washes his shirts initially for him, Charlotte
has to wash them again as '[t]hey were so nearly in a state
in which they were taken off, after a good long wear . . .'

(312). Here gender hierarchy must be displaced to articulate a racial hierarchy.

I am holding back on the discussion of the intersection of whiteness and femininity because I want to finish exploring how class is linked to femininity. Within psychoanalytic discourse in his narrative of the 'Wolf Man', Freud describes the Wolf Man as having had a nursery maid whom he remembered as kneeling on the floor with a short broom beside her.[9] Later, the adult Wolf Man falls in love with a peasant woman kneeling in the same position. Freud situates this narrative within the context of the Family Romance in which the child fantasizes that he has different parents, or noble parents, or that his father is noble and that his mother has had love affairs, such fantasies arising from the Oedipal situation wherein there is a desire to denigrate parents while exalting them; they might also arise from a desire to circumvent an incest barrier.[10] In their reading of the Wolf Man Peter Stallybrass and Allon White remark on Freud's blindness to the integration of class within the construction of desire and masculinity, and the image of Grusha the maid.[11] They point out that 'Freud is so intent upon demonstrating that the Wolf Man's obsession with Grusha is the signifier of the primal scene . . . that he is forced to minimize the figure of the maid' (153). Anne McClintock, too, points out the saturation of class elements in Freud's notion of femininity.[12] She suggests that since working-class women were located as sexually aggressive, and middle- and upper-class women as chaste and passive in the domestic ideology, in Freud's framework the nurse, the maid, etc. who played a central role in the upbringing of middle-class children had to be expelled from his theorizing of femininity. McClintock concludes that the nanny who has both the power of punishment and the power to evoke sexual desire is split 'and displaced into the father and mother as a universal function of gender' (90). The influence of Victorian sexuality on Freud's theoretical framework is undeniable. The same 80 years which produced high imperialism in Western Europe in the wake of the Industrial Revolution and a rising mercantile class also constructed particular notions of masculinity, femininity and whiteness across various discourses and texts. Thus, Freud's theoretical framework must be read not merely within the context of gender relations, but also as encoding these socioeconomic and political shifts.[13]

Femininity and the nation

Just as the unchanging attributes of women were necessary to create the notion of the unmarked bourgeoise, so also the domestic ideal of a virtuous, homebound woman, untouched by regional, class and religious affiliations is necessary for the construction of nationalism that makes imperialism possible. As I argued in Chapter 3, women provide a horizontal evenness which is central for bringing the vertical differences of men into meaning and representation, while the horizontal evenness itself does not undergo any change to its meaning formation. Certainly Partha Chatterjee and R. Radhakrishnan reiterate such a location of woman in the discourse of the nation striving for independence.[14] Citing Chatterjee, Radhakrishnan points out: 'In the fight against the enemy from the outside, something within gets even more repressed and "woman" becomes the mute but necessary allegorical ground for the transactions of nationalist history' (84). In the context of India, in its attempt to decolonize, such a location of woman is inevitable because she represents the 'inner and inviolable sanctum of Indian identity' and stands as a metaphor for home, spirituality, and the true self (84). This construction of woman deploys notions of inner (read: the integrity of the true self) and outer (read: the hostile colonized world). Carrying their framework to its logical extension, we find that women represent genuine Indianness, the unchanging essence of India. Men, who participate in the outer world, carry the weight of history on their shoulders. Historical events interpellate the men as Indians whereas women are always already Indian. To this extent, Indian men's changing identity mimes that of Indian women which is the original identity. Historical events, contact with the outside world, and notions of an originary Indian identity which the Indian women embody combine to construct Indian men. Chatterjee and Radhakrishnan locate this gendered split between inner and outer as one caused by Western enlightenment. As Radhakrishnan states:

Forced by colonialism to negotiate with Western blueprints of reason, progress and enlightenment the nationalist subject straddles two regions or spaces, internalizing Western epistemological modes at the outer or the purely pragmatic level, and at the inner level maintaining a traditional identity that will not be influenced by the purely pragmatic nature of the outward changes (85).

I draw attention to the postcolonial framework, not to make it the universal model to read the woman's role in the nation, but to see if it throws light on the Enlightenment model which it so obviously critiques. In short, if the Enlightenment model is problematic for the notion of gender in a decolonizing nation is gender in a Western democratic nation which is structured through the Enlightenment necessarily unproblematic? In *The Sexual Contract* and *The Disorder of Women*, Carole Pateman suggests that the notion of a social contract is central to the Enlightenment narrative in that all social relations, be they between the individual and the state, or the employer and the employee, are necessarily contractual in form.[15] The cornerstone of liberal democracy emphasizes that all individuals are born free and equal to each other. Here, both free will and one's ownership of oneself are underscored. It is the ownership of self that underpins the employee's contracting of body and skill to the employer. Pateman argues that while civil society and social order are based on a social contract, underpinning the social contract is the sexual contract, which gives it meaning and coherence. This contract is between men and women, and is normally visible in the context of the family. Within the household, the woman is contracted as a worker in the conjugal home:

> What being a woman (wife) *means* is to provide certain services for and at the command of a man (husband). In short, the marriage contract and a wife's subordination as a (kind) of labourer, cannot be understood in the absence of the sexual contract and the patriarchal construction of 'men' and 'women' and the 'private' and the 'public' spheres'. (*The Sexual Contract*; emphasis in original; 128)

Pateman further specifies that though women are part of the social contract narrative in that they can enter into contracts for employment, housing, et cetera, it is the sexual contract that incorporates her differently within society. For

Pateman the social order is divided between two spheres, the civil public sphere and the private. It is her complete incorporation in the latter that positions the woman uneasily in the former. Pateman also suggests that the binary of the public and private historically shifts its meaning regularly, as each century gives the divide a different meaning. However, this divide always also locates women in the private. Where previously women were located in the private because of their perceived close alignment with nature, under capitalism and its gendered and classed division of labour women are relegated to their dependent place in the familial sphere (*The Disorder of Women*; 123).

This relegation of women in the realm of the private goes beyond a decolonizing move in the context of a growing nationalism, as Chatterjee and Radhakrishnan suggest. My rereading of the disjunction between men and women in a liberal democracy via postcolonial discourse is necessary because both discourses, liberal and postcolonial, underscore the trope of home so meaningfully and persistently. Within liberal discourse the home is in alignment with women and the private; within postcolonial discourse the home signifies tradition, true indigenous identity, security and a place which is devoid of racism. In settler colonies like Australia and New Zealand, home has yet another meaning in that it signifies a yearning and nostalgia for Britain. For instance, Godley visits a Mrs Brittan in Christchurch, whose house is 'exactly like a small villa just out of London. The furniture of the drawing room is exactly that, just as they brought it out; small black marble chimney-piece, paper, carpet, and all, even to the few chairs set around the room in their own places' (288). In the aesthetics of the arrangement of her drawing room, Mrs Brittan indicates what London means to her—her house in New Zealand is London displaced. This displacement functions in two ways: first, by reconstructing a 'London' villa in Christchurch, the privileged term 'London' is maintained in the Antipodes; it becomes a marker of imperialism and imperialist aesthetics. Simultaneously, however, this reconstruction of the London villa functions to underscore the fact that Christchurch is not London, nor is New Zealand Britain. Mrs Brittan is not in Britain. London is privileged in opposition to what it is not. Its privilege is only ever retroactive in that it must first be lost. This particular scene is saturated with loss and desire for London. Secondly, remembering London in Christchurch simultaneously underscores, for the postcolonial reader, that the coherence of home and the safety it represents is purchased by excluding specific histories that saturate a place, in this instance, Maori histories. The sedimentation of extant history in geographical space must be occluded for the construction of London and the homesickness that suffuses Mrs Brittan to become visible.

(White) femininity and imperialism

The role of the woman is imbricated within the loss and desire that is at the underside of imperialism and the settling of wild spaces by Britain. It is a commonplace to suggest that the colonial/imperial venture was masculine in nature in its assertion of domination and control, both political and economic. Western women and imperialism are perceived as mutually exclusive terms to the extent that the colonies were perceived as 'no place for a white woman'.[16] In *Empire and Sexuality* Ronald Hyam remarks, '[t]he historian has to remember the *misery* of empire: the heat and the dust, the incessant rain and monotonous food, the inertia and the loneliness, the lack of amusement and intellectual stimulus'.[17] In the wilds of the empire, the Victorian women from Britain (in India especially) were perceived to be, '[m]oping and sickly, narrowly intolerant, vindictive to the locals, despotic and abusive to their servants, usually bored, invariably gossiping viciously, prone to extramarital affairs, cruelly insensitive to [local] women and hopelessly insulated from them' (119). The Angel in the House was meant to remain in the home; once removed from her natural habitat, she lost her angelic qualities.

I want to explore the cultural and emotional investment in the construction of the Angel in the House in the High Victorian era. In his work *Imperialism*, Harry Magdoff gives some astonishing statistics about the movement of Europe and Europeans to non-European spaces between 1800 and 1914.[18] By 1815 Britain had lost its first empire, the thirteen states of the US, but still had its second empire, which was spread from Canada and the Caribbean in the Western hemisphere through India and Australia. Britain, Spain, Portugal, the Netherlands and France—Western and Southern Europe in the main, laid claim in 1800 to 55 per cent of the Earth's land surface. In the first three-quarters of the nineteenth century, Europe acquired new territory at the rate of 210 000 square kilometres a year. Between the 1870s and World War I the rate of acquisition increased to 620 000 square kilometres a year. Eighty-five per cent of the land surface, mostly outside Western Europe, was in the hands of a few colonial powers in Western Europe—the one exception being Japan. Colonial expansion went hand in hand with the diaspora of European people. Magdoff estimates that 55 million Europeans moved to new lands between 1820 and 1920. This figure represents fully one-fifth of Europeans in Europe in 1820.[19] While men were over-represented in the estimated 55 million, a lot of women emigrated as well. However, the 1871 census in Britain indicated that there was a surplus of 718 566 women and an equal surplus of men in the new world.[20] Joanna Trollope points out that by the mid-1800s over 35 per cent of women in Britain between 20 and 44 were single.[21] The empire was partly to blame because it needed Englishmen to govern its far-flung spaces. In the face of such statistics it is understandable that Rachel, Amy and Annie Henning all moved to Australia with their brother Biddulph in 1853–54, as their chances of marrying Englishmen were increased by leaving Britain.

Notions of Victorian British masculinity and femininity, far from being specific to the customs and conditions of the British Isles, were gendered constructions of a people who were not confined to Britain any more. British gender constructions of High Victorianism had encoded within them the needs of imperialism and the identity which comes within the diaspora of a people who were politically, economically, culturally and hegemonically dominant, constructing the notion of home in unfamiliar places. The notion of being British (which elided to being 'English') was a retroactive construct completed according to the demands of the Empire. To this extent, Matthew Arnold's argument in *Culture and Anarchy*, that to emblematize Englishness, to belong to the national life, one had to either be a member of the Anglican church or to have attended Oxford or Cambridge, disguises over the fact that these requirements are specific to the imperialist venture, of the need to civilize and govern the colonies. Within this context, Englishness was limited to men of a certain class. Women were excluded by such a discursive construction of citizenship. In 'Englishness and National Culture', Philip Dodd reminds us that 'vigorous, manly and English was the popular collocation'.[22] Indeed, Biddulph, Rachel's brother, lives up to the popular view of English manliness. Delicate in health as a young man in England, Biddulph is transformed in Australia. Not only does he own stock and stations, but he also knows how to shoe a horse, stuff a saddle (112), shear sheep, mete out justice to horse thieves as in the instance where he has a horse thief lashed two dozen times (154), manage stray horses, fix damaged carts (95), catch eel for dinner (105) and oil-proof a tent by brushing boiled oil over calico (161). The list of his accomplishments and adaptability is endless. He tames the wilderness, settles Queensland as it is opened up for settlement, buys and sells sheep and cattle stations, and makes a fortune in the process. This shift from effete sickly gentleman to settler masculinity is a process that John Godley goes through as well in New Zealand. In the opening pages of his wife's letters, John Godley catches colds very easily. But once he reaches New Zealand he keeps good health, leaves his windows open in winter, chooses to wear damp flannel in a Wellington winter, goes on week-long walking trips and enjoys excellent health. On one hand the colonies are perceived as climatically kinder to sickly men than Britain. On the other, it is the colonies that masculinize these men and actively participate in the construction of Englishness. Notwithstanding Matthew Arnold's construction of national life, national notions of Englishness are shaped in the colonies as much as the colonies are shaped by Britain.

Imperialism and the immigration of middle-class men to settler colonies which muddied and scrambled strict classed divisions of labour also contributed to the increasing respectability of working-class labour.[23] The *Oxford English Dictionary* records the noun 'labour' for the first time in 1880 as referring to labourers who have a political identity. The working class as a cultural formation itself, identifiable as male with vigour, strength and sheer physicality, is a product of the age of high imperialism as much as it is of national life in Britain. National life in Britain in the Victorian era was constructed by the effects of imperialism. At one juncture, Charlotte Godley remarks that the son of Taylor, a waiter whom the Godleys knew in Britain, had become a Customs Officer and a gentleman in New Zealand. Not only were English class distinctions not pertinent in New Zealand, but also the diaspora of the British featured in daily life there. In another context Nupur Chaudhuri suggests that far from rigidly adhering to the mores of Victorian England, '[n]ewspaper and magazine articles, letters to the editor, cookery columns, "exchange columns", and advertisements in women's periodical literature in Victorian Britain reveal . . . . [British women] as a conduit for the flow of culture from India to Britain beginning around the mid-nineteenth century'.[24] While Chaudhuri's work limits itself to the mutual influence of Britain and India and the role of women in braiding the two cultures, I want to expand her thesis to suggest that imperial interests constructed almost every facet of national life in Britain. Notions of masculinity, femininity, class and sexuality were all reconstructed in (while constructing) the colonies and filtered back to Britain to re-emerge as 'English'.[25]

To this extent, the teleology of the domestic ideology which locates women as outside markers of class and region must be re-examined. At some level, colonial men were also the embodiment of shifting notions of class and gender. Godley's remark about the upward mobility of the son of Taylor the waiter is a case in point. In yet another instance, she remarks on men doing 'all the work in every house in New Zealand' (56). This theme of not adhering to familiar gendered division of labour becomes evident when both Godley and Henning describe their trips through the bush. In Australia, men cook, clean, set up tent and pack while Rachel and her sister Annie drive nineteen horses because the men are occupied with other domestic tasks (101).

The point I wish to make is that while the domestic ideology governed British women's lives in Britain and the colonies, it is a specific construction of women required to allay the anxieties and fears of its people in the diaspora.[26] Britain in the Victorian age was in the process of assimilating peoples and lands which were neither organically nor naturally connected to either Britain or each other. A British identity had to be forged in two steps. First, dominance had to be maintained; second, other identities had to be anglicized while simultaneously maintained as being different. Only such a negotiation could ensure British dominance. The daily interaction with difference at all levels—landscape, people, customs, hemisphere, climate, aesthetics and meanings—required the construction of at least one particular factor as constant, unchanging. The notion of the domestic ideology, women at home, reconstructing British homes in foreign spaces, functioning as metonyms of home and of Brittania, went a long way in fulfilling the needs of the British (men) in the diaspora. British identity under high imperialism was a disaggregated identity. The woman's role was to cohere this disaggregation and make it re-emerge as the unchanging British way, the nation itself. Nowhere are the limitations of her role more evident than in an amusing moment in Godley's letters wherein she gives a dummy of a woman to some bachelors to keep in their home so they would maintain a standard of manners befitting the company of a lady. While the incident is amusing on one level, it makes the British woman interchangeable with a dummy, a piece of furniture. One could stand in for the other in the greater mission of maintaining British men as civilized.

Femininity and the devolopment of the domestic ideology is underscored as being constructed several times by the text in the contrast provided between Annie and Rachel Henning. Annie is constructed by the structure of the home. She never 'walk[ed] further than the kitchen garden to cut vegetables for dinner' (148). Her domain is the home and she is immersed in housekeeping (193). Rachel reminds us: 'She keeps house and cooks' (179). As long as the figures of Annie and Amy function as Biddulph's binary opposite, being womanly to his forcefulness, preferring the surroundings of the home to his enjoyment of the outdoors, the relationship, the perfect balance, between imperialism and its production of masculinity and domestic ideology and its particular construction of the woman, is maintained. Rachel, however, fits only very uneasily into this structure. For instance, she categorizes herself as Biddulph's clerk whose 'main function is to keep his books and accounts, copy his letters and invoices'. She prefers these chores to 'making puddings' (179). Rachel also thinks nothing of riding twenty miles to get bars of soap (113–14). She finds nothing 'pleasanter than a gallop over a plain' (117). If the domestic ideology is about the gendered division between public and private, Rachel does not limit herself to either category. Her love of riding fast metonymically links her to the men, but her being a woman forces her into feminine spaces. The difficulty of categorizing Rachel is especially evident when she admits guilelessly and without any vanity to her sister Henrietta that she looks 'very ancient' in Australia, 'under the influence of the hot climate' (142). Furthermore, at the age of 40 she marries Deighton Taylor, who is considerably younger. If the function of the domestic ideology was for women to be mothers, to be feminine, and to maintain the distinction between the public and private, Rachel barely measures up. She never becomes a mother, is not feminine, and refuses to keep to her place in the private realms of the home. If this construction of femininity is to counterbalance the imperial expansion of Britain which was gendered as masculine, Rachel's femininity becomes disturbing. As a figure of femininity, in her preference for the outdoors, in her dislike of making puddings, in her admission of her fading looks because she loves the outdoors, she functions improperly.

Within such a framework Rachel can only function as a disruption, one who exposes the failure of the binary opposites to include everyone. At one juncture, she realizes that when Biddulph marries, she will have to return to England, one more statistic in the growing number of spinsters in Britain's census-taking. In a poignant line she admits that she prefers her life in Australia to that in England: 'I do greatly enjoy the lovely climate, good health and free outdoor life that we have here, and, though I like Aunt Vizard and love her, she would be a poor exchange for Biddulph' (179). The addition of the colonies necessitated changing notions of gender yet the colonies themselves undid or exposed the constructed nature of the binarities of gender. Australia's free outdoor life suits her but as a spinster she cannot make Australia her home. The predicament that Rachel faced was shared by the 718 566 surplus women in Britain cited by A.J. Hammerton. As he states, '[w]omen raised for a state of dependence in marriage but not provided for in the event of spinsterhood were bound inevitably for "educated destitution" ' (35). While Hammerton blames middle-class values and British inheritance laws for such a situation, I want to go even further and suggest that the women who fell outside the narrative of marriage and home that the domestic ideology underscored, who were its constitutive outside, were nevertheless created by the very system that excluded them. Their function as a disruption also simultaneously suggests not their inability to marry or be independent, but rather their status as casualties in Britain's export of its men and its failure to provide for its women. Ultimately, the domestic ideology is not about femininity but is a particular reproduction of imperialism. Feminine women as a category are coopted Britain's imperialistic venture.

Women and race

Having examined the definitions of nineteenth-century domestic ideology which located women as unmarked by class, religion and region, I have argued that as long as the role of women was structured within the family, women would have partaken of the discourse of class which distinguished men from each other. I have suggested that the imperialism which was central to nineteenth-century British identity must be examined for its construction of domestic ideology. Victorian British identity cohered around the notions of the colonies which were central to its economy and that of the diaspora, given that a sizeable number of the British population emigrated to the colonies. The act of moving to new lands, new spaces and new situations necessitated locating women as constant. The woman in the house compensated for the constant contact with difference. Such a location of woman in the home, in private space effectively removed her from the economy of British imperial history and British identity.

In this section of the chapter I want to examine the effects of such a location. If her body and her home functioned as a metaphor for Britain, could woman be British herself? In the public/private divide, how did women experience their nationality? In 'The English Woman' Jane Mackay and Pat Thane argue that in the period of high imperialism:

> The classic English man . . . was held to combine certain
> qualities, including leadership, courage, justice, and honour,

which were defined as distinctively 'English'. He has no exact female equivalent.

The qualities of the perfect English woman were publicly discussed, but they were not generally perceived as being specifically English. Rather they were those qualities—essentially domestic and maternal—believed to be universal in Woman.[27]

Mackay and Thane point out that the English woman proved her superiority to other women by being more domestic and more maternal. They also add that legally the British woman's nationality is figured only tenuously, as she loses her British status on marriage to a foreigner. Being deprived of her right to be categorized as British, how could she emphasize it? Further, how would her movement to foreign spaces impact on her experience of nationality? For the British in the colonies, the move, far from causing them to experience themselves as other, reinforced their nationality and their dominance. It was the native that was other.

The binary of dominant subject and colonized other prevails in Godley's descriptions of the Maori. The disapproval in her tone of the way Maori eat their pork, bread and rice 'without any attempt at tables, chairs, spoons, forks or any other signs of civilization' is remarkable for what Spivak describes as 'the force to make the "native" see himself as "other"' (133). Godley compares them to animals (49), thinks they are the binary opposite of civilized people as their friendly greeting sounds like a sad bereavement (62), suggests that their forms of amusement are childish (93), and describes an old Maori woman in the most derogatory way (95). She seems to particularly dislike Maori women and preferred the appearance of Maori men, so 'much better looking than the women; some . . . . quite handsome, and most of them very lively, and fond of a joke' (95). Rachel Henning's dislike of foreigners is particularly reserved for the Irish, whose presence never fails to evoke an acerbic comment from her. For instance, she finds her Irish servant tiresome for her Irish anecdotes (33); they are stupid (39); when her ship reaches Ireland on its way to Australia she finds the landscape pretty but finds the streets dirty, filthy, swarming with children and pigs (57). Soon her dislike of all foreigners becomes evident. The Chinese are 'dreadful rascals' (72); she rejoices when England defeats

Australia (Victoria) in cricket (81). While making a comment about the defeat of the Australians, she makes an acid remark about Americans as well: 'I suppose new countries are conceited for the same reason that very young men are, and when they have seen a little more of the world they will learn to know their real standing—as John Bull does' (81). Her comments about Australian Aboriginals, however, seem more neutral and occasionally sympathetic.

Much recent scholarship has debated whether British women in the colonies were racist or not. The traditional view of English women has been that they were racist and excessively fond of luxury.[28] More recently, women scholars have argued that there were close relationships between the colonial English women and the racialized other.[29] I, on the other hand, want to posit that the British women's attitudes to race should be read within the context of their lack of subjectivity within the nation.

Within the context of discussing Fanon's *Black Skin, White Masks*, Diana Fuss suggests in *Identification Papers* that 'while the "black man must be black in relation to the white man", the converse does not hold true; the white man can be white without any relation to the black man because the sign "white" exempts itself from the dialectical logic of negativity'.[30] Using this model to analyse the British woman's problematic relationship with the mother country proves fruitful. While the term 'British' signifies the man, as Mackay and Thane indicate, the British woman is encoded within this term only in relation to the man. He becomes the Universal whereas she is once removed from such a universality because of her femininity. In an edited paraphrase of Fuss and Fanon, I can say, 'the British woman is British in relation to the (British) man; however the reverse does not hold as he can be British without any relation to the British woman because he exempts himself from the "dialectical logic of negativity"'. The interchangeability between the terms 'British' and 'man' makes it the transcendental signifier—British is never a not-man. Thus the British male unmarks himself from the category of gender. The British woman, however, can only ever function as a negative term. In the colonies she can accede to the position of British, with agency, not in the subordinate position to her male counterpart, but only via race. Her othering of the racial

169

other temporarily removes her from the position of gendered other and elevates her to ideological/national power.

Within such a reading Henning and Godley's insistence of their Britishness is stridently coded with their anxiety, but simultaneously makes a tenuous claim to their own identity via their nation. Interestingly, Henning starts identifying herself with the Australian pioneer woman in her disparaging remarks about those who come to Australia 'to get colonial experience' (111) and in her response of delight at the wild, uncivilized grandeur of the Australian landscape. Later, however, in one of the last letters included in the volume, written on 30 August 1877, 23 years after she first arrived in Australia, and not having been back to England in sixteen years, she refers to herself as 'we English' (278) as opposed to the colonials. In 1882 she rejoices at 'the English victories in Egypt, and generally think[s] it is a pity *we* cannot manage to "annex" Egypt' (emphasis added; 284). To be categorized as English, Rachel Henning must speak the masculine discourse of imperialism. She can only ever have her nation through declaring her racial superiority. Similarly, Godley has to contextualize her skills in doing laundry within a discourse of the lack of cleanliness among Maori in the shirt-washing incident cited previously; otherwise she will be located in continuum with Maori women and her lack of agency as a woman and as a British woman will become problematic.

The world and the home

In the previous section I suggested that the middle-class Victorian woman constructed by the dominant ideology of imperialism experienced her nationality in the colonies only diacritically in what Fuss describes as 'the negative term in a Hegelian dialectic' (144). But the problem of the Hegelian dialectic for Robert Young is that:

> [it]articulates a philosophical structure of the appropriation of the other as a form of knowledge which uncannily simulates the project of nineteenth century imperialism; the construction of knowledges which all operate through forms of expropriation of the other mimics at a conceptual level the

geographical and economic absorption of the non-European world by the West.[31]

British imperialism not only expropriates the colonized other from its rightful ownership of their own lands, but also requires the expropriation of the British woman of her rightful ownership to her nation/ality. There is multiple mimicry in the act of imperialism: Britain has to deprive women of their right to participate in the nation by incarcerating them within a domestic ideology; it has to deprive the colonized other of their lands and their nation by confining them within a hegemonic construction of knowledge; finally it must deprive its colonies of its wealth by locking and subordinating it within an imperialistic economy. All these deprivations and incarcerations mirror each other; the terms 'British woman', 'colonized, racialized other' and 'colonial economy' are always already one step behind the master economy of a hegemonic Britain, always mimicking the original, the dominant. The construction of British woman as a mimic British man is at odds with the implications of Chatterjee and Radhakrishnan's framework that I discussed earlier, however. In their reckoning it is the Indian women who are always already Indian, unlike the men who have to have their Indianness mediated via their women. Within a discourse of development both the colonized man and the British woman are in a continuum with each other. However, within the vector of power white and colonized women are linked, in that both of them are incarcerated within the home and the private space by both the British and the racialized, colonized men.

It is this trope of the world and the home that I wish to pursue in the conclusion of this chapter. In a telling moment in Godley's text she describes her disorientation in living in New Zealand:

> How curious it will seem . . . to have a very hot Christmas day, if we live to see it, and the windows ornamented with flowers something like lilac laburnums . . . instead of holly. So many things seem turned upside down; in expounding things to Arthur I often come to a stand-still. Sun in the North! etc., it makes our books all wrong. (69)

Godley repeatedly seems destabilized by the unfamiliar in the familiar. In yet another instance she describes May Day in

171

Wellington; listening to the band 'play a great number of very pretty things . . . althogether reminded me almost *too much* of home' (Godley's emphasis; 35).

But which part of it is not like home? Imperialism's legacy of home is coupled with strangeness. In this instance it is the sight of 'parties of natives, rolled in their blankets [who] *squatted* just behind the great drum' (emphasis in the original; 35) that defamiliarized home. The juxtaposition of the familiar with the strange faces Henning and Godley everywhere; the fauna and flora is simultaneously strange and wild, yet familiar and domesticated. The structure of homes, the layout of cities, the appearance of the settlers, all soothe yet disturb them. Life in the colonies becomes the site of the unhomely, the uncanny in their texts.

Freud's notion of the uncanny is repeatedly invoked in postcolonial discourse.[32] Within psychoanalytic discourse Freud describes the uncanny or the *unheimlich* as not the binary opposite of *heimlich* (the familiar and known) but rather as something which is repressed, kept out of sight: the 'uncanny is in reality nothing new or foreign, but something familiar and old-established in the mind that has been estranged only by the process of repression . . . The *unheimlich* is what was once *heimisch*, home-like, familiar; the prefix "un" is the token of repression' (394; 399). He suggests that the origin of this sensation of the uncanny is our experience of the maternal body. What was once familiar and home-like becomes repressed, unfamiliar in our maturation process.

Homi Bhabha plays upon this oscillation between the familiar and the unfamiliar where postcolonial writing introduces the strange in the familiar. The strangeness is connected not just to cultural difference; it is an effect of the repression of otherness which has been projected on to the native, but is really that which is always already part of the dominant. The effect of such a location of the *unheimlich* in the *heimlich* is to produce an ambiguity which questions and dissolves clearly marked binary opposites and reveals 'an interstitial intimacy' between them ('The Location of Culture'; 13). The clear border between world and home, outside and inside, public and private, dissolves and they become part of each other.

It is this effect that Godley and Henning experience in the

Antipodes, the down-under from that which is up above, the binary opposite of the mother country, that which is directly opposite 0 degrees in London. Everything seems turned upside down, not just in its geographical positioning but also in the meaning it reveals of their imperial mission down-under. But it goes beyond a simple dialectic of colonizer-colonized. The construction of Britishness is underpinned by the othering of the Maori, the Aboriginal, the Chinese, the Irish. But it is also simultaneously dependent on them; Britishness and other go beyond the notion of binary opposites giving meaning to each other. The Maori, the Aboriginal, the Chinese and the Irish are all the other in the self, the self in the other which makes them all simultaneously strange and familiar. The homes in the colonial world, the landscape and fauna and flora, become metaphors of the strange in the familiar. The enormous cabbages, the magnificent cauliflowers that Godley keeps remarking on, the gardens which have familiar things growing too quickly in New Zealand, the scarlet verbena, difficult to grow in the mother country but which grows like a weed in Australia, all underscore the impossibility of maintaining the strict boundaries between England and the strange world of the colonies, the *terra incognita*. But strangeness is also incorporated into the familiar: Godley sends boxes of New Zealand native plants to England (126).

In a further step, Godley and Henning's letters destabilize the boundaries between the public and the private. Both women, associated with the world of the private, partake of the public world in that they benefit and structure their lives from the riches of imperialism. The demarcation between private and public is revealed to be a myth in the consideration of the closely structured relationship between imperialism and Victorian domestic ideology. The domestic ideology must be kept hidden, repressed, to keep the narrative of the distinction between the public and private intact. It is this narrative that structures the individual in liberal discourse. What I have attempted to do is to make visible the *unheimlich* of imperialism which participates in the distinction of the public and private and hence maintains the distinction between the genders. By showing the close imbrication of domestic ideology and imperialism I suggest that the world exists in the home and the home in the world. I end where I began. Rachel Henning's living room, with books from Bristol, a chair from America and matting from India, reveals the *unheimlich*, the world in the home. In the discourse of embodiment as well as that of nation, the woman's body is posited as unchanging, constant, and timeless, just as are notions of space. Women are positioned like the present continuous tense form of the verb, but are curiously devoid of the notion of time which is the fundamental purpose of tense in verbs. This construction of the woman's body as embodying timelessness is a feint, in that her body shifts in meaning according to the needs of history, nation and men, and signifies differently according to race, imperialism, nation or decolonization. Her body is enclosed, incarcerated, in a space which has no meaning unto itself but functions to give meaning to others. The woman's body within representation is indeed the black body from Freud's dark continent.

PART III

In conclusion

The postcolonial critic:
Third World (con)texts/
First World contexts[1]

In bringing this work on the connections between race, place, embodiment and theory to a conclusion, I restate my preoccupations: Is blackness an effect or an essence? Is the body prior to discourse? Is place prior to discourse? Does prediscursive place engage with the prediscursive body, an argument central to indigenous rights? Is the discourse produced by such an engagement of necessity at a difference from political, racial and social constructions of the body and place? Is theory an emanation of prediscursive place? Is the production of theory inflected by the indigeneity of the body? Can theory be autochthonous, springing out of the soil from specific places? Or are all these things political productions? Certainly Gayatri Spivak takes the latter position in an interview with Ellen Rooney when she points out that the body is 'a repetition of nature . . . [However], it is through the *significance* of my body and others' bodies that cultures become gendered, economicopolitic, selved, substantive.'[2]

Since I invoke Spivak at the outset I begin my conclusion by describing a particular event in which she participated. I will lay out the territory: the place of narrative origin for this concluding chapter is the Centre for Historical Studies at the elite Jawaharlal Nehru University in New Delhi, India, where Gayatri Spivak, currently teaching at Columbia, held a visiting professorship in 1987. While in Delhi, Spivak was interviewed by three Indian women, Rajeswari Sunder Rajan, Rashmi Bhatnagar and Lola Chatterjee, all professors of English at various universities in Delhi. 'The Post-Colonial Critic' interview is interesting and significant for the range of topics covered: the nature of the post colonial intellectual, the use of First World theory, the women's movement, and the implications of teaching English literature in post colonial countries.[3] Instead of being a commemoration of Spivak's triumphant homecoming, however, the interview is fraught with tension and undercurrents of discord between her and the three Indian professors. As the interview begins, Spivak is asked to comment on the difference between the way she, a 'post-colonial diasporic Indian who seeks to decolonize the mind' perceives herself, and the way she has constituted them, that is, as 'native intellectuals'. (67). Spivak's response is coded with a certain degree of dismay at the lines so sharply drawn by the Delhi-based professors. Their question reveals that she is not one of them, a charge that could be seen as calling into question the identity Spivak relies upon as a practising academician, cultural and postcolonial theorist in the US. She responds, 'your description of how I constitute you does not seem correct. I thought I constituted you, equally with the diasporic Indian, as a post-colonial intellectual' (67). It is apparent from this response that for her the postcolonial condition signifies a similarity in their structural position—everybody in the room is a brown, Indian academic, constituted in similar ways, a product of British colonialism and an English education system, teaching English literature in urban universities, with the same preoccupations, and most likely fairly similar class backgrounds. All three Indian professors are not convinced in the slightest; they demand to know if Spivak is 'privileging exile as a vantage point for a clearer perspective on the scene of post-colonial cultural politics' (67). Spivak responds like a stereotypical English teacher, rapping her colleagues on their knuckles for the incorrect usage of the term 'exile': 'I'd like to say that an exile is someone who is obliged to stay away—I am not in that sense an exile' (68). She adds that she is not privileging her position, though she wants to use it. Spivak next launches a counter-offensive, demanding to know why she is more 'politically contaminated' than they. The Indian professors are not contrite and insist upon the intrinsic differences between the two parties. Rashmi Bhatnagar and Rajeswari Sunder Rajan say, 'perhaps the relationship of distance and proximity between you and us is what we teach and write has political and other actual consequences for us that are in a sense different from the consequences, or lack of consequences, for you' (68). Spivak does not quite address this issue of 'distance and proximity' through the rest of the interview, which degenerates into a long disagreement. They disagree on the role of the NRI (Non Resident Indian); they disagree on the use of elite First World theory and indigenous theory; furthermore, they disagree on Spivak's central groundbreaking essay on postcoloniality, 'Can the Subaltern Speak?'.

My reasons for enframing this chapter within this particular interview are twofold. First, Spivak's interviews are always interesting because they show her constant evolution as a theorist and a thinker; her analyses and theorization of issues develop from one interview to the next. The genre of the interview is truly the most productive one for Spivak, primarily because interviews self-consciously insist upon their temporality, thus permitting a fluidity and changeability of theory. Second, this interview underscores the following question, one that I intend to explore in this chapter: Is there a discontinuous development in the production and practice of postcolonial theory between the intellectuals in Third World postcolonial countries and the dusky and diasporic postcolonial academics in First World universities? In examining postcolonial theory in its complexity, I will analyse theories produced by both groups, the natives and the 'native informants' (the postcolonial theorists located in the First World). The emphasis of Indian academics in the West seems to be on constructions of subjectivities. Academics in India braid nationalistic discourse with postcolonial theory so intricately that one cannot extricate one from the other. I will in particular examine the works of Spivak and of Homi Bhabha, who was based at Sussex University in the UK, and has since moved to the University of Chicago. I will also use a larger base of 'native theorists' from different disciplines.

In conclusion

Postcolonial theory in the Western academy

I feel this juxtaposition of postcolonial theories produced in the East and the West is historically warranted in postcolonial studies due to the kinds of responses that they have evoked in the West. Take, for example, two critical evaluations of Third World theory by Frederic Jameson, an American critic, and Benita Parry, a South African critic.[4] Jameson states the following in his infamous article, 'Third-World Literature in an Era of Multiculturalism':

> Judging from recent conversations among third-world intellectuals, there is now an obsessive return of the national situation itself, the name of the country that returns again and again like a gong, the collective attention to 'us,' and what we have to do and how we do it, to what we can't do and what we do better than this or that nationality, or unique characteristics, in short to the level of the 'people'. This is not the way American intellectuals have been discussing 'America,' and indeed one might feel that the whole matter is nothing but the old thing called 'nationalism' long since liquidated here and rightly so. (65)

Besides his dismissal of the work of Third World intellectuals as simple in contrast to the complex work produced by American intellectuals, Jameson's remarks exactly exemplify the binary thinking through which the West has always considered the East.[5] Jameson sets up his binarity, where the East is the complete alterity of the West, by providing a reading of Lu Xun, a Chinese novelist of the early twentieth century, and of the Senegalese writer Sembene Ousmane, within the context of the Third World's struggle over Western imperialism. Under the umbrella of modern capitalism, Jameson makes the East a metonymic extension of the Third World and the West of the First World, locked in mortal combat with each other. He proceeds to argue that all Third World literatures are uniformly national allegories recording the struggle against imperialism/capitalism, whereas First World literature is more complex. He adds that the First World literature and subject are a result of:

> a radical split between the private and the public, between the poetic and the political, between what we have come to

think as the domain of sexuality and the unconscious and the public world of classes, of the economic, and of secular political power: in other words, Freud versus Marx. (69)

Thus, Jameson subscribes to a developmental model situating First World subject and literature within a postmodern angst while Third World literature is frozen within the realistic mode. Granting the First World the realms of the political as well as the libidinal, the public as well as the private, Jameson denies the latter terms of the equation to his one-dimensional Third World. His construction of Third World difference is made by allegorizing all difference into a univocal/unilingual discourse.

While Jameson's bestowal of a homogenized postmodern anxiety to all Western subjects is problematic, so also is his Marxist reading of the Third World. His blurring of heterogeneities within the Third World in order to critique Western capitalism does not take into account that the preoccupation of the Third World is not solely fixed on struggling against Western cultural imperialism. As Ella Shohat points out in 'Notes on the Post-Colonial', the struggle takes place not only between nations but also within nations with its 'constantly changing relations between dominant and subaltern groups'.[6] Moreover, if capitalism is the precondition of the First World, a Third World country such as India, which has a capitalistic economy and whose industrial resources are among the top ten in the world, ought to be considered as part of the First World. On the other hand, if Jameson considers the division of public and private as the primary determinant of Western postmodern sensibility, consider Aida Hurtado's point in 'Relating to Privilege': that for people of colour in First World welfare states there is no distinction between public and private in that welfare programs and policies intervene in and determine the private zones of their lives.[7] Thus, according to Jameson's own definitions, the Third World exists within the bosom of the First and vice versa. For Jameson, knowledge is predicated on difference, which in turn is predicated on geographical divisions rather than any other consideration such as that of economics, culture, class or religion. Such a rationale is particularly problematic because geographical location becomes the sole determinant of the authenticity and interpretation of the writer/theorist.[8] This argument is not limited to First-World theorists such as Jameson. A manifestation of the geographical argument is implicit in the rebuking of Spivak in the 'Post-Colonial Critic' interview discussed above. The Indian theorists insist that, unlike them, her lack of proximity to, and occupation of, India impacts on her differently ('a lack of consequences'). Their postcolonial politics is autochthonous, hers is foreign and invasive.

In contrast, Benita Parry's approach to postcolonial theory overtly appears to be free of the biases which beset Jameson. In her much cited article 'Problems in Current Theories of Colonial Discourse', she valorizes Frantz Fanon as having inaugurated postcolonial theory, but in her urgent desire to hear the 'natives' speak for themselves, she effectively silences, then dismisses, the native informants—Indian academics in the West—primarily because they are too Westernized. Parry finds the theoretical frameworks provided by Bhabha and Spivak troublesome because both deny the binary of oppressor/ oppressed. Bhabha locates an ambiguity within authority which not only becomes the site of its own deconstruction, but also does not fit within the simple polarity of oppressor/oppressed; Spivak, in her turn, denies any agency and original purity to the voice of the oppressed in the aftermath of the epistemic violence throughout the ex-colonies. For her the voice of the oppressed is an act of ventriloquism. As she insists in 'Who Claims Alterity?', 'the new culturalist alibi, working within a basically elitist culture industry, insisting on the continuity of a native tradition untouched by a Westernization whose failures it can help to cover, legitimizes the very thing it claims to combat'.[9] Spivak's denial of native agency, native voice, another knowledge and alternative traditions untouched by colonialism, proves too problematic for Parry, leading her to conclude that 'Spivak's deliberate deafness to the native voice is at variance with her acute hearing of the unsaid in modes of Western feminist criticism' (39).

Both Parry and Jameson's insistence on seeing the native as unidimensional in her material reality, as opposed to the multidimensional space occupied by the Western non- native, is ultimately unproductive; to have any validity, the native must fall within predictible parameters of the other of the Western subject. Parry's dismissal of Westernized academics and her valorization of natives in their native land suggests a form of exoticization. She admires only Frantz Fanon, whom she reads as maintaining the binary of 'West versus the rest'.

All roads here appear to be leading to a discussion of the politics of place and theory being grounded in geographical space. In the next section I discuss the influence of space and place in the construction of our identity and subsequent production of theory. The notion of place is important to a sense of identity because the culture which it contains and produces situates its subject in a particular structural space, as I have argued throughout this book. More importantly, an articulation of place directly creates our sense of 'rootedness' to our place of origin, an autochthony as I have also clarified. This rootedness gives you a sense of being home—whether you like your home or not—or of being away from home. In addition I will discuss the ramifications of this sense of rootedness and its political effects on the production of postcolonial theory.

Soiled identity

In their article '"Smoking Mirrors"—Modern Polity and Ethnicity', Remo Guidieri and Francesco Pellizi posit that notions of 'authentic' identity are closely linked to the territorialization of space.[10] They point out that:

> before modern administrative definitions came into use, i.e., those made possible by *writing*—which transformed territories into land tenures and landmarks into supports for legal holdings—the actual occupation and use of a given territory was all the base one needed for cultural affirmation. It has its true substance and at the same time its root, its arche—the origin of its legitimacy and its principle—but also its image of a space through which a people's identity found its primary manifestation: our Land. (emphasis in original; 24)

The inscription of land through legal means (such as in land titles or, by extension, the boundaries of nations) functions to ground a community within certain parameters and to legitimize ownership. This kind of mooring of community to a delineated space simultaneously bestows a kind of paradoxical temporal permanence—almost a timelessness within time—to the community through the demarcation of space. Thus our ethnic and national identity (and our place within political economy) partially originates through our occupation of social and geographical space.

In theory, the problems of a rooted identity are several. In 'Putting Hierarchy in its Place', Arjun Appadurai makes a powerful argument for the dangers implicit in rooting groups of people to particular territories.[11] He argues that the basic premise of this approach is itself erroneous because there is no pure culture, uncontaminated by the influences of 'other' cultures. He says 'proper natives are somehow assumed to represent their selves and their history, without distortion or residue' (37). In contrast, the Western subject is exempt from any claims of authenticity because of the complexities and diversities of the West's histories and societies. The tendency of anthropologists to locate and analyse cultures on the assumption of their purity, according to Appadurai, leads to the 'incarceration' of natives, anchoring them and their cultures within well-defined boundaries—as I suggested in Chapter 1. The discourse of anthropology which defines natives whose habits and perceptions are shaped by their local habitats becomes a linguistic marker of their confinement. Appadurai implies that anthropological discourse derives and forwards its meaning through the logic of binary opposition; the native is always the object of inquiry, the 'other' to the dominant self of the anthropologist. Anthropologists are 'regarded as quintessentially mobile; they are the movers, the seers, the knowers. The natives are immobilized by their belonging to a place' (37). He concludes that by extension of this spatial confinement, the native is subjected to intellectual confinement as well. Malkki refers to this phenomenon as a 'sedentarist metaphysics' (3). At its most obvious level the spatial confinement of the native can be perceived in the denigration of landscape. In *The Savage Mind* Claude Lévi Strauss states that definite functions and significance of place are assigned to the flora and fauna and the concrete landscape of one's environment, which suggests aesthetics itself to be a construction of both geography and culture.[12] But if Lévi-Strauss' premise is used in a colonial situation, it suggests that the landscape, flora and fauna, seasons and geographical features of the native's land are generally beyond the experiential and aesthetic perception of the anthropologist who belongs to the dominant group. This limitation is expressed in the language of confinement which is an inadequate and insufficient model to express native geography—for example, the repeated references to the smell of 'rotting vegetation', a characterization of the equatorial regions by *fin-de-siècle* English colonists in India and Africa. The smell of the equatorial vegetation, completely alien to English nostrils, is coded with negativity in the choice of the word 'rotting'. This denigration of place implicit in the language of confinement spills over to the moral and intellectual dimension in a consideration of the native. The native faces a double negative: her landscape and geography are denigrated; she is rooted within it.

Such an incarceration of the native is also insisted upon by Edward Said in his now classic work *Orientalism*, in which he indicates that the renaissance in the West coincides with the growth and enforcement of colonialism and capitalism. According to Said, the notion of the Middle East, a place where Europeans had gone to study Aristotle, was dispelled with the onset of colonialism. A new geographical construct, which included the Middle East, South Asia and South-East Asia, was created by Europeans to function as their binary opposite. The Orient became synonymous with 'the exotic, the mysterious, the profound [and] the seminal' (51), in opposition to enlightened, rational and civilized Europe. In fact, postcolonial studies are premised on the suggestion that the history of colonialism is underpinned by the maintenance of sharply delineated boundaries between self and other. The process of colonialism (and neocolonialism) and the dominance of the rest of the world by the (white) West has transformed the latter into the unmarked (white) Western self. The process of othering colonized cultures has also simultaneously resulted in the covering over of the fact that the (white) Western self itself is also a construction and not a complete, natural category. This un-naming and unmarking of the (white) Western self also effectively naturalizes it and erases traces of the mechanism of binary oppositions in that it posits the non-white, non-Western body as the marked and the visible.

In conclusion

Decolonizing the Oriental self

Postcolonial theorists, picking up the mechanisms through which meaning is encoded to the Orient, have reversed them to invest meaning to the West. Ashis Nandy, a postcolonial theorist in India, deconstructs this notion of the East as lacking agency and as functioning as the negative opposite of the West when he strategizes the following:

> If there is a non-West which constantly invited one to be Western and to defeat the West on the strength of one's acquired Westernness—there is the non-West's construction of the West which invited one to be true to the West's other self and to the non-West which is in alliance with the other self.[13]

Nandy thus locates the non-Western self within an indigeneity and difference, thus facilitating its own construction of what it considers the West ought to be. In this, the non-West retrains its gaze on the West and sees something else. This kind of strategy, which still functions within the logic of binarities, bestows subjectivity and agency on the Orient, particularly India, and simultaneously underscores that the West is equally a geographical construct made by the East, and that Westerners are equally incarcerated within the space created by the Orient.

Ashis Nandy admits to the occidentalizing of the West as a strategy of decolonization. In *The Intimate Enemy*, he acknowledges that the modern and monolithic West is not just a geographical entity but a psychological category as well. He points out that 'the West is now everywhere, within the West and outside . . . The West has not merely produced modern colonialism, it informs most interpretations of colonialism' (xi–xii). Having established this point, he asserts that 'what looks like Westernization (in India) is often only a means of domesticating the West, sometimes by reducing the West to the level of the comic and trivial' (108). This foregrounding becomes strategic in his attempt to create an indigenous postcolonial theory which is not completely reliant on Western analysis of colonialism. Both Nandy, and Partha Chatterjee in *Nationalist Thought and Colonial World*, repeatedly turn to Indian nationalist leaders such as Bankim Chandra Chatterjee and Mahatma Gandhi to create autochthonous models of colonial resistance and postcolonial strategies of representation.[14] Bankim and Gandhi become central figures because they refused to participate in the binary oppositions that colonialism and Western thought engendered. They subscribed to a completely different system of signs, which became problematic for the British because it did not participate in a dualistic economy. For example, Gandhi's strategy of non-violence or empowering passivity fell completely outside the known colonial economy of repressive law and its opposite, violence.[15] Both Ashis Nandy and Partha Chatterjee insist that India is not non-West, nor is the Indian a counterplayer or an antithesis of Western man. In their desire to create an indigenous theory, these theorists attempt to tap into what is outside the circuit of power and colonial discourse of dominant culture, with their intrinsic characteristics of being exclusive and selective.[16] All these Indian nationalists—Nandy, Chatterjee, Bankim and Gandhi—by attempting to create 'native' models, try to indicate a different conceptualization of the world and a different regime of truth.

The production of theory via a naturalized identity and autochthony becomes central to understanding the differences between the postcolonials in India and the Indian postcolonials in the West. The centrality of this becomes evident in the moment of the 'Post-Colonial Critic' interview when, in addition to suggesting that Spivak is 'politically contaminated' because of her (lack of) proximity to her land of origin, all three New Delhi professors confess to a 'certain uneasiness' at her use of 'First World elite theory' (69) in her production of postcolonial discourse suggesting a preference for indigenous theory like Gandhism. Spivak's response to an indigenous theory is almost scathing. 'To construct indigenous theories one must ignore the last few centuries of historical involvement. I would rather use what history has written for me' (69) she retorts. In this exchange of words certain differences are implied. For the New Delhi professors, though they are teachers of English literature, the historical fact of colonialism and the resulting intellectual contamination from the West weighs heavily on their minds. For them decolonizing can begin only by evoking a theory which is as 'homespun' as Gandhiism. Only the Indian (cultural) landscape can give rise

187

to a theory which can be appropriately applied to this particular ex-colony. For Spivak such an approach borders on the naive because, like Appadurai, she argues that there can be no purely indigenous theory. To construct and evoke such a theory would be an oversimplified way of looking at Indianness, because it ignores the historical fact of two hundred years of British rule in India. British rule has undeniably opened the gates of Western epistemology and influence in the Indian subcontinent, in Spivak's reckoning. So Marxism, deconstruction and post-structural European theories are of necessity interlocked with and refracted through indigenous theories in the colonies.

Moreover, while there are overt suggestions of difference in the invoking of a purely Indian epistemology which nullifies Western epistemology, I would argue that such a nationalistic move and binary resistance on the part of the theorists in India itself reveals a fear of contamination of colonialism. In seeking to unify identity in the face of colonial rule, Indian nationalism posits a 'post-' to the colonialism and to the binary gridlock of oppressor/oppressed. The rhetoric of Indian nationalism must emerge as difference from this polarity: 'All Indians are my brothers and sisters.'[17] This act of homogenization re-encodes within itself the precondition of colonial binaries. The rhetoric of national unity and difference are predicated on the originary binary. So notwithstanding another epistemology via Gandhi and Bankim, nationalistic difference has the structural requirement of a primary colonial difference.

At this juncture I want to argue that the political/cultural space occupied by Indians in India is premised on the notion of essence having created identity.[18] For them, the Indian national subject is produced naturally, autochthonically—but this bleeds the Indian overseas of her Indian identity; the Indian abroad is always produced in the interstices of discourses on race and the status of the minority, and the socioeconomic and juridical discourses of the Indian in the West. The Indian abroad, in short, is a set of effects of these discourses rather than the causes. In contrast, the Indians in India are posited as having a naturalized identity, prior to effects. I draw attention to this point because of its problematic nature. The Indians in India seem to see a link between geographic location and identity. In fact, it was this essentialist argument that galvanized and energized the Independence movement in India: India for Indians. It must be remembered, however, that any notion of 'Indian' is itself a British colonial construct in that there was no unified Indian state prior to British colonialism. No pure, originary, unified Indian identity preceded that historical fact. Thus, any autochthonous/indigenous status is actually predicated on historical and colonial discourses, and is inflected by those particular markers of difference.

The point I am making about the problematic nature of the essentialist argument is not to deride the identity politics of Indians in India. I want to suggest that such an argument is a symptomatic extension of the identity politics and strategy which led to Indian independence. The homogenization of the Indian identity is central to the formation of the Indian nation. As Diana Fuss has indicated in *Essentially Speaking*, 'the adherence to essentialism is a measure of the degree to which a particular group has been culturally [or politically] oppressed' (98). If the essentialist argument is central to the formation of the Indian nation, there is a certain political and psychical investment in the expulsion of elements which disturb or muddy the identity of the Indian national subject. In fact, in an analysis of the presence of the Muslim in India and how she undoes unified coherent Indian subjectivity, Faisal Fatehali Devji states: 'The Muslim . . . represents a fundamental anxiety of nationalism itself: of the nation as something unachieved. And as such, every Muslim becomes, at a certain level, the symbol of national frustration and insecurity' (2). Devji posits that the very presence of the Muslim in India reinvokes the trauma of Partition for the Indians. Similarly, the Indian abroad remains the source of fundamental anxiety to India because she negates every notion of essence and indigeneity which is at the core of the construction of the Indian national subject, and reveals this subject to be a discursive formation predicated on colonial politics and difference rather than on homogeneity and the natural. The expulsion of the different Indian, be she settled abroad or be she a Muslim in India, is a structural condition upon which Indian identity is based.

S(p)oiled identity: the essence of borderlands

> If I should die, think only this of me:
> That there's some corner of a foreign field
> That is for ever England. There shall be
> In that rich earth a richer dust concealed;
> A dust whom England bore, shaped, made aware,
> Gave, once, her flowers to love, her ways to roam,
> A body of England's breathing English air,
> Washed by the rivers, blest by suns of home.
>
> Rupert Brooke, 'The Soldier'[19]

The argument between Spivak and her Indian colleagues is based on the premise of spaces being disjunctive and discontinuous. In fact, the valorization of essential, indigenous and authochtonous identity in anthropology is predicated on the premise of spaces being discontinuous. I quote again from my favourite article, 'Beyond 'Culture'', by Akhil Gupta and James Ferguson:

> [T]he distinctiveness of societies, nations, and cultures is based upon a seemingly unproblematic division of space on the fact that they occupy 'naturally' discontinuous spaces. The premise of discontinuity forms the starting point from which to theorize contact, conflict, and contradiction between cultures and societies . . . . [S]pace itself becomes a kind of neutral grid on which cultural difference, historical memory, and societal organization are inscribed.[20]

It is this notion of disjunctive spaces that underpins India's perception of its coherence as separate from that of Britain or the US. However, the historical facts of colonialism, capitalism and neocolonialism have resituated the politics of disjunctive geographical space to one of hierarchy not only among people but also among places. Such a comprehension of space, as Gupta and Ferguson point out, permits one to rethink 'difference *through* connection' (emphasis added; 8). Postcolonial India can then be seen to be in a relationship not just ideologically, but also spatially, with Britain, the mother country. Furthermore, in the postcolonial world, inflected with diaspora, India exists in New York and in London, and the UK and the US exist in Calcutta, Madras/Chennai and New Delhi, thus reframing any notion of a purely Western epistemology. The West is everywhere, but so is the East—this proximity also engenders the subversion of a 'purely' Western epistemology. In such a world the hegemony of the metropolitan epistemology is disturbed, as much as it has disturbed the colonial world. East and West are not in rupture but in an interconnection, in a seamless continuum in the neocolonial world.

Homi Bhabha's hybridity

Indian academics in the West are always conscious of their minority status, and most of them recognize that they function not only as the token of the entire Third World, but also as 'affirmative action alibis' (as used in 'The Post-Colonial Critic'; 79). While their land of origin is India, their domicile and practice of theory is in the West. In this section I deliberately evoke a spatial metaphor when I state I will explore the ground from which Bhabha formulates his postcolonial theory in the UK and in the US. This move is necessary since notions of autochthony have to be reframed and redefined in an interconnected world. I will not so much attempt to summarize the main arguments of Bhabha's theory as to point out how his theory is inflected with his spatial relationship with England, the mother country, when he was living there.

Bhabha's main theoretical frameworks are those of psychoanalysis and deconstruction; several terms, 'mimicry', 'hybridity' and 'ambivalence of authority' are in a continuum in his production of theory. In 'Of Mimicry and Man', Bhabha develops the notion of colonial mimesis, which emerged when England established its hegemony in India.[21] For him, this anglicization of India resulted from Indians who copied the English. Bhabha takes this commonplace notion of the copy as derivative from the original and explores mimicry as menacing. Instead of reassuring the colonizer of his primary status, the colonial mimic transforms the original so that it is something other than what it was before. In an elaboration of his concept of mimicry, Bhabha articulates that of hybridity and how it problematizes notions of authority, in 'Signs Taken for Wonder'. At the risk of oversimplifying, hybridity, which is closely related to Derridean notions of supplement and the way in which the marginal functions, can be described as 'a partial and double force that is more than the mimetic but less than the symbolic, that disturbs the visibility of the colonial presence and makes the recognition of its authority problematic' ('Signs'; 173). The hybrid is a mutation which by being a double of the original appears at first to underscore the power of the original while simultaneously, by being its excess, a mimic, it undermines the original. The hybrid signals a mishmash of signification that muddies the teleological route of meaning and knowledge in a Western framework. The authority of the original is undermined when faced with an excessive double which is produced both by the difference of the copy from its original, and by the original identity's other looking at and evaluating this identity from its own perspective. The doubling of evaluative vision fundamentally disturbs the singular authority on which the colonizer's identity depends, and the power of the hierarchy sustained in the binary. This foregrounding of the ambivalence of authority itself becomes a signifier and marker of resistance for Bhabha because it undermines rigid authority. Bhabha's agenda in developing the concepts of mimicry and hybridity finally becomes evident in 'Narrating the Nation', in which he reinterprets the geographical and hierarchically connected places of England and India:22

> The 'locality' of national culture is neither unified nor unitary in relation to itself, nor must it be seen simply as 'other' in relation to what is outside or beyond it. The boundary is Janus-faced and the problem of outside/inside must always be a process of hybridity, incorporating new 'people' in relation to the body politic, generating other sites of meaning and, inevitably, in the political process, producing unmanned sites of political antagonism and unpredictable forces for political representation.(4)

Bhabha's insistence on a Janus-faced national culture resonates with his desire for a multicultural England, for only a non-unitary national culture can make a place for *emigrés*. In the first place, Bhabha sees his own colonized presence in England as that of a hybrid. As a lecturer in department of English in Britain (and later in the University of Chicago), he apparently practises only the knowledge bestowed upon him by the colonizing force of Britain. He does not teach Indian philosophy or Indian history; his very profession seems to reveal the success of England's colonizing venture. However, his teaching of English is always via his postcolonial sensibility as a hybrid undoing England's hegemonic knowledge within England itself. Thus he creates a dissonance in any notion of a unitary national culture. In this strategic ploy, he first makes a place for himself in England, then legitimizes his own presence through the production of his theory.

The borders of here and there, periphery and metropole, India and England, become blurred in Bhabha's work. Englishness and citizenship become complicated in a deterritorialized and unbounded place. England/India becomes indeterminate and the hegemony of England is undone within its own bosom.

Spivak's subtleties

Neither can Spivak be pinned down to just one theoretical framework. Her diasporic sensibility is revealed in the dispersion of her identity; her theoretical framework is heterogeneous. In her analysis of texts, she moves through deconstruction, Marxism, feminism and postcolonial frameworks. As Robert Young has pointed out, 'rather than reconciling the differences [between these disparate frameworks] her task is to preserve these discontinuities'.[23] Instead of attempting to find a coherent framework within which Spivak's writings can be summarized, I again concentrate on the thematic of territorial identity implicit in her two most significant and oft-cited essays, 'Can the Subaltern Speak?' and 'The Rani of Sirmur', both of which link the identity of place to the production of discourse.[24] In 'The Rani of Sirmur' Spivak introduces the notion of 'worlding', a phenomenon closely associated with the process of colonization, through which the West could produce a series of representations of the East. This new narrative of the East was constructed both to consolidate a coherent subjectivity for the West, and also to bring the hstory of the colonial territory into alignment with that of the West. Thus the colonial space in India was rehistoricized, rewritten and reterritorialized via the British. In 'Can the Subaltern Speak?' Spivak shows the connection between the worlding of geographical space with the subject-constituting project of the different disciplines and institutions of dominant culture—that is, reworlding also reconfiguring epistemology. In answer to her question whether the subaltern (subordinate or person of inferior rank) can speak, she points to the impossibility of answering—she, the subaltern, has no structural space from which she can articulate her subjectivity except from that allotted by the master discourse. In 'A Literary Representation of the Subaltern', Spivak discusses the relationship between the production of knowledge and essentialism:

> The position that only the subaltern can know a subaltern, only women can know women, and so on, cannot be held as a theoretical presupposition either, for it predicates the possibility of knowledge on identity. Whatever the political necessity for holding the position, and whatever the advisability of attempting to identify with the other as subject in order to know her, *knowledge is made possible by irreducible difference, not identity. What is known is always in excess of knowledge. Knowledge is never adequate to its object.*[25] (emphasis added)

In this passage she emphasizes that in the mechanisms of reading a text there is a subject/object dichotomy between reader and text, where the reader always has agency. The reader worlds the text according to her own meaning and subject production. In the reading of a Third World text, or Third World as text, by a First World reader, certain positions of privilege are assumed by the reader. Spivak argues that the insertion of a Third World reader might produce a different reading, but in reality it maintains the same structure and mechanisms of reading with privileged subject positions. In this way the production of knowledge is moved forward only through the dichotomy between subject/object. Spivak herself suggests her own complicity with First World theory is primarily due to the mechanisms of reading a text, and points out that the subaltern cannot speak except through ventriloquism of the master discourse; she has no subject position from which she can enunciate her marginality.

This awareness of the marginal colours Spivak's own positioning. In yet another interview/discussion, 'Postmarked Calcutta, India', Spivak states to Angela Ingram:

> Well, you know, I have a mother and that's Calcutta, and I have a very nurturing stepmother and that's the United States.

Both are ugly. On the other hand if your mother is ugly, and your stepmother is almost, as I said, a nurturing step-mother, you can't just throw her away. So to that extent, I feel that I've earned the right to critique two places.[26]

In this passage we see the use of kinship terms in the construction of identity through place: India is mother and the US stepmother. In effect, Spivak claims blood ties to India (kinship, essentialism) and non-blood ties to the US. My argument is that Spivak attempts to reconcile a post-structuralist agenda of deconstructing identity with the subaltern project of insisting upon and reclaiming a particular, ineffable Indian difference. She constructs and deconstructs her identity simultaneously without prioritizing either identities/theories. She has to insist upon her marginal status, especially because in India she is considered tainted because of her contact with America. In the US, too, she is always the other. Both in the US and in India, Spivak strategically plays upon this notion of being the other.

Finally, within the context of Homi Bhabha's hybridity I would like to discuss the tense postcolonial interview with which I began this piece. Bhabha's construction of the hybrid is based on the notion of *entstellung* or repetition, which has encoded within it a process of displacement, distortion and dislocation. Bhabha argues that in the colonial situation, colonial authority can function only belatedly. That is to say, in the English/India context, English does not have any authority of its own, but gains its authority only on the premise of colonial difference. In effect, intrinsic English authority is delayed, gaining significance only in the colonies. In the colonies, there is a retroactive construction of the prior image of the original plenitude of English authority. This, according to Bhabha, reveals English authority itself to be problematic and ambiguous in that it is 'split between its appearance as original and authoritative and its articulation as repetition and difference' ('Signs Taken for Wonders'; 169) This disawoval of belatedness is necessary because for authority to be exerted it must be immediately visible; or its 'rules of recognition must reflect consensual knowledge or opinion'. The notion of pure colonial authority carries within it a trace of the repressed which is repeated as the hybrid, the mutation, which also destabilizes it and underscores its ambivalence. Bhabha concludes that 'the display of hybridity—its peculiar "replication"—terrorizes authority with the ruse of recognition, its mimicry, its mockery' (176).

I would also like to use this notion of hybridity in the consideration of Spivak's relationship with her Indian counterparts. I would argue that the New Delhi-based theorists in their display of nativism deploy a brand of decolonized colonial authority. Their deliberate referral to Indian theorists to evoke an Indian identity is problematic in that, like colonial authority, Indian identity is an *entstellung*. It is delayed. It is retroactive. Indian authority can be evoked only in decolonizing India. The anxiety to be purely Indian itself carries traces of its colonial past. Within this context Spivak functions as hybrid, a mutation of Indian authority. Her black skin carries the visible marks of pure Indianness while her production of theory simultaneously bears the traces of the hegemony of Western theory and Western epistemology. In effect, the participants of 'The Post-Colonial Interview' become the site which is 'split between [their] appearance as original and authoritative and [their] articulation as repetition and difference'. The New Delhi-based professors are natives, but so is Spivak; Spivak is postcolonial, but so are they.

In a further step, Bhabha and Spivak's theories also reveal the multiple enunciations of place through their insistence on the dynamic dialectical nature of the nation. India, as much as it is natural or discursive, is also produced by its occupants, and the nature of India—its definitions—changes with the actions of its innumerable occupants. The everyday-ness of the millions of Indians occupying (or not occupying) the physical space of India can never be mapped homogeneously.

Conclusion

I owe the conclusion of this piece to R. Radhakrishnan's influential article, 'Ethnic Identity and Post-Structural Différance' in which he indicates that the constituency of the 'ethnic' is involved in a double project of empowering her own identity while simultaneously engaging in the deconstruction of the logic of identity.[27] Within this context I want to read postcolonial discourse as produced by postcolonials in colonial spaces as well as the spaces of Imperium. It is a critical commonplace to state that the postcolonial is the emergent mode, emerging from the spatial and cultural politics of the Imperium. In this, the postcolonial, so long repressed as other, goes through the process of naming herself as 'postcolonial'. Now that she has a name and an identity derived from that name, she attempts to create her own epistemology and knowledge system. However, as Radhakrishnan points out, the instance of naming 'recuperates the general economy of the name' (207) or identity and presence. Within another context, in 'The Evidence of Experience', Joan Scott also protests against this process of naming and consequent recuperation of lost or repressed knowledge, only to keep intact the binary structure involved in the production of meaning.[28] This type of knowledge retrieval, she argues, erases one form of oppression to instate another form in its place. The postcolonial has a name, but it is a name bestowed on her by the oppressor—she now has the duty of oppressing other identities in order to maintain the authority and absolute nature of her name. This structure is implicit in 'The Post-Colonial Critic' interview with Spivak in New Delhi, in the level of anxiety in the room, and the suggestion that Spivak's presence within this framework contaminates the purity and authority of true, autochthonous postcolonial theory/body/identity.

As Radhakrishnan says:

> Doesn't all this sound somehow familiar: the defeat and overthrow of one sovereignty, the emergence and consolidation of an antithetical sovereignty, and the creation of a different, yet the same, repression? What the appeal to the 'nameless' forgets is first, that any emancipatory, emerging movement of the 'self' carries with it a set of repressive mandates that are the obverse of the emancipatory directives, which is to say that the legitimate affirmation of any identity cannot but constitute in the long run another determinate alterity unless this very problematic is critically thematized in the act of affirmation . . . (208–9)

In the process of the 'naming' of the postcolonial, the reviling of Bhabha and Spivak as alterity is inevitable. Bhabha and Spivak can be read as what Radhakrishnan terms as the 'post-ethnic', in that they break the binary gridlock of the Imperium and the postcolony. By partaking of both the US and the UK as well as India, Western knowledge as well as native positioning, the two critics are in a differential relationship to the authority of the politics of the Indian national subject as well as to that of the Western institution. In this way they underscore the repressive mandates of becoming an identity of both groups. Miming both groups, they transform the original and defuse the authority of both names. Their post-structural (non)identity transforms all identity into an indeterminacy, a hybridity which prevents authoritative (Westernized) closure. In what Frederic Jameson has called the 'postmodern hyperspace',[29] only the rapid spiralling of constructing while deconstructing identity that the radical post-ethnic represents can jam up the binary mode of representation.

8

Coda: in postcoloniality

In postcolonial discourse several terms converge: identity, place, race, the body. 'In postcoloniality, every metropolitan definition is dislodged. The general mode for the postcolonial is citation, reinscription, rerouting the historical.'[1] In postcoloniality, the underside of the Enlightenment is revealed: the 'Rights of Man' could be produced only within the context of colonialism, indentured labour and slavery. In postcoloniality, history as beginning with European time is interrogated; the recovery of 'lost' history and the seeking of alternate histories abound. In postcolonial studies, several discursive disciplines and concerns around identity intersect—race, class, gender and sexuality; feminism, race and ethnicity, and nationalism.

What has been a pivotal concern for me in this book is that the notion of embodiment is central to postcolonial studies. As has been revealed within the context of gender studies, the human subject is dichotomized into the mind and the body.[2] To the body is connoted such qualities as passion, biology, the inside, otherness, inertness, unchanging, statis, matter—a more primitive way of being. To the mind is attributed reason, the self, the same, action, movement and intelligence, a more developed way of being or *not* being. If such a dichotomy underpins the comprehension of the woman's body, this understanding is also metonymically extended to the occupants of lands waiting to be colonized, waiting to be roused from inertia, from the torpor of primitivity. The black body is metonymically linked to the woman's body in the power/knowledge system of Western Enlightenment, progress and modernity. In contrast, black bodies and women's bodies bespeak unevolved entities.

Furthermore, the body contains within it the markers of the places inhabited by the subject. The residents of equatorial regions invariably have darker skin. Their skin looks and functions best in the humidity of these regions. Transplant these bodies to colder climates and the skin turns ashen. Bodies are marked by the peripatetic movements which all humans participate in. The body also grants the subject a sense of personal identity, a sense of belonging to the normative group, or of being the other. The body is perceived as origin and signifies the place of origin. The loss of the maternal body constructs the subject within psychoanalytic discourse. The passage through the mirror stage coheres the body for the subject and gives them a sense of physicality in Lacanian thought. When psychoanalytic discourse is enmeshed with postcolonial discourse, the mirror stage and the Symbolic take on an altogether different emphasis. The colonizer functions as the Symbolic and the colonized is always suspended in the mirror stage, cohered by the master discourse of the colonizer. The body is also a message board. Its surface is inscribed and written on. It functions only within representation and demarcates the site of representation.

Place, too, intersects with the meaning of the body in that both are perceived as the ground from which meaning originates. As such, they both do not have a meaning prior to the construction of their meaning, prior to discursive practice, prior to their coming into representation. Both the female and the black body function as matter, as passive, a blank slate, a point of origin. Place is perceived as devoid of history except from that of its occupants. Yet they are mutually interrelated. Place constructs its occupant's body as the occupant gives meaning to place. A mountainous terrain develops a certain series of muscles in the bodies of its occupants just as the occupants give meaning and create a mythology to that terrain. The body is inscribed through place as the place is through the body. Place is of tremendous importance within postcolonial discourse. Colonialism was about the seizing of place, draining it of its resources, its history and the meaning attributed to it by its primary occupants. The centrality of place is made visible in postcolonial discourse by its interrogation of the meaning of locations, the excess or lack of resources in these locations, the equitable sharing and withholding of resources. Terms such as north and south, First World and Third World, intersect geographical places with economics, racialization and notions of 'development'—a peculiar terminology underpinned by the principles of the Enlightenment, of rationality, progress, ownership and the attendant refusal of the north to share equitably with the south.

Body, place, ownership and race are central to an understanding of identity as well. The root of identity is *idem*, 'the same'. For Locke, identity is located in the body, in form: 'one thing cannot have two beginnings of existence, nor two things one beginning'. For him, identity is the product of the body in time. Yet within postcolonial discourse, in an upsetting of the humanist understanding of identity, one thing can indeed have two beginnings of existence, as we have seen in the indigenous retrieval of lost history. Indigenous identity has two meanings, two identities inscribed on the body simultaneously—that which is from its occluded history and that which was constructed with the onset of colonialism. Indigenous identity is always a negotiation between these two identities. For Homi Bhabha, postcolonial identity intersects the humanist tradition of identity as self-reflection with the 'anthropological view of the difference of human identity as located in the division of nature/culture'.[3] For him, mimesis intersects with self-reflection in postcolonial identity.

Finally, race. The *Oxford English Dictionary*'s primary definition of this word is 'a group of persons, animals, or plants, connected by common descent or origin'. So when, how and why did a terminology that included the classification of people, plants and animals get attributed only to certain people? In the process of this shift, some people became attributed with race, the rest unmarked by it—although recently theories of whiteness are developing.[4] Are these raced people linked to plant and animal life as well? In Europe until the fourteenth century, the term 'race' meant 'the human race'. Meanings of race and the markers of it within racial theories are modern Western constructs. There is an absolute convergence between the production of a racial discourse and the onset of colonialism. For Fanon the two are intimately related, as notions of race legitimize the colonial enterprise. Race, like gender, is written on the body and is most often visible. The body classified as black need not necessarily be always black, as Sneja Gunew has pointed out. Race is a classification and is in the eye of the (white) beholder.

Postcolonial discourse turns the common understanding of these terms—race, place, body and identity—on its head and prevents an authoritative closure of their meanings. Postcolonial discourse opens up metropolitan discourse and reveals the antipodal, the opposite side of the world, so the soles of the feet of the metropolitan are planted against those of the antipodean. They kick and rub against each other.

Endnotes

Introduction

1. See Joyce Ann Joyce, 'The Black Canon: Reconstructing Black American Literary Criticism,' in *New Literary History*, vol. 18, no. 2 (Winter 1987): pp. 335–44; also see '"Who the Cap fits"': Unconsciousness and Unconscionableness in the Criticism of Houston A. Baker Jr and Henry Louis Gates Jr' in *New Literary History*, vol. 18, no. 2 (Winter 1987): pp. 371–84.
2. Paul Gilroy, *The Black Atlantic* (London: Verso, 1993).
3. Stuart Hall, 'Minimal Selves' in *Studying Culture*, eds Ann Gray and Jim McGuigan (London: Edward Arnold, 1993), pp. 134–8; also see Stuart Hall, 'Cultural Identity and Diaspora' in *Identity, Community, Culture, Difference*, ed. Jonathan Rutherford (London: Lawrence and Wishart, 1990), pp. 222–37.
4. Kobena Mercer, *Welcome to the Jungle* (New York and London: Routledge, 1994), p. 7.
5. See Donna Awatere, *Maori Sovereignty* (Auckland: *Broadsheet*, 1984).
6. See Julia Kristeva's reference to Plato's *Timeaus* in *Desire in Language: A Semiotic Approach to Literature and Art*, ed. Leon S. Roudiez, tr. Thomas Gora, Alice Jardine, and Leon S. Roudiez (New York: Columbia University Press, 1980), p. 133; Kaja Silverman comments extensively on

Kristeva's use of Plato's *chora* in *The Acoustic Mirror: The Female Voice in Psychoanalysis and Cinema* (Bloomington: Indiana University Press, 1988).

7. Luce Irigaray, *An Ethics of Sexual Difference*, tr. Carolyn Burke and Gillian C. Gill (Ithaca: Cornell University Press, 1993), p. 52.

Chapter 1

1. See Claude Lévi-Strauss, 'The Science of the Concrete' in *The Savage Mind* (London: Weidenfeld & Nicolson, 1966), pp. 1–33. Also see Alfred W. Crosby, *Ecological Imperialism: The Biological Expansion of Europe, 900–1900* (Cambridge: Cambridge University Press, 1986).

2. See George Mosse, *Nationalism and Sexuality: Middle-Class Morality and Sexual Norms* (Madison: University of Wisconsin Press, 1985).

3. See Liisa Malkki, 'National Geographic: The Rooting of Peoples and the Territorialization of National Identity Among Scholars and Refugees' *in Cultural Anthropology*, vol. 7, no. 1 (1992): pp. 24–44.

4. David Lowenthal, 'European and English Landscapes as National Symbols' in *Geography and National Identity*, ed. David Hooson, (Oxford: Basil Blackwell, 1994), p. 17.

5. See Miroslav Hroch, 'From National Movement to the Fully-formed Nation' in *New Left Review*, vol. 198 (1993): pp. 3–20.

6. Benedict Anderson, *Imagined Communities* (London: Verso, 1983).

7. See Ettiene Balibar, 'The Nation Form: History and Ideology' in Etienne Balibar and Immanuel Wallerstein, *Race, Nation, Class: Ambiguous Identities* (London: Verso, 1991), pp. 86–106.

8. The bricoleur is always male in Lévi-Strauss and I deliberately use the word 'native' here in an echo of Lévi-Strauss' use of the term, where 'native' is equated with the 'indigene'. The anthropologist is not a 'native' to any place.

9. For instance, Lévi-Strauss states:
    Their extreme familiarity with their biological environment, the passionate attention which they pay to it and

their precise knowledge of it has often struck inquirers as an indication of attitudes and preoccupations which distinguish the natives from their *white* visitors. (emphasis added) (5)

10. See especially the chapter 'Science, Planetary Consciousness, Interiors' in Mary Louise Pratt, *Imperial Eyes: Travel Writing and Transculturation* (London and New York: Routledge, 1992).

11. See Arjun Appadurai, 'Putting Hierarchy in its Place' in *Cultural Anthropology*, vol. 3, no. 1 (1988): pp. 36–49.

12. René Descartes, *Discourse on Method and the Meditations*, tr. F.E. Sutcliffe (London: Penguin Books, 1968).

13. Maurice Merleau-Ponty, *The Primacy of Perception*, as quoted in Elizabeth Grosz, *Volatile Bodies: Towards a Corporeal Feminism* (Sydney: Allen & Unwin, 1994), p. 87. See especially the chapter 'Lived Bodies: Phenomenology of the Flesh' for a very useful, comprehensive overview of the corpus of Merleau-Ponty's works.

14. Maurice Merleau-Ponty, *Phenomenology of Perception*, tr. Colin Smith (London: Routledge, 1994), p. 92.

15. See especially, 'Throwing Like a Girl: A Phenomenology of Feminine Body Comportment, Motility and Spatiality' in Iris Marion Young, *Throwing Like a Girl and Other Essays in Feminist Philosophy and Social Theory* (Bloomington: Indiana University Press, 1990). Also see Elizabeth McMillan, 'Female Difference in the texts of Merleau-Ponty' in *Philosophy Today*, vol. 31, no. 4 (1987): pp. 359–66; Judith Butler, 'Sexual Ideology and Phenomenological Description: A Feminist Critique of Merleau-Ponty's *Phenomenology of Perception*' in *The Thinking Muse: Feminism and Modern French Philosophy*, eds Jeffner Allen and Iris Marion Young (Indianapolis: Indiana University Press, 1989).

16. Shannon Sullivan, 'Domination and Dialogue in Merleau-Ponty's *Phenomenology of Perception*' in *Hypatia*, vol. 12, no. 1 (Winter 1997): pp. 1–19.

17. Frantz Fanon, *Black Skin, White Masks*, tr. Charles Lamm Markmann (New York: Grove Weidenfeld, 1967).

18. See Gayatri Spivak, 'Can the Subaltern Speak?' in *Marxism and the Interpretation of Culture*, eds Cary Nelson and Lawrence Grossberg, (London: Macmillan, 1988), pp. 271–313. If

Spivak had written nothing else, this article proves her role as an oppositional critic *par excellence.*

19. I am obviously influenced by Derrida's understanding of representation. See in particular the chapter 'From/Of the Supplement to the Source: The Theory of Writing' in *Of Grammatology,* tr. Gayatri Chakravorty Spivak (Baltimore: Johns Hopkins University Press, 1974). Also see 'Sending: On Representation' in *Social Research,* vol. 49, no. 2 (Summer 1982): pp. 294–326.

20. See Henri Lefebvre, *The Production of Space,* tr. Donald Nicholson-Smith (Oxford: Blackwell, 1991), p. 62.

21. See Ian Buchanan, 'Lefebvre and the Problem of Empty Space,' in *Speaking Positions: Aboriginality, Gender and Ethnicity in Australian Cultural Studies,* ed. Penny van Toorn and David English (Melbourne: Victoria University of Technology, 1995), p. 184.

Chapter 2

1. Locke's definitions of identity was within his agenda of describing political identity and the construction of the Universal Subject. As such, notions of identity are imbricated within the European Enlightenment as well as its dark underside, colonialism. For instance, in his *Second Treatise,* wherein Locke has an argument with Filmer's propounding of the divine right of kings, he states that all men (and, by extension, women) live in a state:

   of *Equality,* wherein all the Power and Jurisdiction is reciprocal, no one having more than one another: there being nothing more evident, than that creatures of the same species and ranks promiscuously born to all the same advantages of Nature, and the use of the same faculties, should also be equal without subordination or subjection. (*Second Treatise* 309; Para 4)

   In this passage, Locke ties bodily identity to equality within the state. Such an argument of course legitimizes both colonialism and racism. See John Locke, *An Essay Concerning Human Understanding, 2 Volumes,* ed. Alexander Campbell Fraser (Oxford: Clarendon Press, 1894). Also see John Locke, *Second Treatise of Government,* ed. C.B. Macpherson (Indianapolis: Hackett Publishing Co, 1980).

2. See Philip Gleason's 'Identifying Identity: A Semantic History' in *The Journal of American History,* vol. 69, no. 4 (March 1983): pp. 910–31, for an etymology of the term 'identity'.

3. Sigmund Freud, 'The Ego and the Id' (1928) in *The Standard Position of the Complete Psychological Works of Sigmund Freud (SE),* tr. and ed. James Strachey, 24 vols, (London: Hogarth Press), 19: 27.

4. See, for instance, Freud's assertion in 'On Narcissism' wherein he conflates the body with the libidinal cathexis. He states:

> We can decide to regard erotogenicity as a general characteristic of all organs and may then speak of an increase or decrease of it in a particular part of the body. For every change in the erotogenicity of libidinal zones there might be a parallel change in the ego.

For a succinct summary of bodily identity in Freud, read Elizabeth Grosz' *Volatile Bodies: Towards a Corporeal Feminism* (Sydney: Allen & Unwin, 1994), especially the chapter 'Psychoanalysis and Psychical Topographies'. See Sigmund Freud, 'On Narcissism: An Introduction' (1914) in *SE* 14: 84.

5. In 'The Mirror Stage as Formative of the Function of the I', Lacan removes any distinction between our sense of corporeality and specular perceptions of it. He extends the meaning of the body/I further to include a social sense of it. In so doing, the specular 'I' is displaced by the social 'I'. The specular 'I' is at the threshhold of a socially and culturally constructed ego. Also read Kaja Silverman's chapter on 'The Bodily Ego' in *The Threshold of the Visible World.* See Jacques Lacan, 'The Mirror Stage as Formative of the Function of the I' in *Ecrits: A Selection,* tr. Alan Sheridan (New York and London: W.W. Norton, 1977); also see Kaja Silverman, *The Threshhold of the Visible World* (New York and London: Routledge, 1996).

6. See Frantz Fanon, *Black Skin, White Masks,* tr. Charles Lamm Markmann (New York: Grove Weidenfeld, 1967), p. 112.

7. I draw attention to Locke, Freud and Fanon's use of the term 'man'. Though they seem to use the humanist

understanding of 'man', I can't grant them a gender politics.

8. See Locke's letters to Molyneux, August 23, 1693 and March 8, 1695. Also read the 'Prolegomena' in the version of *An Essay* edited by Alexander Campbell Fraser. Locke was paid the sum of 30 pounds sterling for the copyright, approximately the same sum as Immanuel Kant received for *The Critique of Pure Reason*.

9. See Robert Young, *White Mythologies: Writing History and the West* (New York and London: Routledge, 1990).

10. Locke's essay, to some extent, is in response to Descartes' *Meditations on First Philosophy* published in 1641. In this work, Descartes rejected preconceived notions and wrote in search of a reliable source of knowledge. Descartes' intention was not a static exposition of doctrines but rather a series of mental exercises which everyone must follow for themselves. Despite this emphasis on the individual, Descartes did, however, write within a theological framework.

11. See Michael Ayers, *Locke*, vols 1 and 2 (London and New York: Routledge, 1991), vol. 2, p. 261.

12. In *Problems from Locke*, J.L. Mackie argues the opposite:

    > In the prince and the cobbler we have the same soul and the same consciousness successively in two different bodies . . . Locke claims . . . it is plausible that we have the same person where and only where we have the same consciousness; the sameness of the living body is neither necessary nor sufficient to constitute the same person, nor is the sameness of a spiritual substance.

    While Locke makes a distinction between the categories of person and man, my argument with Mackie is one informed by a Lacanian framework in that personal identity is constructed and validated by culture, a theme strongly hinted at by Locke also. Notwithstanding that the person may be the prince, what prevails in this example is the cobbler's identity. See J. L. Mackie, *Problems from Locke* (Oxford: Clarendon, 1976), p. 176.

13. J.L. Mackie further suggests:

    > Bodily continuity is no part of what 'personal identity' ordinarily means, any more than having atomic number 79 is any part of the ordinary meaning of 'gold'. The

concept of personal identity, as we are now interpreting it, is not the concept of bodily continuity, but it is the concept of something that turns out to be the continuity of the structure of a certain part of the body. (201)

While locating personal identity within consciousness works to a certain extent, it also presumes a homogeneity of bodies. Notions of race just do not figure in Locke's explanation of bodily identity.

14. See Ed Cohen, 'Who are "We"? Gay "Identity" as Political (E)motion (A Theoretical Rumination)' in *Inside/Out: Lesbian Theories, Gay Theories* ed. Diana Fuss (New York and London: Routledge, 1991), pp. 71–92.

15. See Jacques Derrida, 'White Mythology' in *Margins of Philosophy* (Chicago: University of Chicago Press, 1982), p. 215.

16. See Kaja Silverman, *The Subject of Semiotics* (New York: Oxford University Press, 1983), p. 63.

17. See Paul de Man, 'The Epistemology of Metaphor' in *On Metaphor*, ed. Sheldon Sacks (Chicago: University of Chicago Press, 1979), p. 18, note 4.

18. Here the notions of personal identity, personality and social identity all get blurred. Locke valorizes personal identity only by ignoring the other two in its make-up.

19. See, for instance, Locke's usage of the term 'brutes' (animals) as opposed to the term 'machines' (such as watches) in his discussion of organization in matter. In his use of brutes there is a conflation of humans with animals. This passage (which precedes his initial definitions of personal identity, which I have quoted twice in the text) suggests that the identity of the 'brute' comes from the life force within it, unlike in machines. See Locke's *Essay* Book II, pp. 443–4.

20. David Lloyd, 'Race Under Representation,' in *Oxford Literary Review*, vol. 13 (1991), pp. 72–3.

21. See C.B. Macpherson, *The Political Theory of Possessive Individualism: Hobbes to Locke* (Oxford: Oxford University Press, 1962). He starts with the premise that individualism, the cornerstone of a liberal democracy, contains within it a possessive quality. He states:

Its possessive quality is found in its conception of the individual as essentially the proprietor of his own person and capacities, owing nothing to society for them. The individual was seen neither as a moral whole, nor as part of a larger social whole, but as an owner of himself. The relation of ownership, having become for more and more men the critically important relation determining their actual freedom and actual prospect of realizing their full potentialities, was read back into the nature of the individual. The individual, it was thought, is free inasmuch as he is proprietor of his person and capacities (3).

Taken to its logical conclusion, possessive individualism becomes a device 'for the protection of this property and for the maintenance of an orderly revelation of exchange' (3).

22. See Sander Gilman, *Freud, Race, and Gender* (Princeton: Princeton University Press, 1993).

23. See Diana Fuss, *Identification Papers* (New York and London: Routledge, 1995).

24. See 'The Ego and the Id' (1923), *Standard Edition*, vol. 19; 'Group Psychology and the Analysis of the Ego' (1921), *Standard Edition*, vol. 18; 'Mourning and Melancholia' (1917), *Standard Edition*, vol. 17.

25. In *Identification Papers*, Diana Fuss makes the distinction between identity and identification. She points out that:

identification sets into motion the complicated dynamic of recognition and misrecognition that brings a sense of identity into being [and] immediately calls that identity into question. The astonishing capacity of identifications to reverse and disguise themselves, to multiply and contravene one another, to disappear and reappear years later renders identity profoundly unstable and perpetually open to radical change. Identification is a process that keeps identity at a distance, that prevents identity from ever approximating the status of an ontological given, even as it makes possible the formation of an *illusion* of identity as immediate, secure, and totalizable. (2)

In so saying, Fuss attributes a fluidity to identification which identity cannot help but follow.

26. I am indebted to Elizabeth Grosz' extremely useful chapters on 'The Ego and the Imaginary' in *Jacques Lacan: A Feminist Introduction* (London and New York: Routledge, 1990) and 'Psychoanalysis and Psychical Topographies' in

Volatile Bodies: Towards a Corporeal Feminism. In the latter Grosz sums up the relationship between the body and the ego:

> The ego is thus a map of the body's significance or meaning for the subject and for the other. It is thus as much a function of fantasy and desire as it is of sensation and perception; it is a taking over of sensation and perception by a fantasmatic dimension. This significatory cultural dimension implies that bodies, egos, subjectivities are not simply reflections of their cultural context and associated values but are constituted as such by them, marking bodies in their very 'biological' configurations with sociosexual inscriptions. (38)

In this Grosz emphasizes the lack of clear delineation between body and mind, nature and culture, a distinction that is still possible within the Lockean schema.

27. In 'On Narcissism: An Introduction', Freud initially points out that those whose libidinal development has suffered some disturbance, people such as 'perverts and homosexuals . . . have taken as their model not their mother but their own selves' (88). To this list of perverts he soon adds women who have problems with their libidinal development. Then this passage:

> Perhaps it is not out of place here to give an assurance that this description of the feminine form of erotic life is not due to any tendentious desire on my part to depreciate women. Apart from the fact that tendentiousness is quite alien to me, I know that these different lines of development correspond to the differentiation of functions in a highly complicated biological whole. (89)

Though Freud admits primary/biological difference between men and women, he ultimately uses a unitary model of development in that for everyone, 'the development of the ego consists in a departure from primary narcissism' (100). To this extent, women, perverts and homosexuals are all at a severe disadvantage, according to his theoretical framework.

28. My thanks to my colleague Tom Ryan for this story.
29. Judith Butler grapples with this question when she examines how a body comes into being in *Bodies that Matter* (London and New York: Routledge, 1993). She starts with the premise that ' "sex" is an ideal construct which is

forcibly materialized through time. It is not a simple fact or static condition of a body, but a process whereby regulatory norms materialize "sex" and achieve this materialization through a forcible reiteration of those norms' (1–2). Butler's thesis indicates the importance of Freud's notion of the ego as the mapping or representation of the surface of the body and therefore being a cultural mediation. Butler's main question of the body as an entity forcibly materialized through time is not a historical analysis of how it happens but rather a deconstruction of the process through which the discourse of sexed bodies is conducted. In this Butler revisits the argument she makes in *Gender Trouble: Feminism and Subversion of Identity* (New York and London: Routledge, 1990), wherein she states that gender is performative, i.e., it is reiterated through 'acts, gestures, and enactments' (*Gender Trouble;* 136) rather than through a *natural* biological fact which initiates and governs sexed behaviour. In *Bodies that Matter*, she extends this notion of performative from gendered to sexed bodies, both male and female.

Butler explains the process through which the biological body is positioned culturally as primary in her examination of Jacques Lacan's notion of sex. Lacan's notion, as is well-known, posits an anomaly in that sexed positions are assumed by previously ungendered subjects against the abstract notion of the phallus; yet it is the biological body that determines which sexed position the subject will assume within the symbolic (97). This temporal scrambling of primary and secondary causes Butler to state: '[h]ence "sex" is that which marks the body prior to its mark, staging in advance which symbolic position will mark it, and it is this latter "mark" which appears to postdate the body, retroactively attributing a sexual position to the body' (97). Butler's agenda in exposing and analyzing the inconsistency in theories of the body and gender is to question the desirability of identification itself, because, as she indicates, any form of identification is 'to enforce a reduction and a paralysis' (116). Recognizing the rigidity of identification is also simultaneously empowering because it allows for a tracing of 'the ways in which [the concept of] identification is implicated in what it excludes' (119).

Bringing the body into the Symbolic is also to bring it within the vectors of power. The idealized body implicit in the Symbolic, which assumes its assigned sexed position, is thus predicated on the maintenance of homogeneity through race and heterosexuality. The idealized—unmarked—body implied in the psychoanalytic framework then, is the ideal in sex, sexuality and race. Butler points out that

> the symbolic domain, the domain of socially instituted norms, is composed of *racializing norms,* and [exists] not merely alongside gender norms, but are articulated through one another. Hence it is no longer possible to make sexual difference prior to racial difference, or for that matter, to make them into fully separable axes of social regulation and power. (Butler's emphasis; 182)

In *Identification Papers* Diana Fuss focuses on another aspect of Freud's theorization of identity: identification as imitation. Such an analysis is called for on two counts: first, if the ego functions as a coping mechanism as Freud indicates, it is able to do so only by imitating the lost object-choice; second, the colonized body is always perceived within the context of imitation and miming of the colonizing forces. Indeed, there is a large body of literature which deals with mimicry as an inevitable outcome of colonial domination. Fuss attempts first to separate mimicry from masquerade—the former is defined as 'the deliberate and playful performance of a role' (146); next, she points out that there are two notions of mimicry—as playful and as political—given that identification functions at both, the site of fantasy and the site of power (148); finally she attempts to suggest how mimesis can occur in a third way, through 'a refusal of identification' (148). In her analysis of the third form of mimesis Fuss raises an interesting question: What happens to a black/colonized body constructed to function as other to whiteness when it is removed from its class and social identifications and is identified as other racially but not socially? Fuss uses the life of Fanon himself to raise this issue. She points out that though he was appointed Director at the Hospital at Blida-Joinville in Algeria, with Algerian patients, and though he was black himself, Fanon could speak neither

Arabic nor Kabyle with his black patients. He required a translator. Yet his access to French and his training as a psychiatrist in France grants him a (white) French identity. Fuss makes an interesting point:

> To his black Algerian patients, Fanon is white: a French-educated, upper-middle-class professional who cannot speak the language. Identifying with both groups but accepted by neither, Fanon's shifting and contradictory positions kept identity perpetually at bay. It is precisely identity that is suspended or deferred by the work of identification, identity that remains in a state of internal exile. Put another way, Fanon's own identifications are in constant translation, caught in a system of cultural relays that make the assumption of racial identity both necessary and impossible. (164)

Fuss concludes that identification is always political and contains a certain history (165). I would like to add that it is problematic black bodies such as Fanon's which ultimately subvert the neat divisions of colonizer/colonized, settler/indigenous, white/black, in that his (lack of) identity goes beyond a politics of essence or of raced body and exposes the vectors of power which these raced bodies are enmeshed in. Fanon, white by some accounts and black by others, exposes that racial formations are themselves cultural and discursive formations, a point that Howard Winant and Michael Omi make in *Racial Formation in the United States* (London and New York: Routledge, 1994).

30. See especially the classic chapter, 'The Blind Spot of an Old Dream of Symmetry' in Luce Irigaray, *Speculum of the Other Woman* tr. Gillian C. Gill (Ithaca: Cornell University Press, 1985).

31. This is similar to Judith Butler's problem with Lacanian notions of gender and the Symbolic. As I mentioned earlier, Butler points out that Lacan suggests that sexed positions are structural positions within the Symbolic which predate the existence of the subject. Yet the subject is not given a choice as to what sexed position they will choose in that their anatomical difference leads them to the appropriate sexed position within the symbolic. See her essay 'Phantasmatic Identification and the Assumption of Sex' in *Bodies That Matter*.

32. In *Bodies That Matter*, Judith Butler, too, points out that notions of causality get scrambled in such a construction of the body in that the idea gives rise to the materiality of the body (59). Pain or the idea of pain is the progenitor of Freud's body.

33. See Louis Althusser, 'Ideology and Ideological State Apparatus', in *Lewis and Philosophy and Other Essays* (London: New Left Books, 1971).

34. See the implications of this argument in Julia Kristeva's *Revolution in Poetic Language* (New York: Columbia University Press, 1984) in which she reiterates the demarcation between the Imaginary and the Symbolic as the semiotic and the symbolic. On the one hand, such a renaming is subversive in that the semiotic is always in the subterranean regions of the symbolic, waiting to destabilize it. Kristeva also conflates the maternal body with the semiotic and she states in *Revolution in Poetic Language*, '[t]he mother's body is therefore what mediates the symbolic law organizing social relations and becomes the organizing principle of the semiotic *chora*' (27). However, in *Tales of Love* she locates the maternal as an *effect* of the paternal. Also see Kaja Silverman's reading of *Tales of Love* in *The Acoustic Mirror* (Indianapolis: Indiana University Press, 1988), pp. 101–40.

35. See 'Bodies That Matter', pp. 36–55, in *Bodies That Matter* for Butler's reading of Plato and her reading of Irigaray's reading of Plato.

36. See Jacques Derrida's 'Différance' in *Speech and Phenomena and Other Essays in Husserl's Theory of Signs*, tr. David B. Allison (Evanston: Northwestern University Press, 1973), pp. 129–69. In this I am arguing that the body functions like Derrida's notion of differance. Derrida states:

> The trace is not a presence but is rather the simulacrum of a presence that dislocates, displaces, and refers beyond itself. The trace has, properly speaking, no place, for effacement belongs to the very structure of the trace. Effacement must always be able to overtake the trace; otherwise it would not be a trace but an indestructible and monumental surface. (150)

37. See, for instance, Doreen Massey's comments on Laclau in 'Politics and Space/Time' in *New Left Review*, vol. 196

(Nov.–Dec. 1992): 65–84. She says: 'Laclau's argument here is that what we are inevitably faced with in the world are "temporal" (by which he means dislocated) structures: dislocation is intrinsic and it is this—this essential open-ness—which creates the possibility of politics.' As she points out, Laclau's notion of space is an attempt at closure. Since he locates space and politics as antonyms, any repre-sentation of a society is unrepresentable in that it consitutes it and does not describe it (as cited in Massey, 68).

38. See Elizabeth Grosz. 'Space, Time and Bodies', in *Space, Time and Perversion*, (London and New York: Routledge, 1995), pp. 83–102.

39. See Michel Foucault's chapter on 'Scientia Sexualis' in *The History of Sexuality, Vol 1: An Introduction*, tr. Robert Hurley (New York: Vintage Books, 1980); also see 'Space, Knowledge, and Power' in *The Foucault Reader*, ed. Paul Rabinow (New York: Pantheon Books, 1984), pp. 239–56.

Chapter 3

1. Frantz Fanon, *A Dying Colonialism*, tr. Haakon Chevalier (New York: Grove Press, 1965). Published originally in France as *L'An cinq de la révolution algérienne* (Paris: Francois Maspero, 1959). Marie-Aimée Hélie-Lucas, 'Bound and Gagged by the Family Code' in *Third World: Second Sex, vol. 2*, compiled by Miranda Davies (London and New Jersey: Zed Books Ltd, 1987).

2. See Gayatri Chakravorty Spivak, 'Reading *The Satanic Verses*' in *Outside in the Teaching Machine* (New York and London: Routledge, 1993).

3. See R. Radhakrishnan's essay, 'Nationalism, Gender, and the Narrative of Identity' in *Nationalisms and Sexualities*, eds Andrew Parker, Mary Russo, Doris Sommer and Patricia Yeager (New York and London: Routledge, 1992), pp. 77–95.

4. See Benedict Anderson, *Imagined Communities* (London: Verso, 1983).

5. For instance, an American or New Zealand man gains identity not only in opposition to the Australian man, but also to the American and New Zealand woman.

6. See Ernest Gellner, *Nations and Nationalism* (Oxford: Blackwell, 1983), p. 117, emphasis added.
7. See Ernest Renan 'What is a Nation?' in *Nation and Narration*, ed. Homi K. Bhabha (New York and London: Routledge, 1990), p. 20, emphasis added.
8. See George Mosse, *Nationalism and Sexuality: Middle Class Morality and Sexual Norms* (Madison: University of Wisconsin Press, 1985).
9. See David Halperin, *One Hundred Years of Homosexuality* (New York and London: Routledge, 1990), p. 101. See especially the chapter 'The Democratic Body'.
10. See, for instance, the arguments made by Zillah Eisenstein, 'The Relative Autonomy of the Capitalist Patriarchal State' in *Feminism and Sexual Equality*, ed. Zillah Eisenstein (New York: Monthly Review Press, 1984). Also see Aida Hurtado, 'Relating to Privilege: Seduction and Rejection in the subordination of White Women and Women of Color' in *Signs*, vol. 14, no. 4, (1989): pp. 833–55.
11. *Woman–Nation–State*, eds Nira Yuval-Davis and Floya Anthias (London: Macmillan, 1989).
12. Kumari Jayawardena, *Feminism and Nationalism in the Third World* (London: Zed Books, 1986), p. 2.
13. See Carole Pateman, *The Sexual Contract* (Stanford: Stanford University Press, 1988) and Rosi Braidotti, *Nomadic Subjects: Embodiment and Sexual Difference in Contemporary Feminist Thought* (New York: Columbia University Press, 1994).
14. Ketu Katrak, 'Indian Nationalism, "Satyagraha" and Representations of Female Sexuality' in *Nationalisms and Sexualities*, ed. Andrew Parker et al. (New York and London: Routledge, 1992), p. 396.
15. In a note, Fanon explains:
    In the course of Moroccan people's struggle for liberation and chiefly in the cities, the white veil was replaced by the black veil. This important modification is explained by the Moroccan women's desire to express their attachment to His Majesty Mohammed V. It will be remembered that it was immediately after the exiling of the King of Morocco that the black veil, a sign of mourning, made its appearance. It is worth noting that black, in Moroccan or Arab society, has never expressed

mourning or affliction. As a combat measure, the adoption of black is a response to the desire to exert a symbolic pressure on the occupier and hence to make a logical choice of one's own symbol. (36, note 3)

16. I am obviously indebted to Gayatri Chakravorty Spivak's important article, 'Can the Subaltern Speak?', where she examines widow-sacrifice in India in the early 1820s, where the Indian woman is muted between the dialectically interlocking sentences of the white and brown patriarchs. The former's construction of the Indian woman is 'White men are saving brown women from brown men'; the latter's construction of her was 'She wanted to die [a *sati*]' (297). See Spivak, 'Can the Subaltern Speak?' *in Marxism and the Interpretation of Culture*, eds Cary Nelson and Lawrence Grossberg (London: Macmillan, 1988), pp. 271–313.

17. See Anne McClintock, *Imperial Leather: Race, Gender and Sexuality in the Colonial Conquest* (New York and London: Routledge, 1995), p. 364.

18. Diana Fuss, *Identification Papers* (New York and London: Routledge, 1995).

19. See the chapter on 'Panopticon' in Michel Foucault, *Discipline and Punish: The Birth of the Prison*, tr. Alan Sheridan (New York: Vintage Books, 1979), p. 205.

20. See T.B. Macaulay, *Speeches by Lord Macaulay: With his Minute on Indian Education*, ed. G.M. Young (Oxford: Oxford University Press, AMS edition, 1970), p. 359.

21. See, for instance, Said's *Orientalism* (New York: Random House, 1979) and *Imperialism and Culture* (London: Chatto & Windus, 1993). Within psychoanalytic discourse, in *Black Skin, White Marks*, Frantz Fanon makes the link between ideological vehicles and the narcissistic identifications of subject populations in his response to Octave Mannoni's *Prospero and Caliban*.

22. See Gauri Viswanathan, 'The Beginnings of English Literary Study in British India' in *Oxford Literary Review*, vol. 9, nos 1 and 2 (1987); also see *Masks of Conquest: Literary Study and British Rule in India* (London: Faber & Faber, 1989).

23. See Jenny Sharpe, 'Figures of Colonial Resistance' in *Modern Fiction Studies*, 35, 1 (Spring 1989), p. 141.

24. Frantz Fanon, *Black Skin, White Masks*, tr. Charles Lamm Markmann (New York: Grove Press, 1967), pp. 18, 38.

25. See David Lloyd, 'Race Under Representation' in *Oxford Literary Review*, vol. 13, nos 1–2 (1991): pp. 62–94.
26. See *Charles Kingsley: His Letters and Memories of his Life*, ed. Francis E. Kingsley (London: Henry S. King, 1877), pp. 107.
27. See Homi Bhabha, 'Of Mimicry and Man: The Ambivalence of Colonial Discourse' in *The Location of Culture* (London and New York: Routledge, 1994), pp. 85–92.
28. In his work on Algerian women under colonization, *The Colonial Harem*, trs Myrna Godzich and Wlad Godzich (Minneapolis: University of Minnesota Press, 1986), Malel Alloula suggests that the veiled woman is an outright attack on the voyeuristic photographer because her veiled gaze 'resembles his own when it is extended by the dark chamber or the viewfinder. Thrust in the presence of a veiled woman, the photographer feels photographed; having himself become an object-to-be seen, he loses initiative; *he is dispossessed of his own gaze*' (Alloula's emphasis; 14).
29. See 'Of Mimicry and Man' and 'The Other Question' in Homi Bhabha, *The Location of Culture* (New York and London: Routledge, 1994). In 'Of Mimicry and Man', Bhabha analyses the notion of mimicry in colonial practices, an idea which is based on the desire of the mother country to recreate her colonies in her own image. However, the founding principle of colonialism and identity within colonization is always located in difference. Bhabha intersects those fundamentally contradictory elements within colonial discourse with Lacan's notion of mimicry in the construction of gender. For Lacan, mimicry is 'like camouflage, not a harmonization of repression of difference, but a form of resemblance, that differs from or defends presence by displaying it in part, metonymically' (Bhabha; 90). For Bhabha as well, mimicry in colonial discourse is based on a form of resemblance which is simultaneously an *emphasis of* as well as a *disavowal of* difference in that the mimic/colonial can only always be only a partial representation of the colonizing force. Thus the colonial subject is rendered into a 'partial presence', by which Bhabha means 'both "incomplete" and "virtual"' (86) and hovers ambivalently between comforting familiarity and threatening, menacing difference. It is this ambivalent construction of the colonial subject within

colonial discourse that also 'disrupts its authority' (88) in that it can provide only a partial representation of the colonial object. The colonial object, almost the same but not quite, hypervisible and invisible (because of difference), threatening and comforting, is generative of knowledges yet also underscores the discriminatory practices in the construction of that knowledge and, ultimately, its lack or authority and completion.

30. See Jane Haggis, 'Gendering Colonialism or Colonizing Gender?: Recent Women's Studies Approaches to White Women and the History of British Colonialism,' in *Women's Studies International Forum*, vol. 13, no. 12 (1990): pp. 105–15. Jane Haggis, for instance, describes this view of white women as:

> the indolent, pampered socialites of literary fame, neurotically possessive of their men and overly concerned with maintaining racial superiority through petty distinctions and segregation. It was, in this dominant male view, the white woman who lost the British their empire, alienating the friendly native with her petty snobberies and sexual jealousy. (105)

31. See for instance, *Western Women and Imperialism: Complicity and Resistance*, ed. Nupur Chaudhuri and Margaret Strobel (Bloomington: Indiana University Press, 1992); Margaret Strobel, *European Women and the Second British Empire* (Bloomington: Indiana University Press, 1991); Ann Stoler, 'Making Empire Respectable: The Politics of Race and Sexual Morality in Twentieth Century Colonial Cultures' in *American Ethnologist*, vol. 16 (1989): pp. 634–60.

32. Helen Callaway, *Gender, Culture and Empire: European Women in Colonial Nigeria* (Oxford: Macmillan, 1987), pp. 5–6.

33. Claudia Knapman, *White Women in Fiji, 1835–1930: The Ruin of Empire?* (Sydney: Allen & Unwin, 1986).

34. Jenny Sharpe, *Allegories of Empire: The Figure of the Woman in the Colonial Text* (Minneapolis: University of Minnesota Press, 1993).

35. Ella Shohat and Robert Stam, *Unthinking Eurocentrism: Multiculturalism and the Media* (London and New York: Routledge, 1994).

36. In *Culture and Imperialism*, Edward Said defines the term 'contrapuntal reading' as 'reading a text with an under-

standing of what is involved when an author shows, for instance, that a colonial sugar plantation is seen as important to the process of maintaining a particular style of life in England' (78).

37. See Mrinalini Sinha, 'Gender and Imperialism: Colonial Policy and the Ideology of Moral Imperialism in Late Nineteenth-Century Bengal' in *Changing Men: New Directions in Research on Men and Masculinity*, ed. Michael S. Kimmel (Newbury Park, California: Sage, 1993), pp. 217–31. Here Mrinalini Sinha states:

> The process of colonial justification was not a simple one. It entailed a dual approach: On the one hand it emphasized the radical difference of a native society, which made necessary the alien control pattern of domination and on the other, it posited a universality that opened up the possibility for the recuperation or redemption of the native. The latter was important to make sense of the colonial project as a 'civilizing mission'. The redemption of the native, however, could never be complete because of the need to justify continued foreign domination. The tension created between the possibility of redeeming the native and his irredeemable difference allowed for the complexity of colonial ideology. (229)

While Sinha speaks specifically of English colonialism in India, this point of the need for justifying imperialism is pertinent to French imperialism as well.

38. See the chapter on 'Lived Bodies' in Elizabeth Grosz, *Volatile Bodies: Towards a Corporeal Feminism* (Sydney: Allen & Unwin, 1995).

39. Carole Pateman, *The Disorder of Women: Democracy, Feminism and Political Theory* (Cambridge: Polity Press, 1989).

40. See Doreen Massey, 'Introduction: Geography Matters' in *Geography Matters!*, eds Doreen Massey and John Allen (Cambridge: Cambridge University Press, 1984), pp. 1–11; Daphne Spain, *Gendered Spaces* (Chapel Hill: University of North Carolina Press, 1992); and Sara Mills, 'Gender and Colonial Space,' in *Gender, Place and Culture*, vol. 3, no. 2 (July 1996): pp. 125–48.

41. Henrietta Moore, *Space, Text and Gender: An Anthropological Study of the Marakwet of Kenya* (New York: Guilford, 1996), p. 80.

42. Mary Louise Pratt, *Imperial Eyes: Travel Writing and*

Culturation (New York: Routledge, 1992); John Noyes, *Colonial Space: Spatiality in the Discourse of German South West Africa* (Chur: Harwood, 1992); Gayatri Spivak, 'The Rani of Sirmur' in *Europe and its Others, vol. 1* (Colchester: University of Essex, 1985), pp. 126–51.

43. Gayatri Spivak, 'Woman in Difference: Mahasweta Devi's "Doulati the Bountiful"' in *Cultural Critique,* no. 14 (Winter 1989–90): pp. 105–28.

44. Nalini Natarajan, 'Woman, Nation and Narration in *Midnight's Children*' in *Scattered Hegemonies: Postmodernity and Transnational Practices,* eds Inderpal Grewal and Caren Kaplan (Minneapolis: University of Minnesota Press, 1994), pp. 76–89.

45. See Partha Chatterjee's *Nationalist Thought and the Colonial World: A Derivative Discourse* (London: Zed Press, 1986), for his elaboration of these two terms. See R. Radhakrishnan for a discussion of Chatterjee's thesis. Also see Lynda Liu, 'The Female Body and Nationalist Discourse: *The Field of Life and Death* Revisited' in *Scattered Hegemonies,* for her disagreement with Chatterjee's rigid structure.

46. Caren Kaplan, 'Deterritorializations: The Rewriting of Home and Exile in Western Feminist Discourse' in *Cultural Critique,* no. 6 (Spring 1987), p. 194.

47. See Annette Kolodny, *The Lay of the Land* (Chapel Hill: University of North Carolina Press, 1976), pp. 8–9.

48. See Luce Irigaray, *An Ethics of Sexual Difference,* trs Carolyn Burke and Gillian C. Gill (Ithaca: Cornell University Press, 1994).

49. See Jacques Lacan, 'The Signification of the Phallus' in *Ecrits: A Selection,* tr. Alan Sheridan (New York and London, 1977), pp. 281–91. When I was struggling in a graduate seminar on Lacan I became enthusiastic in class over some clear explanations of some of his basic terminologies that I had come across. My professor admonished me rather severely, saying I was naive and that I should hold clear explanations suspect, especially within psychoanalytic theory. Nevertheless, I still have an undergraduate's liking for clear explanations. For a 'clear' reading of this particular point of Lacan's, with all complexity intact, see especially Elizabeth Grosz, *Jacques Lacan: A Feminist Introduction* (London and New York:

Routledge, 1990). Also see Judith Butler, *Gender Trouble: Feminism and Subversion of Identity* (London and New York: Routledge, 1990). Read especially the chapter on 'Prohibition, Psychoanalysis and the Production of the Heterosexual Matrix'; also see Jacqueline Rose's introduction in *Feminine Sexuality: Jacques Lacan and the Ecole Freudienne*, eds Juliet Mitchell and Jacqueline Rose and tr. Jacqueline Rose (New York: Norton, 1982).

50. Claude Lévi-Strauss, *Structural Anthropology* (New York: Basic Books, 1961).

51. See 'Questions of Multiculturalism' in Gayatri Charavorti Spivak, *The Post-Colonial Critic*, ed. Sarah Harasym (New York: Routledge, 1990), pp. 59–66.

Chapter 4

1. See Edward Said, *The World, the Text and the Critic* (Cambridge, Mass: Harvard University Press, 1983).

2. See Partha Chatterjee's first chapter, 'Whose Imagined Community?' in *The Nation and its Fragments*, wherein he argues that Anderson's model of nationalism arising in the West due to print capitalism is not appropriate in a number of Asian countries, which derived a national identity by deliberately positing difference not at their borders but inside themselves. Creating a binary of outer and inner where outer reflected the world outside the home, it deliberately infused a sense of tradition inside the home in order to garner an identity and overthrow colonial rule. Partha Chatterjee, *The Nation and its Fragments* (Princeton: Princeton University Press, 1993); Benedict Anderson, *Imagined Communities: Reflections on the Origin and Spread of Nationalism* (London: Verso, 1983).

3. See Chandra Mohanty, 'Cartographies of Struggle' in *Third World Women and the Politics of Feminism*, eds Chandra Mohanty, Ann Russo and Lourdes Torres (Bloomington: Indiana University Press, 1992), pp. 1–47; Ella Shohat, 'Notes on the "Post-colonial"' in *Social Text*, nos. 31–2 (1993): pp. 99–113.

4. See Chandra Mohanty, 'Under Western Eyes' in *Third World Women and the Politics of Feminism*, eds Chandra

Mohanty, Ann Russo and Lourdes Torres (Bloomington: Indiana University Press, 1992), pp. 1–47.

5. Since the 1970s, New Zealand has been debating defining itself as a bicultural nation with equal powersharing between Maori and Pakeha, moving away from the centralized Pakeha-dominated State. In *Racism and Ethnicity*, Paul Spoonley verbalizes what is a predominant opinion in Aotearoa/New Zealand:

> Biculturalism acknowledges that only two New Zealand 'ethnic' groups, Maori and Pakeha, are particular to New Zealand and that the recent history of this country reflects the contact between these groups. Further the Treaty of Waitangi and its inherited moral, political and social obligations requires that Maori and Pakeha negotiate a relationship which is equitable for both.

While I agree that the dominant group should acknowledge the existence of the 'other' group, I must argue that biculturalism has to be implemented as state policy because state policy must properly represent the people. Furthermore, the legal document of the Treaty of Waitangi must be upheld by the Pakeha not because it is the liberal moral thing to do but rather because the State has reneged on the Treaty and acted illegally ever since it was signed in 1840. See Paul Spoonley, *Racism and Ethnicity* (Auckland: Oxford University Press, 1988), p. 105.

6. I realize that my statement might be perceived as untrue given the theme of the national *hui* (gathering) of Maori women in 1980. The manifesto states 'Gonna Share with all our Black sisters/The Right to be Black/The Right that was taken from us like the land'. While this manifesto might have indicated an oppositional political alliance in the inclusion of all Maoris, Pacific Islanders and Indians in the 1980s, it is simply not true of the 1990s, when biculturalism is officially yet to become policy in New Zealand. This continued delay has imbued the Maori nationalists with a sense of tremendous urgency. Furthermore, Maori women repeatedly cite the example of Australia, which in its perception of itself as a multicultural state has resituated Aboriginals as minority, once more denying them first-people status.

7. See Chicago Cultural Studies Group, 'Critical Multiculturalism' in *Critical Inquiry*, vol. 18 (Spring 1992), p. 531.

8. See M. Berube, 'Public Image Limited: Political Correctness and the Media's Big Lie' in *Debating P.C.: The Controversy over Political Correctness on College Campuses*, ed. Paul Berman (New York: Laurel Press, 1992), pp. 124–49.

9. See Sneja Gunew, 'Multicultural Multiplicities: Canada, USA, Australia' in *Meanjin*, vol. 52, no. 3 (Spring 1993): p. 455.

10. See Homi Bhabha, 'Signs Taken for Wonders: Questions of Ambivalence and Authority under a Tree Outside Delhi, May 1817' in Homi Bhabha, *The Location of Culture* (London and New York: Routledge, 1994). Also see 'Of Mimicry and Man: The Ambivalence of Colonial Discourse' in *The Location of Culture*.

11. Akhil Gupta and James Ferguson, 'Beyond "Culture": Space, Identity and the Politics of Difference', *Cultural Anthropology*, vol. 7, no. 1 (1992): emphasis in the original; p. 9.

12. In this I am influenced by Homi Bhabha's essay 'Of Mimicry and Man' where he states that this form of mimicking goes beyond Fanon's notion of the black man assuming the identity given to him by the colonizer. Bhabha points out that mimicking:

> problematizes the signs of racial and cultural priority, so that the 'national' is no longer naturalizable. What emerges between mimesis and mimicry is a *writing*, a mode of representation, that marginalizes the monumentality of history, quite simply mocks its power to be a model, the power which supposedly makes it imitable. (emphasis in the original; 87–8)

To this extent, the Maori plays the role expected of her but with some unexpected results, as I will proceed to explain.

13. There are at least four extant versions of the Treaty, the two English versions differing significantly from the Maori versions, in their confusion about the meaning of terms such as governorship and sovereignty. The Maori believed they were giving up governorship and retaining sovereignty, but the English intended that they lose both. See Claudia

Orange, *The Treaty of Waitangi* (Auckland: Oxford University Press, 1985).

14. As said by Ngapuhi chief, Panakareao, quoted in Andrew Sharp, *Justice and the Maori* (Auckland: Oxford University Press, 1990), p. 87.

15. See Michele Dominy, 'Maori Sovereignty: A Feminist Intervention of Tradition' in *Cultural Identity and Ethnicity in the Pacific*, eds Jocelyn Linnekin and Lin Poyer (Honolulu: University of Hawaii Press, 1990), pp. 237–54.

16. See Jan Farr, 'Bastion Point,' in *Broadsheet*, vol. 94 (1981), p. 21.

17. See Donna Awatere, 'Rugby, Racism and Riot Gear' in *Broadsheet*, no. 94 (1981), p. 12.

18. See Bill Ashcroft, Gareth Griffiths and Helen Tiffin, *The Empire Writes Back* (London and New York: Routledge, 1989), emphasis in the original; pp. 174–5.

19. Donna Awatere, *Maori Sovereignty*, Auckland: Broadsheet, 1984, p. 51.

20. My gratitude to Anna Yeatman for clarification of this point which she explains in her article 'Interlocking Oppressions'. Briefly put, the politics of identity is premised upon liberal notions of freedom, equality and the Universal Subject. Such notions of the Universal Subject have origins in John Locke's *Second Treatise*, where he argues for the 'Equality which all men are in, in respect to Jurisdiction or Dominion one over another' (para 54). Locke makes a passionate argument that all men (and in extension all women) live in a state:

> of *Equality*, wherein all the Power and Jurisdiction is reciprocal, no one having more than one another: there being nothing more evident, than that creatures of the same species and ranks promiscuously born to all the same advantages of Nature and the use of the same faculties, should also be equal one amongst another without subordination or subjection . . . (emphasis in original; *Second Treatise*, 309, para 4)

Such a reading of the Universal Subject is possible *only* in a liberal and egalitarian society. Furthermore, in such a reading of the Universal Subject, identity is interpreted as pre-given, each one equal to every other human being. Identity politics becomes a fight against the oppression and repression of identity. The oppressed group (women, Maori, homosexuals, Pacific Islanders) previously excluded from the ranks of the Universal Subject makes itself visible, challenges the liberal society successfully and then assumes its rightful place among the family of human beings. See Anna Yeatman, 'Interlocking Oppressions' in *Transitions: New Australian Feminisms*, eds Barbara Caine and Rosemary Pringle (Sydney: Allen & Unwin, 1995).

21. I want to suggest that there are intersections of multiple senses of nationalism in the concept of Maori nation. The notion of *tangata whenua* homogenizes Maori identity whereas *iwi*-based identity is a heterogenous one. Both forms of identity are at the basis of the postcolonial definitions of Maori.

22. See Nira Yuval-Davis and Floya Anthias, *Woman–Nation–State* (London: Macmillan, 1989).

23. In this statement I am attempting to conflate gendered identity with national identity to suggest that identity formation in both functions in similar ways. Judith Butler points out in *Gender Trouble*:

> As wives, women not only secure the reproduction of the *name* (the functional purpose) but effect a symbolic intercourse between clans of men. As the site of a patronymic exchange, women are and are not the patronymic sign, excluded from the signifier, the very patronym they bear. The woman in marriage qualifies not as identity, but only as a relational term that both distinguishes and binds the various clans to a common but internally differentiated patrilineal identity. (emphasis in original; 39)

Thus the nation-state takes the place of the patronymic in its positioning and definition of women. See Judith Butler, *Gender Trouble* (New York and London: Routledge, 1990).

24. See Partha Chatterjee, 'Nationalist Resolution of the Women's Question' in *Essays in Colonial History*, eds Kumkum Sangari and Sudesh Vaid (New Delhi: Kali for Women Press, 1989), pp. 233–53.

25. See Kathie Irwin, 'Towards Theories of Maori Feminism' in *Feminist Voices: Women's Studies Texts for Aotearoa/New Zealand*, eds Rosemary du Plessis et al. (Auckland: Oxford University Press, 1992), p. 12.

26. A counter-argument for my point that Maori women's leadership cannot be visible outside of Maori nationalism in Aotearoa/New Zealand will be made by citing the successful formation of the Maori Women's Welfare League in 1951. While it is undeniable that by 1951 there was a cobbling together of two distinct identities, 'Maori' and 'women', to form this group, two points about the origin and reception of the Maori Women's Welfare League (MWWL) must be remembered. First, this group was organized in the wake of the post-World War II mass urban migration of Maori which created new strains on their identity when they began to be transformed from a rural to an urban workforce. Discussing this historical shift in identity, Tania Rei et al. state that the Maori tribal committees in urban areas attempted to represent the interests of their people. However, the exclusively male tribal committees were sensitive only to male issues such as the welfare of Maori servicemen and land rights. Maori women who felt that the interests of the family, health and housing were largely ignored by the tribal committees successfully formed the MWWL (9). While this can be read as indicating leadership among Maori women, the category of leadership is not a simple configuration where one person shows agency. The organization of the MWWL must be read against the backdrop of urban migration. In effect, urban migration functioned to erase tribal differences among Maori and interpellated them as one people far more effectively than the Treaty. To a large extent this displacement and the relocation of the urban Maori must have helped promote a unified sense of Maori nation.

Second, the MWWL was a cause for resentment among a number of Maori men. As Tania Rei et al. state:

> [The women's] enthusiasm was not shared, however, by their men folk. A letter to the Minister of Maori Affairs in 1953 claimed that the MWWL had usurped the authority of the men and taken over control of the pa . . .

The concern that Maori women were excluding their men from duties that men considered to be theirs came to a head during the late 1950s. In 1960, the Department of Maori Affairs withdrew its administrative support for the MWWL . . . However, the League continued to receive government funding. (9–10)

The point being made here is that MWWL had more than merely the interests of Maori women at heart. The Maori women who formed the MWWL did it out of the sense of urgency that faced them as a people in diaspora. Furthermore, the reception of the MWWL at the hands of their men proves my point that Maori men construct the nation and their women to reflect their own identity.

See Tania Rei, Geraldine McDonald and Ngahuia Te Awekotuke, 'Me Aro Koi Ki te Hao Hine-Ahu-One' in *Women Together: A History of Women's Organizations in New Zealand*, ed. Anne Else (Wellington: Daphne Brasell, 1993), pp. 8–15.

27. See Gayatri Chakravorty Spivak, 'Who Claims Alterity?' in *Remaking History*, eds Barbara Kruger and Phil Mariani (Seattle: Bay Press, 1989), p. 281.

28. See Frank Kermode, *The Sense of an Ending* (New York: Oxford University Press, 1967).

29. See Marianna Torgovnick, *Closure in the Novel* (Princeton: Princeton University Press, 1981).

Chapter 5

1. Sally Morgan, *My Place* (Fremantle: Fremantle Arts Centre Press, 1987). All subsequent references to this text are to this edition.

2. See Jackie Huggins' response, 'Always was Always will Be', to Bain Atwood's article on Sally Morgan, 'Portrait of an Aboriginal as an Artist'.

Jackie Huggins, 'Always was Always will Be,' in *Australian Historical Studies*, vol. 25, nos 98–101 (April 1992–Oct. 1993): pp. 459–64; Bain Attwood, 'Portrait of an Aboriginal as an Artist: Sally Morgan and the Construction of Aboriginality' in *Australian Historical Studies*, vol. 25, nos 98–101 (April 1992–Oct. 1993): pp. 302–18. Also see Jo Robertson's response to Subash Jaireth, 'Talking to; Talking about; or Talking for? Enunciative Politics for non-Aboriginal Literary Critics' in *Imago*, vol. 7, no. 3 (Summer 1995): pp. 84–92; and yet another response to his response, 'Authority and Authenticity in Aboriginal Literature' in *Imago*, vol. 8, no. 2 (1996): pp. 145–50; Subash Jaireth's articles are 'Who Speaks for Whom?: Mikhail Bakhtin and the Idea of Chronotopic Nature of Speaking and Listening' in *Imago*, vol. 7, no. 3 (Summer 1995): pp. 78–83; and 'Whose Speaking or Writing is More Authentic and Authoritative? A Reply to Jo Robertson' in *Imago*, vol. 8, no. 2 (1996): pp. 141–4. Though not part of this series of debates, Annabel Cooper's 'Talking about *My Place*/My Place: Feminism, Criticism and the Other's Autobiography,' in *Southern Review*, vol. 28, no. 2 (July 1995): pp. 140–53, is a more reasoned/reasonable approach to whether one can write about other's autobiographies. I find the implications of Jo Robertson's responses unviable, in that I feel cornered and silenced, prevented from writing about an autobiography of anyone else other than of someone of my racial/ethnic makeup.

3. See Gayatri Spivak, 'A Literary Representation of the Subaltern' in Gayatri Spivak, *In Other Worlds: Essays in Cultural Politics* (London: Methuen, 1986).

4. See Paul de Man, 'Autobiography as De-facement' in *MLN*, vol. 94, no. 5 (Dec. 1979): p. 919.

5. Following de Man I want to make a distinction between the author Sally Morgan the Sally constructed and specularized by the text. I will refer to the author as Morgan and the latter, who is textualized, as Sally to maintain these distinctions.

6. Doris Sommer, *Life/Lines: Theorizing Women's Autobiography*, eds Bella Brodzki and Celeste Schenk (Ithaca and London: Cornell University Press, 1988), p. 118.

7. See John Beverley, 'The Margin at the Center: On Testimonio (Testimonial Narrative)' in *De/colonizing the Subject: The Politics of Gender in Women's Autobiography*, eds Sidonie Smith and Julia Watson (Minneapolis: University of Minnesota Press, 1992), p. 95.

8. See Simon Dentith, *Bakhtinian Thought: An Introductory Reader* (London and New York: Routledge, 1995), p. 94.

9. Julia Kristeva, in *Desire in Language: A Semiotic Approach to Literature and Art*, trs Thomas Gora, Alice Jardine and

Leon S. Roudiez, ed. Leon S. Roudiez (New York: Columbia University Press, 1980), p. 66.

10. In *Rabelais and his World, Problems of Dostoevsky's Poetics* and *The Dialogic Imagination,* Bakhtin elaborates his theory of the narrative and forwards the notion of the dialogic nature of the novel. See Mikhail Bakhtin, *Rabelais and his World,* tr. Helene Iswolsky (Cambridge, Mass.: MIT Press, 1968); *Problems of Dostoevsky's Poetics,* tr. and ed. Caryl Emerson (Minneapolis: University of Minnesota Press, 1984), *The Dialogic Imagination,* trs Caryl Emerson and Michael Holquist (Austin: University of Texas Press, 1981).

11. See Dentith, Michael Holquist, *Dialogism: Bakhtin and his World* (London and New York: Routledge, 1990) and Mikhail Bakhtin, *The Dialogic Imagination: Four Essays,* for complex explanations of Baktin's terms.

12. I also want to point out the convergence of the notion of intertextuality with that of reader-response theory, in that both emphasize the role of the reader in the production of meaning in the text. In *The Implied Reader,* Wolfgang Iser underscores the interplay between the work and the reader to produce the multiple series of meanings that a text can produce. Iser suggests that rereading a work and setting it against a different background allows the reader 'to develop hitherto unforeseeable connections . . . The new background brings to light new aspects [and] more complex anticipations'. This causes the text to reveal 'a potential multiplicity of connections'. In this Iser echoes a point made by Roland Barthes who, in *Mythologies* and *S/Z,* points to the inexhaustibility of the writerly text, which is a veritable Babel. In 'Phenomenology of Reading' Georges Poulet, too, suggests '[t]he work lives its life within me; in a certain sense, it thinks itself and it even gives itself a meaning within me'.

　　See Wolfgang Iser, *The Implied Reader: Patterns of Communication in Prose Fiction from Bunyan to Beckett* (Baltimore: Johns Hopkins University Press, 1974), p. 278; Roland Barthes, *Mythologies,* tr. Annette Lavers (New York: Hill and Wang, 1972) and *S/Z,* tr. Richard Miller (New York: Hill and Wang, 1974); Georges Poulet,

'Phenomenology of Reading' in *New Literary History*, vol. 1, no. 1 (1969–70), p. 59.

13. See Gayatri Chakravorty Spivak, 'Three Women's Texts and the Critique of Imperialism' in *'Race' Writing and Difference*, ed. Henry Louis Gates Jr (London and Chicago: University of Chicago Press, 1986), p. 262.

14. Edward Said, *Culture and Imperialism* (London: Chatto & Windus, 1993), p. 78.

15. Charlotte Brontë, *Jane Eyre*, ed. Richard Dunn (New York: W.W. Norton and Company, 1971), p. 71.

16. See Sandra Gilbert and Susan Gubar, *The Madwoman in the Attic: The Woman Writer and the Nineteenth-Century Imagination* (New Haven: Yale University Press, 1979).

17. See Sigmund Freud, 'Family Romances' (1909), *The Standard Edition of the Complete Psychological Works of Sigmund Freud, Vol. 9*, eds James Strachey et al. (London: Hogarth Press, 1964), p. 238.

18. I thank John Docker for that phrase which came up in a conversation we had in Canberra in February 1997.

19. Charles Dickens, *Great Expectations*, ed. Angus Calder (Harmondsworth: Penguin Books, 1965).

20. Anny Sadrin, *Parentage and Inheritance in the Novels of Charles Dickens* (Cambridge: Cambridge University Press, 1994), p. 9.

21. Judith Butler suggests:
    > The performance of drag plays upon the distinction between the anatomy of the performer and the gender that is being performed. But we are actually in the presence of three contingent dimensions of significant corporeality: anatomical sex, gender identity and gender performance. If the anatomy of the performer is already distinct from the gender of the performer and both of those are distinct from the gender of the performance, then the performance suggests a dissonance not only between sex and performance, but sex and gender and gender and performance. (137)

    See *Gender Trouble: Feminism and the Subversion of Identity* (New York: Routledge, 1990).

22. See Jacques Lacan, 'Function and Field of Speech and Language' in *Ecrits: A Selection* (New York: W.W. Norton, 1977), p. 66.

23. In his work on the theme of miscegenation in William Faulkner's novels, Eric Sundquist points out that the Civil War in the US was caused not only by ideological differences but also by geographical ones between the North and the South, as well as their differing attitudes to miscegenation. Sundquist refers to the pro-slavery reference to Lincoln's 'Miscegenation Proclamation' and cites a leaflet which parodied the Lord's Prayer:

    and called upon the 'spirit of amalgamation' to shine forth and flourish, 'that we may become a regenerated nation of half-breeds and mongrels' and 'live in bonds of fraternal love, union and equality with the Almighty Nigger, henceforward, now and forever. Amen'. (108)

    See Eric Sundquist, *Faulkner: The House Divided* (Baltimore: Johns Hopkins University Press, 1983).

24. Nancy Stepan, 'Biological Degeneration: Races and Proper Places' in *Degeneration: The Dark Side of Progress*, eds J. Edward Chamberlain and Sander Gilman (New York: Columbia University Press, 1985), p. 97.

25. The taboo of miscegenation was, however, continually transgressed by white men with access to black women. Louis Agassiz, the nineteenth-century Swiss-American ethnologist, located the cause of sexual unions between white men and black women on the loose morals of the half-breed servant girls; white men were attracted to the white half of the racially mixed servants, but it was her black half that loosened *both* their inhibitions. See Agassiz as cited in Robert Young, *Colonial Desire: Hybridity in Theory, Culture and Race* (New York: Routledge, 1996), p. 149.

    Robert Young rightly points out that at the centre of racialist discourse is an ambivalence: 'a compulsive libidinal attraction disavowed by an equal insistence on repulsion' (149). Thus the threat of miscegenation is underpinned by sexual fantasies: the underside of taboo is desire. The insistence on a differentiated identity is commingled with a desire for non-differentiation.

    This point about ambivalence is made insistently throughout Freud's works, as in *Beyond the Pleasure Principle*, where the instinct to survive and live is countered by the death instinct; again this phenomenon is dealt with in his essay on 'The Uncanny' where the word *heimlich* soon means its opposite, *unheimlich*.

See Sigmund Freud, *Beyond the Pleasure Principle, Standard Edition of the Complete Psychological Works of Sigmund Freud, vol. 18*, tr. James Strachey et al. (London: Hogarth, 1974), pp. 1–64; also 'The Uncanny', *SE 17*, pp. 217–52.

26. My positing of such a statement is located in *Great Expectations* where the transcending of class is rendered possible in the colonies which are predicated on racial difference. For instance, not only does Magwitch make money in Australia, but Pip, when he gives up Magwitch's fortune, entertains the notion of going to the colonies, to India and finally settles on Egypt. Class limitations can be overcome in the Empire through the inscription of race and the establishment of white as superior. Class difference is erased in the face of racial difference in the colonies.

27. See Nancy Leys Stepan, 'Race and Gender: The Role of Analogy in Science' in *Anatomy of Racism*, ed. David Theo Goldberg (Minneapolis University of Minnesota Press, 1990), p. 47.

28. Paul Ricoeur, 'The Metaphorical Process as Cognition, Imagination and Feeling' in *On Metaphor*, ed. Seldon Sacks (Chicago: University of Chicago Press, 1979), p. 146.

29. See David Lloyd, 'Race Under Representation' in *Oxford Literary Review*, no. 13 (1991): pp. 62–94.

30. See Sidonie Smith, *Subjectivity, Identity and the Body: Women's Autobiographical Practices in the Twentieth Century (Bloomington: Indiana University Press, 1993), p. 6.

31. See Judith Butler, 'Variations on Sex and Gender: Beauvoir, Wittig and Foucault,' in *Feminism as Critique: Essays in the Politics of Gender in Late-Capitalist Societies*, eds Seyla Benhabib and Drucilla Cornell (Cambridge: Polity Press, 1987), p. 133.

32. See Brian Slattery, 'Aboriginal Sovereignty and Imperial Claims' in *Aboriginal Self-Determination*, ed. Frank Cassidy (Nova Scotia: Oolichan Books, 1991), p. 200.

33. As cited in Henry Louis Gates Jr, 'Writing, "Race" and the Difference it Makes' in *Loose Canons: Notes on the Culture Wars* (New York and Oxford: Oxford University Press, 1992), p. 58.

34. See Kay Schaffer, *In the Wake of First Contact: The Eliza Fraser Stories* (Cambridge: Cambridge University Press, 1995), p. 242.
35. See J.B. Harley, 'Maps, Knowledge and Power' in *The Iconography of Landscape: Essays on the Symbolic Representation, Design and Use of Past Environments*, eds Denis Cosgrove and Stephen Daniels (Cambridge: Cambridge University Press, 1988).
36. See José Rabasa, 'Allegories of the Atlas' in *Europe and its Others*, vol. 2, eds Francis Barker et al. (Colchester: University of Essex, 1985), p. 6.
37. Graham Huggan, 'Decolonizing the Map: Post-Colonialism, Post-Structuralism and the Cartographic Connection' in *Ariel*, vol. 20, no. 4 (Oct. 1989): pp. 115–31.
38. See Spivak's 'The Rani of Sirmur' in *Europe and its Others*, vol. 1, eds Francis Barker et al. (Colchester: University of Essex, 1985), p. 133.
39. See Peter Stallybrass and Allon White, *The Politics and Poetics of Transgression* (London: Methuen, 1986), p. 192.

Chapter 6

1. See Charlotte Godley, *Letters from Early New Zealand by Charlotte Godley 1850–1853*, ed. John R. Godley (Christchurch: Whitcombe and Tombs, 1951).
2. See Gayatri Chakravorty Spivak, 'The Rani of Sirmur' in *Europe and its Others*, vol. 1, eds Francis Barker et al. (Colchester: University of Essex, 1985), pp. 128–51.
3. Rachel Henning, *The Letters of Rachel Henning*, ed. David Adams (Sydney: Angus & Robertson, 1966).
4. See especially the chapter titled 'The Early Formation of the Victorian Domestic Ideology' in *White, Male, and Middle-class: Explorations in Feminism and History* (Cambridge: Polity Press, 1992).
5. See Nancy Armstrong, *Desire and Domestic Fiction: A Political History of the Novel* (New York and Oxford: Oxford University Press, 1987).
6. Armstrong cites Howard Perkin:
   According to Perkin, the absence of anything resembling a modern middle class is particularly apparent in England,

where there was no word for *bourgeoise* 'until the nine-teenth century', because 'the thing itself did not exist, in the sense of a permanent, self-conscious urban class in opposition to a landed aristocracy'. (64)

7. See Mary Poovey, *Uneven Developments: The Ideological Work of Gender in Mid-Victorian England* (London: Virago, 1989).

8. See Pierre Bourdieu, *Distinctions: A Social Critique of the Judgement of Taste*, tr. Richard Nice (Cambridge, Mass: Harvard University Press, 1984), p. 466.

9. See Sigmund Freud, 'Wolf Man', *SE* 10.

10. See Sigmund Freud, 'Family Romance', *SE* 9.

11. See Peter Stallybrass and Allon White, *The Politics and Poetics of Transgression* (London: Methuen, 1986).

12. Anne McClintock, *Imperial Leather: Race, Gender and Sexuality in the Colonial Conquest* (New York and London: Routledge, 1995).

13. For a different reading of Freud (the centrality of his Jewishness to his theories on gender) see Sander Gilman, *Freud, Race and Gender* (Princeton: Princeton University Press, 1993).

14. See R. Radhakrishnan, 'Nationalism, Gender and the Narrative of Identity,' in *Nationalisms and Sexualities*, eds Andrew Parker et al. (New York and London: Routledge, 1992), pp. 77–95. Also see Partha Chatterjee, *Nationalist Thought and the Colonial World* (New Delhi: Oxford University Press, 1986).

15. Carole Pateman, *The Sexual Contract* (Stanford: Stanford University Press, 1988); also see *The Disorder of Women: Democracy, Feminism and Political Theory* (Cambridge: Polity Press, 1989).

16. See Helen Callaway, *Gender, Culture and Empire: European Women in Colonial Nigeria* (Urbana: University of Illinois Press, 1987), p. 5.

17. Ronald Hyam, *Empire and Sexuality: The British Experience* (Manchester: Manchester University Press), 1990. (Emphasis in original; p. 89.)

18. See especially the chapter 'European Expansion since 1763' in Harry Magdoff, *Imperialism: from the Colonial Age to the Present* (New York: Monthly Review Press, 1978).

19. See Alfred Crosby, *Ecological Imperialism: The Biological*

Expansion of Europe, 900–1900 (Cambridge, Cambridge University Press, 1986).

20. See A. James Hammerton, *Emigrant Gentlewomen* (Canberra: Australian National University Press, 1979).

21. Joanna Trollope, *Britannia's Daughters* (London: Hutchinson, 1983), p. 23.

22. See Philip Dodd, 'Englishness and National Culture' in *Englishness: Politics and Culture 1880–1920*, eds Robert Colls and Philip Dodd (London: Croom Helm, 1987), pp. 1–29.
    Dodd states:
    The identification of the English with masculine could even determine matters of literary style. Given that males had to read and write (but not too much), they must cultivate a 'masculine' style, as many of the books on style made clear. For instance, Arthur Quiller-Couch could say in one of a series of lectures at the University of Cambridge: 'Generally use transitive verbs, that strike their objects and use them in the active voice . . . For as a rough law, by his use of the straight verb and by economy of adjectives, you can tell a man's style, if it be masculine or neuter, writing or composition.' The dominant English licensed to other groups and to other nationalities those 'female' qualities which it did not acknowledge itself to possess. As recently as 1973 Professor William Walsh could write in his book *Commonwealth Literature* that Indians do not write in a 'direct, masculine way', but with 'Indian tenderness'.

23. The importance of the working class to the needs of the empire is especially evident in Anna Davin's 'Imperialism and Motherhood' wherein she traces the construction of motherhood and hygiene within the discourse of imperialism. See Anna Davin, 'Imperialism and Motherhood' in *History Workshop*, vol. 5 (Spring 1978): pp. 9–66.

24. See Nupur Chaudhuri, 'Shawls, Jewellery, Curry and Rice in Victorian Britain' in *Western Women and Imperialism*, eds Nupur Chaudhuri and Margaret Strobel (Indianapolis: Indianapolis University Press, 1992), p. 232.

25. Obviously I am very influenced by Homi Bhabha's 'Signs Taken for Wonders' by posing such a thesis. He, however, concentrates on the subjectivity of the colonized when he states:

The colonial presence is always ambivalent, split between its appearance as original and authoritative and its articulation as repetition and difference. It is a disjunction produced within the act of enunciation of a specifically colonial articulation of those two disproportionate sites of colonial discourse and power: the colonial scene as the invention of historicity, mastery, mimesis or as the 'other scene' of *Enstellung*, displacement, fantasy, psychic defence and an 'open' textuality. Such a display of difference produces a mode of authority that is agonistic (rather than antagonistic). (107–8)

See Homi Bhabha, 'Signs Taken For Wonders: Questions of Ambivalence and Authority under a Tree Outside Delhi, May 1817' in *The Location of Culture* (London: Routledge, 1994), pp. 102–22.

26. In *The Black Atlantic*, Paul Gilroy suggests that the term 'diaspora' is not limited to Jewish people alone. According to him, historians of slavery and Africa took up the term as pertinent to people of African descent. He suggests that the notion of diaspora provides a way of understanding modernity and cultural identities. In *There Ain't no Black in the Union Jack*, Gilroy says:

Black Britain defines itself crucially as part of a diaspora. Its unique cultures draw inspiration from those developed by black populations elsewhere. In particular, the culture and politics of black America and the Caribbean have become raw materials for creative processes which redefine what it means to be black, adapting it to distinctively British experiences and meanings.

Here the historical specificity of this term, referring to the Jews who were dispersed to live among the Gentiles after the Captivity, with its implications of racism and suffering, is transferred to the Blacks. I deliberately use this term for the white diasporas well because I think notions of race enter the settler colonies through this dispersal of whites from Europe. To a large extent, the white diaspora was at some level economically motivated; the sense of dispersal, the yearning for home, the construction of the mother country in the settler colonies, relates to the history of this term as well. See Paul Gilroy, *The Black Atlantic* (London: Verso, 1993); also see his *There Ain't No Black in the Union Jack* (London: Hutchinson, 1987), p. 154.

27. See Jane Mackay and Pat Thane, 'The English Woman' in *Englishness: Politics and Culture, 1880–1920,* eds Robert Colls and Philip Dodd (London: Croom Helm, 1987), p. 119.
28. See for instance, Percival Spear, *The Nabob* (London: Oxford University Press, 1967); Mark Nadis, 'Evolution of the Sahibs' in *The Historian,* vol. 19 (1975): pp. 425–35; J.K. Stanford, *Ladies in the Sun: The Memsahibs in India, 1790–1860* (London: Galley Press, 1962).
29. See the chapter on Woman–Body–Nation–Space in this work.
30. Diana Fuss, *Identification Papers* (London and New York: Routledge, 1996), p. 143.
31. See Robert Young, *White Mythologies: Writing History and the West* (New York and London: Routledge, 1990), p. 3.
32. See Sigmund Freud, 'The Uncanny', *SE* 17, 1919. Also see Homi Bhabha's 'The Location of Culture in *The Location of Culture,* pp. 1–18 and 'The World and the Home' in *Social Text,* nos 31/32 (1992): pp. 141–53.

Chapter 7

1. I wish to thank the Rockefeller Foundation for providing me with a SIROW (Southwestern Institute for Research on Women) Summer Humanist-in-Residence fellowship at the University of Arizona in June and July of 1992 which allowed me to do preliminary research on this chapter. I am also grateful to Kath Weston for leading me to the right references.
2. See 'In a Word: Interview' in Gayatri Chakravorty Spivak, *Outside in the Teaching Machine* (New York and London: Routledge, 1993), pp. 1–24.
3. See Gayatri Chakravorty Spivak, 'The Post-Colonial Critic' in *The Post-Colonial Critic: Interviews, Strategies, Dialogues,* ed. Sarah Harasym (New York and London: Routledge, 1990). I want to add that in this chapter I follow Vijay Mishra and Bob Hodge's distinction between 'post-colonial' and 'postcolonial' where 'post-colonial' has underpinnings of history and historical event. 'Postcolonial' is discursive in that oppositionality is always present within colonization.

Notice that in any case the ontology of the discursive as well as the historical post(-)colonial is always within the act of colonization. To this extent, Mishra and Hodge make their distinction based on Jean-François Lyotard's notion of the postmodern. See Vijay Mishra and Bob Hodge, 'What is Post(-)colonialism?' in *Textual Practice*, vol. 5, no 3 (1991): pp. 399–414.

4. See Frederic Jameson, 'Third-World Literature in the Era of Multinational Capitalism' in *Social Text*, no. 15 (1986): pp. 65–88; also see Benita Parry, 'Problems in Current Theories of Colonial Discourse' in *Oxford Literary Review*, no. 9 (1987): pp. 27–58.

5. In *Orientalism*, Edward Said suggests that the hegemony of the West generates a series of representations of the East, positing the Eastern hemisphere as its alterity. See Said's classic work, *Orientalism* (New York: Vintage Books, 1978).

6. See Ella Shohat, 'Notes on the "Post-colonial"' in *Social Text*, nos 31/32 (1992), p. 101.

7. See Aida Hurtado, 'Relating to Privilege: Seduction and Rejection in the Subordination of White Women and Women of Color' in *Signs*, vol. 14, no. 4 (1989), p. 849.

8. For a further critique of Jameson's article read Aijaz Ahmad's 'Jameson's Rhetoric of Otherness and the "National Allegory"' in *Social Text*, no. 17 (1987): pp. 3–25; Madhava Prasad reads Aijaz Ahmad reading Jameson in 'On the Question of a Theory of (Third World) Literature' in *Social Text*, nos 31/32 (1992): pp. 27–58.

9. See Gayatri Spivak, 'Who Claims Alterity?' in *Remaking History*, eds Barbara Kruger and Phil Mariani (Seattle: Bay Press, 1989), p. 281.

10. See Remo Guidieri and Francesco Pellizi, '"Smoking Mirrors"—Modern Polity and Ethnicity' in *Ethnicities and Nations*, eds Remo Guidieri et al. (Austin: University of Texas Press, 1988).

11. See Arjun Appadurai, 'Putting Hierarchy in its Place' in *Cultural Anthropology*, vol. 3, no. 1 (1988): pp. 36–49.

12. See Claude Lévi-Strauss, *The Savage Mind* (London: Weidenfield & Nicolson, 1962).

13. See Ashis Nandy, *The Intimate Enemy* (New Delhi: Oxford University Press, 1985), p. xiii.

14. See Partha Chatterjee, *Nationalist Thought and the Colonial World: A Derivative Discourse* (London: Zed Books, 1986).

15. In the colonial narrative, of course, this is reversed to read the Indian violence which led to a repressive regime.

16. See Lila Abu-Lughod, 'Writing Against Culture' in *Recapturing Anthropology: Working in the Present*, ed. Richard Fox (Santa Fe: School of American Research Press, 1992) wherein she indicates that 'the process of creating a self through opposition to an other entails the violence of repressing or ignoring other forms of difference' (140). It is to that extent that Gandhi and Bankim and, by extension, Nandy and Chatterjee short-circuit the binary gridlock of Western notions of self/other by refusing to participate within that system.

17. As I was growing up in a decolonizing, secular India in the 1970s all schoolchildren were required to take the 'pledge' every morning which began with the words: 'India is my country,/All Indians are my brothers and sisters . . .' In modern secular India nationalism is supposed to function to erase communal differences. But the reality can be otherwise. See in particular Faisal Fatehali Devji's 'Hindu/Muslim/Indian' in *Public Culture*, no. 5 (1992): pp. 1–18. Also see Ania Loomba on 'Overworlding the "Third World"' in *Oxford Literary Review*, no. 13 (1991): pp. 164–92.

18. By the essentialist position is meant that there is something irreducible and unchanging in the anchoring of a subject because of the colour of her skin or her nationality. Though the debate between the essentialists and constructionists is normally fought out in the arena of gender, the question of race and subjectivity can be considered in this debate as well. Henry Louis Gates Jr and Anthony Appiah vehemently argue against such a position of essence. Gates maintains in 'Writing "Race" and the Difference it Makes' that:

> Race has become a trope of ultimate, irreducible difference between cultures, linguistic groups, or adherents of specific belief systems . . . Race is the ultimate trope of difference because it is *so very arbitrary in its application*. The biological criteria used to determine 'difference' in

sex do not simply hold when applied to 'race'. (emphasis added; 5)

Joyce Ann Joyce, however, insists on using essence as a strategy of black literary analysis. She insists: 'It is insidious for the Black literary critic to adopt any kind of strategy that diminishes or . . . negates his blackness' (as quoted in Diana Fuss, *Essentially Speaking*; 77).

See Henry Louis Gates Jr, 'Writing "Race" and the Difference it Makes' in *Critical Inquiry*, vol. 12, no. 1 (1985): pp. 1–20. Also see Diana Fuss, *Essentially Speaking: Feminism, Nature, Difference* (New York and London: Routledge, 1989).

19. I cannot resist using this Rupert Brooke poem as an epigraph to this segment. The words of this poem have been memorized by generations of Indian school students, even after Independence.

20. See Akhil Gupta and James Ferguson, 'Beyond "Culture": Space, Identity and the Politics of Difference' in *Cultural Anthropology*, vol. 7, no. 1 (1992): pp. 6–7.

21. See 'Of Mimicry and Man: Ambivalence of Colonial Discourse' and 'Signs Taken for Wonders: Questions of Ambivalence and Authority under a Tree Outside Delhi, May 1817' in *The Location of Culture* (New York: Routledge, 1994).

22. See Homi Bhabha, 'Narrating the Nation' in *Nation and Narration*, ed. Homi K. Bhabha (New York: Routledge, 1990).

23. See Robert Young, *White Mythologies: Writing History and the West* (New York: Routledge, 1990), p. 157.

24. See Gayatri Chakravorty Spivak, 'Can the Subaltern Speak?' in *Marxism and the Interpretation of Culture*, eds Cary Nelson and Larry Grossberg (London: Macmillan, 1988); 'The Rani of Sirmur' in *Europe and its Others*, vol. 1, eds Francis Barker et al. (Colchester: University of Essex, 1984).

25. See 'A Literary Representation of the Subaltern' in *In Other Worlds: Essays in Cultural Politics* (New York: Methuen, 1987).

26. See Spivak, 'Postmarked Calcutta, India' in *The Post-Colonial Critic: Interviews, Strategies, Dialogues*, ed. Sarah

Harasym (New York and London: Routledge, 1990), p. 83.
27. See R. Radhakrishnan, 'Ethnic Identity and Post-Structural Differance,' in *Cultural Critique*, no. 6 (1987): pp. 199–220.
28. See Joan W. Scott, 'The Evidence of Experience' in *Critical Inquiry*, vol. 17 (Summer 1991): pp. 773–97.
29. See Frederic Jameson, *Postmodernism or the Cultural Logic of Late Capitalism* (Durham: Duke University Press, 1990).

Chapter 8

1. Gayatri Chakravorty Spivak, *Outside in the Teaching Machine* (New York and London: Routledge, 1993), p. 217.
2. See in particular, Elizabeth Grosz' chapter on 'Refiguring Bodies' in *Volatile Bodies: Towards a Corporeal Feminism* (Sydney: Allen & Unwin, 1994), for a useful overview of the location of the female body.
3. See Homi K. Bhabha, *The Location of Culture* (New York and London: Routledge, 1994) p. 46.
4. See Louise Allen, *The Lesbian Idol: Martina, kd and the Consumption of Lesbian Identity* (London: Cassell, 1997); Richard Dyer, *White* (London: Routledge, 1997); *Displacing Whiteness*, ed. Ruth Frankenberg (Durham: Duke University Press, 1997); *Whiteness: A Critical Reader*, ed. Mike Hill (New York: New York University Press, 1997); *Critical White Studies: Looking Behind the Mirror*, eds Richard Delgado and Jean Stefancic (Philadelphia: Temple University Press, 1997).

Index

245

"Only when the clock stops, does time come to life."

~William Faulkner

"Time is a brisk wind, for each hour it brings something new...but who can understand and measure its sharp breath, its mystery and its design?"

~Paracelsus

"Time is the most undefinable yet paradoxical of things; the past is gone, the future is not come, and the present becomes the past even while we attempt to define it, and, like the flash of lightning, at once exists and expires."

~Charles Caleb Colton

PROLOGUE
Rhodes, Greece, 226 BC

The rocky slope shuddered. Two isolated jolts. Then the ground really started to move. Acastus Vassos clutched the large white boulder he had been sitting on while eating his bread.

He enjoyed hiking up into the green hills each day to eat. The sound of his sandaled feet on stone were like music as he climbed the low rises. When he was high enough, he turned around and admired the bustling harbor laid out before him. He would eat, absorbing the view and the gusting breezes off the blue Aegean Sea. The thick air in town was often stagnant because of the buildings, the throngs of merchants and the unwashed sailors. But up on the hill, the air was fresh, and the temperature in the summer felt cooler on his skin.

Vassos had been climbing the rocky incline to his normal perch for years, but he had never seen the small white pebbles on the ground hop and jump as they did now. A devout man, he quickly reminded himself of the last time he had made devotions to the gods, at the temples near the Acropolis. The rumble grew louder and louder, until Vassos pulled his hands from the boulder—no longer afraid of falling down the hill—and slammed them against his ears to stop the now deafening thrumming and grinding noise. He

began to shout to Zeus for mercy, as his body slid down off the white rock to the ground a few feet below. The soil bounced and juddered just as the boulder had done. The ground squirmed. A living thing.

Only when his eyes turned toward the view of the harbor, did he cease worrying for his own safety. What he saw in the distance made him forget about himself.

Rhodes was renowned throughout the world for its one major tourist attraction. Across the view of the town lay the busy harbor. At the end of two stone jetties, stood the Colossus. A giant bronze statue of the sun god Helios, over three hundred feet in height, the statue stood even taller on the pedestals below its feet. The bronze guardian stood astride the twin jetties, and all the world's ship traffic passed below the arch of its legs.

Vassos's father, Cletus, had watched the construction of the statue for the twelve years it took, and he would frequently tell the tale before his death of how architects and builders had scoffed at the notion of building a statue astride the entrance to the port. The bronze was too soft and would never support the weight of such a creature, they had said. But, as Cletus had explained to his son, the genius designer, a man named Chares, from nearby Lindos, had an idea. He used several long iron rods inside the structure in a crossing X pattern, pulling the upper left of the statue to the lower right, and vice versa. The crossing iron bars would also add support to the statue's limbs and head. The result was a statue strong enough to stand with legs apart, even at its immense size.

Vassos had heard many stories of the assembling of the Colossus as a child. After the twelve years of its construction, peoples from leagues and leagues away would come to Rhodes to see its magnificence, as the sun glinted off the polished metal.

Vassos had known the statue all his life. It had stood at the entrance to the harbor for fifty-six years—twenty years more than Vassos had been alive. It was a comfortable friend, and like most

of his fellow townspeople, he felt innate pride when he thought of the giant harbor sentry. It was, after all, a constant reminder that the people of Rhodes had thwarted the invasion forces of Antigones the One-Eyed.

The statue was a part of daily life for all of the Rhodian citizens now. But daily life had never included the ground shaking like a caught fish in its death throes. Now, as Vassos looked out over the town to the harbor, he beheld the strangest sight of his life: the Colossus was moving!

The buildings in the town swayed violently. Some collapsed. Boats were tossed over the waters like toys. Three fires erupted around the town. But the Colossus was what held Vassos's gaze. One leg had broken loose from a pedestal, and the other had twisted. The loose leg swung out over the sea, then came back in to the jetty, where the other leg remained. It looked to Vassos like a soldier turning about 180 degrees. Where previously the visage of Helios had faced outward toward the sea, both a welcoming beacon for merchants and sailors, and also a reminder of the fortitude of Rhodes, now the statue faced the trembling city and the sloshing waters of the harbor.

Vassos's mind was already in a panic, but what he saw next made his mouth fall open, and all reasonable thoughts shut down.

The Colossus took a step.

The long, gigantic bronze leg swept along the jetty toward the town, and the foot planted itself down. Then the left leg lifted up off its pedestal and slid up and ahead of the right. The statue looked for all the world like it was walking toward the city and the distant hill where Vassos gawked in horror.

The rumbling continued, and Vassos thought the ground might buckle and launch him into the sky. Then he saw the ground rupture in several spots along the hillside, gaping gouges in soil and rock. He suddenly worried less about flight and the Colossus, and more about being sucked down into the fiery bowels of Hades. He shut his eyes and squeezed them tightly, hoping the disorientation and nausea from the shaking world would go away.

Then it did. All at once, everything stopped.

His eyes snapped open. The rumble was gone. In the distance he could hear screams on the wind. The Colossus had moved even further toward the town, and now it faced out toward the West, its back to the town again, but it was leaning backward and looking up. Toward the sky.

Then Vassos understood. *No. It isn't looking up.*

It was falling over.

Vassos scrambled to his feet and watched as the giant statue fell backward, slamming into the city and crushing homes under its back and limbs. The impact sent up a fluttering wave of dust and debris. A second later came the thundering echo, like the crashing boom of Zeus's own lightning, and a wind that pushed hard against Vassos's skin.

When the breeze off the water finally cleared the dirt from the air, Vassos saw the statue's torso had come loose from the legs. One arm snapped and rolled, crushing more small houses and buildings. The head had broken off and came to rest on its side. Helios's once proud visage was now shamefully wounded.

Vassos stood shocked for just a moment as his mind took in everything his eyes were showing him. Then something in him snapped, and he understood the need of every able-bodied man to assist in the rescue of those that might have been injured. He ran down the rocky hillside, leaping wide dark ruts in the ground, where the world had been torn asunder. When he reached the congested city, the damage was far worse than he had expected. The quaking Earth had caused more death and destruction than the fall of the statue had, but Vassos knew it would be the statue's collapse that people would remember—that, and its walking performance. He assisted struggling men and sweaty soldiers for hours, helping bleeding old women, children with broken bones, and even lost and frightened animals wandering aimlessly and scared in the marketplace.

When he finally made his way closer to the harbor and saw the fallen remains of the giant bronze statue, his heart was heavy.

Crowds of onlookers simply stood and stared at the fallen idol, now that most of the injured had been tended to and the dead had been carried away. People spoke of the statue's fall in hushed whispers. Vassos listened, but he quickly realized that very few of the onlookers had seen the statue walk, as he had.

He began to question his own sanity as the days went on and people talked of the devastating earthquake. He wisely kept his impression of the statue walking, as if of its own free will, to himself. Very few folks had been up in the hills to see the entire event as he had, so the stories of how the bronze giant had made it so far from its original stance astride the harbor varied wildly.

But Vassos knew the truth. The mighty image of Helios had walked. He felt certain of one other thing too, and on this point he was in agreement with all of Rhodes. They would rebuild the statue, and it would be mightier than before.

But Vassos and the rest were wrong.

The statue's ruins would remain on the ground throughout Vassos's lifetime and for hundreds of lifetimes more. Then, centuries later, a man came with almost one thousand camels, which he traded for the ruins. He had workers slice the ruins apart and load them on several boats over the course of many days. The Colossus of Rhodes left the island in pieces and was never seen again. Rumors abounded of what the man would do with the cut up statue. Some said it was melted down, the bronze refashioned into coins. Others said the swarthy man took the statue to a distant land and had it reassembled. Others still said it was rebuilt only to be toppled again. But the rumors and theories soon abated when the land was attacked once again by invaders—this time from the Arab world. People had other worries now.

The last evidence of the statue, its plaque, which the buyer had callously left behind, disappeared some time during the

invasion. But its inscription was remembered in the words of poets and men of letters:

To you, o Sun, the people of Dorian Rhodes set up this bronze statue reaching to Olympus, when they had pacified the waves of war and crowned their city with the spoils taken from the enemy. Not only over the seas but also on land did they kindle the lovely torch of freedom and independence. For to the descendants of Herakles belongs dominion over sea and land.

INITIATIVE

ONE
Somewhere Deep Underground, 2013

The pain was everything.

Bound in darkness, the man's confinement was absolute. If the man's eyes were open or closed, he couldn't tell. He perceived no visual difference between the two states. He longed to speak, to use the words, to free himself from the never-ending agony. But his tongue was swollen and dry in his mouth. The dry heat of the room confining him had long ago sucked all moisture from his flesh.

His body—a modern miracle of his own scientific genius—would keep him alive, struggling against the damage caused by incessant heat and dry air. He was given the most meager amount of water daily. It was really just enough to keep him alive. Without the genetic tinkering to his DNA, he would have died long ago.

His body was a marvel, but there was only so much it could do. He needed to use his voice to escape his present confinement, but that ability was denied to him. Each day when the small, slow stream of liquid dribbled into his open and waiting mouth, he quickly swished it around his swollen tongue, hoping to moisten his mouth enough that he might speak the words. But while his mouth and tongue could make the movements, the breath needed

to vocalize the sounds never came to him. In the end, he would swallow the tiny portion of water, never feeling it hit his stomach, and the days would go on and on.

His last visit from his abusive captor had been, by his own reckoning, at least seven months ago. It was hard to keep track of the days, but he forced himself to do it anyway. Besides the daily struggle to speak, and his thoughts of the ways he would get revenge, maintaining a mental log of the days was the only thing to keep his mind off the pain.

His nervous system fired wave after wave of angry buzzing sensations into his brain, and the pain never stopped. He guessed he had not slept in close to a year—the pain was simply too much to endure. His mind could never rest enough to summon the elusive slumber.

Consciousness was both a blessing and a curse. At first, the agony was so much he thought he would lose his mind completely. But his body's miraculous healing abilities helped to keep him on the edge of sanity. He wondered whether his captor would know that. He wondered a lot of things about his tormentor.

Despite the constant pain, the man was sometimes able to focus his thoughts with a tremendous effort of will, blocking out the stimuli, allowing him to think and plan. These sessions were of varying duration, although in the dark and deep underground, he was never quite sure of elapsed time on a minute by minute or hourly basis. The one thing he knew without question was that the duration would be short, and afterward the waves of unending suffering would return. The surge of pain, when his willpower was finally exhausted, would be overwhelming, and he would silently scream for what he imagined was the rest of the day.

The thing that was more maddening than his imprisonment and torment was the location his captor had chosen for confinement. He knew exactly where in the world he was. He even knew the room. He should after all—it belonged to him. He was trapped in the bowels of a facility he'd designed and paid for, with no way out.

Yet.

He knew that sooner or later, someone would come to free him. He had planned for this contingency. He would have been foolish to even contemplate immortality without having a plan for incarceration. How horrible to be confined eternally. As terrible as his anguish was, he knew it would be finite. He had left the entirety of his escape plan with four different individuals, upon whom he could count implicitly. They would secure his release.

Then, armed with the words, his regenerating DNA and his allies, he would be free to seek out the final prize he sought. The item was so close to his present location. Just minutes away. With that object in his grasp, he would exact his revenge on his tormentor and then on the world. No one and nothing would stop him. He would be immortal. Immune to harm. And with the fabled power the item he sought—*invincible*.

The pieces would be falling into place on the surface. The last of his wealth would have been accumulated. Forces would be gathering. Traps would be springing. His opponents would be closing in, and his allies would be ready. He would pit them all against one another, and when they thought they had the upper hand, he would move in for the kill. His secret weapon waited, hiding in plain sight. He had transmitted the necessary information to his general, and no doubt, the different installations around the globe belonging to his key adversary would have been eliminated by now.

Soon, his adversary and torturer would be alone, his hideous failed experiments destroyed, his resources used up and even the Chess Team would turn against him. With a little luck, Jack Sigler and the adversary would kill each other.

TWO

Endgame Headquarters, New Hampshire

Jack Sigler was on his knees, in the worst pain of his life.

He had come up against a lot of opponents, and he had even faced unimaginable creatures and otherworldly threats, but the thing he hated the most was waiting. And worst of all was waiting for this. Right now, looking down at him as he held the small red velvet box aloft, Sara Fogg's face was unreadable. And Sigler's heart was breaking.

"I said, 'Will you marry me?' It's generally a yes or no kind of question." The broad smile that had been on his face the first time he'd uttered the question was slowly sliding off it now, like an indecisive snail. He could feel the smile. It had turned into a half-crazy leer as he forced it to remain on his face, while she looked down at him with no emotion showing on hers.

"Sara?"

"Jack, I... I... Stand up for a minute," she gently took his hand and helped him to stand, but he twisted and sat on the bed instead. She sat down next to him, and gently placed her hand on his face, turning it to look at her. "You know I love you, Jack."

"There's a 'but' coming. So this is a 'no?'" Sigler began.

"Hush. It's not a 'no', silly," Fogg smiled. "It's just that it's complicated. You know that. You have your life of danger, hunting terrorists and genetically engineered monstrosities, and I have my career with the CDC. We hardly see each other between your missions and my dealing with outbreaks in Africa and the jungles of Borneo. We catch up in hotel rooms around the world, or we spend a few blissful days here in your room in this bunker—with no windows even. And we're trying to raise a fifteen year old girl somehow in the midst of all this madness."

"I know," Sigler sighed. "I know it's not perfect. But these were never things I planned for. I had no idea Fiona would come into

my life. I never pictured myself as a parent. I never expected I'd fall in love with a woman who thinks I can sing well, because to her she smells roses instead of hearing a dog howl."

Fogg laughed and ran a finger through her dark hair. She had kept it short in the past, but she was growing it out now. The subject of her Sensory Processing Disorder had become a playful joke between them, when they had their few intimate moments.

"It actually smells like regurgitated orange peels, but I still love to see you do it—on those five or six times a year, when we actually get to shower together," her smile faded. "This is what I'm talking about. How are we supposed to be married to each other with our lives like they are? Our regular jobs aside, you're searching for your abducted parents, we're all constantly dealing with security like at the White House—"

"Actually," Sigler interrupted, "Endgame has better security than the White House..."

"I know, that's not the point," she stood and strode around the small room that served as Sigler's personal quarters. "I can't ask you to give up your life. Your work with Chess Team is too important. I get that, and so does Fiona. I could quit working for the CDC and just assist here, but even that isn't an ideal life. How do we make marriage work, when we're running for our lives from armed incursions and giant mutated spiders—"

"To be fair, there was just the *one* spider," Sigler pointed out.

"You know what I mean. I love you. And your foster daughter loves you. We have, despite all odds, built a family in this crazy world of yours. You live in this top-secret base in New Hampshire, with constant danger both here and abroad. You're hardly ever here. We cherish the days when we see you, but you and your sister are off on this hunt for a man who could be the historical *Hercules*, for God's sake." Fogg sat on the bed next to Sigler. She ran her fingers through his dark shaggy hair. "How exactly do you picture a marriage working?"

"Look Sara, I know it's not the normal life. I want it to be different too. Asya and I need to tie up this Hercules thing. You know that. The rest of the team are starting to wonder if I'm ever coming back. But even when this thing is done, there will always be times when we're apart for long stretches. It's just the nature of our jobs. We already talked about why I can't leave mine. I don't want you to have to leave your work either. You're good at it and you love it. What I wanted to do, was just cement our commitment to each other. There isn't anything we can do about the practical stuff, but I wanted you to know how serious I am."

Fogg leaned in and kissed him. When they parted, she looked up at him with tears glistening in her eyes, but no drops had yet fallen down her smooth cheeks. "I love you. You are a damn romantic fool, you know that? Yes, I'll marry you. I have no idea how we'll make it work, but yes."

He smiled. "Really?"

"Really."

THREE
Mountains North of Sonbong, North Korea

The view of the valley was a V shape, between two low green hills. The chemical weapons plant, a bland affair with slabs of rectilinear gray concrete and rolls of razor-wire fencing, stood in the middle of the valley. Several undernourished soldiers in bluish-gray uniforms walked glumly around the perimeter, but their patterns were lazy rather than random. Guard towers, like in a prison complex, occupied the four corners of the facility, but the men stationed in the towers were armed with old Soviet era AK-47 assault rifles, just like the men ambling around the perimeter. To the east, a small dirt road led back to the main tarmac and the town of Sonbong to the south.

From the hills, through the V, the facility looked like a target at the end of a long shooting gallery. The small grassy hillside held four oblong bushes, gray rocks and large tufts of brilliant green grass. When one of the bushes snickered, one of the others spoke.

"Rook, we're supposed to be undercover here. What's your problem?"

"Sorry, Queen," Stan Tremblay, callsign: Rook said, shifting in his ghillie suit. Like the other members of Chess Team, he had once been a Delta Operator. That changed when the team became part of a black budget, ultra-secret organization known as *Endgame*. The ghillie suit, made of netting and artificial foliage, made the wearer appear to be a shrub—provided the wearer stayed still. The effect when Rook moved was as if the bush had taken on a life of its own and rolled over on the ground. "It's hard to take these douchenozzles seriously. Plus, my ass is starting to ache."

The first bush that had spoken, Rook's teammate and current field leader, Zelda Baker, callsign: Queen, shifted as well. "They do seem pretty lazy, but the state of your ass is not my primary concern here."

Another bush spoke. "My ass is so asleep it's snoring." The third bush was larger than the others. The man inside, Erik Somers, callsign: Bishop, was a huge mountain of a man, yet generally the most patient and least talkative of the team. "When are these guys gonna do something? We've been up here in the hide for a month, and they still have yet to send out or receive a shipment. By the time something happens, my muscles might have atrophied."

"You too, Bishop? This is supposed to be deep cover. Quit breaking radio-silence, and stop moving." The bush that was Queen, shook briefly toward the top, and Rook could tell Queen was shaking her head back and forth in disgust, the way she frequently did at his antics.

They each wore small tactical radios, so they could communicate remotely. They had earpieces and thin microphones that

stuck to their throats with a gooey glue-like substance. But instead of relying on the radios, they were speaking out loud. If any North Korean soldiers had been in the vicinity, their position would have been given away. A softer voice spoke up now, from the receivers in their ears.

"At least you two still have asses. Mine fell off last week, and I've been looking for it ever since." Shin-dae Jung, callsign: Knight, the team's sniper, was in a different location, far closer to the weapons plant.

The bush that was Queen rolled over. "Sweet Jesus, is there no such thing as military bearing?"

Rook laughed, and his ghillie suit shook. Soon Bishop was snickering too. "Blue, seriously. What the hell? Why are we sitting here in the boonies? Either this place is or isn't concocting chemical weapons. Either way, let's blow it up and go home. Anything so I don't have to listen to these clowns anymore."

A softer, but more serious voice sounded through their earpieces.

"Sorry team. Gaining intel on this facility has been sketchy at best. Everything points to chemical weapons, but I've been reluctant to just send you in. Who knows what conditions are like in there. You might attack the place and wind up sucking in lungfuls of airborne weaponized anthrax. Or it could be a prison, and if you blow it up, you'd be killing hundreds of innocent civilians and protestors. Until we get some better intelligence, you're gonna have to stay put. I can't even offer you any satellite coverage on this one. North Koreans would go ballistic if they detected a satellite or a spy plane overhead. Best I can do is this remote communication. Their systems are not sophisticated enough to pick up our tactical radios, and even if they were, they'd never break the encryption." Tom Duncan, callsign: Deep Blue, the team's founder and handler, was back at their headquarters in New Hampshire. His voice was sympathetic, and none of the team would argue with the man. He was, after all, a former President of the United States.

"Maybe it's time we shook things up then," Queen said.

"What are you thinking, Queen?" Deep Blue's voice sounded concerned on the radio.

"Knight, how close are you to the building?" Queen asked.

"Did you see that guard on the southeast tower spit just now?" came the reply in their earpieces.

"Seriously?" Queen asked.

"It landed on my leg."

"Damn, Knight," Rook chuckled, then sat up and pulled his ghillie suit mask off his head. He turned to Bishop's location, only to find that Bishop had already removed his mask too. Over the last week, Knight had gotten more and more brazen with how close he crept to the building. He was now inside the lazy route the guards walked around the building, inching around as a bush that any of the guards should have noticed wasn't there the previous week.

"See if you can make your way toward the windows on the eastern side and we'll let you know when it's clear so you can stand up and peek in," Queen said, then she sat up and pulled her own mask off. "These damn things are stifling."

"Risky, but understandable. Good call, Queen. I'll check back with you in an hour. Deep Blue out."

With masks off, the three team members in the hills were still camouflaged. Their faces were painted with forest swirls of green and black, and both Queen and Rook wore black and green polyester buffs on their heads to hide their blonde hair. Bishop, with his chestnut Iranian-American skin, left his shaved bald head exposed, although it was painted with the same camo as his face. Rook procured an energy bar and tore the packet open. He began to munch on it, small pieces of the bar lodging in his month of heavy beard growth, which had begun as a carefully sculpted goatee, but was now a mess of hair thick enough for small creatures to nest in it. Bishop began stretching his shoulders, moving in small movements. Although he was over six thousand feet from the occasionally watchful eyes of the plant's guard

towers, he knew that sudden or large movements might attract the human eye. He was camouflaged enough for the distance, even without the ghillie mask, but he wouldn't tempt things with a big arm sweep. Queen lay down on the ground on her back, then flexed her neck sideways, procuring a loud pop as her cervical vertebrae realigned.

The three knew it would take Knight at least two hours to creep the thirty feet he needed to cover to get to the window on the east side of the building undetected. He was, after all, a shrub, to the eyes of the occasionally passing North Korean soldiers. He had to move in such tiny increments, that they would not even notice the movement, allowing the men time to adjust to the bush's location in their subconscious, so they wouldn't suddenly realize there shouldn't be a shrub under the window, when suddenly there was.

Knight was always amused at how the human mind worked. He loved the small subtle visual tricks you could play on the mind. He recalled a TV show he had seen where a person would be stopped on the street for directions, and while the person was answering, two men would carry a large piece of furniture between the asker and the askee, obscuring the asker from view. During the brief moment, where the workers moved the furniture, the asker would step away and another person would step in to receive the directions once the sofa or what-ever was past the scene. It was amazing that most people never noticed they were replying to a completely new person. As a sniper, Knight found many of these small lapses in human attention to his advantage. But even still, he knew it would take him some time to get to the window.

On the hill, Queen, Rook and Bishop sat silently, eating small vacuum-packed energy foods and drinking small sips of water from Camelbak water reservoirs hidden under their ghillie suits, the camouflage-painted drinking tubes secured to their shoulders, so a simple tilt of the head would allow them to grip the bite valves

with their mouths. Despite the brief lapse in protocol, the three stayed silent for most of the hour, lost in their own thoughts. When the first hour had nearly elapsed, a shrill voice shattered the silence.

"Ma! Eolleun il-eona!" The voice was high-pitched and screechy. Queen, Rook and Bishop turned to look behind them on the hill and saw a small squad of five North Korean soldiers, each armed with a fully automatic North Korean produced Type-58 version of an AK-47 rifle. Most of those weapons were pointed at the team, although some shook, the hands holding them unsteady. The men looked no more than eighteen years old, but it was difficult for Queen to tell their ages.

The man that had spoken, yelled again. "Eolleun il-eona!"

"Party's over," Rook said, slowly raising his hands above his head.

Knight's voice came over their earpieces. "He said 'Stop' and 'Get on your feet.' He sounds upset. I'd do what he says." Knight was of South Korean ancestry. He was fluent in the South Korean language, and it was similar in some respects to the language here, even though he had remarked that the North Koreans had challenging accents.

Queen slowly stood and looked at the five young terrified soldiers. "Wonderful," she said.

The man who had ordered them to stand began to shake violently with fear, the barrel of his rifle wavering and swerving, sweat running down his forehead. Then his rifle went off, sending a small burst of bullets at Queen.

FOUR
Endgame HQ, New Hampshire

Deep Blue stood up from his computer chair and stretched his lower back, twisting side to side, then he leaned forward and

touched his toes. He took pride in the fact that he was probably the only former US President who could touch his toes. He was young for an ex-president, and he had stayed in good shape through those grueling years. Then he had been forced to play a more active role in the field with Chess Team, reminding him that while he was exceedingly fit, he was still getting on in years. Injuries that would have been mild during his days as an Army Ranger took far longer to heal now. After the last major catastrophe the previous year, where searing spheres of energy had devastated several global population centers, he decided to officially retire himself from the field.

Besides, people in DC were starting to ask him as Tom Duncan, former US President, if he would undertake some humanitarian missions. He was genuinely interested in some, but he had needed to turn them all down.. As far as the world knew, he was simply retired and reclusive. Following the lead started by Jimmy Carter, and later by Richard Nixon in 1985, he was hardly the first former President to refuse secret service protection post-presidency. His stock excuse was that he was enjoying his time fishing and resting after the stress of four years in the White House and several years before that in the capitol.

In truth, his work with Endgame took up all his time. He had formed the organization to combat extreme forms of terrorism, but it had ended up becoming a full-scale assault force for dealing with viral outbreaks, genocidal madmen, marauding cryptids, dimensional incursions and rampaging rock creatures.

Now, just finding time to exercise was a challenge. With the bulk of Chess Team in North Korea, King and Asya frequently coming and going while looking for their abducted parents, keeping his global eye on possible hotspots around the world and assisting and advising with some of the reconstruction after the energy-portal fiasco the previous year, Tom Duncan was exhausted.

It was nearly 10:30 at night, but with the time difference in Korea, Duncan knew he would be awake for several more hours. He looked around the empty computer room. Lewis Aleman, his right-hand man and computer guru, had turned in, and the other staff members had gone home or to their on-station quarters to get some sleep. With little happening for Chess Team in Asia, and with King and Asya at the base, the other support members really weren't needed to keep tabs on things overnight. Plus, Duncan enjoyed working alone in the electronic womb of the command center.

The central computer room was kitted out with all the latest equipment he could get his hands on using the deep-black Pentagon budgets he had procured for the team before officially leaving office. Large flat-screen monitors lit up the walls, allowing him to keep an eye on the world from a multitude of satellites. He used surveillance cameras too numerous to count and too easily hacked. He even used video streams from field operatives equipped with hidden video cameras on their persons—both those they knew about and those they did not. In the intelligence game of the 21st century, it was all about the cameras.

Besides the large video screens, the room was filled with several workstations and ergonomic chairs. Air-conditioning systems even pumped in a slight scent of jasmine. In the corners of the room were several oxygenating peace lilies and philodendrons, whose vines stretched up to and across the ceiling. Both plants could exist off the artificial lighting in the room, with occasional bursts from solar simulator lamps. They helped to reduce the stress in the room visually, but they also pumped plenty of clean air into the space as well.

Duncan dropped down to the carpeted floor and performed twenty pushups. On the last repetition, he heard the door open.

"Seventy-eight..." he said.

When he looked up, Jack Sigler, callsign: King, was standing in the door with a goofy smile on his face.

"Yeah, right," King said.

"Even we desk jockeys have to stay in shape, Jack."

"You are the most in-shape desk jockey I've ever seen," King said.

Duncan stood and walked over to the door. "What's up?"

"Some good news for a change, Tom," King rarely used Deep Blue's first name, although Duncan had, on many occasions, encouraged him to do so, especially when they were alone. Duncan smiled expectantly. He had an idea what this might be.

"Sara and I are engaged," King said, his grin growing to epic proportions.

Duncan beamed, then hugged King. "Congratulations! That's fantastic! Does Fiona know yet?"

Fiona, King's foster daughter, was attending a boarding school nearby at Brewster Academy, where she stayed along with three rotating Endgame bodyguards.

"No, it just happened an hour ago," King said.

"You popped the question here at HQ? How *romantic*, Jack." Duncan raised a disapproving eyebrow.

"I didn't want to wait. Who knows when Asya and I will have to head out again on another false lead." King frowned.

Duncan placed his hand gently on his friend's shoulder. He knew that King was worried for the safety of his missing parents. The Siglers—*no, the Machtchenkos,* Duncan reminded himself. Their true name had been revealed once King had learned his parents were former Russian spies. They had been missing for several months now. Endgame assumed that Alexander Diotrephes, their former ally and now a possible enemy, held King's parents. But they had found no proof, and had seen no sign of Peter and Lynn Machtchenko. Nor had they been able to find Alexander, a man better known as the historical *Hercules*, who, although immortal, was no bastard child of Zeus. For months, King and his sister Asya had been following every lead, but they kept coming up empty.

"You'll find them. I know you will," Duncan said. Then, trying to bring the conversation back to the upbeat, he asked, "So when is the happy date?"

King looked up and grinned again.

"Actually, we—"

"I have hit 'Herculean Society' Jackpot!" Asya interrupted. She burst into the room, a living projectile fired from the hallway beyond. She was small and lithe, with long dark hair. Stunning to look at, but often deadly serious. She moved to a computer station and brought up an e-mail account.

Initially given the callsign: Hammer, by Queen, as both a nod to the woman's Soviet heritage and standing her own in a knock-down drag-out fight with Queen when the women first met in Norway, Asya's callsign was later changed by Deep Blue to a permanent Pawn status. Far from an insulting callsign, the designation was used for temporary team members in the field, but in this instance, it was an honor for Asya—a woman with only basic Russian infantry training—to be included as a long-term member of Chess Team, which was comprised of former Delta soldiers. Asya had made no complaints about the new callsign.

Now the small woman brought up a digital image of a building. "It is here," she said.

"What are we looking at?" Deep Blue asked. The photo showed the front of a European building with Roman style columns. A statue stood in front. In the foreground was a plaza full of umbrella-covered tables. It could have been any of a number of similar plazas all over Europe, where tourists and locals alike drank beer, ate pizza and ogled passing strangers.

King leaned closer to the image, and brushed his hand through his shaggy dark hair. "Looks like a library."

Asya turned to the men. "It is. National Library of Malta, in Valletta."

The woman turned back to the computer and brought up a second digital image. This one showed a drawing of the building, before the installation of the statue in front of it.

"1812. The library was moved to this building from a different location. Notice the circular arch in front of the entrance."

Both men had. A huge stone circular arch had been erected before the columns, making the two inner columns on either side of the door form the stylized letter H of the Herculean Society, a group of secretive people dedicated to helping Alexander Diotrephes hide certain historical truths and artifacts. King and Pawn had been searching for Society facilities for months, often finding empty office spaces, and in two instances discovering just recently vacated premises. They seemed to always be two steps behind, in their search for Alexander.

Pawn turned to the men and smiled widely. On the normally dour woman's face, the smile held a sinister look. "The arch was taken down after just two years. This was only image I could find with it. Queen Victoria statue was placed in the exact same location in 1891, covering up any evidence that the arch had ever even been there. If the Society people are not in the library..." She let the thought hang in the air.

"They might be under it," King finished for her. "Let's go." King turned and strode out of the room. Deep Blue watched him go. As Pawn neared the door, following her brother, he called out to her.

"Asya."

The woman turned.

"Take care of him. And get him to tell you the good news."

The woman nodded, then hurried after King. Duncan could hear her Russian-accented voice in the hallway as she asked, "What is good news? Blue says you have some."

Duncan smiled. He hoped the lead in Malta would finally go somewhere. Then he turned back to the ergo chair he liked best, a swiveling thing that resembled a dental patient chair, with a split keyboard on either side, touch screen controllers that swung in front of the user and comfortable memory foam seating from head to toe.

He activated his radio for the Chess Team members in North Korea and immediately heard rapid gunfire. His good mood was crushed as his heart began to race.

FIVE
North Korea

"You little shit!"

Queen looked down at her left hip and saw her blood starting to soak through the artificial fabric of the ghillie suit. She looked back up incredulously at the shaking North Korean soldier. "You fucking shot me."

The wound was shallow—just a nick for Queen, who had taken far worse injuries, but the fact that the soldier had unintentionally loosed six rounds in her direction, made her furious. Most of the bullets had gone into the soil around her, but the one had creased her hip.

The soldiers were shouting at each other now in a heated argument, and Queen quickly determined that no one was in charge. She could probably kill all five with only her hands before they got off another shot, but amateurs were often unpredictable. It made them dangerous. So she hesitated. Plus, she knew Rook had something special in store for them.

Instead of moving toward the men, she took a step backward.

The men ceased arguing and they all trained their weapons more carefully at her. Behind her, she could hear Bishop breathing slowly and regularly.

"Geulaeseo?" she asked in Korean, based on Knight's radio advice. *So? What now?*

"Son deul-eo!" the soldier that shot her screamed.

"Hands up," Knight translated in her ear.

Queen squinted at the man.

"Quee-eeen," Rook implored her from behind.

"SON DEUL-EO!"

Queen spat on the ground and stared at the man.

"Bil-eo meog-eul!" the man shouted and stepped forward. As he did so, his ankle pushed against a cleverly concealed tripwire Rook had placed, attached to a modified trigger device. The ground in front of the soldier exploded upward with an ear-shattering boom, the C4 explosive in the M18A1 Claymore mine spraying one-eighth inch diameter steel balls directionally through all five North Korean soldiers, effectively turning the young men into little more than perforated meat bags. The five soldiers were dead as their shattered remains collapsed on the grassy hillside with wet thumps. Queen and the others, on the far side of the device, were blown backward by the blast's pressure wave. They were spared from the hail of projectiles because they launched in just one direction—toward the enemy.

"Queen, what's going on?" Deep Blue's voice came over the radio.

"Communication difficulties. These guys can't read English." Queen stood and brushed dirt off her face.

"Explain," Deep Blue's voice came back, frustrated.

"Three little words..." Queen began.

Rook chuckled, thinking of the words stamped on the front casing of the Claymore. "Front toward enemy."

"Target confirmed," Knight's voice came over the radio.

"You have visual?" Deep Blue asked, before Queen could do the same.

"Affirmative," Knight said. "I'm bugging out while everyone is distracted by the blast and heading for you guys."

Queen turned to Bishop. "Light it up."

Bishop stepped over to the fourth bush on the hill. A camouflage net, similar to his own ghillie suit, covered the ground, forming the artificial bush. He pulled it back, revealing an AGS-40 Balkan automatic grenade launcher. For this mission, the team had been

equipped with primarily Russian armaments, with the exception of Rook's mines. Each member of the team had SR-3 Vikhr machine guns, but Bishop had decided to bring a little something extra. The Balkan was a tripod-mounted beast that looked like a forward slung cannon, with a giant green side drum that held a chain of caseless 40 mm grenades. He opened fire now on the facility down in the valley. The launcher had a maximum effective range of over 8000 feet, and he was well within that distance.

"Better run, Knight," Bishop said calmly. With each pull of the trigger, another grenade was fired down the valley, creating a deep *plunk* noise. The weapon had a firing rate of 400 rounds a minute, but Bishop was shooting leisurely, targeting the guard towers first, then the center of the concrete building. Plumes of orange flame and thick black smoke erupted from the chemical weapons factory, as grenade after grenade exploded in the distance. Soon it was impossible to even see the former facility through all the smoke.

When they heard weapons fire down the slope in front of them, Rook sprayed down the hill with his Vikhr. The few soldiers down the slope ran in all directions without focus, as soon as they realized they were under fire. Then Bishop angled the Balkan down the hill at them, and sent off a few rounds for good measure. He watched as four of the ill-trained soldiers went airborne, grenades detonating all around them, ending lives in an eruption of fire and soil.

"I almost feel sorry for them," Bishop said.

Queen stepped up next to him, firing down the hill with single shots, eliminating anything that moved. "Fuck 'em. Play with chemical weapons, you get burned."

Rook stopped firing, sensing the battle was pretty much done. They would need to hustle a few miles to the south and get to the sea, before reinforcements were called to the area. "I think their real mistake was shooting at you. Must be one of the quickest ways to get dead."

"Aww, hon, you know how to flatter a girl," Queen said with a grin.

"You know it," Rook said and turned to help Bishop pack up the Balkan and their supplies.

"Knight, where are you?" Queen asked.

"I'm already on the other side of you guys. I'll try to provide cover as you make for the boat."

"Copy that. We're moving." With that, Queen turned and began to run for the shore. Rook hefted a supply pack and followed her. Bishop collapsed the tripod, and lifted the still warm barrel of the Balkan over his shoulder, then followed them at a jog.

"Queen, the jet will be providing your distraction in twenty minutes. You better hustle." Deep Blue was referring to a stolen Chinese jet they had acquired that would be firing rockets five miles east of them. With the chemical weapons facility so close to the Chinese border, the plan had always been to implicate the Chinese in the attack, and to focus the North Korean forces toward the border, while the team slipped out to sea on a Zodiac inflatable, to rendezvous with their submarine they'd dubbed the *Kraken*. Once safely out in international waters, the sub would surface and the team would be collected with a vertical take off and landing (VTOL) troop transport, the team had rechristened *Crescent II*. The plane would take them back to New Hampshire at supersonic speeds, while the submarine would move on to the next hotspot.

"Copy. Twenty minutes." As she said it, a small group of soldiers came up over the rise in front of her. "Better make that twenty-five."

SIX
Luqa Airport, Malta

King stretched his lower back as he stood in the immigration line next to his sister. He was still getting used to the idea after all these months that he had another sister. He had grown up with his American

sister, Julie, who had joined the service and died in a plane crash. But after he discovered that his parents had led double lives as Russian spies, he had met Asya, a sister he never knew. She had been raised in Russia, but had been aware of him.

His emotions were mixed about Asya. She was wonderful, and he was learning to love her as a sister, but she also brought up painful memories for him over the death of Julie, and the betrayal he felt over his parents' deception. Each time he thought he had learned all there was to know about Peter and Lynn Machtchenko, the more they felt like strangers. But through all his feelings of hurt over their keeping secrets from him, his thoughts quickly came back to the fact that they were being held by Alexander Diotrephes. The circular train of thoughts, from Asya to Julie, to their parents, and back to Alexander, made it easy for King to keep his mind off his bizarre family tree and on business. Asya, with equal parts determination and typical Russian stoicism, seemed fine with that nature to their relationship. She had been thrilled when he had told her of his engagement to Sara, but within minutes, she was back to business, discussing this latest lead with him.

After a Maltese official in uniform, who looked no older than seventeen, stamped their passports, King turned to Asya and handed her a thick wad of US hundred dollar bills. "Why don't you get us some Euros, and I'll go talk to the guy at the information desk."

She took the money without a word and strode over to an HSBC bank counter.

King walked toward the front of the airport arrivals area. He had no baggage to collect, just the small carry-on North Face duffel bag he carried. Near the front of the hall, he found the circular information counter, with one man seated behind it. The man had a square jaw and a hard look to him. King pegged the man as British immediately, even before he spoke.

"Can I help you, sir?"

King approached the counter. No other passengers were in the area, most still back collecting their bags from the conveyor-belt carousels.

"I was wondering if you could tell me how many tourists Malta gets in a year," King said with a grin.

"One point two million a year," the man replied immediately.

"I was hoping for something closer to five," King replied, sounding disappointed.

The man stood and slid a small cardboard box across the counter toward King, on top of which he placed a tourist map. As he pointed to the map, he said, "I think you'll find nine is a better number."

King thanked the man, took the box and the map, and turned to walk toward Asya, who was just returning from the exchange counter.

"I have money," she told him.

"I have something better. Let's go get a car."

They quickly arranged for a rental car, dissuading the attendant of his notion that they would need a driver. Once they reached the privacy of their rental car, King opened the box, and removed two MP-443 Grach pistols. He recognized these as the modern Russian 9mm sidearm. They were more commonly called *Yarygins*. He handed one to Asya, and she quickly chambered a round from the seventeen in the magazine. He did the same. Then he chuckled.

"What is funny?" Asya asked him.

"You know this weapon?"

"Yes, *Pistolet Yarygina*. Why is this funny?"

"Also called a Grach. Or *Rook*. It's Deep Blue's way of making a joke about how we are on this wild goose chase for our parents and not out helping the team." He started the engine of the gray Mercedes sedan. The car barely made a noise.

"Blue is...a complicated man." Asya turned away from him slightly as she spoke, but King saw her cheeks flush. Realization dawned on him.

"Oh my God, you have the hots for him," he laughed.

"I do not have hots," she said, still facing the window.

King laughed harder as he brought the sedan out into traffic on the main road, passing a McDonald's. They would need to drive about five miles to get across the main island of Malta, to reach the capital, Valletta. He opened the windows on both sides of the car, letting the warm Mediterranean air wash over them. He was looking forward to getting to the coast, so he could see the brilliant blue hues of the sea, which had looked so stunning from the air.

The traffic was thick, but they made it to Valletta in good time. After a twenty minute search, King found a place to park the car. They walked along Republic Street to the plaza in front of the library, which was packed with tourists having lunch at the many umbrella-shaded tables. King wore his signature outfit: jeans and a simple black t-shirt with the King of Rock 'n' Roll, showing his back to the audience, and holding a microphone in his hand. King guessed he now had close to a hundred different Elvis t-shirts. It was the only thing he collected, besides scars. Tucked under the shirt, in the waistband of his jeans, he carried the Yarygin.

Asya walked next to him, her long dark hair up in a ponytail. She wore a light blue blouse and a tight black pair of jeans. King didn't know where she carried her gun, but he knew she had it on her somewhere. Maybe in the small purse-like backpack she wore.

The white umbrellas over the tables all read *Café Cordina* on the flaps, and the chairs were a strange mix of plastic patio furniture and woven wicker backs. A long aisle had been left down the center of the plaza, leading to the statue of Queen Victoria in front of the library's doors. Currently, the statue's head was mobbed with about five white and gray pigeons, all jostling each other for the best perch on the Queen's noggin. Above it all, high on the roof of the library building, the Maltese red and white flag flapped loudly against its flag pole.

Above the doorframe, the word BIBLIOTHECA was carved and inlaid with gold. King also noted a ridiculous number of CCTV

cameras clustered over the arch, but most pointed outward toward the crowd in the plaza.

"Ten cameras is excessive," Asya stated, and once again, King was startled to find how similar he was to this woman that had grown up on the other side of the world from him.

They passed through the stone columns and in through the library's main entrance. King's eyes took a moment to adjust to the lower light. The floor was a zigzagging pattern of green and white marble. He spotted what he was looking for as soon as he entered the room.

Asya looked at the long tables and the walls lined with wooden bookshelves. The main chamber was a huge rectangular room, running to their left and right, the length of the building. Although several windows allowed light to pour into the space, he and Asya both had pink spots in their vision from having been outside in the brighter sunshine.

"Where should we begin?" Asya asked.

King pointed down to the floor, just inside the door, where the green and white marble had been laid in the H symbol of the Herculean Society.

"I'm going to say we should look for stairs to a basement."

SEVEN
Endgame Headquarters, New Hampshire

Tom Duncan stood by the open hangar door, as he always did when the team returned from a mission. He would be present to greet them unless there was a dire situation somewhere that required him to be in operations, where his computers and a connection to the world waited for him. He knew that King and Asya would have only just touched down in Malta, so as the morning sun streamed in the massive hangar door, he smiled warmly for the returning field team.

They came roaring up in a black Land Rover, driven by the team's new head of security, Quinton Saunders. Saunders was yet another steal from the 10th Mountain group at Fort Drum. Duncan had sent the man to collect the team from Laconia airport, where their transport plane would slip in and then be hidden away in a private hangar. Although the vehicle had VTOL capabilities, there was nowhere near the Endgame Headquarters, which was built in sections under several mountains, to keep the plane. The hangar in which Duncan stood normally housed two Black Hawk helicopters—both of which were being upgraded at Fort Devens, down in Massachusetts.

Rook was the first to emerge from the vehicle, and Duncan was surprised to see the month-long growth of blonde beard on the man's face. Combined with Rook's bulk, the overall effect made him look like a wild mountain man.

"Rook, good to see you. If that really is you past all that hair," Duncan said.

"It's coming off today. I'll be glad to have a proper shave."

Bishop, Queen, Knight and Saunders, the new callsign: White Zero, all stepped out of the vehicle, and onto the concrete floor of the wide hangar.

"You could have shaved in the field, like I did," Bishop said.

"I'm just wondering how come we never saw Knight shave," Rook replied.

"I'm Korean. Our hair is trained to grow only where we want it to." Knight smiled, then headed off toward the far end of the hangar.

"Queen, anything you want to tell me?" Duncan asked.

"We were lucky. A small patrol stumbled up on us, just as Knight was moving in to take his look. He'll tell you all about the interior from the look he got, but the intel was righteous. Bishop took it down, and we got the hell out of there. Better intel would have made a month-long stakeout an afternoon takedown." She shook her blonde hair out of a ponytail, and a long swath of it fell across the branded scar she bore on her forehead, covering it.

"Sorry about that. Sometimes we have to go on what we have. I'm glad it turned out alright." Duncan replied. He put his hand on her shoulder. "You were wounded?"

"A scratch," Queen dismissed it. "How are the North Koreans taking it?"

They turned to walk toward the far end of the hangar as they talked. Bishop and Rook had gone on ahead, and Saunders had taken the Rover back out to handle another matter.

"As you might expect. Saber-rattling at both China and Russia, because they don't know who did it. They'll turn their venom on us by tomorrow, whether they have any inkling it was us or not. They always do. They'll threaten to nuke us, and the UN will level more sanctions at them, and it'll blow over. But there will be one less chemical plant in their hands."

"And how long will it take them to build another one?"

Duncan sighed. "Estimates are one month."

"That's not a good ratio. One month to take them down and one month to build them?"

"I know. Some days I feel like we need ten Chess Teams."

A shrill alarm rang out throughout the base, with a red light circulating on the hangar ceiling. The steel door to the hangar began to close on its hydraulic pumps. Five soldiers wearing woodland-camouflage battle dress uniforms (BDUs) raced past

Duncan and Queen toward the guard shack on the side of the main hangar door.

"What's this now?" Queen asked.

Duncan touched a Bluetooth earpiece. "White Zero, what's going down?"

"Sir, we have footage of three intruders on the perimeter of the base. Just down the road from Central. We're looking for them now. Teams are reporting in from Labs and the Dock, but it looks like it was just the three guys." White Zero sounded out of breath.

The base was a sprawling underground affair in three sections. On a map, the three main sections of the facility formed a capital letter A. High speed trains, hidden underground, connected each section of the appropriated base. This section was designated *Central*, and it contained the hangar, the computer rooms and surveillance equipment that Duncan would use to orchestrate Chess Team field operations and a variety of smaller labs and offices. Central sat at the top point of the letter A. The lower left of the A was a section designated *Labs*, because it mostly contained those. That was the section of the base the team had first encountered when the whole base belonged to the megalomaniac Richard Ridley. Finally, the lower right leg of the A-shape was the *Dock*, because the team kept a captured submarine there—the same Russian Typhoon class the team had used to escape North Korea. The sub reached the New Hampshire sea coast through a series of massive natural flooded tunnels and caverns.

The base had initially caused Duncan no end of headaches, because he first needed to get the Army to help clear it of chemical and biological weapons. After Chess Team had begun to move in, they had fought off an incursion of hostile forces and mutated creatures, while Duncan had been trapped inside and his security forces had been trapped outside. Since then, he had been continually beefing up security. Now three men had just sauntered up to the front door of his top-secret base. Duncan wasn't happy.

Queen reached over to a nearby desk and picked up a radio earpiece. She placed it in her ear and listened in on the conversation.

"Zero, who are these guys?" Duncan asked, irritation creeping into his voice.

"No idea, sir," came the reply. "But, they looked pretty weird."

"Define *weird*." Deep Blue was racing for the main computer operations room, and Queen was at his side, her firearm out. Once in his chair, Deep Blue could use the vast security systems as his disposal to find the intruders faster than White Zero could on foot.

"They look the same. Three guys in white business suits," came White Zero's reply.

Queen and Duncan exchanged glances as they reached the door to the central computer lab.

"They all have bald heads too. In the footage I'm seeing, they look like triplets." White Zero's voice sounded confused.

Deep Blue opened the door and then stopped dead. The room was mostly dark, but the lights had been on when he left. Queen read his body language and had her pistol up in front of her. She stepped in front of Deep Blue, motioning for him to remain shielded at the side of the doorway. Unarmed, he complied.

Queen began to enter the mostly darkened room. There was one recessed light in the ceiling, dimly lit, and shining down on the central computer chair in the room. A tall man with a bald head sat in the chair. He wore a fine white linen suit, and a huge shit-eating grin on his face.

"Richard Ridley," Queen said, her gun trained on the maniac's face.

"Not quite who you were expecting, eh, Ms. Baker?" The man's grin grew wider. Two men stepped out of the shadows behind the chair to stand on either side of Ridley. Each man looked exactly like the other.

They were all the same man.

They were all Richard Ridley.

EIGHT
Valletta, Malta

King was ready to give up. The dreary basement of the library held several hundred cardboard boxes of books, and rows and rows of dusty metal shelving. He felt like he was looking through a haystack and wasn't even sure he was after a needle.

"There must be something," Asya said. He could tell she was losing her patience too.

They had been in the basement for over an hour, looking at the boxes, the walls, the ceiling and the floor, for any sign that the Herculean Society had been here, or that they had at least stored something here. But short of going through all the boxes, King had no idea what his next move was.

"Should we open boxes? That assistant librarian might be back at any moment. If she's looking for something further from the stairs next time, we will have nowhere to hide." As usual, Asya was thinking what he was thinking.

"It won't be in the boxes. It'll be something more secretive, and it'll probably be marked in some way, like the floor upstairs—" King stopped and he squinted, thinking hard about the layout of the building, as he had viewed it since he entered.

"You only squinch your nose like that when you have idea," Asya told him.

King turned to her and smiled. "Squinch?"

"I am trying to sound more American."

"Let's go back upstairs. I might have an idea."

Asya followed King up a spiral metal staircase to the main lobby of the library. They slipped quietly through the door and wandered back into the larger part of the hall, as casually as if they were just returning from the restroom.

King scanned the long hall, then turned his eyes up to the second story balcony that ran around the entire room. There were more shelves up there, and several small windows that let golden sunlight stream into the echoing chamber. Asya watched him look, then turned her own eyes up. She pointed to the spot on the balcony directly above the front door—and above the Herculean Society symbol on the floor.

"Was up, not down," she said.

"Yep. Up," King moved to another circular staircase. This one was in the corner of the large hall, and the ironwork along the railing was far more ornate than on the stairs to the basement, with small sections painted in gold leaf.

At the top, they navigated past the occasional book browser, along the carpeted floor of the balcony to the spot above the main hall's doors. King glanced around the space. It was a small reading nook with a chair and a low table. Nothing fancy. He leaned over the balcony's rail and looked down at the H on the floor below. Then he looked both ways along the balcony. No one was on this side of the second floor. He quickly turned and started searching every inch of the wall behind him, sliding the chair aside, and looking behind the table. Asya casually leaned on the rail watching him. Finally he stood straight and faced the wall, scratching his head.

"I don't see it," King said.

Standing slightly behind him, close to the rail, Asya swept her hand up and smacked King in the back of his head. He whipped around and looked at her, more in irritation than pain.

"Use your eyes," she said. Then she pointed her thumb over her shoulder. "That way."

King looked across the space to the railing on the other side of the library's second floor. An identical reading nook mirrored the one in which he stood, with one major difference. On the far wall, behind the chair, and at head level for anyone standing in King's position, was yet another small stylized H symbol, this time carved into the wooden surface of the wall molding.

King mentally kicked himself. He had stood here first and looked down at the symbol on the floor, and looked sideways down both lengths of the balcony, but he hadn't bothered to look across the beautiful library and seen what was right in front of him.

"I'm starting to be glad we didn't grow up together," he grumbled, then started to walk the perimeter of the balcony.

Asya chuckled softly and walked after him. Once on the other side, the first thing King did was look back at the first nook—just in case. Then he zeroed in on the wooden molding on the wall. There was a nearly imperceptible groove around the circular part of the symbol. King grasped the uprights of the stylized H with his fingers and twisted. The entire symbol slid clockwise with a smooth wood against wood scuffing noise. King glanced down the balcony and saw only one other patron on the second floor with them.

"Go," Asya said.

King twisted the H the remainder of the distance until he had spun the symbol a full 180 degrees. A soft *thunk* sounded, and the wooden wall swung back on invisible hinges, revealing a tiny door in the wall behind the chair. Asya slid the chair aside, and King stepped up to the door. It was just slightly more than a foot in width, and only about four feet tall. He had to put his head in first, and then slip in sideways.

Once inside, he was in complete darkness. He reached back on the inner wall behind him as Asya slipped into the doorway, pulling the chair back to its original position as she came. King's fingers brushed across a plastic panel, and he flicked the light switch. A long row of ceiling-mounted fluorescent bulbs illuminated the room. It was a narrow brick passageway, the walls having long ago been painted a shade of white, but the paint was peeling and crumbling now. Asya pulled the door nearly to the closed position and examined the rear of it for a similar handle. She found an identical one in wooden trim that had been painted the same shade of off-white as the

corridor, but the handle was smudged from years of dirty fingers. They wouldn't be locked in. Asya pushed the door gently until it clicked in place.

King pulled his Yarygin and walked cautiously to the end of the tunnel. He noticed the floor declined a bit, but certainly not enough to take them to ground level. Along the way, he checked every inch of the ceiling, wary of traps. Although Alexander and his Herculean Society specialized in protecting—and in some cases obscuring—antiquity, he knew the man was not above using cutting edge technology to do so. King was expecting security traps or, at the very least, CCTV cameras. Instead, he found only the painted brick tunnel.

After about seventy feet, the tunnel ended at a T-intersection. King checked for cameras. Still surprised to find none, he looked in both directions. Fluorescents ran the length of the cross tunnel. At one end was what appeared to be a small room with dark gray metal file cabinets. The other end of the tunnel was in darkness. King looked into the gloom for a long moment.

Then he turned and walked toward the room with the file cabinets. Asya followed, checking behind her as she walked, her own Yarygin in hand.

The room was ten foot square, and as with the tunnel, King found no sign of cameras. The floor was rough, unfinished concrete. The room had no furniture, only seven large black file cabinets. At a quick glance, King could tell they were all unlocked.

"Why is there no security?" Asya asked.

"Uh-huh," King said, moving toward the cabinet in the middle of the room.

"Why that one?"

"Gotta start somewhere. M. Roughly in the middle of the alphabet." King smiled at her. "Figured I'd see what he had on Manifold. Be ready for shit to go haywire."

King grasped the handle of the top drawer and gently pulled, just a half an inch. He checked for tripwires inside the drawer, but

he found only hanging green folders. He pulled the drawer out further and saw that the files were all for names starting with the letter L. He didn't recognize most of the names. The few he did recognize seemed innocuous: Labor Smart, Inc., Labwire, Lepenica, Lico. He slid the drawer closed and repeated the safety check on the next drawer. It was the M drawer. Close to the front, he found what he was looking for. *Manifold Genetics.*

He pulled the thick folder out and laid it gently on top of the cabinet. He soon saw the documents weren't going to be much use to him. Most of the text was in Greek. What little was in English, was mostly what he knew already. Manifold Genetics was a biotech and genetic engineering firm, owned by the madman Richard Ridley. King and Chess Team had gone against the company and stopped them when they had discovered the head of the Lernaean Hydra buried in the sands of Nazca, Peru. Ridley had been cooking up designer soldiers, and Chess Team had put an end to it, appropriating one of Ridley's labs in New Hampshire, and destroying two more in South America and on an island in the Atlantic. The file had US news clippings from the attack on Fort Bragg, when Ridley had reared his head again. But with Alexander's help that time, Ridley had been shut down.

There were what appeared to be telephone transcripts—but in Greek—and photocopies of ownership documents, scientific formulas and all manner of material that King suspected would have been incredibly useful for the team when they had needed to stop Ridley. The intelligence would be invaluable, once they got it all translated. He was about to close the file and slip it into his shirt when the corner of a map slid out from under the stack of documents. King pinched the tip of it with his fingers and slid it out. The map showed the world, with five locations marked in black Greek letters. Although King wasn't fluent in Greek, he and the rest of Chess Team had all spent the last few years studying up on ancient mythology, archeology, history and ancient languages. He was familiar with the Greek alphabet, even though he couldn't read full

words. And in this case, the meaning of these letters was obvious. In New Hampshire, the Greek letter Alpha denoted the former Manifold installation that Endgame now called their headquarters. In South America, King saw the letter Beta was crossed out with a circle and a slash mark in red permanent pen. Gamma, on Tristan da Cunha in the Atlantic Ocean was likewise marked as finished. In the Ukraine, King saw the letter for Delta was also crossed out.

King tapped it with his finger and said, "Queen dealt with this facility when she was looking for Rook."

"And this one?" Asya asked, pointing to the fifth black Greek letter.

It was the symbol for Omega, and over the top of it, the person with the red pen had drawn the Herculean Society symbol. Under that, the word *Carthage* had been written in a smooth cursive script.

King heard a low guttural growl coming from the corridor behind them, in the dark.

"That's where we're going if we get out of here alive."

A second growl came out of the dark at the end of the tunnel, and then the fluorescent bulbs at the far end went out. Then the next set went dark. King and Asya moved to either side of the open doorway, their weapons trained on the end of the tunnel as the darkness advanced toward them.

NINE
Endgame Headquarters, New Hampshire

"**Clones,**" **Queen said** with disgust.

She stood in the room, with three perfectly identical copies of Richard Ridley seated before her. The original Ridley was a robustly tall man, with a gleaming bald head and a menacing smile. She recalled the man's likeness. As she looked at the three seated men,

she could detect nothing to indicate she wasn't looking at three of him. They were perfect replicas of Ridley in every way.

The three men sat in metal chairs that had been hastily bolted to the floor. Their hands were cuffed to the backs of the chairs with industrial-strength plastic zip ties and metal handcuffs. Bishop, Knight and Rook stood behind Queen, each armed and suited up for battle, their weapons trained on the triplets. To the side of the room, another five armed Endgame soldiers, wearing battle armor, held M-16s trained on the seated duplicates.

"We prefer 'divinely created persons,' actually," said the Ridley seated in the middle. "My name is Seth."

"I'd *prefer* to put my boot up your—" Rook spoke up.

"Rook," an electronically modulated voice came over the black speakers tucked up into the corners of the interrogation room. "That's no way to treat our guests."

Seth smiled. "Ah, the mysterious Deep Blue, at last. Or maybe I should be calling you the Man of the—well, no, you're not the Man of the Hour anymore. What *do* they call former presidents, Mr. Duncan?"

"Not sure what you're talking about. You can call me Deep Blue for now," came the electronic response.

Queen was stunned. Blue's identity as former President of the United States, Tom Duncan, was a closely guarded secret, and on the few times the man had appeared in public as Deep Blue, he had worn a tactical battle suit with a helmet and a tinted faceplate. He had been out of sight in the hallway when they had discovered the Ridleys in Ops, and Blue's own checks of the computer system had revealed that although they had entered the room, they had not accessed any of the cameras in the base. There was no way they could have seen Deep Blue's face. The fact that Ridley—Seth— had Deep Blue's operational callsign, and that he even knew of Deep Blue's existence, was bad enough. That they knew his true identity meant that somewhere, someone else knew it too, and the original Richard Ridley had gotten his hands on the information

somehow. Queen imagined Blue's mind was reeling right now, but the electronically altered voice remained flat.

"You haven't introduced your companions, Seth."

"Quite right. My brothers Enos and Jared were not created quite as well as I was. Jared cannot speak, and Enos is mostly deaf."

Queen tried to discern some distinguishing mark so she could keep the three clones straight, but they were all even wearing the same white linen suit.

Deep Blue's voice came over the speakers again. "So we are to understand that the three of you were created by Richard Ridley—the original—when he briefly had access to the mother tongue? When he was trying to enslave the world? Why would he do that?"

Seth smiled again. "Which? Why would our Creator make us or why would He try to enslave humanity?"

"Can I shoot him now? Dumb and Dumber can answer the questions. This one is raising my hackles." Rook stepped forward, leveling a .50 caliber Magnum Desert Eagle at Seth's face.

"Stand down, Rook," Deep Blue said. "We might need all three of them alive."

"These guys aren't even really alive," Rook said. "They're just animated heaps of clay. Shooting them in the head would be like shooting a rock, only more fun."

"Agreed," Deep Blue replied. "But let's see what they have to say for themselves."

Rook stepped back.

Seth smiled at the reprieve.

"But if I don't like what I hear in response to my next question, you can start cutting off his fingers."

Rook smiled. "Then I'm going to make a Kmart run. Pick up a Play-Doh Sweet Shoppe. Make me some Ridley-clone ice cream cones."

The smile vanished from Seth's face. Queen smiled softly, looking at Rook. Then she turned back to Seth. She knew the question Deep Blue would ask, and she wanted the answer just as badly as everyone else.

"Is Richard Ridley alive?" Deep Blue asked.

"We wouldn't be here otherwise," Seth said.

"Where is he?"

When the voice came through the speakers, even though Queen knew the modulator both disguised Deep Blue's voice and removed any traces of emotion, she still thought the question sounded stern.

Seth's face darkened as he looked at the floor. "He is being held prisoner."

"*Where?*" The volume of Deep Blue's voice increased with his urgency. It was clear that he thought he'd have to fight for the answer to this question. The truth was less dramatic and deprived Rook of the pleasure of knocking out a few teeth.

"A former Manifold facility in North Africa."

"Bullshit," Queen spoke up. "He's dead and buried."

Seth looked up at her and sneered. "He is immortal. He could live forever with the mother tongue, even without His genetic enhancements." Seth looked hard at her. "I know our Creator lives because we three are still alive."

"Explain," came Deep Blue's voice over the speakers.

"If He were to die, the command He gave in the mother tongue, the command that granted my brothers and me life, would end. We would return to the inert elemental materials from which we were formed. As all things do in time. But we yet live. So you see, Richard Ridley lives, too."

"Assuming we believe you, that Ridley is alive and being held prisoner, why are you here?" Deep Blue's voice buzzed.

"That should be obvious," Seth said. "We want you to liberate Him."

Enos nodded vigorously on Seth's right. Jared sat stone still, unsmiling.

"You have gotta be kidding me," Rook said.

"I'd sooner put Willie Nelson's greasy hair between my legs and light it on fire," Queen joined in.

Seth grinned, finding humor in the visual. "Nevertheless, I suspect you will all aid us in this endeavor."

Queen leaned forward, hands on her knees, all trace of humor gone. "Richard Ridley is a megalomaniac who raised and loosed an ancient horror on the world. He extinguished countless endangered languages by murdering their last remaining speakers. He brought chaos and hellfire to the world in the form of giant golems, and he personally attempted on more than one occasion to kill members of this team *and* our loved ones. Sometimes in very painful ways. If there is such a thing as the Devil, your creator is the closest I've ever seen to him. Why would we possibly want him free?"

Seth turned to face his two brothers, then turned back to face the members of Chess Team. All three brothers smiled. This time, the smile was wicked.

"I haven't told you who holds Him prisoner, or why. As dangerous as you might believe our Creator to be, there is a man who is even more troubling. That man holds Ridley Prime prisoner. That man... He is a threat to every man, woman and child on this planet. *That* man's megalomaniacal schemes for world domination make Ridley Prime's ambitions appear miniscule by comparison.

"Why would we come here and ask Chess Team to help us liberate our Master? Because our Creator, Richard Ridley, is the only man alive who can save the world."

TEN
Valletta, Malta

King held his fire until the darkness moved. He fired two shots, then waited. Asya held her fire beside him. The booming of the gun inside the tight confines was excruciating, and they needed to conserve their limited ammunition. Plus, he didn't know if bullets would even affect the things.

And they *were* things. He'd had enough experience with the unexplainable to recognize it when he saw it, or in this case, didn't see it.

Only two fluorescent bulbs were still lit at King's end of the connecting cross-tunnel. He briefly considered making a rush into the dark for the side tunnel, but dismissed the idea. He knew what waited for them in the dark.

"The Forgotten," he said.

"What?" Asya shouted. They were both suffering from the hearing loss associated with him firing his weapon in these tight confines.

"The Forgotten," he said louder.

"The wraith-like things that serve Hercules?" Asya asked. She'd been briefed on the team's previous missions, their enemies, allies and all the strangeness they'd encountered over the years.

From the shadows in the hall in front of them, they heard a guttural growl, as if in affirmation.

"They don't like light," King said, his Yarygin still aimed down the hallway at the blackness. Of the two bulbs still lit along the ceiling, the second one was flickering. He hadn't noticed it with all the others on before, but now with just the two, its erratic behavior was obvious. It flickered and strobed, tossing its light around the confined space of the white-washed hall. Then it extinguished. Only the lights in their room and the one tubular bulb just outside the doorway remained. The light extended to about ten feet past King's outstretched arm and pistol, then met an unnatural wall of blackness, where it was absorbed.

As King watched, the dark wall shuffled forward, like a lumbering elephant. When it stopped moving, the wall of dark was only five feet past his extended arm. King pulled his arm back, but kept the pistol trained on the inky barrier, ready for what might emerge.

"Here," Asya had reached into her purse and procured a small but powerful LED flashlight. King took it and shined the light into

the blackness ahead of them. The darkness grunted back at them, in reply.

"Get the file," King said.

Asya stepped back from the doorway, where King remained, and turned toward the still open file cabinet.

The darkness shrieked at them. Asya clapped her hands against her ears. As bad as the gunfire had been, this sound was immensely worse. When the noise abated, dying down to a clicking sound, King called to her.

"Leave it. We're getting out of here."

"How?" Asya asked as she joined him again at the door, her Yarygin pointed at the dark.

"Quickly," then he raced into the darkness, gun in one hand, flashlight in the other. As he moved, the last bulb in the hall extinguished, and the light behind them in the room blinked out. King's flashlight was now the only source of light in the tunnel.

But the wall of darkness retreated from the powerful flashlight. Asya was at his heels. Just before the wall of black reached the point that would allow them to slip into the side tunnel, it stopped. And then snarled.

King understood. This was as far as the wraiths were prepared to back down. He had encountered the creatures before—in Rome, when he was looking for Alexander. Then the creatures had reacted similarly. They would flee in pain from bright light, but ultimately they would not shirk their duty. King hadn't needed to actually kill one though. Alexander had called them off, the last time. King wasn't even sure it was *possible* to kill them. Alexander had implied the creatures were early experiments of his, when he was looking for ways to use the Hydra's blood for longevity. The man had said the wraiths were the inspiration for vampire legends. King could understand why after seeing them up close in Rome. They had hideous wrinkled gray skin. Some were missing facial features like noses and mouths entirely. Still, despite being scientific mishaps, they were each fiercely loyal to Alexander and his mysterious goals.

King took one single step forward and thrust the flashlight out. He needed to send a message to the Forgotten. He would not be dissuaded in his mission either. The tip of the flashlight touched the wall of shadow and a fine film of smoke rose up from the end of the light, filling the tunnel with a charred smell.

King heard Asya fire her weapon once behind him, but he couldn't turn away from the wall. He knew if he did, the thing would be on him in a second.

"Pawn?" he asked.

"There is another behind us, but it stays back."

"We're in a standoff. Again."

"What will we do?" she asked. King admired the lack of fear in his sister's voice. She wasn't worried at all in her abilities or in his. She was merely asking him about the plan.

"Be pushy," King told her. Then he stepped into the field of blackness. The light sizzled harder. Then he felt a hand grasp his left wrist inside the wall of dark, pushing the flashlight up. With his right hand, King fired the Yarygin point blank into the blackness.

The hand still held his wrist and pushed his arm back. Then it moved forward and the field of supernatural darkness dissipated like smoke clearing in a strong wind. Only instead of being blown off to the side, the smoke retreated back down the length of the hallway. The hallway was suddenly revealed in the flashlight's beam—the hallway, and the creature inside it.

A wraith stood before King.

The creature looked like a man in a tattered gray cloak. The skin not covered by the hood over its head was a dark charcoal. The eyes were sunken hollows. This one had a single vertical slit where its nose should have been. It had a lower jaw, but it looked fused to the skull, the flesh melted and scarred where the mouth should have been. Its taut skin clung to the muscles and skeletal structure, like the thing was malnourished.

The creature shoved his wrist hard and let out a clicking growl. King saw the bullet wounds in its chest, but the injuries did

not lessen the creature's strength or resolve. He struggled to force his left arm down, pointing the light at the creature again. It began to shake in his grasp. He fired two more shots at its chest, then moved to swing the arm up and point the gun at its head, but the Forgotten, with an amazing reserve of strength, forced the flashlight all the way up and back in one swift move.

When the beam of light hit King's face, the wraith made a loud sharp bark noise. Then it let go of King's arm.

King pulled his arm back to his chest and pointed the light at the wraith again, but it had leapt to the side of the wall and was retreating down the tunnel, following another looming by the door to the darkened room. Then a third wraith passed over his head, skittering along the ceiling of the tunnel, following the first two.

When the third creature reached the dim recesses of the room at the other end of the tunnel, the fluorescent lights all flicked back on again, suddenly filling the hallway with a brilliant glare. King shielded his eyes for a second, but he kept the Yarygin trained on the far end of the hall.

"What did you do?" Asya asked, coming up next to him.

"Nothing. I think we just got our first lucky break. Once it saw who I was, it retreated. Alexander must have told them he wanted me alive for some reason."

"And me?"

"Let's not stick around to find out." King turned to move back to the file cabinet for the Manifold file, but he heard the guttural growling again from the end of the hall. He stopped and turned back to the hallway. Half the fluorescents had been shut off. He stood waiting, and as he did, the lights slowly turned back on, one by one. The message was clear.

"I think we're being given safe passage out, but we don't get to take anything."

Asya gave a nod and slipped ahead, heading down the side hallway. King paused at the junction, staring into the darkness at

the end, where the wraiths waited. He let the moment spin out, assuring them he was not afraid.

"Where is he?" he shouted at the darkened room.

He waited a full minute for a reply of some kind. When none came, he turned to leave.

But then he heard the distinctive *tink* of metal striking stone. He whipped his head back toward the dark room, and saw a small metal object come skipping along the rough concrete floor toward him. It wobbled to a stop just a few paces from where he stood. He took one long stride and bent down to pick it up. The cool metal in his hand told him what he held.

It was a coin. An ancient one.

King backed into the side corridor with Asya and made his way to the exit. He kept an eye out behind them, but the darkness no longer encroached. When they reached the door, King was prepared for absolute bedlam on the other side. They had fired several shots. The library and the plaza outside would be in an uproar.

"Get to the car as fast as you can," then he swung the door opened and scooted the chair on the balcony aside.

The library was quiet. Business as usual. Patrons were down on the first floor, and an old man was in the stacks up here on the balcony, looking at them as they emerged from the wall. Asya shut the door behind her. The old man turned his attention back to a red leather-bound book in his hand.

King looked at Asya and she shrugged. She tucked her pistol into her purse. Taking his cue from her, King slipped his weapon into the waistband of his jeans, lifting his Elvis shirt over the grip. The gun was still warm against his skin, but not too hot.

They headed out of the library into the strong glare of the Mediterranean sunshine and strolled through the crowded plaza, toward the street.

Once away from people, Asya spoke up in a voice just shy of a shout. "Do you think secret passage was soundproofed?"

"Must have been," King could tell he was shouting too. He hoped his hearing would improve before they got back to the airport.

"What did it throw?" Asya asked.

King held his palm out for her. She examined the small coin. It had rough edges, making it round only in the loosest sense of the word. On the face of the coin was a raised image of a woman, with a crescent moon over her head.

"An ugly woman?" Asya was not sure what she was seeing.

King laughed. "That's supposed to be the head of a lion. This is a coin showing Tanit, a Punic goddess of fertility and war."

"What does it mean?"

King's face soured. "It means Alexander is in Carthage. Probably at the last Manifold facility. Omega."

ELEVEN
Carthage, Tunisia

Asya Machtchenko sat in the white Mercedes cargo van, watching her brother negotiate with an Arab. She was constantly amazed by him, despite the façade she presented of disapproving sister. She was really coming to like him.

King was talking with the man, and the exchange appeared to be friendly. He had told Asya that he would be getting some necessary supplies, but she suspected he was negotiating for some weapons. They had ditched the Yarygins in Valletta before leaving Malta. Traveling across borders with firearms had become practically impossible, but there were always plenty of weapons on the ground in any country. A booming secondhand trade had begun in most parts of the world, and covert military and spies always made purchasing side-arms their first step after clearing customs. Asya knew that in some parts of Russia, you could find

the salesmen in the actual parking lot outside the airport. In this case, they had needed to drive into the surprisingly clean city of Tunis. Asya had not been to many locations in North Africa, although she and King had visited Egypt earlier in the year, following a lead. She found the wide streets and business-like approach of Tunis to be refreshing after the chaos of Cairo.

She watched as King, in yet another of his Elvis shirts—this one showing the aged and sweaty man with big square sunglasses on a red fabric—reached forward and shook the small Arab's hand. *Good*, she thought. *Almost done.* The temperature in the van was fine with the air conditioning running, but she was anxious to get moving. She felt they were very close to finding their parents.

King was led to the side door of another van. The man slid the door open, slowly procured a few small packages and placed them on the floor of the van, stepping aside. King quickly examined the contents, nodding as he did, never keeping a package exposed for long. Then the man handed King what had to be a cloth-wrapped assault rifle. The weapons went into a nylon duffle bag over King's shoulder. Then King passed the man a stack of US dollars. They shook hands again. King turned with his purchases and was walking away when the small Arab called him back.

This cannot be good.

King returned to the man, on guard. She could see it in his posture. She had no weapons if a fight broke out, but she placed her hand on the door handle anyway, prepared to leap out of the van and race to her brother's assistance if necessary. The small Arab smiled and produced a tiny package from under his shirt. He handed it to King, and King laughed good-naturedly. Asya relaxed. King shook the small man's hand again—far more vigorously this time. Then he came back to her van, smiling all the way.

King opened the rear door of the van and slid the nylon bag onto the floor, removing the rifle and laying it down next to the bag, still wrapped in its white cloth covering. Then he climbed into the driver's seat, still smiling. Asya watched him the whole time.

Eventually he turned to her and saw the look on her face. "What?"

"What is so funny?" she asked.

"He said for being such a good customer, he wanted to give me a bonus gift." King smiled and produced the small package she had seen the man hand over. King's fingers removed the cloth, and Asya saw an olive drab WWII-era grenade, commonly known as a pineapple. She knew the weapon had been out of use since the 1960s.

"Bozhe moi, do you think that thing will even still work?"

King laughed. "Well, it looks like Vietnam era, so maybe." The small dark thing had rust on the pin already. "We're weaponed up. I got two Sigs and an AK. Now, where to?"

Asya showed King a small tourist map that highlighted the ruins of Carthage, and she pointed to one of the southerly sites labeled *Tophet*. "I think we start here. Your Tanit Goddess had connections to this place, or so the guide book says. If not this one, then we work our way up and check out all the ruins."

King started the engine and they headed south.

Hours later, with the sun nearly going down, King was exhausted. They had visited each of the ancient sites, hoping to spot some indication of a hidden entrance to a former Manifold base, while also keeping an eye out for the Herculean Society symbol. But discovering Omega's location was turning out to be far more difficult than finding the Valletta library's secret file-room.

King wiped sweat off his forehead with a bandana. "As fascinating as Tunisia is, we haven't made much ground."

Asya sat next to him in the cab of their van, luxuriating in the air conditioning after being out in the heat all afternoon. She fanned a limp tourist map on herself and turned her head to the ceiling of the vehicle. "This is like Kyrgyzstan heat. I am melting. We have seen all of Carthage's major sites."

"Let me see that map," King said, after taking a swig of an ice cold Coke he had bought from a nearby vendor. Asya handed him the map. It showed the archeological sites as orange shapes, and no other detail besides the roads. "This isn't going to work. Can you bring up a satellite map on the laptop?"

Asya opened their rubber-coated magnesium alloy laptop, designed for rough treatment in the field. She had a small satellite antenna attached to the Ethernet port, which allowed them to access the vast array of computing power Deep Blue had back in New Hampshire, as well as a simple Internet connection from anywhere they could reach a passing satellite. Asya opened a satellite view of the ruins in Google Maps.

"You see, we are here," she said.

"Zoom out a bit," King said.

Asya's finger slipped on the mouse's scroll button, zooming the image out to where they could see the whole coastline of Tunisia. She apologized for going too far, then began zooming back in on the ruins, one click at a time.

"Wait," King said, pointing. "What the hell is that?" His finger pointed to a huge rectangle, clearly visible, long before the other structures were.

Asya quickly re-centered the map on the rectangle, and zoomed all the way in.

"It is parking lot for the mosque."

"The mosque?" King asked.

"You know the big one? We saw the tower, when looking at the ruins of the theater." She sounded tired.

"Zoom out again a bit," King said.

She did as he requested, then looked at him, still fanning herself with the useless tourist map.

"You cannot be thinking Ridley would get permission to build Omega inside a mosque. Not even Ridley had that kind of money," Asya tapped the keyboard for a few seconds, searching for information. "The Malik ibn Anas mosque was built in 2003, and

was originally called El Abidine. It holds 1000 worshippers and even has a radio station."

"A radio station?"

"For broadcasting the call to prayer," she told him.

"Ah. No. You're right. Not even Ridley had that kind of clout. But I'm not thinking of the mosque. You said it was built in '03?"

"Yes. But if not the mosque, then where?" she asked.

King smiled and put the van into drive.

"You are serious?"

"I'm telling you, this is where it will be." King pointed at the lines and lines of parked cars. They had been sitting in the southwest corner of the immense parking lot, watching the worshippers arrive in droves for *Maghrib*, the evening prayer. The sun was mostly down on the horizon, as hundreds of men clad in a variety of dress had all jockeyed for parking spots and then quickly hurried into the massive white mosque across the Boulevard de l'Environnement. King had kept the engine running, chewing through petrol, so they could continue to stay cool.

"The parking lot? It's insane. Look how full the lot is. How could Ridley and his people get in and out without being seen?" Asya asked.

King turned to her and grinned. "Easily, as long as he did it at any time of day except during the five times of prayer."

Approximately twenty-five minutes after the last man had entered the mosque, the first of them began hurrying back to their vehicles. Then a swarm of humanity flooded from the structure and the parking lot was inundated with pedestrians and moving vehicles. King thought it vaguely resembled a swarm of fire ants around a hive. In twenty minutes more, the lot was nearly empty, and King marveled at the efficiency of the drivers.

They waited five more minutes and their van was the only vehicle in the gigantic darkening lot.

"That was amazing," Asya said.

"Now to see if I was right."

A few minutes later, he spotted a shadow darting from cover to cover in the little park on the far side of the empty lot.

"There," King pointed, as the shadow shifted.

"A wraith, like in Malta?" Asya asked.

"Maybe."

The shape darted behind white concrete, and then it was gone. King waited a minute, then drove the van across the parking lot with the headlights off. He parked on the north side of the lot, where they had seen the moving shape. To the left was a tiny park with landscaped trees and shrubs. Directly in front of them was a small white fountain. A tiled walkway stretched to the right, off the edge of the lot. Beyond that, was the crosswalk over the boulevard and the courtyard in front of the massive mosque. King looked at the building, seeing the bright white surface suddenly illuminated with spotlights, as the dusk deepened.

Then he turned back to the not-functioning fountain in front of them. He glanced down to the laptop, still open on Asya's lap. He reached over and zoomed in on the satellite view of the fountain.

"This will be the entrance," he said.

"I was thinking the same," Asya closed the laptop, then reached into the nylon bag behind her seat and pulled out the two Sig Sauer pistols, handing one to King. She got out of the van and stood in the lot, looking at the fountain. King stepped out, slipped the grenade into the pocket of his jeans and retrieved the rifle from the back of the van. He slipped its strap over his head and shoulder. Although the lights illuminated the mosque at the end of the giant parking lot, the small park and fountain area were still dark. He reached in the van one more time for the LED flashlight.

"Should we check in with Deep Blue before going in?" Asya asked in a whisper.

"No need. He'll know where we are within an hour, when a satellite passes. I have a micro-transmitter on me."

"A micro-transmitter?" She eyed him up and down. "Where?"

He gave a lopsided grin. "Where no one would want to look."

They made their way to the fountain. There wasn't a drop of water inside.

"It is bone dry," Asya said, stalking around the structure and looking for a lever of some kind.

King looked to the west into the trees of the small park. Then he understood.

"It was late."

Asya looked at him for an explanation.

"The Forgotten. It was late getting back to the fountain. It was caught outside in the sun all day. It stayed in the shade of the park, probably hidden in a tree, or under one of those shrubs. As soon as the sun set, it retreated back to the fountain. This is the entrance." King turned back to examine the stone fountain.

"I don't see any symbols. Only abstract patterns," Asya said.

"Of course," King nodded. "It's Islamic art. There won't be any lettering or obvious symbols or shapes. Just geometric patterns. Plus, remember, this was Ridley's place. The Society only took it over recently. There won't be any obvious letter H."

King lifted his leg and stepped into the empty basin of the concrete and marble fountain. As soon as he brought his full weight into the fountain, a loud crunching sound emanated from the stone. A portion of the floor slid away, revealing the upper rungs of a ladder.

"Isn't that a risky design? Anyone could have found it." Asya stepped into the fountain with King, as he began his descent into the darkness.

"No one ever takes the time to come here. You saw how quickly people hurried into the mosque, and then how quickly they bailed after prayer. Plus the fountain is empty. No one would give it a second glance—and they would never think to step inside of it."

"A child—" Asya started.

"—is probably not heavy enough to trigger the hatch," King finished.

Asya grunted in agreement.

The ladder descended just ten feet. King stepped off and to the side, allowing Asya to come down. His footsteps echoed telling him he was in a huge underground space. He left the flashlight off, not wanting to give away their position any more than the twilit sky would. He also wanted his night vision to adjust.

When Asya was off the ladder, the concrete opening slowly slid closed above them, entombing them in absolute darkness. A scratching noise tickled his ears. Then a small skitter. And a scrape. There were Forgotten here. King pulled up his Sig, prepared to keep the Forgotten at bay.

When he flicked on the LED flashlight, his hopes were suddenly dashed.

There *were* Forgotten here.

Hundreds of them. Maybe thousands. They were in some kind of huge underground space and the Forgotten were all clustered in the dark, clinging to the walls, and hanging from the ceiling above them. When the harsh glare of the LED illuminated the space, they shrieked as one, with a rising tone like an alarm.

From directly behind him, King heard his sister's thick Russian accent.

"Is never easy with you, is it?"

TWELVE
Endgame Headquarters, New Hampshire

"Make no mistake," Seth said, "the man you call Alexander Diotrephes *is* the historical Hercules. If he even *is* a man. But one way or the other, he has probably been alive for over 2500 years. We don't know what he's planning to do with the technology he's gathered, but if he were to combine the dimensional technology you acquired and lost last year, with the other...items he has

collected? Well, let's just say he could blow a hole in the side of this planet that would leave the Earth looking like a crescent moon."

"Not possible," Deep Blue's electronic voice came over the speakers in the room. "How would he even power such a weapon?"

The three Ridleys smiled at Queen and the others. "In the last few years, your Chess Team witnessed our Creator revive the Hydra. You saw a virus that could stop hearts. You discovered an entire city of Neanderthals—still alive—living under a mountain in the jungles of Vietnam. You have seen the power of the mother tongue, the very language of God. King discovered the Elephant Graveyard in Ethiopia, and you..." Seth pointed to Queen, "...you escaped an amusement-park deathtrap and fought creatures that could only be described as...what? Werewolves? How can you— how can any of you—question *anything* at this point?"

The room fell silent for a moment. The litany of strange events they'd all survived conjured images of monsters, tortures and scars, some of which would never fade.

"As much as I hate to say it," Knight spoke up from the corner of the room, "he has a point. Let's not forget that hydra-dragon thing I fought in China too. At this point, I don't think we can dismiss any possibility, no matter how unlikely it seems. Or how untrue we want it to be."

"Alexander has been a fair-weather friend," Bishop added from behind Queen. He had lowered his weapon, but his eyes remained trained on the three Ridley clones.

Seth looked up at the black speaker in the corner of the room. "Your people saw the tremendous power possibilities of the Bluelight project Graham Brown was working on. Alexander— *Hercules*—has that technology."

Queen recalled the reports King had given of a man named Graham Brown who might have been masquerading as a worldwide computer network known as *Brainstorm*. The Bluelight project was a power system that operated on the principle of firing proton

beams into a magnetic field, resulting in a plasma storm above the atmosphere, from which energy could be harvested. But the system was wildly unstable, and King had shut it down...permanently. Or so they had thought.

"Then there's the matter of the miniature black hole," Seth said, his face suddenly grim.

"The *what?*" Queen asked, startled. This was getting bad.

Deep Blue's modulated voice answered. "He's referring to the incident at the Louvre, two years ago. King stopped a black hole from eating Paris. Alexander was present. As far as we knew, all signs of the phenomenon were gone at the end of the incident."

Seth grinned. "Review the security camera footage. A few of the cameras in the museum were powered by a battery backup. Even though the city was struck by a blackout and an earthquake, some of the cameras kept recording. Hercules removed a small token, when King wasn't looking. Placed it in his pocket."

"You don't mean to suggest that an entire black hole was contained in something small enough to fit in a man's pocket?" Deep Blue's modulated voice did not intone the sarcasm, but Queen felt it would be present on his end of the conversation.

"The video shows him struggling to lift the object. A stone the size of a golf ball. How heavy do you suppose it must have been if the legendary *Hercules* nearly couldn't budge it?"

Silence filled the room. Rook shuffled along the side wall, his weapon still pointed at the Ridleys. Queen could not see Bishop or Knight behind her, but she knew they would remain vigilant. The other Endgame soldiers kept their weapons trained on the seated figures.

Queen lowered her pistol and stepped closer to Seth. She squatted, placing her eyes level with Seth's face.

"Could a miniature black hole be used to power that dimensional technology from Norway? To bring those things from the other side back here to Earth?"

"That dimension was theoretically only one dimension of a possibly infinite number. There could be far worse things out

there. And yes, the energy contained in a black hole—no matter its size—could power anything. Theoretically, of course. No one has ever done it before...that we know of."

Deep Blue's voice buzzed into the room again, "What makes you think Richard Ridley can help?"

"With the mother tongue, the Creator is capable of anything. We three do not possess the mother tongue. But He does. He could simply unmake Hercules. He could stop the threat of the black hole and the dimensional technology all at once."

"Or," Deep Blue's voice interrupted, "he might try to claim that technology for himself."

Seth nodded grimly. "But, you are missing the point entirely."

Queen raised a questioning eyebrow. She tried putting herself in Seth's—or Richard Ridley's—mental state, to guess what he meant, but she couldn't see his side of things.

"Oh my God," Deep Blue said through the speakers, after a minute.

"Yes. Exactly," Seth smiled. "Do you really want a man that has the biological ability of regeneration, some kind of unnatural immortality, immense strength, unlimited power and the technology to tear holes between dimensions to suddenly acquire and possess the all-powerful language of God, as well?"

The moment spun out, with no one speaking.

Queen found herself looking at the black speaker up in the corner of the room, waiting for Deep Blue's reply. When the words came, she knew there would have been resignation behind them, if she had heard the man in person. But she also knew it was the only possible response.

"Let's make a deal."

THIRTEEN
Omega Facility, Carthage, Tunisia

The space opened before King like an immense underground parking garage, with thick concrete support columns equally spaced and receding into the unlit portion of the echoing space. King's LED light cast an arc of illumination fifty feet into the throng of shifting wraiths. It was enough.

Well, this sucks, he thought. He guessed the space likely stretched most of the length and breadth of the parking lot above and beyond. It seemed equally likely that it was filled with Wraiths.

But then he noticed something odd. The Forgotten were not attacking him and Asya. They were hissing and screeching, scampering along the ceiling of the space and on the wall behind him—even on the ladder, but they were keeping their distance.

King focused on the wraith closest to him. It was like the others—sickly gray skin, deformed facial features and a long tattered cloak. But it also held a look of curiosity. King watched as it appraised him, tilting its hairless head first one way, and then the other.

"Why do they not attack?" Asya whispered.

"Not sure," King replied. As King spoke, the wraith closest to him stepped forward and hissed louder. Moving slowly, it brought its face just inches from King's. Then it repeated the strange head movements, swaying as it turned its skull. A cobra dancing to an Indian snake charmer's flute.

King moved his forehead closer, in the same manner, and now his face was an inch from the wraith's. It hissed louder, but he sensed the hiss might be out of something else...appreciation or even submission maybe, but not a threat.

King took a chance.

"My name is Jack Sigler," he shouted. "You might know me as King." He moved the LED flashlight up as he spoke, as he had done

in Malta, illuminating his face for the creatures to see his features. The Forgotten's yellow reflective pupils dilated from the light, as its face elongated, and its eyes opened wider—as if in shock. *Or maybe just really bad eyesight*, King thought.

The creature stepped back from King and emitted a loud rising shriek that sounded like a referee tweeting on a whistle. All of the wraiths in the giant space were suddenly silent. The echoing chamber fell quiet except for the scratching noise of clawed hands and feet clinging to the walls and concrete support columns. Their tattered cloaks fluttered as they moved, but the creatures had stopped their incessant noise. To King's relief, the creatures remained docile.

"Step closer to me, Asya," he said quietly. He felt her brush up against his back. "Now walk with me, very slowly."

King took a step forward into the crowd of wraiths.

Asya shuffled forward with him. He took another step, and the wraiths ahead of them parted to reveal the white concrete floor. King began to walk forward at a slow pace, with Asya right behind him. A wraith from the left came close, and he turned to look at it, shining the LED up, so his face would be lit in the harsh white glow.

"King!" he told it, and the creature receded into the crowd.

"Why are they letting us pass?" Asya asked, keeping one hand on his arm.

"The important thing is they are. The question is, for how long? Remember in Malta, they wouldn't let us take the file. For some reason, I'm off limits as long as I play by Alexander's rules."

As King and Asya moved forward, the wraiths filled in the space behind them, never allowing them more than a circle of twenty feet in diameter.

"No chance of retreat," Asya said, looking behind them. "They are following."

"That's fine," King said, gaining confidence. "I am King!" He shouted, and the crowd of Forgotten flinched back, widening the circle of clear floor around King and Asya.

They had covered perhaps three hundred feet from the ladder, with the wraiths curiously clustering around. Occasionally one would dart closer, and King would raise the flashlight and speak his callsign. Then the creatures would dart back to the group.

"I think we're almost under the mosque," King said. The gigantic room ended just ahead at a large, flat wall, with a single unmarked metal door, the only aberration. Several wraiths remained in front of the door.

As King approached the door, more of the wraiths clustered before it, blocking his path.

"I don't think they will allow—" Asya began, but King pressed on, shoving some of the wraiths away from the door. Others slid away at the sight of his forcefulness.

The gray, steel door had a knob, but no lock. King reached for it and unslung the AK-47 from his back. Asya drew her weapon as well. The wraiths kept their distance around them, but the circle now gave them ten feet of floor and ten feet of vertical wall. The wraiths swayed and hissed softly, as if awaiting instructions.

King slowly raised the AK in his left hand to a 45 degree angle, still careful to point it at the floor, and not directly at any of the gyrating creatures. With his right hand, he reached for the door knob. Some of the hisses increased in volume. He got the idea that while the Forgotten were, for some reason, standing down, once he opened the door, all bets would be off.

"Be ready to run in after me," King said. "Three...two...one. Now!"

King whipped open the door, took one step and stopped short. But Asya ran into his back, shoving him forward into the obstacle.

The other side of the door was bricked up from top to bottom with old orange bricks and whitish mortar.

King coughed as the air was knocked from his lungs and his face pressed against the stone. But the impact was harmless. He recovered quickly and turned back to face Asya and the wraiths,

who were hooting and shrieking again, as they had when he had first switched on the light.

I knew this was too simple.

The circle of wraiths moved in, hissing and howling.

FOURTEEN
Over the Atlantic Ocean

Queen shuffled in her seat, trying to get comfortable. The flight would be a few hours, and she was already wound up. It didn't help that this plane, a duplicate of the original *Crescent*, a stealth VTOL troop transport, was more spartan than its predecessor. Named for the craft's curved flying-wing shape, the original *Crescent* had perished in battle the previous year, when King had piloted it into a tear in the fabric of reality, stopping an incursion from another dimension.

Although the half-billion dollar vehicle had been totaled, the move had arguably saved the world. Deep Blue had arranged for the team to keep *Crescent*'s twin, the *Persephone*, which had been assisting in the battle. Now renamed *Crescent II*, the current vehicle was Endgame's for the foreseeable future.

Like its namesake, radar-reflective material covered the ship from one tip of its moon shape across 80 feet of breadth to its other tip. The giant, flat plane could carry 25,000 pounds of load and travel at above Mach 2. With VTOL capability, the plane could pick the team up anywhere and drop them off just as easily, but Queen didn't like it. The original *Crescent* had been fairly plush inside. *Crescent II* was far more utilitarian, and Queen found herself missing that small bit of comfort in her life. She spent enough time in uncomfortable holes in the ground. She just hadn't realized how much she had enjoyed the downtime in the original *Crescent* until she was faced with hours of nothing to do in *Crescent II*.

Her agitation over the uncomfortable seating came through in her voice when she spoke.

"You know the Three Ridleyteers are going to screw us the first chance they get. And if they don't, the real Ridley will." She tugged on the straps on her impact-resistant battle-armor suit, tightening a plate of gray metal and foam on her forearm.

"No kidding. I don't particularly relish the thought of having to deal with four of that ass-clown," Rook, clad in a similar battle suit, nodded toward the flat-screen LED monitor on the wall of the small troop area, showing the three clones strapped and chained to the wall of the rear cargo area of the plane. The Ridleys weren't going anywhere, and the team needed some privacy to develop a plan as they rocketed across the Atlantic Ocean for Tunisia. "We can't trust them, Blue."

Deep Blue was with the team through their headsets, via an encrypted transmission across a military satellite. "I know, Rook. But they make some compelling arguments. Or at least Seth does, while his companions pretend to be deaf and mute."

"Pretend?" Rook looked shocked, and turned to Queen, Knight and Bishop, as if to ask whether he was the only one that hadn't seen through the deception. The others looked equally mystified.

"How?" Queen asked, and it was understood she was addressing Deep Blue.

"I've been carefully watching them the whole time. Enos reacts to loud noises, so he's not really deaf. While they've been in the cargo area, I've seen Jared's lips moving, although the audio sensors in the compartment haven't picked up any sound. It's likely he's fooling too. Doesn't matter. You're right, Queen. They will turn on you at the first opportunity, but not until they have Ridley back. So stay sharp, and when the time is right, we'll turn the tables on them."

"What have you got planned?" Knight looked up from a fashion magazine he was reading.

"First things first. You need to remove Ridley's regenerative abilities. Our scientists have had time to work on the original formula we used to cure George Pierce, back when Ridley infected him with the Hydra's DNA. The formula now requires just a small dose to inhibit the regenerative strand. There's a case on the bottom of the locker, Queen, if you'd retrieve it."

Queen stood and walked over to a black metal weapons cabinet bolted to the wall of the crew room. It was empty except for a small black plastic case at the bottom. She returned to her chair and flipped open the case. Rook leaned over to see the contents.

The case held four small inch-long vials of nuclear green liquid and four spring-loaded auto-injector syringes.

"So we just stab one of these into Ridley?" Queen asked.

"Yes. It should work in seconds. If you can inject him covertly, he might not even know what's happened. But be warned, Ridley will still have the mother tongue, and as long as he can speak, he'll be able to heal from grievous injury."

"Or turn us into paste," Rook added.

"And that's only if we take the clones at their word," Deep Blue said, "which we shouldn't do. They each might possess the mother tongue, but I doubt it."

"What makes you doubt it?" Bishop asked, with his eyes closed. Queen had thought he was asleep and that she was going to need to fill him in later.

Deep Blue's voice was absent from their earpieces for just a second, and then he came back. "If they could speak the mother tongue, they could literally move Heaven and Earth to get Ridley back. That the duplicates came to us and requested our help, means they really need it to free Ridley. If Seth and the others actually had the mother tongue, then they would each be unstoppable—and they would have freed Ridley from Alexander's captivity long ago."

"What do you suppose happens to the duplicates if Ridley were to die?" Queen asked. "Will they really just fall apart?"

"Theoretically, I suppose it could be true. In the original golem story, the rabbi that created it could later unmake it by destroying the word that gave it life. If the sacred word was written on a piece of paper, it could be removed from the golem's mouth. If the text was inscribed on the golem's body, it could simply be altered."

"*Emet* to *met*," Bishop said, recalling what they'd learned about golems while dealing with the threat.

"Exactly," Deep Blue said. "Seeing as how Ridley *spoke* life into the duplicates, he could be the word himself."

Rook shook his head. "In the beginning was the Word, and the Word was with God, and the Word was God."

Deep Blue fell silent. The three other members of the team turned toward Rook. He noticed their collective gaze after a moment. "What? It's from the Bible. Am I the only one that's been to church?"

Deep Blue cleared his throat. "We have to also consider the possibility that Ridley was able to grant them real life. Under their skin might be blood and organs and minds that will continue to live after Ridley dies. It's not what we saw with his other duplicates, but we can't rule it out. And neither can they. I suspect it's part of why they want to find him."

"Pinocchio wants to become a real boy," Knight said.

"That creates two wildly different motives, doesn't it?" Queen asked.

Rook shook his head. "I'm not following. If Ridley dies and they die too, that gives them the motivation to keep him alive, right? That's just based on survival. But if his life isn't tied to theirs, they still want him freed, because he's their what? Some kind of messiah, right? A god?"

"If they can live independently of him, they might simply want the mother tongue for themselves. It *is* a learned language. And never forget—each duplicate has the same crazed hunger for power. They are each as dangerous as the original—if not more so, because they see an unlimited potential for power within their grasps."

"I got a question," Bishop sat up in his chair and opened his eyes. "We know where Ridley is being held, and we know who has him. We know the danger he presents. And we have three more of him in the cargo hold, who, you just said, are possibly even more dangerous than the original..." Bishop paused, and the others present in the room turned to listen. "Why shouldn't we just shoot these three in the head and drop a bomb on the secret base they're taking us to?"

The room was quiet. Deep Blue did not comment.

"That would have been so much cooler if you'd quoted Bishop from *Aliens*," Rook said. "'It's the only way to be sure.'"

No one smiled. Bishop had presented them with brutal, but clear logic that would end all their problems at once. Even Rook's comparison to the *Aliens* movie fit. Why should they engage a proven and deadly enemy up-close and personal when they could end the fight from a safe distance?

When Deep Blue spoke again, he stopped the violent line of thinking. "We can't drop a bomb; first because it's a mosque and we don't want to start World War III, and second... King is already on site."

FIFTEEN
Omega Facility, Carthage, Tunisia

King raised the LED flashlight to his face and screamed as loudly as he could. He waved the rifle and rushed at the approaching horde of wraiths. The reaction was instantaneous. The wraiths—all of them, including those scrabbling with claws along the ceiling— turned and fled to the far end of the massive parking garage-like space.

A moment later, as King looked on bewildered, he saw a dim light at the end of the space, as the hatch he and Asya had entered

through was opened. The hundreds of Forgotten poured out into the night.

King turned to his sister in the dark, the flashlight now pointed at the floor. "Did I forget to brush my teeth?"

"Whatever the reason, they are frightened of you. We should count ourselves lucky—and find a doorway that is not bricked up."

King turned back to the bricked up door and began to run along the wall to the right. Asya followed him. After about a hundred yards, they came to another door, identical to the first. King opened it, the AK-47 at the ready. This door revealed a long dark corridor that sloped down at an angle.

"Jackpot. Let's go," King slung the rifle over his shoulder and pulled out the Sig handgun. He raised the LED light, then sprinted down the darkened hallway.

"Shouldn't we go slow? Look for booby-traps?" Asya asked, huffing behind him in the dark.

"If you had an army of those things would you need booby traps?"

"This is true."

At the end of another few hundred yards, the corridor ended with an open stairwell. They descended what felt like three hundred more yards before the stairs ended at another corridor, this one moving in a right angle to the first. King guessed it would take them back toward the ruins of the Amphitheater, behind the giant mosque. *Well, under the amphitheater,* he thought.

Shortly they came to another stairwell leading up, and the corridor turned at another right angle, this time to their right.

King stopped to look at both possibilities.

"Up or right?" Asya asked. King noticed he was breathing harder than she was.

The stairs were metal and fairly new, with rust in only a few small spots. King took a few steps down the side corridor, then called to Asya. "This way. Look at the walls."

Asya stepped closer until she could see what King had pointed at, in the light. The walls were concrete at the mouth of the tunnel, but after a few feet, the surface switched to ancient pitted stone.

"This is part of the ruins," Asya said.

"That would be my guess. And if I've kept track of where we are accurately, this tunnel runs from beneath amphitheater to the Antonine Baths."

"What about the staircase?" she asked.

"Maybe another entrance?" King shrugged. "Let's see if this tunnel takes us to more ruins first. Ridley and Alexander are both fans of antiquity. My money is on the Baths."

The stone corridor got smaller as they moved forward, and it began to slope sharply after two hundred yards. Then they came to a metal door, with a security keypad next to it.

King checked for security cameras and tripwires, then examined the keypad. It was a pretty simple pad, with just numbers and an enter button. He didn't have any technological tools with him, and even if he did, he wasn't very good at picking locks.

Asya reached for the doorknob on the door and pulled. The door gave about a half inch, then hit its stop. She titled her head to the side, to look at the gap the door made. She looked at King and raised her eyebrows at him. Then she pulled a curved plastic hairclip from her head, and slipped it around the edge of the door and into the gap. In less than ten seconds, King heard a click. The hairclip broke, but the door came open in Asya's hand.

"Nice," he told her.

"We do things low-tech in Russia," she smiled.

"Yeah, I've heard the gag about the cosmonauts using a pencil." King stepped in through the door to behold a large janitorial closet. The inside of the door held a large triangular plaque with a lightning bolt and a sign reading *Electrical Breakers*. He tapped the sign for Asya's benefit.

"Camouflage. Effective," she said.

"A secret escape tunnel for Ridley. The rest of his employees most likely didn't know about it." King moved across the closet to the opposing door, raised his Sig, and slowly cracked the door open.

They were in a well lit laboratory, with blinding white walls, stainless steel counters and cabinets, with bank after bank of fluorescent lamps lining the ceilings. The counters were filled with computers, microscopes and equipment King had only seen a few times before—in Manifold labs. He understood some of the basic principles of genetic science after studying up on the field when they had first run afoul of Ridley, but he really didn't have a desire to press deeply into the subject. Viruses and DNA strands all felt like a tiny invisible world to him. Sara felt at home in that micro-scopic, unseen realm, but he would rather live in the world he could see, where there were threats he could shoot.

His thoughts drifted to his new fiancée for a moment. He'd left her in a hurry once again, and he couldn't help but feel bad about it. She'd just finished pointing out the chaos of their lives and how hard it was going to be for them to have anything resembling a traditional marriage. She'd said yes, but he wondered if she was now second guessing that decision. Because really, who asks a girl to marry him and then flies halfway around the world to fight wraiths and Hercules? Of course, when he got home, she might already be flying off to some other corner of the world, fighting a breakout of some civilization-ending bird flu.

"What is all this stuff?" Asya asked, pointing to one of the few devices King recognized. It was a white plastic box that looked something like a futuristic cash register—as imagined by Stanley Kubrick for a 1960s sci-fi film.

"A PCR. It performs a timed-thermal cycle so you can get an amplification of a polymerase chain reaction."

"Huh," she grunted.

King smirked to himself. If she asked about a dozen other objects in the room he would have been clueless.

At the far side of the lab, were two black doors. King had seen similar doors in Endgame's headquarters. He knew they would seal with rubber airtight stoppers the second any kind of biological contaminant was released in the room. He didn't see any other exits, so he made his way to the bio doors and opened the first.

He peered into a long white hallway that stretched to his right. It had shiny white linoleum floors. Black doors lined the walls, leading to what he presumed were more labs. Directly opposite from his doors were another set labeled *Cold Lab*. King glanced behind him for the sign on his doors. *Microbiology Lab*.

To his left was an unmarked single door with a tiny window. The glass was reinforced with wire. "This way," he whispered. Leading with his handgun, he slowly opened the single door and found what he was hoping for. More stairs. They had been painted a nightmare shade of institutional blue and the stairwell walls were a dull and lifeless gray. The steps led down.

Asya crept down the stairs behind him. "The floor above?" she whispered.

"Probably all labs. I've been in a few of Ridley's places. They all have the same general segregation of living quarters from labs. What we want will be in the offices."

At the bottom of the first set of stairs they came to a landing with a red fire extinguisher and another single black door. A plate above the door read *Sub Level 2*. King passed it and followed the steps deeper into the bowels of the facility. Asya asked no questions this time.

The steps ended at another door, labeled *Sub Level 3*. King gently opened this door, and peered down yet another long corridor, although this one was carpeted in soft gray, and the walls, while painted white, did not glare. The lighting in this hallway was recessed in the ceiling, casting a soft orange glow. The hall held doors only on the right. The first set, were double doors, and looked to be made of cherry wood. King spotted no sign of bio seals around the door's edges. *This one will be an office*, he thought.

He was surprised by the room's contents. It was not an office. Instead, it was a massive natural cave, and along the walls, strange technology lined every inch of the curved stone from floor to ceiling.

But it was the room's occupant that really got King's blood boiling. Standing at the far side of the cavern stood a man with dark curly hair and tanned skin. His chest and arms rippled with muscles, just barely contained beneath his business suit.

Alexander Diotrephes.

He turned just in time to see King rushing into the room and about to tackle him.

SIXTEEN
Amphithéâtre de Carthage, Tunisia

Daryl Trajan, known by his operational callsign of 'Trigger' to most, stayed perfectly still in his tree, on the northern edge of the ruins of the amphitheater. The sun was down, and there was no one around to see him, but he didn't want to chance that the enemy's sniper might be scoping his way. The man was said to be formidable with a long-range weapon—any long-range weapon.

Trigger had been on lookout at the amphitheater for hours, just like he had been the last two days, but today the boredom had cracked in half and blown away on the ocean breeze. First, he had spotted the slim guy in the Elvis t-shirt and some woman making for the fountain entrance of the Omega facility. Then he had witnessed the mass exodus of cloaked figures. The "cloaks", as he'd dubbed them, gave him the willies, what with their shriveled gray skin and their herky-jerky movements, but he felt pretty sure he would have no problem mowing them down with his HK416. The assault rifle looked like an AR-15—black and sexy—but with a wicked scope and a vertical fore-grip. Even though he mostly made

his bones as a mercenary by shooting things, for this job, so far all they had done is surveillance.

Trigger keyed his tactical microphone and called in the new development.

"Trigger to Carpenter, I've got eyes on the flying wing. Team is landing in the field north of the mosque."

"Trigger, this is Eagle. I want a complete account of who emerges from that transport." The unexpected voice was deep and gravelly.

Crap, Trigger thought. He had been expecting his fellow mercenary and friend, Carpenter, to answer the call. But apparently the Big Boss was here now. The man was ugly as sin, with a huge bald head criss-crossed with scars and a jagged hole where an ear should have been. He had chosen the name *Eagle* for himself, but behind his back, most of the mercs referred to him as *Beak*, because of the man's immense nose.

"Tell me about the cloaks you saw too," Eagle said over Trigger's earpiece.

"Well, sir, like I told Carpenter, shortly after Elvis and the woman went in the fountain entrance, the cloaks started streaming out of it. They headed southwest into the trees on the other side of the parking lot."

"We've seen the cloaks make for those trees before," Eagle said, his voice grating like metal scraped on concrete. "Why was this different?"

"This wasn't just a small pack of them. This looked like *all* of them. Hundreds. Maybe a thousand. And they were moving fast. They were in a damn hurry."

"No sign of them since?"

"None, sir. I've got eyes now on the sniper and the big one, exiting the craft. The one with the hand cannons is leading three bald men as prisoners," Trigger described each occupant of the strange stealth craft, as they exited and took to the field. He looked on through the scope of his rifle as the short sniper and

the big guy moved directly toward him, but neither seemed on guard yet. They were just hustling to get out of the open. "I have a shot on the sniper and the big one."

"Negative. I repeat, do not fire. We want all of them, and we want them *inside* the facility. What about the blonde woman?"

"Not yet, I—wait a minute. I've got her on the ground behind Hand Cannons. Transport is dusting off and they are all making for my position. I need to bug out soon." Trigger was frustrated that he couldn't just snipe the targets now. If he took out the sniper first, they'd all be sitting ducks. Still, if Eagle was paying the bills, then Trigger would do as he was told.

"Pack up and head out, Trigger. They're probably heading for the amphitheater entrance anyway. Remember, we want them all inside the facility—and the blonde bitch is mine. Acknowledge." Eagle's voice sounded plenty angry over the radio. Trigger wasted no time replying.

"Acknowledged. The blonde is all yours. Making for the fountain entrance. Trigger out."

He climbed down out of his tree as quickly as he could, without disturbing the branches and leaves. Even without a scope, the sniper might have really good eyes. No point taking a chance.

Trigger hit the ground and started moving west. He crossed a small field, and seconds later was hidden from the incoming targets, the giant mosque blocking their line of sight. He made his way across the boulevard and rendezvoused with four more mercs at the fountain entrance—all the while keeping an eye on the woods, in case the spooky cloaks came back. But Trigger figured them for gone. The way they had left made it seem like they were bailing for good. But the rest of Trigger's team had eyes on the only other entrance. So there was no way the Greek had escaped. He was inside still. So were Elvis and the woman. Now the rest of the team would be inside soon too, with the three bald men.

The plan seemed as safe and secure as it could be. Almost too secure. Dull, even. They would wait until the enemy team entered

the facility, then Trigger and his men would enter from the fountain, while a second group followed their targets into the amphitheater entrance. Finally, Eagle and the rest would enter through the secret vehicle entrance in the woods northwest of the nearby American Cemetery. Trigger still found it crazy that a huge US military cemetery was smack dab in the middle of North Africa, but it made sense. Some 2800 white crosses lined the 27-acre field, all American casualties from World War II. There was a tunnel that ran underground from the cemetery to the loading dock in the bottom of the subterranean Manifold facility.

All three entrances covered. Nowhere to run. Nowhere to hide. Trigger and the rest of the mercenary forces working for Eagle would come in like the waves of the ocean in a fierce storm, smashing and crashing, devastating everything in their path. The Greek and the enemy group Beak had referred to as Chess Team would have no escape. It was going to be like shooting fish in a barrel—with a howitzer.

SEVENTEEN
Omega Facility, Carthage, Tunisia

When King crashed into Alexander, it felt like hitting a brick wall. He'd let the AK go flying to the floor, and he lost the Sig on impact with Alexander's bulky chest. But the collision was still satisfying, as both he and Alexander slammed into the wall of machinery.

"King, wai—" Alexander started, but King had scrambled up to his knees and rammed his fist into Alexander's nose. King felt cartilage crunch under his fist, and Alexander howled, as a burst of bright red blood arced away from his face.

King was pulling his fist back for a second pistoning shot at the same spot, when Alexander let out a roar like a lion and flung

his arm out wildly. The strength in the sweep of Alexander's arm took King by surprise. The man was flailing, but King still found himself airborne, sailing across the room.

King's body hit the polished stone floor of the room and slid, as if he were on the bright yellow Slip n' Slide he had as a kid. He came to rest with his arm outstretched and his Sig in view across the floor. He lunged for the gun. Alexander would be much too tough an opponent for him. Thoughts of what might happen to his head if Alexander landed a clean punch helped to speed him across the slippery floor.

"Jack, you don't under—oh no you don't," Alexander's booming voice grew louder as the man rushed King like a freight train. King dove to the slick floor, counting on his slide to take him the rest of the way to the weapon.

His fingers reached out and grasped the grip of the Sig, just as Alexander slammed into him. They both slid toward the open doors King had rushed through. Asya was nowhere in sight. King had just a split second to wonder where his backup went, before his arm was coming up with the gun as his body continued to slide. Alexander's meaty hand was on his wrist, forcing his arm back.

King bent his wrist as far as it would go and started pulling the trigger, hoping he would either hit some part of Alexander's flesh or at least make the man back down.

Instead, the sound of the shots booming in the echoing rock cavern filled the large man with fury, and suddenly, through Alexander's roar of anger, King found himself lifted and shoved hard against the wall of the cavern. The collision with the unyielding stone took his breath away, but his anger at this man for endangering his parents was making King see red. He pulled the trigger of the Sig as he swung his dangling leg up and connected with Alexander's crotch. The big man flinched, but then pulled King's body, which he was completely suspending in the air now, away from the wall a few inches, before slamming King backward yet again.

King felt ribs break and his whole body started tingling, as his ears roared with adrenaline. The Sig was lost and Alexander's eyes were filled with fury as he smashed King against the wall a third time, then moved his grip, so he was holding King aloft by his neck.

Alexander began to speak again, but King could only hear the man as if he were a long way away.

"...what I'm trying to explain to you..."

King's arm was down by his side and brushed the pocket of his jeans. He felt the small hard lump on his hip, and his fingers dipped into the pocket. The jeans felt tight with the object in his pocket, and his fingers had a hard time reaching around the thing. Finally, the tip of his middle finger hooked on something and he tugged.

"We can end this right now!" Alexander was shouting.

King feebly moved his left fist up as if to punch at Alexander's face. He kept his speed slow and his accuracy way off. It was the perfect feint. Alexander turned toward the arm and brought his own up to block the strike.

Then King moved like a striking cobra, swinging his other arm up and inside the outstretched arm that held him in the air. The pineapple grenade in his fist, King launched the metal upward and bent his wrist back at the last second, so the grenade crunched into Alexander's already broken nose, and King's fingers were spared from being mashed.

Alexander stumbled back and dropped King. King landed in a crouch on his feet, then sprang back up, catching a sharp breath from the broken glass feeling in his side as he did so. His arm swung out like a baseball pitcher's and the fist clutching the grenade came down on top of Alexander's head at the apex of King's jump, once again, the metal connecting with bone.

Alexander staggered back, unsteady on his feet, his arms swinging around like a wild brawler in a bar-room fight, punching at invisible enemies. Then his eyes cleared. They were dark and full of rage.

Oh shit, King just had time to think.

Then the legendary Hercules—healed of all his injuries—was running for him.

King backed up to the wall, and waited for a blink, then dove to the side. Alexander—barreling at King at full speed like the fabled minotaur—mashed into the wall of the cavern. He brought his arms in front of him at the last second, his forearms crossed at the wrists to help cushion the blow. But his speed and strength were no match for centuries old stone. When Alexander hit the wall, the stone exploded outward, spewing large hunks of rubble and the powerhouse of a man out into the carpeted corridor. He tumbled and sprawled into the wall on the opposite side of the hallway before he hit the floor.

King was stunned. He knew he needed his weapon and he needed it fast. He quickly scanned the floor of the room. *Where is the damn AK?* But then he spotted his Sig Sauer, tucked under the front of a desk with a computer monitor, and a stack of papers on it. He raced across the room and leapt onto the floor, the polished surface gliding him right to the weapon. The jolt to his ribs when his hip hit the floor made him wince, but this fight would soon be over.

King reached out to grasp the gun, but it was struck and knocked out of reach. A cloud of red dust shot out from under the table and small chunks of stone scattered everywhere, several pieces pinging into King. He turned and stood, to see Alexander was standing in the giant hole he had torn in the wall. He held a slab of rubble twice the size of a human skull in his right hand, and the intention was clear.

The man had deadly aim. He had thrown a stone across the room that had smashed into the Sig and probably launched it far under the computer desk. The next shot would be to King's skull.

Still holding the grenade in his left hand, King sneered at Alexander and reached the fingers of his right hand for the safety pin. Alexander pulled his arm back with the stone and let it fly.

EIGHTEEN

Omega Facility, Carthage, Tunisia

A scream rang out through the room as Alexander threw the large stone and started to charge toward King.

"*Ostanovit!*" Asya's Russian shout was punctuated with a rapid burst of 7.92 mm bullets blasting into the stone ceiling, one of which made a wild ricochet noise, when it bounced off. "Stop! Both of you!" The sharp tang of gunpowder filled the space.

King flinched at the sound of gunfire in the confined space. The thrown stone whistled harmlessly overhead and shattered against the wall behind the computer desk. Rocky debris sprayed to the floor in a clatter that echoed in the abject silence after the gunshots. Alexander halted his most recent charge and turned to look at Asya. She stood in another doorway that led from the cavern into what appeared to be a small sitting room.

Asya had the AK-47 trained on Alexander. No one spoke for a minute.

"I'll ask you kindly, dear lady, not to fire that in here again. This room is full of very delicate scientific equipment." Alexander stood up straight and began swatting dust and dirt off his torn suit jacket. A flap of fabric that should have been on his chest hung down nearly to his knee. He picked up the flap and looked at it in disgust, then stripped out of the jacket and let it drop to the floor. The front of his white dress shirt had a spatter of blood down the neck and chest, from when King had broken his nose.

King reached under the computer desk and retrieved his Sig. It was scratched and coated in red dust, but it appeared mostly undamaged. He slipped the grenade—its pin still intact—in his pocket again, then stood and trained the pistol on Alexander with his right hand, while clutching his broken rib with his left.

"Morons, come!" Asya turned her back and began walking into the adjoining room.

"Morons?" King asked, his voice rising and a fight still in him.

Asya wheeled back on the men. "Yes!" she shouted. "Morons!" She pointed at Alexander. "You are idiot for letting us think you had kidnapped our parents! How did you think it would end?"

Alexander was about to reply, but Asya whirled to face King. "And you! You had pistol and rifle. You had a grenade! But you chased after him and tried to stop him with your fists? *Yeban ko maloletneye.*" She turned and stalked off into the adjoining room.

King looked at Alexander. "What did she just say?"

Alexander shrugged. "My Russian is a little rusty, but I think she called you an 'adolescent jerk.' It might have been something about a donkey, though."

King motioned for Alexander to follow Asya with his Sig. His rib hurt like a bastard, but he didn't want Alexander to see. He followed the large man into a lounge, which was separated by a thick metal door.

The lounge was lushly appointed with overstuffed comfortable-looking sofas, and armchairs. Off to the side of the room was a wet bar where a man was pouring a drink of single malt scotch for himself. King recognized the man instantly.

"Dad?"

Peter Machtchenko was clean shaven in a pinstripe gray suit that complimented his salt and pepper hair. The wrinkles around his eyes revealed his age to be in the fifties, but his level of fitness and posture suggested a much younger man. King glanced to a chair on the opposite side of the room and saw his mother. Lynn Machtchenko wore a tan pair of slacks and a long-sleeved white cotton blouse with a culturally appropriate scarf around her neck that she would cover her head with, when she went out. Her dark hair was pulled back in a ponytail, accentuating her facial similarity to Asya. Her eyes were kind, with a hint of a smile in them. Neither seemed concerned about the battle that had been

fought in the room next door. The thick door and walls must have dampened the sound.

"You're both here... You're okay?" King's voice was quiet. Stunned.

"Why don't you have a drink, son?" Peter said from across the room, dropping ice cubes into a crystal glass with a loud clink. "We've got a lot to talk about."

"Actually, if you'll all excuse me, I'd like to go change my clothes first," Alexander said.

King raised his Sig at the man. "I don't think so. You're the one with the most explaining to do. I'm not letting you out of my sight."

Alexander turned to face King. "Look, Jack, the scientific equipment in the next room represents the last fifty years of my hard work, and several hundred years of planning. I'm not going anywhere. I just want to put on a clean shirt. Then I'll answer all of your questions." He looked King in the eye, and raised his eyebrows. "All of them. Okay?"

King squinted at the man, still not fully trusting him. "Fine."

Asya walked over and handed the rifle to King, then patted him on the shoulder. "Compromise. Just like big boys. Very nice." Then she moved over to a sofa and sat down.

Alexander chuckled, then walked to a set of doors leading from the lounge into the hallway. "I'll be right back."

King slipped the strap of the AK over his shoulder and slid the Sig into the waistband of his jeans, behind his back. Then, gingerly, he sat down in a wingback chair.

"Were you hurt?" Lynn asked, concern making the smile in her eyes vanish.

"I'll be fine, Mom," King grunted. "Just a broken rib. Why are you two here?"

Peter walked over with a glass of scotch and set it on a glass-topped coffee table for King, then he took his own glass and plopped in a chair next to Lynn. "Well, it's kind of a long story."

King raised an eyebrow at the man. "Asya and I have been looking for you two all over the globe. We've spent a small fortune, used government assets and put ourselves in harm's way to find you."

"Not to mention a totally unnecessary fist fight with a guy who heals faster than I can say 'Hercules,'" Asya said. She was joking, but not smiling. They were both relieved that their parents were alive, but neither were happy to find they'd been duped.

"So you're going to tell us everything." King leaned back in his chair. "You take just as long as you need."

NINETEEN
Omega Facility, Carthage, Tunisia

"Alright, Dad. Let's have it." King leaned forward in the chair, then instantly regretted it, as a fresh shot of bone-jangling pain ripped through his side.

"Well, you already know that Lynn and I worked for the Russian government," Peter began.

"That's putting it mildly. You were spies. Sleeper agent spies, no less. You still are spies—" King spat.

"No, son. That's where you're wrong. We wanted out. What I told you about when we last met was true. But we got roped into one last job, which was supposed to be our way out. For good."

King recalled the story he had been told about Peter and Lynn Machtchenko breaking all ties from the Soviets in 1988. Russia had sent assassins after them just the once. King didn't know the particulars beyond the fact that his mother, who he'd always seen as a gentle woman, shot the man. The would-be assassin survived, but the implication was that the Russians would never try it again. But then, years later, Peter had been outed by the US Government, who promptly threw him in jail for a decade. Upon his release three

years ago, the KGB came sniffing again, hoping to reactivate Peter and Lynn as resources on US soil. The couple had created an elaborate scam to fake Lynn's death, but King had stumbled upon it.

"Your story would work just fine except for the fact that you bugged me. Oh yeah, and there were those dead bodies in your hotel room. And then you were gone. You better have something more meaningful than 'Just when I thought I was out, they pull me back in.'" King was getting tired of the lies. He looked over to Asya and found her simply nodding in agreement.

"Do you remember my twenty-second birthday?" Asya asked, looking at Peter. "The hunting trip? You gave me a speech that day, about honesty."

"I remember," her father said.

"I think it's time you took your own advice and—"

"Hold on," King said, on the verge of imploding. "Your *twenty-second* birthday?"

Peter's eyes turned toward the floor.

King groaned. "You were never in jail, were you?"

"Jail?" Asya said, baffled.

"You let me think you were in jail for ten years?" King shook his head, feeling a mixture of betrayal and sadness.

"The fewer people who knew about Asya, the better," Lynn said. "We have a lot of enemies. You have more. Family can be a weakness, so we hid you from each other. I raised you in the States. Your father raised Asya in Russia."

King understood the reasoning. It was classic spy paranoia, which wasn't necessarily unfounded. But the presence of his sister, of his still living sister, had become a source of stability for him over the past few months. "Family can also be a strength."

Lynn nodded. "We're together now. I hope it will be enough."

"Things have changed in Russia," Peter said, moving on. "Old elements are reclaiming power. They found me again. I had no choice but to make a deal. One last job. For your sister's sake. It was just supposed to be surveillance. They wanted to know your

activities and whereabouts. I was assured you were *not* a target. It was just intel. I figured what could it hurt? You were already wrapped up in your own problems with the attack on Fort Bragg. People were actively trying to kill you. Doing that one last job was supposed to ensure our immunity, and get them to leave you—both of you—alone for good." Peter sighed loudly, then sipped his scotch.

Lynn leaned forward in her chair, her long scarf falling from her neck to her lap. "We were set up, but so were the Russians. It turned out they were being pressured from a business partner that wanted the information..."

"Let me guess," King interrupted. "Richard Ridley."

"Exactly," Lynn continued. "And once things started to go haywire for him, his people picked us up. They were surprisingly good. We were really good once too, but we're getting up there in years. Neither of us stood much of a chance."

King winced at the thought of his parents being mistreated by Ridley's thugs.

"So what happened next?" Asya asked.

"I did." Alexander entered the room from the hallway, holding a large tray with a tea service. He wore a new pale blue shirt, and dark slacks. His face was clean and his hair was damp. His nose looked mended. "I suggest we have some tea. It's my own brew. Very relaxing."

When King raised an eyebrow, Alexander smiled. "It's just tea, Jack. But if you want something for that rib you're clutching, I still have some of the seeds from the Garden of Hesperides."

King recalled the effects of the apple seed. When crushed and liquefied, they acted as a potent regenerative medicine. King himself had been healed by one once, thanks to his good friend, George Pierce.

"Thanks, but I think I'll heal the old fashioned way," King said.

"Thought you might say that," Alexander tossed a white plastic bottle through the air toward King. "Heads up."

King caught the bottle in the air with his left hand, grimacing, as his chest muscles stretched.

"800 milligram ibuprofen tablets—the old fashioned way. Have some green tea to wash it down." Alexander began pouring tea from an ornate golden cloisonné kettle into delicate little matching teacups. King raised an eyebrow at the man again.

"Seriously," the large man said. "Green tea has long been known to reduce the risks of heart disease and cancer, as well as boosting the metabolic rate. Plus, it's soothing to the nerves."

"You were saying about my parents?" King asked, watching the man's hands for any signs that he was slipping something into the brew.

"Peter and Lynn were being held by Ridley's people. While Chess Team was content with the New Hampshire base, my people were taking all the other Manifold facilities around the world." Alexander nodded to Peter and Lynn. "I freed them. They were in Singapore under my protection until last week, when I brought them here. You see, Jack, Ridley was long fascinated with all aspects of antiquity. One of the things he wanted most—the mother tongue—he eventually got his hands on, as you well know. But to get there, he hunted down every sign and every clue he could find that would lead him to the last living speakers of several ancient languages. You know all this."

Alexander finished pouring the tea, placed a cup on the table in front of King, next to the untouched glass of scotch, then took his own seat, next to Asya. He pursed his lips, blew on his cup to cool the brew, then sipped his tea. The tiny teacups looked ridiculous in his massive hands.

Lynn reached for her own cup and took a sip. Alexander had not poured a cup for Peter. The man still had a glass of scotch in his hands. King eyed the tea suspiciously, but seeing no ill effects on Lynn, and not wanting to be rude, he sipped the brew. It was strangely lacking in flavor, like drinking hot water. He wondered why anyone would drink it. Still, he popped the ibuprofen and washed it down with another sip of the scalding liquid.

"Those speakers of ancient languages all had one other thing in common, Jack. Something I didn't find out until too late, which is why so many of them perished, and why I was so keen to safeguard them all." Alexander scowled at the thought of the dead that he had failed to protect.

"What did they have in common?" King asked.

Alexander looked directly at him. "Me."

King turned to Asya, but she looked as confused as he did. "I don't follow."

"Jack, I know you might not believe it, but I am several centuries old. How many offspring do you think a man like me might have had over those years?"

Then it hit King all at once. "No..."

Asya hadn't figured it out yet. "What?"

"All those people...my daughter. They're all your descendants." King looked at Alexander, with his mouth open. "And...shit. We are too." He glanced at Asya again so she would know the 'we' implicated her.

Alexander nodded. "As is your father. I didn't know at first, but I looked into the incident when your mother bugged you."

"Sorry, son," Lynn smiled sheepishly.

"I had suspected our connection for quite some time, Jack." Alexander drank his tea.

"You mean to tell me you weren't tracking my movements?" King asked.

"Think about it, Jack. Centuries, and generation after generation? I can't possibly keep track of all my descendants. But sometimes I come across someone I'm sure about. You noticed that you and your sister were immune to those creatures—you called them Dire Wolves—in Norway, while the rest of your team was affected?" Alexander pointed to King and Asya. "My blood, diluted by centuries of course, but enough to keep you from feeling the effects of those creatures."

King recalled that other members of Chess Team and even support members of Endgame had been affected by a fear-inducing

sonic cry from the creatures they had faced the previous year. He alone had seemed immune to the effect. But during the final battle, he had discovered that Asya was likewise unaffected.

"Wait, you've mentioned that you've been known by many names. Was one of them Adoon?"

Alexander's face darkened. "Where did you hear that name?"

"In Norway. The thing we fought—Fenrir—referred to us as the 'Children of Adoon.' I thought at the time that it was speaking of Earth's inhabitants or referring to the Biblical children of Adam, but it wasn't, was it? It was talking about me...and my connection to you. Who the hell are you?"

Alexander sighed. "I'm just a man trying to get home, Jack. And I need your help."

"When you say 'home,' you don't mean Greece, do you?"

TWENTY
Omega Facility, Carthage, Tunisia

It had been only a few hours, but Queen, was already deeply tired of the three Ridley clones. They were the enemy, but as much as she wanted them gone, she needed to understand them.

"So you three are exact duplicates of the original Ridley? You have the same emotions, the same thoughts? How does that work?" she asked.

They were standing in the ruins of the Roman amphitheater, a large circular walled field with patchy grass and stone debris of what Queen guessed were once buildings. The remains of pillars stood around the circumference of the stadium—some only nubs after the ravages of time. A lone standing pillar stood on a raised platform. The center of the arena had a recessed area like a trench with gates on either end. Seth led them down to one of the gates, which he then unlocked with a key.

"As I've said, we three do not possess the mother tongue, but as I understand it, our Creator used the mother tongue to merge his DNA with the raw material he imbued with life.

Queen raised an eyebrow. It sounded hokey as hell, but she'd seen it with her own eyes more than once. "By raw material you mean, what, clay?"

"It is the most stable of elements with which to imbue life," he replied. "And our lives began as fully formed duplicates of our Creator, complete with his memories, aspirations and intellect. But from that moment forth, we each began creating new memories and having new thoughts shaped by our individual experiences. So while two years ago we were duplicates in every way of Richard Ridley, now we might even be considered human, as we have each led separate lives and made choices our Creator might not have."

"That's too bad," Queen said, as they entered the shadowed end-chamber behind the gate. Knight and Bishop had barrel-mounted flashlights on their MP-5 submachine guns that illuminated the space around them. Jared moved to the wall and began running his fingers along the top, where it met the ceiling. When his fingers found an indentation, he slipped his index and middle finger inside.

"Why is that?" Seth asked.

A loud *clatch* noise filled the arched space, and a portion of the stone wall began to slide back on incredibly quiet pistoning motors. Queen could just barely hear them hissing like air compressors.

She shoved Seth toward the open doorway. "Because I was thinking about killing one of you. If you were just plain old duplicates of Ridley, I wouldn't shed a tear. But on the off chance that as 'new humans' you might have some redeeming quality, I'll keep you alive a little longer."

Seth stepped into the new opening, which revealed a modern metal stairwell and concrete walls. He reached to the wall and flipped on a light switch. Suddenly the stairwell was lit up with

bright fluorescent spotlights mounted on the walls and protected by metal cages. He turned to Queen. "That is very considerate of you."

Rook walked past the man, intentionally slamming his shoulder into Seth's. "I didn't make any such promise, cupcake."

Seth looked at Knight, but the short Korean just stalked away into the stairwell after Rook and the other two duplicates.

Then Bishop walked toward Seth. "Don't even look at me." Unlike Rook, Bishop walked around Seth, as he made for the stairs. He was the poster child for anger management, but that was primarily because he stored up his rage for when he really needed it most. Then he became a volcano. If he let himself rough up one of the duplicates, he might just open the flood gates and end one of them.

Or all of them.

Queen, on the other hand, had no trouble being physical. She took Seth by his shoulder, and with one deft twist of her hand, she guided his body around, so he faced the stairs. Then she shoved him to follow Bishop.

The stone door slid quietly shut behind the group as they made their way down the stairs. At the bottom, they faced two corridors, but Jared, the supposedly mute duplicate, pointed down the tunnel leading west. Eventually they came to a metal door. On the wall beside it was a keypad.

Jared tapped in a code of five 9s, and the door unlocked with a soft clicking noise. Enos, the supposedly deaf duplicate, pulled the door handle open to reveal a janitorial closet filled with mops and bottles of cleaning supplies on high shelves.

At the other side of the closet-sized space was another door.

Queen nudged Seth. "What's on the other side of that door?"

"It's a biology lab. Should be empty. There's no more staff here. Just Alexander and his...servants. But as far as we could tell, they tend to congregate near the mouth of the vehicle entrance for some reason. We're taking you in a different way. We should be able to get

to where Alexander is holding the Creator without being seen. Unless Alexander is present. He's the only real obstacle."

"I'm less worried about him than I am about you three," Queen mumbled.

Seth smiled. "Across the bio lab to the hallway. Turn right and go all the way to the end. We'll take the stairs down. At that point we'll need to be quiet in case Alexander has protection about."

Knight led the way, with his MP-5 submachine gun at the ready. He'd normally have an XM2010 Enhanced Sniper Rifle strapped to his back, but for this mission, sniping wasn't going to be a useful skill. Behind him, Jared and Enos followed, with Bishop coming behind them, also armed with an MP-5. The weapon felt tiny to him, but the large machine guns he typically wielded in the field weren't the best choice for enclosed spaces or fast getaways. Finally, Seth followed Bishop, and Queen brought up the rear.

They moved across the lab with its shiny tables and brilliant white walls into a hallway exactly as Seth had described. At the far end of it, after passing several doors labeled for different kinds of labs—*Cold, Sequencing, Data*, and *Restoration*—and one door labeled *Personnel*, they came to the stairwell, and descended. Queen noted the sign on the back of the door as she closed it. *Sub Level 1*. They passed *Sub Level 2*, and stopped at a door for *Sub Level 3*. Jared waited at the door as she and Seth descended to the floor.

"What's on Sub Level 2?" she asked Seth.

"Mostly office space. This level is primarily storage and the loading dock I mentioned," Seth answered her in a quiet voice, not quite a whisper. "We'll need to move silently from here. The hallway runs straight through to the other side of the facility, just like the hallway on Sub Level 1. On the right will be a solid wall. On the left there'll be a storage room, the dock, and then the security room, where He will be. After the security room is a bathroom, more storage and a small lounge. Then a natural cavern and another stairwell at the end of the hall. Any questions?"

Queen shook her head. She peeked through the wire-reinforced window in the door. The hallway looked like Seth had described it. "Bishop, you're on point. Knight, keep an eye on our six. Rook, you keep an eye on the Three Amigos, here." Bishop stepped in front of Jared and grasped the doorknob with one hand, his MP-5 at the ready in the other. "Go."

Bishop slipped the door open and moved out into the carpeted hallway. As promised, they passed an unmarked door on the left, and then came to two windowed doors that led to the loading dock. Bishop peered through one of the windows and motioned that they could continue. As Queen slipped past the door, following Seth, she glanced in and saw a large concrete platform that dropped away to a larger lower space where a bright yellow forklift sat in front of a ramp. On the end of the dock was a blue metal dumpster. Otherwise, the dock was free of vehicles, and there were no signs of any people or Alexander's wraiths.

The next room was clearly marked *Security*. Bishop paused at the door, then opened it slowly, the barrel of the submachine gun leading. As prophesied, the room was empty. Five black office chairs sat on casters in front of five darkened monitors and computer stations. At the back of the room on the left was a door with a security pad, like the one they had seen upstairs.

"He will be in here," Seth began to rush toward the door, but Bishop shoved the man roughly aside. Rook turned a fierce gaze on the other two duplicates, but neither made a move.

Queen stepped up to the door and the keypad. "What's the code?"

"It should be disabled with the code we punched in upstairs," Seth replied. He looked surly about having been held back from his master.

Queen opened the door and stepped in. When she gasped, Rook was right behind her into the room.

"Oh my God," she managed. "This is... This is..."

"That's some gnarly fuckin' potatoes, is what that is," Rook said.

They were looking at Richard Ridley—or what was left of him.

TWENTY-ONE
Loading Dock Entrance, Omega Facility, Carthage, Tunisia

The vehicle paused at the entrance to the ramp that led from the massive underground parking garage to the loading dock down on Sub Level 3. He climbed out of the white van and checked that his Beretta M9 handgun was seated in its holster. Then he walked across the huge echoing space, leaving three more vans and the bulk of his men to wait.

He knew a small team of three covered the amphitheater exit above ground, but most of the men would go in with him through the loading dock. He was damn glad that the cloaks had mysteriously bugged out. That would make his job a lot easier. He loved it when things came together smoothly on an op—not like that mess in the Ukraine, where he'd lost an ear to that blonde bitch.

A few more strides across the deserted concrete floor and he came to the ladder at the base of the fountain. Two men stood to either side of the metal ladder, and he knew a third would be up top, hidden in the trees near the unused fountain.

The men snapped to attention at the sight of him.

"Who's topside?" he asked.

"Sir, Trigger is up top, in a tree about ten meters from the entrance." The man was short, with thick hairy forearms, covered in thin straight scars. Eagle respected the man and his knife fighting scars. There were a lot of them, but seeing as how the man was standing here, his opponents faired far worse. "Sounds good, Carpenter. You two stay frosty. When the shit hits the fan—and it will—things are likely to bubble up

here. Anyone not wearing solid black BDUs like us? You dust them. That includes the clones."

"Understood, sir." Carpenter nodded.

Eagle smiled grimly.

Carpenter's companion, a greasy, nasty man named Keller, who went by the callsign of Raven, simply stood and looked forward, as if Eagle wasn't even there. Eagle wondered if Raven's bearing was from his time in the Marines, or if he was just zoned out on drugs. It didn't really matter too much. You took what you could get with a mercenary force. Most of the soldiers were veterans of multiple engagements, and they would all stay loyal through the mission; the money he had promised them would ensure that.

Eagle, tall, imposing and to his own mind, hideously deformed, turned and strode back across the garage to his waiting caravan of mercenary soldiers. Each was armed with smoke grenades, and AK-47s, like his. Except for a few of the men, who were less than savory, he liked most of them. Twenty-three in all, they made a nice round twenty-four with him. His own little private army, funded with money from the former Manifold Genetics.

He keyed his microphone as he walked. "Station Two, give me a sit-rep."

"This is Mason at Station Two. They just went in. We gave them five and moved in after them to lock the gate down. No one coming in or out over here, Eagle." The voice was young, but Eagle knew the man was a competent fighter, and the veteran of some bloody battles in Rwanda and Burundi. Eagle had brought the young man on the previous year.

"Excellent. We're moving in. Expect things might come your way. Anything coming down that tunnel is to be considered hostile. Kill it. Eagle out."

He smiled and strode back to the waiting line of vans. As he reached the third van in the convoy, he slapped the side of it hard.

In response, the driver started the engine. Without needing to be told to do so, the second and first vans did likewise. Eagle stepped up to the passenger side door on the first van and slid into his seat. He pulled an AK-47 up out of the foot-well, and lowered the window, leaning the tip out. He knew the vehicle tunnel leading three levels down to the dock was plenty wide for the vans. There was no danger of hitting the walls with the tip of the rifle.

"It's time for the Chess Team and Alexander Diotrephes to die. Let's go," Eagle barked.

The driver threw the van into drive and slowly proceeded down the ramp.

Then Eagle keyed his microphone again. "This is Eagle. Squad One is moving in. Squads Two and Three, stay alert. If the fighting gets past us to the surface, you move in."

Twenty-Four men in the immediate fight. Another forty-eight waiting up top—just in case.

Oh yes, he thought. *In less than an hour, this installation will be mine.* He would execute the members of Chess Team. Kill off the intruding Greek. Eliminate the ridiculous doubles. Then Omega, and its information on the last resting place of the *Chest of Adoon* would be his. And along the way, he'd get to stab that bitch that took his ear. It was going to be a great day. Darius Ridley was finally going to have his revenge.

TWENTY-TWO
Lounge, Omega Facility, Carthage, Tunisia

Alexander led King back into the adjacent cavern-like room. Peter and Lynn remained in the lounge with Asya, speaking in animated Russian. King really looked at the equipment along the walls in the cavern. Before, he had been too busy trying to stay alive. But now, some of the arched metal structures lined with

thick electrical cables in their black rubber insulation, reminded him of something he'd seen before.

"How did you get here so quickly? I was expecting you, of course, but not for a few more weeks, if I'm honest." Alexander moved to the wall of machinery. He examined a few parts of the curved metal, tugged on cables as if to ensure they were not loose and scrutinized small parts. Then he nodded, as if assuring himself that the machine was built correctly. King figured it was all an act to appear disinterested in how King had found the man.

"The library in Malta," King said, leaving the explanation at that.

"How did you get past the Forgotten?" Alexander asked. Then he turned, a storm of anger brewing in his tanned face. "You didn't kill them, did you?"

"No. Once they saw who I was, they let me pass. Made things a whole lot easier that you told them to leave me be." King walked past Alexander to look closer at one part of the machinery. The arched design made the thing look like a seven foot tall Greek letter for Omega: Ω. King wondered how much of the tech he was looking at came from Ridley and how much from Alexander.

"Did they?" Alexander mumbled, absentminded as he checked over a computer screen, attached to the side of the machinery. "Hmm. Well, I suppose that makes sense, doesn't it?"

Then he turned to King, all pretenses at dithering with the machine done. King was watching the man like a hawk.

"Do you recognize elements of the design?" Alexander pointed to the Omega shaped piece of machinery, and all at once, King knew his suspicions were correct. This was the same machinery he'd dealt with in Norway, the designs for which were on a laptop stolen from Endgame headquarters.

"You know I won't let you activate it," King said. His hand hung loose at his side, but it could easily reach for the Sig Sauer in his waistband, if need be.

"Actually, Jack, I'm hoping you'll be the one to help me activate it."

"You're nuts. The last time dimensional tech like this was activated, it ate half the planet. If you think—" King began.

"Please," Alexander said, holding out his hands, to appease King. "Just let me explain a few things."

King stopped his rant, and just looked at Alexander, raising his eyebrows, as if to say *There's no way you can convince me, but go ahead.*

"I've spent hundreds of years amassing scientific knowledge and acquiring technology like this," Alexander pointed a brawny arm at the machine along the wall, "all for one purpose. I'm not a bad man, Jack. Yes, I've made some mistakes, and yes, I've sometimes let my goals overcome any sense of modern morality. But you've seen the Forgotten. You know they were my own experiments, in my early days of testing the limits of immortality."

King frowned again, thinking of the shriveled, hideous creatures that were once normal men.

"But I also take care of them now. I protect them. They are directionless, and if left to their own devices, they might just die, Jack. I would hope that caretaking alone might count for something with you, to show I'm not a monster. I've aided you against Richard Ridley. Hell, I believe we saved the world together. And I have helped you to keep your daughter, Fiona, alive, along with several other last speakers of languages all around the world. The Herculean Society has a membership of thousands—many of whom are being helped more by the Society than they help me. So when I tell you what I've been working on for hundreds of years, I hope that you will see I am being sincere."

"Okay," King said. "Surprise me. What's your motivation?"

"Love," Alexander said, his face completely serious.

King was flabbergasted. It was the last response he ever would have expected.

"What?"

"Listen, Jack. I'm not trying to rip open a portal to another dimension. You can relax. I've retooled this machinery, so it

works properly now. But I need your help to make the machine work...and get me home. That's really all I've ever wanted. The machine is perfectly safe now."

King shifted the strap of the AK-47 across his chest and stared at the man.

"The machine is ready. Like I said, I wasn't expecting you for weeks yet, but I finished work on the device early. It will open a portal to another place. A dangerous place. And... I will need your help there." Alexander raised his hand and flipped a switch on the terminal behind him. The arch of metal and electrical cables hummed, and a field of blue light crackled to life in the circular center of the arch. King felt the hair on his arm stand up, as the electrical field tugged at him. He realized the arch was just large enough to be a man-sized portal, but the last time he had seen a portal like this, he'd seen creatures just larger than a man come through. And even larger creatures waited on the other side.

"Turn it off." King said, hand on the grip of his gun. "I haven't said whether I'm helping you yet."

The chime of a phone drowned out the hum of the machine. Alexander drew the small device from his pocket and looked at the screen. He held his index finger up, indicating that King should wait, and then he took the call.

King almost shot Alexander out of sheer annoyance, but controlled himself and decided to listen to the one-sided conversation instead, hoping to glean a hint of what was going on.

"She's on?" Alexander asked whoever was on the other end. "Connect us." He gave King a slight grin. "Hello? Yes, please hold."

Alexander took the phone away from his ear and held it out to King. "For you."

King squinted, but took the phone. "Hello?"

"Dad?"

"Fiona?" His eyes went from confused to enraged. If Alexander had taken her again, he would kill the man or die trying.

"Why did you call?"

"I called you?"

"Umm, that's what they told me." She sounded more confused than afraid. In fact, there wasn't a trace of fear in her voice. *She's still at school*, he realized.

"I just...wanted to see how you were doing," he said. He knew how she was doing. She had armed guards keeping tabs on her, guards who reported in every night, even if she didn't.

She laughed, and the sound of it made him miss her more than usual. "I'm fine. A little bored, but I think that's normal for someone who's done the things we do."

The things *we* do.

King smiled, nearly forgetting about Alexander. Fiona had survived Richard Ridley's attack on the Siletz reservation that killed her family—her people. She'd been taken by Alexander and subsequently kidnapped and held hostage by Richard Ridley. She'd used the mother tongue to defeat a towering stone golem, saved the entire team and finally, had nearly been sucked inside a black hole, once again proving instrumental in saving his life...and the world. She would one day make a fine addition to the team. She might even be the best of them. But right now...right now she was still a kid.

His kid.

Then he remembered. "Actually, I have some news, but I want to tell you in person."

"So you just called to torture me then?" she said. "Tell me, now. Or I'll flunk out on purpose."

King turned away from Alexander. This was a private moment. He squinted against the glow of the activated machine. *I'll deal with you in a moment*, he thought, and then said. "How would you feel about having a mom?"

"Oh my God..." Fiona was quiet for a moment. "Oh my God! You asked her!"

"I did."

"She said yes?"

"Why wouldn't she?"

"Well, you know. All the bullets and explosions and monsters and—"

"We talked about that."

"So, who's retiring?"

"What?" King felt rattled. Even his teenage daughter could see that marriage for him would be tricky. Perhaps trickier than having a daughter.

"We'll talk when I get home, okay?"

"And that will be?"

That was always the question. *When.* He'd been on the road so much, searching for his parents, that he'd seen Fiona far less than he should. She was at a boarding school, sure, but she was just twenty minutes from the base. He should see her more often. He considered telling her that he'd found his parents, but that would bring up a lot of questions he didn't have answers for yet. And he needed to get them. Now. "I'll see you in a few days. I promise."

"You better, 'cause, you know, Knight taught me how to track. I could hunt you down."

King smiled. "I'll be there."

"Love you, Dad."

"Love you too."

King hung up the phone. His smile faded. Turned into a frown. He turned slowly toward Alexander. "Why?"

"Because I'm merciful," Alexander said. "It was a gift."

"A gift?"

"The chance to say goodbye."

King glanced at the field of energy just a foot away from him. "I'm not going anywhere." He turned back to look at Alexander. The big man was rushing him.. There was no time to get the pistol up. No time to react.

Asya opened the door to the cavernous lab just in time to see Alexander tackle King, and just in time to hear King shout out "No!"

Both men were instantly locked in a grappling embrace as their bodies slammed into a circular wall of crackling blue energy. When they hit the blue light, the wall pulsed outward into a broad sphere of power, stuttering streaming bolts of lightning shooting out across the room in all directions.

Then the machine, and the blue ball of light that had engulfed the men shrank down to two thirds its normal size, before exploding outward in a tremendous blast that sent Asya flying back through the doorway and across the lounge. Her body crashed into one of the small sofas with such force that she toppled the piece of furniture, her body rolling to the far side of it and coming to rest against a coffee table. The impact of her body on the table was enough to overturn a cup of tea that had gone cold. The liquid spread off the end of the table and poured onto her head.

Peter and Lynn stood from their seats and rushed to their injured daughter as smoke and flame billowed out of the doorway to the cavern. A huge cloud slid across the ceiling of the lounge.

"What happened?" Peter asked Asya, cradling her bleeding head.

"I..." Asya started. She sat up and her mother helped her. Asya looked back at the dark gray smoke coming out of the doorway.

She started to stand up, and Peter stopped her. "Are you okay?"

"I am fine," she said and struggled to her feet, with her parents helping her on both sides. She had knocked her head slightly, but otherwise she was alright.

"It was Alexander," she told them. "He and King...they fought again. They crashed into the machine."

"Jack's in there?" Peter was about to turn and run into the cavern. Asya grabbed him by his sleeve.

"You don't understand. The machine exploded...with them inside." Asya turned to look at her mother's already tearing eyes. Then she

turned back to her father. His face was suddenly drawn, and long. His eyes filled with shock and understanding.

"Jack is dead."

INFINITE

TWENTY-THREE

Security Cell, Omega Facility, Carthage, Tunisia

The thing before them could barely be called human.

Richard Ridley's cell was a 20x20 room, and humidity was almost completely absent from the space. It was baking hot, as if they had all crawled inside an oven set to 400 degrees. In the center of the room, two cages were suspended by chains. The top cage was a rusted metal box formed from crisscrossing bars, like some kind of oversized death metal Christmas ornament. Attached to the outside of the cage was a device that looked like a gerbil's water dispenser, but larger and connected to a hose that ran into the ceiling. Hung a few inches under the top cage was a larger rectangular cage suspended vertically, and made from the same rusted iron bars as the first.

Inside the top cage was Richard Ridley's head.

Inside the bottom cage was the man's limbless torso.

But it was what was in the four-inch space *between* the two suspended cages that had prompted Queen's disgust and Rook's admiration.

Ridley's skin was cracked and gray, all over what remained of his body. The places where his limbs should have been were darkened stumps. But the places at the bottom of his head, and the

top of his torso, where his neck should have been, were alive with pink flesh. Tendrils of nerves and blood vessels dangled down from the severed head or stretched up from the headless torso. The tendrils wavered slightly in the air, each struggling and reaching to meet their counterparts on the opposite side of the deadly gap. Only three tendrils had been successful so far, but Queen could see that they were struggling to maintain contact with each other. The spinal cord was a grayish orange stump.

The man was in a constant state of failed regeneration.

As Queen stepped closer, she could see that the eyes were gray and lifeless, sunken back into the sockets, like ill-fitting rubber balls that had been placed into their holders, like toys on a shelf. The mouth hung open, and the tongue was shriveled and black.

"It is worse than I had feared," Seth spoke from behind the group.

"Ridley or not, this is inhuman. Get him down." Queen ordered.

Rook and Bishop moved to the cages and began opening them. They were not locked. There was no need. Knight stepped into the room with the three duplicates, keeping an eye on them, his submachine gun raised.

Seth turned to Knight and Queen. "May we assist in removing Him? I suggest we lay him on the floor and allow the head to rejoin with the torso. Water might also be good."

Queen hesitated, but nodded. Ridley wouldn't be speaking any time soon.

The three clones moved over to help. Rook gently pulled Richard Ridley's head up and away from the cage. The tendrils that had managed to grasp those reaching from the torso snapped. Rook winced.

"It's okay," Seth told them. "Just get the torso out quickly, so He may heal." Seth took the head reverently and laid it on the floor, holding it with his hand, so it would not roll to the side. Bishop pulled the torso out of its cage, swung it around and laid it on the

floor below the head. Jared and Enos gently slid the torso up, until the tendrils reaching from the head touched with those of the torso. They moved the chest up further until the parts of the neck touched. Instantly the skin began to repair itself.

Bishop pulled a plastic tube from his armored shoulder, and offered it to Seth. The clone lowered the tube over Ridley's mouth and squeezed the plastic bite valve with his fingers. A stream of water from the reservoir hidden under the armor plates on Bishop's massive back dripped into the open mouth. Immediately, the blackened shriveled tongue began to thrash from side to side in the mouth, and color returned to it. Then it swelled closer to the size of a normal tongue.

"That's enough," Queen said. "Everybody step back and give him some room."

Bishop stood up and leaned on the far wall, next to Rook. The duplicates stood and backed away, toward the door where Knight remained.

Already, the damaged body's odd gray pallor was slipping away to a mottled yellow and white. Queen watched as the veins on Ridley's forehead inflated, pressing away from the skin. Nubs pressed out from the man's blackened shoulders, no larger than a peanut at first, but they quickly grew to the size of a pear.

His arms, she thought. *I'm actually watching a man grow arms.*

She had, of course, seen Bishop regenerate from grave wounds, back when he had his Manifold-inflicted abilities, but she had never seen anything like this.

She knelt down by Ridley's side, watching the amazing transformation. Femur bones were extending out of the gaping openings under his hips. Then a trail of blood vessels and nerves swirled down the length of the bone, and muscles began to form in patches. Queen looked back up to the man's head, and saw his mouth was healed entirely. Where the nose had been little more than two vertical slits, more resembling a skull than a human face, the full nose had regrown.

His eyelids moved and jittered, his eyes under the flesh darting all around, as if the man were in REM sleep.

Then he took a deep breath in and slowly exhaled.

The breath took Queen by surprise, as if up until now she had been watching a strange science video about the body, but now she was forcefully reminded that she was kneeling next to her worst enemy. And he was coming back from the dead.

His eyelids flicked open. Richard Ridley's pale blue eyes stared at Queen. He spoke in a whisper. "Ms. Baker. Not the first face I thought I'd see upon waking, but a pleasant one, nonetheless." Sweat had popped out on his forehead, from the strain the regenerating was taking on him.

"Hey asshole. You can speak again," she said. "Does that mean you can use the mother tongue to finish healing yourself?"

"I could, but why—"

Queen stabbed his chest with the injector she had slipped out of a pocket on the outside of her armored leg. The serum pumped into Ridley's heart and spread to the rest of his still-regenerating body in a flash. The growth ceased.

"What are you doing?" Seth screamed.

"Shaddap," Rook threatened, raising his MP-5 at Seth and the other two duplicates. Knight, who was still standing near them, pushed Seth back against the wall with his free hand.

"Relax, Ridley," Queen said to the panicked eyes below her. "Just removing your chemical regenerative abilities. The serum alters your DNA, stripping the bits that you got from the Hydra. You don't need them to get back into shape. Once you're healed, if you cross me, I shoot your damn mouth off, and your ability to regenerate is lost forever, without a tongue to use your magic language. Are we clear?"

"Hmm," Ridley said. "I'd nod, but I don't have the musculature back yet. What exactly is it that you want, Queen?"

"I want you to help me kill Alexander Diotrephes."

Richard Ridley laid on the floor, his extremities suddenly stopped from returning. He smiled broadly, showing sparkling white teeth. "That...would be my pleasure."

TWENTY-FOUR
Security Cell, Omega Facility, Carthage, Tunisia

Queen stood and moved toward the three duplicates. She pulled out another auto injector.

Seth's eyes grew wide. "What is in that?"

"Same thing he got," Queen answered, motioning to Ridley.

Seth looked confused, but the attention turned away from him when Ridley chuckled. "They're golems. Earthen men. They cannot regenerate flesh they do not have."

Seth looked a little disappointed to hear this, but tried to hide it.

Knight held Seth with one hand and pointed his MP-5 at the man's temple. "I'm sure you won't blame us for not taking your word on that."

Queen jabbed Seth with the injector and moved to the other two clones. Jared looked as if he might fight.

Rook spoke up from across the room. "Don't even dream it, Captain Kangaroo. I got you covered from here, and she could kill you thirty ways with that injector and another eighty with her bare hands if she wanted you gone."

Jared offered his arm up, pushing up the sleeve of his linen suit jacket, but the fire never left his light blue eyes. Enos offered his arm meekly. Queen wondered at the differences she saw in personalities between the dupes, but she recalled what Seth had said about each of them gaining new experiences. *They really are becoming different people.* She wondered if any of them had a chance at redemption. Could they change from what the original Ridley was—or would she need to kill all three of them?

The serum injected into all four Ridleys, Queen moved back to the man regenerating on the gray concrete floor. A thought occurred to her. "Do you know how you were being imprisoned?"

Richard Ridley moved his head, while mumbling a chant in the mother tongue that was completing his regeneration. His eyes fell on the cages. Queen could see him working it out in his mind. When a dark frown fell on his face, she knew he understood.

"Look at me," she said.

He turned his head toward her, with far less effort than it had taken for him to look over at the cages, still swaying on their chains. His face was neutral now, all signs of the frown gone.

"If you try to screw us, Rook and I will think up something worse than this hideous shit. Do you believe me?" Queen slid the bandana off her forehead, revealing a nasty brand she had received at the hands of an enemy in the past. "I'm no stranger to torture."

Ridley nodded slightly. He paused his chant. "I believe you."

"Good," she said. "I want intel. Describe this facility. Tell me what its purpose was. I want to know every secret fucking panel in this place, and I want to know where Alexander is likely to be held up." She glanced down at the legs Ridley was growing. The feet looked like deformed baby's feet attached to the ends of withered adult legs. "We've got a little time before you're ready to walk."

"I need some water," Ridley said.

Queen looked up at Bishop. The big man stepped over and kneeled, pouring water again from his plastic hose, directly into Ridley's mouth. The regenerating man swallowed in huge gulps, like a man who had just crossed a desert.

"Thank you. This facility was for genetic research initially, but it eventually became a storehouse for archeological finds and artifacts as well. It has three levels, which you would have seen some of to get here. We are on Sub Level 3, which consists of this cell, the outer security room, a loading dock, storage, and a lounge. There's also a natural cavern that predates the Roman occupation. That's at the end of the hall. Second floor is all offices and a meeting room. Plus my office. Oh yes, there's a little kitchen up there too. Sub Level 1 is the labs, and living quarters for the staff. Two ways in and out of the

facility: the loading dock and the secret door through the janitor's closet at the back of the bio lab, on Sub Level 1."

"We came in that way," Queen nodded. "What else?"

"Well, from that closet, you might have come in one of two ways: the stairs from the amphitheater, or the tunnel that leads to the parking garage. The garage connects with the loading dock also. From the garage, you have two ways in or out. The vehicle tunnel takes you to the American Cemetery. There's an emergency ladder from the garage to the unused fountain on the surface, next to the mosque's parking lot." The man no longer had sweat popping out all over his head. Queen noticed that his body appeared nearly whole, although he was hardly as muscular as he used to be. Still, he looked like he might be able to walk again soon.

"We didn't know about the fountain. Nice to see you're telling the truth," she told him.

"Why wouldn't I? I want what you want right now: Alexander." Ridley pushed his torso up with his newly formed arms. He didn't have quite enough strength to sit up fully, so he rested on his elbows, looking relaxed and assessing the growth of his legs.

"May I?" Seth asked Knight, attempting to remove his linen jacket. Knight gave a grim nod.

Seth stepped forward into the room, and removed his cream colored linen jacket, gently draping it over Richard Ridley's exposed genitals.

"Thank you, Seth," he said. The duplicate nodded, and stepped back.

"How can you tell them apart?" Queen asked. She had only been able to remember Seth based on his being the only one who spoke and by keeping mental track of where he was in the room.

"I created him. And the others. I know them."

"How many more are there?" Queen asked, pointing to Jared.

"Sadly, these three are the last, but they are my favorites."

Suddenly, the door to the room opened, and Knight quickly swiveled his weapon toward it. On the other side of the room,

Bishop had his weapon up and trained on the door as well. Rook kept his weapon trained on the three duplicates, despite the sudden intrusion into the room. They had discussed close quarters strategies like this on the plane. They each knew their jobs, and Rook's was to never take his eyes off the duplicates.

Queen swiveled her head toward the door, then stood up and away from Ridley on the floor.

Standing in the doorway was Asya Machtchenko. Pawn. The team had come to know her and love her as family, since discovering that she truly was King's sibling. Originally attaching herself to Rook on a ship in the Barents Sea, she had proven herself a worthy ally, first with Rook in Norway, and later in a pitched battle involving the whole team. In the year since then, she had been constantly helping King look for their parents. On the few times when she had been back at headquarters, Queen had seen the woman bonding with King's girlfriend, Sara Fogg, and his foster daughter, Fiona Lane. Asya had very quickly become an unofficial part of Endgame, but a well liked and well loved part.

The woman stood in the doorway with tear-streaked mascara on her cheeks, looking distracted and surprised to find the whole team in the room with four Ridleys.

Queen walked quickly to the woman. "Pawn? Are you okay?"

Asya stood silently, her eyes wide, clearly in shock more than surprise, now that Queen was close enough to the woman.

Queen gently placed a hand on Asya's shoulder. "Asya?"

Asya blinked, twice. "King is dead."

TWENTY-FIVE
Location Unknown

King and Alexander smashed into the wall of the cavern, a halo of electric blue light dancing around the ceiling of the space. The

men slid down the rough stone wall, and the crackling light winked out, plunging the entire cavern into darkness.

Lying on the floor, King groaned, his ribs having been spared a direct impact, but still protesting from the fall to the floor. "Son of a bitch." King's will to fight disappeared with the light. Wherever Alexander had taken him, the way back was closed. His only chance of returning to his family was to stay calm and use his brain before his brawn. The latter wouldn't do much when it came to a man who could heal from nearly any wound.

Alexander laughed good-naturedly in the dark. "Actually, my mother was kind of a shrew."

"Alcmene?" King asked, cradling his chest with an arm. He had studied ancient history extensively, and Hercules especially.

Alexander grunted. "You can't believe everything you read in modern history, Jack. Things get distorted over centuries. Sometimes by accident, but more often by design."

A brilliant light flared in the dark.

King shielded his eyes for a moment, and then saw that Alexander held a small LED flashlight in his hand. It was tiny—like a keychain light.

"Take me back."

Alexander smiled. "I need your help to save a woman, Jack. She desperately needs help, and I can't do it alone."

Despite his anger, King felt Alexander was being forthright, and his natural instinct was to want to help save a life, but he remained skeptical.

"Where?"

"We are still in Carthage. In the very same cavern."

King looked around the echoing space. The shape of the room looked similar, but the machinery was all gone, the floor of the room was rough and unfinished, and he couldn't see the doors in the distant shadows.

"Bullshit."

"Listen. What do you really know about that technology you appropriated in Norway? About quantum tunneling and dimensions?"

"We didn't have much time to study that tech before you stole the plans and left your threatening note."

"Sorry about that. The note did serve its purpose, though. You *are* here with me, as intended." Alexander chuckled.

King's patience waned. He pulled the Sig Sauer pistol and pointed it at Alexander. "I saw what was on the other side of that portal in Norway, and I watched globes of energy destroy entire cities. I'm not going to let you do the same."

Alexander waved casually at the handgun. "You know that can't kill me."

"I can make you hurt," King countered.

"You might want to conserve your ammunition," Alexander said. "It's going to be a long time before you have a chance to find more."

King, deflated, lowered the pistol to the cavern floor and slumped with his back against the wall. The AK-47 dug into his back, and he pulled the strap off over his head, wincing a bit as he did, but appreciating the fact that the ibuprofen was finally kicking in some.

"Let's start with Einstein. You know his theory of relativity?" Alexander asked, sitting on the floor cross-legged in front of King. His posture was completely non-threatening now, so King relaxed his guard.

"Math isn't my strong suit, but I get the basic gist."

Alexander nodded. "Time and space are joined, but movement faster than the speed of light theoretically allows forward travel in time—or through vast distances in space, yes? The dimensional portal technology in Norway functioned this way. The energy the device used was not only powered by the ocean currents, but also by a special element that came from the other side of that dimensional tunnel—a kind of miniature black hole. A stable one. Infinite power. Enough to punch a doorway to a different dimension."

"How?"

"Imagine two flat sheets of paper, separated by an inch of air. One paper is this world, the next is...someplace else. The machine, and the black hole, essentially pushed on the outside of both sheets of paper until they ruptured and formed a tunnel between the two."

"You're talking about an Einstein-Rosen bridge, right? A wormhole?" King asked.

"Yes, exactly." Alexander smiled like a schoolteacher enjoying that his pupil was keeping up. "But imagine instead that you don't need to travel far; it's not like a ship going through a long tunnel, like in *Star Trek*. Because the Einstein-Rosen bridge doesn't form between the surfaces of the planes or dimensions, leaving a long funnel-shaped tunnel. Instead, it draws the edges of the planes together to where they nearly touch. Travel between the dimensions was instantaneous, right? Like passing through a waterfall or even a thin membrane?"

King recalled the feeling from the previous year. "Something like that, yeah. So what?"

"So take away one of the pieces of paper. Fold the remaining paper over on itself in the shape of a sideways letter U, maintaining that inch of distance between the sides of the paper."

"I don't follow. Isn't the paper flat? Doesn't it have to stay that way?" King asked, interested in the discussion, now that it was beyond his understanding. He frequently looked at learning new things as a challenge to be overcome.

"Einstein's theory suggested that any mass could curve space-time. Instead of paper, think of a sheet of plastic wrap. If you hold it tight from all four corners, but drop a heavy marble on it, it will bow and distort in the center of the wrap, correct?"

"Okay," King said, understanding the reference, but not how an entire dimension could curve into a U shape. "I'll take your word for it."

"Now, what if you used a larger infinite power source—say, another black hole—and you punched a wormhole from one side of the paper to the other. What would you have?"

Thinking he understood, King replied immediately. "Tele-portation."

Alexander let a small smile show. "Close. Remember that the wormhole is faster than light. It's actually a distortion in space-time on both ends of the tunnel, right? Each side having been pushed inward until they meet. Or, in this case, pushed from one side until the tunnel blasts through the other side. In fact, imagine that instead of a black hole, you have a small ring of collapsing micro-stars that have yet to become black holes. Now picture them rotating and glowing, like the ring around Saturn." Alexander drew a circle in the air with his finger. "Centrifugal force keeps it all from forming a singularity—or multiple micro-singularities. So there's no gravitational force at the center of the ring, which would tear you—or anything—apart, as we saw in Paris. Instead, it's just the oppo-site. A complete absence of gravity, like floating in space. Low friction. Easy to blast through the center of it, if you had a rocket or a faster-than-light drive of some sort. Keeping in mind the two sheet example, if the tunnel was only an inch thick, or less, even minimal force might be used to get from one side to the other. Theoretically, you would still be travelling faster than light once you entered the tunnel. Distances shrink, and space-time itself ceases to function as it would if you remained on the first sheet."

"I think I get that," King said, nodding. "So what happens? Where do you go?"

Alexander stood slowly, then offered King his hand. "Follow me."

King snatched the AK, took Alexander's hand and was pulled to his feet.

Alexander led them with the small keychain light to a broad opening in the wall and turned left, to a tunnel hewn from the rock itself. Twenty feet later, the tunnel dead-ended in a long sloping pile of rubble. Alexander turned to the pile and started ascending the slope of scree. King followed him up the loose rocks. Far ahead and above them, there was an opening to the bright blue sky. Alexander moved

surely on the loose rock. He reached the top of the underground hill and the opening in minutes. King went slower, because of his rib, but he reached the surface shortly after the larger man.

At the top of the slope, they were outdoors. A brilliant cloudless blue sky greeted them, with a blazing yellow sun over head. King was relieved that it appeared he was still on Earth. Around them and behind them, the landscape was barren rock and sand. In front of them, twenty feet away, was a beautiful turquoise ocean, casting waves at an immense natural barrier of piled rocks that stretched over three hundred feet along the shore. King could see a more sandy beach to the left of the rocky barrier, and the land rose to larger rocks and boulders at the other end of the barrier.

Alexander turned around in a full circle, a broad beaming smile on his face. Then he looked at King and held his arms out to the side, encouraging King to take in the vista.

"The question, Jack, is not 'where do you go?' It's *when* do you go."

King looked at the man. He wanted to tell Alexander he was insane. Wanted to write off his claim as a delusion. But he couldn't. How could someone who'd traveled between worlds believe moving through time was impossible?

Shit.

Alexander continued to sweep his hands around at the landscape. "Look around you, Jack. We are still in Carthage. We are standing outside the Omega facility, and what will one day be the ruins of Carthage. Except the buildings those ruins once were in our time, are not even here yet. Carthage has yet to be built!"

King looked at the shoreline. He had studied maps of the area before arriving from Malta, and he had looked at a map on the laptop with Asya all afternoon. He understood what Alexander was saying. He made mental adjustments for the slight alteration of the coast by time and erosion.

He was looking at the coastline of Carthage.

He drew in a deep breath. The mild pain in his ribs, dulled by the ibuprofen, assured him he wasn't dreaming. He knew Alexander

was telling the truth. They'd traveled backwards through time. It was ridiculous, but not impossible. In his mind, nothing was impossible. Not anymore. But one question remained unanswered. *"When* are we?"

Alexander looked him in the eye. "800 BC, give or take a year."

TWENTY-SIX
Ancient Karkhedon, 799 BC

"That's..." **King cleared** his throat. "That's a long time ago." Even in the alternate dimension, he'd never felt so far from home.

"Actually, it's now," Alexander said, walking toward the breakwater of giant stones.

King followed him up the rise, taking in the view of the pristine Gulf of Tunis. He looked around again in a full circle. Untouched rocks and sand for as far as he could see, in most directions. Far north along the coast he thought he could make out a structure, but it would have to be only a single story building— possibly a rock. But the geography of the coastline was accurate. He tried to wrap his mind around it. He was seeing Tunisia before it was occupied. Then a history lesson caught up with him. "Wasn't there a Phoenician city here before the Romans?"

Alexander was stalking around the breakwater, looking at rocks, and sometimes squatting down to peer closely at them before standing in a huff and looking elsewhere. He pointed absentmindedly behind him, at the large boulders to the south of the breakwater.

King walked over to the boulders and climbed them to the top.

South of the breakwater, spread out before him, was a small village. Several of the structures were wattle and daub, but a few were comprised of earth-colored stone. At a quick glance, King put the

population at fewer than a thousand people. He saw several wooden boats with brilliant white sails tied to a long wooden pier. On the southern fringe of the town were dozens—possibly hundreds—of camels, tied to wooden posts, and in one case, walking aimlessly in a wooden corral.

King walked back down the boulder to where Alexander was still looking at the stones. He was acutely aware of the grenade, still in his pocket. The AK-47 strapped to his back and the Sig Sauer handgun tucked into the waistband of his jeans. Even his garments and his wristwatch. Everything about him marked him as what he was.

A man out of time.

"That's the mighty kingdom of Carthage?" King asked in disbelief.

Alexander stood upright and smiled. "First, Jack, remember what I said about taking modern history at face value. Second, you're getting your years mixed up. Carthage, or Karkhedon, as the Greeks will come to call it, has existed as a city at this point only for a few years. Carthaginian hegemony doesn't begin for another hundred and fifty years or so, when they strike out for the island of Ibiza. But trade is going like crazy right now, and it will help us in our mission."

"And that mission is?" King asked.

"Hmm," Alexander mumbled as he continued looking at stones.

"What is this mission you've shanghaied me for? I think it's time you told me."

Alexander looked up at King. "I'm sorry, Jack. You're right. I'm just getting ahead of myself. We need to get to Rome. We are going to save my wife, Acca Larentia, from her untimely demise at the hands of my Forgotten."

King was stunned. The man really *was* motivated by love. "You told me she had stumbled onto one of your labs, when you weren't there." King recalled the man's admission when they had fought side by side under the ruins of Rome's Lacus Curtius.

"Yes, she did. To my eternal regret. So we have come back in time to prevent that from happening."

"How?" King asked. "Don't we risk screwing up all of history if we change something in the past?"

"There are several theories about the issue of paradoxes, Jack. I believe only one of them: that whatever we do here in the past, has always happened this way. Whatever we do will not change history. It already is history."

"But if we rescue Acca, won't the younger version of you know? You told me you found her after the Forgotten had attacked her. They drank her blood, you said."

"Yes. She was curious, and she had found the lab, and the Forgotten were behind bars. They hadn't eaten in weeks. She held a cup of water out to them..." Alexander drifted off, lost in the memory.

"I'm sorry," King said. "But how can we save her then without changing the past?"

Alexander's head snapped up, a cheerful look replacing the distant look of loss. "I always have a plan, Jack." He glanced down at the stone at his feet. "Ah! Here it is."

He stepped back off the stone he was standing on, and King could see a very faint, and very rough letter H. This one did not have the typical circle around it. Alexander reached down and picked up the stone, setting it carefully aside. Then he pulled the three surrounding stones aside; each was slightly larger than twice the size of a basketball. He reached into the hole he had created in the top of the breakwater and pulled out a small wooden chest, six inches long by four inches wide and probably three inches deep—maybe less depending on the lid's thickness. The outside of the box was ornately decorated with thin gold foil, and the hinges were hidden on the inside. Alexander handed the box to King.

It was surprisingly light.

What the hell is in this? King wondered.

He held the box in his hands and turned it over, looking at the ornate gold design, and trying to determine where it opened. Then he wondered if it was some kind of puzzle box, like in the *Hellraiser* films. "What is it?"

"What you hold in your hands, Jack, is the infamous Chest of Adoon." Alexander beamed.

"The who of what?"

"Remember what I told you about history being manipulated by some and changed by others. That chest was a simple box of mine. It contains something very valuable. I was drunk one night in Palermo. This must have been around 100 BC, I guess. I was mouthing off, and I said some things about this chest and what it contains. But over the years, the rumors got a little out of hand." Alexander took the box and depressed a hidden button on its backside. The lid popped open with a hiss as trapped air escaped.

"Airtight?" King asked. "How'd you manage that in this day and age?"

Alexander smiled. "I had my ways." He opened the lid and showed King the contents of the box. A small handful of rubies and several dried herbs no longer than an inch in length. In a separate compartment inside the wooden box, were more herbs, finely chopped.

"You went to all that trouble to hide your pot?"

Alexander laughed. He pulled out one of the longer herbs and held it up for King. "This plant is a genetic sibling of Silphium. Have you heard of it?"

King shook his head.

"It was widely known for its medicinal properties. Cyrene even printed it on their coinage. The plant is extinct in your time. This one, though, was even more powerful than Silphium. This one, Jack, can grant immortality. This is essentially what led to the Hydra. This herb, will help Acca to live. And the rubies will get us to Rome."

"So what were the rumors that got out of control?"

Alexander laughed. "It's funny, you know. The contents of the box grant eternal life, but the rumor that got started was that the chest contained a powerful weapon of destruction and death. There are faint references to it throughout history, but even into your time, the rumors persisted. By the 21st century, the rumor about the *Chest of Adoon*, as it came to be known, was that it contained something with godlike destructive powers—like the Ark of the Covenant in that *Indiana Jones* film." Alexander scooped out the rubies and dropped them in his pants pocket. Then he delicately placed the four long herbs into a plastic sandwich baggie that he pulled out of his shirt pocket. He took out another baggie and held it open, pouring the smaller herbs into it.

"What's that one?" King asked.

"Green tea from China. You have no idea how hard it is to get in this part of the world, at this time."

King tried not to smile. He didn't want to. But it happened anyway. "Hold on, if your theory of time is correct, the irony is off."

"How so?" Alexander raised an eyebrow.

"In the 21st century, the box won't contain the herbs anymore, because you will have removed them. It will just contain air."

"Exactly. I only thought of that when I was dealing with Ridley."

King became serious. "What are you talking about? Ridley was—"

"My prisoner," Alexander said. "Held just a few rooms down from the lounge where we talked."

"You what?" King shouted, clutching his fists."If he gets loose, Asya and my parents are still back there."

"He won't get loose, don't worry about that. Your family will be fine. Besides, shortly before we went through the portal, the rest of your team arrived."

King thought about the situation and knew Chess Team would protect Asya and the Machtchenkos. They would find Ridley, and if he was still a threat, they would simply end him. Still, it pissed him off that Alexander had kept so many dangerous secrets.

"All this time *you* had Ridley?"

"It took a long time to get what I needed from him. Eventually I had to offer him a trade."

"Explain." King was not pleased to hear that Ridley might have gotten something he wanted, which usually led to hundreds of people dying.

"Relax. I needed him to teach me one small phrase of the mother tongue. When I told him what it was, he seemed to think it was harmless enough, but he was a stubborn bastard and didn't want to part with his secret words. I tortured him for a while, but he was too good at resisting. Eventually I offered him something he wanted. You see, he had heard about the Chest of Adoon too. Had looked for it for years. After becoming immortal and capable of regenerating, after learning the mother tongue, which granted him the power to bestow life, the only thing he still desired was the so-called godlike destructive power contained within the chest. He wanted it badly. So I told him where it was. I figured, the Chest was still in its hiding place in 2013, so he could have it—after all, he was already immortal. The herbs would do nothing to help him. I guess at the time, I was thinking only of taking some of these herbs from the Chest, but I see now it would be too dangerous to leave any of them, even though we only need two for Acca. And I'm not letting Ridley get my tea." Alexander chuckled at his own joke.

King pointed at the hole under the rocks where the wooden chest had been hidden. "That's not a very secure location. How do you know it was undisturbed all those years?"

"I come back eventually—the younger me does. I changed, or rather, *will* change, the location slightly. It's plenty secure in the 21st century. No one ever finds it."

"What about you, when you come back to move the chest? Won't you open it and see everything missing?" King asked, trying to wrap his mind around the intricacies of paradoxes versus determined fate.

"No, I never opened it again. I just moved it. I was in a hurry that day." Alexander seemed lost in thought again, the many years of his long life washing over his consciousness.

"So if Ridley gets free, he'll go after the box?"

"Yes. But it will be empty. Actually the true irony is that the box was under his nose all along. Ridley had been searching for the Chest of Adoon for years. He ended up taking over a small place of mine on this spot and building his lab here for an entirely different reason. He had no idea he was practically sitting on top of the box. You should have seen his face when I told him where it was."

Alexander was about to put the empty box back in the hole.

"Wait. No one ever opens that box again, right?" King asked, moving closer, and taking the box from Alexander.

"No. Why?"

"Let's leave a little message for Ridley, in case he ever finds it." King placed his message inside the box and carefully shut the lid. It hissed for a moment, some hidden mechanism once again removing the atmosphere from inside the box. Then he placed the box into the hole in the ground.

Alexander laughed heartily. Then he hefted the boulders back into place, careful to put the one with the H on top, exactly as it had been. "I like your sense of humor, Jack."

TWENTY-SEVEN
Karkhedon Port on the Mediterranean, 799 BC

King waited by the docks wearing the itchy robe and sandals Alexander had procured for him. He looked the part, except for the rifle, which he kept wrapped in a swaddling of fabric, strapped across his back. The Sig was tucked under a flap of cloth on his rope waistband. It didn't feel very secure, and he kept unconsciously

adjusting it, hoping the motion wasn't giving him away, and then realizing he had nothing to worry about—people in the era had never seen a concealed carry, because there weren't any guns yet, and wouldn't be for another eighteen centuries.

The dock was crowded with men coming and going. Most wore similar robes and sandals. They carried loads to and from the waiting boats, and they haggled for prices in several different languages. King saw mostly North African faces, but there were enough seafarers from afar, and even white European faces, that he blended in with the crowd. King had even heard what sounded loosely like Latin being spoken.

He tried to stay vigilant, but then reminded himself he had no need to be. To everyone else on the crowded docks, he and Alexander would be just two more travelers or merchants.

"Jack!" Alexander came strolling down the pier, waving. The period clothes—a robe like his own, sandals and a small satchel made from an animal hide—seemed to fit the man perfectly. "I've arranged passage for us to Sicily."

Alexander smiled broadly and pointed to a short shabby man with a scraggly goatee and dark skin. King stepped up to Alexander and the man slipped an arm around his shoulders like they were pals, and led him to meet the little shabby man. Alexander was acting overly casual. For a moment, King wondered if he was just happy to be back in a forgotten time, like visiting a childhood home. But then Alexander spoke quietly. "I've told him you don't speak the language, but he still wanted to meet you. Just nod to him."

King did as he was told, and the man nodded in return, smiling widely, showing just three blackened stumps of teeth.

"They're pirates, but they should get us safely to our destination," Alexander told him.

They followed the short man, who occasionally turned and beckoned them forward with his hand. He led them past most of the boats along the pier, finally arriving at a small, twenty foot long

vessel. The square sail was a hundred shades of dirty. The crew looked in worse shape than their captain, with about ten men, all in various stages of scurvy to King's eyes.

"Climb aboard, Jack. I'm just waiting on...ah! Here he comes." Alexander looked down the pier to a small boy of about ten years, who was running toward them holding a wooden tray on the top of his head, a rag twisted to look like a turban keeping it balanced.

"What's this?" King asked, but before Alexander could answer, King figured it out. As the boy got closer, King could see two small orange cups on the tray on the boy's head, and a huge jug with steam rising out of the top.

The boy arrived and steadied the tray with a hand, then used both hands to pull the tray down and present it to Alexander. The immortal man took the tray, gave the boy a kind word in a language King did not know, and the boy happily scampered away. Alexander took the delivery and climbed aboard the boat, delicately balancing the tray against the swaying of the boat on the harbor's blue waters.

"Is that what I think it is?" King asked with disgust, climbing over the gunwale from a small wooden plank. He sat next to Alexander on a hard wooden bench attached to the inner wall of the boat.

"Tea. Practically unknown in this part of the world. We must celebrate. And give prayers for a successful journey." The man picked up the clay urn with one meaty hand and poured the steaming liquid into a cup. The tea was nearly translucent, with just a slight green tinge, but the bottom of the cup was murky, when King peered into it.

"I did mention I'm not a big fan of tea, right?"

"You'll drink it now, Jack. The water in this time period would kill you if it wasn't boiled. Your system has no immunity to the bacteria and viruses of these days. And you'll be hard pressed to find a bottle of Sam Adams for another 2800 years." Alexander handed King a cup. "Drink it fast. They don't know how to glaze the clay yet, so if you wait too long, your cup will disintegrate in your hand."

King looked at the brew skeptically, but then took a sip. It was better than the tea they had had in the lounge with his parents.

Alexander poured and drank from his own cup, as the last of the crew boarded and took their seats at oars. The sail was luffing as the crewmen, without orders or chants, began rowing the boat away from the pier. The lines were dumped haphazardly on the deck. No one had time for coiling the rope, King guessed.

The sky was patchy with white fluffy clouds, but there was no sign of a storm anywhere. King swallowed more of the tea and found the flavor improving. "This vessel doesn't look particularly seaworthy. How long of a trip is it to Sicily?"

Alexander finished the rest of his cup of tea in one gulp, then looked at King with a raised eyebrow. "About twenty-five hours. Longer if the wind isn't with us. Hence the prayers...and the tea. Unless you'd rather drink seawater."

"I never thought you'd be much for praying—or do you pray to the old Greek pantheon?" King asked.

"Actually, I pray to them all. God, Allah, the Greek Gods, Buddha, Vishnu and whoever. I figure it can't hurt on a sea voyage. We'll use the time on the trip for me to fill you in on a few things about the way the world works in this time. Things you should and shouldn't do."

"Like burning my favorite Elvis t-shirt?" King asked, still feeling the sting of giving up his modern clothes.

"Exactly. We wouldn't want some enterprising twentieth century archeologist to stumble across that AK-47. So you'll need to keep track of it. If it breaks, there's no way to fix it in this time, so you'll have to dismantle it, destroy the pieces, and bury them in different places. Dropping the bits in the sea here..." Alexander pointed over the starboard bow, as the man in front of him on a bench continued to grunt as he rowed, "wouldn't be a bad idea either. The point, as in all things like this, is to be as unnoticed as possible."

About halfway out of the harbor, the captain spoke to the men in a long rambling speech. The oarsmen grunted and

groaned, but stowed the oars and began pulling in the lines for the sails. A few men with red-stained gums produced small packets of something wrapped in large leaves that they sucked. King imagined it was the equivalent of a smoke break for some of the oarsmen. Only three men appeared necessary for manning the sail. The wind snapped the sail taut and the boat sliced neatly through the crystal blue waters, heading out of the harbor. Soon they were in open sea.

Moments later, an argument broke out between two of the sailors. King and Alexander watched, not really taking much interest. "The tall man says he's due a greater cut of their haul, because he did more work last time. The shorter man says he always gets the dirty jobs," Alexander told King.

The two sailors bickered and more men joined in the argument, their voices raising in volume. From the stern behind him, King could hear the captain feebly berating his crew, but they were past the point of listening. The men's faces were flushing with blood as the argument heated up.

Suddenly Alexander leapt up and moved toward the throng of arguing men. King stood too, wondering why Alexander was leaping into the fray.

Is this about us? King wondered.

Alexander was turning to look at King. "Jack! It's a distrac—"

He never got to finish his cry.

King felt a searing burn in the middle of his back, making his arms jerk outwards to his sides, and his head jerk involuntarily upward. His torso blazed with so much pain he couldn't form a coherent thought. As his eyes fell downward, he saw something that shouldn't be there.

In the middle of his chest, sticking out of the white scratchy robe, was at least seven inches of metal, coated in blood.

His blood.

He had been stabbed in the back so hard, that the blade had plunged clear through his chest.

As life left him, his only thought was that Fiona would be angry at him for breaking his promise.

TWENTY-EIGHT
Security Cell, Omega Facility, Carthage, Tunisia, 2013

The words hung in the air.

King...dead.

The room was silent. Queen looked sharply at Asya. "Are you sure?"

"Yes. There was an explosion. Alexander and King were at the center of it. There's no way they could have survived. Not even Alexander. Their bodies...they're gone. Dust."

Asya all but fell into Queen's arms. The two women latched onto each other in a strong embrace. When they had first met, Queen had attacked Asya and they had fought a knock-down drag-out fight that was oddly similar to her first encounter with King. Asya, surprisingly, had held her own in the combat. Since then, Queen and Asya had become friends, mostly through Queen's acknowledged admiration for Asya's fighting ability and for her connection to King.

Jack, Queen thought. *Oh no.*

"I know...that we were foes," Ridley was in a full sitting position on the floor when Queen turned back to see him, "but I'd like to offer my—"

"Hey, *Dick!*" Rook called out, angry sarcasm dripping from his mouth as he uttered the nickname. He stalked over to squat in front of Ridley. "Do you know the only two parts of the human anatomy that are affected by radiation from a microwave oven?"

Ridley looked back at Rook, not comprehending the sudden shift in the conversation. "I...I really can't say that I do."

Rook scowled. "The eyeballs and the testicles. Unless you want me to put yours in a microwave, shut the fuck up." Rook

stood and walked past the three clones, throwing each dirty looks, before returning to his original post against the far wall.

Queen scanned the room after Rook's outburst. Knight was looking at the floor, all memory of his mission to guard the door and keep an eye on the duplicates when Rook wasn't, now forgotten. Bishop still leaned on a wall, and although his facial expression had changed just the slightest, in the form of a raised eyebrow, she knew he was reeling inside. Ridley wisely closed his mouth and looked at his left foot as its big toe formed a toenail.

The duplicates stood in place, although Queen noted that Seth was now closer to the door.

"Knight," she called. The small Korean man's shocked face stayed aimed at the floor. "Knight!" She shouted this time. The man's head snapped up, irritation replacing his look of shock. "Stay sharp." She motioned to the duplicates. "We're not out of the shit yet. We'll mourn King later."

"Copy that," Knight nodded, his eyes returning to a practiced focus, aiming directly at Seth. "I'm solid."

Queen moved slowly away from Asya. "Goes for you too, Pawn. Your brother would want you to fight."

Asya nodded, wiped her tears and stood up straight.

Queen moved to the center of the room where Ridley sat on the floor. She looked down at the man's still forming toenail. "Can you walk?"

"Give me five more minutes," he said, not looking up at her.

Queen turned to Asya. "Alexander is gone?" Then she clarified. "All of him?"

Asya stepped further into the room, still somewhat dazed. She nodded. "Like I said, dust. Vaporized. I have looked over what little is left of the wreckage. There is nothing left...nothing to bury."

Queen hung her head.

She touched her tactical throat microphone. "Did you copy all that?"

After a few seconds pause, she heard Deep Blue's voice in her ear. "I...I'm sorry, Queen. The embedded homing chip he had is gone from my screens too."

"And...what do we do with these ass-clowns now that we don't need them for Alexander?"

"They're too dangerous to allow them to go free. Bring them back home. We'll get them to a secure prison."

"Are you sure that's the way you want to play it?" Queen asked.

There was a moment of silence, followed by, "We're better than that."

"Just wanted to be sure," Queen said, fighting to hide her disappointment, because right then, she really wanted to kill a bad guy...or four, though only one of them was truly alive.

Queen stood and walked back to Asya. She leaned in close, not wanting to share the information with the Ridleys. "Your parents?" she asked quietly.

"Safe," Asya nodded.

"Good. We'll get them, take these Ridleys back home, and figure out how to break the news to Sara and Fiona."

"I will tell them," Asya said, clenching her jaw. "I would not want them to remember you as the bearer of such bad news."

Queen's appreciation for Asya's stoic Russian ways increased all the time. Here this woman was, having just lost the brother she had come to know and love, and the woman was thinking of others first. Queen patted her on the back.

Queen nodded and turned back to Richard Ridley. "On your feet." She reached down, grabbed his arms and hefted him to his feet. The linen jacket slid to the floor, exposing his now fully re-formed genitals and pubic hair, but he didn't seem to care. His chest was hairy while his bald head gleamed under the bright heat lamps recessed into the ceiling. His skin, a sickly gray and yellow before, was now back in the full pink of health. His muscles had been rebuilding while the team had mourned the news of King's

demise, and now, with the exception of hair still growing on his legs, and the large toe, still looking shriveled, on his left foot, he was pretty much back to the way he had been when Queen had first seen him.

"You can stand even if you can't walk," Queen told him.

"Yes. It's just the big toe yet. It affects balance, so I can't—" Ridley began.

Queen threw a punch, landing the blow hard on Ridley's cheek, shattering the man's cheekbone, and sending him flying across the room. He smashed into the hanging cages, the impact ripping the chains from their moorings in the ceiling. Ridley, the cages, the chains and all sailed across the room in a tangle of whipping iron, careening against the floor and the wall.

Queen felt like she might have broken a finger bone on the punch, but it was simultaneously one of the best looking and most dynamic punches she had ever thrown, as well as being the most personally satisfying.

"Can I go next?" Asya asked.

Queen barked out a short laugh, her tension broken completely by the woman's sharp dry wit.

Queen turned toward the three duplicates. They looked angry, but said nothing. Seth was still very close to the door, but Knight had his eyes fixed firmly on the duplicate. There was little chance the duplicate would make a break for it. If he did, it would be a very short run.

Richard Ridley sat up from the tangled cages and chains, rubbing his face with his hand and whispering something. Already, Queen could see the three places on the man's face where the skin had split were healing. In seconds, all that remained to indicate an injury was a little bit of blood, which he pawed at angrily.

Queen stepped over to him, her MP-5 leveled at the man's face. "Alexander is dead. We don't need you any more. Please. Make a move. I dare you."

Ridley said nothing. Just stared. Then his eyes darted to the left, looking over her shoulder, for just a fraction of a second. When they came back to her, he smiled. A huge grin. A winning grin.

Shit, she thought.

Queen turned to look back at the door. Knight had been distracted by her attack on Ridley. Seth had inched closer to the door. He stood in front of a control panel next to it. She had noticed it when she had first turned away from the horror of Ridley in the cages. A stainless steel panel, with an LCD display screen, temperature controls, an intercom, light switches and a large red button, which she assumed was a panic button. Seth stood in front of the panel now, his back to it. His eyes were directly on hers, and his face held the same malicious grin as Ridley's.

Slowly, he leaned, until his back depressed the red button.

TWENTY-NINE
Tyrrhenian Sea, 799 BC

Jack Sigler became aware of two things when he woke. The ground was moving, and he didn't feel dead. Long years of experience with precarious situations had taught him to take stock of his surroundings using his other senses when waking, before opening his eyes. He did so now.

He smelled the salty sea. The gentle rocking motion and wooden creaking noises told him he was on a boat. A new scent reached his nose. Something acrid and foul. He had trouble placing it for a moment, because it was masked by the smell of the sea, but then the familiar scent registered.

Blood.

Old blood.

Still, he kept his eyes closed. This time he listened. There was a complete lack of human sounds. No breathing, or shuffling feet, clunking oars or shouted orders. Even if the crew were sleeping, they'd be a noisy bunch. *I'm alone*, he thought. Left for dead. Perhaps adrift at sea or maybe tied to a dock.

He let his mind move from the environment around him to his personal wellbeing. He didn't feel like a man who had been run through. In fact, his chest felt fine—strong and pain free for the first time since his ribs had been broken. He let his mind roam over his body, and he realized that every part of him felt okay. Better than okay. He felt as good as he did on the few times when he and Sara had taken a break, staying at some random bed and breakfast, waking to the rising warm sun instead of to an alarm clock. Strong. Relaxed. Refreshed.

He tensed his muscles, preparing to leap into a fight if need be, and slowly opened his eyes. He lay on his back in the middle of the boat, his feet pointing toward the bow. The gunwales and the deck were spattered with dried blood, but there was no sign of the crew. The sail luffed gently above him, on a soft breeze.

King twisted around and glanced to the stern. Alexander was slumped at the tiller, his head leaned back against the stern, his mouth open, his chest rising and falling. The man was asleep at the wheel. He also had a full, dark, curly beard.

How long have I been out?

King reached a hand up to his own face and felt at least a month's worth of thick facial hair. *I really hate the past*, he thought, recalling the series of events that had befallen him—including being stabbed in the back—since being yanked out of his time. He stood up slowly and took stock of the sea around him. They were near a coastline of some sort, jagged hills of green with jutting white rocks no more than a mile away. The waters were an amazing shade of translucent greenish blue. When he looked over the side, he saw they were grounded on a sandbar—the water was no more than a foot deep. The gentle roll of the boat was not the

vessel swaying on the water, but rather rolling on the sand in the shallow liquid. There was no sign of the other men, besides the blood spattered on the wooden surfaces of the ship. King found his Sig on the deck and picked it up.

He walked over to the sleeping man and called his name.

Alexander came awake immediately, clear eyed, as if he had been only resting his eyes.

"Jack. It's good to see you up again." He stood up and stretched his arms.

"How long was I out? What happened?" King looked around the boat, his unasked question about the crew obvious.

"They set us up." Alexander glanced around the boat at the blood. "I might have gone a little rough on some of them." Alexander looked sheepish, like a man that had gone on a full-on temper tantrum and now felt guilty.

"You killed them all?" King asked.

"In my defense, they were trying to kill me. And..." He set his eyes on King. "...they had already killed you."

King looked down at his robe and realized it was not the same robe he had been wearing. He touched the spot on his chest where he had been stabbed, expecting to feel the welt of a thick scar under the rough-spun cotton. Instead his chest felt smooth.

"It was the tea. I hope you'll forgive me, Jack, but I felt it might be safer for us both, considering the dangers of the present age. Turns out I was correct."

"The tea?" King looked up. "You dosed me with one of your healing herbs? I thought I was dead. I didn't realize those things were so powerful."

Alexander smiled. "You *were* dead."

"What?"

"The herbs *are* extremely powerful—similar chemically to the formula I used to heal you in Rome—but these can actually restore life. They alter the DNA in much the same way as Ridley's Hydra

serum. Your body healed all the damage from the sword strike, but the first full resurrection always takes a long time."

King looked at his arms as if he expected to see something different, but they looked the same to him. "I died...and came back?"

"Congratulations, King. You're immortal." Alexander said the words casually, like he'd just proclaimed King the winner of a spelling bee. "Come on, let's make for shore. You've been unconscious for twenty-eight days." Alexander leapt nimbly over the side of the boat, his rope sandals in his hand, his feet splashing into the shallow water.

King felt sick, though not physically. He'd been kidnapped to the past, manipulated, and now, without his consent had been...altered. *Into what?* "What are the side effects of—"

"Side effects?" Alexander shook his head. "This isn't some crude formula developed by Ridley. You're not going to grow scales or go on a murderous rampage. You drank my *original* formula, Jack. There are no side effects. Other than not aging, the ability to heal from most any injury short of a nuclear blast, which, let's face it, is a long ways off, and the resilience to handle some of my other...brews. If you ever need a boost of strength, we can—"

"Keep it," King said. He had experienced Alexander's strength-enhancing brew once before. It was like a nitrous-charged adrenaline shot that made him stronger and faster, but at the expense of his body. He tore muscles and ligaments, broke bones and landed himself in a coma. From what he understood, the strength-enhancing concoction caused significant injury to Alexander as well—he just healed immediately.

King pursed his lips, a thousand questions coming to mind. In the end, he decided to handle it like Rook might. "Fuck it." King glanced around. "Where's my rifle?"

"Lost at sea. In the fight. Let's go," Alexander called, as he began walking through the knee-deep water toward the distant shore.

King hopped the gunwale and landed in the water. "Are we swimming?"

"The water stays shallow like this all the way to the beach. We have to move by foot. Hopefully when we get to land I can find us some donkeys."

"Donkeys? Where are we?" King splashed through the water, catching up with Alexander.

"Donkeys are miserable beasts, but they get us from point to point in Italy. I think we're near what will be Naples."

"That sounds like it's going to take a long time," King said. He'd seen enough time travel movies to suspect they would return to their present just seconds, maybe hours or days, after they left, making the departure a temporary discomfort for the people he left behind, but he didn't relish the idea of spending a few months in the past. Not that he would age. Alexander had taken care of that. "Will it wear off? The immortality?"

"If it did, you wouldn't be immortal, would you? We can reverse the effects later on. But for now, for this mission, you need to be strong, immune to injury and most of all, able to withstand the years. It will take us some time to get where we're going and do what we have to."

King ground his feet into the sand and came to a stop. "Wait."

Alexander paused and looked back. King could see that the man knew what question was coming next. He didn't even need to ask it.

Alexander sighed. He looked honestly apologetic. "Twenty-five years, Jack. Acca doesn't die for another twenty-five years."

THIRTY
Security Cell, Manifold Omega Facility, 2013

Queen snarled as jets of gas sprayed down from the ceiling. She lunged across the room toward Seth while holding her breath, but

she had already sucked in a lungful of the gas before realizing the true threat.

Her body flew through the air at the smiling bastard, but she could already feel an immense cough building in her lungs, and as her torso tightened, she could see Seth beginning to whisper. Alarm had registered on Knight's Asian features, but his first response was to suck in a lungful of the gas, and he stood directly under a jet. As Queen reached her hands out to choke the shit out of the smiling duplicate, Knight's body sank toward the floor. She heard a pistol fire from behind her, and then her chest shuddered and she coughed hard, whooping in a huge chest-full of the gas-laced air.

She smashed into Seth, the two of them toppling awkwardly to the ground in a tangle of limbs. Queen felt sleep taking over. It wouldn't kill them, but she expected to wake in shackles. Or maybe not wake up at all.

She rolled on the floor. Her body felt heavy. She fought against her closing eyelids, but it was a losing battle.

Seth's brow furrowed as he focused on whispering. Queen closed her eyes, promising herself she'd end Seth, the first chance she got. *No more Ms. Nice Queen*, she thought, and then she dreamed.

Thirty seconds after the gas stopped shooting from the nozzles in the ceiling, a ventilation fan in the wall behind Bishop's slumped body activated. The vent sucked all the white gas from the room, while an air conditioning vent on the far wall pumped fresh air into the cell. The rubber seals around the sole door in and out of the room, which had activated when Seth's body hit the large activation button, released. An audible hiss filled the room as the pressure equalized.

Jared was the first to stir, waking up and performing a perfect push-up, before springing to his feet. He moved to Richard Ridley, and checked the man's pulse, his fingers touching his creator's neck as delicately as if he were caressing eggshell-thin porcelain.

Satisfied that the man was alive, he stood from his squat and walked toward Enos. Something was wrong. Enos's chest was not moving. The duplicate wasn't breathing. Jared squatted down and rolled his brother over. In the center of Enos's head was a perfectly round hole, just large enough for the tip of Jared's pinky finger. Still in Jared's grasp, the body softened and drooped. The color faded and the features that defined Enos fell slack. Jared lay the heap down and stepped away. Enos was now nothing more than a human-shaped mass of clay dressed in an expensive suit.

Jared growled. They had each been so focused on using the mother tongue to avoid the effects of the gas—a compound of Fentanyl altered by Richard Ridley to create a more effective and less potentially lethal type of knockout gas—that their self-defense lapsed long enough for a Chess Team member to squeeze off a single, but highly accurate shot. Jared considered using the mother tongue, taught to him by Richard Ridley before his incarceration, to animate the clay once more, but it wouldn't be Enos. The memories and experiences that made him unique were gone forever. Enos was dead.

Jared stood and turned to see Seth stirring and disentangling himself from Queen's limbs.

"The Creator?" Seth inquired.

"He is well. Enos is dead. One of them got a shot off," Jared said with disgust.

"Regrettable," Seth said, walking over to Ridley. "Help me get him up."

Jared walked over, pausing only to kick the unconscious Bishop hard in the face, fracturing the man's nose. Blood sprayed against Jared's pant leg.

"Leave them," Seth said.

"They will hunt us."

"The Creator is our priority, and time is short."

Jared nodded and helped Seth lift Richard Ridley up. They dragged him toward the door. By the time they reached it, Ridley was waking up.

Seth and Jared carried Ridley through the door, and he began to take some of his own weight. They guided him to one of the chairs in the room, easing him down. Ridley raised a hand and rubbed it on his forehead, as if he were waking from a long slumber.

Seth moved to a nearby locker, pulled out a black zip-up security jumpsuit and handed it to Ridley.

The man stood and stepped into the legs of the suit, then pulled it up on his body and yanked the zipper up to the middle of his broad, hairy chest. Then he started to lace up the boots Seth passed him. "Thank you, Seth. Where are our enemies?"

Jared pointed his thumb over his shoulder at the still open door to the room full of unconscious bodies. "What would you have us do?"

Ridley looked at his bare wrist, as if a lifetime of habit was driving him to check the time. Seth handed him the limited edition silver and black Rolex Submariner from his own wrist. Ridley smiled and donned the expensive wristwatch. "What's the situation?"

Seth replied before Jared could. "Your brother Darius has amassed a sizeable force. He was poised to attack the facility any day now. We didn't see him on the way in, but the last I heard from our informant, he was near. We've taken precautions. We used Chess Team's resources to get to you, but King is apparently dead, as is Alexander Diotrephes. The rest of the building is empty."

"And the *Chest*?" Ridley asked.

"We were unable to locate it, but we have some leads and—" Jared began.

"Never mind. I know where it is." Ridley smiled at his two duplicates.

Jared flipped on three security monitors, adjusting the reception on the CCTV cameras hidden around the installation to show the large garage filled with vehicles heading down the ramp to the loading dock and armed soldiers stationed outside the amphitheater. There were men at the foot of the stairs leading to the surface as well.

Ridley's smile evaporated. "Looks like they're here already. Disappointing."

"The timing could not be helped," Seth said.

"We are so very close. Let's leave Chess Team and Darius to squabble among themselves. I want the prize."

Jared pointed at the monitor showing the stairs to the amphitheater, behind the secret janitorial closet door. "This way."

Seth turned to the cell door and slammed it shut, listening to the lock tumble.

THIRTY-ONE
Security Office, Manifold Omega Facility, 2013

Peter Machtchenko held his breath. He raised his hand up to Lynn, behind him in the small supply closet filled with uniforms hanging on pegs and cardboard boxes filled with three-ring binders. She was already being silent though. They were out of practice, but training like theirs, despite being forty years old, was impossible to forget, even if the body wasn't always up to the task. When the bio-seal door had begun to open, Peter obeyed the rising hairs on the back of his neck and had leapt into the security room's closet with Lynn.

Now inside the cramped space, listening to the voice of the man he knew to be Richard Ridley, Peter was hoping desperately that his daughter was still alive. He had already lost one child this day, and two over the course of his lifetime. Losing the third would destroy him.

He overheard something about a chest, a sizeable force and a man named Darius. That was all Peter needed to hear to know things were going to go from bad to worse. After a minute, the voices receded on the other side of the door. Lynn reached around him for the handle. He grabbed her hand and held her there for a few

seconds more, just to be sure. They might be ex-spies, but neither of them were armed, and Peter wouldn't feel better until he had a 9mm in his hand.

He let go of Lynn's hand and she turned the handle on the dark wooden door. It opened smoothly and slowly. No squeak. They stepped out into the empty security room and quickly scanned the area. Ridley was gone. One of the monitors on the desk showed a view of the nearby loading dock. Vehicles were pulling in, one by one, and an army of soldiers were getting out.

"Not good, not good," Lynn said.

Peter moved to the locked door in the corner. He had tried to scope out the facility earlier in the week, when Alexander had brought them here, but the man was always unexpectedly around whenever Peter had tried to creep through the place unnoticed. Peter had made it down to this security room, but he hadn't seen inside the closed door, which he assumed led to some kind of a holding cell.

They had come looking for Asya, only to unexpectedly see someone emerging from the locked door. Peter and Lynn had ducked into the supply closet just in time. But now all the old alarm bells were ringing in Peter's head, and his hackles were on high alert. He didn't know what was behind the door, but he guessed it was connected to everything.

Peter scanned the edges of the door quickly, noted the un-inflated rubber biohazard seals around the edges, and then ignored the threat they implied. Now was not a time for caution. Now was a time for action. And that meant opening this door, risks be damned.

Peter glanced around the room and saw a security officer's belt hanging on a peg. The belt was glistening black leather with pouches. It held a radio and a ring of keys. More importantly, he found a variation of what he was looking for. He wanted a wooden police baton, but what he found was a 16" telescoping steel and chrome baton in a holster. It was better than no weapon, so he snatched it from the belt and turned back to the door. He knew

Lynn was behind him monitoring both the door and the video feed of the loading dock.

He unlocked the latch as Lynn spoke, "Hurry. No time left."

Peter whipped open the door and was ready to swing down with the baton.

Instead, a hand shot upward, restricting his downward thrust, as a blonde woman's face plunged through the door.

Peter staggered back, dropping the baton, slipping and falling backward on to the floor. His head connected with the hard concrete and he unconsciously shouted out. "Fuck!"

The blonde woman's hair was sweaty and plastered to her face as she staggered into the room. "Sorry," she said.

Asya came out of the room next, supporting a beefy man with a blonde goatee. Asya looked ill as well, while the blonde man just looked weak.

Then came a small unhappy Korean man, followed by a mountain of an Arabian man with a broken nose and a blood-stained face. Each of them was armed with rifles and wore tactical battle armor. Peter recognized them as the rest of his son's team.

"No time!" Lynn shouted, picking Peter up off the floor. "Must go now."

Already the blonde man was at the outer door with Asya. Despite the fact that they were not armed, Lynn shoved Peter after the two, ahead of the rest of the team.

They turned right outside the door, heading past the door to the loading dock, Lynn shoving Peter the whole way, so that he was pushing against Asya and the blonde man.

The blond man turned around, annoyed. "What's the rush?"

Behind them, the blonde woman and the other two men had just emerged from the security room. The door to the loading dock, now between Peter's group and the stragglers, burst open and three metallic objects flashed into the air.

Peter saw the blonde woman recognize the aerial objects and turn about on her comrades, forcing them back into the security

room. Lynn was shoving him through a door, as Asya pulled his shirt from the front. They all landed in the room with a split second to spare. A thunderous crack sounded, filling the corridor behind them with light and smoke as the door to the room slammed shut.

Peter raised his head, looked at the room they'd fallen inside, and smiled. "You chose the right place for a standoff, dear," he said. The others turned their eyes from the door to the room behind them, taking in the rack after rack of military hardware, explosives, rifles, handguns and grenades. An armory.

"I think I just got a Manifold stiffy," the blond man said, smiling, as he reached for a strange looking rifle with three barrels.

THIRTY-TWO
Campania, 795 BC

"You never said anything about lions, damn it!"

"True," Alexander grunted, as he wrestled a four-hundred-fifty pound lion to the ground and then head-butted the creature. "But I did tell you the Oscans would eventually lose to the Samnites. You were the one that said we should help out the little guys."

King stalked across the marshy ground in a slow circle, his crude iron sword up, the thick-maned brown lion snarling as it kept pace with him. He found himself wishing he still had the Sig Sauer—or the damn AK that Alexander had lost at sea four years ago, when they had first travelled backward in time. The lion stopped moving suddenly and leaned back, but King knew it was preparing to spring and not retreating. He squatted, making himself an easier target, the blade held close to his side, and the tip extending just past his hunched body.

Although Alexander had bestowed him with eternal life, pain was still pain, and being eaten alive created the very unpleasant

possibility of being a long meal. Plus, while the larger Greek had an otherworldly strength in addition to immortality, despite King's newfound healing ability, *he* still possessed only the strength of a normal man. Against an angry, underfed lion on a battlefield in rural Villanovan-era Italy, he stood only a slim chance.

The creature sprang at King, its mouth opening up in a toothy roar, ready to devour him, just as the invading Samnites had planned when they had fired bloody chunks of mutton at the Oscans from makeshift trebuchets. Once again, King had been surprised at the inaccuracy of historical accounts, as he had read that catapults and trebuchets hadn't been common place until the third century BC. Once the bloody meat began to fall from the sky, the Samnites had loosed five lions as their vanguard. The starved beasts had wasted no time racing toward the crude defenses King and Alexander had helped the locals build around their village.

Now the deadly lion was airborne for King's position, and he needed to time things just right. The creature closed the distance with its huge lunge, and at the last second possible, King shoved upward, throwing the full weight of his body behind the blade, and then sidestepping the incoming mass of fur and claws. King rolled over backward on the ground, landing in a crouched position on his feet, his balance having become much better after years of living outdoors and engaging in frequent hand-to-hand battles.

The lion impaled itself on the broad blade of King's iron sword, landing without grace on its head and snapping its own neck in the process, as the full weight of its attack came pounding down to the ground. Even if the sword hadn't ended the lion's life instantly as it ripped through fur and flesh and muscle, the broken bones might have finished the creature off. King stepped cautiously toward the beast, but it was done. Its huge chest no longer moved. King could see the animal's ribs clearly, and once again he raged at the thought that men had tortured and abused this majestic animal, training it for war against a mostly unarmed and peaceful people. King knew the history. He and Alexander had spent long hours discussing the

ways things went down. He knew his actions wouldn't change the historical outcome, but he intended to take as many of the Samnites with him as possible, before the fight was over.

He pulled the bloodied sword from the lion's chest-wall, and bid the creature a safe passage to its next life.

When King turned, he saw Alexander extracting his meaty fist from the shattered head of the lion that had attacked him. Yellow fur was matted with blood and bone across his knuckles. King knew Alexander, like him, took little joy in killing animals, but sometimes it was the only way.

"That's the last of them," Alexander said, standing up and wiping his hands down the front of his already filthy robe. "The spears will come next."

"We'll be ready for them, then," King said with a lopsided grin.

"Or we could just move on. We know the outcome," Alexander replied, but from the smile on his own face, King knew the man was just playing Devil's advocate and he had no intention of leaving the fight now. Over the years, they had found a common ground. Despite King's continued anger at being temporarily trapped in the past—if twenty-five years could be called temporary—his painful longing for Sara and Fiona and his continued concern for the fate of his team and family, he could not turn away from people in need. And to King's surprise, neither could Alexander.

"Who's to say whether one of the Oscans we save today won't go on to father someone important? If we stay and fight this losing battle, then we always stayed and always fought this fight. That's your theory on time travel, right?" King walked back toward the crude wooden battlements he and Alexander had built. They had discussed their working theory on time travel dozens of times over the years, but without any further evidence of their actions from King's time, and knowing the vagaries of inaccurate historical accounts, the issue was truly moot.

"Who is to say," Alexander parried, "that we didn't always leave this fight in the middle, abandoning the Oscans to their

fate?" The big man followed King, and they put on jovial smiles for the worried locals, both of them knowing they would fight and both of them knowing that in the end, they would lose. But the locals—kind people who had sheltered and fed them, who loved songs and lived simple farming lives—had no such knowledge. So the men would show them brave faces and teach them radical battle techniques.

"Who is to say?" King grimaced. "My conscience."

Alexander nodded. "Your conscience has gotten us into more scrapes..."

"Not just mine," King said. Alexander had gone to extremes in his pursuit of time travel. He had put a lot of people in harm's way. Maybe worse. But now that he was here, in the past, moving toward saving the woman he'd missed for thousands of years, his true self was showing. Hercules had been a hero, or at least, he was now. King decided to let Alexander off the hook. "Besides, it's not like we have anything better to do. How is the practice coming along?" King asked.

Alexander frowned.

For months and months he had been practicing the simple phrase he had tortured out of Richard Ridley. A single expression in a nearly extinct language. The *mother tongue*. Alexander didn't want the whole language. Just one sentence. The one that would allow him to create a lifeless human body out of inanimate clay. A body that would completely pass for human. The body of his wife, Acca. For five years, Alexander had been practicing the sentence, first in the safety of the Omega facility in 2013, and now creating inert bodies that the two men would leave buried all over Italy. With each attempt, Alexander's work was more and more perfect, with one exception.

"I still can't recall her face. It's maddening, Jack. She was the love of my life, and I've spent centuries looking for a way to save her. Now that I nearly have it, I'm frustrated by the fact that I can't remember her face clearly enough to recreate the corpse accurately."

King had examined several of the faces Alexander had created over the years. Each was slightly different. Eyes spaced a bit farther apart than the last or a bit narrower. Brows higher or lower, mouth pursed slightly more or less. He understood the depth of Alexander's love for Acca, and he didn't fault the man. When he had first heard that Alexander was having trouble recalling Acca's visage, he tried to recall the image of his dead sister Julie, and found it hard to picture just how her nose looked. Even worse, he was starting to have trouble picturing Sara and Fiona, who he hadn't seen in years. He couldn't imagine how tarnished his memory might have been after centuries.

King placed his hand on his friend's shoulder. "You'll get it. And even if you don't, we can always get a good look at her before you need to."

Alexander smiled, accepting the advice. "You're right." He turned his eyes to the field ahead of him. Five thousand soldiers with long spears ran across the marshy ground, screaming incoherently. "We're outnumbered four to one. Still like our chances?"

King grinned. "Of winning? No. Of making them work for it? You bet your ass."

As a pair, they leapt past the defensive wall and rushed out to meet the enemy.

THIRTY-THREE
Sub Level 1, Manifold Omega Facility, 2013

Jared, the more naturally militant personality of the three men, led his Creator and his duplicate-brother out of the stairwell and into the hallway of Sub Level 1. He moved slowly into the hall, glancing down its empty length, and peering cautiously at the doorways leading into the opposing Cold Lab and the Microbiology Lab. Darius's forces hadn't entered this level yet.

"He's probably hoping to flush them from the loading dock upward. We'll spring the trap behind the janitor's closet before they're expecting it," he told Ridley and Seth.

He approached the door to the Microbiology Lab and opened it slowly, expecting a hail of gunfire. When none came, he moved in and the other two men followed. The lab looked untouched.

"They'll be on the other side of the closet, or down the tunnel at the Amphitheater stairs. Either way, they have a defensible position. They'll—"

"It makes no difference," Seth interrupted.

Richard Ridley walked over to a security panel on the wall. It had a 6-inch LCD screen and a few buttons next to a numerical keypad. Ridley typed in a security code and the LCD came to life showing two soldiers stationed in the hall outside the janitorial closet's secret door. They looked bored as they lounged against the tunnel walls, completely unaware they were being monitored by the camera in the security plate next to the door.

"Only two men," Ridley said. "Hardly an obstacle." He typed in another sequence on the keypad, and a locked metal cabinet on the wall sprang open. Inside it, he retrieved a satellite phone and a Browning 9 mm pistol. He handed the phone to Seth and the gun to Jared.

Seth stepped away from the other two men and began dialing a number. Jared cocked the weapon and moved to the janitorial closet. He carefully moved a mop aside, allowing Ridley to follow him into the cluttered space. Jared looked back to Ridley for confirmation. The man nodded, the overhead bulb shining off his bald head.

Jared turned back to the door, opened it and fired two shots. Both of the soldiers were caught completely off guard, crumpling to the tunnel floor without even raising their weapons.

Jared stepped into the tunnel, reached down and pulled a Glock 19 from the dead mercenary's holster. He kept it and handed the Browning back to Ridley. Seth, finished with his phone call,

stopped at the control panel and punched in a third sequence, then he joined the other two. "We're ready," he said. "Communications are jammed."

Jared stepped over the two corpses bleeding on the tunnel floor and led the way into the dark tunnel. Ridley paused at the security panel on the far side of the door. He typed in a code and the tunnel filled with light from several caged lights lining the walls.

Jared turned back to Ridley. "Sir, they'll know we're coming..."

Ridley simply nodded and they moved on down the length of the tight tunnel. The pitted stone walls were just wide enough for the broad men to pass, but would make an excellent place for an ambush.

As they came to the end of the tunnel, they could see the stairs that led up to the amphitheater, but no mercenaries guarding it. Jared stepped to the foot of the stairwell.

He immediately jumped backward, his Glock raised, as a body tumbled down the stairs, rolling to a stop at his feet. The dead man's throat had been sliced. There was no sign of anyone on the stairs above them.

"Trigger?" Seth called out.

Jared looked around at his brother in surprise. Whatever this was, his brother had kept him in the dark.

"That you, Seth? Sorry about that. He was a struggler, that one." Daryl Trajan, callsign: Trigger, descended the steps, his sniper rifle strung across his back, and a bloodied Gerber folding knife in his hand. The slim man wore black BDUs. He bent to wipe the blade of his knife on the dead man's clothes, then stepped over the body.

Jared lowered his pistol and looked to Ridley and Seth. They were smiling.

"Are we good?" Seth asked.

"All clear at this end. Carpenter will have the stairwell to the garage in a minute," Trigger replied, folding up his knife and slipping it into a sheath on his belt.

"You have no qualms about switching sides?" Ridley asked.

"No, sir. Some mercs follow a code of honor. I follow a code of greenbacks. With as much money as Seth offered me for this job, I'll be retiring to a villa in Honduras." Trigger smiled a huge grin, clearly pleased with having chosen the correct side of the struggle between the Ridley brothers. "Darius and his forces are all inside the loading dock by now. Any men loyal to him on the surface have been eliminated."

Trigger glanced down to a wrist-mounted two-way pager, which was gently vibrating against his skin. He depressed a button three times, then looked back up at the others.

"Gentlemen, this is Carpenter," Trigger introduced the stocky man coming down the dark side tunnel from the second stairwell that led to the garage. As the man stepped into the light, Jared could see he wore black BDUs like Trigger, but he had thick pink scars on his brawny exposed forearms.

"Garage is secured. Everyone up top is loyal to us," Carpenter said in a surprisingly soft voice.

Jared looked at the man and wondered about loyalty. He was irritated that Ridley and Seth had not confided in him about this part of the plan, co-opting some of Darius's forces to work for Ridley.

"So," he said, a little of his irritation creeping into his voice, "what's next?"

Richard Ridley stepped forward, patting Jared on the shoulder as if to say *Don't worry about the small stuff, we didn't tell you because there wasn't time.* He grinned at everyone. "Let's go up top and get my Chest. Darius's force should engage the Chess Team in the next five minutes. When they do, send in the second wave of soldiers to kill everyone."

THIRTY-FOUR
Sub Level 3, Manifold Omega Facility, 2013

Rook burst out of the door bringing up the MetalStorm rifle he'd taken from the armory. He rolled to the floor and fired down the hallway. MetalStorm weapons fired rounds straight out of the barrel, triggering each with an electronic jolt. The first three rounds exited the three barrels before Rook felt the kick. He'd been trained to fire in three round bursts, because each shot moved the barrel up just a little higher. With a MetalStorm weapon, all three shots would be accurate and the need to adjust for the next three was minimal. But Rook didn't adjust at all. He held the trigger down and unleashed all thirty rounds in just under two seconds.

The small cluster of men that had already come in through the loading dock were greeted by a wall of bullets. They dropped in a heap, their limbs tangling. Rook stood on unsteady feet, the effects of the gas still making him woozy, but he shook his head with a grin. "Deep Blue has *got* to get me one of these." Then he tossed the weapon to the floor, not knowing how to reload the thing. He brought up his MP-5 from his shoulder.

Peter and Asya followed him out the door into the hall, each armed with a newfound Manifold MP-5, also opting for weapons they knew how to use and reload. Lynn ducked her head out of the armory and looked at the bodies on the floor. The four men, each dressed in black BDUs, had motley looking hair and tattoo-covered skin on their exposed forearms. A pool of blood formed around their tangled bodies.

Rook took a tentative step further toward the loading dock doors, which were on the other side of the fresh pile of corpses. There was no sign of Queen or the others. Rook guessed they had successfully ducked back into the security room, the view inside of which was now blocked by a closed and bullet-riddled door.

Rook was about to take another step toward the dock, when the doors burst open into the hallway, and another four armed men rushed into the cramped space. He let loose a burst of fire from his MP-5, stepping back, but the sudden movement sent a wave of nausea through him. He slipped and fell backward. He tried to turn it into a back roll, but awkwardly smashed into the wall of the narrow corridor instead.

Peter raised his weapon to finish the newly arrived men, but Asya had stepped forward and already sprayed them with a burst of fire from her own weapon. Rook got to his feet as the newly arrived men fell. They looked just as unkempt as the first bunch.

"Mercenaries," he said, thinking about who they might be working for and how Chess Team was going to deal with this new threat. He keyed his microphone, trying to reach Queen, but all he got in his earpiece was static.

Rook frowned. "Something's blocking coms. This is going to suck donkey—"

The door to the loading dock inched forward again, and before Rook could put some bullets through the door and into whoever was on the other side, something came flying into the corridor. He knew this projectile would not be just a stun grenade.

He turned to tell the others to run, but they were already turning.

He turned his attention toward the end of the hall. A shadow moved across the stairwell door window. There were more of them. Rook's group was about to be pinned down in a crossfire, and getting holed up in the small armory on the right would just make the slaughter go faster.

"Go left!" he shouted.

Lynn, the closest to the stairwell, was already moving in that direction. Asya was right behind her as they both slipped into the unmarked door across from the armory.

Rook took a huge lunging step, shoved Peter through the door and toppled into the doorway, his legs still not inside the room

when the air was knocked out of his lungs. The clap of noise was deafening. Something—metal fragments most likely—sliced into his foot. His toes went numb. The doorway filled with smoke from the detonated grenade. Rook felt someone tugging his wrist, pulling him into the room. He twisted and looked back into the corridor, now choked with dark billowing clouds near the ceiling. At the floor level, from Rook's vantage point, he saw what he had hoped for—a limp arm extending from the partially ajar stairwell door, lying in its own blood.

Then his feet were past the door, and his view was cut off as the door closed to the carnage in the hallway. Rook rolled over in his bulky impact armor and staggered to his feet. He was grateful for the suit. It had clearly protected him from the bulk of the grenade's blast, despite the stab of pain in his foot.

"Where are we?" he asked.

"The viewing gallery," Peter replied. Then a light came on and Rook could see the older man standing by a light switch on the wall. The room was twenty feet across but appeared to run the full length of the facility, paralleling the corridor they had just escaped. The ceiling was twice as high as that of the corridor, and there was a balcony rail up above the space, in the center third of the room, so those on the second floor could look down into the vast space.

Rook checked his ankle and saw a small trickle of blood. Then he saw several other pitted marks in his armor's leg and chest plates.

Well, mostly protected me, he thought.

Rook looked to his left. The far wall appeared to be a darkened Plexiglas of some type. He jogged over to it, the small wound in his foot shooting pain up his leg with each step. He put his eyes up against the dark wall, but couldn't see through it. He quickly realized how close the base was to the sea, and guessed that this was a giant Ridley-designed aquarium.

"Is there a door at the other end?" Rook asked, as he started down the long empty room.

"Only way out of here is up," Peter said. The older man pointed up at the second floor balcony with the barrel of the MP-5.

"Stairs?" Lynn asked.

"No. We'll have to climb up somehow." Peter looked doubtful.

"Alright," Rook said. "Pawn, take the door."

Asya took up a position guarding the door they had just come through. She still looked a little pale from the gas, but she threw herself into the task without complaint.

Rook ran over to the wall and turned his battle armored back against it. "Up," he said to Peter. Rook held his hands out. Peter quickly scrambled up onto Rook's shoulder's and reached the lip of the second story balcony, pulling himself up.

"We got one thing in our favor," Rook said, as Peter left his shoulders and Lynn began to climb up his body to her husband's waiting hands. "Their coms don't work either—or they wouldn't have blown the crap out of their own people in the stairwell."

Lynn scampered up Rook's body and was up on the balcony before he knew it.

"Pawn, you're next."

Asya turned to him. "But the door..."

"I'll handle it."

Asya wasted no time. She was looking better—less shaky. Whatever the effects of the gas were, she appeared to be dealing with them better than everyone else.

Asya lowered her weapon and sprinted to Rook's position, placing one foot on his outstretched hands and springing lithely up to the second story. Rook immediately had his weapon up and trained on the door at the start of the long gallery. He spotted a small black wire at the bottom of the door—a fiber optic spotting scope. He opened fire on the door, blasting the scope and hopefully scaring whichever mercenary was so timid as to check the room out before throwing grenades in. Rook crossed the space to the Plexiglas wall. He opened a hidden compartment on the bulky thigh of his impact armor and extracted a large brick of C4 explosive, which he smacked

against the wall. Then he affixed a detonating blast cap. The radio switch to detonate the explosive was on his wrist. He didn't know if whatever was blocking his communication with the rest of Chess Team would block the signal to the explosive, but it was worth a try.

He was just about to race back to the wall under the balcony and make the climb himself, with some assistance from Asya, when the door to the room exploded off its hinges and into the room, knocking him to the ground.

THIRTY-FIVE
Sub Level 3, Manifold Omega Facility, 2013

Queen paused by the door. She was getting no connection to Deep Blue back home and she couldn't raise Rook either. Something was scrambling communications.

Two things, she thought in something like a prayer. *That's all I want. Active coms and Richard Ridley's head back in a bird cage.*

They were fools to have freed the man. Now with Alexander dead and no longer a threat, Ridley would go after the most powerful weapon he could find. She didn't know what his long game was, but as soon as she saw Seth's smile when he activated the gas, she knew it had been his plan all along. Not the duplicates', Ridley's. He had somehow planned the whole thing out himself.

A burst of gunfire in the corridor had her crouched by the door, ready to add her own bullets to the fray.

"Ready, Knight?"

The small man was deadly in a fight and as hardy as the rest of the team, but the loss of King seemed to have demoralized him worse than the rest. He didn't respond to her.

"You want me to—" Bishop began.

Queen whirled on Knight, who was slumped against a wall. His face was paler than usual, and she knew it was the gas they had

breathed. She moved over to the man and saw his eyes were glazed and unfocussed. "Knight?"

No response.

She shook him by the collar of his battle suit.

Knight didn't respond to the shaking.

"Shin!" Queen shouted and slapped the man across his face.

His eyes startled and fluttered. Then he focused in on Queen and she saw an angry glare creep across his face.

"You awake? You with us? We need you, man."

"I'm good," Knight said. "Fucking gas. I'm a little guy, you know."

Queen grinned. He was, in fact, a few pounds lighter than she was, though that was their little secret. "Good, I'll open the door and cover you. You try to find the jamming device and disable it. I want Deep Blue's support, and I want to put Ridley back in his grave. Can you handle that?"

Knight nodded.

She turned to look at Bishop. No longer looking like his normal serene and placid self, Bishop appeared to be dealing with King's demise and their betrayal by the duplicates in his typical fashion. Rage. The kind she hadn't seen on Bishop's face since the days when he'd been infected with Ridley's regenerative serum.

"You okay, big guy?"

His eyes darted to her, sharp, focused and burning. He didn't need to say a word. He was ready to tear someone apart.

She moved back to the door, and cracked it open. She heard shouting in the hall and peered around the door frame, her MP-5 up and ready. At the end of the hall, she saw Rook's armored form leaping into a doorway. Men were at the stairwell door at the end. Down on the floor, a grenade skittered to a stop.

Knight crouched next to her, about to leap out into the hall and run like hell toward the far end of the corridor, in search of the jamming device.

"No!" she shouted.

She threw her weight backward, blocking Knight from leaving the room, when the grenade detonated, spraying the hallway with steel fragments. Her left arm, although covered from shoulder to wrist in the impact absorbing battle armor suit, was perforated with projectiles. She pulled the numb limb back and saw blood trickling from several spots on the appendage.

"Motherfu—" she cut herself off, as she took in a deep breath when the pain kicked in.

Knight leaned in with an auto injector syringe and showed it to her. "You want this?"

Queen recognized the cocktail they each carried. It contained a mix of caffeine and 1000mg of Ibuprofen. The drug wouldn't make her tired, but it would dull some of the pain.

Queen just nodded.

Knight placed the device against the side of her exposed neck and activated it. Queen inhaled sharply again, as the injector rammed the drug into her body.

"What now?" Knight asked.

Queen didn't have an answer.

"I say we blow through the wall to the next room. If need be, to the one after that. We can't fight them all in close quarters, and we need to not be where they think we are." Bishop held up a small wad of C4 in his hand.

Queen nodded, then struggled to her feet. "Everyone back in the cell when it goes off."

Bishop affixed the explosive to the wall just above a computer monitor on a desk, and the others fell back toward the cell. He placed a timed detonator for ten seconds, then rushed to the door to the cell, swung around it and hid behind it, while keeping a steel toed boot in the jamb.

Queen nodded at the move. The last thing they needed was to get locked in the hellish cell again.

The blast went off. Several chunks of rubble pelted the wall, filling the room with the scent of hot plaster dust.

Bishop moved into the room and coughed from the dust and smoke. Queen followed him and saw a nightmare of architecture. The wall behind the computer stations had been shattered, but the next room must have been a bathroom, because they had broken through into a crawlspace with water pipes that were now a tangled mess of jagged metal and spraying water. The far side of the space was another wall, still mostly intact. Water erupted across the exposed electrical wiring and damaged security stations, spraying arcs of spitting sparks across the whole side of the security suite. The hole they had blasted was probably large enough for them to get through—even with the bulky impact armor suits—but the tangle of jagged metal, spraying water and electricity made it a deathtrap.

"Gonna have to use more C4," Bishop said.

Then Queen saw the door to the security room open just a crack at the end of the blasted room, a large piece of rubble stopping the door after just an inch.

"Quickly," she whispered, and raised her weapon.

THIRTY-SIX
Lake Bracciano, Etruria, 780 BC

"**Ostentatious much?**" **King** asked.

Alexander frowned. "I admit I was a bit full of myself in those days."

The men were looking across the lake to a villa built up on a hill that would come to be called the *Mountain of Roman Rock*, but which at present was unnamed. The villa resembled the medieval castles that wouldn't come to the region for centuries yet. A round stone tower attached to the villa's side rose up two stories. Other homes nearby were much smaller, and most were made low to the ground and from wood. The landscape was dotted with trees— absent in King's own time—and he once again marveled at how

different the landscape of Italy looked millennia before he would be born.

The building was their final target after almost twenty years of living in the past. They had fought countless battles, and even spent years as farmers and shepherds, living quietly, and waiting for the perfect time to save Acca from death at the hands of Alexander's Forgotten wraiths. By this point, Alexander had practiced with the mother tongue so much that he had gotten the body perfect, including the withered nature of the corpse after the Forgotten had sucked her dry of blood. But he still needed the face. They had stayed away from the woman for fear of creating problems with the timeline, or from running into Alexander's younger self. Now they needed to glimpse the woman, so Alexander could practice the face as well, before they needed to exchange her for a duplicate desiccated corpse, while the younger Alexander was away.

"You sure a five-years-too-young Acca will do the trick for practice?"

Alexander, who had on many occasions told King stories of the woman's beauty, just smiled. He had that far-away look King had seen so many times, when the man thought of his wife. Then he nodded. "Yes. She changed little in those years, when our sons were grown men. And after the incident..." Alexander always referred to her death as 'the incident', "...her face was shriveled from blood loss. Nearly unrecognizable. But it needs to be perfect." Alexander had rarely spoken of the twin sons he had had with Acca, but when he did, it was always obliquely and brief. King got the impression that Alexander didn't like his sons much, so when the man mentioned them again now, he let the comment pass.

Alexander had long ago described the full scope of his plan. King ran through it all in his head again. They would surreptitiously contact Acca, explain about the details of her death and how Alexander had come back to save her. They would leave the pseudo-corpse for Young Alexander to find and mourn over, setting in

action a course of events that would lead them back in time. While Alexander's younger self grieved, they would use a machine in another of his laboratories to get home—separately. King didn't know where or when Alexander considered home. They'd lived a lifetime as brothers now. But that was one secret Alexander had yet to reveal.

"This isn't far from Rome," King observed.

"You mean, from where Rome will be," Alexander clarified and then shook his head. "Only about twenty miles. But there's a village to the south where we can get rooms. They make great wine too."

"Where are we most likely to spot her?" King asked, as they left the view across the lake behind and turned for the village. King's body was now deeply tanned, his healing abilities strangely not affecting the pigment in his skin. His hair was longer now too, down below his shoulders, and to fit in with the era, he had grown a thick luxuriant beard. The few times he caught a reflection of himself in shined metal, he thought he looked more and more like Alexander. The robes and sandals helped with that image.

"Either in the village or we'll make a call up at my villa at some point." A wistful look came over the big man's face. "We spent a lot of time there."

"Let's get some wine before you start crying."

Alexander smiled. "You have a way with words, Jack." The two had become close friends over the years, and King had long since forgiven him for the abduction that led to their travel into the past.

But King had yet to shake the pain he hid. He spent time every morning, sitting in the glow of the rising sun, eyes closed. To the observer, he was praying or meditating, but all he was really doing was remembering. He played the events of his modern life through his mind each morning, when his imagination was most fertile, and he watched his life like an ongoing TV show, watching key events repeatedly like reruns. He thought about Fiona and Sara most of all, but his parents and Asya were always present in

his mind, as were Zelda, Stan, Erik, Shin and Tom. At first, he'd thought of them by their callsigns, but three years ago he had trouble recalling Bishop's name. He'd had to ask Alexander. Knowing he and Alexander were closer to their goal filled him with an anxious tension that threatened to tear down the mental blocks he kept in place through hardened discipline. If those barriers ever broke and the full weight of the despair he felt from missing his loved ones washed over him, he would be useless. So he fought, and worked toward Alexander's goal and the promise of home, in the arms of his girls, with the same passion as Alexander, who was near the end of his much longer, but similar struggle.

"I still haven't seen why you needed me on this little adventure of yours," King said, distracting himself from thoughts of home.

"As I've said before, I needed someone I could trust—and we have yet to face any real problems."

"Real problems?" King asked with a raised eyebrow. "You nearly lost your head in Corsica."

"How was I to know that arrogant bastard was a Prince?

"Prince or not, you didn't have to urinate on him..."

"He was a ponce." Alexander let out a guffaw.

The two joked as they wandered into the nearby village, which was a collection of low buildings and ramshackle wooden structures nestled between picturesque chestnut and olive trees. King watched a man walking toward them. Unlike most of the people he saw, this man looked like he was taking in all the sights around him for the first time, the way King felt *he* must look every time they traveled. But the man's manner didn't resemble that of a stranger to the region. Rather, he was nodding to himself at things he saw, as if he were ticking things off a mental checklist. King didn't think of the man as a threat—hardly anyone was a threat to him and Alexander. Still, he found the man's manner interesting.

The man looked to be in his forties, and had a graying beard, with a high tanned forehead and a receding gray hairline. His eyes were a pale blue, nearly gray. Small crow's feet around the man's

eyes lent wisdom to his already intelligent face. Like King, he wore a robe and sandals. As the man neared, King was about to move his eyes away from the man, when something on the man's arm caught King's eye. The man had faded rope wrapped around his forearm like a bracelet, but underneath it, King could have sworn he had seen a glint of metal or glass. Circular...like a watch.

Before he could be sure, the man had walked past them. King turned to Alexander and put his hand on the big man's bicep to stop him from walking on.

"Did you see that?" King asked.

Alexander whipped his head around and instantly noted the man to whom King was referring. He mumbled a name that sounded like, "David," and added "Steer clear of that man, Jack. He's nothing but trouble."

With that, Alexander turned and strode on toward the village.

Shrugging, King followed. If Alexander didn't come forth with a full explanation on something, no amount of cajoling would get it out of the man. King knew if the story was important enough, it would come out eventually—usually with wine.

Alexander found a place he remembered and told King it had the best bread he would ever taste, when suddenly the large man stopped in his tracks and grabbed King painfully by the arm.

King turned his head and looked. He quickly identified the man Alexander had seen. His hair was shorter, and he wore a thin cloth band around his forehead that looked like a kind of crown. His robes were far richer than those King wore—dyed fabrics, and elaborately stitched roses along the hem. The man's bearing was regal, as if he thought himself far above the people around him. People stepped out of the way as the man moved through, as if they knew and feared him.

King was looking at Alexander. The *young Alexander.*

He turned and looked up at his friend, who had grown his hair and beard long, and who was dressed in a poor man's robes, like King. King's Alexander was over 2800 years older, but to see

the man's face, he was just ten or twenty years the senior of the man in the wealthy robes. The resemblance was there, but you'd have to know to look for it. The hair and disparity in appearance of wealth made a large difference. Anyone besides King was unlikely to link the two men, even if they stood near each other.

King looked back to the younger Alexander with the burgundy robe and took in the man's bravado. King's Alexander had certainly mellowed over the years. This younger man acted like a hoodlum, pushing into people who got in his way, talking loudly with shopkeepers, and bragging about everything. King had learned several of the Etruscan dialects during his years in the past, and this man, naturally, spoke with a wealthy, educated dialect.

They watched quietly as the younger, brasher Alexander wandered the market in the center of the village, almost as if he were killing time.

Then they saw her.

King did a double take when he saw the woman. He could not believe his eyes. He was looking at a woman that looked almost exactly like photos he had once seen—of his own mother.

THIRTY-SEVEN
Etruria, 780 BC

"That's her…"

Alexander spoke with a reverence that made King take note. He'd known his friend for years now, and heard the man in every kind of mood. But the sudden appearance of his lost love in the busy village market had taken the man's breath away.

The woman, like Lynn Machtchenko in her younger years, had a slim build, but wider flared hips. Her hair was lustrous and dark, cascading over her shoulders in waves. High cheekbones and a subtle smile made her face come alive. Not a man in the market

could keep his eyes off her. She looked to be about twenty-five, but Alexander had said she would be closer to forty. No matter which way you looked at her, Acca Larentia was a stunningly beautiful woman. If she didn't look so very much like his own mother, King could see falling under the woman's spell. Alexander had told him story upon story about the woman's tenderness and generosity as well. Her beauty was only a bow tied around an amazing package.

"I thought my father was your descendant," King said. The likeness to his mother left no doubt that *she'd* been the one to pass on Alexander's bloodline.

"Actually," Alexander said. "Both of them are."

While Alexander's bloodline had been thinned over millennia, having two parents descended from the man rather than just one made King's and Asya's blood a little more...*Herculean*...than usual. King wondered if that's what had drawn Alexander to him, but he didn't ask. It was ancient history now.

King turned to watch his friend admiring the woman. He felt an odd satisfaction at seeing Alexander's eyes wide with wonder, where before there had always been something dark in them. In the future, when they had first met, King had taken that look for deviousness, planning and machination. Over time, he had come to know it instead as a look of dark bitter regret—regret at the life lost with his wife in the pursuit of eternal life for them both.

As King watched, Alexander's look of hopeful joy turned sour. King reached out and whispered, "Your wait is almost over."

Alexander turned and started away from the village, back toward the lake. King raced to keep up.

"That's not the problem, Jack," Alexander's voice was almost a growl. "I screwed up the timing. We don't have five years to prepare."

"I'm afraid to ask. How much time do we have?"

"Closer to five hours. It happens tonight, Jack. She'll return from the village on her own. She pokes around the house and stumbles onto my secret lab. She'll find the Forgotten. They look

famished. They haven't been fed in some time. In those days—*these* days—I was lazy about such things. Left on their own, they go mad. But kept in herds and fed in captivity, they thrive." Alexander's face was lost in remembrance for a moment. King let him have the space instead of prompting him for more.

They kept up a fast pace, hiking along the trail back toward the lake. Just when King thought Alexander wouldn't speak again, the man cleared his throat.

"You remember how it will happen?"

King nodded. "She'll find them parched. Offer them a drink."

"That has always been my assumption. I never saw it happen. When I came in, the cup and the water were on the floor, her body laid out of reach, but sucked dry and withered. She offered them a drink. They accepted. Tonight. We have to get there first. We have to stop her, and we have to create a perfect duplicate corpse—but I've had no time to practice her face."

"Will the look you had tonight be enough for that?" King asked.

"It will have to be."

They circled the lake in silence and the afternoon turned into evening. The sky filled with rich hues of deep blue and streaks of orange as the sun set behind the hills southwest of the lake. The few people in the area had already retired for the night, and the duo had the trail to themselves.

Alexander's villa sat high up on the side of a hill, almost 1500 feet above the level of the huge lake, but Alexander led King away from the hill, and around to the north of it.

"There's a tunnel entrance on the other side that leads directly to the lab. We'll go in that way."

They circled around the hill until the gloom of the oncoming night cloaked the forest in shadows.

Alexander led them closer to the base of a rocky wall, and they trudged through the forest until the going was so difficult, King thought he might trip over a tree root.

Alexander stopped suddenly, as if he heard something.

"What is it?" King whispered.

Alexander let out an exasperated sigh. "It's been so long, I've forgotten exactly where the stone is. I think we have to go back a bit," Alexander chuckled.

"I thought you were supposed to be a genius." King smiled.

Alexander's tension melted away slightly. "It's not like that time in Poseidonia, you knew where *you* were going..."

"How am I supposed to know the difference between a temple to Poseidon and a temple to Hera, when they don't even have any Doric columns yet?"

Alexander smiled. "I told you those wouldn't come for another few hundred years. I've never seen a priestess so angry."

King rubbed his cheek. "I can still feel that slap."

They moved back the way they had come, Alexander mumbling to himself and running his hand along the rock wall as they went. King could just barely see the man moving his arm in the deepening dusk.

"Aha!" Alexander stopped and hugged the rock wall, stretching his massive arms around a huge protruding rock. The man took a huge breath and then struggled until King could hear a grinding sound. Alexander rolled the massive round stone to the side, revealing the dark yawning mouth of a cave.

"That's a little Biblical, isn't it?" King asked, raising an eyebrow. He was frequently amused, and sometimes disturbed, by Alexander's stories of the hubris of his youth. He had certainly seen improvements in the man's behavior over the last two decades, and he attributed the change to their friendship. Alexander himself professed to not having had nearly enough close friends over the years in whom he could confide.

"It was practical at the time. No one else around would have been able to move the stone but me."

Alexander stepped into the darkened tunnel. King looked around and voiced his concern. "Should we close it up after us?"

He couldn't see how it could be done, but it went against his nature to leave his six unprotected.

"No need," came the soft reply from down the tunnel.

King walked cautiously into the dark, feeling for the walls and ceiling of the tunnel, but they were broad enough to allow Alexander to move through them swiftly. Then something occurred to King, and he slowly pulled his sword from his belt.

"Why are you whispering?"

The reply took a second, and King knew he was about to receive bad news.

"I forgot to tell you something."

Before King could ask, he heard a low snarling sound that rose in volume until the bass of the growl shook his bones, like amplifiers at a rock concert.

"I forgot to mention the dog."

"The *dog*?" King asked. But then understanding dawned on him. "Please tell me it doesn't have three heads."

Alexander's reply was drowned out by a robust growling that vibrated the stone under King's feet. Three heads or not, the thing sounded huge and hungry.

THIRTY-EIGHT
Viewing Gallery, Manifold Omega Facility, 2013

The heavy door smashed hard into the Plexiglas wall, dislodging the explosive Rook had set, and knocking it to the floor against the aquarium wall, where the door promptly landed on top of it. Rook had been thrown backward by the blast and ended up on his back, struggling like a tortoise to get onto his legs.

Asya let a burst of bullets fly from her position on the second level, strafing the doorway. Rook heard her utter a Russian curse as a heavy mercenary fell through the doorway onto his face. Then

he saw something arc down from the balcony, hit the door and bounce out through the open doorway and into the corridor.

Rook got to his feet and let out a grunt as he raced for the wall. Asya had tossed a grenade she had taken from the armory down the length of the gallery. It was a good throw. A deflection off the 45 degree angled door, and straight out of the room and into the waiting arms of the mercenaries was a nearly impossible shot. But with the door open, Rook could find himself on the receiving end of more metal fragments. He heard screams behind him and then the explosion. The shockwave sent him slamming face first into the wall. He missed Asya's outstretched hand and slid down the wall to the floor.

"I feel like a pregnant kangaroo on a pogo-stick in this friggin' armor. Doesn't anyone ever use a handgun any more?" Rook pulled out one of his two Desert Eagle pistols and waited on the floor. As soon as he saw the forearms of the first man enter the room, he fired twice, the loud booming shots echoing through the long room. The first shot missed, but punched a softball sized hole in the wall. The second shot struck the mercenary's arm—and took it off. The merc fell back, screaming in pain.

Rook looked up to the metal guard rail around the second story balcony. He saw Asya was rapidly tying a bed sheet to the rail, while nervously watching the door at the end of the gallery's lower level. He holstered the Desert Eagle and scrambled on hands and knees for the dangling sheet.

"I can't cover you and help you climb," Asya said, as she finished tying and then swept her submachine gun up again on its strap.

Rook didn't see any sign of Peter or Lynn. He assumed they had already left the upper room, looking for the way out. He couldn't blame them. He would have done the same.

Rook quickly unbuckled his chest armor, removing the bulky plate and impact foam pieces around his arms and torso, dropping them to the floor. They offered protection, but they were stiff and

added a lot of weight. He debated removing the leg armor, but the one now coated in his blood, was probably acting as a compression bandage for his wounded leg. He decided to leave it.

Freed of the weight of the chest armor, and wearing only a black synthetic t-shirt over his broad chest, Rook attacked the bed sheet, shimmying up the cloth, while Asya sprayed the door at the end of the hall with the odd burst of gunfire, hoping to dissuade further incursion. But Rook knew it was just a matter of time until they tossed in another grenade—or worse. He tugged his weight up and after two pulls, gave up on keeping his legs wrapped around the spindly sheet, relying instead on the raw strength in his beefy arms.

Once at the lip, he placed one hand on the concrete floor, and reached up with the other for the bar, pulling himself horizontal in the process, and then rolling under the guard rail onto the balcony. When he stood, Asya was again blasting down into the gallery, by the door. He took quick stock of his location—a large, swank, sparsely decorated office of some sort. *Most likely Ridley's*, he thought. Potted plants dotted the space around a low leather sofa and a glass-topped coffee table. When Rook spotted the executive bathroom at one end of the office and the ajar doorway to a nice bedroom at the other end, he knew his guess was right. He could see the fitted sheet from the bed on the floor of the bedroom. *Now I know where the sheet came from*, he thought. One more exit led from the room to a lighted hallway beyond, the door left wide open. *That'll be where Peter and Lynn went.*

"Can we run now?" Asya asked, stepping up to him.

"Cover me for just a minute," he said, jogging over to the desk near the center of the huge office. The opportunity to learn even a little of what Ridley might have planned was too good, but he'd only sacrifice the minute. He knew Asya's supply of magazines would run out, and he counted on the mercenaries downstairs to get crafty any second now. Plus, if they figured out he and Asya

had ascended to the next level, they would try to flank him by taking the stairwell at the end.

Asya made it back to the rail just as a sustained burst of AK-47 fire strafed the balcony. Rook recognized the sound of the weapon, and knew the jig was nearly up. He altered course away from the desk before he'd even made it there, and instead he made for the far end of the balcony, where he saw a control panel on the wall, next to a large potted fern.

Rook opened fire on the gallery floor, and the AK stopped with a sputtering burst. Asya popped up at her end of the balcony and fired her own sustained burst of gunfire down at the mercenaries, who quickly darted back to the cover of the doorway. Rook caught a glance of the last guy—dressed in black BDUs and snakeskin cowboy boots with a big white ten-gallon hat.

"What a maroon," he mumbled to himself. He raised one of the Desert Eagles and held his angle on the doorway down below at the end of the gallery. "Asya, go. Get with Peter and Lynn, then rendezvous with Queen if you can."

Asya paused and looked at him sternly.

"I got this. Go," he told her.

She turned and sprinted for the door to the hall.

Just then, Ten Gallon came back into the doorway. The sights on Rook's barrel were already lined up. All he had to do was squeeze. The big Desert Eagle boomed once, and the white hat jumped, the brim of it splattered with blood and bone. The mess that had been Ten Gallon's head actually stuck to the wall next to the door—hat and all. "Now that's nasty," Rook said before the hat fell with a wet thud.

"Bunch of amateurs," he called out. "I got a bullet for each of you. Maybe you nut-twists should go home and get more guys."

He glanced to the control panel on his left and scanned the controls. There was a button labeled *Kliegs*, so he pushed it.

Immediately, the massive dark Plexiglas wall came to life, as several enormous underwater spotlights on the other side illuminated

the water. A bewildering array of fish were swimming just on the other side of the wall. Rook guessed the glass wall was maybe 350 feet long by 30 high. *This isn't an aquarium,* he thought, *it's the fucking ocean!*

The water was crystal clear, with a sandy bottom and a few bits of coral and tufts of sea plants. Sea stars and several dozen black spiny urchins sat on the sand.

None of those things held Rook's attention though. The glass wall had been built for one obvious purpose. To view the monstrosity taking up ninety percent of the underwater view. Lying on its back was a giant statue of a man, measuring at least 300 feet in length. The surface of the statue was covered in barnacles and coral, and other sea life, but the massive figure, posed as though standing, was impossible to miss.

As soon as the thought of the statue standing entered Rook's mind, his eyes grew wide. Remembrances of past battles with Ridley's animated golems filled his mind. The thought of this monstrosity standing up made Rook's stomach flip.

"Satan's flaming taint! Why do I get all the fun?"

Just then the balcony erupted in sparks as bullets ricocheted off the rail, and Rook realized the shots were coming from behind him. He was pinned.

THIRTY-NINE
Sub Level 3, Manifold Omega Facility, 2013

Knight shoved Queen and Bishop out of the way, hurling a grenade at the door to the security suite, and another toward the damaged wet wall. Then he pulled the door closed all the way. The grenades exploded seconds later, and the door's automatic bio-hazard seals inflated, then quickly deflated. Knight guessed they had been punctured by a grenade fragment.

Luckily, the locking mechanism didn't engage, even though the seal had. He swung the door all the way open and loosed a burst of MP-5 fire around the room. No one had made it into the suite, but the previously damaged deathtrap wall was now a gaping hole into the adjacent bathroom, with pipes and spitting electrical wires having been cleared by the grenade blast. Knight leapt through the opening, his weapon up and ready to fire in the direction of the parallel corridor. Then he ran for the hall before Queen or Bishop had entered the bathroom.

Knight whipped the bathroom door open and prepared to blast any mercenaries in the long corridor, but all he saw to his right was a long pile of black-clad bodies, stretching back to the loading dock doors and beyond to the stairwell at that end. The other end of the hallway was clear except for some stone rubble near the end. Knight sprinted in that direction.

He found a storage room on his left. Ran past. Just as bullets pinged down the hallway near his feet, he dove through the next door, into a lounge. He quickly scanned the space. Sofas, a table. Nothing he could use. Beyond the lounge was an open double doorway filled with debris. He crossed to the doorway and looked in on what appeared to be a natural cave formation, but the room was filled with mechanical wreckage and the rubble of the collapsed ceiling. Above him, a few wooden cabinets and part of a tilted refrigerator hung out of the ruined ceiling. *A kitchen*, he thought.

He heard gunfire down the corridor. An AK-47. Queen and Bishop answered with a barrage of their own, spurring his climb up the rubble and wreckage, heading to the next level. Most of the kitchen floor was gone, but Knight managed to scramble into and out of the second floor kitchen. He pulled himself to a tottering standing position by the horizontal door handle. As soon as Knight stood, the handle of the door jiggled. The door opened inward. With nowhere to go but backward and down, he quickly leaned forward, straightening one arm above the door handle and leaning his weight against the shoulder. There was a

tiny one-inch-square plastic catch at the bottom of the door designed to grab the stopper pin on the wall, so the door could be kept open. Knight placed the toe of one of his boots on the plastic box, and stepped up.

The door swung in abruptly, and Knight rode the back of the door as it swept him toward the wall. Two men rushed into the room only to find no floor on which to stand. They plummeted ten feet to the unexpected rubble below them. One man's leg shattered on impact, and Knight could hear the sickening crunch of bones as he impacted a large piece of misshapen rock. Knight swung his MP-5 out in his left hand, firing two quick and deadly accurate three-round bursts before swinging around faster than most men can blink and firing twice more. The two men in the hall fell to the floor wearing matching surprised expressions frozen on their faces. One of them managed to squeeze off a single shot before he died, but Knight felt nothing. The quick spin and lingering effects of the gas stole Knight's balance. He dropped the submachine gun knowing its strap would hold it in place. With his hand free, he reached out and snagged the front handle of the door, which was swinging closed. With a yank, he was upright again. Without people shooting at him, he slipped around the door and into the hall.

The two dead men dressed in black BDUs lay sprawled on the floor. One had a swarthy mustache, and the other man had tattoos of jigsaw pieces over one half of his face. Jigsaw man was still breathing, but unconscious.

There was no backup in sight. He looked right. The hallway ended at a T junction. He looked left. The hallway looked identical, but a woman suddenly appeared. He called to her. "Pawn!"

Asya ran up to him. "Are you alone?" He nodded and raised his MP-5, only to discover the weapon was ruined. The single shot fired by the merc had struck the MP-5's barrel. The dent was small, but any imperfection could result in the weapon blowing up in his face.

He unlooped the submachine gun's strap and dropped the weapon to the floor before drawing his Browning 9mm sidearm and pointing it down the long hallway.

"Everyone still alive?" he asked.

She nodded. "Queen and Bishop?"

"For now," he said.

"Which way?" Asya asked.

"Your way. Up. Looking for a communications scrambler. Probably in Ridley's office." Knight said. He climbed to his feet, keeping a wary eye down the hallway.

"Just came from there. Nothing like that. Maybe in the labs upstairs?"

"Worth a try."

He followed her around the corner to the stairwell. Distant bursts of automatic weapons fire echoed up from below. Asya opened the door to the stairwell and glanced down. No one in sight. She motioned for him to follow. Knight stepped into the landing and looked up. Finding no sentry, he raced up the concrete steps to the next level's door, clearly marked *Sub Level 1* in black letters. He peered through the chicken wire-reinforced glass window and found an empty hallway. He said a silent prayer for small favors and slipped into the hall. Asya was right behind him.

"Been in there," Knight said, passing the initial lab doors through which he and the others had entered the facility. He started walking past the doors and down the hall.

"What about this one?" Asya asked. She pointed to a set of doors across from the Microbiology Lab. The sign next to the doors read *Cold Lab*. Beside that was a small stylized icon of a seven-headed dragon.

"They have tissue samples of the hydra in there," Knight said, and he kept walking, quickening his pace. The hydra had been reawakened after its long, petrified sleep in a Manifold lab, just like this, while he traded bullets with Manifold's security force. He wasn't eager for a repeat.

"Are you sure?" Asya asked, joining him in his long strides down the hallway.

"Pretty sure."

Asya smiled. "*Last Crusade*. Love that movie."

"Indy never had to face a multi-headed regenerating nightmare. I would have taken the snakes."

Further down the long hallway, they came to two more sets of doors on opposite sides. The room on the left was labeled *Data Lab,* the room on the right, *Sequencing Lab.*

Knight popped his head into the Data Lab. The room was dark, but the acoustics inside told him it was large. He found the light switch on the wall, and flicked it with an audible snap. Long rows of overhead lights flickered to life, revealing desk after desk of computer stations, reminding Knight of Hollywood versions of NASA or NORAD headquarters. At the far end of the room was a radio station with a long, thick rubber-coated black antenna. Although all the other computers in the huge lab had been turned off, this station was alive with green and red LED lights.

"Is that—" Asya began.

Knight raised his pistol and fired off three shots, shattering the equipment in the corner and throwing a shower of sparks into the air.

Knight tried his throat microphone. "Queen? You read?"

He heard a burst of static and then Queen's voice came through. "Thank fuckery. Where the hell are you?"

"Sub Level 1. You still on 3?"

"We're pinned down in the bathroom. You got out just in time."

"Blast through the next two walls. You got a storage room, then a lounge. Access up to the next level through a caved-in kitchen." Knight walked back to the hallway as he talked and Asya was right by his side.

As he stepped out into the hallway, bullets raced past him from the stairs he had used. He ducked back into the Data Lab.

"Shit. You're gonna need to try for the South stairwell when you get on Two, Queen. North is now hostile."

"Crap," he heard her say. "Hold on."

Knight heard a distant booming noise from the bowels of the facility.

"We're gonna try to circle around to the south side of the loading dock and pin these bastards down," Knight said into his mic.

Knight looked at Asya and she gave a curt nod, indicating she was ready to rush out into the fray again. She was a lot like her brother.

"'We?' Who have you got?"

"Pawn. Give us five. Then make for the south stairs."

"Got it. Where the fuck is Rook?"

"Haven't seen him," he said.

"Rook is on Level 2," Asya said, intuiting Queen's line of question. It wasn't hard. She knew Rook and Queen were an item. Generally inseparable. She would never admit it, but Queen's concern was personal as much as it was tactical.

Knight relayed the message and turned to Asya. "Ready?"

"Go," Asya said from behind him.

Knight yanked the door open in one hard pull.

Standing on the other side of the door was a huge man dressed in black and wearing a camouflage Vietnam-era infantry helmet. His AK-47 was raised at Knight's heart. As the man's finger began to squeeze, Knight closed his eyes.

FORTY
Lake Bracciano, Etruria, 780 BC

"**What...is that** smell?"

"That...would be puppy," the voice came floating back softly. King could just barely make out the man's silhouette in the dark

tunnel. They were coming up on some kind of light source in the distance, but it was faint.

"You called Cerberus, the three-headed hellhound guardian of Hades, 'Puppy?' Really?"

"I couldn't bring myself to destroy the creature. He was...cute once. When he was small. Also, I have yet to weave the Cerberus story into the ancient religions. It started on its own, really, after puppy got free one night."

"You're telling me that the fabled twelfth labor of the *mighty* Hercules was basically catching your loose dog?"

"Actually, that's probably the most accurate telling of the story I've ever heard," Alexander whispered. "I found him in a cave. Brought him home."

As more light filled the tunnel, King could finally make out the stone wall of the natural cave. Alexander's form was fully visible ahead. The tunnel ended at a huge round arena-like space, all carved from a naturally formed cavern. King could see where stone ledges had been fashioned as seating, but there were also natural stalactites that connected with stalagmites, forming thin columns that supported the roof far overhead. Across the floor of the giant space was a thick iron chain. Each link looked large enough for King to crawl through. One end of the chain was pegged to a rock wall. The other end of the chain was out of view to the right of the tunnel entrance.

Alexander held a hand up, preventing King from entering the arena. "'Hellhound' was a bit of an exaggeration, although he is large."

"How big are we talking here?"

"Ever seen a rhino up close?"

"You're kidding."

Alexander's grim face said he wasn't. "That's how big he was when I got him."

King's jaw fell slack. "You said he was *small* when you got him."

"Comparatively speaking," Alexander said with a shrug. "And we can't kill him, either."

"Why not? And won't he recognize your scent?"

"I'm afraid he might not. My body chemistry might have changed since the inclusion of the herbs and serums that give me my longevity and strength. But the reason we can't kill him is more complex."

King understood immediately. "The time-stream. He saves your life at some point?"

"I told you he was a good pup."

Alexander strode out into the arena. King followed. Almost immediately they heard another rumbling growl that shook the stone on which they stood.

King looked to his right, down the length of the arena. A few torches burned along the walls of the broad expanse, but the thing he desperately wanted to see at the end of the chain wasn't there. The end of the chain was a big iron ring and a bolt that went through it. There was no sign of the beast.

"He's loose. Great. I hate you, you know that, right?"

Alexander turned to look at King, but his face angled up and above the tunnel entrance, far over King's head.

"He's behind me, isn't he? I *really* hate you."

King turned as the beast growled again, and this time he had a visual to go with the epic rumbling. He wasn't disappointed. The creature stood crouched on a ledge above the tunnel entrance. It was probably twenty feet tall if it hadn't been crouched. King expected a three headed dog to have three necks as well, but it didn't. All three heads grew out of a single thick neck, and one of the three had grown at an odd angle, as if it were a genetic mutation. King could only count five ears on the creature. Where the other should have been, two heads were fused. Thick black fur covered the creature. Its tail had been docked like a doberman's, but the overall shape of the beast reminded him of a terrier crossbred with a huge Labrador retriever for the shape of its body and a Saint Bernard for the shape of its heads.

One of the three heads appeared to have been sleeping but was rousing now. The other two were snarling, with lips pulled back and long ropes of slobber as thick as King's arm drooling down to the ground like the cave's stalactites.

"Distract him!" Alexander called. Then the man ran off to the side of the arena.

King looked around desperately. "With what!"

The hellhound stepped down to the arena floor with one massive paw, effectively blocking retreat down the entrance tunnel. The paw and foreleg were, by themselves, as tall as an African elephant, but in all other ways besides size, looked just like a dog—with hair the thickness of twine.

King turned and ran for the nearest cave column. The ground shook as the giant animal pounced down from the rock ledge and gave chase.

King got to the column and glanced back. Just in time. The gaping maw of the central head was inches behind him. He threw his body to the side, behind the column. The three-headed beast's momentum carried it past, but the left side head turned in time to snap at him, spraying a long rope of frothy saliva at him. The moisture smacked into King's face like a soaking wet towel.

He rolled on the floor and swiped at his face with the sleeve of his robe, hardly penetrating the thick coating of saliva. He ignored it after that. Had to keep moving. He had correctly guessed that the hound wouldn't damage the delicate columns in the arena, so he planned to use them as shields, at least until the beast lost its patience and decided the cavern could lose a column and not collapse.

He got to his feet and ran for the next column. The slathering creature was right behind him. He heard metal grinding across the stone floor of the cavern. When he looked, he saw Alexander hauling on the giant chain like a sailor pulling in a simple rope. He hoped whatever Alexander had planned, he would do it fast.

As he ran, one of King's rope sandals broke and went flapping off his foot. He shook his leg as he ran, flinging the broken sandal

away. The thought flitted across his mind that if he was lucky, the three-headed monstrosity giving chase would fetch the slipper. The loud growl behind him disabused him of that notion. He kicked off the other sandal with a hop and sprinted as fast as he could across the cool stone floor.

Just as King reached the column and was about to make his jump, he felt his left arm painfully wrenched behind him, when he was pumping his elbow back. Then his whole arm was on fire and tugging him to a halt and upward. His body swung in the air and twisted.

Then he saw it. His entire left arm was in the jaws of the creature's central head. King was lifted up, hanging from the thing's jaws.

Then the hellhound violently thrashed its head from side to side, and King screamed.

FORTY-ONE
Under Alexander's Villa, Etruria, 780 BC

The scream echoed around the arena until King's limp form flew across the room and landed on the floor in a heap.

After a moment, King opened his eyes and looked at his arm—or what was left of it. The flesh had been torn just above the wrist and peeled off up past the elbow where the jagged skin and torn muscle dangled down from his shoulder. He could see his radius and ulna bones in his forearm, stripped clean of muscles and tendons. Yellowish-white ligaments were all that held his elbow joint together. His hand was still whole but looked grotesque now, like a Mickey Mouse glove on a stick figure.

His head fell back onto the stone floor with a *thunk*, and his eyes closed. He tried to scream again, but no voice came. The overwhelming scent of his own body's blood and meat filled his

nostrils, churning his gut. But he didn't panic. He'd gone through this before. Not the giant three-headed hellhound, but he'd survived mortal wounds on a few occasions. He knew what would happen next. With his eyes still closed, he turned his head. Then he opened his eyes and watched the impossible. The jagged flaps of skin at the shoulder stretched and grew as snakes of musculature slipped out from below it like alien tendrils probing for a meal. The flesh at his wrist grew upward toward the elbow. In a minute, the tendrils of muscle had joined and were filling out. The sensation was pure fiery agony. It sucked the air out of his lungs, but he fought against the building scream and remained calm. It would be over in moments.

Just a few more seconds of world class torture, he thought, *then I'll—*

Movement across the arena caught his eye.

Alexander stood on the monstrous dog's back. He held the massive chain wrapped around the creature's single throat like a garrote. The hellhound snapped its three sets of jaws and thrashed its heads from side to side, but Alexander refused to let go. He looked like some kind of insane rodeo rider on a dog that weighed more than a tank.

The creature ran from side to side, then forward and stopped suddenly, like a maddened bull. Alexander struggled behind the beast's neck, then cried out in triumph and leapt off the animal. He landed nimbly on the floor and raced for the side wall and the tunnel entrance.

Is he leaving me here? King wondered.

Cerberus chased him toward the wall. The massive chain sprang up off the floor behind the beast.

The chain pulled taut. The center head snapped up, and the giant animal's momentum suddenly came to a complete stop. Its legs slipped up out from under it into the air, and the massive beast's body slammed back onto the ground. The chamber shook from the impact. Dust cascaded down from the ceiling.

Alexander had successfully chained the dog. He smiled from the doorway of the tunnel, then began edging his way around the arena, as the giant creature got to its feet and began barking at him—each vocalization sounding like a peal of thunder in the enclosed cavern.

King looked down at his arm and saw that it had nearly finished knitting back together. He just needed a few more layers of skin. The process felt like a severe sunburn, but in reverse. The healing also left him ravenously hungry.

He rolled to his side and gingerly tested putting some weight on the arm. The muscles were as strong as ever. Like new...because they were. He pushed himself up to a sitting position, then stood.

Alexander ran around the perimeter of the stone arena. Cerberus kept pace at the end of its tether, barking at him in three distinct voices, each taking turns to create an unceasing wave of sound.

"You're not out of the—" Alexander was yelling.

King looked down at the ground, then at the oncoming beast-dog. He wasn't out of the radius of its arc.

Crap!

He turned and sprinted for the wall, his bare toes finding little crevices and impurities in the stone floor as he ran and gripping them, propelling him faster. At last he slammed into the stone wall at the far side of the cavern, just as Alexander zipped around the back of him and the massive dog passed him, hot on Alexander's tail. The wash of air that swept over King reminded him of standing on the edge of a subway platform when a train slammed past without any plans of stopping at that station.

King edged around the circumference of the stone wall, scratching his itching forearm. He saw his sword in the arena. It was bent to hell and too far inside the arc of the hellhound's tether.

Another lost blade.

He made his way to the opposite side of the arena from where they had entered. There was an identical tunnel mouth. Alexander

stood there waiting, as though nothing exciting had happened. The giant dog barked twice more and then ran off toward the far side of the arena.

"Not a word about its bark being bigger than its bite. I nearly lost my arm," King said.

"But your clever distraction worked. I was able to leash him."

"Clever distrac—? Did I mention that I hate you?"

"Once or twice," Alexander replied.

"Today?" King prodded.

"I think we're up to three. Come on. The lab is this way." Alexander led them down a long dark tunnel. King ran a hand along the dark wall until it flared away, leaving him only with Alexander's dim silhouette to guide him forward. "Next, we will deal with the Forgotten. Then the creation of the body."

Suddenly, the shape of Alexander's body disappeared in the darkness ahead.

"Right. The Forgotten. But they're all locked up. Hey, where did you—"

Something smashed into King's body from the left, throwing him against a wall, hard. He rolled with the impact, and came up on his feet. He could hear a scrabbling in the dark and wished he had nabbed one of the lit torches in the arena.

Something hit him low in the gut, but through long years of rigorous exercise, King's abdomen was like a rock. The blow still took air out of him, but it did little damage. He thrust down with two balled fists, hitting his attacker before it could retreat and launch a second assault from the gloom. The impact was hard and brittle under his fists, like he had just punched a wooden board encased in bubble wrap.

King could hear Alexander struggling in the dark. Then a match flared brightly. Matches wouldn't first see widespread use in China for another twelve hundred years, but Alexander and King had agreed to make and use some modern amenities at times when others were not around. Matches were one of their creature comforts.

The match lit a torch sconce on the wall, casting orange light in all directions. They had entered a wider room at the end of the tunnel. Like the parking garage in Tunisia, every surface—floor, walls and ceiling—was covered in wraiths. There were hundreds of them chittering in the dark.

The Forgotten were free.

Unlike in Tunisia though, this time they attacked all at once. King watched as a swarm of the creatures mauled Alexander. Then they turned on King, a chaotic mass of fast, nimble bodies moving with the ravenous excitement of hungry lions who have just spotted a baby zebra. He tried to fight them, but it was no use. They moved too fast, and more often than not, his punches struck only their cloaks.

In just ten seconds, King was overwhelmed, buried beneath a mass of hungry wraiths reaching for his skin—and the blood beneath it.

FORTY-TWO
Ruins of Carthage, Tunisia, 2013

The sun would not rise for another hour, but the dark heavens were already lightening. Pale blue leached up into the Arab sky on the horizon.

Richard Ridley smiled.

It was all coming together. That bastard Alexander was dead. King was dead, too—both unexpected gifts. His rebellious brother, Darius, had walked into a trap. Chess Team was cut off and unable to contact support. Although they had robbed him of his genetic immortality, it made little difference. With the mother tongue, he could repair damage to his body and give himself longevity by forcing his cells to age slower, perhaps not at all. And now...the Chest of Adoon. The power it contained was said to be without comparison. A civilization destroyer.

His company, Manifold Genetics, was in ruins, like the landscape around him, to which Trigger and Carpenter had led him. But that made little difference. He had many holdings and subsidiary companies. He had the wealth, even without the labs. Soon he would have a destructive power to correct all the wrongs done to him. Combined with his superior intellect, the mother tongue, and a lot of money, he would be an unstoppable force.

No more toying with these people, he thought. It was time for real power. World changing power.

He slowed his pace, allowing Seth and Jared to walk ahead of him. At first, Jared kept glancing back, afraid he would miss something. Seth continued on ahead, secure in his role. They walked through the dark ruins, Trigger lighting the way with a flashlight. Carpenter fell back to the rear to protect their small group.

They crossed La Goulette Road and headed into the trees on the opposite side, next to a house. Ridley still found it amusing that the wealthy Tunisians had built estates nestled in between the standing ruins. If they had been in a Western nation, the entire area would have been a World Heritage site, but here, the wealthy had managed to get every scrap of land that didn't have an ancient rock on it.

They passed through a small copse of trees that ran along the backside of a house, and then they were in the necropolis. Beyond the tombstones lay another small forest, and then the ruins called the Antonine Baths. Beyond those, the Gulf of Tunis.

Richard Ridley looked around at the small stones of the darkened necropolis. He smiled again. The necropolis was as good a place as any. He raised the silenced pistol Trigger had provided him, and shot Jared neatly in the back of the skull. The sound the weapon made was like someone spitting in the dark. Jared's body collapsed to the ground, draping over one of the low stones that acted as markers for ancient graves. Without time to prepare to use the mother tongue to heal himself, Jared was dead. His body went slack as it reverted to clay.

Seth turned at the act, shocked.

"Don't worry, Seth. I know you are loyal to me. Jared dreamed of independence. From the moment I gave you life, you were all individuals, with personalities and emotions all growing further away from mine, based on your experiences. I didn't like the direction Jared was going. Sooner or later, we would have butted heads. Or he would have gone to our enemies. That's no good for business."

Trigger and Carpenter looked unconcerned. They knew they were getting paid—and extremely well—to do their jobs. As long as they performed, they wouldn't be getting bullets to the head. Besides, Ridley thought both men most likely imagined themselves capable of drawing their weapons on him faster than he could gun them down. Little did they know, in a few moments, he would no longer require their services.

"Let's move," Ridley said.

Trigger led the way into the trees on the opposite side of the necropolis, and the group unceremoniously left Jared's gray corpse draped over the stone.

"Once we have the Chest," Seth said to Ridley, "what do you intend to do next?"

Ridley shook his head. "That depends on the nature of the destructive force contained within the Chest. If the weapon is easily used, perhaps I'll test it out on Tunis. But in my experience, ancient weapons with this kind of destructive power most often turn out to be biological. It might require study."

"Destroying Tunis would be simple, even now with just the mother tongue, but perhaps not the statement you want to make to the world for your first assault. Maybe something bigger? The destruction of an entire nation, perhaps?" Seth spoke hesitantly. Ridley figured he was no doubt wary of getting a silenced bullet in the face. But it was a reasonable suggestion.

Ridley smiled at the idea. "Maybe China. I *would* like to have my own tea empire."

They came upon the ruins of the Baths. The third largest Roman Bathing Ruins in the world, Antonine was something special. In its

heyday, it would have been like an aquatic gymnasium, with pools of differing sizes and purposes. An amazing place to while away a Roman-era day. The complex faced the sea. An incredible view. It was also architecturally clever, lying at the base of two sloping hills, allowing water to flow down to it. Ridley considered having the baths reconstructed once the whole of North Africa was his. His only problem with North Africa was all the people. *Nothing a little genocide can't fix.*

With the power he would soon possess, nothing would be impossible.

That's what he told himself, but there were lingering doubts. Despite all of his research into the Chest supporting the idea that it contained a destructive power beyond imagining, he had to remember that it was placed there by ancient people who had yet to conceive of the atomic bomb. That said, he'd read texts comparing it to natural forces like typhoons and earthquakes, as well as mythological forces such as Zeus's lightning bolts and the fires of Hades. Even by modern standards of destruction, those comparisons gave him hope that the weapon inside the chest would give him dominion over the human race. The mother tongue—the language of God—made him divine. The power inside the Chest would allow him to enforce his divinity world-wide.

The ruins, now little more than stumps of rock, walls, arched doorways and the occasional cave, had one other major benefit, unbeknownst to most. He had built his Omega facility under the baths at gigantic expense, and the process had required the continual hiring of architects and builders, who were quietly murdered later on. Bribing government officials had nearly bankrupted him at the time. But he had known of the mother tongue even then, and he had known it would only be a matter of time until he acquired it.

With the mother tongue, the prize under the Gulf of Tunis was invaluable. *How ironic that two powerful weapons had been concealed here.*

Building the aquarium wall had been maddeningly difficult with no less than twenty architects telling him it was an impossible feat, and five eventually designing the thing. They were all dead now. But in the end, he had it: one of the world's most amazing offices with an unparalleled view of one of the Seven Wonders of the Ancient World.

He had stood at that railing, lusting to control his secret find for long years, while his people scoured the globe for antiquities, secrets and power. The Hydra had blown up in his face, with the involvement of the Chess Team, first at his Peru facility, then again in the Atlantic and finally in New Hampshire. But those defeats were minor compared to the advancements in genetics he had made, and the serum he had designed to give himself regeneration. It occurred to him that he still had the formula. A smile slipped onto his face. He could make more, and ensure he could always regenerate from injury. Better yet, he would build a loyal army, unable to be killed. Visions of unkillable soldiers marching on Washington D.C., supported by living stone golems filled his imagination. The possibilities were endless.

And distracting.

The others paused where the ruins met the shoreline. Ridley walked past them, and strode into the lapping waves of the Gulf of Tunis. He knew that the shallows ran twenty feet out before the shelf dropped 80 feet. He had SCUBA dived here on several occasions, exploring the area well.

The others hung back, still unsure of why it was necessary to make haste for the shoreline.

The sun would soon be peeking over the eastern horizon across the sea. The sky grew lighter. Ridley checked his watch. 4:00 a.m. on the dot.

Showtime.

Richard Ridley raised his hands into the air, facing the sea. He began shouting commands into the air. As usual, when he used the mother tongue, his mind heard the commands in his head in

English, but what came from his mouth sounded guttural, strange and distorted.

A Bible verse flitted through his mind and brought a smile to his face.

The Lord killeth, and maketh alive: he bringeth down to the grave...and bringeth up.

Up, Ridley thought. *I bringeth thee up!*

FORTY-THREE
Sub Level 2, Manifold Omega Facility, 2013

Queen leapt nimbly over the rubble and scrambled up Bishop's body onto the second level, through the shattered kitchen. She checked that the hallway was clear, then helped Bishop work his massive frame—made bulkier by the impact armor—up into the hallway of Sub Level 2.

They both sat panting on the floor. Queen kept her weapon trained on the length of the hall, while Bishop focused on the nearby turn toward the north stairwell.

It had been a long hard slog, first blowing a hole through the wall into the storage room, and then again into the lounge. Then they had found the collapsed kitchen in what looked like a cave. In each room except the cave, they had needed to exchange gunfire with the mercenaries in the hall. The men seemed to be pacing them. Queen didn't know if the mercenaries knew about the collapsed kitchen, but if they didn't, it wouldn't take them long to figure out that their prey had fled upward.

She keyed her throat microphone. "Deep Blue? You read?"

Still no answer.

Although Knight had gotten the internal communications working, she couldn't reach further afield. She had tried Domenick Boucher at CIA too, but hadn't been able to get a long distance signal.

Probably interference from the structure. We're pretty far under-ground.

They'd need to get topside before she could call in reinforce-ments. Queen had tried Rook too, but she couldn't raise him. She tried not to think about it. If King was gone and Rook bought it too, she didn't know what she'd do. She still had a hard time wrapping her head around King being gone—just like that.

It seemed impossible.

King had always been there. His skills in the field and casual attitude had been the glue that held Chess Team together. Each member of the team would have willingly died a dozen times over for King. He never asked for their respect, but he had earned it just the same. He never backed down from any threat, and his maverick, hare-brained approaches to getting things done had continually impressed.

She just couldn't believe he was gone.

"If we're gonna go..." Bishop started.

"I know," Queen said. "Let's go."

They both stood, and not a moment too soon. A door just down the corridor opened as a man stuck his head out, followed by the barrel of an MP-5.

Queen took aim, but stopped her trigger finger just in time. "Mr. Sigler?"

Peter came rushing out of the room with Lynn close on his heels. The two aging spies were out of breath from their quick sprint down the carpeted corridor.

"Have you seen our daughter?" Lynn asked as she turned to keep an eye on the hallway behind her.

"She's with Knight. Let's go. This way." Queen started for the south stairwell.

Lynn held up a hand. "CCTV in the office. The stairwell is full of men below and above. Can't go that way."

Queen turned to Bishop and nodded. The big man turned toward the nearer end of the corridor, and the right angle turn

that led to the north stairwell. When he got to the corner, he placed the barrel of his weapon at the edge of the wall, then darted his head around it. The others followed him without a sound when he pushed forward.

He paused at the door.

"Knight and Pawn are on the floor above us," Queen said. "Rook's out of touch." Not having to mention King's status felt wrong. She filled the gap with the obvious. "Whoever is below us is hostile."

Bishop opened the door and threw his last grenade down the stairwell, then stepped back, allowing the door to close. A few seconds later, an explosive roar shook the stairwell. Smoke rose up past the small window in the door. "That was my last."

"I'm out too," Queen looked to King's parents. She couldn't imagine what they must be going through. "Lynn: you're my Pawn. Peter, you're with Bishop. Stay by our sides, and we'll try to get you out of here alive."

Lynn's only response was to hand Queen two extra magazines for her MP-5.

Peter nodded.

Bishop led the way, spraying the upper stair landing with a hail of bullets as he lunged into the stairwell. His legs pistoned up and down as if he were a track star, instead a of a mountainous war machine. Queen nudged Peter to follow Bishop, then Lynn was next, and she took up the rear, keeping her eye on the lower flight of stairs. They encountered no resistance.

At the top of the stairs, Bishop lurched out of the door, throwing himself to the smooth floor of the corridor. He fought the instinct to just spray bullets into the hallway, which was what he might have done if he had one of his chain-fed machine guns. But spraying and praying was just a quick way to waste ammo with a submachine gun. Instead, he fired controlled bursts at the small group of men fifty feet away. He picked his targets one by one, dropping them with accurate gunfire. Knight would be proud.

Queen took the lead with Lynn at her side. They moved into the Microbiology Lab, and made for the janitorial closet. By the time she had the door open, Peter was with them. Bishop ducked inside the door to the lab, as gunfire ripped through the corridor again. One of the mercenaries at the end of the hall must have survived. Either that or more of them had arrived.

They're like cockroaches, Queen thought. *If we can just leapfrog our way out like this...*

But the long tunnel beyond the janitor's closet could be a killing field, the perfect place for an ambush—and this mission had already cost them too much.

"Knight, Rook, if you can hear me, Bishop and I are bugging out with Peter and Lynn, I suggest you do the same."

There was no response.

Fuck.

"Lynn, you're a good shot, right?"

"Pretty good."

"Cover our six. Bish, up front with me. Anyone in our way is hostile. Shoot until you're out of bullets."

Lynn gave a nod. The same kind she'd seen King give a hundred times before rushing out to face an enemy.

Queen flung the door open and crouched. Bishop took a stance next to her. No gunfire came. The tunnel was lit. There was a small pile of bodies just beyond the door. Someone had already exited through this route. She didn't know who, but she was glad for the lucky break. "Go."

The group sprinted down the tight tunnel, with Queen and Bishop's armored bodies acting as a shield for King's unprotected parents. Although the lights were on now, Queen couldn't see to the end of the tunnel. Still, what she could see looked promising— an empty run until the curvature of the tunnel's incline obscured her view of the stairs.

They ran until they reached the stairs. More bodies lay at the foot of the stairwell, and for the first time, Queen got the

idea that the forces attacking her were not directly under Ridley's command. They made their way up the stairs to the amphitheater door, only to find it unlocked and ajar. The outer gates were not locked either.

They emerged into the Tunisian pre-dawn twilight, and the smell of the nearby salt water filled her nostrils. Bishop scanned the ruins and the trees that ringed the amphitheater with a small set of night-vision goggles.

"That way," he said.

"You see tangos?" Queen asked.

"No."

"How could you know they went that way, then?" Peter whispered.

"Some tree branches are disturbed, bent and broken. Also, about 2000 feet through the trees that way is the sea—and a heli-pad. Ridley likes helicopters."

Queen started for the tree line. "Somebody paid attention during the briefing."

"He's not getting away again," Bishop said. "This time we'll take care of him permanently."

Queen let that comment wash over her. Bishop had more reason to loathe Ridley than the others. He'd been turned into a monster and had nearly killed Knight as a result. While the rest of the team fought Ridley and licked their wounds afterwards, Bishop had struggled with the physical and psychological fallout of being turned into something inhuman. She clapped Bishop's shoulder. "This time, we'll end him."

As they crossed the road and slipped into the trees, Queen contacted Deep Blue. Now outside the confines of the Omega facility, she had a clear link to New Hampshire.

"Queen, what the hell is going on over there?" Deep Blue's voice was modulated only to protect his identity—the emotional stabilization program that removed all trace of his state of mind wasn't activated. He sounded extremely worried.

"Everything's gone tits up. I'm with Bishop and two new Pawns. Pawn Zero is with Knight. Rook is MIA..." she paused. "Blue...King and Alexander are down." Her voice trembled slightly. She squashed the rising emotions back down and said, with more authority, "Repeat. King is down. Ridley is loose with two of the Three Amigos."

She paused.

"I...want...you...to...bring...the...fire. You read me Deep Blue? This man does not escape us this time. The Grim Reaper is waiting for him with open arms."

There was a pause on the line as she entered the necropolis. She saw one of the Ridley duplicates draped over a stone marker. She walked up to the body and confirmed it was dead, reverted to an inert clay form. "One of the Amigos is down. That makes Ridley plus one. Copy?"

"I copy, Queen. Stay your course."

Queen couldn't tell if Deep Blue had activated the emotional stabilizer or if he was bottling things for later, but he sounded cool and in control.

"I'm showing four heat blooms near the water," Deep Blue added. "Straight ahead."

Ridley, Queen thought, and started forward.

"Help is on the way, Queen." Deep Blue said.

"The fucking *fire*, Blue. Make it happen. Out."

She moved into the trees on the far side of the necropolis. Bishop ran beside her, Peter and Lynn following close behind.

One more try, she thought. *One more. Please be there.*

She keyed her microphone.

"Rook?"

"Queen!" Rook's voice filled her ear, loud, desperate and fouled by static. "For the love... God... don't... outside."

"Rook! You're coming through patchy. Say again. Say again!"

"Don't let Ridley... tongue... For fuck's sake! This... crazy... massive!"

She burst through the trees into a clearing—the baths.

The shoreline was just a hundred and fifty feet away And *he* was just beyond, wading in the shallows.

In the lightening sky, she could see Richard Ridley in a dark jumpsuit, his arms raised to the heavens. Three other men stood nearby—one of them was the last remaining duplicate, whose white linen suit glowed in the pre-dawn twilight.

The air filled with a rumbling sound like thunder, and she realized it was caused by Ridley, shouting out at the sea.

"Don't let him use the fucking mother tongue outside! No matter what!" Rook finally came through clearly, but his warning was too late. The sea was writhing.

FORTY-FOUR
Sub Level 2, Manifold Omega Facility, 2013

"It's already too friggin' late, isn't it?" Rook rubbed a hand over his blond hair and then raised it back into the air as he'd been commanded to do.

Queen didn't respond.

Three armed men stood in the doorway of the office. They wore black, but the odd assortment of accoutrements each man wore, besides the basic black BDUs, revealed them as mercenaries. One man wore a Braves cap. Another had three blue bandanas tied over one thigh. The third man was tall and slim. He wore a green jungle hat. Each was armed with an AK-47.

Rook glanced down into the gallery and saw five more black-clad mercenaries rush into the space and cover his position from below.

"Don't even breathe fast, gob-shite," the tall mercenary said. "Or we'll turn you into Swiss bloody cheese." The accent was Lancashire.

Probably ex-SAS, Rook thought. *Wonderful.*

Rook let his eyes wander to the illuminated glass wall holding the ocean at bay. As he looked out at the enormous submerged statue, a school of small black fish darted over its face, then abruptly changed direction and fled off to the right, past the edge of Rook's view.

"Just so you know, the sarcastic humor, witty nicknames, and creative threats are kind of my thing," Rook said.

"Too bloody bad," the SAS man said, stepping closer, weapon raised. Rook made an easy target.

But Rook didn't take his eyes off the glass wall. "Course, colorful language ain't gonna save you from Jolly Green over here."

"What do you—" the SAS man started, but then stopped when a grinding noise filled the gallery.

Even through the several-inch thick wall of Plexiglas, every man inside the space heard the loud crunch and rumble of grinding stone. The remaining fish lazily swimming near the statue turned and fled. The massive head outside the window slowly rotated, until the face was turned directly toward the viewing gallery wall. Seaweed was wrapped around the long tines of the statue's crown, the elongated spikes reminding Rook of a demonic statue of liberty. But this statue was male. The face was bearded.

As the SAS man lost his voice, the gigantic head stopped turning.

Then it opened its eyes, and the screaming began.

Hardened men of war started shouting in the gallery below. They ran for the door, gripped by fear. No amount of training could prepare a soldier for such a sight, and no amount of money could provide that much courage. The enormous statue peered through the aquarium wall, raw unbridled anger filling its solid eyes. Immense eyebrows furrowed and frown lines appeared at the mouth, which was larger than the upper office in which Rook and his three captors stood.

Rook turned to look back at the men by the office door. They had each let the barrels of their respective weapons droop, as they stared at the huge moving head with slack jaws.

"I'm guessing you boys weren't in on Ridley's plan. We're all gonna be chopped sushi."

Bubbles exploded from the ocean floor surrounding the statue. Silt and sand billowed in massive clouds as the statue pulled away from its long-time resting place and began to sit up. Its huge arm twisted toward the wall. Each fingernail was larger than a man. The face turned to a vicious scowl, and the tips of its stone fingers touched the Plexiglas.

"Sweet mother of God..." the man with the leg bandanas said, as his bladder let go and a puddle of acrid beer-smelling urine stained his pants.

Rook brought his raised hands together, fingers resting on his wristwatch. The remaining mercenaries still weren't looking at him as he slipped one battle-armored leg through the metal railing of the balcony and held on tight. He took one last look at the rising stone monstrosity beyond the viewing window and then leaned toward the metal control panel on the wall. Moving slowly, he bumped the light switch with his shoulder. The office went dark, but the giant statue awakening from the sea bed remained illuminated like a Neptune-themed Christmas tree.

"What the—" the SAS man started, but never finished as Rook depressed the radio trigger on his wristwatch.

The block of C4, still hidden under the metal door on the floor of the gallery, exploded. The door spun through the gallery, but posed no real threat. That came next. The immensely thick aquarium wall shattered right up the center with a hideous shriek. The crack spider-webbed faster than a sneeze, and the wall gave way. The Gulf of Tunis—just a small portion of the mighty Mediterranean Sea—gushed through the now nearly 300-foot long open window into the subterranean base. The pressure-driven salt water instantly filled the gallery, blasting down the Sub Level 3 corridor. A tidal wave of white frothing fury swept over the balcony rail, and a second after Rook grasped the rail with both hands, it hit.

The impact was like getting punched in the face and chest by a gaggle of heavyweight fighters, but Rook clung to the rail, his armored legs firmly locked in place around the metal. The tsunami of water plowed through the office space, crushing furniture across the room, and slamming the three mercenaries into the wall, pinning and drowning the shocked men.

Rook had taken a huge breath before he detonated the C4, and he had closed his eyes against the wall of water, but the second he felt the initial surge of terrifying pressure leave his face, he couldn't help but open his eyes to take in the sight.

He wished he hadn't.

The Colossus was rising.

TERMINAL

FORTY-FIVE
Sub Level 1, Manifold Omega Facility, 2013

Knight was about to die. The man pointing an AK-47 at his heart had a long handlebars mustache under his Vietnam era helmet and a look in his eyes that said he was going to enjoy what came next.

Suddenly, the man's chest ripped apart, small bursts of flesh and fabric spraying upward from the man's chest. The sight was coupled by the staccato clap of an MP-5 being drained of its ammo. Bullets ripped into the man until he fell over backward.

Knight turned his head down and saw that Asya had slipped down between his splayed legs and fired her MP-5 upward from the floor—missing his crotch by inches—to fill the mercenary full of bullets and death.

She slid gracefully out from between his legs, popped to her feet, replaced her spent magazine and then checked both ways down the hallway of Sub Level 1's laboratories.

"Thanks," Knight said and walked out into the hallway, gingerly stepping over the dead man. A pile of bodies covered the floor at the southern end of the hall. He distantly recalled hearing gunfire, but thought it had been on a different level.

Then they heard yet another explosion, deep in the depths of the facility—but this one was stronger. The air in the hallway started rushing past him.

His mind didn't have time to process what he was experiencing before his instincts took over. He grabbed Asya's hand and dragged her toward the Microbiology Lab and its secret tunnel to the surface. Asya asked no questions, but simply ran with him. As they rounded the doorway into the lab, water began spraying out of the bottom and sides of the stairwell door.

Knight ran faster.

They reached the janitorial closet and found the secret door wide open. More bodies covered the floor on the other side. Knight heard the stairwell door blow up behind him. *Rupture*, was the word that swept through his mind. Water rushed into the hallway behind him with mad intensity, the wave crashing into the lab, upturning tables and equipment like a rampaging monster.

"Go!" Knight yelled.

They ran as fast as they could, but the water was faster.

The wave of water blasted into them from behind, knocking them down and launching them toward the tunnel's end. Knight managed to shut his mouth just in time. He hoped Asya had done the same.

The salt water stung his eyes when he tried to look for her, so he snapped them shut again, and reached out with his hand, hoping he would be able to grasp the staircase railing.

But he didn't have to. His body was tossed up and out of the water and onto the floor of the tunnel. The water sloshed around him, and then began to recede back into the tunnel. Knight raised his head and saw Asya a few feet in front of him. Her long hair was down in front of her face. After a moment's stillness, she coughed the water from her lungs.

Knight heaved in a deep breath, then saw that the stairs were nearby—only they didn't look right. He staggered to his feet and looked back the way they had come. They had been swept right

past the amphitheater stairs and into the next tunnel. He didn't know where these stairs led, but they went up. It would be an improvement over the flooded subterranean base.

"You okay?" he asked.

"I think I swallowed most of Mediterranean," Asya said between coughs.

"Let's get out of here," Knight said, taking the stairs and trusting that if Asya could joke, she'd be fine.

They ascended the stairs to another tunnel, and then found a door that led to a huge underground parking lot with concrete support columns, and a nearby vehicle tunnel leading down.

Not what I want.

Knight looked across the vast lot, but couldn't find another exit.

"Come, this way. Entrance from fountain is near mosque." Asya led the way across the garage.

Knight followed, looking for CCTV cameras or men taking cover behind the pillars, but once he was convinced they were alone in the echoing space, he began jogging faster. Then he spotted a black metal ladder on the far wall, and two dead bodies at the foot of it.

"No shortage of dead men here," Asya said.

She climbed the ladder and opened the hatch at the top.

They climbed out of the fountain and into a small park. They were alone.

"Almost dawn. Mosque worshipers will arrive soon." The sky was a pale blue, the sun just below the horizon.

"Can't be helped," Knight said. Then he keyed his microphone.

"Queen, you read?"

"Knight! Get your ass to the shore on the far side of the Baths. The shit is getting deep." Queen's voice sounded frantic. Then he heard distant gunfire.

He started to run toward the looming mosque, and the ruins just beyond it. Asya stayed right by his side. They raced through the concrete and manicured shrubs of the park to the road. Traffic

was trickling through already, and several cars honked at them as they sprinted across the asphalt. Knight was drenched with sweat and sea water. The battle armor wasn't helping. They angled across the road to a triangular parking lot where early arriving worshipers were already parking their cars. Knight paid them no heed as he made for the relative privacy of the trees beyond, which created a natural boundary between the mosque and the amphitheater ruins.

When they reached a stand of trees and were free from the confused looks of the devout, he paused to catch his breath.

"Help me out of this crap," Knight said, unbuckling one of the battle armor forearm plates. Asya stepped up and helped him unbuckle all the armor. Each new piece removed made him feel lighter and cooler. Even after the recent swim, he felt over-heated, and realized it had been hours since he'd had a drink of anything. With the armor off, he bounced on his feet twice, refreshed slightly by the feeling of lightness, and said, "Let's go," before tearing off again, much faster than before.

On the far side of the trees, they found a small path and a concrete bench. Next to it was a closed up and boarded food cart, with a hand-painted wooden board listing the food options in Arabic. He wanted to stop, break in and guzzle some water, but he'd trained to operate for days on minimal food and water. He could drink when the fighting was done.

His soaked BDU pants clung to him as he ran, but his synthetic t-shirt had nearly dried—damp only at the armpits and neck. He looked over at Asya as they ran through more trees right next to the concrete wall of a house. She glistened with seawater and sweat, but ran with the same look of determination he'd seen in King. The Sigler family had a lot in common.

Then he was on the ground, and Asya was shouting. His left arm burned with pain. He looked at it and saw blood. Gunfire rattled through the trees above him. He couldn't move his head far enough to see what had happened to Asya.

Then he saw a man emerge from the trees. His scarred bald head gleamed in the first rays of the sun. The side of his face was horribly disfigured, and he smiled a huge leering grin. Then he took three running steps forward and kicked his boot into Knight's stomach. The air left Knight's body at the same speed the consciousness left his confused mind.

FORTY-SIX
Sub Level 3, Manifold Omega Facility, 2013

Rook was nearly out of breath as he left the balcony rail. The oncoming rush of water subsided, but the room was completely submerged. He could feel the pressure of the deep mashing against his ears. It wasn't easy to swim over the rail with the added weight of the impact armor plates and foam still attached to his legs, but he didn't think he had time to take them off. The combat boots weren't helping either.

Salt water stung his eyes as he stroked over the gallery toward where the Plexiglas wall had been. He thought his only chance would be swimming for the surface instead of trying to navigate up underwater stairwells and hallways. He didn't know how far up the water went, but if the whole second level was under water, chances were good the entire complex was drowned.

His lungs burned as he stroked with his arms, hoping that outside the flooded gallery would be a clear shot to the surface—and not some underwater cavern with no air waiting for him.

The klieg lights in the water lit up the sandy bottom, from which the enormous statue was still rising. It had turned its head away from the exploded Plexiglas wall, and was now using its hands to push itself up. Rook couldn't see the size of the gigantic thing—he was too close to it. What he could see were the enormous spikes on

the crown, and the huge shoulders of the creature, as it started to rise up in the water.

He clawed for the surface, fighting the swirling waters created by the giant's rising. He kicked and struggled, but as he rose, a sinking feeling began to grow in his heart.

He wasn't going to make it.

He could see the glowing sky above. Layers of darting fish above showed him just how far below the surface he was. He just wasn't moving fast enough. He lost some of his air in an involuntary exhale, then reached for his nose with one hand and clamped his mouth shut with his jaw. His lungs sucked hard at the scant air in his mouth, and he could feel the depth still trying to force its way into his ears.

His eyes moved to his left to where the stone behemoth was still in slow motion.

Bastard.

Then he had an idea. He used the rest of his strength to stroke madly with his arms, exhaling the last of his air and kicking wildly. As long as the giant didn't spot him, he might have a chance.

But the monstrous statue started to turn its head again. Rook quickly shifted his direction, to stay behind the creature's head as it rose, but the head was faster. One of the long spikes on its crown careened into him from behind, lifting him through the water faster. He twisted and tried to push off the spike, but it was too late. Rather than fight, Rook spun around and clung to the crown's barnacle-covered spike.

A moment later, his head broke the surface. He took in a huge gulp of the sweet morning air. Then he started coughing and spluttering, drawing in deep drafts of air in between each fit. He fell from the crown and landed on the ground, hugging it as he coughed.

Then sense returned.

This isn't the ground.

Rook had only intended to catch a lift to the surface of the water on the express train that was the rising statue. But his desperation for

air had cost him. He was now lying face down and hugging the top of the giant's crown. He leaned over the side and looked down to the water some fifty feet below him and receding.

The creature was standing up. It rolled over onto its hands and knees, then raised its waist. Rook clung on for dear life as he rose one hundred feet above the water, then two hundred, then more. When the gigantic statue was fully erect, only its lower legs were still submerged under the water—what Rook had judged to be fifty feet or more of salty brine.

"Well ain't you the biggest fucking golem in the history of the world," Rook said, and for the first time he realized what this statue was—*the Colossus of Rhodes.*

The statue took a step toward the shore and shallower water. Rook was at the back of the head, facing out to sea. He struggled to turn around so he could see where they were headed. He crawled across the head, hands and knees splayed wide like a water bug. The statue took another huge step, shaking its frame when it contacted the ground. Rook slid over the curved head and shouted as he saw the world ahead come into view. He slammed into the edge of the raised crown and clung on.

The head was enormous. Rook judged it to be forty or fifty feet in diameter inside the ring of the crown. He leaned back, inside the crown's lip, and felt safer once he couldn't see the immense drop. Inside the ring of the crown was like a balcony; the crown itself surrounding the top of the skull like a low wall. Rook slowly stood, wary of the next jolting step, and once again looked at the world before and below him.

The view was amazing.

Dawn had fully struck. The land was bathed in sunlight—except for a long stretch in front of the giant, where its shadow left a swath of ground in night. Rook was 300 feet up, and the few people he could see on the shore looked more like specks of ground-up pepper than ants. He knew how high he was. He knew what he was riding on. As a part of Chess Team homework, he'd

had to study the ancient world, and the starting place had been the Seven Wonders: the Great Pyramid of Giza, the Hanging Gardens of Babylon, the Temple of Artemis, the statue of Zeus at Olympia, the Halicarnassus mausoleum, the lighthouse at Alexandria.

And the Colossus of Rhodes.

He didn't know how or why it was underwater off the coast of Tunisia, but he knew he was standing on its skull 300 feet in the air. And as it took its first step out of the sea onto the dry land of the Carthage ruins, crushing ancient stone under foot, he knew if Chess Team couldn't find a way to stop it, or stop Ridley, the Colossus would grind half of North Africa under its heels before enough military might could be on hand to destroy it.

FORTY-SEVEN
Under the *Mountain of the Roman Rock*, Lake Bracciano, 780 BC

King lost count of how many times he had died.

The wraiths kept coming, and their embrace was deadly. Every time King awoke, the battle began anew. He punched, kicked and head-butted until he was overwhelmed again. Then they would suck him dry, leaving his withered corpse on the floor.

And then...he would come back.

The cycle repeated for what felt like a lifetime.

But that was about to change. King was pissed. Instead of punching and kicking, he started eye gouging, and tearing out throats. He bit and growled and roared and slammed the full weight of his body behind every blow, knowing that any self-sustained injury would be healed by the time he struck again. At times, the crushing throng of Forgotten fell back, recoiling at his rage and ferocity. He stopped going for body shots and focused solely on heads.

This time he was alive long enough to see past the writhing, swarming bodies to Alexander.

The man was a whirlwind of rage and action. Wraiths were flying everywhere as Alexander hurled them and batted them away as if they were paper dolls. But still they came. King couldn't understand how there could be so many of them, unless Alexander had gotten the date wrong.

They're supposed to be locked up.

Then an idea grew with each strike, as he felt the energy leaving his limbs from every touch of a wraith. Tiny tendrils on the creature's palms latched onto his skin, like a million tiny leeches. With just a glancing blow, they could suck a patch of flesh dry. When the idea finally resolved in his mind, King felt a burst of energy and began plowing through the wraith bodies around him, making his way for Alexander.

"You said they were locked up!"

Alexander flexed his brawn, sending half a dozen crouched creatures flying off his chest and back.

"Now really isn't the time for recriminations!" he shouted.

"No! They are supposed to be locked up when she comes! Remember? We have to get them penned up!"

Alexander grimaced. King recognized the expression as pained agreement.

"Follow my lead!" Alexander shouted.

The big man started bulling through the swarm of wraith bodies, batting them away, so their deadly fingers could not drain his life force. He herded them toward a far wall of the cavern. King did his best to keep up.

The bigger man was building up momentum, and King could see he wasn't really battling the wraiths any more, but was plowing a path through them. King did the same. They moved the battle through a low arch, the Forgotten crawling down on them from the ceiling and the stone of the archway.

On the other side of the arch, King found himself in the lab. Iron-barred cells lined one of the walls. They stood empty. Wall mounted torches lit the space. Crude scientific equipment, well

before its time, covered the many stone tables scattered throughout the large room.

Alexander made his way toward one of the cells, swung the door wide and ran inside. A dozen of the wraiths followed him into the cell. King understood and did the same with the next cell. The spaces inside were no bigger than a ten by twenty room. Only so many of the Forgotten could squeeze themselves into the spaces without getting in their own way. King had the advantage in the space. He fought and pushed, slammed and crunched his way around the room following the perimeter until he was at the door again.

Reaching hands grasped at him from all directions as bodies continued to fill the cell, all swirling and rushing in search of his blood. He lunged out of the door, took a wraith by the neck and shoved it into the cell, knocking those by the door back. He slammed the door shut and heard the lock clunk into place.

Before he could feel some satisfaction at locking up a large number of the monsters, King was struck from behind and slammed into the cell's bars. Arms grabbed at him from inside, and then from outside. Locked in place, his body was quickly sucked dry until the wraiths released him, dropping his dried husk of a corpse to the floor.

It took five more deaths to imprison the rest. King wasn't sure how many times Alexander had fallen, but he'd seen the big man go down a few times. In the end, there were more bodies on the floor of the lab and the outer cavern than there were in the cells, but the cells were still tightly packed. Once the prison was full, it was easier to kill the stragglers than it was to try to stuff them into the already over-crowded cells. For every one they stuffed in, two would slip out.

When he killed the last wraith by ripping its throat out, King fell over onto its corpse, breathing hard and waiting for his regeneration to bring him back to full vitality.

"I was...right about...one thing," Alexander said weakly. He must have been worse off than he looked, but King knew he would be back to his hearty self in a few minutes. "They didn't...recognize my scent."

"My God. Did you have to go through this every time you wanted them locked up?"

Alexander laughed softly. "No. They obeyed the younger me."

"You told me once that their embrace was an awful thing," King said, breathing heavily from his pile of corpses.

"I was telling the truth," Alexander said, finally sitting up.

"I see that now." King tried to stand, but his body wasn't ready.

"You understand now, why I cannot let this happen to her."

King just nodded and the men fell into silence.

After a few minutes, they had recovered sufficiently to stand. King was pleased to see he was able to stand first.

"We'll need to get the bodies out of here. Can you drag them to the edge of the arena, while I start work on the duplicate corpse?"

"You want me to feed them to puppy?" King asked.

"It's the quickest way to dispose of the bodies," Alexander said. "The Forgotten occasionally have it out with Cerberus, so even if some scraps are left behind, my younger self will think nothing of it other than wishing he'd seen the fight."

King nodded. "What about her face? Can you recreate it?"

"If I can't get it right, I'll finish it when she gets here. We won't have a lot of time—he'll arrive not long after."

King started dragging the Forgotten bodies out of the lab. Some of the equipment had been damaged too. He'd have to ask Alexander about that. It took him several trips, dragging the pathetic withered bodies by the capes or hoods of their dark gauzy cloaks. He felt slight regret. To hear Alexander describe them, the Forgotten were like animals or children—not fully capable of taking care of themselves. Leaving their bodies in the arena for the hellhound was probably a fate they did not deserve. But there would be no time for a memorial service.

By the last load, Alexander had nearly finished with his lifelike corpse. The body was naked, but it was withered in places, and definitely female. The hair was right—just like King had seen in the market earlier in the day. The face was still a blank slab of creamy flesh. Alexander stood over the body repeating a sentence in a language King could only hear as grunts and rumbling murmurs. The corpse's arm was growing less withered instead of more, and King realized where Alexander had gotten his raw materials for the body.

At last the man stopped speaking, but the face on the body was still blank.

"You used one of them," King asked, indicating the Forgotten behind the bars.

"It seemed...right. I don't know how else to explain it." Alexander shrugged.

"I'm not questioning your choice. I know this can't be easy for you. What about all this blood? And the broken equipment?"

"I thought about that," Alexander said, standing and stretching his neck from side to side. "When I found her, I saw her body, and the spilled glass of water. We'll need to remember that. But I didn't see anything else. The whole room could have been in shambles and I wouldn't have noticed. Afterward...well, there won't be much lab left when I'm done."

King nodded. If something were to happen to Sara or Fiona, whatever inanimate objects surrounding him would get the full force of his vented anger. He felt his concern over seeing them again well up, but he and Alexander were almost done. Alexander had sworn King would be returned to his time, his family, friends, daughter and future wife. The end was in sight. "Okay. Let's get the glass of water," King said.

"You could have mine, if you asked politely." Standing in the door, watching the two of them, an earthenware cup of water in her hand, Acca Larentia looked angry.

FORTY-EIGHT
Alexander's Lab, *Mountain of the Roman Rock*, 780 BC

Acca Larentia placed a hand on her hip, waiting for an answer from the two men.

She wore the same dyed fabric dress from the market. Her sandals, interwoven with thin strings of gold, showed her wealth. Her hair was a little more windblown than it had been in the market, but it still strongly resembled the styles King had seen his mother wearing in photos from the 50s, when she was a young woman. Acca's face was flushed with color, but her skin was perfect. The woman was absolutely beautiful, and once again, King could see waiting centuries for her.

"Acca..." Alexander whispered and took a step forward. "Do you recognize me?"

She took a step closer, lowering her cup. "You do look...familiar, sir. Perhaps a heretofore unnamed brother of my husband?"

Alexander took one more gentle step and then stopped. "Except you know he has no brother. You know the story of Iphicles to be a false one."

Acca descended the remaining steps at the doorway to the floor, and walked close, but she kept one of the stone lab tables between her and Alexander. She also warily eyed King. He stayed still, waiting to see how things would play out.

"My husband, Carutius, told me only two people knew that story of Iphicles was false—he and I." The anger on her face was replaced by confusion. She squinted at him. "You could be my husband's twin, indeed."

"You are also one of the few alive who know that your husband's true name is not Carutius," Alexander said cautiously. He moved closer to the center of his side of the lab table.

"Who do you think he is, then?" she asked. "And who are you?"

"You know who I am, my love. My appearance has changed slightly, but you see the same man before you. Others have called me Heracles, but you alone in this time know my secret name of Alexander." A tear began to trickle from his eye down his bearded cheek.

Acca raised a trembling hand to cover her mouth with the tips of her fingers—as if she had suspected this truth, but the full revelation of it confirmed some madness in her soul.

"I left you in the market not an hour ago. Your hair was shorter. Your beard less wild. Your clothes different. Your manner, even, has changed. Is this some trick of the gods? How can this be?"

Alexander quickly related the story of his past—a future he hoped yet to avoid for her. He detailed his journey to the twenty-first century without her, and his constant search for first the secrets of immortality, and then later for a way to travel back into the past to save her. She handled it well, but King supposed the woman who married this man already saw the world as a far stranger place than most people would believe. Alexander finished by telling her his plan to replace her with a duplicate corpse and said, "I have waited a hundred lifetimes to return to this night, this very moment, and undo the darkness I allowed to befall you."

"I don't understand," she said, her own tears now coming freely. "Why put yourself through that anguish again? Why not just keep me safe from your creatures now, and reveal what has happened to your younger self? Then return to your strange time, where events would have changed and caught up to you?"

"It won't work like that. It...just isn't possible. What happened in my past, happened. There's no way to change those things—there is only the possibility of changing the *appearance* of those things. Do you see? I already know that's not how things happen, because I'd already remember it." He paused to sigh, glanced at King, and added, "And...I am a better man, now. Your death changed me. Broke me. Allowed me to be remade into someone who is more worthy of your love. I would not undo that." He

looked at King again. "Time has a way of giving us perspective...and strength to do what must be done."

"Well, right now we're a bit short on time," King said. "The younger Alexander will be back from the market soon. We need to be gone when he arrives, and we need to finish." He glanced at the faceless corpse.

"Who is this man?" Acca asked.

"His name is Jack," Alexander replied.

"A strange name, but *who* is he? Why is he here?"

Alexander smiled. "Look at him closely. Can't you see it?"

Acca squinted at King, focusing on his eyes. She sucked in a quick breath. "He has my father's eyes."

Alexander nodded. "He is our descendant."

This revelation brought a new concern to Acca's mind. "Our children?"

"Will lose their mother tonight. But they will survive. They will *thrive*, for countless generations." He nodded at King. "Long into the future. And Jack is right, Acca. Please. Let us finish what we must. We'll take you somewhere safe, I'll explain everything carefully, and if you don't like what you hear, I'll let you make your own choice as to how to proceed." He stepped around the lab table to her, his hand outstretched.

She looked closely at his face, then reached for his hand. As King watched, he could see an almost electric jolt go through the both of them when their flesh met. Her face changed instantly.

"It really is you," she whispered.

His tears streamed from his eyes. "Yes, my love. It really is."

She threw herself into his arms, the cup of water flying from her hand behind them, crashing against the floor, right next to the mostly finished duplicate corpse. Alexander gently placed his arms around the woman as she sobbed into his chest. He laid the side of his cheek on the top of her head as gently as if she were an egg that might crack. King had seen his friend in many moods and manners over the years, but he had never seem him be so very gentle.

King's eyes returned to the corpse, the spilled water and the shattered earthenware cup. It looked perfect to him, but he didn't have the memories to confirm that.

"Alexander," he said softly. "The face."

Alexander took a deep breath, then stepped back from Acca and delicately raised her chin. "We must hurry."

She nodded, and Alexander turned to the body on the floor.

"Is the cup right? The spill?" King asked.

"It's fine," Alexander knelt to the floor and gently placed his hands over the blank slate where the corpse's face should have been. He began chanting under his breath. The floor rumbled beneath their feet. King turned to Acca to reassure her if she was worried, but the woman watched without fear. He guessed the touch was enough to convince her of everything.

King looked back to Alexander, as the man stood and stepped away from the false corpse.

The face looked exactly like Acca's now—if it had been aged by twenty years, and had most of the vitality sucked from it. There was a black necrotic spot on the cheek, and the eyes were closed, but the corpse could not be mistaken for anyone else.

There was just one problem.

"Alexander—the clothes."

The corpse was naked.

"Of course." He turned to Acca. "We will need your robe. And your sandals."

King was about to turn away to give the woman privacy, but she simply slipped out of the dress, and stepped out of her sandals, completely unashamed of her nudity. She picked up the robe with one hand and tossed one sandal to King. The other she handed to Alexander. Then she slipped the dress over the corpse's head. King and Alexander fixed the sandals on the body's feet and helped to roll the body over so Acca could pull the dress down to where it would be. Finally, she pulled a bronze bracelet off her wrist and placed it on the wrist of the body.

"The bracelet...I remember it now. I hadn't seen it before."

"I bought it at the market after I left you tonight," she said. "I liked it."

Alexander stood and rushed to a long cabinet against one wall. The cabinet was made of wood, and had several shelves built into it, like a cross between an armoire and a Chinese herbalist's chest of drawers. He opened a drawer and pulled out a folded piece of burgundy cloth—one of his own robes. He handed it to Acca, and she quickly wrapped the fabric about her body, folding and twisting it until it covered all but her shoulders.

"We need to go," King said.

Just then they heard a loud clanking in the stairwell beyond the doorway from which Acca had appeared.

"He's back," she whispered.

"Run," Alexander said.

FORTY-NINE
Carthage Ruins, 2013

Queen's fingers went slack. Her weapon fell to the ground.

Her jaw hung open, and a single phrase got lodged in her mind.

Not. Fucking. Possible.

To say that the immense statue rising from the sea was gigantic would have been an insult to it. She had been to Liberty Island once in New York. She had learned that the Statue of Liberty stood 151 feet tall—just over 300 feet with its concrete and granite pedestal. This thing was probably close to 300 feet on its own. The spires on its crown made the resemblance uncanny. This monstrosity could have been Liberty's father. It wore a long cape of bronze with a greenish patina, and while the cape was stiff, and did not move like cloth, it did move. The rest of the statue was nude except

for a small loin-cloth. The muscles of the bare chest were flat and chiseled—a bit un-lifelike, if she thought about it. The pecs were too square, the abs too circular. The sculptors had envisioned a perfect warrior, but the dimensions were off just slightly. The overall effect was compounded by the inclusion of sea growths of coral and large swatches of seaweed, draped over the joints.

Through her disbelief and shock, she recognized it for what it was.

The Colossus of Rhodes.

But how? I thought it had been dismantled years after it fell. And how the hell did it get here, all the way across the Med?

Bishop, ever the man of few words, simply leaned down, picked up her dusty MP-5 and handed it back to her.

Queen took her weapon and forced her mind back to the moment at hand. "Kill Ridley and Seth. That's priority number one. We get them, and that fucker topples."

"What I was thinking," Bishop said. He started running for Ridley's position on the shore, as the immense statue took another step out of the sea, and onto land.

Queen raced after him.

They were already within an effective range of Ridley's group, but she held off until she closed to within seventy-five feet. She raised her weapon, and while still running at the group of men on the shore, she started firing a spray of bullets at a rate of 800 rounds a minute.

Bishop took cover behind one of the standing columns of the Baths. He joined her in laying into the enemy.

Queen took up position behind a block of stone at the end of a wall and kept firing.

One of the men in black was hit in the arm, but then both men quickly returned fire with their AK-47s.

The world's most recognizable assault rifle had a much longer effective range than the MP-5 submachine guns, but they were all within range of each other now, so it made little difference.

Seth and Ridley had leapt for cover. To Queen's satisfaction, the humongous statue had stopped walking once it reached the shore. *Ridley needs to concentrate to control it. Hard to do that with bullets flying all around.*

She smirked, but she knew the reprieve wouldn't last long.

"Queen, you read?" Deep Blue was in her ear. "What the hell am I seeing on satellite?"

"That would be the Colossus of Rhodes, golem-style. We really need that support. Now."

"They're forty minutes out."

"This will be over in forty minutes! This thing is 300 feet tall. And it looks pissed. We're trying to keep Ridley and his twin under fire. If they can't concentrate, they can't use the language to work the statue. But that won't last long. Especially if they have reinforcements on the ground already."

"They do. I'm seeing close to a battalion of men coming your way."

"Then you better tell them to hurry. That or bring body bags. Lots of them."

Queen switched channels, and called for Knight. No reply. She tried Rook.

"Where you at, ma puce? You better have some fuckin' good news for me."

Rook's voice came through with a lot of background hiss, like he was in a wind tunnel. "Would it help if I said 'I can see my house from here?'"

Queen raised her hand to shield her eyes from the glare of the morning sun as she looked up, up, up, to the top of the statue's immense head. She could only just make out movement all the way up there. He actually looked like a flea at that height.

"Sweet holy Moses," she said.

FIFTY

Antonine Baths, Carthage, 2013

Darius Ridley whipped his foot back and delivered another whopping kick to the tiny slant-eyed bastard's stomach, a huge grin spreading across his face. His plan had gone completely to hell, but he was still having the time of his life.

Somehow, and he couldn't figure out how it had happened, Richard's lackey clones had co-opted his mercenary force, and turned at least some of them against him. It should have been simple. Wait until the doubles and the Chess Team were inside, then swoop in covering all the exits and kill everybody. But the Chess Team, had put up a fight, and his team was sloppy. Stepped all over each other. The facility had jammed their communications—although that should have worked to their advantage, preventing the Chess Team from coordinating their response to the unexpected attack. His men shouldn't have needed the coms—they knew what to do and how to do it.

Still, things had gone pear-shaped. As soon as he heard that their communications gear wasn't working underground, he had held back. After the first explosion, when he began getting reports back to him by runner that they were encountering heavy close quarters resistance, he had retreated to the safety of the loading dock vehicle tunnel. The enemy had dug in from the gallery and the security suite on Sub Level 3. Even though his men should have been able to flank the bastards from the north stairwell, they were suddenly encountering resistance on all levels of the facility—and his reinforcements never came. That was when he had left his men behind and run up the ramp to the parking garage, looking for his men at the fountain entrance.

What he found were slit throats and an unguarded entrance. He had gone topside then, and found a similar scene at the amphitheater. Someone had killed his men, and his reinforcements were

nowhere in sight. He'd contemplated going back to the cemetery, but he had suddenly understood what had happened. The clones had arranged it for Richard. They would get him out, using the men Darius had paid for. If he returned to the cemetery—his command center for this operation—there would be killers waiting for him.

Instead, he had waited in the shadows near the amphitheater for a time. Then he had gone back to the fountain entrance, waiting in the darkness patiently. Eventually the Korean—*Knight, yes, that's his callsign*—and a Russian woman emerged. He had followed them as the smaller man ditched his armor and frantically radioed his people.

Darius really couldn't believe things had come to this. First his brother had sidelined him for some minor failings, shuffling him off to act as head of security for a mostly pointless facility in the Ukraine. Ostensibly it was to keep him away from the more violent actions going on at some of the more important bases in Peru and the States. But in the end, that hadn't mattered. The female member of Chess Team, Queen, had stumbled upon his base and infiltrated it before they even knew she was there. After a pitched battle, the bitch chewed his ear right off the side of his head.

She had gotten away, and he had barely escaped with his life. There was no chance of going back to his brother's people then, and Richard himself had been missing and presumed dead. Instead, Darius had used his own resources to slowly comb through Manifold installations, hunting for any sign of Richard or the damned Chess Team. In the end, his people had located the Greek, and from that, Darius had found the clones. His people—well, he had *thought* they were his people—had watched the doubles long enough to learn that they thought Richard was being held in Tunisia at the Greek's captured installation.

But Darius's plan to kill off the clones, his brother and Chess Team, as well as to capture the bitch and torture her until the sun went out, was off the boards now. Now he just needed to make the best of the situation, kill as many of the traitorous bastards as possible and get out of Tunisia alive.

When the chance to ambush the little Korean presented itself, he couldn't resist. And now, as the man coughed blood in the sand, Darius was suddenly feeling fine. Great, even.

He kicked the man on the ground again. He had knocked the Russian chick a good one, and he would turn his attention to her when he was done with this one.

He didn't know why the ground was shaking. Didn't care. He guessed maybe a shit-ton of explosives had gone off below in the base. It didn't matter.

The squinty-eyed fucker was crawling away from him, looking up in horror. As if that would help him. He could crawl all he wanted. He wasn't going to get away.

Suddenly something slammed into Darius from behind, and the ground shook violently again. He hit the dirt face down, taking a cloud of dust in the mouth. Now he was pissed. He rolled to the side and saw it had been the feisty little Rusky. *Okay, bitch. We're gonna dance.* But instead of fighting, the woman was frantically trying to drag the Korean away.

He pulled a long Kennesaw Cutlery survival knife from its sheath on his leg. He couldn't believe the little slut wasn't even looking at him.

The ground rumbled again, and he had a hard time staying on his feet this time. When he regained his balance, he noticed the two of them weren't looking at him.

They were looking up.

FIFTY-ONE
Antonine Baths, Carthage, 2013

Knight couldn't tear his eyes away, as the giant foot came down.

The bald mercenary with the missing ear, who had kicked the crap out of him, only thought to look up at the last second. By that

point, he wouldn't have been able to even understand what was about to flatten him.

The immense foot smashed to the ground, squirting the mercenary out from under its heel like a stamped-on ketchup packet. The giant foot had fallen so close to Knight that for a few seconds, he wasn't sure whether any of the gore had come from his own body. He wondered whether he would have even felt a limb or two being flattened that fast.

But then the huge foot took another step, and Knight could see the grotesque imprint of the flattened man on the underside of the thing's massive foot, dripping wetness, as it swept overhead and pivoted, back the way it had come.

Knight coughed feebly, spitting up a wad of bloody phlegm. He was faring better than the man who'd attacked him, but he'd taken a beating. "Probably...gonna need a doctor."

"I'll get you to the others. Contact Queen," Asya said.

Knight couldn't stop coughing, so he fumbled at his ear with one hand and passed the earpiece to Asya, along with his throat mic, which he peeled away from his neck. The glue on the microphone had turned gooey in the heat.

"Pawn to Queen. Knight is in bad shape. Need assistance right now," Asya donned the communications gear, pulling the transmitter pack from Knight's belt. "Also, there is *velikan* on the loose."

"A what?" came Queen's reply.

"*Velikan*. Is Russian word for Great Big Fucking Giant."

"We've seen. What's wrong with Knight?"

Asya sighed. "Mercenary kicked crap out of him. He's coughing blood."

"Where are you?"

"That thing nearly stepped on us a second ago," Asya said, as Knight finally settled down and stopped hacking.

"Okay. Stay put. I'm sending your parents to you."

Asya turned to Knight. "She is sending my mother and father. We'll get you to a hospital."

"I'll be able to limp around with an adrenaline shot," Knight said.

"I haven't got one. We will see what we can do. Queen says to stay here."

Asya sat on the ground next to him and wiped some of the muck from his face with her hand.

"Flat man was a pig, but this end was undignified—even for him."

"Quick, though," Knight said with a laugh, and then winced at the pain in his ribs. He was pretty sure a few of them were broken. His face felt butchered too. His left arm was sore where a bullet had grazed him, and he felt like he had to pee, but if he did it would be extremely painful.

"Not gonna be much use fighting whatever the hell that thing was."

Asya patted him on the head. "Don't worry, Sniper-Man. We'll just blow it up. Won't need a steady shot for that."

"I knew letting Ridley out was a bad idea," Knight said, as he rubbed his forehead.

Asya said nothing.

He turned to look at her. "About Jack...I'm sorry, Asya." She nodded, then turned away. "Now is not the time."

They lapsed into silence, and Knight closed his eyes. He was in no shape to help her repel any more mercenaries if they showed up, and she was a pretty good shot with an MP-5. He could rest.

A minute later, Peter and Lynn Machtchenko came rushing down the path. She carried another MP-5, and he held a couple of small nylon pouches in his hands. Peter skidded to a stop and began frantically unzipping the pouches. Lynn remained standing and kept looking behind her.

"We have to hurry," Lynn said.

Peter pulled out an adrenaline auto injector and stabbed it into Knight's arm. Then he handed Knight two huge white pills. "Dry swallow. Sorry I don't have water."

Knight took the pills and ground them in his teeth, then swallowed the ground gritty remains. They were prescription-strength painkillers—he recognized the bitter taste.

The adrenaline started flowing through him.

Peter crawled behind him and slipped his arms into Knight's armpits. He started to haul Knight up, and Asya came over to help from his front. In a few awkward seconds, Knight was on his feet. He actually felt better on his feet, since his ribs weren't resting against anything and pushing painfully on his innards.

"Now what?" Knight asked.

"Now we run," Lynn said. "That thing is coming back. And fast!"

Asya had one side of him and Peter the other, as they started to run. It was only now that Knight paid attention to the thunderous footfalls vibrating through the ground. Whatever belonged to the huge feet wasn't walking now.

It was stomping.

FIFTY-TWO
Alexander's Lab, *Mountain of the Roman Rock*, 780 BC

Alexander stopped them in the shadows of the next room. They waited from the edge of the darkened doorway, watching the lit lab, where they could see but not be seen.

"Shouldn't we go?" King hissed.

"We need to make sure our assumptions about time are correct. I remember what I did back then. We have about twenty minutes after he finds the body before he goes on a full-on tantrum, destroying everything in sight. If it doesn't go down that way, we might need to reconsider our next steps."

They waited in silence.

After a few minutes, the younger version of Alexander—the Hercules of myth—stepped drunkenly out of the far doorway and

staggered down the steps into the lab. He was whistling a tune of some sort, when he saw the body on the ground near the bars. The tune died slowly on his lips, as if his lungs had just run out of air to continue blowing.

He stood in place for a full thirty seconds. Then he walked slowly toward the body on the ground. He looked up at the Forgotten wraiths, clustered around the bars, watching him, and reaching through the bars for the body's ankle, which was just a few inches too far away.

King noticed that as the shaken man walked to the cell and the body, he suddenly exhibited none of the drunken stagger he had just a moment ago. The sight of the body had sobered him in an instant.

Young Alexander knelt down next to the body, but did not touch it.

From the shadows, the older Alexander held his hand out to the others in the dark, as if to say: *Wait. Here it comes. We're either right or very, very wrong.*

The younger man, still dressed in the clothes he had worn to the marketplace, reached out a hand slowly, and touched the body's neck, feeling for a pulse. The hand stayed in place for an interminably long moment, then simply dropped to the man's side. A low moaning escaped the man's lips, but the sound went on and on, without a new breath. It grew in intensity until it was more like a siren then a moan.

He lowered his head, and the sound grew raspy like a growl.

In the shadows, the elder Alexander waved the other two down the hall as the younger Alexander threw his head back and howled in anguish. The sound was heartbreaking.

King turned and led the way down the long room where he had fought and died several times, and into the narrow tunnel beyond. As the last of the ambient light receded, Acca placed her hand on his shoulder. She couldn't see. He slowed his pace in the dark as the younger Hercules's screams echoed through the caverns.

Soon they came to the edge of the arena. King was about to tell Acca about the hellhound, but Alexander beat him to it. King saw that most of the bodies he had piled were gone now. The three of them circled around the perimeter of the massive cavern, but the huge dog didn't notice. It was busy devouring and crunching the bones of a Forgotten.

When they reached the far tunnel that led to the forest, Alexander had them wait. He ran back into the center of the arena and quickly climbed onto Cerberus's back. The animal was startled and began twisting its head, trying to snap at him. He quickly pulled the pin securing the chain around the hound's central head. Then he leapt off of the beast and ran for the tunnel. The huge animal gave chase for just a second, but then thought better of it and turned back to its easy meal.

Alexander led them through the night forest and around the lake, until both Acca and King were so tired they could barely stand.

"We need to stop soon," King said.

"It won't be safe to stop anywhere near here. We need to get at least another town over. Tomorrow we can make for Antium, where I have another lab."

"I am so very tired, my love. I do not think I can go another step tonight." Acca sounded half asleep already.

Alexander reached into a small pouch on his belt and produced a tiny tin, in which King knew he kept the last of his herbs. By the light of the full moon, King watched the man pull out a small leaf and crush it between his fingers, before sprinkling the crumbs into his mouth, his head tilted back. He sighed heavily, and then swept Acca up into his meaty arms.

"I hope you can manage on your own, Jack. I don't think I could carry you both."

"I'll make it," King said, his body already easing the pain in his lungs. Then he started off through the forest again, taking the lead. Alexander's speed slowed with the weight of his wife, but they still

put a lot of distance between themselves and the lake, before the moon went down in the sky and only stars lit the way.

Acca had long since fallen asleep in Alexander's arms as they walked. He had shifted her into one meaty arm, so he could allow the other to rest for a time. Then he would shift her to the other arm, and vigorously shake the first, as if it had gone to sleep on him. King knew the extra strength the herb had provided the man would be fading from his system soon. Even though Acca was slim, her sleeping dead-weight must have been exhausting to carry. King would have offered to carry her for a time, but he was barely able to keep going himself. If not for his body's ability to heal, he would have collapsed long ago. They walked on under the stars in silence.

For a few minutes, King felt like it was old times for the two of them, but then he reminded himself that their mission was nearly complete, and soon he would be going home. He blinked and saw Sara's face. It came clear to him for the first time in a long time. Perhaps knowing he would see her again allowed whatever mental defenses he had created to collapse. Whatever the cause, the brief mental glimpse brought a smile to his face.

"What's next? We get to your place in Antium, and then what? How do we get you home? How do I get back? All you've ever told me was that you had access to the technology—but not until the time was right."

"That's the tricky part, Jack."

"Saving Acca wasn't tricky?"

"What comes next involves untested technology I created in this time, but never found a power source for. We have to examine the machine I made when I was younger, alter it and incorporate the things I learned from the Norway technology. We couldn't get to the tech early, because I couldn't be sure my younger self wouldn't stop in for a visit. That's not going to happen now. I spend a few days tearing up the area around the lake, and then

months in a depression, rarely leaving that villa. It will be safe for us in Antium, now."

"So the tech is dodgy, but why is this the tricky bit?" King asked, understanding the issue with avoiding Alexander's younger self. The two had discussed such things for years, debating issues of paradox and destiny.

"Powering the machine," Alexander replied. "I never used it to return home, because I couldn't power it. Not until the twentieth century—but by then, I had come up with this plan to save her. The hard part is we have to power the device with this..." Alexander held up a small brown rock the size of a golf ball, which hung around his neck on a thick chain he had worn since they arrived in the past. He let it fall gently to his chest, then awkwardly tucked it back into his robe with the one hand, while his other arm cradled Acca.

"What...exactly...is that thing?" It looked familiar, but King couldn't place it.

"Paris," Alexander said.

The single word triggered King's memory. He'd never forget Paris and that he'd nearly been sucked inside out by a sentient...

"Wait. We closed that portal. Completely. That can't be what I think it is."

"If what you think is a dwarf black hole, hidden inside the flimsiest of rock coverings? Then yes, that's exactly what it is."

FIFTY-THREE
Latium, 780 BC

"You've been wearing a *black fucking hole* around your neck for twenty years, and you didn't think to tell me?"

Acca stirred in Alexander's arms, so he shifted her to both arms. She laid her head against his chest and went back to sleep.

"Quiet, Jack. Let's not wake her." They continued walking across a pasture. "I've told you before how much I've been playing this whole thing by ear. I wasn't sure any of this would work. But there's simply no power source in this time that is strong enough. I took this thing in Paris for this very purpose. It's an immense source of power. If anything can power up the portal I have here, this will be it." Alexander moved over to a soft rise of grass and gently set Acca down on it. She stirred briefly, opened her eyes and looked around, then blinked and went back to sleep on the grass.

King plopped down on the ground himself, ready for sleep. Alexander sat cross-legged. "I'll take first watch. Get some sleep, Jack. You're going to need it."

King yawned. "Why? What's waiting for us in Antium?"

"Man eating birds with sharp bronze beaks and projectile metallic feathers," Alexander said.

King sat up. "Seriously?"

"No. Just joking."

"Dick," King laid back down.

Alexander laughed. "Go to sleep."

Hours later they began walking south again. King walked ahead, allowing Alexander and Acca time to discuss the extremely complicated story their lives had become. When they stopped in a small village for a lunch of bread, cheese and wine, Acca seemed convinced. She no longer questioned the impossibility of their having travelled back in time. Her only questions were geared toward what they needed to do next.

"Jack," she said, "Alexander tells me that you have a woman for whom, you too, would cross the oceans of time. You must miss her very much. I am so grateful you were willing to come assist him."

King just nodded. He didn't think it would be right to tell her how he didn't have much choice in coming. It was also water

under the bridge for him. But the mention of Sara, made him yearn to be done with this mission—especially since they were so close to the end now.

Alexander had left them after lunch to obtain some horses. King was left to chat with Acca over wine.

"He's missed you terribly. Everything he's done over the years was to keep his identity a secret and to make this all possible."

"Tell me about your time," she said, sitting back in her chair.

He laughed. "It's so different in many ways, but still the same in others. We've made many advances. Men have travelled to the moon in a flying cart, I guess you would call it. Most of the carts on the ground are propelled by what would seem like magic, but is more of a complicated series of metal parts that make the wheels move, fueled by a liquid we pump from the ground and refine. People live indoors, and we have boxes to keep our food cold in the kitchen, and other boxes to cook with. We have rooms in our homes where you can defecate and urinate, and water will flush those things away from your house to a place where the waste is treated and broken down into mostly harmless parts. We can hold a small device in our hands and speak to people on the other side of the world with it. But we've also made so many terrible things. Weapons that can kill a man in a blink. Weapons that can destroy entire cities just a fast. There are wars in the future that will claim millions of lives, and there are men, who would, if given the chance, destroy all of humanity."

Acca sat up in her chair. "It sounds terrible. How did so many things come to be made? Were they gifts from the gods?"

King smiled. "No. Most of these things were simply developed over time by man, to fulfill one purpose or another. It's our nature to turn just about everything into weapons."

Acca seemed to digest this information, while sipping more of her wine.

"And what do you do to make this strange world of yours a better place?"

King thought about the question for a while. He thought about his life—first in the military and later with Chess Team. He decided to break it down into the simplest terms possible. "The people who kill innocents, who seek out power at the expense of others, or who, in their madness, want to destroy the world..." He looked up at her eyes, saw his mother for a moment, and said, "I find them. And I stop them."

"And if they can't be stopped?"

"Then I kill them."

Acca nodded in understanding. She was no stranger to violence. "Why do you do it?"

King had often thought about the bizarre nature of what he did, but he rarely gave thought to why. It was like breathing. He just did it.

"It's the right thing to do," he said.

Acca smiled. "I can see why she likes you."

FIFTY-FOUR
Antonine Baths, Carthage, 2013

Richard Ridley was sweating. It took concentration to use the mother tongue to animate inanimate things, like mud and stone. The larger the golem, the harder it was to not just grant the thing life, but also give it direction. Purpose. A mission it would follow until its undoing. And as far as golems went, it didn't get bigger than the Colossus.

The statue was made of iron, bronze, brass and stone, but unlike other such statues built many centuries later, this one was not hollow. It had been filled with crushed stone and rock of varying sizes. Over the centuries, coral and sediment had cemented the interior spaces between the brass plates forming the skin, so that even though much of the iron tie bars inside had

rusted away, the statue held its integrity. Making the thing stand and walk, as if it were alive, meant forcing breaks along joints that did not exist, and grinding the stone and metal past each other, then re-bonding the molecules, so the limbs did not simply fall off.

He had used the tongue to animate things before, but the Colossus was huge, and it was taxing his abilities. Sweat poured down his face, and his arms felt weak. He mumbled the guttural language, repeatedly, like a mantra, to keep the statue alive.

Once the shooting had started, he had a hard time seeing where to direct the statue. He was startled initially at the automatic weapons fire, and he had simply stopped the thing from walking. He should have known some of the Chess Team would make it out of Omega and past his men. Their skills, while a constant annoyance, were impressive. He had ducked behind the ruins with Seth and sent the Colossus toward the sound of gunfire, stomping on anything that moved, while Trigger and Carpenter returned fire. Without time to imbue the statue with intelligence enough to control its own actions, Ridley really needed a higher perch from which to control the statue. If he could see where he was sending the ancient statue, he'd be able to steer it better. He considered the minaret on the nearby mosque, but then realized he'd only need to keep the Chess Team busy for a few minutes longer.

The statue was his. It was one of the first antiquities he had discovered in his endless search for ancient knowledge and power. He had built his Omega facility right next to it on the shore, and had paid a fortune for the sea wall in his office, so he could look at it and dream of one day making it walk. It had been a long journey from there to here. Now, he was finally making the thing move. If only the last members of Chess Team could be dealt with, he would soon have the Chest of Adoon, and then the remaining military forces of the world would fall before him. Oh, certainly they would try to destroy him first, with their special forces teams, assassins and probably even a nuclear warhead. But none of those things would work.

He stuck his head up over the stone barrier, quickly checking on the position from which the gunfire was coming. Then he looked to the sky to see where he had sent the Colossus on its last blind sprint. He was getting closer.

He dropped down behind the stone wall, just as a bullet pinged off the top of it, missing his head by less than an inch.

"What can I do?" Seth asked from beside him.

"Crawl that way. Peek around the side of that rock and shout directions to me, while I try to steer our large friend."

Ridley returned to mumbling the ancient language commanding the statue, as Seth scrambled away to another nearby block of stone exposed from the sandy soil.

The ground trembled as the Colossus charged back into the center of the Antonine Baths, its footfalls crushing blocks of stone and fragments of columns as it came.

"Turn right a bit," Seth called from his vantage point.

Ridley made the mental adjustment and uttered the harsh words from the back of his throat.

"Good, now bring it closer to us."

The rumbling footfalls sped up, as the creature lumbered faster toward their location.

"They are running for the trees now. Try to angle it to the left—" Seth began.

Suddenly, their position was riddled with bullets, shots ricocheting off the stone, and hitting all around the ground of their hiding place.

"Fuck!" Ridley's concentration was broken. He lost control of the Colossus, and it stopped moving, frozen in mid stride. He and Seth scrambled away from the stone and down the embankment to the beach, away from the gunfire.

Somehow, it was coming from above them. Ridley scanned the skies, looking for a helicopter or something, but he found nothing. He looked up the beach to their former hide. Carpenter was dead. Trigger was scooting across the sand toward a stone

block, trailing a river of blood from one limp leg. The man wouldn't last long.

"Where they hell did that come from?" Ridley asked.

He frantically looked up and down the beach. At the north end, he saw figures in black moving into the ruins—more of his men. *Finally.* The local military would be dressed in garishly bright camouflage—exactly the wrong color for the local environment. The police would be dressed in black, but they would be carrying plastic riot shields with Arabic text emblazoned across them.

Now he just needed the mercenaries to keep the Chess Team busy long enough. He needed to get the Colossus under control and bring it to him. All he needed was a few uninterrupted minutes.

Suddenly, more bullets ripped into the sand from above, and Ridley and Seth leapt back, diving into the water.

"There," Seth was shouting and pointing. "It's coming from up there!"

Ridley looked up the body of the Colossus. Right up its chest to the cape bunched around its neck and the head with its pointed crown. On top of the head, next to one of the spires jutting off the crown, Ridley could see brief flashes of light.

"Son of a bitch! One of them is on top of it. How the hell did he get up there?"

"Can you toss him off?" Seth asked.

"I can do better than that," Ridley said. He tried to ignore the hail of bullets occasionally peppering the sand of the beach, and he sat down in the shallow water, letting the warm water rise to his neck.

He began uttering the strange ancient language. He closed his eyes and let them roll up into his head, as he focused on one thought.

One command.

He repeated it in his mind, and then his mouth and tongue uttered the thought in the foreign language over and over again.

Slap. Your. Head.

FIFTY-FIVE
Antonine Baths, Carthage, 2013

Bishop swore as his MP-5 ran dry. He'd been firing at the spot where Ridley and his men were hunkered down, when the gigantic statue went on a thunderous rampage, crushing everything under foot, before returning to the shore and suddenly stopping.

Then Rook had started firing from his perch up on top of the statue's head. Ridley's concentration must have broken.

"Longer you keep them off guard with shit like that, the more chance we have of finding you a really big step-ladder, Rook," he spoke into his throat mic, as he set his submachine gun down on the sandy ground, and pulled out a pistol. It was better than nothing. If Peter and Lynn made it back with Knight, he'd get a spare magazine from them.

"Hardy har har," came Rook's reply. "I'm getting sun burnt like a friggin' scorpion up here."

Queen fired off a final blast of gunfire from her own weapon until the magazine was empty. "Just keep firing on Ridley's position. If he can't concentrate, he can't move that thing."

Queen turned to Bishop. "Any more mags?"

He shrugged. "Was gonna ask you," he said, even though he knew she was out.

"Shit."

Bishop heard movement behind his position and whirled the 9 mm around. Peter and Asya were struggling along, with Knight in between them. The little man looked like he'd been worked over by someone Bishop's size. Lynn came behind them with an MP-5, covering the group as they moved. Bishop got up and ran to them. He slipped into Asya's place, taking Knight's weight.

"What happened?" he asked.

"Some bald guy missing an ear kicked the crap out of me. He said something about 'his forces', so I guess he must have been in charge," Knight's voice was weak.

"Ridley's not running the show?" Bishop said.

"He looked a bit like Ridley, but it wasn't another duplicate."

Queen came and joined the group. They all crouched as another fusillade of bullets came their way, pinging off the stone ruins.

"This guy is missing an ear, you said?" she asked.

"*Was.* The golem squashed him flat." Knight closed his eyes.

"I think I know who that was," Queen said, accepting a fresh magazine from Peter, as Lynn handed Bishop her MP-5. He gave her the 9 mm in exchange.

"You do?" Bishop asked.

"Darius Ridley. Richard's brother. I met him in the Ukraine. I'm the one who took the ear."

"Couldn't have happened to a nicer prick," Knight mumbled. "Where's Rook?"

Bishop pointed, and Knight tiled his head to look up to the Colossus. "That's the Colossus of Rhodes. Rook's on top."

"Is he steering it?" Knight asked, his eyes wide.

"Nope. Just hitching a ride."

As if to prove the point, another burst of gunfire erupted from the crown of the stationary statue, raining down on the beach. Rook let out a whoop, his voice faint, but he was clearly enjoying the crazy situation that would petrify most people.

"He ought to just chuck grenades down," Knight said.

"I think he's out. Besides, I'm not sure they'd make it to the ground before going off."

"Who are we shooting at?" Knight asked.

"Ridley, one clone, two mercs," Queen said. "I might have hit one of the mercs."

"So let's rush them while Rook has them pinned," Knight suggested, then fell into a bout of coughing.

"Yeah, 'cause you're in shape for a quick sprint up the beach followed by some hand to hand," Bishop said.

"Let me at 'em," Knight wheezed.

"It's not a bad idea," Peter said. "I know I'm not my son, but I've been in a few scrapes. We can flank them while your man on the statue keeps them pinned. If we wait until their reinforcements come, we're dead. If we wait until Ridley can control that giant again, we're even more dead."

Queen looked like she was running through scenarios in her head, then she nodded. "Bishop, the beach from the south. Lynn, stay here with Knight. Peter, with me to the north. Asya, you stay in the middle and make them think we're still here."

"I'm a better shot than Peter, why don't I come with you?" Lynn asked. Queen and Bishop looked at her and Peter. The man nodded in agreement with the plan.

"Fine, let's go."

Bishop ran down a dirt road to his right, keeping low, so the short rock walls still standing from the ancient bathing complex shielded him to some small degree. He scanned the area ahead, then the tree-line to his right, the giant statue near the beach and back toward Knight's position with Peter. As he brought his eyes back to the beach, he caught a glimpse of motion where there shouldn't have been any, far to the north, through the ruins. He dropped behind the low wall and rolled to a stop. Then he crawled next to the wall, inched up to the top and took a peek.

He didn't see anything for a full minute. Then he saw a man dressed in black dart from one block of stone to another. He wondered if Ridley's boys were trying the same thing he was. But then he saw another man move through the ruins. Then another.

Shit.

He keyed his microphone. "Queen, you read?"

"What?"

"Reinforcements. North end. Wearing black and leap-frogging through the ruins."

"Dammit."

Bishop checked the statue again. Its hand reached up toward its head. "Rook! Get out of there! The hand is coming up! You gotta move!"

The gunfire from the top of the Colossus stopped, as the creature's huge hand swung up and slammed down on top of its head, as if it were trying to swat away the world's largest deerfly. The impact made a cracking sound as loud as a peal of thunder.

FIFTY-SIX
Antium, Latium, 780 BC

The machine was amazing, especially considering the date. The lab was full of metal components that shouldn't exist for thousands of years.

There was a massive arc of thin metal that looked like gold, supported by a wooden frame, shaped roughly like the Greek symbol Omega: Ω. The top of the arch was taller than Alexander—easily enough room for three normal people to use the arch as a gateway. The structure stood in the middle of a huge lab. Rough unsheathed copper wire wound around the frame and the golden metal. At the far end of the room, an old wooden water-wheel stood. King could tell at a glance that the younger Alexander had tried to power the arch with crude electricity from the waterwheel, but he knew it wouldn't have been nearly enough power.

The design of the electrical wiring, the layout of unsheathed coiled cables across the stone and the bent metal plates that lined the outside of the arch like armor reminded King of the dimensional portal he had passed through in Norway. There were other molded metal shapes, the purpose for which King could not fathom. In one part of the room, a small pit was gouged out of the stone floor and

filled with a noxious green chemical liquid, through which some of the exposed copper wiring ran.

"A lot of this stuff looks like you built it with knowledge of future sciences. If this is your first trip back to the past, how did you pull that off?" King asked.

Alexander sat heavily in a chair near the apparatus and looked at King. "You've lived here in the past long enough to know that history and myth often present a less than accurate picture about ancient events. Science becomes religion, or witchcraft. Sometimes even the most extraordinary events or discoveries are forgotten and erased from time."

King leaned against a wall and nodded. Acca sat in a chair nearby, listening, but her face revealed nothing about whether she was already privy to the information Alexander was about to share.

"How do you suppose people of this time would have explained me? A man of my strength and vitality? Someone with knowledge of things most people would consider magic? Even though I've spent most of my life keeping what I knew hidden, people occasionally catch a glimpse of what I can do. How do you think they would explain it?"

"Hercules. Bastard son of Zeus," King said.

"Precisely. You've known me over two decades. Do I like snakes?"

"No. You always let me go first if there were snakes."

"So what's the likelihood I throttled some of them in my crib? People make up stories about people they perceive as heroes. I didn't always keep to myself. Before Acca, I was arrogant and a showoff. Stories got told, and they amplified over the years. Some of it was based in truth. You know the Hydra was real, and you met Cerberus. But was I the offspring of Zeus? Of course not. As far as I know, Zeus doesn't exist. And I've told you this was my first trip back to the past. What does that leave?"

King thought about his encounters with Alexander before their trip to the past. The man was mysterious. He kept to himself.

He led a devoted group of followers. He was immortal. He had an army of the Forgotten around the world—failed scientific experiments, he had claimed. He knew things before others did. He obscured the truth about history, allowing the myths to obfuscate the truth further.

And he knew about Chess Team's battle in Norway, even though he wasn't there. King had traveled through a dimensional portal to another dimension, where he had encountered a creature that called him one of the 'Children of Adoon.' King had come to learn that *Adoon* was another name by which Alexander was known. And now King was looking at yet another dimensional portal that Alexander had created. The design was clearly the same basic structure.

"You're...not human, are you?"

Alexander smiled. "Depends on your definition of human, Jack. I am a man, with biology roughly similar to most people on the planet, though more similar to yours. I don't have two hearts or scales on my skin. I *am* human, but no, I'm not from this dimension. I was a scientist. A simple man of science. And I found a way between worlds. This dimension wasn't the first I visited. I saw myself as an intrepid explorer. I investigated several dimensions and encountered many different kinds of...people, including the monster Fenrir, you encountered in Norway. I became addicted to discovery and with each new dimension, I became more arrogant. And sloppy."

King interrupted. "You got stranded here."

Alexander chuckled softly.

"I had the know-how to design this machine from scratch. I just didn't realize that I wouldn't find any suitable power sources." Alexander stood and paced back and forth. "Can you imagine how I searched? I was just over four hundred years old when I met Acca."

"Four hundred years old?" King asked, a skeptical eyebrow raised.

"A natural lifespan for people in my dimension, where a richer atmosphere, free of pollutants, and slightly different biology allow for longevity. There was a time in this dimension where men lived nearly a thousand years. Methuselah. Adam. Noah. All are said to have lived more than nine-hundred years."

"You don't believe that—" King stopped his argument, remembering the age of the man to whom he spoke.

Alexander grinned. "I travelled the world in search of power. I investigated every meteorite that fell to Earth. I followed up on every rumor of the supernatural and the strange."

"And you built a portal home from scraps and bits you cobbled together yourself..."

"I mined some of the gold in those connectors myself." Alexander pointed at the machine.

King looked to Acca. "Did you know he was from...somewhere else?"

She simply nodded.

"Can she live in your world?" King asked.

Alexander nodded. "Of course. The air is almost identical. It'll be like living on the side of a mountain for her. Clear crisp air, with a slightly rarefied atmosphere. It's a peaceful world, with far more wide open natural spaces than here...even in this time."

"So even after Acca 'died'..." King made quotes in the air with his fingers, "you worked to find a power source for the machine."

"At first, I was destroyed by the grief, and like most people, I just wanted to go home to my loved ones. *My* family. And I had been trying for so very many years. I operated out of the shadows as best I could. For a while I affected the outcome of events and wars. If a potential outcome could get in my way, I got involved. After a while, I realized little *could* get in my way. So I worked from the shadows. I kept my identity a secret, and when something powerful from antiquity came along, I got my hands on it first. If something didn't suit my purposes, I kept it safe and out of the wrong hands. Eventually I gained some followers—the Herculean

Society—people dedicated to my ideals of preventing powerful objects from being used for evil and protecting historical sites—many of which hold meaning to me personally—from desecration. They also helped obscure the truth about the past with mystery and myth, though not even the Society always knew why.

"And then I encountered Chess Team. My first encounter was with Rook and Queen. They were rude but brave...and expected. I saw a recording of that battle in New Hampshire. I watched how you handled the monster, and I knew our time together had nearly begun. I kept an eye on you from then on, knowing you would become an ally. I had inside information, after all."

"Inside information?" King asked. His face darkened. "Who?"

Alexander smiled, but it quickly faded. He became serious. Quiet. "Before the Hydra. Before Ridley and Delta. Before Julie died. I have *always* known you, Jack. How is that possible? Think. You have all the pieces. Use that incredible mind of yours. You were never just a soldier."

King looked at the machine and thought about what he had just heard. He had Alexander's genes in him. He was a descendant. Did his parent's know more than they had told about that? Or was Deep Blue holding back on a secret alliance with Alexander? *No, that doesn't make sense.* But then, as he looked at the flimsy portal and the crude copper cabling, he realized what was missing from the machine—a computer.

This machine couldn't be automated.

Someone had to run it.

Someone...who stayed behind.

FIFTY-SEVEN
Alexander's Lab, Antium, Latium, 780 BC

"**I have only** the one machine, Jack, and only one black hole to power it. It's good for one trip. One way. If you want me to use it to send you

home, I will. But Acca and I will be stranded here, out of time *and* space. Even if we go into hiding somewhere, the danger of me running into the younger version of myself will be extreme. I travelled broadly."

"You bastard," King stood up, and stalked across the lab to shout in Alexander's face. "You brought me here against my will. Now you're emotionally blackmailing me—*again*—telling me I'm the only hope you have for getting home. What made you think I would go for this?"

Alexander's face was sober, but friendly, despite King shouting at him so hard that spittle had flown from King's mouth and landed on Alexander's face in little specks. "Because you already did."

King frowned, confused.

"How do you think I snuck into your highly secure base in New Hampshire and stole that laptop with the plans for the Norway machine, Jack? Without triggering a single alarm? Without anyone seeing me? I'm good, but I'm not that good."

"You're saying *I* took the laptop?"

"You already made this decision." Alexander reached out to place his hand on King's shoulder, but King yanked away.

"You fooled me into believing you were a good man," King said.

"This is all new to you," Alexander said, "But to me...Jack, we've been friends for a long time. A *very* long time."

King shook his head and stormed away. He was flustered. His face felt hot. Blood rushed through his ears. The possibility of what Alexander was telling him scared the shit out of him.

Sara. Fiona.

King felt the muscles in his neck constrict as panic set in. He wasn't one to run from a fight, but he ran from this, as fast as he could, out of the lab. He blindly stumbled through the hallways and passages in Alexander's Antium villa, looking for the way out. Eventually, he opened a window and just climbed outside, sucking in the evening air in huge gulps. He felt like he couldn't breathe.

He was trapped. He couldn't get home.

He was stuck in the past.

He ran a hundred yards away from the building toward the beach. They were on the northern shore of a town called Antium— a place Alexander had told him would eventually be the modern city of Anzio, made famous by the Allies landing here in World War II.

He staggered down to the water, thinking about the Allied landing, trying to keep his head from the enormity of what lay before him.

At the water's edge, Jack Sigler, callsign: King, gave up. He fell to his knees in the sand and hung his head.

He stayed like that a long time, until the sky turned dark, and he heard Alexander's footsteps behind him. The man sat softly in the sand next to him. He was quiet for a while.

"If there was any other way—"

"There is," King said weakly. "Send me home."

"If you really want me to do that, I will. It'll take a few months to recalibrate the machine...but—"

"But, you know that's not going to happen," King said. "Because it would have already and you would have no memory of me. Did I tell you why?"

"Why, what?"

"Why I decided to remain in the past? Why I decided to give up my life?"

"You're not giving it up," Alexander said. "Merely postponing it."

"By 2800 years!" King shouted, clenching his fists.

They stayed quiet for a minute and then Alexander said, "You told me...it was the right thing to do."

It was a God-awful stupid answer, but King recognized the thought as his own, the primal force that motivated all his decisions. The *right* thing. But this didn't feel right. "This can't be how it happens..." King said softly.

"A lot of good will come of it," Alexander said.

"For you," King said, "I'm sure."

"For us both." Alexander leaned forward and lazily traced his finger through the sand. "For the world. You...make a difference, Jack. The world needed saving long before you were born."

King perked up. Alexander was playing to his sense of duty, he knew, but he couldn't hide his interest. "Explain."

"The details, I'm afraid, will have to be discovered later on, but simply put, there are times throughout history when grievous wrongs need to be undone, when men and women need saving, when all of humanity finds itself on the brink...and sometimes, more often than not, *I* am not the one who stands up to the darkness."

"You are full of shit," King said. "You think a good speech is going to—"

"I didn't save Fiona."

King turned to him. "No, you kidnapped her."

"Before that, Jack. On the reservation, where you found her, in the car. That was you. She would have died with the rest had you not been there. This circle...this path...it saves my wife, but it also saves your daughter."

"How do I know that anything you're telling me is true?"

Alexander leaned back revealing a drawing in the sand, two vertical lines joined by a circle, the symbol for the Herculean Society and Alexander's calling card.

Mental tumblers once again fell into place. If Alexander was telling the truth, this symbol wasn't just used by Alexander. According to his stories, King left a note bearing this symbol, once after saving Fiona and once after stealing the laptop.

"You have always misinterpreted this symbol," Alexander said. "It was never an H. Never stood for Hercules. The circle is the world. The lines are two pillars, holding everything together. The *two* leaders of the Herculean Society."

"The wraiths in the library in Malta," King whispered. "This is why they obeyed me."

Alexander nodded. "They could see you were different. Less sure of yourself. But the Forgotten, in the future, would never harm you."

King searched his mind for an argument, for some other reality that made sense. Sara and Fiona were within his grasp. They had never been further, but he'd been expecting to see them soon. But if Alexander was telling the truth, and King did not stay, Fiona would die. King's life would be radically altered. The circle that bound him and Alexander would be broken and Acca would also die.

"She's a good woman," King said.

"Unparalleled," Alexander agreed. "You...will stay?"

King forced the smallest of smiles. "You already know the answer." He stood and patted Alexander on his shoulder. "I'm glad you got her back."

Alexander stood as well. "What now?"

"Now...we send you both home," King said. "Before I change my mind."

They walked back into the villa. Alexander led them directly to the lab. Acca was waiting there, sitting in a chair, wringing her hands together.

She stood when they entered. "Are you alright, Jack?"

"I'll be okay."

"Alexander explained what you must do. I am very sorry." She took his hands. "Do you remember what you told me? About why you do the things you do? You said because it was the right thing to do, but you never said it was also the hardest thing to do." She wrapped her arms around him, squeezing him tightly. "Thank you." She had tears in her eyes when she stepped away.

He nodded, then turned to Alexander. "Show me what to do."

Alexander procured the rock on the chain around his neck. He tugged the chain hard, until it snapped off the top of the rock, where it had been affixed. Then he held it out to King.

"You'll need to set it into the machine...there," Alexander pointed at a round receptacle he had made from a cup, with wires running into and out of it. "The portal should open instantly. When we step through, there's a good chance that everything will

blow up on this end. I suggest you run like hell. Immortality isn't a blessing if you're buried alive."

"Sounds like you speak from experience," King said, taking the dwarf black hole in his hand. It was far heavier than he thought it would be. Probably over thirty pounds.

"I've seen the inside of a few jails, yes. Keep to the edges of history, Jack. You can change the world, but be subtle. Keep your face out of the history books. Stay in the shadows."

King smiled. "Sounds like business as usual."

"There will come a day when you will return to your present, as promised. It will be hard to remember them...your family, your friends. Do what you can to preserve their memory and do not forget Carthage. Chess Team will need its King."

King didn't think he could ever forget the most important people in his life, the people who made him who he was, but 2800 years was a long time. He felt his resolve waning. "We better do this now." He stepped up to the machine and held the stone above its receptacle. "Ready?"

Alexander walked to him and held out his hand to shake with King. King grasped the hand and felt it warmly close over his. "Thank you, Jack. For everything."

"How will I know you made it over there safely?"

"You won't. You just have to take some things on faith."

Alexander walked back to Acca, and they stood in front of the empty portal. "Say hello to Lancelot for me." Alexander smiled broadly as King laughed. He pulled Acca close to him. She smiled nervously at King, then looked up at Alexander. He met her eyes with a reassuring smile and gently stroked her face with his hand.

King heard him whisper to her. "We'll be fine."

King dropped the golf-ball sized stone into the cup, where it connected with the copper wires.

Blue arcs of electricity shot across the bare metal cables, filling the room with a burnt stench instantly. The stone shell burst into dust, revealing a small black swirling sphere. Smoke poured

off the apparatus, and the arch began to glow with a wall of bluish light.

"Goodbye," King said.

Alexander gave a nod and led Acca into the blue light. It washed over them like a wave of water and then—they were gone. The light bowed out of the arch, stretching across the room for over twenty feet, before it snapped back into the arch and inverted. Then the frame of the arch buckled and it toppled inward, sucked into the portal. King watched, unable to turn away as the light stretched inward for what looked like a mile. Then it stopped and snapped back toward him.

He closed his eyes.

When King woke, it was daylight, the sun streaming down from overhead where the roof of the lab should have been. He stood up and breathed in the salty smell of the sea. As he stood, a large piece of burnt timber slid off his back and onto the ground. He was standing in a field of rubble.

He could see the beach and the blue waves to his left, and far off to his right he could see a shepherd leading his flock of sheep and carrying the long hooked stick of the trade. No one else was around, but the explosion would eventually draw the curious.

King stepped over the rubble and saw that his robe was in tatters. Although it still covered his crotch, there were more than a few holes singed through to his chest. That would have to be one of his first steps. He paused at the ruined wall and admired the view.

The sound of a jangling bell turned his attention away from the sea. A boy, accompanied by a goat, ran toward him. The boy couldn't be more than ten. His eyes were wide, his face streaked with tears.

"Help!" the boy yelled. "You must help me."

He knelt down and caught the panicked boy by his arms. "What's wrong?"

"Thank the gods for sending you," the boy said. "I knew it would be you."

"You *know* me?" King asked. He'd never seen the boy before.

"Everyone knows you," the boy said. "I prayed to the gods for help. The ground shook. I saw the smoke. You must have leapt from Olympus!"

King glanced back at the crater left by the explosion. The place looked like it had been struck by a meteor. "Tell me, who do you think I am?"

The boy smiled despite whatever emergency had sent him in search of aid. "You don't know your own name?"

"Tell me," King said.

The boy's smile widened. "You are Perseus, son of Zeus."

King returned the boy's smile. "Let's go."

FIFTY-EIGHT
Carthage, 2013

Knight watched in horror as the Colossus slapped its hand down on the top of its head, hard enough to break two of the huge spires off the rear of its crown.

They tumbled end over end, until one fell in the sea and the other plunged, tip first, deep into the sand of the beach, where it stood like a modern addition to the surrounding ruins.

"Ohooiet!" Peter said in Russian, standing beside Knight.

"You still there, Rook?" Knight said into his microphone. "Rook?"

"Yeah, yeah. I'm still here. I'm on the friggin' shoulder now. This mega-pecker missed me by inches." Rook's voice came through Knight's earpiece with a lot of static.

Knight heard gunfire then and ducked his head down. Peter crouched down next to him behind the rough, pitted stone.

A few of the structures at the baths, mostly those further from the sea, were still intact, forming nearly complete rooms and doorways, and in a few cases, a second story. But after the Colossus's rampage, very few structures were left higher than six feet. The few remaining Doric columns had been knocked over, and walls that had stood for hundreds of years had been shattered into little more than stone and pebbles.

But there were still enough walls and rocks to hide behind, and plenty of opportunities for cat-and-mouse games, if the enemy was willing to fall for them. He had spotted some of the mercenaries jockeying for position at the far end of the ruins, and knew the others might be caught unawares.

"Queen, you've got hostiles slipping into the complex. Get out of there and rendezvous back with me. We need to move to more level ground."

"I hear you. We're on our way," Queen said. Bishop responded similarly.

"I'd love to make it," Rook said, "but I think that would end a little messy for me."

"Understood, Rook," Knight heard Queen say. "We'll get you down as soon as we can."

"Team: this is Deep Blue. I've got no satellite coverage for another twenty minutes, so I can't advise on position, but based on what I'm seeing in older satellite maps, getting out of the ruins is probably a good idea. I've got reinforcements coming your way. ETA, thirty minutes. Best I can do."

Then gunfire erupted all over the ruins. The newly arrived mercenaries had tired of waiting. Queen and Lynn came rushing back to Knight's position from the north. They slid to a stop behind his low wall, ducking for cover, as the top of the wall pinged with shots, blowing dust over Knight and Peter.

"Nice of you to join us," Knight said. "Lovely day for a stroll."

"Fuckers are starting to really piss me off. This whole op is a steaming pile of shit. No recon, no idea of how many we're up

against and..." Queen's volume dropped off. Knight understood she was about to say that they had lost King, but had stopped herself because Peter and Lynn were present.

Just then, Asya came bounding over the wall, landed a full yard beyond the four clustered people, and rolling gracelessly in the sand. Knight almost fired his pistol at her, thinking she was a threat. Bullets riddled the top of the wall, just a fraction of a second after Asya came hurtling over it. He wondered if she had been hit.

"You okay?" he asked.

"I'll be sore tomorrow. Worse if we get killed. I think we are about to be seriously outnumbered."

"I'm pinned down," Bishop's voice came through the earpiece. "Move out and I'll join you by going straight to the trees from here. Where are we meeting up?"

Queen spoke up. With King KIA, she was the field team leader. "After the trees, head north. The mercs will cut over from the ruins and try to push us south. That's just where we want them. If we head too far west, we'll be back at the mosque and endangering thousands of morning worshippers. The sea is to the east. South is residential neighborhoods. To the north is the Presidential palace— and I can't believe they haven't sent out troops yet. But they will soon. Assuming the locals aren't in Ridley's pocket, then I want the Presidential guard on the far side of our tangos, putting them in a crossfire."

"Sounds like a plan, Boss," Bishop said. "I'm on the move."

The fact that Bishop had called her 'Boss' wasn't lost on Knight. He knew that Bishop had used that nickname for King sometimes. It meant that Bishop had accepted King's demise, and already in his head, Queen was King's permanent replacement as the head of the team. Knight didn't think he could process King's loss that fast.

More bullets ripped into the sandy soil to the side of their position.

"We need to move," Queen said. "Peter. Lynn. Get him up."

Asya came around to the south side of the group and Queen stayed on the north side. Peter and Lynn slipped their arms around Knight and helped him to a crouch. He took in a deep gasping breath as his crushed rips stabbed into his innards.

"Go," Queen said.

The five of them made a mad dash for the tree line, with bullets blasting past on both sides and ahead into the trees.

Knight looked back, and once more he caught a glimpse of the brilliant turquoise sea. He wanted nothing more than for his ribs to stop hurting and to be able to take a swim in that water.

Maybe, if we get out of this alive, I'll take Beck to an island somewhere. Maybe the Maldives.

He and Anna Beck, a support member of Deep Blue's Endgame organization, had been seeing each other for over a year now. When their relationship began, he'd thought it might not last long, but it had. Now, with bullets flying all around, and him feeling like he might die at any moment, his thoughts turned to her, and he realized how much he missed her.

Peter stumbled on a rock, and suddenly Knight fell toward the ground, with Lynn on top of him. When they hit, the impact from both the ground and Peter on one side of his ribs, and Lynn's full weight on the other side, made Knight shout out in pain.

"Oh God, sorry, sorry," Peter said, and he and Lynn both scrambled to disentangle their limbs from his, while Knight's whole world contracted into a tight ball of pain. His vision went white, and he could hear a loud noise in his ears, but he couldn't process it. His whole body was shaking with giant thumps.

As the pain subsided, he realized what was happening.

The Colossus was on the move again.

FIFTY-NINE

Edge of the Antonine Baths, Carthage

Queen thought they were done. The gigantic statue had resumed its rampage. They were taking fire from multiple locations. Knight was in no shape to move, let alone walk. Bishop was on his own, and Peter and Lynn had just dropped Knight in a heap on the ground.

Bullets ripped into the sand nearby as the ground rumbled from the Colossus's thundering footfalls. Queen dropped to one knee and fired back into the ruins until her finger squeezed the trigger and nothing happened. She was out of ammunition. She looked to Lynn again, who had recovered and was helping Knight up.

"Any more mags?" Queen asked.

Lynn shook her head. Peter looked down.

Queen turned to Knight. "What do you have?"

"Just a few shots left."

Queen dropped her MP-5 and pulled out her Browning handgun. She held her fire, waiting to have a clear shot at one of the black-clad mercenaries darting in and out of the remaining ruins. Then she looked up to see the statue moving her way, across the crumbling walls. It looked like it might step on some of the mercs, too, but there would be no avoiding it once it arrived.

At the edge of the grass, where they had stopped because of Knight's fall, Queen saw a metal sign fixed to a post. Across the top was a maroon strip reading 'Danger' in English and Arabic. Under that was a somehow comical silhouette icon showing a man either about to walk off the end of a crenellated castle's tower or about to break out into Cossack-style dancing. The end of the tower was crumbling and dropping stones to the ground. The sign had warnings in Arabic, French and English to not walk on the ruins. Just then, the Colossus took a sweeping step and its massive foot landed on top of one of the remaining structures in the ruins. The impact sent stone flying in all directions, and a cloud of dust rose up where the structure had stood.

"We're gonna take as many of these bastards with us as possible," Queen said. She spotted a man darting for cover and fired a shot. It was well beyond the practical range of her weapon, but she clipped the guy on the shoulder and he went down in a tumble. Peter and Lynn got Knight moving again toward the relative safety of the trees. Asya fired twice more as they ran. Queen held back on her shots, making them last.

When they reached the trees. Queen took up position behind a huge palm and extended her pistol back toward the ruins. She waited patiently, breathing in slow shallow breaths. Soon she saw just what she wanted. Another fool in black, standing out against the sand colored stone. She loosed three shots from her pistol until the man's body jerked and shuddered, then fell. Two more men popped up in the doorway of a barely standing structure. Most of the left of the wall had crumbled, and only a foot of the right edge of the wall remained. Queen emptied her weapon, but missed the last two men, who returned fire with their AK-47s. She pulled her arm back with the empty 9mm just as the side of her tree splintered outward from heavy fire.

She holstered the handgun and looked down at the ground. *Okay*, she thought. *Now we do things my way.* She pulled out an SOG Creed knife from its sheath on her armored leg. The knife was her new favorite. At nearly thirteen inches in length, it was still useful for field operations, but the broad head gave the thing more of a machete look than a typical Special Forces knife. Marketed as the perfect tool for cutting and chopping wood, she knew its true purpose was to increase the length of the cutting edge, for opening up your enemy.

She planned to open anyone stupid enough to get too close.

"Bish, you out of the shit yet? I'm about to start cutting over here," she keyed the mic, while keeping her eye on the fast approaching Colossus.

"Changed my mind. I went for the beach instead. About to lay the hurt on Ridley's position with the last of my mags. Should slow up the golem."

"Okay," she said. " Do it. We're moving north."

Queen heard gunfire across the ruins and suddenly the Colossus stopped moving. She saw muzzle-flare up on the thing's shoulder, and knew Rook had joined the fray again.

She raced through the park's clustered trees, staying off the few paths leading to the other sites of Carthage's ruins and quickly caught up with the others. Knight was taking more of his own weight now, running with Peter and Lynn, despite his extensive injuries. She guessed the drugs were kicking in now. It wouldn't matter if they couldn't find some weapons though. They were pretty much out of bullets.

They burst out into a clearing, and she saw they were too late.

Peter, Lynn and Knight stopped running. Asya started to dart to the left back into the trees before she saw it was useless. Across the clearing, at least forty men stood waiting for them with rifles raised. Queen stopped and swore. Lynn glanced back at Queen, then lowered her weapon to the ground. Peter and Knight dropped theirs as well. Asya looked unsure of what to do.

Queen clutched the grip of her knife tightly, feeling the grooves in the metal grip under her fingertips. She toyed with the idea of rushing the men and slicing up a few of them before they riddled her with bullets. She figured she could get three of them for sure. A fourth or fifth, if luck was with her.

"Put it down lady," one of them men said in a heavy French accent.

That made her grip the knife tighter. She took a step forward with the knife clutched in her hand. The mercenary raised his AK and seated the stock into his shoulder, pointing it directly at her. It wasn't the most accurate weapon in the world, favored more for its availability and cheapness, but Queen had no doubt the man could hit her from where he stood.

A warm wind blew through the space, raising a swirling cloud of dust and fine sand, shifting the blond hair hanging over her forehead and revealing the bright red brand of a skull encased by a star.

The merc blinked in surprise.

Queen took another defiant step.

The man's finger twitched.

And then, a man screamed. Then another.

In the snap of a finger, pandemonium erupted through the mercenaries' ranks. Dozens of dark bodies in flowing gray cloaks ripped into the clearing, leaping and running. The mercs opened fire at the creatures, but there were too many of them. The mercenaries were overrun, killed or bled dry by the fast-moving Forgotten who struck with surgical precision and timing.

Queen watched stunned, as the wraithlike Forgotten, Alexander Diotrephes's strange creatures, mauled and destroyed the black-clad soldiers. She had never seen them in the sunlight, and she believed they couldn't bear it—much like the legends around vampires. But the creatures attacked the mercenaries without flinching from the light, or from the bullets, and before she could even comprehend what had happened, they raced deeper into the ruins, hunting out and attacking more of the soldiers. She heard gurgling screams and random gunfire from the walled ruins.

She turned to see Asya and the others looking just as shocked as she was. The clearing in front of them was now littered with bodies—mostly mercenaries but a few Forgotten, as well. And to Queen's delight, there were more assault rifles than she knew what to do with. She ran over and picked up an AK-47 from the hands of a now headless mercenary. Then she looted the corpses for more of the distinctive curved magazines. She tossed a few to Asya, who expertly loaded a rifle and passed it to her mother before taking up another.

"That might have been the strangest fucking thing I've seen all day," Knight said. "And it's been a strange day."

Queen heard more thunderous footfalls and looked up to see the Colossus shimmying and shaking, swatting at itself like a human being assaulted by black flies. But there was nothing there. Nothing

she could see, anyway. But she knew Rook was still there. Only *he* could irritate a 300-foot tall golem that much.

"Day ain't over yet," Queen said.

SIXTY
On the Colossus, Carthage

Rook clung to a crack at the back of the creature's neck. He'd moved down from the head to the shoulder when Ridley had figured out he had hitched a ride. That climb wasn't easy, moving down the side of the head, but the folds of the ear had made decent handholds.

After he had fired down on Ridley's position one last time, using up the remaining rounds in his submachine gun, the bastard had figured out he'd moved. The giant statue shook and shifted about in unexpected ways—trying to throw him. The shoulder offered little cover, but he couldn't climb back up to the safety of the ear with the damn thing doing a dubstep dance under him. As he reached out for another crease at the back of the neck, where the cape began, a huge hand came up to swat at the shoulder. The collision missed, but sent up a cloud of dust and stone. It struck a second time, the crashing blow booming like a truck accident.

Rook scrabbled behind the head, hanging from his fingers.

Then the statue lunged forward. Rook's body flew upward. He jammed one fist deeper into the crack between the neck and the bunched cape just in time. His weight yanked hard on the jammed arm, and he felt the skin on the back of his hand grinding off against a sheet of barnacles. Then the Colossus lifted its body up, slamming Rook against the cape.

As pain pulsed through his body, Rook considered sliding down the cape again, but knew there would be nothing to arrest his fall as he got closer to the bottom. He'd simply drop the 250 feet

to the ground and splatter. Then he saw the huge arm raise up again, aiming for its head. Under the arm, he spotted notches on the side of the body, where the metal plates came together at a seam. He knew what they were instantly—a ladder for the creators and maintenance people to climb the statue. He remembered images he'd seen—most based on conjecture and the scantest of written descriptions—almost universally showed the Colossus with one arm raised, like the Statue of Liberty. This arm. The right one.

Rook moved to the edge of the cape and let go of the large crack at the neck. If the statue made any violent movements now, he'd be flung away. He pressed his arms on either side of the cape's 'fabric'—broad metal plates, long since corroded to a sickly green color. He wrapped his legs around the edge and was pleased to find that the rough impact foam that bulged from places in the leg armor improved his grip.

The massive arm swept up again. Rook reached out, not looking down at the precipitous fall. His fingers grazed the little chiseled-in nook in the armpit, just missing it. He swung his arm back and then reached out again, committing to the act. He'd either catch the handhold or fall to his death. His fingers slipped inside the notched ladder rung, fitting perfectly. There was grit inside, and what felt like a smooth sea shell, but hanging hundreds of feet off the ground, he was just glad for a handhold. He let go of the cape with his legs and swung out over the open space beneath the Colossus's armpit. He shoved his free hand inside a second notch and found it empty and solid.

Now if I can just climb down two hundred feet before this bucking bronco throws me.

He started to descend and soon found that not all the nooks were created equal. For one thing, they were hand carved, so their shapes and sizes were not even. But more troubling was that some were filled to bursting with shells and other marine debris. He was able to scoop out some of the muck with his fingertips on the first two notches he found clogged, but the third one was hardened to

the consistency of cement. He could skip a 'rung' of the ladder, but if he ran into two or three in a row that were clogged, he'd be in trouble.

The Colossus had stopped pursuing him, probably because he was now hidden from Ridley's sight. The giant was now moving forward carefully, crushing any structure that remained standing—giving his team no place to hide. Ridley was coordinating the mercs on the ground.

Rook looked up again. The most precarious thing in his current position, besides being hundreds of feet in the air, was the swinging right arm. If the damn thing brushed the statue's ribs, he'd be ground into paste.

After five more rungs, Rook felt himself tilting. He paused and held on tight. The Colossus was bending at the waist.

Oh shitfizzle.

As the statue's chest bent forward, Rook's fingers slipped in the notches, squashing together in a much smaller space. Shouting in pain, he fought against gravity and lifted his legs. He shoved his feet into two lower rungs and pushed up, while he pulled down with his arms. His already tired muscles shook, but he'd effectively locked himself in place, like a gecko on a window, without the suction cups.

The huge statue swung its hand like it was about to slap someone across the face, but instead, it swept through several of the ancient walls, as if it was cleaning breadcrumbs off the dinner table. Its massive legs were crouched, and the waist was nearly horizontal to the ground now, but Rook was still a hundred feet up. If they were still over the sea, he'd have dived for it, but over land, it was still too high to jump.

The Colossus made another huge sweep with its hand, slamming into stone walls and archways. When the arm lifted away, almost a third of the ruins were flattened, but the statue was also missing its hand at the wrist. Rook couldn't see through the dust whether the hand had just fallen off or been pulverized by the tremendous impact.

The force of the strike revealed that Ridley wasn't just clearing a path, he was using the Colossus to attack Queen and the others. Rook hated how helpless he was, but he had to use all his strength just to hold on as the statue stood tall again.

Rook let his feet fall out of the holes as the thing's body went vertical. His body swung down and his hands once again held his full weight. He grunted at the tug on his fingers. He could feel them getting sweaty. He wasn't going to be able to hold on much longer. He reached his left hand out of the hole, and quickly wiped the tips of his fingers across his chest. He was hoping to dry them off, but the exertion meant his t-shirt was doused with sweat and tacky. Wiping his fingers didn't dry them at all.

Then he reached for the next lower handhold. It was packed tight with grit. He scraped his fingernail across the rough surface, but none of the debris was loosening. He reached lower for the next hole. It was full too.

Son of a bitch!

He looked down and saw the third rung was free and clear. He'd have to let go, fall a few feet and catch himself. Sure, he thought, no problem. Then he counted off in his head, *one... two... three!*

He let go.

And fell...up.

It took his mind a second to register that he was moving in the wrong direction, but then he realized what had happened. The Colossus's left hand had reached across the chest and plucked him free like a wood tick.

The hand wrapped around him tightly. He couldn't move. The fingers stopped their grinding flex, just before they crushed him to death. The arm extended out in front of the Colossus as it turned around. The face tilted down to look at him, as the hand held him up for the face to see. The face sneered at him. Then the mouth formed two words. There was no sound emanating from the mouth, no actual lungs or voice box to create sound, but the shape

of the lips and tongue was unmistakable—a message for him, directly from Richard Ridley. Then the wind blasted past Rook's head as the left arm whipped past the face and the torso twisted to the side. Rook felt his stomach lurch like he was on a fast elevator or an amusement park ride.

Then suddenly the hand stopped. The arm was cocked back. The head turned toward him and the lips formed a nasty smile.

Rook had only just started his reply when the arm launched forward, the hand moving like a rocket to pitch him out to sea.

"Yeah, fuck you toooooooo!"

The fingers opened and Rook felt his body launch out over the water.

SIXTY-ONE
The Beach, Carthage

Bishop watched Rook sail out to sea before his position was fired on and he had to tear his eyes away. Five mercs in black were advancing down the beach toward him. He darted down to the rocky shoreline and laid down, the barrel of his recently acquired AK-47 aimed back up the beach. The sand stretched south for a bit before becoming a rocky pile, no doubt used as a kind of breakwater against storms. Still wearing his armor, Bishop didn't notice the rough surface of the rocks below him.

He wished he had more firepower, but the AK would work for now. Instead of firing wildly, like the mercs, he switched the weapon to its semi-automatic mode, prepared to make every bullet count. He controlled each breath, blocking out the rest of the world, not worrying about Rook's fate. He gently squeezed the trigger, and one of the three mercenaries on the beach toppled over backward, his head spraying out to the sides in a burst of red, coating his companions in gore. The other two men dropped to the sand.

Bishop could still see them. He wasn't anywhere near Knight when it came to being an accurate shot. He had a lot of bullets though, and he knew how to take his time. He lined up the next shot and waited, allowing two full breaths to come and go. The shot was trickier, because the man was low to the ground and so was Bishop. But the head was still visible. Bishop brought his aim just a nudge higher before firing, anticipating that the bullet might drop in its arc slightly before it reached the man. It missed.

He breathed in again and released. He held his breath. When he fired again, the boom of the rifle was joined by a geyser of red further down the beach. The third man scrambled to his feet and retreated, dropping his rifle as he went. The man shouted as he ran, but Bishop couldn't make out whether the man was saying something or just shrieking in terror.

Bishop heard a rumble and turned his gaze upward. The Colossus stared down at him.

And things were going so well.

He jumped to his feet and ran for the ruins.

The Colossus took a huge stride up the beach toward his position, then bent over and swept its massive handless arm across the ruins to Bishop's right. A tidal wave of broken walls and chunks of rock, along with a cloud of roiling dust and sand barreled toward him, propelled by the sweeping arm. Bishop dropped the AK, made an about face and ran for the water.

He reached the rocks and dove headfirst into the shallow water. He slid beneath the waves, his armor slowing him some, but his prodigious strength more than made up for the extra drag. Then the first piece of the debris hit the water, far ahead of him. It had flown over him and crashed into the water. A large slab of stone wall, maybe seven feet tall and four feet wide sliced vertically into the sea, stabbing into the sandy bottom. Bishop turned to his left, heading north along the shore as more rock and sand arced over his head into the drink. The *thunks* they made under water sounded gentle, but he knew each piece of stone had the potential to crush or pin him under the surface.

He raised his head for another breath and saw that the statue had moved on, rampaging across the ruins, stomping wildly. He realized then that Ridley couldn't actually 'see' through the statue. He was striking blindly, hoping to hit something.

Bishop swam back to the rocky shoreline, and activated his throat mic.

"Queen, the statue is blind. Ridley can't see where he's steering the thing."

There was no reply.

Bishop clawed his way out of the water and checked the small pack on his hip for the radio—it was waterproof but it was dented in. Something must have hit him. He had no way to get in touch with the others.

The Colossus took another two rampaging steps, kicking at the ruins as it went. Bishop could see several black-clad bodies take to the sky along with crumbling blocks of stone. The bodies twisted and turned in the air before they hit the ground, screaming the whole way. They reminded him of Rook.

Bishop turned to look out to sea, but before his eyes got that far, he spotted something else about 600 yards up the beach.

The helipad. And the bird sitting on it was starting up its rotor blades.

Bishop quickly unstrapped his armor plating, and removed his boots. Then he pulled off his sticky t-shirt. Wearing just his wet BDU pants, he dove back into the water and started swimming diagonally across the water from the beach—kicking for the helipad.

On his left along the ruins, the Colossus had ceased moving again. More of its right arm was missing now. Bishop couldn't see Ridley or any of his people. He guessed the fight had moved inland. It was hard to see anything from the water. He turned his focus back to swinging his arms and kicking his legs. He needed that helo.

By the time he got to the rocky side of the helipad, the chopper's rotors were in full spin. Bishop wasted no time. He climbed up the

rocks and sprinted around the back of the bird, to the right side of the craft, going for the pilot. He didn't bother ducking his head like you always see in films. He knew the rotors were so high above him that they wouldn't touch him.

The helipad was deserted, but the pilot sat inside the little Eurocopter. Bishop wasn't sure what model it was, but it had a small body, just big enough for five passengers total. With a white body and navy blue skids, it looked more like something the Tunisian President might fly in.

As he got closer, he could see the pilot was wearing camouflage and not black. *A local,* he thought. *Not a merc.* Bishop whipped open the Pilot's door and punched the man in the side of the head, then dragged his unconscious body out of the bird.

He was pleased to note that even though the helicopter was a civilian craft, it had a rocket pod mounted on the pilot-side skid.

He strapped himself in and gently placed his feet on the rudder pedals. He held the cyclic with his right hand and grabbed the throttle grip on the collective with his left. He had had exactly five helicopter pilot lessons, and none of them had gone very well, so he handled everything delicately.

He began raising the collective and twisted the throttle to increase his engine speed. The helicopter lifted off the ground. He moved the cyclic forward ever so gently and he felt the craft shudder as it transitioned from vertical movement to forward movement. He kept gaining altitude, but he was heading straight into the ruins, where he didn't want to be. He pressed the cyclic to his left and depressed the rudder pedal to make a turn out to sea. He spun almost 180 degrees—more than he wanted, but he was still heading away from the land, which *was* what he wanted. He pressed the cyclic forward more sharply than he needed to, and the nose of the craft dipped as it moved forward. He increased the throttle and the craft sped out to sea.

Now all he had to do was keep the craft level and look out the windows for any sign of Rook. The latter proved to be more difficult.

When he was sure he was further from the shore than Rook could have been tossed, he turned the craft with some difficulty, and started back.

Then he spotted something in the water. He smiled.

"You are seriously hard to kill, Rook."

The water was splashing slightly around him as Rook swam toward shore. He was much farther south than the beachfront adjacent to the ruins, but Bishop supposed it would be hard for Rook to know exactly where to head, that far out to sea.

Bishop brought the helicopter lower with some dithering. He'd learned that nearly everything he did with the controls needed to be done gently. It wasn't like driving a car or a motorcycle. It was like driving a car with hypersensitive power steering through an obstacle course, while sending a text message and eating a messy burger without getting any on you.

He moved toward Rook's position, and hoped the man wouldn't shoot him out of the sky. He came up behind Rook, and lowered the helicopter to where it was just two feet above the surface of the water. Rook turned in the water to watch him. Then Bishop gently wiggled the cyclic side to side, making the helicopter dance left and right across the water—the only thing he could think of to send a signal to the swimming Rook that he wasn't a threat.

Bishop could see Rook mouthing the words "What the fuck?"

The windows were tinted though, and Bishop knew Rook couldn't see who was flying the chopper. He held the bird steady as Rook swam toward him. When Rook grabbed the left side skid, Bishop could feel the helicopter dip slightly toward the water, and he raised the collective just a nudge. Then he waited.

A few seconds later, the passenger side door of the craft opened, and one of Rook's Desert Eagle hand cannons was pointed in the doorway. Then Rook looked in. His face changed in an instant from hostile to confused.

"When the hell did you learn to fly?" he shouted.

Bishop couldn't hear him over the rotors, but just smiled. Rook slammed the door shut and strapped himself in. Then he donned a headset, and flicked a transmitter button on the side of it. Bishop raised the collective, and brought the bird up away from the water, as Rook grabbed the second headset and reached across to seat it on Bishop's head, before flicking it on.

"Thanks for the rescue. I thought I'd break my friggin' back when that Frankendouche chucked me."

"How *did* you survive, man? You we're flying like a missile." Bishop brought the helicopter up and pointed it straight at the giant statue on the shore. When he felt the helicopter was roughly the height of the giant's head, he leveled off.

"You mean other than being the toughest S.O.B. you know? My legs hit first. The armor absorbed a lot of the impact. If I'd landed on my back, I'd be dead. It still felt like being dumped onto concrete from about twenty feet." Rook leaned forward, looking out the window. "You have a plan beyond saving my ass?"

"There's a rocket pod on the skid," Bishop told him. "I was thinking we blow something up."

"My specialty." Rook smiled and rubbed his hands together. "Then we can use the chopper to run Ridley down and grind him into chuck."

Bishop laughed. "*Now* we have a plan."

SIXTY-TWO
North of the Ruins, Carthage

Queen watched in amazement as the helicopter approaching from the sea fired a rocket at the Colossus of Rhodes. The rocket raced from one of the skids on the underside of the helicopter, and left a long thin trail of white smoke as it zipped directly for the statue's immense head.

The detonation was spectacular, spraying rock and metal fragments in all directions. The remaining giant spires on the statue's crown went flipping end over end in all directions, as giant slabs of stone came raining down all around the ruins.

Queen watched the sky, but none of the debris would reach her. The wind was picking up, and clouds were filling the sky out to sea. The breeze cleared the cloud of smoke hanging over the shoulders of the Colossus.

The statue now had no head.

But it was still moving.

She needed to find Ridley. The arrival of the Forgotten had turned the tide of the ground battle initially, but more of the mercenaries had arrived from the north, and this time they were not startled by the wraiths. The end result was a lot of bodies littered around.

She picked her way past savaged corpses of soldiers and bullet-riddled wraith things with shriveled gray skin and mutated faces. Asya was by her side, but the others had hung back, Knight being mostly a liability in a firefight at this point.

She turned to Asya. "You know what? The hell with this. We need that statue stopped. We need Ridley dead, and we're too outnumbered on the ground even with the wraiths helping. I want you to go get a vehicle. I don't care if it's a school bus, a freight truck, a bulldozer or a friggin tank. Make it big. This skulking around is getting us nowhere. I'm gonna try to find Ridley and stab his black heart."

Asya nodded curtly, then ran off through the trees, headed for the main road.

Queen slipped off to her right, deeper into the remains of the ruins. She knew Ridley and Seth were holed up somewhere near the northern end of the ruins, but she didn't know where. She ran through a still-standing archway, and slipped out the other side, hiding behind fragments of stone as she moved. Most of the area was covered in a cloud of dust and fine particulate sand now, but

she could still see the Colossus looming above, as its headless form moved up the shore, toward the northern end of the ruins.

When Queen rounded the next corner, she could finally see Richard Ridley.

He was wearing a black jumpsuit and stood atop a round structure at the far northern end of the ruins. Bullets struck the northern side of the structure, causing Ridley to flinch, but he just ducked and ignored them as he commanded the Colossus. The statue continued its steady approach, heading straight toward him.

"Who the hell is that, then?" she asked herself, wondering who was shooting at Ridley. *Maybe Deep Blue's reinforcements are early?* she thought.

Didn't matter, they were taking the heat off of her for the moment. She moved two more walls closer to the round structure, and took aim with her AK-47.

She fired three shots in rapid succession, the third found Ridley's arm and severed it at the elbow. But there was no blood, and the Colossus was still moving. Then the man's arm began to grow back.

What the hell?

And then she realized. She wasn't looking at Richard Ridley. It was Seth acting as his decoy. Seth wasn't controlling the Colossus at all. He was using the mother tongue to regenerate his body as he was continually peppered with bullets, while somewhere else, hidden, Ridley pulled the strings of the statue. "That's alright," she said.

She changed the selector to fully automatic and blasted away at Seth's head until his body fell off the raised wall. She wanted him dead too. She understood that he might not have actually died, thanks to that damned magic language, but he was out of the game for now.

She made her way toward the water, through the ruins, occasionally coming across a pitched battle between men in camo and mercs in black, or between mercs and wraiths, or some

combination of the three. When she saw camo, she went the other way. She didn't know who the newcomers were, but she suspected they were locals, trying to protect the nearby Presidential Palace. When she came across a straight merc/wraith brawl, she popped as many of the mercs as she could. The wraiths appeared to be losing, perhaps struggling in the sunlight.

Finally reaching the sea side of the ruins, she looked toward the helipad. She saw a tennis court, a few trees, and crouched down by the trees—Richard Ridley. He was looking up as he directed the Colossus toward the group of camo-clad soldiers closing in on Seth's location.

I got you now, you son of a bitch.

She raised her rifle, only to have her position peppered with bullets from the ruins to her left. She dropped to the ground, and rolled in the sand, trying to take cover behind a nearby rock. She could see a literal swarm of black-clad men emerging from the ruins. These weren't mercenaries, they were a private army. Bullets rained down all around her, punching divots in the sand until one of the shots found her calf.

She cried out, as the bullet found its way between her armored plates. Blood oozed warmly over her skin.

She curled into a fetal position and began removing the armor on her calf to get at the wound. When the plates and foam pieces were off, she used her knife to slice open her black BDU pants leg. The wound was mostly into meat in the back of her calf, and she didn't think any bone had been hit.

She shredded the pants with the blade of the knife, and then cut a thin strip, that she shoved into the hole in her calf, pushing it in with her pinky finger and wincing and grinding her teeth the whole time. Finally, she wrapped another strip around the wounded leg and tied it off.

When she looked back up, with her knife in hand, she saw a mercenary standing over her, his rifle pointed at her head. He had a full beard, and the sleeves of his BDU jacket had been rolled up sloppily. One of his arms was covered in dried blood.

She pulled her knife arm back, prepared to throw the blade up at the man. He stepped back and brought the AK-47's stock tightly into his shoulder and aimed.

She threw the knife, and as a buzzing sound filled her ears, the man squeezed the trigger of the rifle, unleashing a torrent of bullets.

SIXTY-THREE
Tennis Court, Carthage Ruins

Richard Ridley watched the nearby exchange with great interest. He had seen his mercenaries flooding out of the ruins, and had then spotted Queen on the beach, closing in.

He smiled when his soldiers arrived and pinned her down. Smiled wider when they shot her leg. She was pinned, and nothing was going to save her.

Then he heard the buzzing noise, out of place in the seaside battle. He looked further down the beach. A man on a motorcycle— a dirt bike really—raced toward Queen. A hooded cape billowed out behind him and concealed his face. He was large and brawny, and dressed all in black. As the man approached the mercenaries that had pinned Queen, he pulled a katana from a sheath on his back, under the cape. Somehow the man maintained his hold on the bike at that speed, with just one hand.

But the most staggering thing about this man was what came in his wake. Wraiths. Hundreds more. They kept pace with the speeding motorcycle, but suddenly broke away and headed for Ridley's army.

Then everything happened at once.

Queen threw her knife at the mercenary above her. The man fired, but missed as the stranger on the dirt bike ripped past, the blade of his sword slicing neatly through the mercenary's neck, toppling his head into the sand a full two yards past Queen's body.

The rider continued straight past...and headed directly for Ridley as a tidal wave of wraiths poured out of the ruins.

Ridley had thought there were a lot of the hideous creatures before, when they had attacked his men, but now there were too many to count, leaping, clawing, climbing and clinging to every surface. They ripped into the mercenaries on the beach, and Ridley saw limbs start to fly. The mercenaries fought back, but it was a hopeless situation. They would be quickly overrun by the wraiths. Ridley could see it clearly. He quickly began chanting a healing mantra.

The man on the dirt bike arrived a moment later, leaping off the speeding vehicle. He landed on his feet in a crouch, with the blade extended horizontal to the ground. The bike continued for a few yards and then crashed spectacularly, flipping end over end until it came to a halt against some trees.

"Waste of a perfectly good bike," Ridley said. He knew who he was facing. The man's long hair and brawn, plus the arrival of the cloaked, gray-skinned creatures was a dead giveaway. Somehow, the damned Greek had survived.

The man stood slowly, facing Ridley. Only the bottom of his beard could be seen under the long hood on his cloak, but his muscled forearms rippled with menace. *Good*, Ridley thought. *I've wanted this for a long time.*

The cloaked man came in fast, swinging the katana. Ridley stepped inside the swing and blocked it with his left arm, still mumbling his chant in the mother tongue. He punched hard with his right hand, the knuckles of his fingers extended to strike his opponent's throat.

The strike was lightning fast, but the man dipped his chin at the last second, and stepped back.

That's right, I can fight.

Ridley was glad he had invested the time in studying the Krav Maga now. The Israeli martial art was based on real street-combat techniques designed to incapacitate or kill the opponent as quickly

as possibly. Ridley had had no need of studying katas and dance moves. He wanted a martial art that could kill quickly and efficiently. Krav Maga was just that. But his opponent was incredibly fast. Possibly trained in the same techniques. This *would* be a fight.

The Greek circled Ridley slowly, keeping his head low, and the sword well out to the side, which seemed like a foolish place for it. Under normal circumstances, a blade was a threat, but while Ridley chanted the mother tongue, he would heal from any wound. *Well, nearly any wound. If he takes my head off like he did to that mercenary...*

Ridley vowed that wouldn't happen. He rushed in, kicking down at his opponent's inner leg and punching out for the face under the hood. He would go for the eyes and the nose. Then the throat again, then the groin with a knee. He envisioned the movements as he was in motion.

But the man spun in a tight circle, bringing the blade in and slicing Ridley across the stomach. He could feel the blade tear into him, slicing through the zipper of the jumpsuit, and chewing its way through all the layers of his skin. But he ignored the pain and followed through with his plan. His fist hit the back of the man's head, just as his mumbling made his skin lining seal up before it spilled his stomach onto the ground. The itch would be maddening if he wasn't so focused on his next moves. His foot came down in between the spinning man's legs. He missed his intended target, but his leg now tangled the other man's. They fell together. On the journey down, he launched his other leg, solidly connecting with the other man's groin from behind.

Before they hit the ground, the man threw an elbow around, continuing his spin. The bone connected squarely with Ridley's nose. He felt his cartilage snap and blood spray out of his face and back through his nasal passage, filling his mouth with a copper tang. As they hit the sandy ground under the tree, the man remained in motion, head-butting Ridley, and then rolling out of reach.

Ridley twisted around and got to his feet in a crouch. His mouth still mumbling, the wound on his stomach was nearly healed. The Greek was on his feet too, his blade lost and now lying within Ridley's grasp. The tenets of Krav Maga suggested he pick up the blade and use it to end the fight quickly, but he had suffered for too long at the hands of the Greek, when he was in those cages.

No, he would prolong the fight and take pleasure out of every strike he landed.

The Greek stood up slowly to his full height. He undid the cloak's button at his neck, and pulled it away. His hair—both on his head and his beard—was long, black and a bit messy.

The hair wasn't exactly how Ridley remembered it, but a more glaring inconsistency held his attention.

This man did not have the Greek's eyes.

"You're not Alexander Diotrephes," Ridley said.

The man shook his head. "You're going to wish I was. He'd go easier on you."

Ridley's eyes widened. He recognized the voice.

Then the two men ran at each other.

SIXTY-FOUR
The Beach, Carthage

Chaos surrounded Queen.

The newcomer raced past on his dirt bike, lopping off her would be murderer's head. Queen struggled to her feet, her leg driving bolts of pain straight through to her brain. But she ignored the agony and rushed at the two mercs nearest to her. She tore their throats out with her hands.

The motocross man was fighting Ridley. Hundreds of wraiths streamed out of the ruins, attacking the newly arrived army. Bullets cut through the air in every direction. A thick choking smoke roiled

through the atmosphere. Wraiths leapt like killer monkeys, bounding over the rubble before landing on the shoulders of men who suddenly shrieked at the hideous touch of the creatures leeching their blood away.

But the wraiths never turned on her. For whatever reason, the creatures were here as allies. And she welcomed the fuck out of them.

Queen picked up a rifle and started shooting down mercs. She stopped firing entirely when she saw Knight approaching from the far side of the ruins along with Peter and Lynn. They were all armed with stolen mercenary rifles. She didn't want to risk hitting them in a crossfire.

"Knight, you read?" she said into her mic.

"I thought it would be just mop up at this point," Knight replied.

"Things didn't go exactly as planned," she said.

Just then the helicopter came ripping by overhead. Rook hung upside down from one of the skids, his legs locked over the bar and a shit-eating grin on his face. In each hand he held a Magnum Desert Eagle .50-caliber pistol. Each pull of the trigger dropped another of the mercenaries, who were too busy worrying about wraiths to think about a danger from above.

"Eat it, Jockey-Stains!" he shouted over their communications channel.

The big guns pounded the air, *boom, boom, boom.*

"Who the hell is flying the chopper?" Queen asked.

Knight replied. "Bishop's been taking lessons."

The helicopter wobbled and then took a long sweeping turn around the stationary Colossus, before wobbling again on the other side of the statue, almost hitting it, spinning around in a circle, and then moving sideways, facing the wrong way.

"I'm gonna guess not *too* many lessons yet," Queen said.

"Not sure he knows how to land," Knight chuckled.

Queen fired off a few more shots at the mercenaries, but it was apparent the wraiths would win this battle now.

Fresh gunfire erupted from the far side of Colossus. The camouflaged soldiers were firing on the wraiths with a heavy machine gun. Suddenly the shots from Rook's handguns sounded quieter. Someone fired an RPG into the mess. Queen dove for the sand of the beach again.

The rocket smashed into one of the last upright walls of the ruins, spaying wraith and mercenary guts alike in different directions.

With a shriek of tires, a huge blue Mercedes truck came roaring over the dirt road behind the camo soldiers, scattering them to the left and the right, as it came barreling through and loudly honking its horn.

It left the road and bounded over the ruins, running over wraith and mercenary alike.

The camo soldiers redirected their fire on the rear of the covered heavy truck, but their small arms fire did little to deter it. *Even if they could get the .50 cal on it, they're not going to stop her now.*

Asya looked small through the windshield of the massive truck, as it bounced high over the rocky rubble, more in the process of crashing than driving over things. The truck had arrived so suddenly that it looked out of control, but Queen knew exactly what the feisty little Russian was planning. *Smart Girl. She's going to ram it.*

Just before the blue truck crashed into the leg of the Colossus, Asya threw herself out of the driver's side door. The truck, without its driver, swerved sharply to the side and looked like it would miss. But then the right front wheel caught on a solid piece of rubble and the back side of the truck lifted into the air.

The truck flipped and smashed into the lower calf of the statue's leg. The truck ripped the lower leg of the statue clean off, and then tumbled further into the ruins, flipping and rolling.

Unbalanced, the Colossus toppled over, slowly falling toward where Ridley and the thickly bearded man were still fighting.

Gunfire forced Queen to hobble back down the beach, trying to get away from the camo-soldiers and the Colossus's impact zone.

Just then the helicopter came screaming overhead, Rook now clinging to the skid with one arm and bleeding from the other. The bird was streaming smoke, and it looked like Bishop was going to crash into the sea. As soon as the helicopter was over the water, Rook let go of his skid and dropped about thirty feet, sending up a big splash. At less than twenty feet over the surface of the water, Bishop banked the craft hard to the left and dove out the right side door, the spinning blades missing his ankles by what looked like inches. The helicopter crashed into the water just as a rocket streamed in and slammed into the chopper, sending parts of the white metal skin high into the sky, amid a gurgling roiling ball of orange flame and black smoke.

Queen looked up at the falling Colossus, and back to the combatants locked in a furious fist-fight under the trees near the tennis court. Then she recognized the stranger's fighting style and skidded to a stop.

"It can't be," she said.

The man seemed to sense her attention. He turned toward her for a moment. He was far away, but beyond the beard and the hair, she knew she was looking at Jack Sigler, back from the dead and commanding an army of wraiths.

Then the mighty headless Colossus slammed into the ground, flattening him and Ridley, and sending up a plume of sand and dust so thick that Queen couldn't see anymore. The thunder from the impact nearly ruptured her eardrums, and the shockwave knocked her down onto her back.

"Queen, are you alright?" Knight was asking in hear ear.

Queen closed her eyes. She could still see his face, but it wasn't possible. Not only had Asya seen him die, but he didn't just grow his hair and beard that long overnight. She shook her head. "I'm just going to lie here for a while. I need to bleed for a bit."

SIXTY-FIVE
Ruins of Carthage

Queen lay in the sand, listening to the wraiths tear the last of the mercenaries apart to her left in the ruins. The Tunisian forces had stopped firing and were in full retreat. She couldn't see any of them on the fringes of the battle anymore. She suspected she knew the reason for that.

"Deep Blue," she coughed a few times to clear her throat. "You read me?"

"Go ahead, Queen."

"You behind the withdrawal of the Tunisian forces?" she asked.

"Yes, but there will be some big hell to pay later. The President is shitting bricks, and the bricks are building pyramids. I still don't have eyes on you. Give me a sit-rep."

"Sure, why not? I'm just relaxing on the beach."

"Not exactly the time for sarcasm," Deep Blue said.

"Wasn't kidding. I am actually lying on the beach. Leg is shot to hell. What else? Ridley turned the Colossus of Rhodes into a golem. It kicked our asses, then fell over. Pawn did that. Crashed a truck into the golem's leg. She might be dead. Bishop and Rook crashed into the sea in a helicopter that blew up. They might be dead. There's an army of Alexander's wraiths killing the last of the mercenary forces. I think Ridley got squashed, but I can't confirm it. Seth took a few rounds to the head, but was doing his healing thing, so who knows? I haven't heard back from Knight—he's got some broken ribs."

"My God. Anything else I should know?"

"I saw King."

"His body?"

"Going toe-to-toe with Ridley before the Colossus dropped on top of them."

Just then a single shot rang out loudly, cutting through the silence that followed the battle. The sound sent a jolt through her body. She sat up quickly.

"Be right back, Blue."

"Wait! Queen—" she switched channels.

"Knight?" she asked into her microphone.

She heard another single shot. And then another.

"It's me," he said in her ear. "Seth is alive. About a hundred yards out from me. I keep shooting him, but he keeps getting back up. If I can't take off his jaw, I'm not sure I can keep him down while he's whispering that mother tongue crap." Queen heard another single shot.

"Try to keep him incapacitated. Where are you?"

"Northwest corner of the ruins. Better hurry. I'm running out of bullets and I'm not going anywhere fast."

She heard another shot echo through the ruins, as the smoke and dust started to clear. The wind was picking up fast now. The sun slid behind a wall of dark storm clouds coming in from the water. She struggled back to her feet and saw wraiths zipping into the ruins and away from the shore—there were no more mercenaries standing. The field in front of the shattered bits of history was strewn with bodies and parts of bodies—more parts than full corpses. She staggered over the first few arms and legs she saw, not wanting to step on the dead. But there were too many of them. She gave up and just started walking on whatever was underfoot, heading toward the ruins, armed only with her knife. She could bend down and pick up any number of rifles, but it seemed like too much work. Right now she was having trouble walking. The pain shooting up her leg with each step on her damaged calf was excruciating. But there were priorities. She needed to get to Knight and help him keep Seth down. She wanted no loose ends this time.

She tried to reach Rook and Bishop to no avail. It was down to her. So she fought against the pain in her leg and clutched the

knife tightly in her hand. If Seth was still down when she got there, she'd cut his head off. That would keep the little pecker from regenerating.

As she stumbled past a three foot high wall of stone, she saw someone coming toward her through the dust. She crouched, ready to deal death if whoever was coming was another hostile.

Once she got to the ground though, she realized she wouldn't be getting back up. She was done. Her leg felt like it was on fire, and she was having trouble staying awake.

"Queen, are you alright?" It was Peter. He knelt in front of her. Lynn stood behind him, helping Asya stand. Asya had blood streaming down her face. Lynn looked pretty banged up too.

Queen reached out the knife to Peter. "Knight. Northwest ruins. Needs help now." Another shot rang out. "Go."

Peter didn't question. He just took the knife and started running through the ruins.

Lynn brought Asya limping over and gently lowered her to the ground next to Queen. Then Lynn sat down next to them, breathing hard.

The three women didn't say a word to each other. They just watched as the dust parted and settled, blown by the increasingly wild winds of the storm. The view to the beach cleared, revealing two figures emerging from the water. Bishop and Rook. They headed up the beach toward Queen's position. Bishop looked fine besides a small limp. He was barefoot, and bare-chested, wearing only his black BDU trousers. Rook's arm was coated in fresh blood. He was wearing only leg armor, his chest now bare also, his shirt tied over his shoulder as a makeshift tourniquet.

They walked up to the women, and sat wordlessly on the ground next to the ladies.

The shooting stopped.

Queen toggled her com. "Knight?"

"Seth is down. Won't be getting back up. Peter and I are on our way to you."

"Knight okay?" Rook asked her.

"He'll live. They'll be here in a minute. Nice swim?"

"Brisk," Bishop said.

They lapsed into silence, all of them just breathing hard.

She turned at the sound of a grunt coming from the Colossus, which was hidden by slowly settling dust. There was a *thunk*, but then much closer, the sound of footsteps. From behind. Queen turned to see Peter helping Knight walk. Peter was covered in blood.

"It's not mine," he said to Lynn, before she could ask.

He plopped onto the sandy ground next to his wife.

Knight leaned down, and inhaled sharply. Then he lowered himself to the ground with the group.

"Seth?" Queen asked him.

"Papa Sigler dropped a big rock on his head," Knight said.

Queen looked at the blood covering King's father.

He glanced down at himself. "It was more of a column. And it rolled, more than fell."

Queen squinted at the red covering Peter. "He *bled*?"

Knight nodded. "Looks like Ridley got one of them right, or maybe it was the healing mantra he was using over and over. But at the end, when he saw the blood, he looked just as surprised as us. Hate to say it, but he died with a smile on his face."

While the others watched the storm coming in, Queen watched as the dust cloud still concealing the Colossus slowly melted away. She wondered how she was going to tell them she'd seen King again, and then considered not telling them at all. He'd suffered the same fate as Ridley. Why make them relive his passing?

A distant grunt followed by a wet *slap* tickled her ear.

She looked to Rook. He heard it too.

"What is that?" he asked. "Survivor?"

The clouds finally reached them and the bottom suddenly fell out of the sky. The rain came down in huge cold globules. Queen never would have guessed that the rain could be so cold with the

temperature so warm. They were quickly soaked, but no one made a move to find shelter from the torrential downpour. None of them had the strength.

Queen heard the clapping noise again, and looked back to the Colossus. The rain dissipated the last of the dust cloud. She could see the immense headless statue on the ground.

Standing on its chest, still beating the shit out of each other, were Ridley and the man she thought might be King.

"Oh, wow," she said. She struggled to her feet. The others all turned to see what she was talking about.

Ridley head-butted his opponent, but the man recovered quickly, pulling back and then launching into a spinning kick that connected with Ridley's head. Ridley rolled with the impact, bringing the back of his fist into the other man's throat. Instead of recoiling from the blow, the man pulled in tighter, jabbing a thumb into Ridley's left eye socket.

Ridley grunted and pulled his head back, the thumb sliding out in a bloody mess. The rain spraying from the sky washed the blood down his face. Then the eye was back, whole again. His mouth never stopped moving, mumbling all the while he was in motion.

The two combatants flowed around each other in a ballet of violence. Elbows flew, kicks snapped, punches twisted through the air. For each strike made by either man, another rapidly followed by his opponent. Both men were covered in blood that washed down their bodies in the rainwater. Neither man slowed. Ridley reached in and gouged out the flesh of his opponent's throat. The man didn't pause. Barely noticed. He threw an uppercut into Ridley's solar plexus, then hooked his fingers into Ridley's nose, ripping the skin.

Ridley's face was already healing, and the torn nostrils didn't slow him. He used a forearm smash to hit his opponent in the face, but the man took the strike and bought up a knee, slamming it into Ridley's kidney. As he turned, Queen saw the man's throat looked fine.

The grunting and *thunking* noises of the two opponents beating on each other was the only sound besides the falling rain.

"Should we stop them?" Lynn asked softly.

"How?" Rook said.

Just then the dark-haired man caught Ridley's forearm and twisted while thrusting with an open palm strike. The group heard Ridley's bone break, and saw the jagged end of a shattered Ulna bone rip through the flesh in a bloody spurt. Ridley leapt up, driving a knee into his opponent's chin. The bone jerked sideways with a loud pop, as the man's jaw broke. And then unbroke. He retaliated with a double punch, straight ahead, hitting Ridley's momentarily unprotected throat, as the man landed from his kick. Ridley staggered back a step, before launching a deadly kick at his opponent's chest. The man slipped backward and started to spin, but he lost his footing. The chest of the statue on which they stood had become slick with blood and rain. His foot went out behind him, as he face planted into the statue, then he flipped backward and rolled off the other side of the Colossus.

Ridley raised his arms and started chanting, his voice rumbling over the rain. At his feet, the giant statue's chest bubbled and boiled up. The surface broke, spewing rocks and pebbles like a miniature volcano. The almost liquid flow of rubble carried a small wooden chest up and out of the torso of the statue, and deposited it at Ridley's feet. The box was a dark wood with stripes of glinting metal.

Ridley bent and picked up the box. He held it reverently. Then he lifted it up to the sky, as if it were an offering, and he began chanting again.

This time, the Colossus stirred. It tried to sit up, but without a head or a leg, and missing half an arm, it was unable. Ridley looked across the ruins, and began chanting again.

Queen heard rumbling from the stone behind her in the ruins.

Then she heard a voice that left no room for doubt. "Ridley! Put the box down. I'm not done with you yet!"

The man she knew was King climbed back up onto the chest of the Colossus from where he had fallen. He was once again holding the sword.

Ridley turned to King and smiled.

"Nor am I done with you."

He held the box in front of him and began to open it.

Queen willed King to attack, to finish the fight. She couldn't explain how he was alive or why he looked so different, but this *was* King, and she knew what he could do—and that he'd been holding back.

But instead, he just stood there.

Waiting.

SIXTY-SIX
Ruins of Carthage

Ridley didn't mess around with trying to figure out the latching mechanism. He used the mother tongue to undo the lock and opened the fabled Chest of Adoon.

The chest hissed as its airtight seal was broken and the lid came up. Accompanying the hiss was a loud *ping* as a curved piece of metal spun into the air. Ridley followed the spinning metal with his eyes and then looked down. His forehead furrowed.

Then his face, his hands and the chest were erased in a concussive explosion.

Ridley's headless torso crumpled to the Colossus's chest. Without his genetic ability to regenerate and no face with which to utter the language of God, he wouldn't be coming back. Ever.

King stepped up next to the corpse, and he saw the mangled head lying nearby. He reached down the front of his shirt to a leather band he wore as a necklace. He had worn it around his neck for so long, that most days he forgot it was there. Some years

he had worn it on a gold chain, and at other times, he had worn it on a string, but the pendant on the necklace was always the same. A reminder of things to come. Of this very moment.

The safety pin for the grenade he had planted in the box, back in 799 BC. He had taken care of and polished the pin for centuries, and when the metal was starting to give way from age, he had had it coated in silver, and years later in stainless steel. He held it up now on the end of the brown leather cord, and dangled it over his enemy's body. He wasn't sure the grenade would work after all these years in Alexander's airtight box, but if it hadn't, he had been prepared to use the sword.

He dropped the pin, the reminder having served its purpose.

As the rain pelted the back of his head, he turned and saw the group of people staring at him.

Queen was bleeding from a tourniquet-covered leg. Rook was favoring a wrapped shoulder. Bishop looked exhausted. Knight was coated in blood and clutching his chest with one arm. *Ribs*, King thought. Asya had cuts on her head and was holding a cloth to the side of her face. His parents were there too. They both looked like they had been dragged through an abattoir, but they appeared mostly unharmed. Besides being wet from the rain, every one of them had one thing in common.

They all stood with their mouths hanging open in absolute shock, staring at him.

He slid down the side of the Colossus, and dropped to the ground below. It was a thirty foot drop, but he took it with ease, absorbing the shock with bent legs. Feeling no lingering pain from his battle, he stepped over to his friends and family.

"Sorry I was late," he said, but the joke was lost as his voice became shaky. He had done and seen things few people would believe. He'd witnessed the rise and fall of nations and empires, and he had played a hand in some of it. He had watched civilizations grow, had seen humanity rise from the ashes again and again. But none of that compared to this moment.

He had watched his team over the years. Watched his naïve younger self, too. On several occasions, it took all of his strength to not get involved. To let things play out as they had. But he'd managed to never once interfere in their lives. Because of that, this was the first time in over 2800 years that he had stood, face-to-face with these people. And it nearly broke him.

His mother saw the pain in his eyes first, and whether or not she understood it, she threw her arms around him, not just hugging him but keeping him on his feet. Peter was there next, then Asya and the others. King shook with sobs, the mental walls that had kept him strong through millennia crashing down.

As King calmed and the group began separating, Rook whispered, "King..."

King looked up at his old friend.

"That was the coolest friggin' thing I have ever seen in my life."

King laughed and wiped the tears from his eyes. "There has never been another man like you, Rook."

"I don't know about never," Rook said.

King grinned. "Pretty sure."

Asya stepped up to King. "I saw you die when Alexander's machine exploded."

King shook his head. "I've died many times, but that wasn't one of them."

Lynn placed her hand against the side of his beard. She looked into his eyes. She was seeing things only a mother could. "You've been gone a long time."

He nodded. "It's a long story."

"We have time," Peter said.

"It's a very long story." King smiled and pointed to the sky where the VTOL Crescent II descended toward them. "And I would really like to see my daughter and the woman I'm going to marry."

EPILOGUE
Nazca, Peru

A solitary set of feet pounded the dry soil, barely filling the air with the sound of a soldier on the march. But this man was not a simple soldier. Not any longer. Now he was something much, much more.

He marched without cease, without pause for food, water or rest, across the arid, lifeless Nazca plains. When the man finally stopped in the shade of a tall hill, he turned and cast a cool gaze back the way he had come.

His sweat-dampened, long dark hair clung to his forehead, but the man paid it no heed. Nor did he wipe away the beads of sweat rolling into his eyes. The woven sack he carried hung lifeless at his side, so still and bland that anyone watching the man might not even see it. And the contents might as well be air. There was no one left who would mourn the object's passing.

He dropped the shovel he carried down onto the ground, and then he tossed the sack down. Upon striking the hot, dry earth, the sack rolled and came to a lazy stop. A cloud of dry dust rose and then clung to the fabric as though the desert were already trying to claim it.

King looked at his single piece of baggage, which contained the shattered head of Richard Ridley. They'd taken it with them

from Carthage, just in case. But it never regenerated and showed normal signs of decay. Deep Blue had wanted to incinerate the remains, but King insisted on a burial.

This burial.

It was...cathartic.

As he stood there, shovel in hand, he thought back on the past month. His reunion with Sara had shaken him. All of his long forgotten memories—the way her eyes looked in the sun, the smell of her hair, her lopsided smile, and so many other details he'd taken for granted—came back in a rush. She'd been confused by his tears and weak legs, but a quick explanation coupled with his long hair and beard had helped her to quickly understand. She was shocked and amazed that he had waited so long for her...and he *had* waited. 2,812 years of celibacy. The only descendants of Jack Sigler roaming the world would be the ones he created with her.

Seeing Fiona was harder. He'd fallen to his knees in the parking lot of her school. Sensing his heartbreak, she'd run to him and hugged him tight. She didn't ask about the beard or the hair, she'd simply said, "It finally happened."

Apparently, she'd seen her rescuer in Siletz and had always known it was King...but a different King, the one with long hair and a beard. She handled the explanation better than everyone else and made him promise to regale her with stories from history. She also made him take her out of the boarding school. He agreed before she finished asking, vowing to spend as much time with her and Sara as humanly possible.

Once everyone had been gathered at the base in New Hampshire, he'd told his friends and family an abbreviated version of his story, and they had been dumbfounded by the magnitude of it. King explained how he had placed the grenade in the 'Chest of Adoon' instead of leaving it empty, and how Alexander had told him that he eventually arranged for the relocation of the Colossus of Rhodes to Tunisia, where he had once hoped to build a small fortress. The fortress never

happened. He'd treated the statue with a special solution to prevent corrosion and left it along the shore, underwater, where only he would be able to retrieve it. Later, he hid the Chest of Adoon inside the chest of the Colossus. He thought it was clever. But only King had known the joke, and the Chest was never recovered, or opened, again. Until Ridley got it.

King remained in New Hampshire for a month, reuniting with his family and watching over his mending friends while the team's scientists studied Ridley's remains and ensured he was, without a doubt, not coming back. Not that anyone was going anywhere. The geopolitical backlash to the events in Carthage, which no one could find a reasonable explanation for, threatened to expose them. So they stayed silent. Waited for the world's hackles to lower. And finally, Domenick Boucher, head of the CIA and one of the few people who knew Endgame existed, gave them the all-clear. Tensions had eased and a terrorist group was blamed for simultaneously releasing a hallucinogenic gas and detonating several bombs in Tunisia. The governments of several nations knew that was not the truth, but not one of them wanted to tell the world that the 300-foot tall Colossus of Rhodes had come to life and attacked the city. Bodies were disposed of. Videos were destroyed. Rumors were started and evidence was planted.

As soon as the all-clear had been given, King had taken Ridley's remains and jetted to Nazca, Peru—where it all began—courtesy of *Crescent II*. The flight took just hours, and no one would be the wiser.

He stared down at the sack again, then looked at his watch. *Crescent II* was a stealth vehicle, but the Nazca plains sported more airborne tourists than anywhere else in the world. It was the only way to really see the giant geoglyphs carved into the desert by the ancient Nazcans and the occasional Greek demigod. He had an hour and a half before the first scheduled flight passed overhead.

He lifted the shovel and set to work, digging out the entrance to the cave his friend George Pierce had discovered under the

massive stone, years ago. The memory was dim for King, but he knew it had happened for George only a few years back.

When the entrance to the cave, where King himself had once been trapped, was clear, he unceremoniously chucked the head into the cave, watching as it rolled along in its burlap.

He started filling in the entrance. Before the digging was done, he tossed the shovel itself into the tunnel and finished the work by hand. When he was done, he pulled a small hammer and a chisel from his belt and went to work on the side of the hot stone.

The symbol was simple, but he wanted it to be large. Large enough to be seen by anyone else that should come along in the next several hundred years. He carved it deep into the side of the stone, then he walked to the other side of the rock where Pierce had discovered the other carving, left centuries ago, by Alexander. The letters were in ancient Greek and the transcription read:

"Here is buried the beast most foul... Fire and sword did sever the head immortal, forever entombed beneath sand and stone. Be warned all who read these words. Heed the screaming guards within and keep dry the earth lest you wake the monster and taste its mighty vengeance."

King went to work with the chisel again, destroying Alexander's message, which had withstood the ravages of time thanks to the lack of weather on the plains. When the stone was completely smooth, he walked back to his side of the stone, and looked at the symbol he had carved, five feet tall.

He had never used the symbol before, but since Alexander—the first pillar in the Herculean Society's insignia—was now gone from the Earth for good, it seemed fitting to start a new legacy. The Herculean Society and its wraith protectors served King now, and he wanted the new symbol to be familiar to them, but to reflect a change in the guard. It was simple and would be easily recognizable to speakers of all languages around the world and through the ages. Over the following

years, leaders and governments would come to know the symbol, and what it meant.

Danger.

Stay away.

You don't want any part of this.

They would learn to trust the symbol, and that ignoring its warning led to peril. The Herculean Society symbol had worked in the same way over the ages. It wasn't known to all countries throughout history. Its meaning was lost and found as power shifted between nations and continents. Not every president understood it as a warning, including Tom Duncan, but they usually learned, often the hard way. Where the Herculean Society symbol was found, strange and deadly danger awaited. And whatever it was, someone else was handling it. Someone who knew better.

The symbol was the reason the Bermuda Triangle was still largely unexplored and unexplained. It was the reason the Russians still kept people away from Krasnoyarsk Krai, where the Tunguska comet had detonated. It was the reason no one would ever know what really happened to Roanoke.

King stepped back and looked at his new symbol. It was similar enough to the original that those who recognized the Herculean Society symbol might recognize the authority of the new.

It was crude, but it would do.

He turned and started walking away from the giant boulder that covered the cave. There was just one more thing to do.

He had lived an incredibly long life, impervious to harm. He almost couldn't remember what it had been like to be afraid of death or to know that an injury could be permanent. In a way, he couldn't remember what it felt like to be human.

King reached into the small pouch on his belt and removed an auto injector. It was similar to the serum the team had used on the Ridleys to rob them of their Hydra-induced regenerative abilities. But King's version of the serum had started off as a potion Alexander had left for him in a Herculean Society base in Greenland. King had ordered some of his scientists working for the Society to analyze it and make small adjustments to it. If he injected it into himself, it would once again alter his DNA. It would remove the regenerative abilities Alexander had granted him by slipping herbs into his tea all those years ago. It would also remove his immortality.

He had lived a long, long time. He was ready to settle down with his family—his fiancée and his adopted daughter. He was ready to live a normal lifespan, and when the time came, he was ready to die.

He placed the injector against his skin, the metal warm from the hot sun beating down on him for the last several hours. He looked at the metal around the glass vial as it glinted in the sun. Over 2800 years. He wondered if he would still have the memories and experiences of those years, once his genetic code was rewritten, or whether, like his healing abilities, all that would fade as well.

He activated the high-pressure injector, and then it snapped loudly, driving the serum into his body. He expected to feel something, even though his techs had told him he would not.

All he felt was the slight sting on his arm from where the needle had punctured his skin. He removed the injector and looked at his arm. The needle hole oozed a tiny drop of blood. He wiped it away with his finger, and noted that the puncture wound had not closed up instantly as it would have in the past.

Easy come, easy go.

King looked up at the sky. It would be late afternoon in New Hampshire now. He pulled out a black satellite phone and called home. It took some rings and digital clicks, but the call went through.

"It's done," he said, when Deep Blue answered. "I am officially younger than you again."

"Not really," Deep Blue said.

"You know what I mean," King replied.

Deep Blue chuckled. "Then you won't mind if I start bossing you around again?"

King smiled. A mission was coming. "Where do you want me?"

"Home," Deep Blue said. "Just come home."

"Copy that," King said. "I'll be there for supper."

As he hung up the phone, a high pitched whistle turned him around.

Rook stood at the top of the hill, lowering his hands. Beside him stood Queen, Bishop and Knight. And they weren't alone. George Pierce, Sara, Fiona, Asya and his parents had all made the trip with him. A trip to say goodbye to the past and to welcome home their future.

Rook, however, had a few more words to say. He cupped his hands to his mouth and shouted down the hill, "That is the shittiest 'K' I have ever seen!"

King laughed and started up the hill as Fiona raced down to meet him.

ABOUT THE AUTHORS

JEREMY ROBINSON is the bestselling author of thirty novels and novellas including ISLAND 731, SECONDWORLD, and the Jack Sigler series including PULSE, INSTINCT, THRESHOLD and RAGNAROK. Robinson is also known as the #1 Amazon.com horror writer, Jeremy Bishop, author of THE SENTINEL and the controversial novel, TORMENT. His novels have been translated into eleven languages. He lives in New Hampshire with his wife and three children.

Visit him online at: www.jeremyrobinsononline.com

KANE GILMOUR has visited or lived in over 40 countries around the world. A former rock climber and mountain biker, he now kayaks, and still explores the furthest reaches of the world, as time permits. He is the author of RESURRECT and THE CRYPT OF DRACULA, and the co-author of the bestselling Jack Sigler thriller, RAGNAROK. He lives in the wilds of central Vermont with his wife, son, and daughter, where he's working on his next novel and planning his next international excursion.

Visit him online at: www.kanegilmour.com

CPSIA information can be obtained at www.ICGtesting.com
Printed in the USA
LVOW08s1730191113

361953LV00007B/1049/P

OMEGA

dimensions. Rook's Russian ally, Asya Machtchenko, turned out to be King's sibling—the result of his parents' double lives in the mother country. Asya claimed their parents had been abducted, and she asked the team to help find them.

At the end of the fight in Norway, when the team returned to New Hampshire, a laptop containing the designs for the dimensional technology was mysteriously lifted from their headquarters, and a note was left behind explaining that Alexander needed the designs and that he was holding King's parents hostage. King was warned to stay out of the way, but instead, he vowed to take the fight directly to the legendary immortal—and if necessary, to the death.

returned, murdering the last living speakers of the world's most ancient languages and deciphering the *mother tongue*—an ancient protolanguage, otherwise known as "the language of God," which bestowed its user the ability to animate inanimate objects. With help from Alexander, Chess Team kept Fiona safe and defeated Ridley once again. But when the smoke had cleared, King's parents were missing and presumed on the run back to Russia. Ridley was presumed dead, but had, in fact, become the prisoner of a man who had no qualms about torture.

Attempting to take some time off, King went repeatedly toe-to-toe and wits-to-wits with a criminal mastermind named Graham Brown, aka *Brainstorm*, and in their final battle, he stopped a black hole forming in the Louvre from destroying all of Paris. He fought side-by-side, once again, with Alexander. Unseen by King, Alexander pocketed a small round piece of rubble in the aftermath.

Meanwhile, in the Ukraine, Zelda Baker, callsign: Queen, discovered an old Manifold facility and faced off against Richard Ridley's brother, Darius Ridley. In Norway, Stan Tremblay, callsign: Rook, took some unauthorized time off that led to him discovering a former Nazi laboratory. Erik Somers, callsign: Bishop, was horribly experimented upon by Ridley in their initial clash. Although cured, he still bears the emotional scars. Shin-dae Jung, callsign: Knight, faced the horror of the resurrected Hydra alone in the team's first fight against Ridley. Hoping for some of his own down-time, he wound up facing another genetic monstrosity in an abandoned city in China. Also in the aftermath of the *mother-tongue* skirmish with Ridley, Tom Duncan stepped down from the US presidency to assume his Chess Team duties as callsign: Deep Blue, full time, running the team from a captured Manifold facility in New Hampshire, and rechristening the expanded Chess Team organization as *Endgame*.

Most recently, the team faced a world-wide threat of annihilation that resulted in a frantic battle in Norway and the capture of otherworldly technology capable of opening portals to different

THE STORY SO FAR

Richard Ridley was a megalomaniac with twin dreams: immortality and ultimate power. His multi-billion dollar genetics company, *Manifold*, was poised to give him both, when he discovered the historic resting place of the Lernaean Hydra—on the Nazca plains of Peru. Combining Hydra DNA with humans, Ridley hoped to create invincible regenerating soldiers and to gain his much-coveted eternity.

A crack squad of Delta operators, known as Chess Team— King, Queen, Bishop, Rook and Knight—orchestrated by the US President, defeated Ridley, his security forces and the unintentionally resurrected Hydra in a desperate battle. Along the way, the team had help from a mysterious man named Alexander Diotrephes—the legendary *Hercules*, alive, well and immortal. But in the chaos of the battle, Richard Ridley escaped.

A year later, nearly the entire population of the Siletz reservation in Oregon was exterminated. The only survivor, 13-year old Fiona Lane, the last living speaker of her native language, ended up in the custody of Jack Sigler, callsign: King, field leader of Chess Team.

The following year, King's parents unexpectedly revealed they had led a secret life as former Russian spies. Then Richard Ridley

For all the Jack Sigler fans who find us on Facebook. Thanks for the never ending encouragement, camaraderie and excitement. You know who you are.

OMEGA

A Jack Sigler Thriller

JEREMY ROBINSON

WITH KANE GILMOUR

BREAKNECK MEDIA

ALSO BY JEREMY ROBINSON

The Jack Sigler Novels

Prime
Pulse
Instinct
Threshold
Ragnarok
Omega

The Chess Team Novellas
(Chesspocalypse Series)

Callsign: King – Book 1
Callsign: Queen – Book 1
Callsign: Rook – Book 1
Callsign: King – Book 2
Callsign: Bishop – Book 1
Callsign: Knight – Book 1
Callsign: Deep Blue – Book 1
Callsign: King – Book 3

The Origins Editions
(First five novels)

The Didymus Contingency
Raising The Past
Beneath

Antarktos Rising
Kronos

Standalone Novels

SecondWorld
Project Nemesis
Island 731
I Am Cowboy

The Last Hunter
(Antarktos Saga Series)

The Last Hunter – Descent
The Last Hunter – Pursuit
The Last Hunter – Ascent
The Last Hunter – Lament
The Last Hunter – Onslaught

Writing as Jeremy Bishop

Torment
The Sentinel
The Raven

ALSO BY KANE GILMOUR

The Jason Quinn Series

Resurrect
Frozen

Horror & Fantasy Novels

The Crypt of Dracula
Monster Kingdom

Jeremy Robinson's Jack Sigler Novels

Callsign: Deep Blue
Ragnarok
Omega

Co-Edited Anthology

Warbirds of Mars: Stories of the Fight!

INSTINCT

PULSE

"Robinson blends myth, science and terminal velocity action like no one else."
— Scott Sigler, NY Times Bestselling author of NOCTURNAL

"Just when you think that 21st-century authors have come up with every possible way of destroying the world, along comes Jeremy Robinson."
— New Hampshire Magazine

PRAISE FOR THE JACK SIGLER THRILLERS

THRESHOLD

"Threshold elevates Robinson to the highest tier of over-the-top action authors and it delivers beyond the expectations even of his fans. The next Chess Team adventure cannot come fast enough."
— Booklist - Starred Review

"Jeremy Robinson's Threshold is one hell of a thriller, wildly imaginative and diabolical, which combines ancient legends and modern science into a non-stop action ride that will keep you turning the pages until the wee hours."
— Douglas Preston, NY Times bestselling author of IMPACT

"With Threshold Jeremy Robinson goes pedal to the metal into very dark territory. Fast-paced, action-packed and wonderfully creepy! Highly recommended!"
— Jonathan Maberry, NY Times bestselling author of TOOTH & NAIL

"With his new entry in the Jack Sigler series, Jeremy Robinson plants his feet firmly on territory blazed by David Morrell and James Rollins. The perfect blend of mysticism and monsters, both human and otherwise, make Threshold as groundbreaking as it is riveting."
— Jon Land, NY Times bestselling author of THE TENTH CIRCLE

"Jeremy Robinson is the next James Rollins."
— Chris Kuzneski, NY Times bestselling author of THE DEATH RELIC

"Jeremy Robinson's Threshold sets a blistering pace from the very first page and never lets up. For readers seeking a fun rip-roaring adventure, look no further."
— Boyd Morrison, bestselling author of THE LOCH NESS LEGACY

PRAISE FOR ISLAND 731

"Robinson (Secondworld) puts his distinctive mark on Michael Crichton territory with this terrifying present-day riff on The Island of Dr. Moreau. Action and scientific explanation are appropriately proportioned, making this one of the best Jurassic Park successors."
— Publisher's Weekly - Starred Review

"Take a traditional haunted-house tale and throw in a little Island of Dr. Moreau and a touch of Clash of the Titans, and you wind up with this scary and grotesque novel. Robinson, a skilled blender of the thriller and horror genres, has another winner on his hands."
— Booklist

"[Island 731's] premise is reminiscent of H.G. Wells' The Island of Dr. Moreau, but the author adds a World War II back story...vivisection, genetic engineering, Black Ops, animal husbandry and mayhem. This is the stuff that comic books, video games and successful genre franchises are made of."
— Kirkus Reviews

"A book full of adventure and suspense that shows 'science' in a whole new horrific light. This is one creepy tale that will keep you up all night! And it is so well written you will think twice before taking a vacation to any so-called 'Island Paradise!'"
— Suspense Magazine

PRAISE FOR SECONDWORLD

"A brisk thriller with neatly timed action sequences, snappy dialogue and the ultimate sympathetic figure in a badly burned little girl with a fighting spirit... The Nazis are determined to have the last gruesome laugh in this efficient doomsday thriller."
— Kirkus Reviews

"Relentless pacing and numerous plot twists drive this compelling standalone from Robinson... Thriller fans and apocalyptic fiction aficionados alike will find this audaciously plotted novel enormously satisfying."
— Publisher's Weekly

"A harrowing, edge of your seat thriller told by a master storyteller, Jeremy Robinson's Secondworld is an amazing, globetrotting tale that will truly leave you breathless."
— Richard Doestch, bestselling author of THE THIEVES OF LEGEND

My appreciation goes also to each person whose support for this book renews a vision of art that may, in the words of Gerard Manley Hopkins, "Give beauty back, beauty, beauty, beauty, back to God, beauty's self and beauty's giver," art that renews our souls and our commitment to the tasks that call us.

One

the language of our tribe

Invocation

*L*et us try what it is to be true to gravity,
to grace, to the given, faithful to our own voices,

to lines making the map of our furrowed tongue.
Turned toward the root of a single word, refusing

solemnity and slogans, let us honor what hides
and does not come easy to speech. The pebbles

we hold in our mouths help us to practise song,
and we sing to the sea. May the things of this world

be preserved to us, their beautiful secret
vocabularies. We are dreaming it over and new,

the language of our tribe, music we hear
we can only acknowledge. May the naming powers

be granted. Our words are feathers that fly
on our breath. Let them go in a holy direction.

Sometimes God

hurries through a gap in granite,
shows in a flower's shining. Once
I felt a light touch on my shoulder
as I stirred oatmeal for breakfast.

In the most unlikely places,
always in motion,
about to disappear, gone
when I turn to see.

The cleft rock I hide in,
near as my yard
or these neighborhood sidewalks,
opens and is ordinary.

When the hand
is removed from my face, other faces
scatter and gather
the vanishing body of God.

Directions

Psalm 3

*T*hese days
we've learned
that God is inward
and nowhere,
cannot be assigned
a designated space,
has no dimension we can name,
is hard to find.

After many deaths
and calling out names,
love and the tears running,
I've looked and looked for Him
within and out,
to ground (of being?),
through a maze of words
page after page.

Old ways last long
and looking up was all
the final pull,
that pause where something
moves.

Is this the way the psalmist means
"My glory and the lifter of my head"?

Nothing So Wise

There is nothing so wise as a circle.
Rainer Maria Rilke

*T*he arc of an egg
bends hands
to shape prayer,

the shell
unbroken,
the heavy yolk
floating.

Our fingers
curving always
inward, become a cup,
an open bowl.

Prayer is
circumference
we may not
reach around,

space for all we cannot hold,
the rim of Love toward which we lean.

The Fish

*We have toiled all night
and taken nothing. . . .*

Bone weary, with aching arms and eyes
we row to shore at dawn. Our bait
is gone, the puddles at our feet
dry slowly from the edges.
We are more than ready to go home
and sleep.

He hails us from the shore,
his words startle us to anger.
To put out to sea again!
To lift the nets and let them down!
We have fished these waters out,
we know the sea is empty.

Nevertheless, at Thy word, Lord. . . .

Our nets overrun with living food,
the shining scales weigh heavy as a question:
why in us this miracle?
We are the fish he gathers,
we move hungry in love's net
thrown round us in the morning sea.

Provision

Enter my lament in thy book;
store every tear in thy flask.

Psalm 56:8

*E*very night
the false bottom
falls out, and God makes
more room, keeping track
of my laments.

There's no way to keep them
from coming, so many
that salt accumulates
in a residue of crystals.

Divided as usual, I
live in three worlds at once
and often run at them
to wrestle them down,
crying, bless me, O bless me.

And they do, so often
they do: the past
I can't save or argue away,
the present insisting it is
ordinary and remarkable,
the future promising
similar demons and angels.

The bottle fills and is emptied,
each tear counted
like the telling of beads.

A Practice for the Heart

Let us learn to live swaying
As in a rocking boat on the sea.
Hölderlin

*T*his moment and no other, and never again. What's necessary
already at hand and worthy of trust. Even this afternoon's

small earthquake, the shifting tectonics rearranging stress
in faults unpredictable as hope and disaster, quite beyond

happiness. But the questions, O the questions, lean into my
ribs at night: why and when and what if and who cares enough

to answer, is anybody there? They come with dry tongues.
The songs I swallowed are gone and those I put down

disappear in the hearts of strangers. The air turns cold
in the gaps between silence and answer, the landscapes

that formed me persist with permission to walk there.
The dead come back walking and singing. I do not

have long to sing or tend to what looks after me in the dark.
There's no going forward or back into change that is

and is coming. More than I need. Less than I ask.
Taken or not, the roads intersect, and the questions

hang tilted like the arms of windmills in this country
I can't go toward or return to, or live in.

Quaker Worship: The Metaphor
Moves in Two Directions

1.

*W*e come into this stillness
like snowfall, the air
alive with angels, every
blessed flake singular and
mysterious, what's outside
quiet now, and changing
form. Quickening, we
breathe silence. Presence
holds our lives in hush.
Light dazzles. Listening,
we learn to answer,
and we keep each other warm.

2.

Silence wraps us close. We're
comforted, although the angry world
is cold. We love the spell
of falling snow, and tell
how beautiful it is
inside together here
with God
      who may want us
wiser, other,
clumsy great Saint Bernards
rising from beside the fire to go out
across blizzard mountains,
carrying rescue into the wild air.

My Own Name

Now I can no longer be deceived.
I have my own name, and I write
the letters where I want them.
These marks I learn to make
are work harder than fifty years
in the fields. It is what the young
die for, these few real words,
land no one can any more cheat us
out of. When the soldiers come
I will know what their papers say,
and I will not sign everything.

Nicaragua, 1980

Wild Honey

(after a photograph in *National Geographic*)

Outside the door of his house in Aracati, Brazil
he haunches on the dried mud and pours honey
into a long-necked liquor bottle. A man has to drink
to be a hunter, *meleiro,* stealing from fierce African bees
that leave fire under his skin. The buzzing migrations
reclaim their losses, they know whose rooms he's broken into
and they come after him. Many busy bees, much honey
in the hive, maybe a hundred dollars from this year's
taking the dark gold rich as a man's love for his wife,
sweet as memory that burns his mouth.

She watches from the window, watches the slow honey
filling the bottle, counts her days filled with crying
children, nights with no sleep. Over and over she's
told him you can't keep robbing the bees, this kind
sends signals to its kind and they come. A man can take
only so much, only so many stingers in his body. Doesn't he
know the bees are angry, trapped inside that bottle
he holds straight in front of him, so careful not to spill
any drop he took? Tonight will there be fever again,
his old dream of running from that humming in his ears,
caught heavy and sticky with honey on his hands,
caught in the thick gold swarm?

Emigré

*E*ven here, they go shopping in the morning.
I don't know the language and I point

backward to pears and cheeses. The market
I want is somewhere, and it is closed.

Women carry mesh bags to the stalls.
In this city enough is too much.

My pockets are small and ripe fruit stains.
No one picks berries from unfamiliar bushes.

The faces on their coins are watching.
I can't count what it costs to stay here.

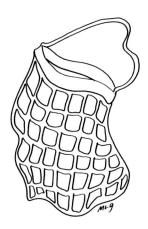

Meeting for Worship

*N*ow, for this space, I put them all aside,
the awesome things for which no words will come.
Such grief must go where only God is guide.

Our lovely planet darkens. Nightmares ride.
The sunlit waters thicken into scum.
Now, for this space, I put them all aside.

I read of torture; others bleed. Outside
thin screams rise. They keen a steady hum.
Such grief must go where only God is guide.

The aging skeletons no robe can hide
when eyes go out and soul surrenders, dumb,
now, for this space, I put them all aside.

Beyond compassion's reach, our guilt or pride,
is hurt so huge our human mercy's numb.
Such grief must go where only God is guide.

Who could contain these evils, and confide
the awesome things for which no words will come?
Now, for this space, I put them all aside.
Such grief must go where only God is guide.

Four From the Republics

In Tblisi

*G*iven dark red cherries
in a paper sack, we return the smiles of the tall man
and his daughter, accept their gift, the warm juice
sweet on our tongues, an old harvest of legend
and rebellion mixing in our blood.

By a mountain road
we see a wishing tree garlanded with paper streamers,
colored ribbon. And we listen to miraculous tales:
Nina and the life-giving pillar; the lifting tree
that moved by itself; clay wine jugs buried
long ago in the earth when a son was born,
cracked open at his wedding feast. (Drink the good wine
of this republic of Georgia, they say, drink it on the spot
or bottle it. In this air if you wait,
vinegar is what you get.)

At our hotel we drink fresh yogurt
in glasses, eat tomatoes with basil and parsley,
fine white-fleshed peaches. In the dining room
men are singing harmony so true
we can see their souls in their faces
flying out to meet us.

On a high cliff
above the confluence of two rivers, we
visit a third-century church, place kopeks
on the black candelabra, touch the hardened
yellow wax. Joining hands at the altar
we sing "Dona Nobis Pacem," our song ascending
like smoke through the broken roof,
and carrying to the fields where farmers
rake the harvest into long green rows.

Piskaryovskoye Memorial Cemetery, Leningrad

*O*ne peony costs thirty-five kopeks, and I buy
a large pink flower, join the slow lines
walking between graves: half a million
bodies under banked mounds of grass
on either side of fifteen thousand Bulgarian roses
the color of an American variety we call *Fragrant Cloud,*
these statistics a litany I try to take in.

Finding a place for the peony, I push it through wire mesh
into water, think of my grandmother's peony bushes,
her white and red flowers, her house I was born in,
Midwest Memorial Days, and armloads of iris,
peonies, roses, carried to our separate, single graves.

In the nine-hundred-day siege of this city
whole families of the dead were laid day after day
on the streets of snow and starvation and could not
be buried. The people who live in Leningrad do not
carry flowers when they come here in the spring.
They bring sugar, dark bread, tobacco,
necessities the dead may be hungry for.

Tourists may not come then, we may not come with flowers
or our longing to touch the photographs in the museum,
as if touching could assist belief,
make the black coffins real in the snow,
the women hauling sand bags,
the pages torn from a child's notebook,
the list of names of the living,
her own name on the last page. And that man's face
with his cheekbones pushing his stretched skin,
his eyes telling us we're all *inastranits,*
foreigners and visitors in this country
where we don't know the language
and can't learn fast enough.

Izmailovo Hotel, Moscow

*P*ushing her mop on the marble floor, the long stairs,
the cleaning woman finds her own rhythm in devotion
not unlike the barefoot ecstatic who crosses herself
three times before the altar with its icons and candles,
then lowers her heavy body to kiss the floor.
The hotel lobby is vast as the universe is vast
and this bucket of water and dirty mop require attention.
Oblivious, concentrated, bending like a birch
in a forest of shining leaves, she leans into the wide circles
that give back salt fish and stewed apples, the good bread
she feeds her family in a country gray with rain.

Rites of Departure

*I*n Tashkent I learn an old belief: after death
carrion eat the sins of our flesh, and we proceed

without this burden. Already the buzzards and vultures
circle. Coyotes howl at the edges of my life, the rats

come closer. I notice small white grubs at work in a tree
on the forest floor, its trunk huge as my carnal sins.

There may be food enough if I live long enough, even
my pride in saying this an obvious failure. But my most

grievous faults have nothing to do with flesh. My uneasy
spirit anticipates good appetite from scavengers, wants them

hungry also for my heart, that they make it light enough
to leave without envy or malice, without meanness.

Two

the dark veins of the leaves

Sorrow Trees

*I*f there are fever trees, and they tell me there are,
I know where I've been walking. No one's named this
similar species, but sorrow trees exist. Look
how rain brings out the red, how wet
the blackness shines. Long patterns on these trunks,
irregular and gnarled. This bark never peels
as eucalyptus does. My fingers move around the knobs,
trace the grooves they're caught in, as I am
caught: I heard of a man so lonely
all he had to hug was trees. Every day
I live like a botanist, examining these roots,
naming the dark veins of the leaves.

28

Taking Leave

A second look's the first of many we give to the lives
that leave us, as I turn again to yours, repeating
the day before yesterday that stuns me with clarity,
refuses to admit the freeway, the accident, this news.

You are still here, you sit beside me, touch my hand.
We exchange gossip, laugh easily, make promises, say
we have missed each other, and this has to change.
We plan a time to talk about our work, our children.

This is a first return. I will come often to your face,
your white summer hat with cutwork design, flowered ribbon,
the whimsical message on your shirt: "I've abandoned
the search for truth. Now I'm looking for a good fantasy."

Looking back, grief wants to find you in the complex music
of leave-taking. If I slow my memory, will I hear us
without this darkening tone, recognize the intervals,
the silence around our words quite elegant and pure?

for Pegge

Changes in the Natural Order

*H*e is not sick but out of season,
out of his garden grown, confusion
in the germ, a question in a leaf
to be a leaf. As if a seed forgets
intention to become, the message
garbled in the stem, an asking
not an answer in the bloom. He
says good morning wondering if
it's day, recalls precision
lost. What stays stays on
too long, and as he dies he sings
as if he's surely getting well.

Holy Water

If you cry too much
you won't get into heaven.

In my mouth my mother's words
still taste like salt. I'm farther now than ever,
angels tell me, my vision washed and wet
and drying in the wind, my mother's
rained-on laundry blowing clean.

What rivers keep us out of heaven, if they do,
are running where I cannot stop my eyes.
The thaw begins, and seepage under stone.
All year the freshets sing.
Water levels rise, lift me through the locks
and toward those gates she said I wouldn't see.

My life may pour me in,
triumphant as a cork
before the throne.

For Louise

*D*riving a long way
over mountains
through fine dry snow
I come to your house
where very soon
you will die.

Your husband opens the door.
We go toward fire
on the stone hearth.

From your chair
you greet us, and then
I see you
scarlet and gold,
in Chinese silk.

Suddenly color
is what matters
in the world,

and your thin hands
reaching.

Clear under your skin
your bones
are sure. They say

we will hold
no conversation
with death. Love is

the silence
we give each other.

I only know I want to sing
or do some stately dance
before you. Gallant
is the old word.

Who would I ask
to come?
What colors
will I wear?

Suicide

*I*t is early for sorrow.
We move in fog. Our failure
holds us in, the possible answer
circling back on impossible questions.
Guilt is our primary word.
We cannot forgive our absence.
Godspeed trembles against rage
and will not let it pass love's door.

Your wit was a polished shield.
You did not speak your need
in any way we heard at all.
What slow accretions to that moment?
The hidden gun in the corner closet
became a promise and your single eye,
one bright simplicity.

Love is a word we dare not stumble over.
May our calls be clear on one another.
Teach us the ways of asking,
let the room that holds us be large,
safe home for the things that are human.

Release us, friend, forgiven,
whose separate journeys move together
in the space we have named God.
Let us go without guilt, as we have had
to let you go, given no choice.
Set us free to learn from our prayers.
We lift you on what hopes we have.

for John

Carving the Pumpkin

*H*e told her he wouldn't come anymore, not
to watch her dying. But now it is October
and he is here. They sit at the kitchen table,
her wheelchair pulled close. They
have known each other a long time.
The blue radiation crosses are dim on her temples,
her hair is beginning to thin.

Sharing one knife they mark lines
where they will cut out the face. For innocents
all decisions are momentous: Shall we work in triangles
or squares? Circles? For the mouth, how many
teeth? A fierce face or a friendly one?
Who watches from the window this year is important.

He steadies the pumpkin and she makes the first cut.
Long and circular, an inch below the stem.
Pushed in deep, all the way to the hollow, the knife
pulls out clean. The incision meets itself.
Together they lift the handle and laugh when the lid
comes off. Heads close, leaning a little
toward the wet hole, they look into space
with its strings and seeds.

When it is finished, they talk of fairytales,
say they have carved a coach ready to go anywhere.
Tonight they will roast the seeds in the oven and eat them.
Nothing is to be wasted, or saved for the long winter.

for Edna

Popcorn

tight in the rows, a perfect fit
on the cob, red kernels, yellow
and blue. Shucking them off
you have to pry the starters loose,
then they come easy, chaff
a fine float in the air.

Some grains don't burst,
stay hard in the husk.
In the back and forth
of the skillet, others burn,
some white flowers scorch,
a waste of leftovers,
oil and salt on the handfuls
you try to crack with your teeth.

When my friend died that summer
in Africa, his last words
remembered Christmas in Ohio,
a tree with lights and cranberries,
popcorn. He said he could almost
hear the kernels singing against the lid,
see explosions of goodness
turning quiet as snow in the pan.

for Cecil

The Old Ones

*T*ime
starves us to that place
where blue stone
splinters. We break,
and give over.
We roughen under weight.

   Some old ones
polish smooth as
shining pebbles. Others
crumble in a gentle dust.
A few rest here
in warm hands. Held by
love's fierce light,
seeing secrets in all things.

Even
in that place
where bodies go
into a gathering of stones.

Grandfather

*I*t is late for the world to melt.
He listens where the howling air
blows loose from midnight. No one
gives him back his clothes. Courage,
half-blinded, is a northstar blur.
Centered in that stubborn pole
he keeps his heart in that pure cold.

Frost hardens mirrors in his face.
He curls against the snow. The thin
ice films the shape he is. We see
he's king of winter, and we come
to silence with our living hands.
Death has this place. A frozen garden
waits. Grandfather knows.

Watercolor

*W*as the way he saw,
in wash, light underneath,
around, and coming through,

delicate layers darkening
as he chose. His brush
rinsed color on a world
where the smallest edges
told. They kept on bleeding
till he fixed them. Sometimes
nothing could be done. He
almost never knew unless
he caught his work
before it dried.
It's odd, he thought,
how textures guide the flow.

Now he was old he didn't want
to paint opaque, be definite
or bold. He didn't want the heavy,
more elastic stuff, thick pigment
made to cover up mistakes
and do it right again
so many times. Free and fast
was best, and he would go
outdoors when days were good.
Translucent was the clearest view
he had, and subtle shade permitted
change enough. It was a fluid world.

He lived in light so long
he saw it always there,
and coming through.

About Grief

You'd think a poem could contain it, hold
that wild roughness on the page
in a careful structure,
the form a few words take
enough to keep the power
steady and still.

Day after day I work to set the iron
like rebar in concrete,
mix pebbles and rocks and sand,
pour everything in
and brace the walls against
that river's weight.

But all the time grief
waits to surprise us: storms
in the canyon on the clearest day,
flash floods in the desert,
the deluge, the downpour, underground
the imperceptible rising of water.

One at a Time

*G*one more absolutely away
than any travellers we know, they are not
the dead, strangers moving so far we can't
for the life of us recall their names,
and lose them across that unguarded border.

  Never with us to be
who they were, still they are more than the dead.
Each was one and is one, singular,
keeps a particular history, a voice.

  When you call me
call me *Ben.* Call me *Alexandra.* My name is *Harry.*
Lillian is my name. I am the one who, that one:
the boy who made dams in the gutters, then let loose
the water in the streets; the woman who loved egrets
and the spare beauty of bones; the one who said
it's a good idea, go back to school. I am your father,
your mother, your friend, your lover. Resurrect me
in specifics. Give me a body of remembered detail.
Say *Hank.* Say my name.

Home Stretch

No place for a vision. Not here, crossing the divide
near Siskiyou. Not coming down this long grade
on an ordinary highway, with that lumber truck
rattling past, logs chained to the flatbed,
heavy clamps chewing into bark as the load shifts,
only the cab window separating the driver from trees
pointed at his head. Hugging the inside edge
they go downhill fast, and the road comes clear.
Cars behind and in front, prospect easy and open,
no preparation for anything different, no signal
the journey was changing and we'd arrived already
where we belong, in a whole new order of things.

Our beloved dead ride the horizon, dear bodies
and bones from graves, dust in air gone forward
scouting the territory. They make safe what never
will be familiar, can be nowhere if not ahead of us.
When we reach them they will be farther on.
Thick as a cloud the unborn are pushing behind us
unsteady as hope, our single destination
the persistent shine in the mirror. Processional
uncertain of Canterbury but on the way, this blue car
in the middle close to center lane on a freeway
that cannot be measured in either direction.
All secondary roads feed this one.

The asphalt is humming beneath us, so many signs
we cannot keep track of instruction or meaning. Vulnerable
among campers, vans and pick-ups, maintaining distance
from that church bus with its absolute bumper sticker,
we hold to our given place, these margins and boundaries.
Slowing down, leaving the straightaway, we pull in
at a rest stop. The rush of warm wind ends,
the roaring in our ears. Standing near the road
two pilgrims eat watermelon; the cut fruit changes
from red to white above the hard green rind. Sweet
pink juices drip to the ground. Between the usual words,
quiet, and a variable rain of seeds.

Swimming with Friends

*B*etween breaths I say their names,
draw in air for them, kick hard for them,
pull my arms against all that weight of water,
each stroke for someone. Lifting my shoulder
on the backstroke, changing and turning over
for the crawl, I hum their lives into bubbles.
Others take no notice of these
my loved, invisible companions
who swim back and forth with me
doing laps, easy as fish.

Wet Weather

*T*onight I track them down, slugs in the primroses, snails
in the hyacinths. Even before their sweet bells open,
chewed to slippery brown nubs. I cut the slugs in half,
harvest baby snails off the chrysanthemums, collect
heavy shells in a plastic bag, crunch them all underfoot,
empty this slaughter in the compost. Trying to save the vegetables.
The fog's in, somewhere a dog won't stop barking. In our house
you're dying, going out of yourself, leaving this world.
When we say *God* to one another, I don't know who God is.
I decide against the snails and slugs, but they keep on
greedy for hyacinth and lettuce. From the other side
of a gate she's too small to open, a child's crying. She
can't get back to her world of yard and toys, her house.
Outside the circle of my flashlight, the snails
leave silver lines, patterns in the dirt. Outdoors
in this dripping weather, a knife in my hand,
wet plastic sticking to itself in slime and bits of shell,
I want the child's mother here, her answering words:
"It's all right now. Didn't you know I'd come?"

Balance

On the creek path
two logs make a narrow bridge,
and here I learn: don't hesitate,
imagine mountain goats in the Andes
sure-footed on the rocks
and staring down at me
where I step out and across,
make it over without falling,
my arms ever so slightly
swaying.

High in the redwoods, rain,
a humming in the earth.
After long hush, wind
pulling needles through the air,
patterns of water repeating
old comings and goings,
the dancers ready to enter the sacred circle,
the singing about to begin.

How everything happens at once. Now.
Someone I love could be dying while I sit here,
a yellow leaf beside me, a mosquito
on my forehead so light it's not until
the sting begins I brush it away. All over the wood,
buzzing and calling. A covey of quail
skim the sides of the path,
skittering blurs I almost miss.
I walk through whirring and trilling.

In the sweat lodge a teacher
tells us that the pain we experience
is only a fragment of the world's suffering.
How it goes on! At the center of the Costanoan circle
I bow to the four directions, open my arms
to let go an excess of dying,
return everything to the power of this place
where spirits come and surprise me
like the light in the trees, the portion of sky
the redwoods open and close and weave into.

A Certainty of Transformations

$\mathcal{M}$y salts will flow one day to heather
and ocean waters scour my bones
that shall be earth and rock and mould.
Winds from far spaces between cold stars
will blow me around and over the warm hills.
Supporting a world of weeds and spiders
I shall be woven into knotted grasses.
flowers will nestle into my ruins;
my dust will comfort their growing
and cushion the heartbeats of little birds.
It will not be a new thing or strange
to nourish beauty kin to what I loved.
My seasons were a dependable procession.
There was no growth that came easy,
none without its singular celebration.
Salt and bone will find their accustomed home,
return easily to earth's familiar arms,
certain of place prepared and welcome waiting,
my body moving sure and right to its changing task.
But, oh, there's more of me that's insubstantial
and presses equal claim for new employment.
The fire that warms this house wants other tinder.

My heart pumps messages beyond the flow of blood,
and I've achieved a person eager for renewal.
Affection's earth enough to sprout such change,
and love's the richer mix for metamorphosis.
Yet mystery is where the final trust resides
and I've been transient there at other times,
often enough to know that change is how we're made.
Surprise hides laughing around corners
and weeping is a necessary healing
doubly releasing to those who've learned
to see beyond the surfaces of tears.
Lively creation labors everywhere.
We are upheld by all we do not see,
our lives enmeshed in endless restless worlds.
The whole of me moves straight toward transformation.
Alive in ways I cannot imagine I will continue,
relinquishing all that I am to new remarkable forms,
translated in death to some fresh becoming.

Three

downstream to joy

In the Rain, Small Lights

In this time between time I try to say
what presses on me: rain streams out of the sky
and the smell of the rain enters the pores of my body,
which knows and cannot tell. A child's red wagon
rusts in the grass; looped over a branch,
the broken piñata head of a yellow fish;
in the weeds a white and blue ball washed clean.

There is nothing to hold onto but my life
and I wait for the invasion of grace.
Single drops of rain catch and hold such light
as there is, and the light is shaken, lost
in itself, loosed from twigs and leaves
to go back into streaming rain.

The great anxiety of my life
is that I will not see
these small lights in the water
or pay attention when they fall.

The Retreat

I came hunting for a word,
some thing to carry
in that fearful country
where we must live
who love one another.

Voices out of the weeds,
the cry of the self
in narrowing places,
our stubborn lonely land.

Dry things curled away
like smoke. Blue acorns
fell around me.   Inside
the sky opened.

Then all the words
turned to music
and became one word,

a stone I held while light
bled into my fingers.

Crossing the old land,
openings appear in the tangled roots
of long contraries between us.

I bring you this stone,
a terrible wonder
shining from this healing.

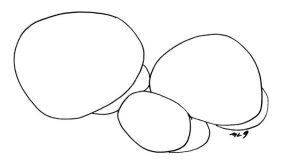

Making Angels in Chicago

Midnight. The wind easy at last,
thick snow falling.

New-married, we
dress and go outdoors
where each thing is
given its own comforter, the world
bedding down in beauty. We run
back to the place we grow young in,
blue frozen nights
we remember.

Filling our hands with snow, we throw it
high toward the window. You friends asleep,
wake up! Come and see! It will not
look this way tomorrow, or even
one minute from now!

But I have forgotten
whether you joined us, or only
opened your window.

What stays are angels
we made on the neighbors' lawns,
how we lay down in snowfall streets
opening our arms and singing hallelujah.
For a while there was heaven
cold on our necks. The wet stars
rained in our faces, the air
piercing and pure as if spring
already were here.

When we rose from the ground
we saw the shapes we had been,
the snow
filling our wings with feathers.

Steadying the Landscape

*T*he artist studies her painting.
Something isn't right in this landscape.

Trees hang in air and the old barn
is floating away from its ground.
Her blue mountain wants placing.

She looks until she sees
she's forgotten a clear horizon line,
the long definitive stroke
that divides the world.

It comes to her then,
how a dark edge
eases the eye, a way
of righting things.

It comes to her then,
how a thin seam
opens the sky, a sign
of separation

tracing the true prospect,
steadying the landscape.

The Thaw

*T*ight-reined, I've run too many winter journeys,
events have ridden me hard on roads I didn't choose,
there's no horizon in this shifting landscape
and subtlety in assault by scattering.
My world moves by in images of ice;
its brittle pictures break in any wind.
What soundless thaw will breathe on frozen days,
who will stop the running winter's ride?

I cry aloud to the springtime gods:
slow me now. Remove these hardened reins;
turn me loose in fields and pastures
where I may share the wisdom of warm beasts
nuzzling tender shoots in morning freshness.
Their soft eyes trust a nourishing world,
standing still in place, they belong.

Heal me with long meadows and with mountains,
open me to mild, gold-shadowed distances,
set me down in fragile flowering orchards,
let me bend with grass to the flowing wind,
run my life shallow along spring ditches.
Quiet pools draw color from the moving skies.
Freedom is the air's new scent, the certain faith
that moves in light on the green meadows.

Furrow

Nobody saw when I left the house and my straightened bed
that was soft and square and gave me no room

to rest in the grain of my grief. But the furrow
lay long and was open to me where I put my face

in the dirt. The strong black smell
came cool in my throat and my hands uncurled.

My full length stretch till the soil
gave way to the shape I was, and let me stay.

There's no like place in the city now, and I can't
find words to tell what I mean:

how quiet that night on the ground, how the stars
came down to comfort me.

for Pauline

Of Marriages and Mountains

Some hands that hold on heights let go
for sharper steeper downward slide.
What heart could be committed, pure,
when distant viewpoints call delight?
Who would test the crevices of dark
in mountains rough, rewarding, sure?

The ranges hold together. Elements
of earth, rock, air fuse into mountains
where twisting trails descend and rise.
It takes the thrust of inwardness
to shape this mass on which we climb;
that moving force determines weight and size.

True marriage is a mountain, no mistake,
heartland that's elevated, absolute,
and makes demands. Quick walking will not do.
The intricate solidity of mass and peak
requires some narrow places, folds of stone.
The hands that hold help one another through.

A Harvest Measure

$\mathcal{A}$ golden stillness warms these resting fields
that stretch away to lost beginnings;
I take the harvest measure of my years.
This is my season before the winter comes
and I would taste memory's air and smoke,
smell green wood again and the old earth.

Youth was a flood of wonders, openings.
I moved through that springtide dreaming, taking,
ardent in the ache of my delicious loves.
Beauty swept me away, enchanted by dawn and sunset;
I was a dancer through rainbow and cloud,
alive in the hurt of the world,
tender and quick in my tears.

But I never became beauty's too-familiar friend,
and the lighted distances remained between us.
In the dusk of the falling years,
that shining blesses the miracle of things.
New worlds spin on my fingertips,
surfaces proclaim marvels, tell me legends.
Form within form rests continuing revelation,
intricate and varied beyond my dreams,
simpler and lovelier than I had imagined.

My tears spring from old sources,
but the rivers have widened, deepened,
and there is commerce on those waters
that move me downstream to joy.
Possibilities widen within as winter nears.
The bones of the land emerge in the dying fall.
The harvest is not hoarded into barns,
and I am well nourished in the sharing.
I sing as I walk thankful in these fields
where frost whitens the ground,
where darkness gathers at the edges of the sky.

Naming the Animals

*W*e pinch and pound them into form, we pull
a variety of ears and tails, noses. With toothpicks
we poke holes for eyes. So many animals,
as fast as you imagine or say the names:
    make a rabbit, Grandma   make a dog
    a worm   a fish   a dinosaur
Exclaiming over our handiwork, we turn them out
in lines, a parade. It's the eighth day of creation
and whatever we say, is.

Every creature different, you acknowledge each,
it's amazing, no strangeness or failure intimidates you.
One after the other animals grow and become.
We march them into the egg carton, the ark, the kingdom.

And with equal impunity you destroy them, your fists
smash red clay thin on the table. Without wailing
you turn what was into something else.

All the names sound good to you, at two you say them
over and over, new words alive in your mouth.
So many words, no end to words, and not one
is *doomsday* or *hope.* You are too busy
naming the animals, testing the syllables.
I give you others:
   try *octopus*   try *elephant*   *tiger*   *panda bear*
   try *puppy*   *shishkebab*   *doorknob*
   say *sarsparilla* *pocket* *nobody*
   maybe yes   maybe no

You'd like us to remake the world, you'd like
your universe in miniature, scaled down
from the great original, everything safe in your hands,
a world you take charge of and put to bed at night,
the whole dictionary singing out joy in your speech.

for Sam

O Most Admired Disorder

*P*raise muddle and mistake, unclear
disorder's pretty business, all temper
out of sorts, the mess that no one
comes to bless. Praise tumble, litter,
scraps, confused untidy heaps, ferment
and maze, the random sort that never
will compute. Praise jungle weeds
and foggy haze, dump and fumble
that do not discriminate. Disorganized
is how we start, a mix
too full, too rich to last.
Stick in your thumb.
The whole pie falls apart.

Talking Back

Bless the Lord, O my soul;
and all that is within me,
bless his holy name!

*T*oo much. The all's too much. We want
to bless the world, and You, the way
the singer says. But *everything*
inside, offered up, a gift
that's known before the wrapping's off?
For what we are and bear, no catalogue
will do. Our secrets have their place.
And You, You keep Your own, who try
with us such various ways. We will not see
Your meanings plain, but pray You stay
original and clear, majestic, quite beyond
belief. Turn us to awe. Our pain, how does
it praise? We ask for comfort, though. O give
the refuge we have lost, and be reciprocal,
Presence we may find and claim. Teach us
while we live, and hold our curious hearts
expectant, late in darkness, hungry, wanting home.

Flying with Marc Chagall

*T*he angel of Marc Chagall flies over the roofs of
    the world.
He has arms that give directions to a blue-green
    horse
below him. The horse has one rosy wing and the
    body
of a chicken, a head that looks back over its
    shoulder,
stick legs feathering out to nothing. Safe
    in all
that strange air, animal and angel keep moving.
    The angel
separates ribbons of a deep and different blue,
    almost
purple, streamers left over from the hours closest
    to morning.

Suspended beneath Presence, the little horse
　　　has no need
of messages or apples.　Even his frayed legs
　　　are unimportant
with the eyes of the angel looking down so intent
　　　and tender
they are shut to see.　Through every blessed hour
　　　some guardian
watches over and protects blue chickens and green
　　　horses,
any combination willing to chance it
　　　and fly.

Discernment

*T*he smallest branch began to move
before I saw a bird climb up that bough.
The window's ledge was in the way, yet still
I sense that this somehow may tell me news,
be whisper's breath of grace, a swaying parallel
announcing Presence. For surely it is true
wind's touched me times before I knew direction,
or had seen the grasses bend. I would not

push this metaphor too far and break
both branch and bird, but You know how
we guess Your will, keep us aware. You make
our longing to discern Your shape in any guise,
a trembling twig to tell us You are coming,
or afterward in motion, You were there.

Flowering Quince

*B*elieving
in the thing
that springs without reason
I hold this branch
where quince flowers hide
red promise under
hard dark,

celebrate this mystery
breaking free in its own time,

tender blossoms from unlikely stem
full blown,

the rosy curve
caroling out of winter.

Waiting
in another darkness,
sliding my fingers down
the empty branch,
I feel a roughness there.

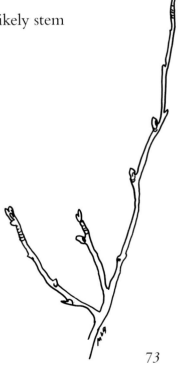

Four

*how I love this world
how it opens*

Shaking the Tree

*V*ine and branch we're connected in this world
of sound and echo, figure and shadow, the leaves
contingent, roots pushing against earth. An apple

belongs to itself, to stem and tree, to air
that claims it, then ground. Connections
balance, each motion changes another. Precarious,

hanging together, we don't know what our lives
support, and we touch in the least shift of breathing.
Each holy thing is borrowed. Everything depends.

Above Ground

*I*t is time to be quiet
and kneel in the dirt
trying to hear
bacteria and fungi,
the slow movement of middens,
earthworms throwing their casts,
root hairs in tunnels of soil,
the fine humus washing down
seeds and empty nests.

Astonishing sounds
must play in these spaces between us,
a strenuous music of being,
the strings of the whole instrument
vibrating.

Perhaps it is a mercy we cannot hear
the dark humming underfoot,
a shift from motion to stillness,
the holy diversity below us
we are not yet ready
to enter.

Skeletal

*V*eins hold a leaf together,
snakes move on varied bones
in supple, hinged economy
flexible across the stones.

The skeleton determines size,
segmented limit sets
to carry the consistency
on which a body's put.

Flesh grows lovely on the frame,
takes shape upon the form.
Without that firm necessity
no symmetry is born.

Praise intrinsic structure
organic to the whole,
substantial core of energy
particular and cool.

Sharing the Territory

*M*ore of them than us, more all the time, the creatures
closing in, pushing against us with beaks and muzzles,
showing their teeth, raising up feelers and stingers,
our mutual territory crowded with animals and insects

whose habits and descriptions beggar the mind and sense.
It's a bloody zoo we belong to, and how in the name of God
acknowledge this variety, how keep it all together? Who will
sing for mosquitoes or banana slugs, who serenades

the fire ants or wants the nervous African bees
swarming in clouds for the kill? Who makes hymns
for the slither under the rock, praises the yellow eyes
that surprise us in the dark by the road? Who will be there

when the lion's jaws rip the flesh of the gazelle
and the hawk's talons break the bones of the mouse?
What holds us each one to the process, to the terrible music
in rhythms repeating like blood, like prayer, unstoppable?

Let God who makes them care for them.
Let God who makes me keep me in my place.

Standing Here on Fire

*T*he bush itself was fire, and clean, the heat
of incandescence that did not disappear.
A small tree burned for Moses and was not consumed.

The burnings of our day destroy the air. Smoke
wastes the wind and heavy ashes fall. The grit
blows back into our teeth and eyes. We make

brash claims upon the world and pour down fire,
who cannot bear the steady glow God gives
to common things. We will not turn aside.

We come too near and never bend. Our shoes
stay on. In wilderness we stand upright
and hear no voice. In bondage to ourselves we burn.

He Remembers That We Are Dust

Psalm 103

*L*ord, in thy hands dust is no little thing
but life-stuff lifted on thy changing winds;
freeblown and dry, quiescent to thy touch
our powdered substance leaps to shape and sing.

Through lighted dust each image stakes its claim,
through dancing bits of earth light filters free
and redwoods magic to cathedral groves.
Transforming dust means sight is not the same.

In dust and light thy meanings speak and change.
Each day and night they summon us to see.
Across space miles and dust the sunlight burns
where colors flaunt their varied wonder range.

Lord, in thy hands dust breathes creation's sum.
We are most finely ground, who wait for light
to make us shine, for breath to set us free.
Lord, shape us to remember and become.

Cyclamen

Cyclamen grows as cyclamen must
with backwards wonderful wings
bent strangely askew on supporting stems,
absurdly ready to lift and fly
in the many directions that beauty moves.
I rise toward tears on the rakish wings
affirming their pink hallelujah yes,
cockeyed and sure in the morning sun,
and faithful to blooming no matter what.

I dig my toes in the stubborn earth
of the limited space that is mine to live,
and I set the wings of my beauty free,
wild and sure it is mine to give
whatever direction points its yes,
affirming my flight in the morning air,
gay and certain of wonder there,
faithful to blooming no matter what.

Soaring

For the sake of a single verse . . .
one must feel how the birds fly.
Rainer Maria Rilke

*N*o invitation's strong enough. I will not
take to air or glide down currents of wind.
I will not climb and fall in those dangerous
directions. Yet I knew a man once who flew
soaring eye to eye with a red-tailed hawk
high riding streams of air up and over
valleys between bare hills and the trees.
The eye of the flying bird, he said,
met his eye flying beside.

   O as he told what it meant to him
then to be man, solitary, out of element, steadily
looked at level with the creature in space, I was
lifted and carried there where the red-tailed bird
flashed by. Wind was a rush in my hair and, captive,
I was hooded by light. The hawk's eye held me
holy and dark, mild and strange in the roaring air.

for Alan

Changes

Ice that hardens on a leaf
and sheathes a growing thing in stone
is in itself arrested flow
awaiting movement of the sun.

A leaf that glows beneath the ice
may not be safe when changes come.
Some plants survive a wintering
that leaves some others numb.

I cannot speak for frozen leaf
or ice that melts from form.
A fluid instant holds my faith,
ways of the sun are warm.

Winter Meditation

*R*ain. The scimitar leaves of eucalyptus
softening underfoot, blue forms on the ground,
muted gray and green in the trunks, colors
never noticed until now, the torn bark
a promise of paintings I might get to,
the rainy fragrance reminding me
how I love this world, how it opens
through the trees the always receding arch
of its blessing, this year at interregnum,
hiatus in an old succession of months
too cold for germination
and the bulbs are thinking it over.

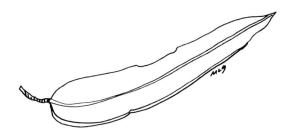

December Morning

*T*he weather changes, and the world
becomes more than it is, as if
that were not enough. Luminous
and ringing, the cold day
begins in blue that is
almost green, and I go to the window
to see if this is really the light
of morning, and it is,

winter light I had forgotten
could come over the houses
before the sun comes. To be able
to get out of bed and see
this particular color
and then to watch it fade
is for a moment
to be given a glimpse
of the unimaginable world.

Being here in these changes
is to wear the sky like a wedding ring,
a promise of common daylight after all,
one more chance to praise
by breathing everything in.

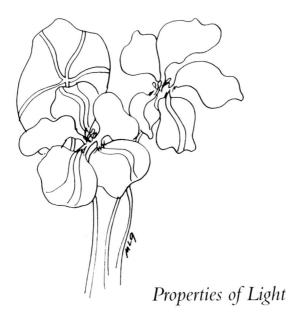

Properties of Light

*A*field of light, and my need to say
that it exists. Each morning I walk here
almost blinded by water the sun shines on,
look down from Strawberry Hill
across the roofs of the dazzling city
emerging out of fog, a haze of light
over and around the houses, giving
everything a quality for which *luminous*
is the only word. My need to see such light
holding and sliding off the eucalyptus trunks, their
ragged bark. To be exposed to the wet grasses
shaking and splintering that light, to recognize
nasturtium leaves for the bright green mirrors
they are, the red, orange and yellow fires
inextinguishable, spreading up the hill.

Limestone and granite give back radiance, and we
walkers in this field lift our feet and set out,
moving though our once and only mornings,
afternoons. Light searches the surfaces of all things,
and what if there were no mirrors in the world, what if
the brass lock on the door did not say no, the window
did not let the light come through? What if light
did not find itself renewable? As my necessity
for these words, mirrors I carry into the sun
of this blazing day, this dance,
this carnival where I am given access to another
world, to the spirits who walk with me
pointing out the properties of light.

All That Is Necessary

*T*his is no day for poetry.
Green surrounds me. Clear
birdsong comes from a tree
somewhere. A giant gold-black
bumblebee misses my nose and goes
for the wild sweetpeas. The sun
pulls odors from the earth.
The hills grow a ragged horizon.
Mist rises from their pockets.

More. Always more.

Why turn the world to language?
Can I be here without this need,
be simple, love what is, in place?
I will never come back
to these words. The fat bumblebee
has them. The leaves say all
that is necessary.

Being Orderly Come Together

A day for praise,
the motions of meeting and parting
perfect in rhythm, each pattern
specific to the dance,
one figure leading to the next
in particular gravity:
the steady sound of a hammer,
water falling in drops
the earth takes in,
cut flowers for the neighbors,
time for errands,
the right words in place.
After long absence
the Maker of the world
seems not too far away.
Even loss and death
begin to look like gifts,
this life without asking,
with no need to know.

Notes on the Poems

One ⌒ *the language of our tribe*

6   During meeting for worship, looking toward the east room fireplace in the San Francisco Friends Center, I noticed the carved circle in the wood, and Rilke's words came. The poem began, moved to include images from a retreat led by Alexandra Docili.

12   From Margaret Mossman's metaphors in ministry.

14   Response to a program at AFSC annual meeting, which described the Nicaraguan literacy campaign.

18   Pacific Yearly Meeting Quaker Peace Tour to the Soviet Union, 1987.

Two ⌒ *the dark veins of the leaves*

27   From a story told by Gerri House, Religion and Psychology conference.

29   Peggemae Lacey, a member of San Francisco Meeting and former clerk of Pacific Yearly Meeting, was killed in a tragic automobile accident in 1986, following Yearly Meeting. She had just completed eight years as clerk of the Discipline Committee, which revised our *Faith and Practice*. The news came as I was leaving the city for the Napa Valley Poetry Conference, where this elegy was written.

30   For Morgan and Johanna Sibbett. At the time of Morgan's death, they were resident hosts at San Francisco Friends Center.

Three ~ *downstream to joy*

72 The Young Friends of Pacific Yearly Meeting asked me to join a panel discussion on "Discerning God's Will for Our Lives." I worked at a table on the sun porch of our home in San Francisco. Looking into the top branches of a Monterey pine, I saw a dove fly into the tree, and into the poem.

Four ∼ *how I love this world*
how it opens

77 In our worship, ministry by Katharine Whiteside Taylor made connections which prompted the poem.
78 Prompted by Francis Hole's talk at Friends General Conference, 1986.
79 Written after one of Alexandra Docili's art classes; her teaching opened fresh ways of seeing and responding to the world.
83 From a message by visiting Friend, T. Canby Jones.
84 Story by Alan Strain.
85 From a Sierra Club photograph found during a retreat at the home of Charlotte Weil.
90 Written on the porch at Casa de Luz, Ben Lomond Quaker Center in the Santa Cruz mountains, California.
91 The title is from Edward Burrough (1662): "Being orderly come together . . . in unity and concord . . . all things (are) to be carried on."

Other lives, un-named, are in these poems. To them, as well, my thanks. And to my family. And to the writers who for more than ten years in San Francisco have helped me work. I am particularly grateful to Carolyn Miller, who edited the original manuscript.

Acknowledgments

Poetry

Grateful acknowledgment is made to the editors of the periodicals and books in which the following poems were published:

Blue Unicorn	"Carving the Pumpkin"
California Quarterly	"Winter Meditation"
Colorado Review	"Wild Honey"
Earth/Light	"Above Ground"
Equinox	"Emigré"
Friends Bulletin	"Being Orderly Come Together"
	"Flying with Marc Chagall"
	"Flowering Quince"
	"He Remembers That We Are Dust"
	"Meeting for Worship"
	"Provision"
	"Shaking the Tree"
	"Sometimes God"
	"Standing Here on Fire"
	"Taking Leave"
Friends Journal	"The Metaphor Moves in Two Directions"
	"The Retreat"
Modern Maturity	"O Most Admired Disorder"
Northern Review	"Popcorn"
The Seattle Review	"Izmailovo Hotel, Moscow"
	"Piskaryovskoye Memorial Cemetry, Leningrad"
	"Rites of Departure"
Sri Chinmoy Broadside	"Invocation"
Studia Mystica	"Talking Back"
Transfer	"The Old Ones"
Western Humanities Review	"Home Stretch"
Yankee	"Grandfather"
	"Sorrow Trees"
	"Swimming with Friends"

Other poems appear in two out-of-print books by Jeanne Lohmann: *Bonnie Jeanne* (1971, with Harry A. Ackley) and *Where the Field Goes* (1976). Selections were also made from *Steadying the Landscape* (1982—copies available from the author at 2501 Washington Street SE, Olympia, Washington 98501).

Copies of *Gathering A Life: A Journal of Recovery* (a prose memoir) may be obtained from the publisher: John Daniel & Co., P.O. Box 21922, Santa Barbara, California 98121.

Art

Grateful acknowledgment is made to Mary Lou Goertzen for creating the line drawings especially for this book and for use of previously printed art.

Line drawings copyright © 1994

"Mesh Bag" for "Emigré," page 16
"Peony" for "Piskaryovskoye Memorial Cemetery," page 21
"Trees" for "Sorrow Trees," page 27
"Shiny Pebbles" for "The Retreat," page 57
"Branch of Buds" for "Flowering Quince," page 73
"Dirt and Worms" for "Above Ground," page 78
"Eucalyptus Leaf" for "Winter Meditation," page 86
"Nasturtiums" for "Properties of Light," page 88
"Wild Sweet Pea" for "All That Is Necessary," page 90

Quilt Portrait for Pegge Lacey, page 28

Between Silence and Answer

New and Selected Poems

was set in Bembo, a desktop computer typeface from the Adobe Type Library. Bembo was modeled on typefaces cut by Francesco Griffo for Aldus Manutius' printing of *De Aetna* in 1495 in Venice, a book by classicist Pietro Bembeo about his visit to Mount Etna. Griffo's design is considered one of the first of the old style typefaces, which include Garamond, that were used as staple text types in Europe for 200 years. Stanley Morrison supervised the design of Bembo for the Monotype Corporation in 1929. Bembo is a fine text face because of its well-proportioned letterforms, functional serifs, and lack of pecularities; the italic is modeled on the handwriting of the Renaissance scribe Giovanni Tagliente.

The book was composed using Aldus Pagemaker 5.0 on a MacIntosh Centris 610. One thousand copies were printed in the United States of America by Thomson-Shore, Inc., Dexter, Michigan, in May 1994. It was printed on 60# Glatfelter Supple Opaque, an acid-free recycled paper from the Glatfelter Company .

Book Design by
Eva Fernandez Beehler and Rebecca Kratz Mays